Visit the Web site for

Understanding Western Society

bedfordstmartins.com/mckaywestunderstanding

FREE Online Study Guide

Get instant feedback on your progress with

- Chapter self-tests
- Key terms review
- Map quizzes
- Timeline activities
- Note-taking outlines
- Chapter study guide steps

FREE History Research and Writing Help

Refine your research skills and find plenty of good sources with

- A database of useful images, maps, documents, and more at *Make History*
- A guide to online sources for history
- Help with writing history papers
- A tool for building a bibliography
- Tips on avoiding plagiarism

CONTEMPORARY EUROPE

ATLANTIC OCEAN

North Sea

Baltic Sea

NORWAY
Bergen
Oslo

SWEDEN
Stockholm
Göteborg

SCOTLAND
Edinburgh
Glasgow

NORTHERN IRELAND
Belfast

IRELAND
Dublin

UNITED KINGDOM
Liverpool
Birmingham
WALES
ENGLAND
Thames R.
London

Cork

English Channel

DENMARK
Aarhus
Copenhagen

Elbe R.

Vistula R.

RUSS
Kaliningra
Gdansk

Berlin

POLAND
Wa

NETHERLANDS
Amsterdam
Rotterdam

Antwerp
Brussels
BELGIUM

Rhine R.

GERMANY
Frankfurt

Prague
CZECH REP.
Brno

Kraków

SLOVAK
Mis

Vienna
Danube R.
Bratislava

AUSTRIA
Innsbruck
Graz

Budapest

HUNGARY

Luxembourg
LUXEMBOURG

Paris
Seine R.

FRANCE

Loire R.

LIECHTENSTEIN
Munich
Zürich
Vaduz
Bern
SWITZERLAND

A L P S

Lyons

Rhône R.

Milan
Po R.

SLOVENIA
Ljubljana
Zagreb
CROATIA

BOSNIA AND HERZEGOVINA
Sarajevo

Belgr
SER

Bay of Biscay

ANDORRA
Andorra la Vella
PYRENEES

Marseilles

MONACO

San Marino
SAN MARINO

A P E N N I N E S

Adriatic Sea

Split

Podgorica
MONTENEGRO
Tiranë

ALBAN

Oporto
PORTUGAL

Madrid
Ebro R.

Barcelona

SPAIN

Lisbon

Seville

Corsica

Rome
ITALY

Naples

Sardinia

Tyrrhenian Sea

Ionian Sea

Balearic Is.

Gibraltar (Gr. Br.)

Algiers

Rabat

Tunis

Palermo
Sicily

Valletta
MALTA

MOROCCO

TUNISIA

ALGERIA

Mediterranean

Tripoli

LIBYA

60°N
50°N
40°N
30°N

20°W
10°W
0°
10°E

60°N

0°

Elevation

Feet	Meters
Over 13,120	Over 4,001
6,561–13,120	2,001–4,000
1,641–6,560	501–2,000
661–1,640	201–500
0–660	0–200
Below sea level	Below sea level

⊛ National capital
• Major city

0   150   300 miles
0   150   300 kilometers

THE CONTEMPORARY WORLD

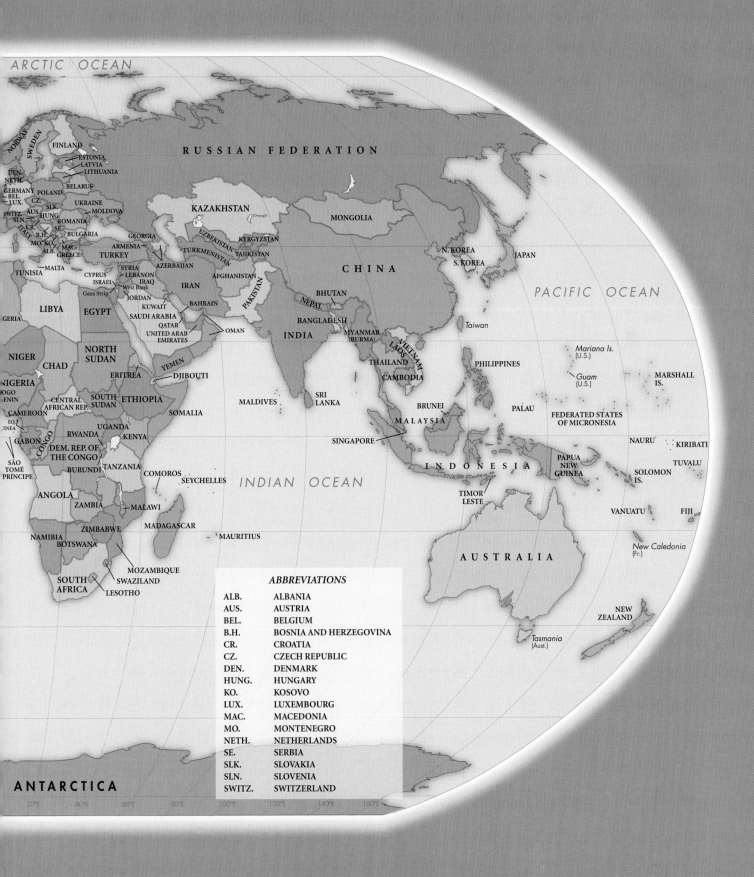

ARCTIC OCEAN

RUSSIAN FEDERATION

NORWAY
SWEDEN
FINLAND
ESTONIA
LATVIA
LITHUANIA
DEN.
NETH.
GERMANY
BEL.
LUX.
POLAND
BELARUS
SWITZ.
AUS.
SLK.
UKRAINE
SLN.
HUNG.
MOLDOVA
ITALY
CR.
ROMANIA
MO. KO.
SE.
BULGARIA
ALB.
MAC.
GREECE
ARMENIA
GEORGIA
TURKEY
AZERBAIJAN
TUNISIA
MALTA
CYPRUS
SYRIA
LEBANON
ISRAEL
IRAQ
West Bank
Gaza Strip
JORDAN
IRAN
LIBYA
EGYPT
KUWAIT
BAHRAIN
SAUDI ARABIA
QATAR
UNITED ARAB
EMIRATES
OMAN

GERIA
NIGER
CHAD
NORTH
SUDAN
YEMEN
ERITREA
DJIBOUTI
NIGERIA
OGO
ENIN
CAMEROON
CENTRAL
AFRICAN REP.
SOUTH
SUDAN
ETHIOPIA
SOMALIA
EQ
INEA
GABON
CONGO
RWANDA
UGANDA
KENYA
DEM. REP. OF
THE CONGO
SÃO
TOMÉ
PRÍNCIPE
BURUNDI
TANZANIA
COMOROS
SEYCHELLES
ANGOLA
ZAMBIA
MALAWI
NAMIBIA
ZIMBABWE
MADAGASCAR
MAURITIUS
BOTSWANA
MOZAMBIQUE
SWAZILAND
SOUTH
AFRICA
LESOTHO

KAZAKHSTAN
UZBEKISTAN
KYRGYZSTAN
TURKMENISTAN
TAJIKISTAN
AFGHANISTAN
PAKISTAN
NEPAL
BHUTAN
BANGLADESH
INDIA
MYANMAR
(BURMA)
MALDIVES
SRI
LANKA

MONGOLIA

CHINA

N. KOREA
S. KOREA
JAPAN

Taiwan

PACIFIC OCEAN

LAOS
VIETNAM
THAILAND
CAMBODIA
PHILIPPINES

Mariana Is.
(U.S.)

Guam
(U.S.)

MARSHALL
IS.

BRUNEI
MALAYSIA
SINGAPORE
PALAU

FEDERATED STATES
OF MICRONESIA

NAURU
KIRIBATI

INDONESIA
PAPUA
NEW
GUINEA
TUVALU
SOLOMON
IS.

INDIAN OCEAN

TIMOR
LESTE
VANUATU
FIJI

New Caledonia
(Fr.)

AUSTRALIA

NEW
ZEALAND

Tasmania
(Aust.)

ANTARCTICA

20°E   40°E   60°E   80°E   100°E   120°E   140°E   160°E

ABBREVIATIONS

ALB.	ALBANIA
AUS.	AUSTRIA
BEL.	BELGIUM
B.H.	BOSNIA AND HERZEGOVINA
CR.	CROATIA
CZ.	CZECH REPUBLIC
DEN.	DENMARK
HUNG.	HUNGARY
KO.	KOSOVO
LUX.	LUXEMBOURG
MAC.	MACEDONIA
MO.	MONTENEGRO
NETH.	NETHERLANDS
SE.	SERBIA
SLK.	SLOVAKIA
SLN.	SLOVENIA
SWITZ.	SWITZERLAND

Understanding Western Society

A BRIEF HISTORY

Understanding Western Society

A BRIEF HISTORY

VOLUME 1 **From Antiquity to the Enlightenment**

John P. McKay
University of Illinois at Urbana-Champaign

Bennett D. Hill
Late of Georgetown University

John Buckler
Late of the University of Illinois at Urbana-Champaign

Clare Haru Crowston
University of Illinois at Urbana-Champaign

Merry E. Wiesner-Hanks
University of Wisconsin–Milwaukee

Joe Perry
Georgia State University

BEDFORD/ST. MARTIN'S
Boston • New York

In Memoriam
John Buckler
1945–2011

FOR BEDFORD/ST. MARTIN'S
Publisher for History: Mary Dougherty
Executive Editor for History: Traci M. Crowell
Director of Development for History: Jane Knetzger
Developmental Editor: Kathryn Abbott
Senior Production Editor: Lori Chong Roncka
Senior Production Supervisor: Nancy Myers
Executive Marketing Manager: Jenna Bookin Barry
Editorial Assistant: Robin Soule
Production Assistants: Laura Winstead and Elise Keller
Copyeditor: Susan Moore
Indexer: Leoni Z. McVey
Cartography: Mapping Specialists, Ltd.
Photo Researchers: Carole Frohlich and Elisa Gallagher, The Visual Connection Image Research, Inc.
Permissions Manager: Kalina K. Ingham
Senior Art Director: Anna Palchik
Text Designer: Brian Salisbury
Cover Designer: Donna Lee Dennison
Cover Art: Joachim Beuckelaer, *At the Market*, 1564. The Bridgeman Art Library.
Composition: NK Graphics
Printing and Binding: RR Donnelley and Sons

President: Joan E. Feinberg
Editorial Director: Denise B. Wydra
Director of Marketing: Karen R. Soeltz
Director of Production: Susan W. Brown
Associate Director, Editorial Production: Elise S. Kaiser
Managing Editor: Elizabeth M. Schaaf

Library of Congress Control Number: 2011931600

Manufactured in the United States of America.

6   5   4   3
f   e   d

For information, write: Bedford/St. Martin's, 75 Arlington Street, Boston, MA 02116   (617-399-4000)

ISBN-13: 978–0–312–66887–7 (Combined edition)
ISBN-13: 978–0–312–66888–4 (Volume 1)
ISBN-13: 978–0–312–66889–1 (Volume 2)

U*nderstanding Western Society* grew out of many conversations about the teaching, study, and learning of history in the last decade. We knew that many instructors wanted a Western Civilization text that introduced students to the broad sweep of history but that also re-created the lives of ordinary men and women in appealing human terms. We knew that instructors wanted a text that presented cutting-edge scholarship in new fields of historical inquiry. We also came to realize that a growing number of instructors thought that their students needed a brief text, either because instructors were assigning more supplemental reading or because they thought their students would be better able to grasp key concepts given less detail. Finally, many instructors wanted a text that would help students focus as they read, that would keep their interest in the material, and that would encourage students to learn historical-thinking skills. We are extremely proud to introduce a textbook designed to address all of these concerns—*Understanding Western Society: A Brief History.*

Narrative

Understanding Western Society presents the broad sweep of the history of Western civilization through the lens of social history. History as a discipline never stands still, and over the last several decades cultural history has joined social history as a source of dynamism. The focus on cultural history highlights the interplay between men's and women's lived experiences. Historical scholarship also has increasingly emphasized the global context of European history, and *Understanding Western Society* reflects that trend. Among the global topics of *Understanding Western Society* are examinations of the steppe peoples of Central Asia, of Muslim views of the Crusades, of the Atlantic world, and of the processes of decolonization and globalization. In addition, scholarship on gender is woven throughout the narrative and in sections on Frankish queens, medieval prostitutes, and female humanists. The politics of gender and gender roles during the French and industrial revolutions are explored as well.

In response to the calls for a less comprehensive text, in developing *Understanding Western Society*, we shortened the narrative of the parent text, *A History of Western Society*, by 30 percent. We condensed and combined thematically related sections and aimed throughout the text to tighten our exposition while working hard to retain topical balance, up-to-date scholarship, and lively, accessible writing. The result is a brief edition that preserves the narrative flow, balance, and power of the full-length work, and that allows students to better discern overarching trends and connect these with the individuals who animate the past.

Pedagogy and Features

In trying to create a text that would help students grasp key concepts, maintain their interest in reading, and help them develop historical thinking skills, we then joined this brief narrative with an innovative design and unique pedagogy. *Understanding Western Society*'s chapter architecture supports students' reading and helps them to grasp key themes and ideas. All chapters open with a succinct statement about the main themes and events of the chapter, designed to establish clear learning outcomes. Chapters are organized into three to six main sections, with **section headings crafted as questions** to facilitate active reading. **Chapter-opening chronologies** underscore the sequence of events, and definitions in the margins explain **key terms**, providing on-the-page reinforcement and a handy tool for review. **Chapter locators** across the bottom of each two-page spread keep students focused on where they are in the chapter and help them see how the material they are reading connects to what they have already reviewed and to what is coming next.

We also reconsidered the traditional review that comes at the end of the chapter. Each chapter includes a "**Looking Back, Looking Ahead**" conclusion that provide an insightful synthesis of the chapter's main developments, while connecting them to events that students will encounter in the chapters to come. Each chapter ends with a step-by-step "**Chapter Study Guide**" that not only helps students with the basic material but also encourages them to move beyond a basic knowledge of what happened in the past to a more nuanced grasp of how events relate to each other, and a better understanding of why the past matters. In essence, the chapter-review sections provide the tools to help students develop the skills of historical analysis and interpretation while also helping them to read and think critically. We hope that this combination of design and pedagogy will help students grasp meaning as they read and also model how historians think, how they pose questions, and how they answer those questions with evidence and interpretation.

Other features of the book further reinforce historical thinking, expand upon the narrative, and offer opportunities for classroom discussion and assignments. In our years of teaching Western Civilization, we have often noted that students really come alive when they encounter stories about real people in the past. Thus, each chapter includes an "**Individuals in Society**" biographical essay that offers a brief study of an individual or group, informing students about the societies in which these people lived. The spotlighting of individuals, both famous and obscure, underscores the book's attention to cultural and intellectual developments, highlights human agency, and reflects changing interests within the historical profession as well as the development of "micro-history." Biographical essays in *Understanding Western Society* include features on Cyrus the Great who in the sixth century B.C.E. founded the Persian Empire; Glückel of Hameln, a German-Jewish widow who lived in the seventeenth century; and Josiah Wedgwood, the eighteenth-century English potter.

Each chapter also includes a primary source feature, "**Listening to the Past**," chosen to extend and illuminate a major historical issue considered in each chapter through the presentation of a single original source or several voices on the subject. Each opens with an introduction and closes with "Questions for Analysis" that invite students to evaluate the evidence as historians would. Selected for their interest and importance, and carefully fitted into their historical context, these sources allow students to observe how history has been shaped by individuals. Documents include Eirik the Red's tenth-century saga of his voyages to North America; Denis Diderot's fictional account of a voyage to Tahiti from the eighteenth century; and the 1959 "kitchen debate" between the U.S. vice president Richard Nixon and the Soviet premier Nikita Khrushchev.

We are particularly proud of the illustrative component of our work—the art and map program. Although this is a brief book, over 400 illustrations, all contemporaneous with the subject matter, reveal to today's visually attuned students how the past speaks in pictures as well as in words. Recognizing students' difficulties with geography, we also offer 87 full-size, full-color maps and 61 spot maps. Each chapter includes a "**Mapping the Past**" activity that helps improve students' geographical literacy and a "**Picturing the Past**" visual activity that gives students valuable skills in reading and interpreting images.

The new directions in format and pedagogy that are the hallmark of *Understanding Western Society* have not changed the central mission of the book since it first appeared in its original format, which is to introduce students to the broad sweep of Western Civilization in a fresh yet balanced manner. As we have made changes, large and small, we have always sought to give students and teachers an integrated perspective so that they could pursue—on their own or in the classroom—those historical questions that they find particularly exciting and significant. We hope students will then take the habits of thinking developed in the history classroom with them, for understanding the changes of the past might help them to handle the ever-faster pace of change in today's world.

Acknowledgments

It is a pleasure to thank the many instructors who read and critiqued the manuscript through its development:

James H. Adams, Pennsylvania State University, Abington
Gemma Albanese, Dawson College
Robert Anxiaux, Eastfield College
Deborah C. Bjelajac, Florida State College at Jacksonville
Eugene Boia, Cleveland State University

Elizabeth Collins, Triton College
Ian Drummond, Gordon College
Bobbie Harris, Hillsborough Community College
John S. Kemp, Truckee Meadows Community College
Peter J. Klem, Great Basin College
James A. Lenaghan, The Ohio State University
Carol Levin, University of Nebraska–Lincoln
Heidi J. Manzone, University of North Florida
David B. Mock, Tallahassee Community College
Wesley Moody, Florida State College at Jacksonville
Ellen Howell Myers, San Antonio College
Laura M. Nelson, West Virginia University
Rosemary Fox Thurston, New Jersey City University

It is also a pleasure to thank the many editors who have assisted us over the years, first at Houghton Mifflin and now at Bedford/St. Martin's. At Bedford/St. Martin's, these include developmental editor Kathryn Abbott; associate editors Lynn Sternberger and Jack Cashman; editorial assistant Robin Soule; executive editor Traci M. Crowell; director of development Jane Knetzger; publisher for history Mary Dougherty; photo researchers Carole Frohlich and Elisa Gallagher; text permissions editor Elaine Kosta; and Lori Chong Roncka, senior production editor, with the assistance of Laura Winstead and the guidance of managing editor Elizabeth Schaaf and assistant managing editor John Amburg. Other key contributors were text designer Brian Salisbury, senior art director Anna Palchik, copyeditor Susan Moore, proofreaders Janet Cocker and Angela Morrison, indexer Leoni Z. McVey, and senior art director–cover designer Donna Dennison. We would also like to thank editorial director Denise Wydra and president Joan E. Feinberg.

Many of our colleagues at the University of Illinois, the University of Wisconsin–Milwaukee, and Georgia State University continue to provide information and stimulation, often without even knowing it. We thank them for it. The authors also thank the many students they have taught over the years. Their reactions and opinions helped shape this book. Merry Wiesner-Hanks would, as always, like to thank her husband Neil, without whom work on this project would not be possible. Clare Haru Crowston thanks her husband Ali, and her children Lili, Reza, and Kian, who are a joyous reminder of the vitality of life that we try to showcase in this book. John McKay expresses his deep appreciation to JoAnn McKay for her keen insights and unfailing encouragement. Joe Perry thanks Andrzej S. Kaminski and the expert team assembled at Lazarski University for their insightful comments and is most grateful to Joyce de Vries for her unstinting support and encouragement.

Each of us has benefited from the criticism of his or her coauthors, although each of us assumes responsibility for what he or she has written. John Buckler has written the first six chapters; building on text originally written by Bennett Hill, Merry Wiesner-Hanks has assumed primary responsibility for Chapters 7 through 14; building on text originally written by Bennett Hill and John McKay, Clare Crowston has assumed primary responsibility for Chapters 15 through 20; John McKay has written and revised Chapters 21 through 25; and Joe Perry has written and revised Chapters 26 through 31, building on text originally written by John McKay.

Brief Contents

Contents

1 Origins
ca. 400,000–1100 B.C.E. 2

2 Small Kingdoms and Mighty Empires in the Near East
ca. 1100–513 B.C.E. 32

3 The Development of Classical Greece
ca. 2000–338 B.C.E. 54

4 The Hellenistic World

336–30 B.C.E.   86

5 The Rise of Rome

ca. 750–31 B.C.E.   112

6 The Pax Romana

31 B.C.E.–284 C.E.   138

7 Late Antiquity

250–600   166

10 The Life of the People in the High Middle Ages

1000–1300 260

11 The Creativity and Challenges of Medieval Cities

1100–1300 288

12 The Crisis of the Late Middle Ages

1300–1450   320

13 European Society in the Age of the Renaissance

1350–1550   352

16 Absolutism and Constitutionalism in Europe

ca. 1589–1725   450

17 Toward a New Worldview

1540–1789   488

Maps, Figures, and Tables

Maps

Figures and Tables

Special Features

Listening to the Past

Individuals in Society

Adopters of *Understanding Western Society: A Brief History* and their students have access to abundant extra resources, including documents, presentation and testing materials, the acclaimed Bedford Series in History and Culture volumes, and much much more. See below for more information, visit the book's catalog site at bedfordstmartins.com/mckaywestunderstanding/catalog, or contact your local Bedford/St. Martin's sales representative.

Get the Right Version for Your Class

To accommodate different course lengths and course budgets, *Understanding Western Society: A Brief History* is available in several different versions and e-book formats, which are available at a substantial discount.

- Combined edition (Chapters 1–31) — available in paperback and e-book formats
- Volume 1: From Antiquity to the Enlightenment (Chapters 1–17) — available in paperback and e-book formats
- Volume 2: From the Age of Exploration to the Present (Chapters 15–31) — available in paperback and e-book formats

The online, interactive **Bedford e-Book** can be examined or purchased at a discount at bedfordstmartins.com/mckaywestunderstanding; if packaged with the print text, it is available at no extra cost. Your students can also purchase *Understanding Western Society: A Brief History* in other popular e-book formats for computers, tablets, and e-readers.

Online Extras for Students

The book's companion site at bedfordstmartins.com/mckaywestunderstanding gives students a way to read, write, and study, and it helps them find and access quizzes and activities, study aids, and history research and writing help.

free *Online Study Guide.* Available at the companion site, this popular resource provides students with quizzes and activities for each chapter, including multiple-choice self-tests that focus on important concepts; a flash card activity that tests students' knowledge of key terms; timeline activities that emphasize causal relationships; and map activities intended to strengthen students' geography skills. Instructors can monitor students' progress through an online Quiz Gradebook or receive e-mail updates.

free *Research, Writing, and Anti-plagiarism Advice.* Available at the companion site, Bedford's **History Research and Writing Help** includes the textbook authors' **Suggested Reading** organized by chapter; **History Research and Reference Sources**, with links to history-related databases, indexes, and journals; **More Sources and How to Format a History Paper**, with clear advice on how to integrate primary and secondary sources into research papers and how to cite and format sources correctly; **Build a Bibliography**, a simple Web-based tool known as The Bedford Bibliographer that generates bibliographies in four commonly used documentation styles; and **Tips on Avoiding Plagiarism**, an online tutorial that reviews the consequences of plagiarism and features exercises to help students practice integrating sources and recognize acceptable summaries.

Resources for Instructors

Bedford/St. Martin's has developed a wide range of teaching resources for this book and for this course. They range from lecture and presentation materials to assessment tools and course-management options. Most can be downloaded or ordered at bedfordstmartins.com/mckaywest understanding/catalog.

HistoryClass for Understanding Western Society. HistoryClass, a Bedford/St. Martin's Online Course Space, puts the online resources available with this textbook in one convenient and completely customizable course space. There you and your students can access an interactive e-book and primary-sources reader; maps, images, documents, and links; chapter review quizzes; interactive multimedia exercises; and research and writing help. In HistoryClass you can get all our premium content and tools and assign, rearrange, and mix them with your own resources. For more information, visit **yourhistoryclass.com**.

Bedford Coursepack for Blackboard, WebCT, Desire2Learn, Angel, Sakai, or Moodle. We have free content to help you integrate our rich content into your course-management system. Registered instructors can download coursepacks with no hassle and no strings attached. Content includes our most popular free resources and book-specific content for *Understanding Western Society: A Brief History*. Visit **bedfordstmartins.com/cms** to see a demo, find your version, or download your coursepack.

Instructor's Resource Manual. The instructor's manual offers both experienced and first-time instructors tools for preparing for lecture and running discussions. It includes chapter-review material, teaching strategies, and a guide to chapter-specific supplements available for the text.

Computerized Test Bank. Each chapter of the test bank includes a mix of fresh, carefully crafted multiple-choice, matching, short-answer, and essay questions. It also contains the Review, Visual Activity, Map Activity, Individuals in Society, and Listening to the Past questions from the textbook and model answers for each. The questions appear in Microsoft Word format and in easy-to-use test-bank software that allows instructors to easily add, edit, re-sequence, and print questions and answers. Instructors can also export questions into a variety of formats, including WebCT and Blackboard.

PowerPoint Maps, Images, Lecture Outlines, and i>clicker Content. Look good and save time with ***The Bedford Lecture Kit***. These presentation materials are downloadable individually from the Instructor Resources tab at **bedfordstmartins.com/mckaywestunderstanding/catalog** and are available on ***The Bedford Lecture Kit*** **Instructor's Resource CD-ROM**. They include ready-made and fully customizable PowerPoint multimedia presentations built around lecture outlines with embedded maps, figures, and selected images from the textbook and with detailed instructor notes on key points. Also available are maps and selected images in JPEG and PowerPoint formats; content for i>clicker, a classroom response system, in Microsoft Word and PowerPoint formats; the Instructor's Resource Manual in Microsoft Word format; and outline maps in PDF format for quizzing or handing out. All files are suitable for copying onto transparency acetates.

Overhead Map Transparencies. This set of full-color acetate transparencies includes 130 maps for the Western Civilization course.

Make History — Free Documents, Maps, Images, and Web Sites. *Make History* combines the best Web resources with hundreds of maps and images, to make it simple to find the source material you need. Browse the collection of thousands of resources by course or by topic, date, and type. Each item has been carefully chosen and helpfully annotated to make it easy to find exactly what you need. Available at **bedfordstmartins.com/makehistory**.

Videos and Multimedia. A wide assortment of videos and multimedia CD-ROMs on various topics in Western civilization is available to qualified adopters through your Bedford/St. Martin's sales representative.

Package and Save Your Students Money

For information on free packages and discounts up to 50 percent, visit **bedfordstmartins.com/mckaywestunderstanding/catalog**, or contact your local Bedford/St. Martin's sales representative.

Bedford e-Book. The e-book for this title, described above, can be packaged with the print text at no additional cost.

Sources of Western Society, Second Edition. This two-volume primary-source collection provides a rich selection of sources to accompany *Understanding Western Society: A Brief History*. Each chapter features five to six written and visual sources that present history from well-known figures and ordinary individuals alike. A "Viewpoints" feature highlights two or three sources that address the same topic from different perspectives. Document headnotes as well as reading and discussion questions promote student understanding. Available free when packaged with the print text.

Sources of Western Society e-Book. The reader is also available as an e-book. When packaged with the print or electronic version of the textbook, it is available for free.

The Bedford Series in History and Culture. More than one hundred titles in this highly praised series combine first-rate scholarship, historical narrative, and important primary documents for undergraduate courses. Each book is brief, inexpensive, and focused on a specific topic or period. For a complete list of titles, visit **bedfordstmartins.com/history/series**. Package discounts are available.

Rand McNally Atlas of Western Civilization. This collection of over fifty full-color maps highlights social, political, and cross-cultural change and interaction from classical Greece and Rome to the post-industrial Western world. Each map is thoroughly indexed for fast reference. Available for $3.00 when packaged with the print text.

The Bedford Glossary for European History. This handy supplement for the survey course gives students historically contextualized definitions for hundreds of terms—from *Abbasids* to *Zionism*—that they will encounter in lectures, reading, and exams. Available free when packaged with the print text.

Trade Books. Titles published by sister companies Hill & Wang; Farrar, Straus and Giroux; Henry Holt and Company; St. Martin's Press; Picador; and Palgrave Macmillan are available at a 50 percent discount when packaged with Bedford/St. Martin's textbooks. For more information, visit **bedfordstmartins.com/tradeup**.

A Pocket Guide to Writing in History. This portable and affordable reference tool by Mary Lynn Rampolla provides reading, writing, and research advice useful to students in all history courses. Concise yet comprehensive advice on approaching typical history assignments, developing critical reading skills, writing effective history papers, conducting research, using and documenting sources, and avoiding plagiarism—enhanced with practical tips and examples throughout—have made this slim reference a bestseller. Package discounts are available.

A Student's Guide to History. This complete guide to success in any history course provides the practical help students need to be effective. In addition to introducing students to the nature of the discipline, author Jules Benjamin teaches a wide range of skills from preparing for exams to approaching common writing assignments, and explains the research and documentation process with plentiful examples. Package discounts are available.

The Social Dimension of Western Civilization. Combining current scholarship with classic pieces, this reader's forty-eight secondary sources, compiled by Richard M. Golden, hook students with the fascinating and often surprising details of how everyday Western people worked, ate, played, celebrated, worshiped, married, procreated, fought, persecuted, and died. Package discounts are available.

The West in the Wider World: Sources and Perspectives. Edited by Richard Lim and David Kammerling Smith, this first college reader to focus on the central historical question "How did the West become the West?" offers a wealth of written and visual source materials to reveal the influence of non-European regions on the origins and development of Western Civilization. Package discounts are available.

How to use this book to figure out what's really important

The **chapter title** tells you the subject of the chapter and identifies the time span that will be covered.

15

European Exploration and Conquest

1450–1650

Before 1450 Europeans were relatively marginal players in a centuries-old trading system that linked Africa, Asia, and Europe. Elites everywhere prized Chinese porcelains and silks, while wealthy members of the Celestial Kingdom, as China called itself, wanted ivory and black slaves from Africa, and exotic goods and peacocks from India. African people wanted textiles from India and cowrie shells from the Maldives in the Indian Ocean. Europeans craved Asian silks and spices but they had few desirable goods to offer their trading partners.

The European search for better access to Asian trade led to a new overseas empire in the Indian Ocean and the accidental discovery of the Western Hemisphere. Within a few decades European colonies in South and North America would join this worldwide web. Europeans came to dominate trading networks and political empires of truly global proportions. The era of globalization had begun.

The **chapter introduction** identifies the most important themes, events, and people that will be explored in the chapter.

Global contacts created new forms of cultural exchange, assimilation, conversion, and resistance. Europeans struggled to comprehend the peoples and societies they found and sought to impose European cultural values on them. New forms of racial prejudice emerged, but so did new openness and curiosity about different ways of life. Together with the developments of the Renaissance and the Reformation, the Age of Discovery—as the period of European exploration and conquest from 1450 to 1650 is known—laid the foundations for the modern world. ∎

416

Memorizing facts and dates for a history class won't get you very far. That's because history isn't just about "facts." It's also about understanding cause and effect and the significance of people, places, and events from the past that still have relevance to your world today. This textbook is designed to help you focus on what's truly significant in the history of Western societies and to give you practice thinking like a historian.

Life in the Age of Discovery. A detail from an early-seventeenth-century Flemish painting depicting maps, illustrated travel books, a globe, a compass, and an astrolabe. The voyages of discovery revolutionized Europeans' sense of space and inspired a passion among the wealthy for collecting objects related to navigation and travel. (National Gallery, London/Art Resource, NY)

Chapter Preview

▶ What were the limits of world contacts before Columbus?

▶ How and why did Europeans undertake voyages of expansion?

▶ What was the impact of conquest?

▶ How did Europe and the world change after Columbus?

▶ How did expansion change European attitudes and beliefs?

The **Chapter Preview** lists the questions that open each new section of the chapter and will be addressed in turn on the following pages. You should think about answers to these as you read.

Each section has tools that help you focus on what's important.

The **question in red** asks about the specific topics being discussed in this section. Pause to answer each one after you read the section.

▼ What were the limits of world contacts before Columbus?

Historians now recognize that a type of world economy, known as the Afro-Eurasian trade world, linked the products and people of Europe, Asia, and Africa in the fifteenth century. The West was not the dominant player before Columbus, and the European voyages derived from a desire to share in and control the wealth coming from the Indian Ocean.

The Trade World of the Indian Ocean

The Indian Ocean was the center of the Afro-Eurasian trade world. It was a crossroads for commercial and cultural exchange between China, India, the Middle East, Africa, and Europe (Map 15.1). From the seventh through the fourteenth centuries, the volume of this trade steadily increased, declining only during the years of the Black Death.

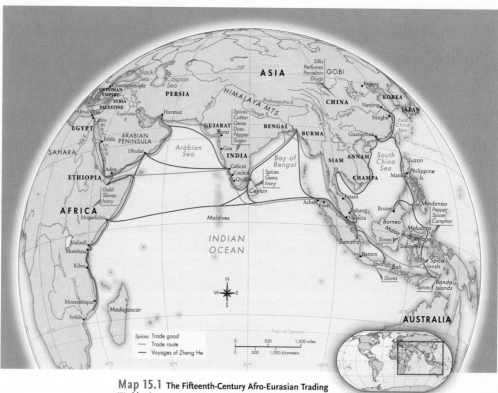

Map 15.1 The Fifteenth-Century Afro-Eurasian Trading World After a period of decline following the Black Death and the Mongol invasions, trade revived in the fifteenth century. Muslim merchants dominated trade, linking ports in East Africa and the Red Sea with those in India and the Malay Archipelago. Chinese Admiral Zheng He's voyages (1405–1433) followed the most important Indian Ocean trade routes, in the hope of imposing Ming dominance of trade and tribute.

Chapter 15
European Exploration and
418   Conquest • 1450–1650

CHAPTER LOCATOR   What were the limits of
world contacts before
Columbus?

The **chapter locator** at the bottom of the page puts this section in the context of the chapter as a whole, so you can see how this section relates to what's coming next.

Merchants congregated in a series of multicultural, cosmopolitan port cities strung around the Indian Ocean. The most developed area of this commercial web was in the South China Sea. In the fifteenth century the port of Malacca became a great commercial entrepôt (AHN-truh-poh), a trading post to which goods were shipped for storage while awaiting redistribution to other places.

The Mongol emperors opened the doors of China to the West, encouraging Europeans like the Venetian trader and explorer Marco Polo to do business there. Marco Polo's tales of his travels from 1271 to 1295 and his encounter with the Great Khan fueled Western fantasies about the Orient. After the Mongols fell to the Ming Dynasty in 1368, China entered a period of agricultural and commercial expansion, population growth, and urbanization. Historians agree that China had the most advanced economy in the world until at least the start of the eighteenth century.

China also took the lead in exploration, sending Admiral Zheng He's fleet along the trade web as far west as Egypt. From 1405 to 1433, each of his seven expeditions involved hundreds of ships and tens of thousands of men. Court conflicts and the need to defend against renewed Mongol encroachment led to the abandonment of the expeditions after the deaths of Zheng He and the emperor. China's turning away from external trade opened new opportunities for European states to claim a decisive role in world trade.

Another center of trade in the Indian Ocean was India, the crucial link between the Persian Gulf and the Southeast Asian and East Asian trade networks. The subcontinent had ancient links with its neighbors to the northwest: trade between South Asia and Mesopotamia dates back to the origins of human civilization. Arab merchants who circumnavigated India on their way to trade in the South China Sea established trading posts along the southern coast of India, where the cities of Calicut and Quilon became thriving commercial centers. India was an important contributor of goods to the world trading system; much of the world's pepper was grown there, and Indian cotton textiles were highly prized.

The Columbian Exchange

The migration of peoples to the New World led to an exchange of animals, plants, and disease, a complex process known as the Columbian exchange. Columbus brought sugar plants on his second voyage; Spaniards also introduced rice and bananas from the Canary Islands, and the Portuguese carried these items to Brazil. Everywhere they settled, the Spanish and Portuguese brought and raised wheat with labor provided by the encomienda system. Grapes and olives brought over from Spain did well in parts of Peru and Chile.

Apart from wild turkeys and game, Native Americans had no animals for food. Moreover, they did not domesticate animals for travel or to use as beasts of burden, except for alpacas and llamas in the Inca Empire. On his second voyage in 1493 Columbus introduced horses, cattle, sheep, dogs, pigs, chickens, and goats. The multiplication of these animals proved spectacular. In turn, Europeans returned home with many food crops that become central elements of their diet.

Disease was perhaps the most important form of exchange. The wave of catastrophic epidemic disease that swept the Western Hemisphere after 1492 can be seen as an extension of the swath of devastation wreaked by the Black Death in the 1300s, first on Asia and then on Europe. The world after Columbus was thus unified by disease as well as by

Columbian exchange The exchange of animals, plants, and diseases between the Old and the New Worlds.

Chapter Chronology

1443	Portuguese establish first African trading post at Arguin
1492	Columbus lands in the Americas
1511	Portuguese capture Malacca from Muslims
1518	Spanish king authorizes slave trade to New World colonies
1519–1522	Magellan's expedition circumnavigates the world
1521	Cortés conquers the Mexica Empire
1533	Pizarro conquers Inca Empire
1602	Dutch East India Company established

Chapter chronologies show the sequence of events and underlying developments in the chapter.

Key terms in the margins give you background on important people, ideas, and events. Use these for reference while you read, but also think about which terms are emphasized and why they matter.

The Chapter Study Guide provides a process that will build your understanding and your historical skills.

■ Chapter 15 Study Guide

Online Study Guide
bedfordstmartins.com/mckaywestunderstanding

STEP 1
Identify the key terms and explain their significance.

Step 1

GETTING STARTED Below are basic terms about this period in the history of Western civilization. Can you identify each term below and explain why it matters? To do this exercise online, go to bedfordstmartins.com/mckaywestunderstanding.

TERMS	WHO (OR WHAT) AND WHEN	WHY IT MATTERS
conquistador, p. 422		
caravel, p. 423		
Ptolemy's *Geography*, p. 423		
Treaty of Tordesillas, p. 430		
Mexica Empire, p. 431		
Inca Empire, p. 433		
viceroyalties, p. 435		
encomienda system, p. 435		
Columbian exchange, p. 437		

STEP 2
Analyze differences and similarities among ideas, events, people, or societies discussed in the chapter.

Step 2

MOVING BEYOND THE BASICS The exercise below requires a more advanced understanding of the chapter material. Examine the nature and impact of European exploration and conquest by filling in the chart below. What were the motives behind expansion? Why did monarchs support overseas expeditions? Why did men like Columbus undertake such dangerous journeys? Identify key conquests and discoveries for each nation. Then, describe the impact of exploration and colonization in the Americas in both the New World, Europe, and Africa. When you are finished, consider the following question: What intended and unintended consequences resulted from European expansion? To do this exercise online, go to bedfordstmartins.com/mckaywestunderstanding.

EXPLORATION 1492–1600	MOTIVES FOR EXPLORATION AND SETTLEMENT	CONQUESTS AND DISCOVERIES	IMPACT IN NEW WORLD	IMPACT IN EUROPE	IMPACT IN AFRICA
Portugal					
Spain					
France					
England					

Visit the FREE Online Study Guide at **bedfordstmartins.com/mckaywestunderstanding** to do these steps online and to check how much you've learned.

Step 3 | PUTTING IT ALL TOGETHER

Now that you've reviewed key elements of the chapter, take a step back and try to see the big picture. Remember to use specific examples from the chapter in your answers. To do this exercise online, go to bedfordstmartins.com/mckaywestunderstanding.

STEP 3
Answer the big-picture questions using specific examples or evidence from the chapter.

WORLD CONTACTS BEFORE COLUMBUS

- How did trade connect the civilizations of Africa, Asia, and Europe prior to 1492? Which states were at the center of global trade? Which were at the periphery? Why?

- Why were Europeans at a trading disadvantage prior to 1492? How did geography limit European participation in world trade? What role did Europe's economy and material culture play in this context?

THE EUROPEAN VOYAGES OF DISCOVERY

- Why were Europeans so eager to gain better access to Asia and Asian trade? How did fifteenth-century economic and political developments help stimulate European expansion?

- Compare and contrast Spanish, French, and English exploration and colonization of the New World. What common motives underlay the efforts of all three nations? How would you explain the important differences you note?

THE IMPACT OF CONQUEST

- What kinds of societies and governments did Europeans seek to establish in the Americas? What light does the nature of colonial society shed on the motives behind European expansion and European views of the indigenous peoples of the Americas?

- What was the Columbian exchange? How did it transform both Europe and the Americas?

- How did European expansion give rise to new ideas about race?

EUROPE AND THE WORLD AFTER COLUMBUS

- What role did increasing demand for sugar play in shaping the economy and society of the New World? Why were sugar and slavery so tightly linked?

- If Europe was at the periphery of the global trading system prior to 1492, where was it situated by the middle of the sixteenth century? What had changed? What had not?

- How did expansion complicate Europeans' understanding of themselves and their place in the world?

■ **In Your Own Words** Imagine that you must explain Chapter 15 to someone who hasn't read it. What would be the most important points to include and why?

ACTIVE RECITATION
Explain the important points in your own words to make sure you have a firm grasp of the chapter material.

449

Understanding Western Society

A BRIEF HISTORY

1

Origins

ca. 400,000–1100 B.C.E.

The civilization and cultures of the modern Western world, like great rivers, have many sources. These sources have flowed from many places and directions. Early peoples in western Europe developed numerous communities uniquely their own but also sharing some features. Groups developed their own social organizations and religious practices, and they mastered such diverse subjects as astronomy, mathematics, geometry, trigonometry, and engineering. The earliest of these peoples did not record their learning and lore in systems of writing. Their lives and customs are consequently largely lost to us.

Other early peoples confronted many of the same basic challenges as those in Europe. They also made progress, but they took the important step of recording their experiences in writing. The most enduring innovations occurred in the ancient Near East, a region that includes the lands bordering the Mediterranean's eastern shore, the Arabian peninsula, parts of northeastern Africa, and above all Mesopotamia, the area of modern Iraq. Fundamental to the development of Western civilization and culture was the invention of writing by the Sumerians, which allowed knowledge of the past to be preserved and facilitated the spread of learning, science, and literature. Ancient Near Eastern civilizations also produced the first written law codes, as well as religious concepts that still permeate daily life.

How do we know and understand these things? Before embarking on the study of Western history, it is necessary to ask what it is. Only then can the peoples and events of tens of thousands of years be placed into a coherent whole. ∎

Life in Early Egypt. The lives of early Egyptians revolved around the seasons and their crops. This wall painting depicts workers picking bunches of grapes for winemaking. (Erich Lessing/Art Resource, NY)

Chapter Preview

▶ What do we mean by "the West" and "Western Civilization"?

▶ What was the significance of the advent of agriculture?

▶ What kind of civilization developed in Mesopotamia?

▶ How did Mesopotamian culture spread in the Near East?

▶ What were the characteristics of Egyptian civilization?

▶ How did foreign invasions alter the Near East?

▼ What do we mean by "the West" and "Western Civilization"?

Most human groups have left some record of themselves. Some left artifacts, others pictures or signs, and still others written documents. In many of these records, groups set out distinctions between themselves and others. Some of these distinctions are between small groups such as neighboring tribes, some between countries and civilizations, and some between vast parts of the world. One of the most enduring of the latter are the ideas of "the West" and "the East."

Describing the West

Ideas about the West and the distinction between West and East derived originally from the ancient Greeks. Greek civilization grew up in the shadow of earlier civilizations to the south and east of Greece, especially Egypt and Mesopotamia. Greeks defined themselves in relation to these more advanced cultures, which they saw as "Eastern."

The Greeks passed this conceptualization on to the Romans, who saw themselves clearly as part of the West. For some Romans, Greece remained in the West, while other Romans came to view Greek traditions as vaguely "Eastern." To Romans, the East was more sophisticated and more advanced, but also decadent and somewhat immoral. Roman value judgments have continued to shape preconceptions, stereotypes, and views of differences between the West and the East—which were also called the "Occident" and the "Orient"—to this day.

Greco-Roman ideas about the West were passed on to people who lived in western and northern Europe, who saw themselves as the inheritors of this classical tradition and thus as the West. When these Europeans established colonies outside of Europe beginning in the late fifteenth century, they regarded what they were doing as taking Western culture with them, even though many aspects of Western culture had actually originated in what Europeans by that point regarded as the East. With colonization, Western came to mean those cultures that included significant numbers of people of European ancestry, no matter where on the globe they were located.

In the early twentieth century educators and other leaders in the United States became worried that many young people were becoming cut off from European intellectual and cultural traditions. They encouraged the establishment of college and university courses focusing on "Western civilization," the first of which was taught at Columbia University in 1919. In designing the course, the faculty included cultures that had long been considered Eastern, such as Egypt and Mesopotamia, describing them as the "cradles of Western civilization." The course spread to other colleges and universities, evolving into what became known as the Western civilization course.

After World War II divisions between the West and the East changed again. Now there was a new division between East and West within Europe, with Western coming to imply a capitalist economy and Eastern the Communist bloc. Thus, Japan became Western, and some Greek-speaking areas of Europe became Eastern. The collapse of communism in the Soviet Union and eastern Europe in the 1980s brought yet another refiguring, with much of eastern Europe joining the European Union, originally a Western organization.

At the beginning of the twenty-first century, Western has certain cultural connotations, such as individualism and competition, which some see as negative and others as positive. Islamic radicals often describe their aims as an end to Western influence, though Islam itself is generally described, along with Judaism and Christianity, as a Western monotheistic religion. Thus, throughout its long history, the meaning of "the West" has shifted, but in every era it has meant more than a geographical location.

4

Chapter 1
Origins
ca. 400,000–1100 B.C.E.

CHAPTER LOCATOR | What do we mean by "the West" and "Western Civilization"?

What Is Western Civilization, and Why?

The topic of Western history leads to the question, "What is civilization?" The word civilization comes from the Latin adjective *civilis*, which refers to a citizen. Citizens willingly and mutually bind themselves in political, economic, and social organizations in which individuals merge themselves, their energies, and their interests in a larger community.

Civilization, however, goes beyond politics to include an advanced stage of social development. Civilized society is refined, possessing the notion of law to govern the conduct of its members. It includes a code of manners and social conduct that creates an atmosphere of harmony and peace within the community. It creates art and generates science and philosophy to explain the larger world. It creates theology so that people can go beyond superstition in their pursuit of religion.

The term *Western* in this context means the ideas, customs, and institutions that developed primarily in Europe, the Americas, and their colonies throughout the world. These ideas, customs, and institutions set Western civilization apart from other civilizations, such as the African and Asian, that developed their unique ways of life as a result of different demands, challenges, and opportunities, both human and geographical. Yet some of the roots of Western civilization lie in western Asia and northern Africa. Mesopotamia, and to a lesser extent Egypt, created concepts that are basic to Western thought and conduct; and they helped to shape European cultures. No civilization stands alone. Each is influenced by its neighbors, all the while preserving the essentials that make it distinctive.

At the fundamental level, the similarities of Western civilization are greater than the differences. Almost all people in Europe and the Americas share some values, even though they may live far apart, speak different languages, and have different religious, political, and social systems. These values are the bonds that hold a civilization together. By studying these shared cultural values, which stretch through time and across distance, we can see how the various events of the past have left their impression on the present and even how the present may influence the future.

▼ What was the significance of the advent of agriculture?

By about 400,000 B.C.E. early people were making primitive stone tools. From that time until about 11,000 B.C.E., an age known as the Paleolithic period, people survived as nomadic gatherers and hunters usually living in caves or temporary shelters. This period was followed by the Neolithic period, usually dated between 11,000 and 4000 B.C.E.,

Chapter Chronology

ca. 400,000 B.C.E.	Primitive stone tools begin to be used
400,000–11,000 B.C.E.	Paleolithic period
11,000–4000 B.C.E.	Neolithic period
ca. 7000 B.C.E.	Domestication of plants and animals
ca. 3100 B.C.E.	Unification of Upper and Lower Egypt
ca. 3000 B.C.E.	Establishment of first Mesopotamian cities; development of wheeled transport and cuneiform writing
3000–1600 B.C.E.	Erection of the Stonehenge monument
2500 B.C.E.	Scribal schools flourish in Sumer
2331 B.C.E.	Establishment of the Akkadian empire
ca. 2000 B.C.E.	Indo-Europeans arrive in the Near East
ca. 1800 B.C.E.	Hyksos people settle in the Nile Delta; Hittites expand eastward
1792–1750 B.C.E.	Hammurabi rules Babylon
1367–1350 B.C.E.	Akhenaten imposes monotheism in Egypt
ca. 1200–1000 B.C.E.	Sea Peoples destroy the Hittite and Egyptian empires

civilization Citizens united in political, economic, and social organizations devoted to a larger community; civilizations include laws that govern, a code of manners and social conduct, and scientific, philosophical, and theological beliefs that explain the larger world.

Paleolithic period The time between 400,000 and 11,000 B.C.E., when early peoples began making primitive stone tools, survived by hunting and gathering, and dwelled in temporary shelters.

Neolithic period The period between 11,000 and 4000 B.C.E., when the development of agriculture and the domestication of animals enabled peoples to establish permanent settlements.

when nomadic peoples began settling into communities sustained by agriculture and domestic animals.

Paleolithic Life

Paleolithic peoples were hunters and gatherers. Hunting in groups, they used their knowledge of the animal world and their power of thinking to plan how to down their prey. Paleolithic peoples also nourished themselves by gathering nuts, berries, and seeds. Some even knew how to plant wild seeds to supplement their food supply. Thus they relied on every part of the environment for survival.

The basic social unit of Paleolithic societies was probably the extended family. Paleolithic peoples depended on the extended family for cooperative work and mutual protection. The ties of kinship probably also extended beyond the family to the tribe—a group of families led by a patriarch, a dominant male who governed the group. Most tribes probably consisted of thirty to fifty people.

Group members had to cooperate to survive. The adult males hunted and between hunts made stone weapons. The women's realm was primarily the camp, but they too ventured out to gather nuts, grains, and fruits to supplement the group's diet. The women's primary responsibility was the bearing and care of children. Part of women's work was tending the fire, which served for warmth, cooking, and protection against wild animals.

Some of the most striking accomplishments of Paleolithic peoples were intellectual. They used reason to govern their actions. Thought, language, and cave paintings—the world's first art—permitted the lore and experience of the old to be passed on to the young. Paleolithic peoples developed the custom of burying their dead and leaving offerings with the body, perhaps in the belief that somehow life continued after death.

Neolithic Life

The real transformation of human life occurred when hunters and gatherers gave up their nomadic way of life to depend primarily on the grain they grew and the animals they domesticated. Agriculture made for a more stable and secure life. Neolithic peoples were responsible for many fundamental inventions and innovations that the modern world takes for granted. First, obviously, was systematic agriculture, the basis of all modern life. The settled routine of Neolithic farmers led to the evolution of towns and eventually cities. Farmers usually raised more food than they could consume, and their surpluses permitted larger and healthier populations. Since surpluses of food could also be bartered for other commodities, the Neolithic era witnessed the beginning of large-scale trade.

The transition to settled life also had a profound impact on the family. The shared needs and pressures that make for strong extended-family ties in nomadic societies are less prominent in settled societies. Bonds to the extended family weakened. In towns and cities, the nuclear family—father, mother, and children—was more dependent on its immediate neighbors than on kinfolk.

For unknown reasons, people in various parts of the world all seem to have begun domesticating plants and animals at roughly the same time, around 7000 B.C.E. Four main points of origin have been identified. In the Near East, people at sites as far apart as Tepe Yahya in modern Iran, Jarmo in Iraq, Jericho in Palestine, and Hacilar in modern Turkey raised wheat, barley, peas, and lentils. They also kept herds of sheep, pigs, and possibly goats. In western Africa, Neolithic farmers domesticated many plants, including millet, sorghum, and yams. In central China, peoples of the Yangshao culture developed techniques of field agriculture, animal husbandry, pottery making, and bronze metallurgy. Innovations in the New World were equally striking. Indians in Central and South America domesticated a host of plants, among them corn, beans, and squash. From these areas, knowledge of farming techniques spread to still other regions.

6

Chapter 1
Origins
ca. 400,000–1100 B.C.E.

CHAPTER LOCATOR | What do we mean by "the West" and "Western Civilization"?

Stonehenge Megaliths (large stone structures) like the one shown here at Stonehenge can still be seen across the British Isles and in France. A Neolithic society laboriously built this circle to mark the passing of the seasons. (© Frank Siteman/Science Faction/Corbis)

Once people began to rely on farming for their livelihood, they settled in permanent villages and built houses. Early farmers chose places where the water supply was constant and adequate for their crops and flocks. At first, villages were small, consisting of a few households. As the population expanded and prospered, villages usually developed into towns. Towns also became vulnerable to outside attack, and the townspeople responded by building walls. Such walls prove that towns grew in size, population, and wealth, for these fortifications were so large that only a big, dependable labor force would have raised them. They also indicate that towns were developing social and political organizations, since they would have been impossible to build without central planning.

Prosperity had two other momentous consequences. First, grain became an article of commerce. The farming community traded surplus grain for items it could not produce itself. Trade also brought Neolithic communities into touch with one another, making possible the spread of ideas and techniques.

Second, agricultural surplus made possible the division of labor. It freed some members of the community from the necessity of raising food. Artisans and craftsmen devoted their attention to making the new stone tools farming demanded. Other artisans began to shape clay into pottery vessels, which were used to store grain, wine, and oil, and which served as kitchen utensils. Still other artisans wove baskets and cloth. People who could specialize in particular crafts produced more and better goods than any single individual could.

Prosperity and stable conditions nurtured other innovations and discoveries. Neolithic farmers improved their tools and agricultural techniques. They domesticated bigger, stronger animals, such as the bull and the horse, to work for them. To harness the power of these animals, they invented tools like the plow, which came into use by 3000 B.C.E. By 3000 B.C.E. the wheel had also been invented, and farmers devised ways of hitching bulls and horses to wagons. Using animals and machines to do a greater proportion of the work enabled Neolithic farmers to raise more food more efficiently and easily than ever before.

Many scholars consider walled towns the basic feature of Neolithic society. Yet numerous examples prove that some Neolithic towns existed without stone or mud-brick walls. For instance, at Stonehenge in England the natives erected wooden palisades for safety. The most

▪ The Impact of Systematic Agriculture
Gave rise to stable societies and considerable prosperity
Made possible an enormous increase in population
Allowed for economic specialization and material progress
Facilitated the accumulation and spread of knowledge
Prepared the way for urban life

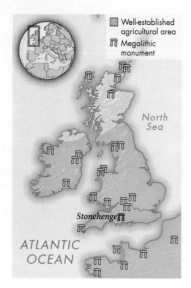

Well-established agricultural area
Megalithic monument

The British Isles, ca. 2500 B.C.E.

concentrated collection of walled towns is found in Mesopotamia. Since generations of archaeologists and historians have concentrated their attention on this region, they have considered it typical. Yet they have failed to properly appreciate circumstances elsewhere. The fundamental point about the Neolithic period is that men and women created stable communities based on agriculture. They defended their towns in various ways by common consent and effort. This organized communal effort is far more important than the types of defenses they built.

Stonehenge presents an example of how the unique context of a Neolithic group influenced the communal efforts of its people. Remnants of this Neolithic society can still be seen today in England. Named after the famous stone circle built approximately 3000–1600 B.C.E., this culture spread throughout the British isles and northwestern France.

Like other similar structures, Stonehenge is a large ring of huge worked stones weighing many tons. It marks the movement of the sun, moon, and stars. It was also a place of ritual ceremony celebrating the renewal of life. Just as the celestial bodies had their annual cycles, the Stonehenge people had their cycles of life and death—and continuity.

The construction of the great circle tells much about the people who built it. Only a relatively large and stable population could have provided a workforce able to devote so many years to its erection. The people first had to quarry the stones and in many cases haul them over long distances. They crossed their neighbors' lands, which indicates shared customs and beliefs. Other circles such as at nearby Avebury housed religious centers in the shape of two large inner circles. Many other structures contained the simple homes of permanent settlers, and still others were fortified enclosures that protected the inhabitants. These sites served various social functions, and they reveal the existence of relatively prosperous, well-organized, and centrally led communities. They also prove cooperation among similarly constituted groups. None of them individually could have built these monuments.

The people themselves lived in the countryside in communities of perhaps fifty families. They farmed the land, kept animals, and made pottery. As in other primitive societies, headmen and groups of elders probably made up a simple communal leadership.

The Stonehenge people enjoyed a surprisingly rich intellectual life. Their stone circles alone prove that they had mastered astronomy, mathematics, and engineering. They intimately knew their environment and cherished a simple religion. Most notably, these people used part of their time over many years to preserve and pass along to future generations the detailed building techniques and mathematics to raise Stonehenge. Yet despite their many wonderful achievements, the Stonehenge people did not develop writing. Without literacy they failed to hand their legacy to others beyond their own culture. Thus all of their learning died with them. Literacy proved one of the supreme advances in history. That breakthrough came in Mesopotamia.

▼ What kind of civilization developed in Mesopotamia?

irrigation A system of watering land and draining it to prevent buildup of salt in the soil; the solution to the problem of arid climates and scant water supplies.

The origins of Western civilization are generally traced to Mesopotamia (mehs-oh-puh-TAY-mee-uh), the Greek name for the land between the Euphrates (yoo-FRAY-teez) and Tigris (TIGH-gris) Rivers. Faced with an arid climate and scant water supplies, Mesopotamian farmers learned to irrigate their land and later to drain it to prevent the buildup of salt in the soil. Irrigation demanded organized group effort. That in turn underscored the need for strong central authority to direct the effort. This led to governments in which

Chapter 1
Origins
ca. 400,000–1100 B.C.E.

8

CHAPTER LOCATOR   What do we mean by "the West" and "Western Civilization"?

individuals subordinated some of their particular concerns to broader interests. These factors made urban life possible in a demanding environment. By about 3000 B.C.E. the Sumerians established the first cities in the southernmost part of Mesopotamia, which became known as Sumer (Map 1.1). The fundamental innovation of the Sumerians was the creation of writing.

Environment and Mesopotamian Development

From the outset, geography had a profound effect on the evolution of Mesopotamian civilization. In this region agriculture is possible only with irrigation. Consequently, the Sumerians and later civilizations built their cities along the Tigris and Euphrates Rivers and their branches. In addition to water, the rivers supplied fish, a major element of the Sumer diet. The rivers also provided reeds and clay, which the Sumerians used as building materials.

Although the rivers sustained life, they acted simultaneously as a powerful restraining force, especially on Sumerian political development. Between the rivers, streams, and irrigation canals stretched open desert or swamp, where hostile nomadic tribes often roamed. Communication between cities was difficult and at times dangerous. City was

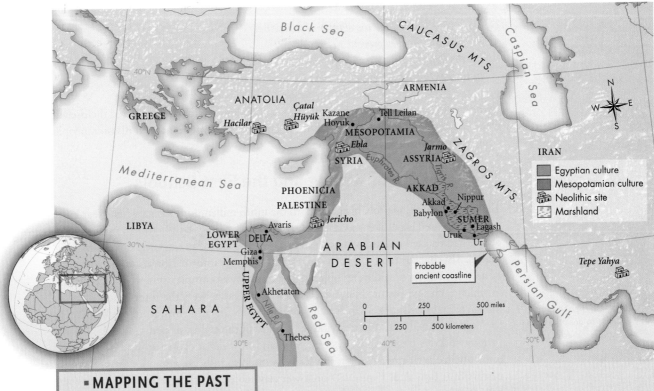

▪ MAPPING THE PAST

Map 1.1 Spread of Cultures in the Ancient Near East, ca. 3000–1640 B.C.E.

This map depicts the area of ancient Mesopotamia and Egypt, a region often called the "cradle of civilization."

ANALYZING THE MAP What geographical features of this region naturally suggest the direction in which civilization spread?

CONNECTIONS Why did Mesopotamia and Egypt earn the title of "cradle of civilization"? Why did the first cultures of Mesopotamia spread farther than the culture of Egypt?

To complete this activity online, go to the Online Study Guide at bedfordstmartins.com/mckaywestunderstanding.

isolated from city, each in its own locale. Thus each Sumerian city became a state, independent of the others and protective of its independence. Any city-state that tried to unify the country was resisted by the others. As a result, the political history of Sumer is one of almost constant warfare. Although Sumer was eventually unified, unification came late and was always tenuous.

The harsh environment fostered a grim, even pessimistic, spirit among the Sumerians and other Mesopotamians. They especially feared the ravages of flood. The Tigris can bring quick devastation. The chronicle of King Hammurabi (see page 16) recorded years when floods wiped out whole cities. Vulnerability to natural disaster deeply influenced Mesopotamian religious beliefs.

The Mesopotamians considered natural catastrophes the work of the gods. The gods, they believed, used nature to punish the Mesopotamians. According to the myth of the Deluge, which gave rise to the biblical story of Noah:

> *A flood will sweep over the cult-centers;*
> *To destroy the seed of mankind . . .*
> *Is the decision, the word of the assembly of the gods.*[1]

The myth of Atrahasis describes the gods' annoyance at the prosperity of mankind and tells how Enlil suggests sending a drought to destroy human life:

> *Oppressive has become the clamor of mankind.*
> *By their uproar they prevent sleep.*
> *Let the flour be cut off for the people,*
> *In their bellies let the greens be too few.*[2]

In the face of harsh environmental conditions, the Mesopotamians considered themselves weak and insignificant as compared to the gods. In response to natural disaster, people could only pray to the gods for relief.

The Invention of Writing and the First Schools

The origins of writing probably go back to the ninth millennium B.C.E., when Near Eastern peoples used clay tokens as counters for record keeping. By the fourth millennium, people had realized that drawing pictures of the tokens on clay was simpler than making tokens. This breakthrough in turn suggested that more information could be conveyed by adding pictures of still other objects. The result was a complex system of pictographs in which each sign pictured an object. These pictographs were the forerunners of a Sumerian form of writing known as cuneiform (kyoo-NEE-uh-form), from the Latin term for "wedge shaped," used to describe the strokes of the stylus, or pen.

cuneiform Sumerian form of writing; the term describes the wedge-shaped strokes of the stylus.

How did this pictographic system work, and how did it evolve around 3000 B.C.E. into cuneiform writing? At first, if a scribe wanted to indicate a star, he simply drew a picture of it (line A of Figure 1.1) on a wet clay tablet, which became rock-hard when baked. This complicated and laborious system had serious limitations. It could not represent abstract ideas or combinations of ideas.

Scribes overcame this problem by combining signs to express meaning. To refer to a slave woman, for example, the scribe used the sign for woman (line B) and the sign for mountain (line C)—literally, "mountain woman" (line D). Because the Sumerians regularly obtained their slave women from the mountains, this combination of signs was easily understandable.

The next step was to simplify the system. Instead of drawing pictures, scribes developed signs that represented ideas. Thus the signs became *ideograms*: they symbolized ideas. The real breakthrough came when the scribes started using signs to represent sounds. For

10

Chapter 1
Origins
ca. 400,000–1100 B.C.E.

CHAPTER LOCATOR · What do we mean by "the West" and "Western Civilization"?

instance, two parallel wavy lines indicated the word *a* or "water" (line E). Besides water, the word *a* in Sumerian also meant "in." The word *in* expresses a relationship that is very difficult to represent pictorially. Instead of trying to invent a sign to mean "in," some clever scribe used the sign for water because the two words sounded alike in Sumerian. This phonetic use of signs made possible the combining of signs to convey abstract ideas.

The Sumerian system of writing was so complicated that only professional scribes mastered it, and even they had to study it for many years. By 2500 B.C. scribal schools flourished throughout Sumer. Most students came from wealthy families and were male. Each school had a master, teachers, and monitors. Discipline was strict, and students were caned for sloppy work and misbehavior. After completing their training, most scribes took administrative positions in the temple or palace, where they kept records of business transactions, accounts, and inventories. But scribal schools did not limit their curriculum to business affairs; they were also centers of culture and scholarship. Topics of study included mathematics, botany, and linguistics. Advanced students copied and studied the classics of Sumerian literature.

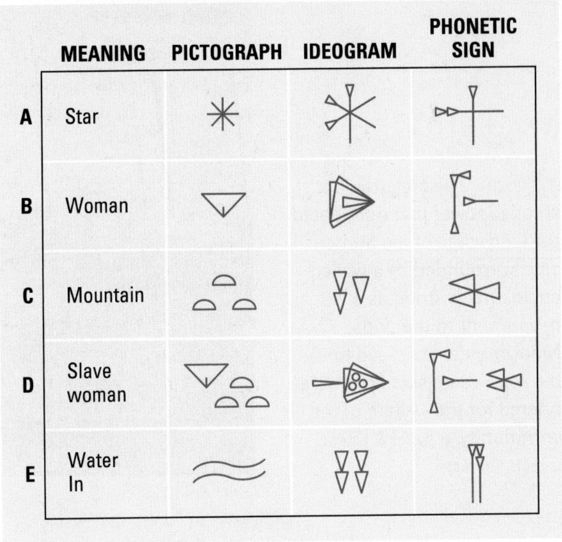

Figure 1.1 Sumerian Writing

(**Source:** Excerpted from S. N. Kramer, *The Sumerians: Their History, Culture and Character.* Copyright © 1963 by The University of Chicago Press. All rights reserved. Used by permission.)

Talented students and learned scribes wrote compositions of their own. As a result, many literary, mathematical, and religious texts survive today, giving a full picture of Mesopotamian intellectual and spiritual life.

Mesopotamian Thought and Religion

The Mesopotamians made significant and sophisticated advances in mathematics, including the development of the concept of place value — that the value of a number depends on where it stands in relation to other numbers. The Mesopotamians did not consider mathematics a purely theoretical science. The building of cities, palaces, temples, and canals demanded practical knowledge of geometry and trigonometry.

Mesopotamian medicine was a combination of magic, prescriptions, and surgery. Mesopotamians believed that demons and evil spirits caused sickness. Physicians could help force a demon out by giving the patient a foul-tasting prescription. As medical knowledge grew, some prescriptions were found to work and thus were true medicines. In this slow but empirical fashion, medicine grew from superstition to an early form of rational treatment.

Mesopotamian thought had a profound impact in theology and religion. The Sumerians originated many beliefs, and their successors added to them. The Mesopotamians practiced polytheism, that is, they believed that many gods ran the world. Mesopotamian gods were powerful and immortal, but otherwise lived their lives much as human beings lived theirs. Like humans, they could be irritable, vindictive, and irresponsible.

polytheism The worship of several gods; this was the tradition of the Mesopotamian and Egyptian religions.

The Mesopotamians worshiped the gods because they were mighty. Human beings were too insignificant to pass judgment on the conduct of the gods, and the gods were too superior to honor human morals. Likewise, it was not the place of men and women to understand the gods. The motives of the gods were not always clear. In times of affliction, one could only offer sacrifices to appease them.

Encouraged and directed by the traditional priesthood, which was dedicated to understanding the ways of the gods, the people erected shrines called ziggurats in the center of each city and then built their houses around them. Their hope was that a god who had a splendid temple might think twice about sending floods to destroy the city.

Ziggurat The ziggurat is a stepped tower that dominated the landscape of the Sumerian city. Surrounded by a walled enclosure, it stood as a monument to the gods. Monumental stairs led to the top, where sacrifices were offered for the welfare of the community. (Charles & Josette Lemars/Corbis)

The Mesopotamians had many myths to account for the creation of the universe. According to one Sumerian myth (echoed in Genesis, the first book of the Bible), only the primeval sea existed at first. The sea produced heaven and earth, which were united. Heaven and earth gave birth to Enlil, who separated them and made possible the creation of the other gods. The later Babylonian culture (page 15) had similar beliefs. These myths are the earliest known attempts to answer the question, "How did it all begin?"

In addition to myths, the Sumerians produced the first epic poem, the *Epic of Gilgamesh* (GIL-guh-mesh), which evolved as a reworking of at least five earlier myths. (See "Listening to the Past: Gilgamesh's Quest for Immortality," page 14.) An epic poem is a narration of the achievements, the labors, and sometimes the failures of heroes that embodies a people's or a nation's conception of its own past. The Sumerian epic recounts the wanderings of Gilgamesh—the semi-historical king of Uruk (OO-rook)—and his search for eternal life. The *Epic of Gilgamesh* shows the Sumerians grappling with such enduring questions as life and death, humankind and deity, and immortality.

Sumerian Social and Gender Divisions

Sumerian society was a complex arrangement of freedom and dependence, and its members were divided into four categories: nobles, free clients of the nobility, commoners, and slaves. Nobles consisted of the king and his family, the chief priests, and high palace officials. Generally, the king rose to power as a war leader; elected by the citizenry, he established a regular army, trained it, and led it into battle. The might of the king and the frequency of warfare quickly made him the supreme figure in the city, and kingship soon became hereditary. The symbol of royal status was the palace, which rivaled the temple in grandeur.

The king and the lesser nobility held extensive tracts of land that were, like the estates of the temple, worked by slaves and clients. Clients were free men and women who were dependent on the nobility. In return for their labor, the clients received small plots of land to work for themselves. Although this arrangement assured the clients of a livelihood, the land they worked remained the possession of the nobility or the temple. Thus, the nobles commanded the obedience of a huge segment of society. They were the dominant force in Mesopotamian society.

Commoners were free and independent of the nobility. They belonged to large families that owned land in their own right. Male commoners, unlike women, had a voice in the political affairs of the city and full protection under the law.

Chapter 1
Origins
12 ca. 400,000–1100 B.C.E.

CHAPTER LOCATOR   What do we mean by "the West" and "Western Civilization"?

At the bottom rung of society were slaves. Some Sumerian slaves were prisoners of war and criminals who had lost their freedom as punishment for their crimes. Still others served as slaves to repay debts. These were more fortunate than the others, because the law required that they be freed after three years. But all slaves were subject to whatever treatment their owners might mete out. They could be beaten and even branded. Yet they received at least some legal protection. Slaves engaged in trade and made profits. They could borrow money, and many slaves were able to buy their freedom.

Sumerian society made clear distinctions based on gender. Sumerian society was **patriarchal**, a system in which most power rests with older adult men. The patriarch of a tribe led the families that made up the tribe, but he cooperated with the heads of other related families. He was supposed to govern wisely and in accordance with custom and family tradition. All members of the tribe and family had various rights and responsibilities. Everyone had a recognized place in the social order. The patriarch generally provided all members with a secure family life.

Patriarchy may have been linked to the private ownership of property for agriculture. Men generally did the plowing and cared for animals, which led to boys being favored over girls for the work they could do for their parents while young and the support they could provide in their parents' old age. Boys became the normal inheritors of family land. Women could sometimes inherit if there were no sons in a family, but they did not gain the political rights that came with land ownership for men.

The city-states that developed in the ancient Middle East, beginning with Sumer, further heightened gender distinctions. Sumer was dominated by hereditary aristocracies, whose members became concerned with maintaining the distinction between themselves and the majority of the population, and by male property owners who wanted to be sure the children their wives bore were theirs. These concerns led to attempts to control women's reproduction. In most states, laws mandated that women be virgins on marriage and imposed strict punishment for a married woman's adultery; sexual relations outside of marriage on the part of husbands were not considered adultery. Concern with family honor thus became linked to women's sexuality in a way that it was not for men; men's honor revolved around their work activities and, for more prominent families, around their performance of public duties.

These economic and political developments were accompanied and supported by cultural norms and religious concepts that heightened gender distinctions. In some places, heavenly hierarchies came to reflect those on earth, with the gods arranged in a hierarchy dominated by a single male god, who was viewed as the primary creator of life. Because other hierarchies such as those of the hereditary aristocracy privileged the women connected to powerful or wealthy men, women did not see themselves as part of a coherent group and often supported the institutions and intellectual structures that subordinated them.

Sumerian Harpist A seated woman plays a simple harp. Her fashionable dress and hat indicate that she is playing at the royal court. Other scenes from art prove that music played a vital part in the lives of all Sumerians. (Erich Lessing/Art Resource, NY)

The human desire to escape the grip of death, to achieve immortality, is one of the oldest wishes of all peoples. The Sumerian Epic of Gilgamesh is the earliest recorded treatment of this topic. The oldest elements of the epic go back at least to the third millennium B.C.E. According to tradition, Gilgamesh was a king of Uruk whom the Sumerians, Babylonians, and Assyrians considered a hero-king and a god. In the story, Gilgamesh and his friend Enkidu set out to attain immortality and join the ranks of the gods. They attempt to do so by performing wondrous feats against fearsome agents of the gods, who are determined to thwart them.

During their quest Enkidu dies. Gilgamesh, more determined than ever to become immortal, begins seeking anyone who might tell him how to do so. His journey involves the effort not only to escape from death but also to reach an understanding of the meaning of life.

The passage begins with Enkidu speaking of a dream that foretells his own death.

" Listen, my friend [Gilgamesh], this is the dream I dreamed last night. The heavens roared, and earth rumbled back an answer; between them I stood before an awful being, the sombre-faced manbird; he had directed on me his purpose. His was a vampire face, his foot was a lion's foot, his hand was an eagle's talon. He fell on me and his claws were in my hair, he held me fast and I smothered; then he transformed me so that my arms became wings covered with feathers. He turned his stare towards me, and he led me away to the palace of Irkalla, the Queen of Darkness [the goddess of the underworld; in other words, an agent of death], to the house from which none who enters ever returns, down the road from which there is no coming back. **"**

At this point Enkidu dies, whereupon Gilgamesh sets off on his own. During his travels he meets with Siduri, the wise and good-natured goddess of wine, who gives him the following advice.

" Gilgamesh, where are you hurrying to? You will never find that life for which you are looking. When the gods created man they allotted to him death, but life they retained in their own keeping. As for you, Gilgamesh, fill your belly with good things; day and night, night and day, dance and be merry, feast and rejoice. Let your clothes be fresh, bathe yourself in water, cherish the little child that holds your hand, and make your wife happy in your embrace; for this too is the lot of man. **"**

Ignoring Siduri's advice, Gilgamesh continues his journey, until he finds the god Utnapishtim (oot-nuh-PISH-tim). Like Gilgamesh, he was once a mortal, but the gods so favored him that they put him in an eternal paradise. Gilgamesh puts to Utnapishtim the question that is the reason for his quest.

" Oh, father Utnapishtim, you who have entered the assembly of the gods, I wish to question you concerning the living and the dead, how shall I find the life for which I am searching?

Utnapishtim said, "There is no permanence. Do we build a house to stand forever, do we seal a contract to hold for all time? Do brothers divide an inheritance to keep forever, does the floodtime of rivers endure? . . . What is there between the master and the servant when both have fulfilled their doom? When the Anunnaki [the gods of the underworld], the judges, come together, and Mammetun [the goddess of fate] the mother of destinies, together they decree the fates of men. Life and death they allot but the day of death they do not disclose."

Then Gilgamesh said to Utnapishtim the Faraway, "I look at you now, Utnapishtim, and your appearance is no different from mine; there is nothing strange in your features. I thought I should find you like a hero prepared for battle, but you lie here taking your ease

▼ How did Mesopotamian culture spread in the Near East?

The Sumerians established the basic social, economic, and intellectual patterns of Mesopotamia, but the Semites played a large part in spreading Sumerian culture far beyond the boundaries of Mesopotamia. The interaction of the Sumerians and Semites, in fact, gives one of the very first glimpses of peoples of different origins coming together. The outcome was the evolution of a new culture that consisted of two or more old parts. In 2331 B.C.E. the Semitic chieftain Sargon conquered Sumer and created the Akkadian empire. Sargon, the first "world conqueror," led his armies to the Persian Gulf. Although

Chapter 1
Origins
ca. 400,000–1100 B.C.E.

14

CHAPTER LOCATOR | What do we mean by "the West" and "Western Civilization"?

on your back. Tell me truly, how was it that you came to enter the company of the gods and to possess everlasting life?" Utnapishtim said to Gilgamesh, "I shall reveal to you a mystery, I shall tell you a secret of the gods." 〞

Utnapishtim then tells Gilgamesh of a time when the great god Enlil had become angered with the Sumerians and encouraged the other gods to wipe out humanity. The god Ea, however, warned Utnapishtim about the gods' decision to send a great flood to destroy the Sumerians. He commanded Utnapishtim to build a boat big enough to hold his family, various artisans, and all animals in order to survive the flood that was to come. Although Enlil was infuriated by the Sumerians' survival, Ea rebuked him. Then Enlil relented and blessed Utnapishtim with eternal paradise. After telling the story, Utnapishtim foretells Gilgamesh's fate.

〝 Utnapishtim said, ". . . The destiny was fulfilled which the father of the gods, Enlil of the mountain, had decreed for Gilgamesh: In netherearth the darkness will show him a light: of mankind, all that are known, none will leave a monument for generations to compare with his. The heroes, the wise men, like the new moon have their waxing and waning. Men will say, Who has ever ruled with might and power like his? As in the dark month,

Gilgamesh from a decorative panel of a lyre unearthed at the Sumerian city of Ur. (The University Museum, University of Pennsylvania, neg. T4-108)

the month of shadows, so without him there is no light. O Gilgamesh, this was the meaning of your dream [of immortality]. You were given the kingship, such was your destiny, everlasting life was not your destiny. Because of this do not be sad at heart, do not be grieved or oppressed; he [Enlil] has given you power to bind and to loose, to be the darkness and the light of mankind. He has given unexampled supremacy over the people, victory in battle from which no fugitive returns, in forays and assaults from which there is no going back. But do not abuse this power, deal justly with your servants in the palace, deal justly before the face of the Sun." 〞

Source: From chs. 3–7 of *The Epic of Gilgamesh*, trans. N. K. Sanders (Penguin Classics, 1960; third edition, 1972), pp. 89–116. Copyright © N. K. Sanders, 1960, 1964, 1972. Reproduced by permission of Penguin Books Ltd.

QUESTIONS FOR ANALYSIS

1. What does the *Epic of Gilgamesh* reveal about Sumerian attitudes toward the gods and human beings?
2. At the end of his quest, did Gilgamesh achieve immortality? If so, what was the nature of that immortality?
3. What does the epic tell us about Sumerian views of the nature of human life? Where do human beings fit into the cosmic world?

his empire lasted only a few generations, it spread Mesopotamian culture throughout the Fertile Crescent. This legacy would be carried on by the Babylonians, who under Hammurabi would unite Mesopotamia politically and culturally.

The Triumph of Babylon

Although the empire of Sargon was extensive, it was short-lived, and within two hundred years it collapsed. The Akkadians, too, failed to solve the problems posed by Mesopotamia's geography and population pattern. It was thus left to the Babylonians to unite the city-states of Mesopotamia politically and culturally.

The Babylonians were Amorites (AM-uh-rites), a Semitic people who had migrated from Arabia and settled on the site of Babylon along the middle Euphrates, where that

Sargon of Akkad This bronze head, with elaborately worked hair and beard, portrays the great conqueror Sargon of Akkad. The eyes were originally inlaid with precious jewels, which have since been gouged out. This head was found in the ruins of the Assyrian capital of Ninevah, where it had been taken as loot. (Interfoto/Alamy)

river runs close to the Tigris. Babylon enjoyed an excellent geographical position and was ideally suited to be the capital of Mesopotamia. It dominated trade on the Tigris and Euphrates Rivers: all commerce to and from Sumer and Akkad had to pass by its walls. It also looked beyond Mesopotamia. Babylonian merchants followed the Tigris north to Assyria (uh-SEER-ee-uh) and Anatolia. The Euphrates led merchants to Syria, Palestine, and the Mediterranean. The city grew great because of its commercial importance and sound leadership.

Babylon was fortunate to have a farseeing and able king, Hammurabi (hahm-moo-RAH-bee) (r. 1792–1750 B.C.E.). Hammurabi set out to do three things: make Babylon secure, unify Mesopotamia, and make Babylon the center of Mesopotamian civilization. The first two he accomplished by conquering Assyria in the north and Sumer and Akkad in the south. Then he turned to his third goal.

Politically, Hammurabi consolidated his power by utilizing the Semitic concept of the tribal chieftain and the Sumerian idea of urban kingship. Culturally, he encouraged the spread of myths that explained how Marduk (MAHR-dook), the god of Babylon, had been elected king of the gods by the other Mesopotamian deities. Hammurabi's success in making Marduk the god of all Mesopotamians made Babylon the religious center of Mesopotamia. Through Hammurabi's genius the Babylonians made their own contribution to Mesopotamian culture—a culture vibrant enough to maintain its identity while assimilating new influences. Hammurabi's conquests and the activity of Babylonian merchants spread this enriched culture north to Anatolia and west to Syria and Palestine.

Life Under Hammurabi

One of Hammurabi's most memorable accomplishments was the proclamation of a law code that offers a wealth of information about daily life in Mesopotamia. Like the codes of the earlier lawgivers, Hammurabi's law code proclaimed that he issued his laws on divine authority "to establish law and justice in the language of the land, thereby promoting the welfare of the people." Hammurabi's code inflicted harsh penalties. Despite its severity, a spirit of justice and a sense of responsibility pervade the code. Hammurabi genuinely felt that his duty was to govern the Mesopotamians as righteously as possible.

The Code of Hammurabi has two striking characteristics. First, the law differed according to the social status and gender of the offender. Nobles were not punished as harshly as commoners, nor commoners as harshly as slaves. Certain actions that were crimes for women were not crimes for men. Second, the code demanded that the punishment fit the crime. It called for "an eye for an eye, and a tooth for a tooth," at least among equals. However, a noble who destroyed the eye of a commoner or slave could pay a fine instead of losing his own eye. Otherwise, as long as criminal and victim shared the same social status, the victim could demand exact vengeance.

Hammurabi's code began with legal procedure. Individuals brought their own complaints before the court. Each side had to produce written documents or witnesses to support its case. In cases of murder, the accuser had to prove the defendant guilty; any accuser who failed to do so was put to death. This strict law was designed to prevent people from lodging groundless charges. Another procedural regulation covered the conduct of judges. Once a judge had rendered a verdict, he could not change it. In this way, the code tried to guarantee a fair trial and a just verdict.

Hammurabi's law code A proclamation in the language of the land issued by the Babylonian king Hammurabi to establish law and justice; it inflicted harsh punishments, but it was pervaded by a sense of responsibility to the people.

Chapter 1
Origins
16
ca. 400,000–1100 B.C.E.

CHAPTER LOCATOR   What do we mean by "the West" and "Western Civilization"?

Consumer protection is not a modern idea; it goes back to Hammurabi's day. Merchants had to guarantee the quality of their goods and services. A boat builder who did sloppy work had to repair the boat at his own expense. House builders guaranteed their work with their lives. If inhabitants died in a house collapse, the builder was put to death. A merchant who tried to increase the interest rate on a loan forfeited the entire amount. Hammurabi's laws tried to ensure that consumers got what they paid for and paid a just price.

Because farming was essential to Mesopotamian life, Hammurabi's code dealt extensively with agriculture. Tenants faced severe penalties for neglecting the land or not working it at all. Since irrigation was essential to grow crops, tenants had to keep the canals and ditches in good repair. Anyone whose neglect of the canals resulted in damaged crops had to bear all the expense of the lost crops. Those tenants who could not pay the costs were forced into slavery.

Hammurabi gave careful attention to marriage and the family. As elsewhere in the Near East, marriage had aspects of a business agreement. The prospective groom or his father and the father of the future bride arranged everything. The groom offered the father a bridal gift, usually money. If the man and his bridal gift were acceptable, the father provided his daughter with a dowry. After marriage the dowry belonged to the woman and was a means of protecting her rights and status. Fathers often contracted marriages while their children were still young, and once contracted, the children were considered to be wed even if they did not live together.

The wife was expected to be rigorously faithful. The penalty for adultery, defined as sex between a married woman and a man not her husband, was death. There was no corresponding law for married men. The husband had the power to spare his wife by obtaining a pardon for her from the king. He could also accuse his wife of adultery even if he had not caught her in the act. If she was found innocent, however, she could take her dowry and leave her husband.

The husband had virtually absolute power over his household. He could even sell his wife and children into slavery to pay debts. Sons did not lightly oppose their fathers, and any son who struck his father could have his hand cut off. A father was free to adopt children and include them in his will. Although the father's power was great, he could not disinherit a son without just cause. Cases of disinheritance became matters for the city to decide, and the code ordered the courts to forgive a son for his first offense. Only if a son wronged his father a second time could he be disinherited.

Prostitution, both male and female, was as common in Mesopotamia as it is today. Though disreputable, it was not illegal in Mesopotamia and was instead taxed. Prostitutes, like Mesopotamians in general, differed in social status. A "temple prostitute" performed sexual acts in the temple as part of her sacred duties. The money went to the maintenance of the temple. Other women lived as courtesans, sexual partners and social companions to wealthy and powerful men, who generally had wives and children as well. Prostitutes and courtesans differed from concubines, who were women who lived with men without marriage. All of them lived under the protection of the law.

Hammurabi's law code took magic as a fact of life. Magic was often associated with religion and medicine. Mesopotamians genuinely believed that supernatural forces could directly and benevolently intervene on their behalf. In devout belief they used chants and incantations to call on higher unseen powers to bring them happiness.

Law codes, preoccupied as they are with the problems of society, provide a bleak view of things, but other Mesopotamian documents give a happier glimpse of life. Although Hammurabi's code dealt with marriage in a hard-fisted fashion, countless wills and testaments show that husbands habitually left their estates to their wives, who in turn willed the property to their children. Hammurabi's code restricted married women from commercial pursuits, but financial documents prove that many women engaged in business without hindrance. Some carried on the family business, while others became wealthy landowners in their own right.

Mesopotamians found their lives lightened by holidays and religious festivals. Traveling merchants brought news of the outside world and swapped marvelous tales. Despite their pessimism, the Mesopotamians enjoyed a vibrant and creative culture that left its mark on the entire Near East.

▼ What were the characteristics of Egyptian civilization?

No other single geographical factor had such a fundamental and profound impact on the shaping of Egyptian life, society, and history as the Nile (Map 1.2). The Egyptians never feared the relatively tame Nile in the way the Mesopotamians feared the Tigris. Instead, they sang its praises:

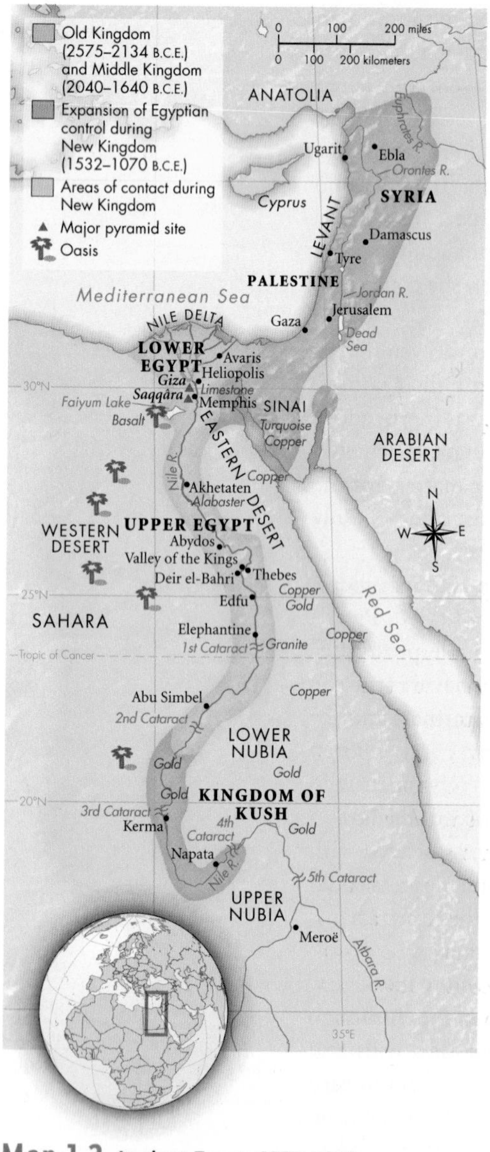

Hail to thee, O Nile, that issues from the earth and comes to keep
   Egypt alive! . . .
He that waters the meadows which Re [Ra] created,
He that makes to drink the desert . . .
He who makes barley and brings emmer [wheat] into being . . .
He who brings grass into being for the cattle . . .
He who makes every beloved tree to grow . . .
O Nile, verdant art thou, who makest man and cattle to live.[3]

To the Egyptians, the Nile was the supreme fertilizer and renewer of the land. Each September the Nile floods its valley, transforming it into a huge area of marsh or lagoon.

The annual flood made growing abundant crops almost effortless, especially in southern Egypt. By the end of November the water retreated, leaving behind a thin covering of fertile mud ready to be planted with crops. The extraordinary fertility of the Nile Valley made it easy to produce an annual agricultural surplus, which in turn sustained a growing and prosperous population. The Nile also unified Egypt. The river was the region's principal highway, promoting easy communication throughout the valley.

Egypt was fortunate in that it was nearly self-sufficient. Besides the fertility of its soil, Egypt possessed enormous quantities of stone, which served as the raw material of architecture and sculpture. Abundant clay was available for pottery, as was gold for jewelry and ornaments. The raw materials that Egypt lacked were close at hand. The Egyptians could obtain copper from Sinai (SIGH-nigh) and timber from Lebanon. They had little cause to look to the outside world for their essential needs, a fact that helps explain the insular quality of Egyptian life.

The God-King of Egypt

Geographical unity quickly gave rise to political unification of the country under the authority of a king whom the Egyptians called "pharaoh." Historians divide Egyptian history into periods. The political unification of Egypt in the Archaic period (3100–2660 B.C.E.) ushered in the period known as the Old Kingdom

Map 1.2 Ancient Egypt, 2575–1070 B.C.E.
Geography and natural resources provided Egypt with centuries of peace and abundance.

18

Chapter 1
Origins
ca. 400,000–1100 B.C.E.

CHAPTER LOCATOR | What do we mean by "the West" and "Western Civilization"?

Ra and Horus The god Ra was the most powerful of the Egyptian gods. Here he takes on the form of Horus, the falcon-god (left). The red circle over Ra's head identifies him as the sun-god. In this scene Ra also assumes characteristics of Osiris, god of the underworld. He stands in judgment of the dead woman on the right. She meets the god with respect but without fear, as he will guide her safely to a celestial heaven. (Egyptian Museum, Cairo)

(2660–2180 B.C.E.), an era remarkable for prosperity, artistic flowering, and the evolution of religious beliefs.

Like the Mesopotamians, the Egyptians were polytheistic in that they worshiped many gods. They developed complex, often contradictory, ideas of their gods that reflected the world around them. The most powerful of these gods was Amon (AH-muhn), a primeval sky-god, and Ra, the sun-god. Amon created the entire cosmos by his thoughts. He caused the Nile to flood and the northern wind to blow. He brought life to the land and its people, and he sustained both. The Egyptians cherished Amon because he championed fairness and honesty, especially for the common people. He was also a magician and physician who cured ills, protected people from natural dangers, and protected travelers. The Egyptians considered Ra the creator of life. He commanded the sky, earth, and underworld. Ra was associated with the falcon-god Horus, the "lord of the sky," who served as the symbol of divine kingship. Horus united Egypt and bestowed divinity on the **pharaoh**. The obvious similarities between Amon and Ra eventually led the Egyptians to combine them into one god, Amon-Ra. Yet the Egyptians never fashioned a formal theology to resolve these differences. Instead they worshiped these gods as different aspects of the same celestial phenomena.

> **pharaoh** The leader of religious and political life in the Old Kingdom, he commanded the wealth, resources, and people of Egypt.

The Egyptians likewise developed views of an afterlife that reflected the world around them. The dry air of Egypt preserves much that would decay in other climates. Thus there was a sense of permanence about Egypt: the past was never far from the present. The

King Menkaure and Queen The pharaoh and his wife represent all the magnificence, serenity, and grandeur of Egypt. (Old Kingdom, Dynasty 4, reign of Mycerinus, 2532–2510 B.C.; Greywacke; H x W x D: 54¹¹/₁₆ x 22³/₈ x 2¹⁵/₁₆ in. (139 x 57 x 54 cm). Harvard University–Museum of Fine Arts Expedition, 11.1738. Museum of Fine Arts, Boston)

Book of the Dead An Egyptian book that preserved ideas about death and the afterlife; it explains that the soul leaves the body to become part of the divine after death.

dependable rhythm of the seasons also shaped the fate of the dead. According to the Egyptians, Osiris (oh-SIGH-ruhs), a fertility god associated with the Nile, died each year, and each year his wife, Isis (EYE-suhs), brought him back to life when the Nile flooded. Osiris eventually became king of the dead, and he weighed human beings' hearts to determine whether they had lived justly enough to deserve everlasting life. Osiris's care of the dead was shared by Anubis, the jackal-headed god who annually helped Isis resuscitate Osiris. Anubis was the god of mummification, so essential to Egyptian funerary rites. The Egyptians preserved these ideas in the *Book of the Dead*, which explained that the soul left the body to become part of the divine after death. It entered gladly through the gate of heaven and remained in the presence of Aton (AHT-on) (a sun-god) and the stars. Thus the Egyptians did not draw a firm boundary between the human and the divine, and life did not end with death.

The focal point of religious and political life in the Old Kingdom was the pharaoh, who commanded the wealth, resources, and people of all Egypt. The pharaoh was so powerful that the Egyptians considered him to be Horus in human form, a living god on earth, who became one with his father Osiris after death. His wife was associated with Isis, for both the queen and the goddess were viewed as protectors. The pharaoh was not simply the mediator between the gods and the Egyptian people. Above all, he was the power that achieved the integration between gods and human beings, between nature and society, and the power that ensured peace and prosperity for the land of the Nile. The pharaoh was thus a guarantee to his people, a pledge that the gods of Egypt (strikingly unlike those of Mesopotamia) cared for their people.

Just as the pharaohs occupied magnificent palaces in life, so they reposed in great pyramids after death. Built during the Old Kingdom, these massive tombs contained all the things needed by the pharaoh in his afterlife. The walls of the burial chamber were inscribed with religious texts and spells relating to the king's journeys after death. The pyramid also symbolized the king's power and his connection with the sun-god. After burial the entrance was blocked and concealed to ensure the pharaoh's undisturbed peace.

The Life of the Pharaoh's People

Egyptian society reflected the pyramids that it built. At the top stood the pharaoh, who was traditionally endowed with absolute power over everyone in the kingdom. In reality he relied on a sizable circle of high officials and their literate staffs to administer his vast lands. High priests also shouldered much of the religious burden of performing necessary rituals and running the lands donated to the various gods. A numerous peasantry made up the broad base of the social pyramid.

The Egyptian view of life and society is alien to those raised with modern concepts of individual freedom and human rights. Yet to ancient Egyptians the pharaoh embod-

Pyramids of Giza Giza was the burial place of the pharaohs of the Old Kingdom and of the aristocracy, whose smaller rectangular tombs surround the two foremost pyramids. (Jose Fuste Raga/Corbis)

ied the concept of **ma'at**, a cosmic harmony that embraced truth, justice, and moral integrity. Ma'at gave the pharaoh the right, authority, and duty to govern. To the people the pharaoh personified justice and order — harmony among themselves, nature, and the divine. They were in effect ruled by a god. If the pharaoh was weak or allowed anyone to challenge his unique and sacred position, he opened the way to chaos. Twice in Egyptian history the pharaoh failed to maintain rigid centralization. During these two eras, known as the First (2180–2080 B.C.E.) and Second Intermediate (1640–1570 B.C.E.) periods, Egypt was exposed to civil war and invasion. Yet the monarchy survived, and in each period a strong pharaoh arose to crush the rebels or expel the invaders and restore order.

In the minds of the Egyptians, the Nile formed an essential part of this cosmic harmony. The river made them farmers and divided their year into three seasons, beginning with its flooding from June to September. During this time farmers were free to work on the pharaoh's building programs. When the water began to recede in October, they diverted some of it into ponds for future irrigation and began planting wheat and barley for bread and beer. From October to February farmers harvested crops. Harvest time generally brought farmers joy, but in Egypt it brought the tax collector. One scribe described the worst that could happen:

> *And now the scribe lands on the river bank is about to register the harvest-tax. The janitors carry staves and the Nubians rods of palm, and they say, Hand over the grain, though there is none. The farmer is beaten all over, he is bound and thrown into a well, soused and dipped head downwards. His wife has been bound in his presence and his children are in fetters.*[4]

That was an extreme situation, but it illustrates the plight of commoners.

The lives of all Egyptians centered around the family. Marriage was a business arrangement, just as in Mesopotamia, arranged by the couple's parents. The couple was expected

ma'at The Egyptian belief in a cosmic harmony that embraced truth, justice, and moral integrity; it gave the pharaohs the right and duty to govern.

Egyptian Home Life

This grave painting depicts an intimate moment in the life of an aristocratic family. As in life, the deceased father sits at the center of his household. Often found in Egyptian tombs are statuettes of cats, family pets and the symbol of the goddess Bastet. (Gianni Dagli Orti/The Art Archive)

ANALYZING THE IMAGE How many different types of people are shown in this scene? How do the depictions of the different groups relate to their status in this household?

CONNECTIONS Based on your reading, do you find this depiction of Egyptian home life accurate? How might an image of a poor family differ from this depiction?

To complete this activity online, go to the Online Study Guide at bedfordstmartins.com/mckaywestunderstanding.

to have children as quickly as possible. They especially wanted boys. Boys continued the family line, and only they could perform the proper burial rites for their father. Yet the family also wanted girls, and the Egyptians did not practice infanticide. The children were especially taught to honor and love their mother. All Egyptians tried to educate their children so that they could prosper, and for that they began with writing. The goal for most ordinary Egyptians was to become scribes.

Wealthy Egyptians lived in spacious homes with attractive gardens and walls for privacy. Such a house had an ample living room and a comfortable master bedroom with an attached bathroom. Smaller rooms served other purposes, including housing family members and servants, and providing space for cows, poultry, and storage. Poorer people lived in cramped quarters. Excavations at Tell el Amarna show that their houses were sixteen and one-half feet wide by thirty-three feet long. The family had narrow rooms for living, including two small rooms for sleeping and cooking. Worst of all, the very poor lived in hovels with their animals.

Life in Egypt began at dawn with a bath and clean clothes. The Egyptians bathed several times a day because of the heat and used soda for soap. Rich and poor alike used perfumes as deodorants. They left the house scantily clad, again because of the heat. Men often wore only a kilt and women a sheath. They all preferred linen clothes because they were cool.

Ordinary women lived a curious combination of restraint and freedom in a male-oriented society. While they obeyed their fathers, husbands, and other men, they possessed considerable rights. Marriage serves as an example. Nothing indicates that any ritual or religious act played any part in it. Marriage seems to have been purely a legal contract in which a woman brought one-third of her family's property to the marriage. The property continued to belong to her, though her husband managed it. She could obtain a divorce simply because she wanted it. If she did, she took her marriage portion with her and could also claim a share of the profits made during her marriage. Women could own land in their own names and operated businesses. The income gave them a strong voice in all family affairs. Women could testify in court and bring legal action against men. These economic factors protected women and gave them an enhanced station in society.

Yet for all of women's economic powers, they held a curious position in marriage. The husband could keep several wives or concubines. One wife, however, remained primary among the others. A husband could order his wife to her quarters and even beat her. But if a man treated his wife too violently, she could take him to court. A man could dispense with his wife for any reason, just as she could leave him. While a husband went unpunished for adultery, the wife suffered death.

Information from literature and art depicts a world in which ordinary husbands and wives enjoyed each others' company alone and together with family and friends. They held parties together, and together accepted invitations to parties. They both participated in the festivities after dinner. Egyptian tomb monuments often show a couple happily standing together, arms around each other. In short, despite constraints that many modern people find distasteful, Egyptian families ordinarily led happy lives.

The Hyksos in Egypt

While Egyptian civilization flourished behind its bulwark of sand and sea, momentous changes were taking place in the ancient Near East, changes that would leave their mark even on rich, insular Egypt. These changes involved enormous and remarkable movements, especially of peoples who spoke Semitic tongues.

The original home of the Semites was perhaps the Arabian peninsula. Some tribes moved into northern Mesopotamia, others into Syria and Palestine, and still others into Egypt. Shortly after 1800 B.C.E. people whom the Egyptians called Hyksos (hik-SOHS), which means "rulers of the uplands," began to settle in the Nile Delta. The movements of the Hyksos were part of a larger pattern of migration of peoples during the First and Second Intermediate periods. The history of Mesopotamia records many such wanderings of people in search of better homes for themselves. Such nomads normally settled in and accommodated themselves with the native cultures. The process was mutual, for each group had something to give to and to learn from the other.

So it was in Egypt, but the historical record, as shown by this description of the events as later recorded by the priest Manetho in the third century B.C.E., depicted the coming of the Hyksos as a brutal invasion:

Unexpectedly from the regions of the east men of obscure race, looking forward confidently to victory, invaded our land, and without a battle easily seized it all by sheer force. Having subdued those in authority in the land, they then barbarously burned

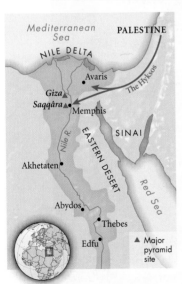

The Hyksos Settlement of Egypt, ca. 1640–1570 B.C.E.

our cities and razed to the ground the temples of the gods. They fell upon all the natives in an entirely hateful fashion, slaughtering them and leading both their children and wives into slavery. At last they made one of their people king, whose name was Salitis.[5]

Although the Egyptians portrayed the Hyksos as a conquering horde, they were probably no more than nomads looking for good land. Their entry into the delta was probably gradual and generally peaceful.

The Hyksos created a capital city at Avaris, located in the northeastern Nile Delta, but they probably exerted direct rule no farther south. The Hyksos brought with them the method of making bronze and casting it into tools and weapons that became standard in Egypt. They thereby brought Egypt fully into the **Bronze Age** culture of the Mediterranean world. Because bronze tools were sharper and more durable than the copper tools they replaced, they made farming more efficient than ever before. The Hyksos's use of bronze armor and weapons as well as horse-drawn chariots and the composite bow, made of laminated wood and horn and far more powerful than the simple wooden bow, revolutionized Egyptian warfare. However much the Egyptians learned from the Hyksos, Egyptian culture eventually absorbed the newcomers. The Hyksos came to worship Egyptian gods and modeled their monarchy on the pharaonic system.

Bronze Age The period in which the production and use of bronze implements became basic to society; bronze made farming more efficient and revolutionized warfare.

The New Kingdom: Revival and Empire

Politically, Egypt was only in eclipse. The Egyptian sun shone again when a remarkable line of kings, the pharaohs of the Eighteenth Dynasty, arose to challenge the Hyksos. These pharaohs pushed the Hyksos out of the delta, subdued Nubia in the south, and conquered Palestine and parts of Syria in the northeast. In this way, Egyptian warrior-

Tutankhamon as Pharaoh This painted casket depicts the pharaoh as the defender of the kingdom repulsing its invaders. Tutankhamon rides into battle under the signs of the sun-disk and the vulture-goddess, indicating that he and Egypt enjoy the protection of the gods. (Egyptian Museum, Cairo)

Chapter 1
Origins
ca. 400,000–1100 B.C.E.

24

CHAPTER LOCATOR | What do we mean by "the West" and "Western Civilization"?

Nefertiti, the "Great Wife"

The long-lost bust of the queen of Egypt. (Bildarchiv Preussischer Kulturbesitz/ Art Resource, NY)

THE EGYPTIANS CALLED the pharaoh's wife the "great wife," somewhat in the way that Americans refer to the president's wife as the "first lady." The great wife legitimized her husband's exercise of power through religious beliefs. The Egyptians believed that she was divinely born and that the god Amon took the human form of her husband, impregnated her, oversaw the development of the child in her womb, and ensured a healthy delivery. Thus the child was the offspring of both the god and the pharaoh. The great wife could not legally be pharaoh, for only a male could exercise that power. Yet only she could make legitimate the pharaoh's right to power. The Egyptians literally and formally considered hers the throne of power, although her power was passive rather than active.

So stood things until Nefertiti, who was an exceptional great wife. Unlike her predecessors, she was not content to play a passive role in Egyptian life. Like her husband, Akhenaten, she passionately embraced the worship of Aton. She used her position to support her husband's zeal to spread the god's worship. Together they built a new palace at Akhetaten, the present Amarna, away from the old centers of power. There they developed and promulgated the cult of Aton to the exclusion of the traditional deities. Nearly the only literary survival of their religious belief is the "Hymn to Aton," which declares Aton to be the only god. It also mentions Nefertiti as "the great royal consort whom he !Akhenaten! loves, the mistress of the Two Lands !Upper and Lower Egypt!"

Until recently historians have thought that Akhenaten divorced and exiled Nefertiti. Scholars now, however, have uncovered a very different and remarkable story of her later life. Instead of rejecting her, Akhenaten made Nefertiti his co-regent. She now jointly ruled Egypt with her husband. After his death, she governed the kingdom in her own right. Yet her rare accession to the sole power came at a dark time in Egyptian history. Hostile neighbors threatened the Egyptian-held Syrian border, among them the Hittites. In a daring move Nefertiti sent a letter to Suppiliuma, the Hittite king, offering to marry one of his sons. The king was stunned, but Nefertiti's move was brilliant. By joining the enemy, she would create a Hittite-Egyptian super-power. Intrigued by the idea, the Hittite king sent her his son Zannanza, but an Egyptian assassinated him, causing the plan to collapse. Nefertiti nonetheless kept Egypt independent and died peacefully, leaving the throne to her son Tutankhamon.

Nefertiti played a novel role in Egyptian art. In funerary and temple art, she is usually depicted with Akhenaten and their daughters. This practice went against the tradition of presenting the royal couple as austere and aloof. Instead, Nefertiti and Akhenaten were portrayed as an ordinary family. Their daughters often appear playing on their parents' laps or with one another. Even Nefertiti's own appearance in Egyptian art was a departure from tradition. As the illustration here shows, the famous bust of her is a realistic, not idealized, portrait. The face is one of grace, beauty, and dignity. It is the portrait of an individual, not a type.

Nefertiti's bust has its own story. When Akhenaten's successor abandoned the palace at Amarna, the site was ignored, except as a source for building materials. Nefertiti's bust remained in the sculptor's workroom, which eventually caved in. There it lay, undamaged, for more than three thousand years. On December 6, 1912, a German archaeological team discovered it intact and sent it to Germany. The authenticity of the bust has recently been challenged, but on flimsy grounds. After World War II, the bust was moved to its current home outside Berlin, where Nefertiti can still be admired today.

QUESTIONS FOR ANALYSIS

1. What were Nefertiti's religious beliefs, and how did she demonstrate them?
2. In what ways was Nefertiti unique among "great wives"?

---

pharaohs inaugurated the New Kingdom—a period in Egyptian history from 1570–1075 B.C.E. characterized by enormous wealth and imperialism. During this period, probably for the first time, widespread slavery became a feature of Egyptian life. The pharaoh's armies returned home leading hordes of slaves who constituted a new labor force for imperial building projects.

What was the significance of the advent of agriculture? | What kind of civilization developed in Mesopotamia? | How did Mesopotamian culture spread in the Near East? | **What were the characteristics of Egyptian civilization?** | How did foreign invasions alter the Near East?

The pharaohs of the Eighteenth Dynasty created the first Egyptian empire. They ruled Palestine and Syria through their officers and incorporated the neighboring region of Nubia into the kingdom of Egypt. Egyptian religion and customs flourished in Nubia, making a huge impact on African culture there and in neighboring areas. The warrior-pharaohs celebrated their success with monuments on a scale unparalleled since the pharaohs of the Old Kingdom had built the pyramids.

One of the most extraordinary of this unusual line of pharaohs was Akhenaten (ah-keh-NAH-tuhn) (r. 1367–1350 B.C.E.), a pharaoh more concerned with religion than with conquest. Nefertiti (nef-uhr-TEE-tee), his wife and queen, encouraged his religious bent. (See "Individuals in Society: Nefertiti, the 'Great Wife,'" page 25.) The precise nature of Akhenaten's religious beliefs remains debatable. Most historians, however, agree that Akhenaten and Nefertiti practiced monotheism; that is, they believed that there was only one universal god—the sun-god Aton, whom they worshiped. They considered all other Egyptian gods and goddesses frauds and disregarded their worship.

monotheism The belief in one universal god.

Akhenaten's monotheism, imposed from above, failed to find a place among the people. The prime reason for Akhenaten's failure is that his god had no connection with the past of the Egyptian people, who trusted the old gods and felt comfortable praying to them. Average Egyptians were no doubt distressed and disheartened when their familiar gods were outlawed, for those gods were the heavenly powers that had made Egypt powerful and unique. The fanaticism and persecution that accompanied the new monotheism were in complete defiance of the Egyptian tradition of tolerant polytheism, or worship of several gods. Thus, when Akhenaten died, his religion died with him.

▼ How did foreign invasions alter the Near East?

At about the same time the Hyksos entered the Nile Delta, the Hittites, who had long been settled in Anatolia (modern Turkey), became a major power in that region and began to expand eastward. The Hittites were the first Indo-Europeans to become important throughout the region. The term Indo-European refers to people who speak a language from a large family of languages that includes English, most of the languages of modern Europe, including Greek and Latin, and languages as far afield as Persian and Sanskrit, spoken in ancient Turkey and India. Around 2000 B.C.E. Indo-Europeans migrated into Anatolia where, after conquering and mingling with the local people, they founded a new kingdom. The Hittites left a lasting imprint on the Near East before the empires of the whole region suffered the shock of new peoples and widespread disruption.

Indo-European Peoples who speak a language from a large family of languages that includes English, most of the languages of modern Europe, Greek, Latin, Persian, and Sanskrit.

The Rise of the Hittites

The rise of the Hittites to prominence in Anatolia is reasonably clear. During the nineteenth century B.C.E. the native kingdoms in the area engaged in suicidal warfare that left most of Anatolia's once-flourishing towns in ashes and rubble. In this climate of destruction, the Hittite king Hattusilis I built a hill citadel at Hattusas from which he led his Hittites against neighboring kingdoms (Map 1.3). Around 1595 B.C.E., Hattusilis's grandson and successor, Mursilis I, extended the Hittite conquests as far as Babylon. Upon his return home, the victorious Mursilis was assassinated by members of his own family, an act that plunged the kingdom into confusion and opened the door to foreign invasion. Mursilis's career is representative of the success and weakness of the Hittites. They were extremely vulnerable to attack by vigilant and tenacious enemies. Yet once they were united behind a strong king, the Hittites were a power to be reckoned with.

Chapter 1
Origins
ca. 400,000–1100 B.C.E.

26

CHAPTER LOCATOR | What do we mean by "the West" and "Western Civilization"?

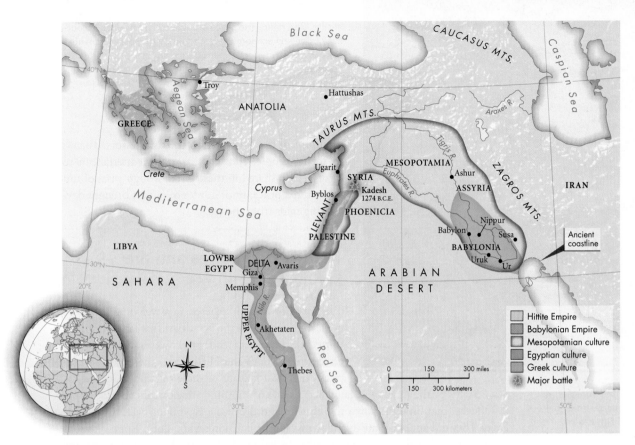

Map 1.3 Balance of Power in the Near East, ca. 1300 B.C.E. This map shows the regions controlled by the Hittites, Egyptians, and Babylonians at the height of their power. The striped area represents the part of Mesopotamia conquered by the Hittites during their expansion eastward.

The Hittites, like the Egyptians of the New Kingdom, produced an energetic and able line of kings who built a powerful kingdom. Perhaps their major contribution was the introduction of iron into warfare and agriculture in the form of weapons and tools. In 1274 B.C.E. the Hittite King Muwattalli attacked the Egyptian army of Rameses II at the Battle of Kadesh in Syria. In hard fighting the Hittites stopped the Egyptian advance, inflicting heavy casualties on the Egyptians. In defeat, Rameses retreated to Egyptian-held territory, leaving the Hittites in control of northern Syria. This battle could have led to further warfare, but instead the Hittites offered the Egyptians peace and then alliance. Formal friendship followed alliance, and active cooperation followed friendship. They next included the Babylonians in their alliance. All three empires developed an official etiquette in which they treated one another as "brothers," using this familial term to indicate their connection. They made alliances for offensive and defensive protection and swore to uphold one another's authority. Hence, the greatest powers of the period maintained peace.

In northwestern Anatolia the Hittites came into contact with Greeks moving into Greece and western Anatolia. The Greeks migrating east were less advanced than the Hittites. They settled among other Indo-European people, such as the little-known Luwians, and established the small kingdom of Wilusa with a capital at Taruisa. The Greeks came under the shaky control of the Hittites, but more important, they became absorbed into the more advanced culture around them. The Hittites thereby helped to bring the sophisticated culture of the East to the emerging culture of the West.

While the Hittites never created a high culture of their own with art and philosophy, they preserved, nourished, and passed on the venerable customs, knowledge, and

What was the significance of the advent of agriculture?   What kind of civilization developed in Mesopotamia?   How did Mesopotamian culture spread in the Near East?   What were the characteristics of Egyptian civilization?   **How did foreign invasions alter the Near East?**

27

traditions of the Near East to their successors. Thanks to them, people from the eastern Mediterranean to Central Asia shared in these gifts through years of uninterrupted peace, until hordes of raiders brought devastating raids from the sea.

The Fall of Empires and the Survival of Cultures

The Battle of Kadesh ushered in a welcome period of peace and stability in the Near East that lasted until the thirteenth century B.C.E. Then, however, foreign invaders destroyed both the Hittite and the Egyptian empires. The most famous of these marauders, called the Sea Peoples by the Egyptians, launched a series of stunning attacks from about 1200 to 1000 B.C.E. that brought down the Hittites and drove the Egyptians back to the Nile Delta. They did not penetrate inland to disrupt the Babylonian kingdom. Nor did the Sea Peoples and other dimly known peoples do serious damage to the social and cultural advances made by their predecessors.

The basic social, economic, and cultural patterns of the Near East not only survived the onslaught but also maintained their hold on the entire area. The disrupted peoples and newcomers followed the same pattern of cultural accommodation as the Sumerians, Hyksos, Hittites, and other groups described earlier in this chapter. Yet it is a mistake to think that the Egyptian and Hittite civilizations survived to face a cultural vacuum.

The Egyptians took the lead in the recovery by establishing commercial contact with their new neighbors. With the exchange of goods went ideas. Both sides shared practical concepts of shipbuilding, metal technology, and methods of trade that allowed merchants safely and efficiently to transact business over long distances. They all—old-timers and newcomers—began to establish and recognize recently created borders, which helped define them geographically and politically. One of the most striking and enduring of these developments was the cultural exchange among them.

When the worst was over, the Egyptians reached beyond their greatly reduced territory to engage in trade with the Semitic peoples of Palestine and Syria whom they found living in small walled towns. Farther north, they encountered the Phoenicians (fih-NEE-shuhnz), a people who combined sophisticated seafaring with urban life.

The situation in northern Syria reflected life in the south. Small cities in all these places were mercantile centers rich not only in manufactured goods but also in agricultural produce, textiles, and metals. The cities flourished under royal families that shared power and dealt jointly in foreign affairs. These northerners relied heavily on their Mesopotamian heritage, which was a product of overland trade with Babylon. While adopting Babylonian writing to communicate with their more distant neighbors to the east, they also adapted it to write their own north Semitic language. Their texts provide a wealth of information about their life. At the same time they welcomed the knowledge of Mesopotamian literature, mathematics, and culture. They worshiped both their own and Mesopotamian deities. The cultural exchange remained a mixture of adoption,

Sea Peoples Foreign invaders who destroyed the Hittite and Egyptian empires in the thirteenth century B.C.E.

28 Chapter 1
Origins
ca. 400,000–1100 B.C.E.

CHAPTER LOCATOR | What do we mean by "the West" and "Western Civilization"?

adaptation, contrast, and finally balance, as the two cultures came to understand and appreciate each other.

Southern Anatolia presented a similar picture. The Hittite kingdom dissolved after repeated attacks. The remaining settlements consisted of trading colonies and small agricultural communities. Thousands of cuneiform tablets testify to commercial and cultural exchanges with Mesopotamia. Here also the Hittite heritage lived on, especially in politics and social relations. In Anatolia, kingship and temple were closely allied, but the government was not a theocracy (rule by a religious authority). A city assembly of adult free men worked together under the king, and a prince administered the cities. Thus some men who were not members of the elite had a voice in political and social affairs. The world of these people rested on a mixture of the Hittite past and their own native achievements. This combination enabled them to create an environment uniquely their own.

← LOOKING BACK LOOKING AHEAD →

THROUGH CENTURIES the peoples of Europe and the ancient Near East progressed from dwelling in caves to dwelling in cities. The development of agriculture allowed Neolithic groups to prosper and to fashion a broad cultural life. The result was more complex and prosperous communities. These developments led to the first genuine urban societies in Mesopotamia. The Sumerian development of writing enabled Mesopotamian culture to be passed on to others. Neighboring peoples adopted their advances in writing, arts and sciences, literature, and religion, thereby spreading it through much of the Near East.

In Egypt another strong culture developed, one that made an impact in Africa, the Near East, and, later, Greece. The Egyptians' pharaonic system and religious beliefs influenced the lives of their neighbors. Into this world came the Hittites, an Indo-European people who learned from their neighbors and rivals. Their political system and alliances would bring peace to the region and influence later peoples.

After a period of devastating raids in the west, the Hittite empire collapsed, leaving a greatly reduced Egypt in the eastern Mediterranean and a stable, but somewhat distant Babylonia in Mesopotamia. The surviving settlements shared the benefits of their societies with the newcomers, who stayed and intermingled with the cultures of the Near East. The newcomers contributed to the advance of Egyptian and Mesopotamian cultures by introducing new technologies and religious ideas. The result was the emergence of a huge group of communities, including the Phoenicians, Hebrews, and Syrians, that enjoyed their own individual character, while at the same time sharing many common features with their neighbors. ■

- **For a list of suggested readings for this chapter, visit** *bedfordstmartins.com/mckaywestunderstanding*.

- **For primary sources from this period, see** *Sources of Western Society*, Second Edition.

- **For Web sites, images, and documents related to topics in this chapter, see Make History at** *bedfordstmartins.com/mckaywestunderstanding*.

■ Chapter 1 Study Guide

Online Study Guide
bedfordstmartins.com/mckaywestunderstanding

Step 1

GETTING STARTED Below are basic terms about this period in the history of Western civilization. Can you identify each term below and explain why it matters? To do this exercise online, go to bedfordstmartins.com/mckaywestunderstanding.

TERMS	WHO (OR WHAT) AND WHEN	WHY IT MATTERS
civilization, p. 5		
Paleolithic period, p. 5		
Neolithic period, p. 5		
irrigation, p. 8		
cuneiform, p. 10		
polytheism, p. 11		
patriarchal, p. 13		
Hammurabi's law code, p. 16		
pharaoh, p. 19		
Book of the Dead, p. 20		
ma'at, p. 21		
Bronze Age, p. 24		
monotheism, p. 26		
Indo-Europeans, p. 26		
Sea Peoples, p. 28		

Step 2

MOVING BEYOND THE BASICS The exercise below requires a more advanced understanding of the chapter material. Begin by filling in the chart included below with descriptions of Mesopotamian and Egyptian society and culture in four key areas: government, religion, economy, and marriage and family life. When you are finished, consider the following questions: How did geography and climate affect the development of each civilization? Why was Egypt generally more stable than Mesopotamia? To do this exercise online, go to bedfordstmartins.com/mckaywestunderstanding.

REGION	GOVERNMENT	RELIGION	ECONOMY	MARRIAGE AND FAMILY LIFE
Mesopotamia				
Egypt				

PUTTING IT ALL TOGETHER Now that you've reviewed key elements of the chapter, take a step back and try to see the big picture. Remember to use specific examples from the chapter in your answers. To do this exercise online, go to bedfordstmartins.com/mckaywestunderstanding.

THE WEST AND WESTERN CIVILIZATION

- What do we mean by "the West"? How has the meaning of the term changed over time?

- What is a civilization? How does a civilization differ from less developed forms of society?

AGRICULTURE AND THE EMERGENCE OF CIVILIZATION

- Compare and contrast Paleolithic and Neolithic society. How did the advent of systematic agriculture help produce the differences between the two societies?

- What role did community play in Neolithic life? How did Neolithic communities differ from Paleolithic communities?

MESOPOTAMIAN CIVILIZATION

- How did geography shape the development of Mesopotamian civilization? How did the environment influence political structures, social hierarchy, and religious ideas?

- How did Mesopotamian culture become the dominant culture of the Near East? Why did it appeal to so many of the peoples of the region?

EGYPTIAN CIVILIZATION AND THE NEAR EAST

- How did geography shape the development of Egyptian civilization? To what extent do environmental factors explain the differences between Egyptian and Mesopotamian society?

- How did New Kingdom Egypt go about building an empire? Why was the Egyptian empire more stable than the empires of the Near East?

- How did Near Eastern civilization survive the fall of the Near Eastern empires? What explains its persistence in the face of political and military disaster?

■ **In Your Own Words** Imagine that you must explain Chapter 1 to someone who hasn't read it. What would be the most important points to include and why?

2

Small Kingdoms and Mighty Empires in the Near East

ca. 1100–513 B.C.E.

The migratory invasions that brought down the Hittites and stunned the Egyptians in the late thirteenth century B.C.E. ushered in an era of confusion and weakness. Although much was lost in the chaos, the old cultures of the ancient Near East survived to nurture new societies. In the absence of powerful empires, the Phoenicians, Hebrews, and many other peoples carved out small independent kingdoms until the Near East was a patchwork of them. During this period Hebrew culture and religion evolved under the influence of urbanism, kings, and prophets.

In the ninth century B.C.E. this jumble of small states gave way to an empire that for the first time embraced the entire Near East. Yet the same ferocity of the Assyrian Empire that led to its rise contributed to its downfall only two hundred years later. The Chaldeans, a Semitic-speaking people who had long dwelt in northern Mesopotamia, now became strong enough to create a new kingdom in Babylon. In 550 B.C.E. the Persians and Medes (meeds), Indo-Europeans who had migrated into Iran, created a "world empire" stretching from Anatolia in the west to the Indus Valley in the east. For over two hundred years, the Persians gave the ancient Near East peace and stability. ■

Life in an Empire. The kings subject to the Persians brought tribute to King Darius at his palace at Persepolis. Here a Phoenician king bears his gift of loyalty. (© Kazuyoshi Nomachi/Corbis)

Chapter Preview

▶ What new kingdoms arose in the Near East after 1100 B.C.E.?

▶ What was unique about Hebrew civilization?

▶ What explains the rise and fall of the Assyrians?

▶ How did the Persian Empire differ from its predecessors?

▼ What new kingdoms arose in the Near East after 1100 B.C.E.?

The fall of empires ushered in a period of cultural diffusion, an expansion of what had already transpired in the broad region. Even though empires expired, many small kingdoms survived, along with a largely shared culture. These small states and local societies had learned much from the great powers, but they nonetheless retained their own lore and native traditions, which they passed on to their neighbors, thus diffusing a Near Eastern culture that was slowly becoming common. The best-known examples can be found along the coast of the eastern Mediterranean, where various peoples created homes and petty kingdoms in Phoenicia and Palestine.

The End of Egyptian Power

The invasions of the Sea Peoples brought the great days of Egyptian power to an end. The long wars against invaders weakened and impoverished Egypt, causing political upheaval and economic chaos. One scribe left behind a somber portrait of stunned and leaderless Egypt:

> The land of Egypt was abandoned and every man was a law to himself. During many years there was no leader who could speak for others. Central government lapsed, small officials and headmen took over the whole land. . . . In the distress and vacuum that followed . . . men banded together to plunder one another. They treated the gods no better than men, and cut off the temple revenues.[1]

No longer able to dream of foreign conquests, Egypt looked to its own security from foreign invasion. Egyptians suffered four hundred years of political fragmentation, a new dark age known as the Third Intermediate Period (ca. 1100–653 B.C.E.).

In southern Egypt, meanwhile, the pharaoh's decline opened the way to the Nubians, who extended their authority northward throughout the Nile Valley. Since the imperial days of the Eighteenth Dynasty (see Chapter 1), the Nubians had adopted many features of Egyptian culture. Now Nubian kings and nobles embraced Egyptian culture wholesale. Libyans from North Africa also filtered into the Nile Delta, where they established independent dynasties. From 950 to 730 B.C.E. northern Egypt was ruled by Libyan pharaohs. The Libyans built cities, and for the first time a sturdy urban life grew up in the delta. Although the coming of the Libyans changed the face of the delta, the Libyans, like the Nubians, eagerly adopted Egypt's religion and way of life. Thus the Nubians and the Libyans repeated an old Near Eastern phenomenon: new peoples conquered old centers of political and military power but were assimilated into the older culture.

Nubian Cylinder Sheath The purpose of this sheath is unknown, but it and many others were found in the tombs of the kings of Kush in the Sudan. The winged goddess at the bottom stands between two figures of the Egyptian god Amon-Ra. The sheath plainly shows the Nubian debt to Egyptian religion and art. (Nubian, Napatan Period, reign of King Amani-natake-lebte, 538–519 B.C. Findspot: Sudan, Nubia, Nuri, Pyramid 10. Gilded silver, colored paste inclusions. Height × diameter: 12 × 3.1 cm [4¾ × 1¼ in.]. Museum of Fine Arts, Boston. Harvard University–Boston Museum of Fine Arts Expedition, 20.275)

Chapter 2
Small Kingdoms and Mighty Empires
in the Near East • ca. 1100–513 B.C.E.

34

The reunification of Egypt occurred late and unexpectedly. With Egypt distracted and disorganized by foreign invasions, an independent African state, the kingdom of Kush, grew up in the region of modern Sudan with its capital at Nepata. Like the Libyans, the Kushites worshiped Egyptian gods and used Egyptian hieroglyphs. In the eighth century B.C.E. their king, Piankhy, swept with his army through the entire Nile Valley. United once again, Egypt enjoyed a brief period of peace during which Egyptians continued to assimilate their conquerors. Nonetheless, reunification of the realm did not lead to a new Egyptian empire.

Yet Egypt's legacy to its African neighbors remained vibrant and rich. By trading and exploring southward along the coast of the Red Sea, the Egyptians introduced their goods, religion, and ideas as far south as Ethiopia. Egypt was also the primary civilizing force in Nubia, which became another version of the pharaoh's realm, complete with royal pyramids and Egyptian deities.

The Rise of Phoenicia

One of the peoples who rose to prominence in the wake of the Sea Peoples' attacks were the Phoenicians, Semitic-speakers who had long inhabited several cities along the Mediterranean coast of modern Lebanon. Although they had lived during the great days of the Hittites, Egyptians, and Babylonians, in this period the Phoenicians came into their own. Now fully independent, the Phoenicians took to the sea. They were master shipbuilders, and with their stout ships, between about 900 and 550 B.C.E. they became the seaborne merchants of the Mediterranean.

The growing success of the Phoenicians, combined with peace in the Near East, brought them prosperity. They began to manufacture goods for export and expanded their trade to Egypt. Moving beyond Egypt, they struck out along the coast of North Africa to establish new markets in places where they encountered little competition. This route led them to establish Carthage, meaning "new city" in Phoenician, which prospered to become the leading city in the western Mediterranean.

Phoenician Ships These small ships seem too frail to breast the waves. Yet Phoenician mariners routinely sailed them, loaded with their cargoes, to the far ports of the Mediterranean. (British Museum/Michael Holford)

CHAPTER LOCATOR | **What new kingdoms arose in the Near East after 1100 B.C.E.?** | What was unique about Hebrew civilization? | What explains the rise and fall of the Assyrians? | How did the Persian Empire differ from its predecessors?

35

HIEROGLYPHIC	REPRESENTS	UGARITIC	PHOENICIAN	GREEK	ROMAN
	Throw stick	T	ʌ	Γ	G
	Man with raised arms	E	ⅎ	E	E
	Basket with handle	▷	↓	K	K
	Water		⌐	M	M
	Snake		⸜	N	N
	Eye	◁	O	O	O
	Mouth		?	Π	P
	Head		9	P	R
	Pool with lotus flowers		W	Σ	S
	House		9	B	B
	Ox-head		K	A	A

Figure 2.1 **Origins of the Alphabet** This figure shows the origin of many of the letters of our alphabet. As peoples encountered a form of writing, each altered the sign without changing its value. (**Source:** A. B. Knapp, *The History and Culture of Ancient Western Asia and Egypt*, 1/e. Copyright © 1988 Wadsworth, a part of Cengage Learning, Inc. Reproduced by permission. www.cengage.com/permissions.)

Although the Phoenicians did not found colonies, as did the later Greeks, they planted trading posts and small farming communities along the coast. From them they shared the vital culture of the more developed Near East with less urbanized peoples. Yet they did not impose their culture, preferring instead to let the natives adopt whatever they found desirable. In this peaceful fashion the Phoenicians spread their trade and something of their customs. Their trade routes eventually took them to the far western Mediterranean and beyond to the Atlantic Ocean.

Phoenician culture was urban, based on the prosperous commercial centers of Tyre, Sidon, and Byblos. The Phoenicians' overwhelming cultural achievement was the development of an alphabet (Figure 2.1): unlike other literate peoples, they used one letter to designate one sound, a system that vastly simplified writing and reading. The Greeks would later modify this alphabet and use it to write their own language.

▼ What was unique about Hebrew civilization?

The fall of the Hittite Empire and Egypt's collapse created a vacuum of power in the western Near East that allowed for the rise of numerous small states. South of Phoenicia arose the land of the ancient Hebrews. Early Jewish history, like that of most other peoples, is compounded of myths, legends, and facts. While the Hebrew Bible preserves many stories of events that defy the laws of nature, historians and archaeologists have

Chapter 2
**Small Kingdoms and Mighty Empires
in the Near East** • ca. 1100–513 B.C.E.

36

The Golden Calf According to the Hebrew Bible, Moses received the Ten Commandments on Mt. Sinai. He descended to find the Hebrews worshiping a golden calf, which was against Yahweh's laws. In July 1990 an American archaeological team found this model of a gilded calf inside a pot. The figurine, which dates to about 1550 B.C.E., is strong evidence for the existence of the cult represented by the calf in Palestine. (Courtesy of the Leon Levy Expedition to Ashkelon. Photo: Carl Andrews)

been able to verify other aspects of the Bible. A conflict has arisen between those who accept the Bible as truth and those who demythologize it. Myth often contains grains of truth, but just as important, myth represents what people believe happened. Pitting myth against history, therefore, is the wrong approach. It is preferable to understand what both contribute to our understanding of the past.

The Hebrew State

Earlier Mesopotamian and Egyptian sources refer to people called the Hapiru, independent nomads who roamed the Near East in search of pasturage for their flocks. According to Hebrew tradition, the followers of Abraham migrated from Mesopotamia around 2184 B.C.E., and Egyptian documents record Hapiru already in Syria and Palestine in 2000 B.C.E. The Hebrews are believed to have been a part of this group. Together with other seminomadic peoples, they migrated into the Nile Delta seeking good land. There the Egyptians enslaved them.

The period of enslavement and the subsequent release of the Hebrews—Passover and the Exodus—form a pivotal episode in their history, though historians have yet to find proof of a large-scale exodus. According to the Hebrew Bible, Moses threatened the pharaoh with the death of all first-born sons of the Egyptians. He instructed the Hebrews to prepare a hasty meal of a sacrificed lamb eaten with unleavened bread. The blood of the lamb was painted over the doors of Hebrew houses. At midnight the Hebrew God Yahweh (YAH-way) spread death over the land, but he passed over the Hebrew houses with the blood-painted doors. This was literally the Passover of Yahweh. The next day a terrified pharaoh ordered the Hebrews out of Egypt. Moses then led them in search of the Promised Land, a period known as the Exodus. During the Exodus Yahweh summoned Moses to Mount Sinai, where he made a covenant with the Hebrews as his chosen people (see page 38). After forty years of wandering in the desert, Yahweh led the Hebrews to the holy land. While the story of their flight has not been substantiated, we do know that the Hebrews finally settled in Palestine in the thirteenth century B.C.E.

In Palestine the Hebrews encountered the Philistines; the Amorites, relatives of Hammurabi's Babylonians; and the Semitic-speaking Canaanites. Despite numerous wars, contact between the Hebrews and their new neighbors was not always hostile. The Hebrews freely mingled with the Canaanites, and some went so far as to worship Baal, an ancient Semitic fertility god represented as a golden calf. Once again, newcomers adapted themselves to the culture of an older, well-established people.

Yahweh The Hebrew god that appeared to Moses on Mount Sinai and made a covenant with the Hebrews; in Medieval Latin he became known as Jehovah.

Possible Route of the Hebrew Exodus, ca. 1250 B.C.E.

CHAPTER LOCATOR | What new kingdoms arose in the Near East after 1100 B.C.E.? | **What was unique about Hebrew civilization?** | What explains the rise and fall of the Assyrians? | How did the Persian Empire differ from its predecessors?

37

Map 2.1 Small Kingdoms of the Near East, ca. 800 B.C.E.
This map illustrates the political fragmentation of the Near East after the death of Solomon.

The greatest danger to the Hebrews came from the Philistines, whose superior technology and military organization at first made them invincible. In Saul (ca. 1000 B.C.E.) the Hebrews found a champion and a spirited leader. In the biblical account Saul and his men battled the Philistines for control of the land, often without success. In the meantime Saul established a monarchy over the twelve Hebrew tribes.

Saul's work was carried on by David of Bethlehem, who pushed back the Philistines and waged war against his other neighbors. To give his kingdom a capital, he captured the city of Jerusalem, which he enlarged, fortified, and made the religious and political center of his realm. David's military successes won the Hebrews unprecedented security, and his forty-year reign was a period of vitality and political consolidation. His work in consolidating the monarchy and enlarging the kingdom paved the way for his son Solomon.

Solomon (ca. 965–925 B.C.E.) applied his energies to creating the nation of Israel out of a collection of tribes ruled by a king. He divided the kingdom into twelve territorial districts, cutting across the old tribal borders. To bring his kingdom up to the level of its more sophisticated neighbors, he set about a building program. Work was begun on a magnificent temple in Jerusalem and on cities, palaces, fortresses, and roads. The temple in Jerusalem was intended to be the religious heart of the kingdom and the symbol of Hebrew unity. Yet Solomon's efforts were hampered by strife. In the eyes of some people, he was too ready to unite other religions with the worship of the Hebrew god Yahweh. The financial demands of his building program drained the resources of his people, and his use of forced labor for building projects further fanned popular resentment.

At his death, the united state of Israel broke into two parts, with one part retaining the name Israel (Map 2.1). The northern part of the kingdom of David and Solomon became Israel, with its capital at Samaria. The southern half was Judah, and Jerusalem remained its center. With political division went a religious rift: Judah worshiped Yahweh alone; while Israel, the northern kingdom, established rival sanctuaries for gods other than Yahweh. War soon broke out between them.

Eventually, in 722 B.C.E., Israel was wiped out by the Assyrians (see page 43), but Judah survived numerous calamities until the Neo-Babylonians crushed it in 587 B.C.E. The survivors were sent into exile in Babylonia, a period of exile commonly known as the **Babylonian Captivity**. In 538 B.C.E., after the Persians defeated the Babylonians, King Cyrus the Great permitted some forty thousand exiles to return to Jerusalem. During and especially after the Babylonian Captivity, the exiles redefined their beliefs and practices and thus established what they believed was the law of Yahweh. Those who lived by these precepts came to be called Jews.

Babylonian Captivity
Period from 587 to 538 B.C.E. during which the survivors of a Babylonian attack on the southern kingdom of Judah were exiled in Babylonia.

The Evolution of Jewish Religion

Hand in hand with their political evolution, the Hebrews were evolving their spiritual ideas. Their chief literary product, the Hebrew Bible, has fundamentally influenced both Christianity and Islam and still exerts a compelling force on the modern world.

Fundamental to an understanding of the Jewish religion is the concept of the **Covenant**, a formal agreement between Yahweh and the Hebrew people that if the Hebrews worshiped Yahweh as their only god, he would consider them his chosen people and protect them from their enemies. The Hebrews believed that Yahweh had led them out of bondage in Egypt and had helped them conquer Israel, the Promised Land. In return, the Hebrews worshiped Yahweh alone and obeyed his Ten Commandments, an ethical code of conduct revealed to them by Moses.

Unlike Akhenaten's Egyptian brand of monotheism (see Chapter 1), Hebrew monotheism became the religion of a whole people. Yet the Hebrews did not consider it their duty to spread the belief in the one god, as later Christians did. As the chosen people, their chief duty was to maintain the worship of Yahweh as he demanded. That worship was embodied in the Ten Commandments, which forbade the Hebrews to steal, murder, lie, or commit adultery. The Covenant was a constant force in Hebrew life. (See "Listening to the Past: The Covenant Between Yahweh and the Hebrews," page 40.)

From the Ten Commandments evolved Hebrew law. The earliest part of this code, the Torah or Mosaic law, was often as harsh as Hammurabi's code (see Chapter 1), which had a powerful impact on it. Later tradition, largely the work of prophets who lived from the eleventh to the fifth centuries B.C.E., put more emphasis on righteousness than on retribution.

The uniqueness of the Hebrews' religion can be seen by comparing the essence of Hebrew monotheism with the religious outlook of the Mesopotamians. Whereas the Mesopotamians considered their gods capricious, the Hebrews believed that their god would protect them and make them prosper if they obeyed his commandments. The Jews felt that magicians, witches, astrologers, and soothsayers harmfully and wrongly usurped powers that properly belonged to Yahweh. The Mesopotamians, however, accepted magic as a natural part of their religious life. The Mesopotamians thought human beings insignificant compared to the gods, so insignificant that the gods might even be indifferent to them. The Hebrews, too, considered themselves puny in comparison with Yahweh. Yet they believed that they were Yahweh's chosen people, whom he had promised never to abandon. Finally, though the Mesopotamians believed that the gods generally preferred good to evil, their religion did not demand ethical conduct. The Hebrews could please their god only by living up to high moral standards as well as worshiping him.

Yahweh is a single god, not surrounded by lesser gods and goddesses; there is thus no female divinity in Judaism, though occasionally aspects of God are described in feminine terms. Though Yahweh is conceptualized as masculine, he did not have sexual relations as Mesopotamian, Egyptian, and Greek male deities did. His masculinity was spiritualized, and human sexual relations were considered a source of ritual impurity. Despite this, sex itself was basically good because it was part of Yahweh's creation, and the bearing of children was seen in some ways to be a religious function. In the codes of conduct written down in the Hebrew Bible, sex between a married woman and a man not her husband was an abomination, as were incest and sex between men. Men were free to have sexual relations with concubines, servants, and slaves, as well as with their wives. The possibility of divorce was also gender-specific: a man could divorce his wife unilaterally, but a wife could not divorce her husband, even for desertion. In general Judaism frowned on celibacy, and almost all major Jewish thinkers and rabbis were married.

Religious leaders were important in Judaism, but not as important as the Torah and the Talmud they interpreted; these texts came to be regarded as the word of Yahweh and thus had a status other writings did not. The most important task for observant Jews was studying religious texts, an activity limited to men until the twentieth century. Women were obliged to provide for men's physical needs so that they could study, which often meant that Jewish women were more active economically than their contemporaries of other religions. Women's religious rituals tended to center on the home, while men's centered on the temple.

Covenant A formal agreement between Yahweh and the Hebrew people that if the Hebrews worshiped Yahweh as their only god, he would consider them his chosen people and protect them from their enemies.

CHAPTER LOCATOR | What new kingdoms arose in the Near East after 1100 B.C.E.? | **What was unique about Hebrew civilization?** | What explains the rise and fall of the Assyrians? | How did the Persian Empire differ from its predecessors?

39

The Covenant Between Yahweh and the Hebrews

These passages from the Hebrew Bible address two themes important to Hebraic thinking. The first is the meaning of kingship; the second is the nature of the Covenant between the Hebrews and their God, Yahweh.

The background of the excerpt is a political crisis that has some archaeological support. The war with the Philistines put a huge strain on Hebrew society. The passage below describes an incident when Nahash, the king of the Ammonites, threatened to destroy the Hebrews. New and effective political and military leadership was needed. The elders of the tribes had previously chosen judges to lead the community only in times of crisis. The Hebrews, however, demanded that a kingship be established, even though Yahweh was their king. They turned to Samuel, the last of the judges, who anointed Saul as the first Hebrew king. In this excerpt Samuel reviews the political, military, and religious situation confronting the Hebrews, reminding them of their obligation to honor the Covenant and expressing hesitation in naming a king.

❝ Then Nahash the Ammonite came up and encamped against Jabeshgilead: and all the men of Jabesh said unto Nahash, Make a covenant with us, and we will serve thee. And Nahash the Ammonite answered them, On this condition will I make a covenant with you, that I may thrust out all your right eyes, and lay it for a reproach upon all Israel. And the elders of Jabesh said unto him, Give us seven days' respite, that we may send messengers unto all the coasts of Israel: and then, if there be no man to save us, we will come out to thee.

Then came the messengers to Gibeah of Saul, and told the tidings in the ears of the people: and all the people lifted up their voices, and wept. And, behold, Saul came after the herd out of the field; and Saul said, What aileth the people that they weep? And they told him the tidings of the men of Jabesh. And the Spirit of God came upon Saul when he heard those tidings, and his anger was kindled greatly. And he took a yoke of oxen, and hewed them in pieces, and sent them throughout all the coasts of Israel by the hands of messengers, saying, Whosoever cometh not forth after Saul and after Samuel, so shall it be done unto his oxen. And the fear of the Lord fell on the people, and they came out with one consent. And when he numbered them in Bezek, the children of Israel were three hundred thousand, and the men of Judah thirty thousand. And they said unto the messengers that came, Thus shall ye say unto the men of Jabeshgilead, To morrow, by that time the sun be hot, ye shall have help. And the messengers came and shewed it to the men of Jabesh; and they were glad. Therefore the men of Jabesh said, To morrow we will come out unto you, and ye shall do with us all that seemeth good unto you. And it was so on the morrow, that Saul put the people in three companies; and they came into the midst of the host in the morning watch, and slew the Ammonites until the heat of the day: and it came to pass, that they which remained were scattered, so that two of them were not left together.

And the people said unto Samuel, Who is he that said, Shall Saul reign over us? bring the men, that we may put them to death. And Saul said, There shall not a man be put to death this day: for to day the Lord hath wrought salvation in Israel. Then said Samuel to the people, Come, and let us go to Gilgal, and renew the kingdom there. And all the people went to Gilgal; and there they made Saul king before the Lord in Gilgal; and there they sacrificed sacrifices of peace offerings before the Lord; and there Saul and all the men of Israel rejoiced greatly.

And Samuel said unto all Israel, Behold, I have hearkened unto your voice in all that you said to me, and have made a king over you. And now, behold, the king walks before you; and I am old and grayheaded; and behold, my sons are with you: and I have walked before you from my childhood until this day. Behold, here I am: witness against me before the Lord, and before his anointed: whose ox have I taken? or whose ass have I taken? or whom have I defrauded? whom have I oppressed? or of whose hand have I received any bribe to blind my eyes with it? and I will restore it to you.

And they said, You have not defrauded us, nor oppressed us, neither have you taken anything from any man's hand. And he said to them, the Lord is witness against you, and his anointed is witness this day,

The Lives of the Hebrews

The nomadic Hebrews first entered Palestine as tribes, numerous families who thought of themselves as all related to one another. At first, good farmland, pastureland, and freshwater sources were held in common by the tribe. Typically each family or group of families in the tribe drew lots every year to determine who worked which fields. But as formerly nomadic peoples turned increasingly to settled agriculture, communal use of land gave way to family ownership. In this respect, the experience of the ancient Hebrews

that you have not found anything in my hand. And they answered, he is witness. And Samuel said unto the people, It is the Lord that advanced Moses and Aaron, and that brought your fathers up out of the land of Egypt. Now therefore stand still, that I may reason with you before the Lord of all the righteous acts of the Lord, which he did to you and your fathers. 🔊

At this point Samuel reminds the Hebrews of their Covenant with Yahweh. He lists the times when they had broken that Covenant, the times when they had served other gods. He also reminds them of Yahweh's punishment for their backsliding. He tells them frankly that they are wrong to demand a king to rule over them, for Yahweh was their lord, god, and king. Nonetheless, Samuel gives way to their demands.

🔊 Now therefore behold the king whom you have chosen, and whom you have desired! and behold, the Lord has set a king over you. If you will fear the Lord, and serve him, and obey his voice, and not rebel against the commandment of the Lord, then shall both you and also the king who reigns over you continue following the Lord your God: But if you will not obey the voice of the Lord, but rebel against the commandment of the Lord, then shall the hand of the Lord be against you, as it was against your fathers. Now therefore stand and see this great thing, which the Lord will do before your eyes. Is it not wheat harvest today? I will call to the Lord, and he shall send thunder and rain; that you may perceive and see that your wickedness is great, which you have done in the sight of the Lord, in asking you a king. So Samuel called to the Lord; and the Lord sent thunder and rain that day: and all the people greatly feared the Lord and Samuel. And all the people said to Samuel, pray for your servants to the Lord your God, so that we will not die: for we have added to all of our sins this evil, to ask us for a king. And Samuel said to the people, Fear not: you have done all this wickedness; yet turn not aside from following the Lord, but serve the Lord with all your

Ark of the Covenant depicted in a relief from a synagogue in Capernaum, second century C.E. (Ancient Art & Architecture Collection)

heart; And do not turn aside; for then should you go after vain things, which cannot profit nor deliver; for they are vain. For the Lord will not forsake his people for his great name's sake: because it pleases the Lord to make you his people. Moreover, as for me, God forbid that I should sin against the Lord in ceasing to pray for you: but I will teach you the good and the right way: Only fear the Lord, and serve him in truth with all your heart: for consider how great things he has done for you. But if you shall still act wickedly, you will be consumed, both you and your king. 🔊

Source: 1 Samuel 11:1–15; 12:1–7, 13–25. Abridged and adapted from *The Holy Bible*, King James Version.

QUESTIONS FOR ANALYSIS

1. How did Samuel explain his anointment of a king?
2. What was Samuel's attitude toward kingship?
3. What were the duties of the Hebrews toward Yahweh? How might those duties conflict with those toward the secular king? How might the Hebrews avoid the conflict?

seems typical of that of many early peoples. Slowly the shift from nomad to farmer affected far more than just how people fed themselves. Family relationships reflected evolving circumstances. With the transition to settled agriculture, the tribe gradually became less important than the extended family. As in Mesopotamia, land was handed down within families, generally from father to son.

For women, the evolution of Jewish society led to less freedom of action, especially in religious life. At first women served as priestesses in festivals and religious cults. Over the course of time, however, the worship of Yahweh became more male-oriented and

CHAPTER LOCATOR | What new kingdoms arose in the Near East after 1100 B.C.E.? | **What was unique about Hebrew civilization?** | What explains the rise and fall of the Assyrians? | How did the Persian Empire differ from its predecessors?

41

male-dominated. Women were seen as ritually impure because of menstruation and childbirth, and as a result their role in religion was much reduced. For the most part, women were largely confined to the home and the care of the family.

The typical marriage in ancient Israel was monogamous, and a virtuous wife was revered and honored. Perhaps the finest and most fervent song of praise to the good wife comes from the book of Proverbs in the Hebrew Bible:

> *Who can find a virtuous woman? for her price is far above rubies. . . . Strength and honour are her clothing; and she shall rejoice in time to come. . . . Her children arise up, and call her blessed; her husband also, and he praiseth her. . . . Favour is deceitful, and beauty is vain: but a woman that feareth the lord, she shall be praised.* (Proverbs 31:10, 25–30)

The commandment "honor thy father and thy mother" was fundamental to the Mosaic law. The wife was a pillar of the family, and her work and wisdom were respected. The newly married couple was expected to begin a family at once. The desire for children to perpetuate the family was so strong that if a man died before he could sire a son, his brother was legally obliged to marry the widow. The son born of the brother was thereafter considered the offspring of the dead man.

The early education of children was in the mother's hands. She taught her children right from wrong and gave them their first instruction in the moral values of society. As boys grew older, fathers instructed them in religion and the history of their people. Many children were taught to read and write, and the head of each family was probably able to write. Fathers also taught sons the family craft or trade.

The development of urban life among the Jews created new economic opportunities, especially in crafts and trades. People specialized in certain occupations, such as milling flour, baking bread, making pottery, weaving, and carpentry. All these crafts were family trades. Sons worked with their father, daughters with their mother. If the business prospered, the family might be assisted by a few paid workers or slaves. Commerce and trade developed later than crafts. Trade with neighboring countries was handled by foreigners, usually Phoenicians. Jews dealt mainly in local trade, and in most instances craftsmen and farmers sold directly to their customers.

Daily life was governed by the law laid out by the Torah and the Talmud, a later work that records civil and ceremonial law and Jewish legend. The dietary rules of the Jews provide an excellent example of both the relationship between the Torah and the Talmud and their effect on ordinary life and culture. According to the Torah, people were not to eat meat that they found in the field. This very sensible prohibition protected them from eating dangerous food. Yet if meat from the countryside could not be eaten, some rules were needed for meat in the city. The solution found in the Talmud was a set of regulations for the proper way to conduct ritual slaughter and to prepare food. Together these two works regulated and codified Jewish dietary customs.

Hebrew Archer Although graven images were taboo to the Hebrews, Israeli archaeologists recently found this black seal depicting an archer shooting an arrow. The inscription beside him means *for Hagab*. The children of Hagab were among those whom King Cyrus returned from Babylonia (Ezra 2:46). (Photo: Clara Amit. Courtesy, Israel Antiquities Authority)

Chapter 2
Small Kingdoms and Mighty Empires in the Near East • ca. 1100–513 B.C.E.

42

▼ What explains the rise and fall of the Assyrians?

Small kingdoms like those of the Phoenicians and the Hebrews could exist only in the absence of a major power. The beginning of the ninth century B.C.E. saw the rise of such a power: the Assyrians of northern Mesopotamia, whose chief capital was at Nineveh (NIN-uh-vuh) on the Tigris River. The Assyrians were a Semitic-speaking people heavily influenced by the Mesopotamian culture of Babylon to the south. They were also one of the most warlike peoples in history. Living in an open, exposed land, the Assyrians experienced frequent and devastating attacks by the tribes to their north and east and by the Babylonians to the south. The constant threat to survival experienced by the Assyrians promoted political cohesion and military might. Yet they were also a mercantile people who had long pursued commerce with both the Babylonians in the south and the peoples of northern Syria in the north.

The Power of Assyria

The Assyrians had inhabited northern Mesopotamia since the late third millennium B.C.E. For over two hundred years they labored to dominate the Near East. In 859 B.C.E., the new Assyrian king, Shalmaneser (shal-muh-NEE-zuhr), unleashed the first of a long series of attacks on the peoples of Syria and Palestine. These events inaugurated two turbulent centuries marked by Assyrian military campaigns, constant efforts by Syria and the two Jewish kingdoms to maintain or recover their independence, and eventual Assyrian conquest of Babylonia and northern Egypt. In addition, periodic political instability occurred in Assyria itself, which prompted stirrings of freedom throughout the Near East.

Under the Assyrian kings Tiglath-pileser III (TIG-lath-pih-LEE-zuhr) (r. 744–727 B.C.E.) and Sargon II (r. 721–705 B.C.E.), the Assyrians stepped up their attacks on Anatolia,

Surrender of the Jews The Jewish king Jahu finally surrendered to the Assyrians. Here his envoy kneels before the Assyrian king Shalmaneser III in total defeat. Although the Assyrian king treated Jahu well, his people were led off into slavery. (British Museum/Michael Holford)

CHAPTER LOCATOR | What new kingdoms arose in the Near East after 1100 B.C.E.? | What was unique about Hebrew civilization? | **What explains the rise and fall of the Assyrians?** | How did the Persian Empire differ from its predecessors?

43

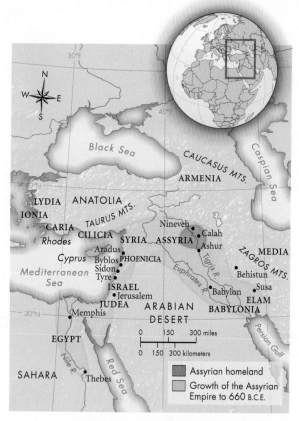

Map 2.2 Expansion of the Assyrian Empire, ca. 900–660 B.C.E. The Assyrian Empire at its height (ca. 660 B.C.E.) included almost all of the old centers of power in the ancient near East.

Syria, and Palestine. The kingdom of Israel and many other states fell; others, like the kingdom of Judah, became subservient to the Assyrians. In 717 to 716 B.C.E. Sargon led his army in a sweeping attack along the Philistine coast, where he defeated the pharaoh. Sargon also lashed out at Assyria's traditional enemies to the north and then turned south against a renewed threat in Babylonia. By means of almost constant warfare, Tiglath-pileser and Sargon carved out an Assyrian empire that stretched from east and north of the Tigris River to central Egypt (Map 2.2). Revolt against the Assyrians inevitably promised the rebels bloody battles and cruel sieges followed by surrender accompanied by systematic torture and slaughter.

Though atrocity and terrorism struck fear into Assyria's subjects, Assyria's success was actually due to sophisticated and effective military organization. By Sargon's time, the Assyrians had invented the mightiest military machine the ancient Near East had ever seen. The mainstay of the Assyrian army was the infantryman armed with spear and sword and protected by helmet and armor. The Assyrian army also featured archers, some on foot, others on horseback, and still others in chariots—the latter ready to wield lances once they had expended their supply of arrows. Some infantry archers wore heavy armor. These soldiers served as a primitive field artillery whose job was to sweep the enemy's walls of defenders so that others could storm the defenses. For mobility on the battlefield, the Assyrians organized a corps of chariots.

Assyrian military genius was remarkable for the development of a wide variety of siege machinery and techniques, including excavation to undermine city walls and battering rams to knock down walls and gates. Never before in the Near East had anyone applied such technical knowledge to warfare. The Assyrians even invented the concept of a corps of engineers, who bridged rivers with pontoons or provided soldiers with inflatable skins for swimming. And the Assyrians knew how to coordinate their efforts, both in open battle and in siege warfare.

Assyrian Rule and Culture

Not only did the Assyrians know how to win battles but they also knew how to use their victories to consolidate their power. As early as the reign of Tiglath-pileser III, the Assyrian kings began to organize their conquered territories into an empire. The lands closest to Assyria became provinces governed by Assyrian officials. Kingdoms beyond the provinces were not annexed but became dependent states that followed Assyria's lead. The Assyrian king chose their rulers either by regulating the succession of native kings or by supporting native kings who appealed to him. Against more distant states the Assyrian kings waged frequent war in order to conquer them outright or make the dependent states secure.

In the seventh century B.C.E. Assyrian power seemed firmly established. Yet the downfall of Assyria was swift and complete. Babylon finally won its independence from Assyria in 626 B.C.E. and joined forces with the Medes, an Indo-European-speaking folk from Persia (modern Iran). Together the Babylonians and the Medes destroyed the Assyrian Empire in 612 B.C.E., paving the way for the rise of the Persians. The Hebrew prophet Nahum (NAY-uhm) spoke for many when he asked, "Nineveh is laid waste: who will bemoan her?" (Nahum 3:7). Their cities destroyed and their power shattered, the Assyrians disappeared from history. Two hundred years later, when the Greek ad-

44

Chapter 2
Small Kingdoms and Mighty Empires
in the Near East • ca. 1100–513 B.C.E.

Assyrian Battle Scene

Art here serves as a textbook of Assyrian warfare. While some Assyrian troops attack the city wall, archers clear the parapets, and Assyrian combat engineers undermine the foundations of the wall. (British Museum. Photo © Michael Holford)

ANALYZING THE IMAGE How many means of attack do the Assyrians use against the besieged city? Can the defenders repel them all?

CONNECTIONS The Assyrians, with their military might, greatly expanded their empire. Yet, they were unable to hold onto their gains. Why do you think their downfall was so swift?

To complete this activity online, go to the Online Study Guide at bedfordstmartins.com/mckaywestunderstanding.

venturer and historian Xenophon (ZEH-nuh-fuhn) passed by the ruins of Nineveh, he marveled at the extent of the former city but knew nothing of the Assyrians. The glory of their empire was forgotten.

Modern archaeology has brought the Assyrians out of obscurity. Excavations have unearthed monumental sculpted figures, numerous Assyrian cuneiform documents, as well as brilliantly sculpted friezes. The latter have proven particularly interesting. Assyrian kings delighted in scenes of war, which their artists depicted in graphic detail. By 668 B.C.E. Assyrian artists had hit on the idea of portraying a series of episodes—a visual narrative of events that had actually taken place. Scene followed scene in a continuous frieze, so that the viewer could follow the progress of a military campaign from the time the army marched out until the enemy was conquered.

CHAPTER LOCATOR | What new kingdoms arose in the Near East after 1100 B.C.E.? | What was unique about Hebrew civilization? | **What explains the rise and fall of the Assyrians?** | How did the Persian Empire differ from its predecessors?

45

Assyrian art fared better than Assyrian military power. The techniques of Assyrian artists influenced the Persians, who adapted them to gentler scenes. In fact, many Assyrian innovations, military and political as well as artistic, were taken over wholesale by the Persians. Although the memory of Assyria was hateful throughout the Near East, the fruits of Assyrian organizational genius helped the Persians to bring peace and stability to the same regions where Assyrian armies had spread terror.

The Neo-Babylonian Empire

The decline of Assyria allowed the Babylonians to create a new dynasty of kings and priests known as the Chaldeans. The Neo- (or new) Babylonian empire they created was marked by the restoration of past Babylonian greatness. The Chaldeans were Semitic-speaking tribes that settled in southern Mesopotamia, where they established their rule, later extending it farther north. They grew up strong enough to overthrow Assyrian rule in 626 B.C.E. with the help of another new people, the Indo-European Medes, who had established themselves in modern western Iran (see page 47). Their most famous king, Nebuchadnezzar (neh-buh-kuhd-NEH-zuhr) (r. 604–562 B.C.E.), thrust Babylonian power into Syria and Judah, destroying Jerusalem and deporting the Hebrews to Babylonia.

The Neo-Babylonian Empire, ca. 560 B.C.E.

The Chaldeans focused on solidifying their power and legitimizing their authority. Kings and priests consciously looked back to the great days of Hammurabi. They instituted a religious revival that included restoring old temples and sanctuaries, as well as creating new ones in the same tradition. Part of their effort was commercial, as they sought to revive the economy in order to resurrect the image of Babylonian greatness. In their hands Babylonia itself became one of the wonders of the ancient world. They preserved many basic aspects of Babylonian law, literature, and government. Yet they failed to bring peace and prosperity to Mesopotamia. Loss of important trade routes to the north and northeast, combined with catastrophic inflation, reduced income. Additional misfortune came in the form of famine and plague. The Chaldean kings had to some degree created a situation that ultimately led to their downfall in 539 B.C.E. It would not come from internal rebellion, but rather from two groups of Iranian newcomers: the Medes and the Persians.

▼ How did the Persian Empire differ from its predecessors?

Like the Hittites before them, the Iranians were Indo-Europeans from central Europe and southern Russia. They migrated into the land between the Caspian Sea and the Persian Gulf. Like the Hittites, they then fell under the spell of the more sophisticated cultures of their Mesopotamian neighbors. Yet the Iranians went on to create one of the greatest empires of antiquity, one that encompassed scores of peoples and cultures. The Persians, the most important of the Iranian peoples, had a farsighted conception of empire. Though as conquerors they willingly used force to accomplish their ends, they normally preferred to depend on diplomacy to rule. They usually respected their subjects and allowed them to practice their native customs and religions. Thus the Persians gave the Near East both political unity and cultural diversity.

Chapter 2
**Small Kingdoms and Mighty Empires
in the Near East** • ca. 1100–513 B.C.E.

46

The Land of the Medes and Persians

Persia—the modern country of Iran—is a land of mountains and deserts with a broad central plateau in the heart of the country. Between the Tigris-Euphrates Valley in the west and the Indus Valley in the east rises an immense plateau that cuts the interior from the sea. Iran's geographical position and topography explain its traditional role as the highway between East and West. Throughout history, nomadic tribes migrating from the broad steppes of Russia and Central Asia have streamed into Iran. Confronting the uncrossable salt deserts of Iran, most of them have turned either eastward or westward, moving until reaching the advanced and wealthy urban centers of Mesopotamia and India. Where cities emerged along the natural lines of east-west communications, Iran became the area in which nomads met urban dwellers, an area of unique significance for the civilizations of both East and West.

The Iranians entered this land around 1000 B.C.E. as part of the vast movement of Indo-European-speaking peoples whose wanderings took them from Europe to India (see Chapter 1). These Iranians were nomads who migrated with their flocks and herds. They were also horse breeders, and the horse gave them a decisive military advantage over the native peoples of Iran. Centuries of immigration saw constant cultural interchange between conquering newcomers and conquered natives.

Two groups of Iranians gradually began coalescing into larger units. The Persians settled in Persia, in southern Iran (Map 2.3). Their kinsmen, the Medes, occupied Media in the north. The Medes united under one king around 710 B.C.E. They next extended their control over the Persians to the south. In 612 B.C.E. they joined the Babylonians to overthrow the Assyrian Empire. With the rise of the Medes, the balance of power in the Near East shifted east of Mesopotamia for the first time.

The Rise of the Persian Empire

In 550 B.C.E. Cyrus the Great (r. 559–530 B.C.E.), king of the Persians and one of the most remarkable statesmen of antiquity, conquered the Medes. (See "Individuals in Society: Cyrus the Great," page 50.) Having united Persia and Media, Cyrus set out to achieve two goals. First, he wanted to win control of the West and thus of the terminal ports of the great trade routes that crossed Iran and Anatolia. Second, he strove to secure eastern Iran from the pressure of nomadic invaders.

In a series of major campaigns, Cyrus achieved his goals. He swept into Anatolia, easily overthrowing the kingdom of Lydia. His generals subdued the Greek cities along the coast of Anatolia, thus gaining him important ports on the Mediterranean. From Lydia, Cyrus marched to the far eastern corners of Iran and conquered the regions of Parthia and Bactria. Internal discord had weakened the Babylonians, and they welcomed him as a liberator when his soldiers moved into their kingdom in 539 B.C.E., overthrowing the Chaldean kings. With these victories, Cyrus demonstrated to the world his benevolence as well as his military might. He spared the life of Croesus (KREE-suhs), the conquered king of Lydia, who then served him as a friend and adviser. He allowed the Greeks to live according to their customs, thus making possible the spread of Greek culture. Cyrus's humanity likewise extended to the Jews, whom he found enslaved in Babylonia. He

Funeral Pyre of Croesus This scene, an excellent example of the precision and charm of ancient Greek vase painting, depicts the Lydian king Croesus on his funeral pyre. He pours a libation to the gods, while his slave lights the fire. The Greek historian Herodotus has a happier ending, saying that Cyrus the Great set fire to the pyre, but that Apollo sent rain to put it out. (Louvre/Réunion des Musées Nationaux/Art Resource, NY)

CHAPTER LOCATOR | What new kingdoms arose in the Near East after 1100 B.C.E.? | What was unique about Hebrew civilization? | What explains the rise and fall of the Assyrians? | **How did the Persian Empire differ from its predecessors?**

47

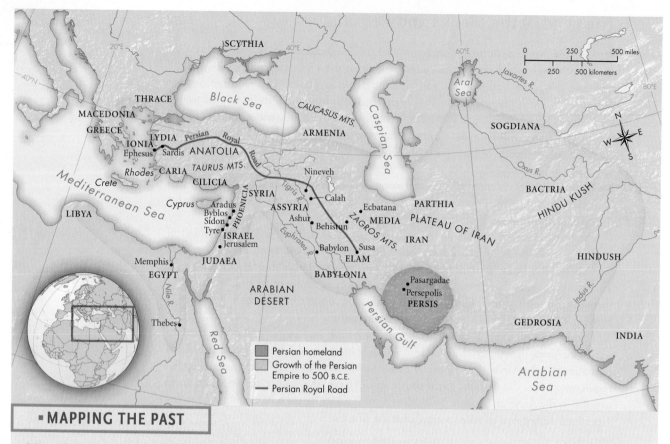

■ **MAPPING THE PAST**

Map 2.3 Expansion of the Persian Empire, ca. 1000–500 B.C.E.

Compare this map showing the extent of the Persian Empire with Map 1.3 on page 27, which shows the earliest political extent of the Near East, and Map 2.2 on page 44.

ANALYZING THE MAP What new areas have opened to the old Mesopotamian cultures shown on Map 1.3? What cultures have been consumed by the growth of Assyria and Persia?

CONNECTIONS What do these maps suggest about the shift of power and the spread of civilization in the ancient Near East?

To complete this activity online, go to the Online Study Guide at **bedfordstmartins.com/mckaywestunderstanding**.

returned their sacred objects to them and allowed them to return to Jerusalem and re-build the temple.

Cyrus's successors Darius (dah-REE-uhs) (r. 521–486 B.C.E.) and Xerxes (ZERK-sees) (r. 486–464 B.C.E.) rounded out the Persian conquest of the ancient Near East. Within thirty-seven years (550–513 B.C.E.), the Persians had transformed themselves from a sub-ject people to the rulers of an empire that included Anatolia, Egypt, Mesopotamia, Iran, and western India. Never before had this region been united in a single vast political organization (see Map 2.3).

The Persians knew how to preserve the peace. Unlike the Assyrians, they did not resort to royal terrorism to maintain order. Instead, the Persians built an efficient ad-ministrative system to govern the empire, based in the capital city of Persepolis (puhr-SEH-puh-lihs), near modern Schiras, Iran. From Persepolis they sent directions to the provinces and received reports from their officials. To do so they maintained a sophis-ticated system of roads linking the empire. The main highway, the famous **Royal Road**, spanned some 1,677 miles. Other roads branched out to link all parts of the empire from

Royal Road The main high-way created by the Persians; it spanned 1,677 miles from Greece to Iran.

the coast of Asia Minor (Anatolia) to the valley of the Indus River. This system of communications enabled Persian kings to keep in close touch with their subjects and officials. They were thereby able to make the concepts of right, justice, and good government a practical reality.

Persian Religion

Iranian religion was originally tied to nature. Ahuramazda (ah-HOOR-uh-MAZ-duh), the chief god, was the creator and benefactor of all living creatures. Mithra, the sun-god whose cult would later spread throughout the Roman

The Impact of Zoroastrianism The Persian kings embraced Zoroastrianism as the religion of the realm. This rock carving at the Persian city of Behistun records the bond. King Darius I (left) is seen trampling on one rebel; other rebels are lined up behind him. Above is the sign of Ahuramazda, the god of truth and guardian of the Persian king. (Robert Harding World Imagery)

Empire, saw to justice and redemption. As in ancient India, fire was a particularly important god. The sacred fire consumed the blood sacrifices that the early Iranians offered to all their deities. A priestly class, the Magi, developed among the Medes to officiate at sacrifices, chant prayers to the gods, and tend the sacred flame. In time the Iranians built fire temples for their sacrifices and rites.

Around 600 B.C.E. a preacher named Zarathustra (zar-uh-THUH-struh) — better known as Zoroaster (zo-roh-AS-tuhr) — introduced new spiritual concepts to the people of Iran. Zoroaster taught that life is a constant battleground for the two opposing forces of good and evil. The Iranian god Ahuramazda embodied good and truth, but Ahuramazda was opposed by Ahriman (AH-ree-mahn), a hateful spirit who stood for evil and lies. Ahuramazda and Ahriman were locked together in a cosmic battle for the human race.

Zoroaster emphasized the individual's responsibility to choose between good and evil. He taught that people possessed the free will to decide between Ahuramazda and Ahriman and that they must rely on their own conscience to guide them through life. Their decisions were crucial, Zoroaster warned, for there would be a time of reckoning. When the battle was over and Ahuramazda had won, those who had lived according to good and truth would enter a divine kingdom. Liars and the wicked would be condemned to eternal pain, darkness, and punishment. Thus Zoroaster preached a last judgment that led to a heaven or a hell.

Under the protection of the Persian kings, **Zoroastrianism** (zo-roh-AS-tree-uh-nihz-uhm) swept through Persia, winning converts and sinking roots that sustained healthy growth for centuries. Zoroastrianism survived the fall of the Persian Empire to influence liberal Judaism, Christianity, and early Islam, largely because of its belief in a just life on earth and a happy afterlife that satisfied the longings of most people. Good behavior in the world, even though unrecognized at the time, would receive ample reward in the hereafter. Evil, no matter how powerful in life, would be punished after death. In some form or another, Zoroastrian concepts still pervade the major religions of the West and every part of the world touched by Islam.

Zoroastrianism
Persian religion whose gods, Ahuramazda, god of good and light, and Ahriman, god of evil and dark, were locked in a battle for the human race; the religion emphasized the individual's responsibility to choose between good and evil.

Persian Art and Culture

The Persians carried on the cultural work of the Hittites, their predecessors in Central Asia. They cultivated native customs and beliefs, while freely adopting aspects of the venerable civilizations of peoples farther west. They both welcomed and respected new

CHAPTER LOCATOR | What new kingdoms arose in the Near East after 1100 B.C.E.? | What was unique about Hebrew civilization? | What explains the rise and fall of the Assyrians? | **How did the Persian Empire differ from its predecessors?**

49

Cyrus the Great

CYRUS (559–530 B.C.E.), KNOWN TO HISTORY AS "the Great" and the founder of the Persian Empire, began life as a subject of the Medes, an Iranian people very closely related to the Persians. Legend records that Astyages (as-TIGH-uh-jeez), king of the Medes, ordered the infant Cyrus killed to eliminate him as a future threat. Cyrus, like the biblical Moses, escaped the plot and went on to rule both his own Persians and the Medes.

Cyrus was a practical man of sound judgment with a good sense of humor. He was merciful but strict with his counselors and generals. He was also broad-minded and keenly interested in foreign peoples and their ways of life. Legend tells how Cyrus's intelligence and good qualities, such as those shown while a boy, later won him the kingship of the Persians. Herodotus tells how Cyrus's playmates chose him king. He assigned them specific duties; and when one aristocratic boy refused to obey his orders, Cyrus had him "arrested." The boy's father later demanded that Cyrus explain his haughty behavior. Cyrus replied that the other boys had chosen him king, and he did his duty justly, as a king should. He told the man that if he had done anything wrong, he was there to take his punishment. The man and the other boys admired his calm sense of duty and responsibility.

Astyages eventually marched against the grown Cyrus and was defeated. Instead of enslaving the Medes, Cyrus accepted them as cousins and included them in the new kingdom of Persia, thus demonstrating his magnanimous concept of rule. Unlike the Assyrians, Cyrus was building an empire based on Persian rule of faithful subjects.

Cyrus's assumption of the kingship was an irreversible step: Persia held too important a strategic position for its neighbors to leave it alone. Croesus, king of the Lydians, who considered Cyrus an immediate threat, planned to cross his eastern border at the Halys River to attack Cyrus. Legend has it that Croesus consulted the Delphic oracle about the invasion, and Apollo told him, "If you make war on the Persians, you will destroy a mighty empire."* Thinking that the oracle meant the Persian Empire, Croesus went ahead and was defeated; the oracle meant that he would destroy his own kingdom.

Cyrus's victory brought the Greeks of Asia Minor under his rule. They had loyally obeyed Croesus and resisted Cyrus, but he won their friendship by treating them mildly. They dutifully paid the royal taxes, in return for which they enjoyed peace, political stability, and prosperity. Greek subjects continued to practice their religion with the same freedom as other Persian subjects. They also enjoyed the liberty to continue their intellectual pursuits.

Cyrus went on to conquer Babylon in 539 B.C.E., where he was received as a liberator. Cyrus wrote of his victory: "When I entered Babylon as a friend, and when I established the seat of government under jubilation and rejoicing, Marduk, the great lord, induced the magnanimous inhabitants of Babylon to love me. . . . My numerous troops walked around Babylon in peace. I did not allow anybody to terrorize the country of Sumer and Akkad."† He restored civil government and religious cult centers that had fallen into ruin. He particularly honored the traditional Babylonian god Marduk. In addition he freed the Jews from their Babylonian Captivity and permitted them to return to their homeland. Cyrus paid for the rebuilding of their temple in Jerusalem and returned sacred vessels that the Babylonians had seized. The Hebrew Bible states that Yahweh made Cyrus his anointed and supported all his efforts.

Cyrus died in 530 B.C.E. while campaigning in Central Asia. Though much of his life was spent at war, he knew how to govern conquered peoples benevolently. He honored and protected their religions and saw to the maintenance of their temples. He allowed them to live according to their own customs and local laws. Like other kings, he taxed them, but without oppressing them. The epitaph on his simple tomb read: "O man, I am Cyrus the son of Cambyses. I established the Persian Empire and was King of Asia. Do not begrudge me my memorial."‡

Cyrus's tomb, though monumental in size, is rather simple and unostentatious. The cylinder (inset) is a historical text, written in Babylonian, that defended the legitimacy of Cyrus's rule and announced the return to traditional political life and religious practices. (tomb: Christina Gascoigne/Robert Harding World Imagery/Alamy; cylinder: Erich Lessing/Art Resource, NY)

QUESTIONS FOR ANALYSIS

1. What were the keys to Cyrus's success as a ruler?
2. How did Cyrus's rule compare to that of the Assyrians?

*Herodotus 1.53.3.

†James B. Pritchard, ed., *The Ancient Near East*, vol. I (Princeton: Princeton University Press, 1958), p. 207.

‡Arrian, *The Anabasis of Alexander*, 6.29.9.

religious beliefs. They saw in the older creeds another long-established way of worshiping the gods. To these older faiths they contributed their own religious beliefs, enriching them with the moral concepts of Zoroastrianism. The importance of truth and the promise of a happy life after death reinforced the precepts of traditional religions like those of the Egyptians and Hebrews.

The Persians made significant contributions to art, culture, and peoples' ways of life. In art they took the Assyrian tradition of realistic monumental sculpture, but ennobled it. Instead of gory details of slaughter, they portrayed themselves as noble and their subjects as dignified. They also depicted foreigners realistically. Their art expressed their power not by portraying bloody warfare but by emphasizing the benign peace shared by all their subjects.

The Persians encouraged their subjects to live according to their own social and religious customs. They did not unnecessarily interfere with their subjects' daily lives. Their rule resulted in an empire that brought people together in a new political system while honoring traditional local ways of life. Although some peoples, notably the Egyptians, sometimes rebelled against Persian rule, most subjects enjoyed uninterrupted lives. Above all, the Persians gave the Near East two centuries of peace and stability.

←LOOKING BACK LOOKING AHEAD →

DURING the centuries following the Sea Peoples' invasions, natives and newcomers brought order to life across the ancient Near East. As Egypt fell, small kingdoms, including Israel and Phoenicia, grew and prospered. These fortunate circumstances enabled a comfortable life to develop once again. Yet a dark side of life emerged when the Assyrians created a cruel military monarchy in Mesopotamia. The Near East saw a period of harshness and oppression that only the triumph of the Persians ended. This Iranian people spread a broad and humane empire across the area. They gave the region general peace and opened avenues to both the West and the East. That to the West became particularly important because it introduced them to the Greeks. This step led to the enrichment of life for Greeks and Easterners alike. The world was becoming much larger.

Since the early Greeks had already settled in the areas of modern Turkey and Greece, they had absorbed numerous aspects of the advanced cultures they had encountered. They learned of Near Eastern religious myths and the sagas of heroic wars. They also acquired many of the advanced technologies that they encountered. They combined these borrowings with their own intrinsic talents to create their own distinct civilization, one that fundamentally shaped the subsequent development of Western society. ■

- ■ **For a list of suggested readings for this chapter, visit** *bedfordstmartins.com/mckaywestunderstanding*.

- ■ **For primary sources from this period, see** *Sources of Western Society,* Second Edition.

- ■ **For Web sites, images, and documents related to topics in this chapter, see Make History at** *bedfordstmartins.com/mckaywestunderstanding*.

CHAPTER LOCATOR | What new kingdoms arose in the Near East after 1100 B.C.E.? | What was unique about Hebrew civilization? | What explains the rise and fall of the Assyrians? | How did the Persian Empire differ from its predecessors?

51

Chapter 2 Study Guide

Step 1

GETTING STARTED Below are basic terms about this period in the history of Western civilization. Can you identify each term below and explain why it matters? To do this exercise online, go to bedfordstmartins.com/mckaywestunderstanding.

TERMS	WHO (OR WHAT) AND WHEN	WHY IT MATTERS
Yahweh, p. 37		
Babylonian Captivity, p. 38		
Covenant, p. 39		
Royal Road, p. 48		
Zoroastrianism, p. 49		

Step 2

MOVING BEYOND THE BASICS The exercise below requires a more advanced understanding of the chapter material. In this exercise, you will compare and contrast the Assyrian and Persian empires. Begin by filling in the chart below by describing some of the factors that contributed to the growth and power of each empire. When you are finished, consider the following questions: What factors were most important in the rise of each empire? How did the leaders of each empire attempt to consolidate their power and react to potential threats? To do this exercise online, go to bedfordstmartins.com/mckaywestunderstanding.

	METHODS OF EXPANSION	ROLE OF MILITARY POWER	ROLE OF TRADE	ROLE OF RELIGION	VIEW OF OTHER PEOPLES
Assyrian Empire					
Persian Empire					

Step **3**

PUTTING IT ALL TOGETHER
Now that you've reviewed key elements of the chapter, take a step back and try to see the big picture. Remember to use specific examples from the chapter in your answers. To do this exercise online, go to bedfordstmartins.com/mckaywestunderstanding.

NEW KINGDOMS

- Why did the fall of the Near Eastern empires lead to a period of cultural diffusion?
- What does the rise of the Phoenicians tell us about the new opportunities open to small kingdoms after the fall of the Near Eastern empires?

THE HEBREWS

- Describe the family and community life of the Hebrews. How did it differ from the norms that prevailed among the Egyptians and the Babylonians?

- Compare and contrast the religion of the Hebrews with that of their Near Eastern neighbors. What were the most important differences? In what ways, if any, did the Hebrews draw on other Near Eastern religious traditions?

THE ASSYRIANS

- In what ways did the establishment of the Assyrian empire differ from earlier efforts at empire building in the Near East?

- Given that theirs was an age of endemic warfare, how did the Assyrians earn a particular reputation for violence and cruelty? Was this reputation deserved? Why or why not?

THE PERSIANS

- In what ways was the Persian Empire unique in the history of Near Eastern Empires? What policies contributed to its unprecedented size and stability?
- Was the diversity of the Persian Empire a strength or a weakness? What evidence can you present to support your position?

■ **In Your Own Words** Imagine that you must explain Chapter 2 to someone who hasn't read it. What would be the most important points to include and why?

3

The Development of Classical Greece

ca. 2000–338 B.C.E.

The people of Greece developed a culture that fundamentally shaped Western civilization. They were the first to explore most of the questions that continue to concern Western thinkers to this day. Going beyond mythmaking, the Greeks strove to understand the world in logical, rational terms. The result was the birth of philosophy and science—subjects that were as important to most Greek thinkers as religion. The concept of politics evolved through Greek philosophy. Greek contributions to the arts and literature were equally profound.

The history of the Greeks is divided into two broad periods: the Hellenic period (the subject of this chapter), roughly the time between the arrival of the Greeks (approximately 2000 B.C.E.) and the victory over Greece in 338 B.C.E. by Philip of Macedonia; and the Hellenistic period (the subject of Chapter 4), the age beginning with the remarkable reign of Philip's son, Alexander the Great (r. 336–323 B.C.E.) and ending with the Roman conquest of the Hellenistic East (200–146 B.C.E.). ■

Life in Classical Greece. Religion was central to Greek life. This detail from a vase shows a man and two women approaching a temple from the left. There, the priestess, with a bough in hand, greets them. (© The Metropolitan Museum of Art/Art Resource, NY)

Chapter Preview

▶ How did geography shape the early history of the Greeks?

▶ What was the polis and what was its role in Greek society?

▶ What were the major developments of the Greek Archaic Age?

▶ How did war affect Greek civilization?

▶ How did Macedonia come to dominate Greece?

▼ How did geography shape the early history of the Greeks?

Hellas, as the Greeks still call their land, encompassed the Greek peninsula, the islands of the Aegean (ah-JEE-uhn) Sea, and the lands bordering the Aegean, an area known as the Aegean basin (Map 3.1). Mountains divide the land, leaving few plains and rivers. Greece is, however, blessed with good harbors, the most important of which look to the east. The islands of the Aegean serve as steppingstones to Asia Minor.

The major regions of Greece were Thessaly (THEH-suh-lee) and Boeotia (bee-OH-shuh) in the north and center, lands marked by fertile plains that helped to sustain a strong population capable of serving as formidable cavalry and infantry. Immediately to the south of Boeotia is Attica, an area of thin soil that is home to the olive and the vine. Its harbors looked to the Aegean, which invited its inhabitants, the Athenians, to concentrate on maritime commerce. Still farther south, the Peloponnesus (peh-luh-puh-NEE-suhs) was a patchwork of high mountains and small plains that divided the area into several regions.

The geographical fragmentation of Greece encouraged political fragmentation. Communications were extraordinarily poor. Rocky tracks were far more common than roads. These conditions prohibited the growth of a great empire like those of the Near East.

The Minoans and Mycenaeans

During the Bronze Age, Neolithic peoples built prosperous communities in the Aegean, but not until about 2000 B.C.E. did they establish firm contact with one another. By then artisans had discovered how to make bronze. With the adoption of metallurgy came even greater prosperity. Some Cretan (KREE-tuhn) farmers and fishermen began to trade their surpluses with their neighbors. The central position of Crete (kreet) in the eastern Mediterranean made it a crucial link in this trade. These favorable circumstances produced the Minoan culture on Crete, named after the mythical King Minos.

The palace was the political and economic center of Minoan society. About 1650 B.C.E. Crete was dotted with palaces, but the palace at Knossus (NO-suhs) towered above all others in importance. Few specifics are known about Minoan life except that at its head stood a king and his nobles. Minoan society was wealthy and, to judge by the absence of fortifications on the island, relatively peaceful.

Beginning around 2000 B.C.E., Greek-speaking peoples began arriving in the Balkans. They came gradually as individual groups speaking various dialects of the same language. They nonetheless considered themselves a related people. More culturally advanced than the natives, they easily took control of the land. By about 1650 B.C.E. one group had founded a powerful kingdom at Mycenae (migh-SEE-nee).

Early Mycenaean Greeks raised other palaces and established cities at Thebes (theebz), Athens, and elsewhere. As in Crete, the political unit was the kingdom. The king and

Minoan A flourishing and vibrant culture on Crete around 1650 B.C.E.; the palace was the center of political and economic life, the most important one being Knossus.

Mycenaean A Greek society that developed around 1650 B.C.E. when a powerful group centered at Mycenae spread its culture over the less-advanced native population.

Dionysos at Sea Dionysos, a Greek god, here symbolizes the Greek sense of exploration, independence, and love of life. (Bildarchiv Preussischer Kulturbesitz/Art Resource, NY)

Chapter 3
The Development of Classical
56 Greece • ca. 2000–338 B.C.E.

CHAPTER LOCATOR │ How did geography shape the early history of the Greeks?

his warrior aristocracy stood at the top of society and the king's palace was the economic center of the kingdom. Within its walls royal artisans fashioned jewelry and rich ornaments, made and decorated fine pottery, forged weapons, prepared hides and wool for clothing, and manufactured the other goods needed by the king and his retainers. The Mycenaean economy was marked by an extensive division of labor, all tightly controlled from the palace. At the bottom of the social scale were male and female slaves, who were normally owned by the king and aristocrats but who also worked for ordinary people.

Contacts between the Minoans and Mycenaeans were originally peaceful, and Minoan culture flooded the Greek mainland. But around 1450 B.C.E. the Mycenaeans attacked Crete, destroying many Minoan palaces and taking possession of the grand palace at Knossus. For about the next fifty years, the Mycenaeans ruled much of the island until a further wave of violence left Knossus in ashes.

After the fall of Knossus, Mycenaean kingdoms in Greece quickly expanded commercially throughout the Aegean. Prosperity, however, did not bring peace, and between 1300 and 1000 B.C.E. kingdom after kingdom suffered attack and destruction as a result of mutual discord.

The fall of the Mycenaean kingdoms ushered in a period that historians usually call the "Dark Age" of Greece (ca. 1100–800 B.C.E.). Even literacy, which was not widespread in any case, was a casualty of the chaos. Nonetheless, the Greeks managed to preserve their culture and civilization. It was a time of change and challenge, but not of utter collapse.

The disruption of Mycenaean societies caused the widespread and prolonged movement of Greek peoples. They dispersed beyond mainland Greece farther south to Crete and across the Aegean to the shores of Anatolia. They arrived during a time when traditional states and empires had collapsed. Economic hardship was common, and various groups wandered for years. Yet by the end of the Dark Age, the Greeks had spread their culture throughout the Aegean basin.

Chapter Chronology

ca. 2000 B.C.E.	Greeks arrive in the Balkans
ca. 1650 B.C.E.	Founding of the kingdom of Mycenae; establishment of Minoan palaces
ca. 1100–800 B.C.E.	Dark Age; Greek migrations within the Aegean basin; poems of Homer and Hesiod
ca. 800–500 B.C.E.	Archaic Age; rise of Sparta and Athens
ca. 750–550 B.C.E.	Greek colonization of the Mediterranean
ca. 735 B.C.E.	Sparta begins expansion by going to war against Messenia
508 B.C.E.	Cleisthenes begins democratic reforms in Athens
500-338 B.C.E.	Classical Period; major intellectual and artistic achievements
499–479 B.C.E.	Persian wars
459-445 B.C.E.	War between Sparta and Athens
447 B.C.E.	Construction of the Parthenon begins
431–404 B.C.E.	Peloponnesian War
404–338 B.C.E.	Spartan and Theban hegemonies; success of Philip of Macedonia
399 B.C.E.	Socrates executed
386 B.C.E.	First Common Peace
371–362 B.C.E.	Thebes, with an alliance of city-states, rules Greece
359 B.C.E.	Philip II ascends Macedonian throne
338 B.C.E.	Philip II wins battle of Chaeronea; gains control of Greece

Homer, Hesiod, and the Epic

Much of what we know of the Dark Age comes from Greek literature. The Greeks, unlike the Hebrews, had no sacred book that chronicled their past. Instead, they had Homer's *Iliad* and *Odyssey*. These epics are poetic tales of the heroic deeds of legendary heroes. They also learned about the origin and descent of the gods from the *Theogony* (thee-AH-guh-nee), an epic poem by Hesiod (HEH-see-uhd). In terms of pure history, these works contain scraps of information about the Bronze Age, much about the early Dark Age, and some about the poets' own era.

The *Iliad*'s tale of war belongs to the Troy of the late Bronze Age. Homer's *Iliad* recounts the Mycenaean Greek expedition to besiege Troy to retrieve Helen, who was

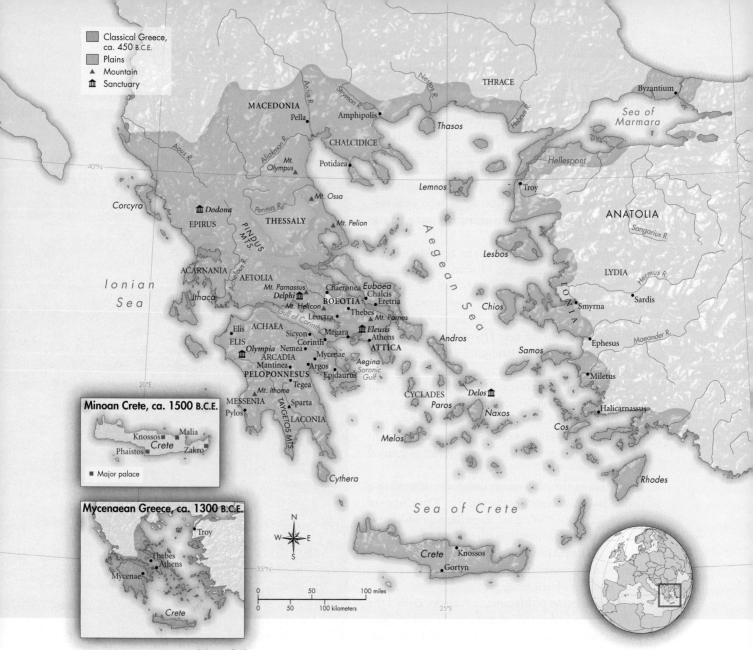

Map 3.1 Classical Greece, 500–338 B.C.E. In antiquity, the home of the Greeks included the islands of the Aegean and the western shore of Anatolia (Turkey in modern times) as well as the Greek peninsula itself.

abducted to Troy by Paris, the king's son. The heart of the *Iliad*, however, concerns the quarrel between Agamemnon, the king of Mycenae, and the tragic hero of the poem, Achilles (uh-KIL-eez), and how their quarrel brought suffering to the Achaeans, the name Homer gives to the Mycenaeans.

Homer's *Odyssey* records the adventures of Odysseus (oh-DIH-see-uhs), a hero of the war at Troy, during his ten-year voyage home to his wife Penelope. He encounters many dangers, storms, and adventures, but with wisdom and steady courage he finally reaches his home.

Both of Homer's epics portray engaging but flawed characters who are larger than life, yet typically human. Homer was also strikingly successful in depicting the great gods, who generally sit on Mount Olympus and watch the fighting at Troy like spectators

Chapter 3
**The Development of Classical
Greece** • ca. 2000–338 B.C.E.

58

CHAPTER LOCATOR | How did geography shape the early history of the Greeks?

at a baseball game, although they sometimes participate in the action. Homer's deities are reminiscent of Mesopotamian gods and goddesses: raucous, petty, deceitful, and splendid.

Hesiod, who lived somewhat later than Homer, made the gods the focus of his epic poem, the *Theogony*. Hesiod was influenced by Mesopotamian myths. Like the Hebrews, Hesiod envisaged his cosmogony—his account of the way the universe developed—in moral terms. Zeus, the son of Cronus (CROH-nuhs), defeated his evil father and took his place as king of the gods. He then sired Lawfulness, Right, Peace, and other powers of light and beauty. Thus, in Hesiod's conception, Zeus was the god of righteousness who loved justice and hated wrongdoing.

▼ What was the polis and what was its role in Greek society?

After the upheavals that ended the Mycenaean period and the slow recovery of prosperity during the Dark Age, the Greeks developed the **polis** (PAH-luhs). The term *polis* (plural *poleis*) is generally interpreted as "city-state." The polis was, however, far more than a political institution. Above all it was a community of citizens whose customs comprised the laws of the polis. Even though the physical, religious, and political form of the polis varied from place to place, it defined Greekness.

polis Generally interpreted to mean city-state, it was the basic political and institutional unit of Greece.

Origins of the Polis

Even during the late Mycenaean period, towns had grown up around palaces. These towns and even smaller villages performed basically local functions. The first was to administer the ordinary political affairs of the community. The village also served a religious purpose in that each, no matter how small, had a local cult to its own deity. The exchange of daily goods made these towns and villages economically important, if only on a small scale. These settlements also developed a social system that was particularly their own. They likewise had their own views of the social worth and status of their inhabitants and the nature of their public responsibilities.

When fully developed, each polis normally shared a surprisingly large number of features with other poleis. Physically a polis was a society of people who lived in a city (*asty*) and cultivated the surrounding countryside (*chora*). The city's water supply came from public fountains, springs, and cisterns. By the fifth century B.C.E. the city was generally surrounded by a wall. The city contained a point, usually elevated, called the acropolis (uh-KRAH-puh-luhs) and a public square or marketplace called the *agora* (AH-guh-ruh). On the **acropolis** stood the temples, altars, public monuments, and various dedications to the gods of the polis. The **agora** was the political center of the polis. In the agora were shops, public buildings, and courts.

acropolis An elevated point within a city on which stood temples, altars, and public monuments.

agora A public square or marketplace that was a political center of Greece.

The countryside was essential to the economy of the polis and provided food to sustain the entire population. But it was also home to sanctuaries for the deities of the polis and the site of important religious rites. The sacred buildings, shrines, and altars were physical symbols of a polis, uniting country and city dwellers.

The average polis did not have a standing army. Instead it relied on its citizens for protection. Rich citizens often served as cavalry, which was, however, never as important as the heavily armed infantry, or **hoplites**, who were the backbone of the army. In some instances the citizens of a polis hired mercenaries to fight their battles. Mercenaries were expensive, untrustworthy, and willing to defect to a higher bidder. Even worse, they sometimes seized control of the polis that had hired them.

hoplites The heavily armed infantry who were the backbone of the Greek army.

The Sanctuary of Apollo at Delphi The Greeks worshiped Apollo at Delphi, a somewhat remote spot on Mt. Parnassus (see Map 3.1). As seen from a higher slope, the theater overlooks the temple of Apollo, which is approached by the Sacred Way that leads up to it. (Steve Vidler/SuperStock)

Governing Structures

monarchy Type of government in which a king rules; common during the Mycenaean period.

tyranny Rule by one man who used his wealth or other powers to seize the government unconstitutionally.

democracy A type of Greek government in which all people, without regard to birth or wealth, administered the workings of government; in practice, only people granted citizenship participated.

oligarchy A type of Greek government in which a small group of wealthy citizens, not necessarily of aristocratic birth, ruled.

federalism A political system developed by Greek states that banded together in leagues and marshaled their resources to defend themselves from outside interference, while remaining independent in their internal affairs.

Greek city-states had several different types of government. Monarchy, rule by a king, was prevalent during the Mycenaean period but afterwards declined. From about 500 B.C.E. Greek states were either democracies or oligarchies. Sporadic periods of violent political and social upheaval often led to a third type of government—tyranny. Tyranny was rule by one man who had seized power by unconstitutional means, generally by using his wealth to win a political following that toppled the existing legal government.

The most popular and lasting of these political ideals were democracy and oligarchy (OH-luh-gahr-kee). Greek democracy meant the rule of citizens, not "the people" as a whole, and citizenship was drastically limited. Greek democracies were in fact little more than expanded oligarchies. Oligarchy, which literally means "the rule of the few," was government by a small group of wealthy citizens. All Greek democracies jealously guarded political rights. Only free adult men who had lived in the polis a long time were citizens. The remaining free men and all women were not active citizens of the democracy. Resident foreigners and slaves were also excluded from citizen rights, except for protection under the law. Still, democracy was attractive because it permitted certain male citizens to share equally in the determination of diplomatic and military policy of the polis.

Many Greeks preferred oligarchic constitutions. Oligarchy was the government of the prosperous but it left the door open to political and social advancement. Greek oligarchy was not generally oppressive, and it possessed a democratic aspect. All members of an oligarchic government held a passive citizenship in which they enjoyed civil rights. If members of the polis could meet property or money qualifications, they could enter the governing circle. Thus oligarchy provided an avenue for political and social advancement.

Although each polis was normally jealous of its independence, some Greeks banded together to create leagues of city-states. Here was the birth of federalism, a political system in which several states formed a central government while remaining independent in their internal affairs. United in a league, a confederation of city-states was far stronger than any of its individual members and was better able to withstand external attack.

Chapter 3
The Development of Classical
60 Greece • ca. 2000–338 B.C.E.

CHAPTER LOCATOR | How did geography shape the early history of the Greeks?

Even federalism could not overcome the passionate individualism of the polis, which proved to be a serious weakness. The citizens of each polis were determined to remain free and autonomous. Rarely were the Greeks willing to unite in larger political bodies. The result was almost constant warfare.

▼ What were the major developments of the Greek Archaic Age?

The Archaic Age was one of the most vibrant periods of Greek history. During this period the Greeks recovered from the downfall of the Mycenaean kingdoms and continued the advances made during the Dark Age. Greeks ventured as far east as the Black Sea and as far west as Spain. Politically these were the years when Sparta and Athens—the two poles of the Greek experience—rose to prominence.

Overseas Expansion

During the years 1100–800 B.C.E. the Greeks grew in wealth and numbers. This prosperity brought new problems. The increase in population meant that many families had very little land or none at all. The resulting social and political tensions drove many Greeks to seek new homes outside of Greece.

Early Greek Warfare Before the hoplites became the backbone of the army, wealthy warriors rode into battle in chariots, dismounted, and engaged the enemy. This scene, from the side of a vase, shows on the left the warrior protecting the chariot before it returns to the rear. The painter has caught the lead horses already beginning the turn. (Courtesy of the Ure Museum of Greek Archaeology, University of Reading)

From about 750 to 550 B.C.E., Greeks from the mainland and Asia Minor traveled throughout the Mediterranean and even into the Atlantic Ocean in their quest for new land (Map 3.2). They sailed in the greatest numbers to Sicily and southern Italy, where there was ample space for expansion. In Sicily they found the Sicels, who had adopted many Carthaginian customs, including a new urban culture. The Sicels welcomed Greek culture but not Greek demands for their land. Nonetheless, the two peoples made a somewhat uneasy accommodation, and there was some intermarriage among them. In southern Italy the Greeks encountered a number of Indo-European peoples. They welcomed Greek culture, and the Greeks found it easy to establish prosperous cities without facing significant local hostility.

Some adventurous Greeks sailed farther west to Sardinia, France, Spain, and even the Canary Islands. In Sardinia they established trading stations for bartering with the natives. Commerce was so successful that some Greeks established permanent towns there. From these new outposts Greek influence extended to southern France.

Colonization changed the entire Greek world, both at home and abroad. In economic terms the expansion of the Greeks created a much larger market for agricultural and manufactured goods. From the east, especially from the northern coast of the Black Sea, came wheat. In return flowed Greek wine and olive oil. Greek-manufactured goods circulated from southern Russia to Spain. During this same period the Greeks adopted the custom of minting coins. Over time coinage would replace the barter system, in which one person exchanges one good for another without the use of money. Thus Greek culture and economics, fertilized by the influences of other societies, spread throughout the Mediterranean basin.

Colonization presented the polis with a huge challenge, for it required organization and planning on an unprecedented scale. The colonizing city, called the *metropolis*, or mother city, first decided where to establish the colony, how to transport colonists to the site, what supplies would be needed, and who would sail. Once an expedition was under

Map 3.2 Colonization of the Mediterranean, ca. 750–550 B.C.E. Though the Greeks and Phoenicians colonized the Mediterranean basin at about the same time, the Greeks spread much farther.

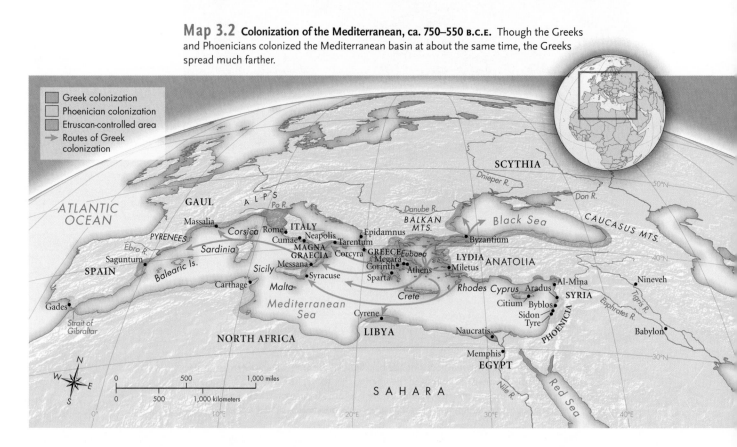

way, an oikist (OY-kist), or leader, was in full command of the band until the colony was established in its new site and capable of running its own affairs. A significant aspect of colonizing ventures was that all free male colonists were considered political equals and were expected to have a voice in the new colony.

Once the new polis was established, the oikist surrendered power to the new leaders. The colony was thereafter independent of the metropolis. For the Greeks, colonization had two important aspects. First, it demanded that the polis assume a much greater public function than ever before, thus strengthening the city-state's institutional position. Second, colonization spread the polis and its values far beyond the shores of Greece. Even more important, colonization on this scale had a profound impact on the course of Western civilization. It meant that the prevailing culture of the Mediterranean basin would be Greek.

The Growth of Sparta

During the Archaic period the Spartans expanded the boundaries of their polis and made it the leading power in Greece. Like other Greeks, the Spartans faced the problems of overpopulation and land hunger. Unlike other Greeks, they solved these problems by conquest, not by colonization. To gain more land, the Spartans set out in about 735 B.C.E. to conquer Messenia (muh-SEE-nee-uh), a rich, fertile region in the southwestern Peloponnesus. This conflict, the First Messenian War, lasted for twenty years and ended in a Spartan triumph. The Spartans appropriated Messenian land and turned the Messenians into **helots** (HEH-luhts), or state serfs.

In about 650 B.C.E. Spartan exploitation and oppression of the Messenian helots led to a helot revolt so massive and stubborn that it became known as the Second Messenian War. Finally, after some thirty years of fighting, the Spartans put down the revolt. Nevertheless, the political and social strain it caused led to a transformation of the Spartan polis. After the victory non-noblemen, who had done much of the fighting, demanded rights equal to those of the nobility. The agitation of these non-nobles disrupted society until the aristocrats agreed to remodel the state. The "Lycurgan regimen," as the reforms were called after a legendary lawgiver, was a new political, economic, and social system. Political distinctions among Spartan men were eliminated, and all citizens became legally equal. Actual governance of the polis

helots State serfs who worked the land.

Spartan Hoplite The bronze figurine portrays an armed soldier about to strike an enemy. His massive helmet with its full crest gives his head nearly complete protection, while a corselet covers his chest and back, and greaves (similar to today's shin guards) protect his shins. In his right hand he carries a thrusting spear and in his left a large round shield. Hoplites were the backbone of all Greek armies. (Bildarchiv Preussischer Kulturbesitz/Art Resource, NY)

was in the hands of two kings who were primarily military leaders. The kings and a group of elders made up a council that deliberated on foreign and domestic matters and prepared legislation for the assembly, which consisted of all Spartan citizens. The real executive power of the polis was in the hands of five ephors, or overseers, elected from and by all the citizens. In effect, the Lycurgan regimen broadened the aristocracy, while at the same time setting limits on its size. Social mobility was for the most part abolished, and instead an aristocratic warrior class governed the polis.

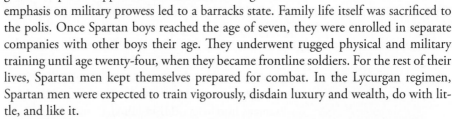

Spartan Expansion, ca. 735–500 B.C.E.

To provide for their economic needs, the Spartans divided the land of Messenia among all citizens. Helots worked the land, raised the crops, provided the Spartans with a certain percentage of their harvest, and occasionally served in the army.

In the Lycurgan system every citizen owed primary allegiance to Sparta. Suppression of the individual together with emphasis on military prowess led to a barracks state. Family life itself was sacrificed to the polis. Once Spartan boys reached the age of seven, they were enrolled in separate companies with other boys their age. They underwent rugged physical and military training until age twenty-four, when they became frontline soldiers. For the rest of their lives, Spartan men kept themselves prepared for combat. In the Lycurgan regimen, Spartan men were expected to train vigorously, disdain luxury and wealth, do with little, and like it.

Similar rigorous requirements applied to Spartan women. They were prohibited from wearing jewelry or ornate clothes. They too exercised strenuously in the belief that hard physical training promoted the birth of healthy children. Yet they were hardly oppressed. They enjoyed more active and open public life than most other Greek women. They were far more emancipated than many other Greek women in part because Spartan society felt that mothers and wives had to be as hardy and independent as their sons and husbands. While nominally under the guidance of a male guardian, the Spartan woman often managed her own financial affairs and owned her own land. Unlike other women in Greece, she could own property. For all of these reasons, Spartan women shared a footing with Spartan men that most other Greek women lacked.

The Evolution of Athens

Like Sparta, Athens faced pressing social and economic problems during the Archaic period, but the Athenian response was far different from that of the Spartans. Instead of creating an oligarchy, the Athenians extended to all citizens the right and duty of governing the polis. The Athenian democracy was one of the most thoroughgoing in Greece.

For Athens the late seventh century B.C.E. was a time of turmoil, the causes of which are virtually unknown. In 621 B.C.E. Draco, an Athenian aristocrat, doubtless under pressure from the peasants, published the first law code of the Athenian polis. His code was thought harsh, but it nonetheless embodied the ideal that the law belonged to the citizens. Nevertheless, peasant unrest continued.

By the early sixth century B.C.E. social and economic conditions led to another explosive situation. The aristocrats owned the best land, met in an assembly to govern the polis, and interpreted the law to their advantage. Noble landowners were forcing small farmers into economic dependence. Many families were sold into slavery; others were exiled, and their land was mortgaged to the rich.

In many other city-states, conditions like those in Athens led to the rise of tyrants. One person who recognized these problems clearly was Solon, himself an aristocrat.

Chapter 3
The Development of Classical Greece • ca. 2000–338 B.C.E.

64

CHAPTER LOCATOR | How did geography shape the early history of the Greeks?

Solon was relentless in his public calls for justice and fairness. The aristocrats realized that Solon was no crazed revolutionary, and the common people trusted him. Around 594 B.C.E. the nobles elected him *archon* (AHR-kahn), chief magistrate of the Athenian polis, and gave him extraordinary power to reform the state.

Solon immediately freed all people enslaved for debt, recalled all exiles, canceled all debts on land, and made enslavement for debt illegal. He also divided society into four legal groups on the basis of wealth. In the most influential group were the wealthiest citizens, but even the poorest and least powerful men enjoyed certain political rights.

Although Solon's reforms solved some immediate problems, they did not bring peace to Athens. Some aristocrats attempted to make themselves tyrants, while others banded together to oppose them. In 546 B.C.E. Pisistratus (pigh-SIHS-trah-tuhs), an exiled aristocrat, returned to Athens, defeated his opponents, and became tyrant. Pisistratus reduced the power of the aristocracy while supporting the common people. Under his rule Athens prospered, and his building program began to transform the city into one of the splendors of Greece. His reign as tyrant promoted the growth of democratic ideas by arousing rudimentary feelings of equality in many Athenian men. But tyranny did not long outlive Pisistratus, for his son Hippias ruled harshly, committing excesses that led to his overthrow.

Democracy took shape in Athens under the leadership of Cleisthenes (KLIGHS-thuh-neez), a wealthy and prominent aristocrat who had won the support of lower-status men and emerged triumphant in 508 B.C.E. Cleisthenes created the deme (deem), a local unit that kept the roll of citizens, or *demos*, within its jurisdiction. All the demes were grouped in tribes, which thus formed the link between the demes and the central government.

The democracy functioned on the idea that all full citizens were sovereign. Because not all citizens could take time from work to participate in government, they delegated their power to other citizens by creating various offices meant to run the democracy. The most prestigious was the board of ten archons, who were charged with handling legal and military matters.

Legislation was in the hands of two bodies, the boule (BOO-lee), or council, composed of five hundred members, and the ecclesia (ee-KLEE-zhee-uh), the assembly of all citizens. By supervising the various committees of government and proposing bills to the ecclesia, the boule guided Athenian political life. It received foreign envoys and forwarded treaties to the ecclesia for ratification. It oversaw the granting of state contracts and was responsible for receiving many revenues. It held the democracy together. Nonetheless, the ecclesia had the final word. The ecclesia could accept, amend, or reject bills put before it. Every member could express his opinion on any subject on the agenda, and a simple majority vote was needed to pass or reject a bill.

Athenian democracy proved to be an inspiring ideal in Western civilization. It demonstrated that a large group of people, not just a few, could efficiently run the affairs of state. Like all democracies in ancient Greece, however, Athenian democracy was limited. Slaves, women, recent migrants, and foreigners could not be citizens; their opinions about political issues were not taken into account or recorded.

▼ How did war affect Greek civilization?

In the years 500 to 338 B.C.E., Greek civilization reached its highest peak in politics, thought, and art. In this period the Greeks beat back the armies of the Persian Empire. Then, turning their spears against one another, they destroyed their own political system in a century of warfare. Some thoughtful Greeks felt prompted to record and analyze these momentous events. Herodotus (ca. 485–425 B.C.E.) traveled the Greek world to

Map 3.3 The Persian Wars, 499–479 B.C.E. Begun initially as a local conflict between the Ionian Greeks and the Persians, the war eventually spread to involve a coalition of Greek forces who were able to defeat the Persians.

piece together the course of the Persian wars. Although he consulted documents when he could find them, he relied largely on the memories of the participants. Next came Thucydides (thoo-SIHD-ih-deez) (ca. 460–ca. 399 B.C.E.), whose account of the Peloponnesian (puh-luh-puh-NEE-zhuhn) War remains a classic of Western literature. Unlike Herodotus, he was often a participant in the events that he described.

This era also saw the flowering of philosophy, as thinkers in Ionia and on the Greek mainland began to ponder the nature and meaning of the universe and human experience. The Greeks invented drama, and the Athenian playwrights explored themes that still inspire audiences today. Greek architects reached the zenith of their art. Because Greek intellectual and artistic efforts attained their fullest and finest expression in these years, this age is called the "classical period."

The Persian Wars

One of the hallmarks of the classical period was warfare. In 499 B.C.E. the Ionian Greeks, with the help of Athens, rebelled against the Persian Empire (Map 2.3, page 48). The rebellion failed, and the Ionians remained under Persian rule. Yet in 490 B.C.E. the Persians struck back at Athens, only to be defeated at the battle of Marathon, a small plain in Attica (Map 3.3). Despite the rebuff, the Persians renewed the attack. In 480 B.C.E. the Persian king Xerxes led a mighty invasion force into Greece. In the face of this emergency, many of the Greeks united and pooled their resources to resist the invaders. The

66

Chapter 3
The Development of Classical Greece • ca. 2000–338 B.C.E.

CHAPTER LOCATOR   How did geography shape the early history of the Greeks?

Statue of Leonidas Found at Sparta, this statue is commonly thought to represent Leonidas, the Spartan king who died valiantly at Thermopylae. With its careful rendering of the muscles and face, the statue reflects the Spartan ideal of the strong, intelligent, and brave warrior. (Vanni/Art Resource, NY)

Spartans provided the overall leadership and commanded the Greek armies. The Athenians, led by Themistocles (thuh-MIHS-tuh-kleez), provided the heart of the naval forces.

The first confrontations between the Persians and the Greeks occurred at the pass of Thermopylae (thuhr-MOP-uh-lee) and in the waters off Euboea. The Greeks at Thermopylae fought heroically, but the Persians won the battle. In 480 B.C.E. the Greek fleet met the Persian armada at Salamis, an island just south of Athens. Though outnumbered, the Greek navy won an overwhelming victory. The remnants of the Persian fleet retired, and with them went all hope of Persian victory. In the following year, a coalition of Greek forces, commanded by the Spartan Pausanias with assistance from the Athenian Aristides, smashed the last Persian army at Plataea, a small polis in Boeotia.

The significance of these Greek victories is nearly incalculable. By defeating the Persians, the Greeks ensured that they would not be taken over by a monarchy, which they increasingly viewed as un-Greek. The decisive victories meant that Greek political forms and intellectual concepts would be handed down to later societies.

Growth of the Athenian Empire

The defeat of the Persians had created a power vacuum in the Aegean, and the Athenians took advantage of the situation. The Athenians and their allies, again led by Aristides, formed the Delian League, a grand naval alliance aimed at liberating Ionia from Persian rule. The Delian (DEE-lee-uhn) League was intended to be a free alliance under the leadership of Athens. Athenians provided most of the warships and crews and determined how many ships or how much money each member of the league should contribute to the allied effort.

The Athenians, supported by the Delian League and led by the young aristocrat Cimon (KEY-muhn), carried the war against Persia. But Athenian success had a sinister side. While the Athenians drove the Persians out of the Aegean, they also became increasingly imperialistic. Athens began reducing its allies to the status of subjects. Tribute was often collected by force, and the Athenians placed the economic resources of the Delian League under tighter and tighter control. Dissident governments were put down, and Athenian ideas of freedom and democracy did not extend to the citizens of other cities.

Athens justified its conduct by its successful leadership. In about 467 B.C.E. Cimon defeated a new and huge Persian force at the Battle of the Eurymedon River in Asia Minor. But as the threat from Persia waned and the Athenians treated their allies more harshly, major allies such as Thasos (THAH-saws) revolted (ca. 465 B.C.E.).

The expansion of Athenian power and the aggressiveness of Athenian rule also alarmed Sparta and its allies. While relations between Athens and Sparta cooled,

Delian League A free naval alliance under the leadership of Athens aimed at liberating Ionia from Persian rule.

The Delian League, ca. 478–431 B.C.E.

- Delian League
- Allied with Delian League, 446 B.C.E.
- Athenian military settlement

Thasos

Corcyra

BEOETIA
Megara · Athens
Corinth · · Delos
· Sparta

PERSIAN EMPIRE

Pericles (PEHR-uh-kleez) (ca. 494–429 B.C.E.), an aristocrat of solid intellectual ability, became the leading statesman in Athens. Pericles was aggressive and imperialistic. At last, in 459 B.C.E. Sparta and Athens went to war over conflicts between Athens and some of Sparta's allies. Though the Athenians conquered Boeotia, Megara (MEG-uhr-uh), and Aegina (ih-JIGH-nuh) in the early stages of the war, they met defeat in Egypt and later in Boeotia. The war ended in 445 B.C.E. with no serious damage to either side and nothing settled. But it divided the Greek world between the two great powers.

Athens continued its severe policies toward its subject allies and came into conflict with Corinth, one of Sparta's leading supporters (see Map 3.3). In 433 B.C.E. Athens sided with Corcyra (kohr-SIGH-ruh) against Corinth in a dispute between the two. Together with the Corcyraean (kohr-SIGH-ree-uhn) fleet, an Athenian squadron defeated the Corinthian navy. The next year Corinth and Athens collided again, this time over the Corinthian colony of Potidaea (pot-eh-DEE-uh), in a conflict the Athenians also won. In this climate of anger and escalation, Pericles took the next step. To punish Megara for alleged sacrilege, Pericles in 432 B.C.E. persuaded the Athenians to pass a law, the Megarian Decree, that excluded Megarians from trading with Athens and its empire. In response the Spartans convened a meeting of their allies, whose complaints of Athenian aggression ended with a demand that Athens be stopped. Reluctantly the Spartans agreed to declare war.

The Peloponnesian War

At the outbreak of the Peloponnesian War the Spartan ambassador Melesippus warned the Athenians: "This day will be the beginning of great evil for the Greeks." Few men have ever prophesied more accurately. The Peloponnesian War lasted a generation and brought in its wake fearful plagues, famine, civil wars, widespread destruction, and huge loss of life.

In 431 B.C.E. the Peloponnesian War began in earnest (Map 3.4). In the next seven years, the army of Sparta and its Peloponnesian allies invaded Attica five times. The Athenians stood behind their walls, but in 430 B.C.E. the cramped conditions nurtured a dreadful plague, which killed huge numbers, including Pericles himself. (See "Listening to the Past: Thucydides on the Great Plague at Athens, 430 B.C.E.," page 70.) The death of Pericles opened the door to men who were rash, ambitious, and more dedicated to themselves than to Athens. Under Cleon (KLEE-on), the Athenians counterattacked and defeated the Spartans at Pylos (PIGH-lohs). In response, the Spartan commander Brasidas widened the war in 424 B.C.E. by capturing Amphipolis, one of Athens's most valuable subject states. Two years later, both Cleon and Brasidas were killed in a battle to recapture the city. Recognizing that ten years of war had resulted only in death, destruction, and stalemate, Sparta and Athens concluded the Peace of Nicias (NIGH-shee-uhs) in 421 B.C.E.

The Peace of Nicias resulted in a cold war. The cold war soon grew hotter, however, thanks to the ambitions of the Athenian aristocrat Alcibiades (al-suh-BIGH-uh-deez) (ca. 450–404 B.C.E.). A shameless opportunist, Alcibiades widened the war to further his own career and increase the power of Athens. He convinced the Athenians to attack Syracuse, the leading polis in Sicily. His only valid reason was that such an operation would cut the grain supply from Sicily to the Peloponnesus. The undertaking was vast, requiring an enormous fleet and thousands of sailors and soldiers. In 414 B.C.E. the Athenians laid siege to Syracuse. The Syracusans fought back bravely and in 413 B.C.E. succeeded in crushing the Athenians.

The disaster in Sicily ushered in the final phase of the war, which was marked by three major developments: the renewal of war between Athens and Sparta, Persia's intervention in the war, and the revolt of many Athenian subjects. The year 413 B.C.E. saw Sparta's declaration of war against Athens and widespread revolt within the Athenian Empire.

Chapter 3
The Development of Classical
Greece • ca. 2000–338 B.C.E.

68

CHAPTER LOCATOR | How did geography shape the early history of the Greeks?

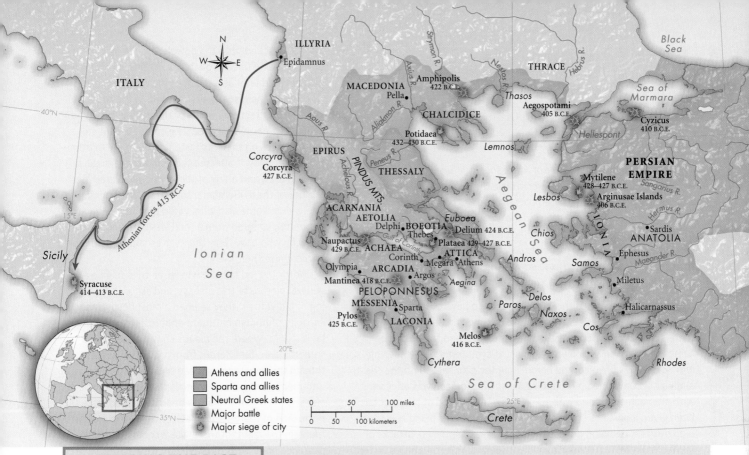

Map 3.4 The Peloponnesian War, 431–404 B.C.E.

This map shows the alignment of states during the Peloponnesian War.

ANALYZING THE MAP Where geographically do the major battles and sieges take place? What does this suggest about the spread of this conflict?

CONNECTIONS What does this map tell us about the growing political disintegration of Greece?

To complete this activity online, go to the Online Study Guide at **bedfordstmartins.com/mckaywestunderstanding**.

Yet Sparta still lacked a navy, the only instrument that could take advantage of the unrest of Athens's subjects, most of whom lived either on islands or in Ionia. Alcibiades, now working for Sparta, provided a solution: the Persians would build a fleet for Sparta, and in return, the Spartans would give Ionia back to Persia. Now equipped with a fleet, the Spartans challenged the Athenians in the Aegean, the result being a long roll of inconclusive naval battles.

The strain of war prompted the Athenians in 407 B.C.E. to recall Alcibiades from exile, but even he could not restore Athenian fortunes. In 405 B.C.E. Spartan forces destroyed the last Athenian fleet at the Battle of Aegospotami, after which the Spartans blockaded Athens until it was starved into submission. After twenty-seven years the Peloponnesian War was over.

Athenian Arts in the Age of Pericles

In the last half of the fifth century B.C.E. and prior to the outbreak of the Peloponnesian War, Pericles appropriated Delian League funds to pay for a huge building program,

What was the polis and what was its role in Greek society?   What were the major developments of the Greek Archaic Age?   **How did war affect Greek civilization?**   How did Macedonia come to dominate Greece?

69

LISTENING TO THE PAST

Thucydides on the Great Plague at Athens, 430 B.C.E.

In 430 B.C.E. many of the people of Attica sought refuge in Athens to escape the Spartan invasion. Overcrowding, the lack of proper sanitation, and the scarcity of clean water exposed the huddled population to virulent disease, and a severe plague attacked the crowded masses. The great historian Thucydides lived in Athens at the time and contracted the disease himself. He was one of the fortunate people who survived the ordeal. For most people, however, the disease proved fatal. Thucydides left a vivid description of the nature of the plague and of people's reaction to it.

People in perfect health suddenly began to have burning feelings in the head; their eyes became red and inflamed; inside their mouths there was bleeding from the throat and tongue, and the breath became unnatural and unpleasant. The next symptoms were sneezing and hoarseness of voice, and before long the pain settled on the chest and was accompanied by coughing. Next the stomach was affected with stomach-aches and with vomitings of every kind of bile that has been given a name by the medical profession, all this being accompanied by great pain and difficulty. In most cases there were attacks of ineffectual retching, producing violent spasms; this sometimes ended with this stage of the disease, but sometimes continued long afterwards. Externally the body was not very hot to the touch, nor was there any pallor: the skin was rather reddish and livid, breaking out into small pustules and ulcers. But inside there was a feeling of burning, so that people could not bear the touch even of the lightest linen clothing, but wanted to be completely naked, and indeed most of all would have liked to plunge into cold water. Many of the sick who were uncared for actually did so, plunging into the water-tanks in an effort to relieve a thirst which was unquenchable; for it was just the same with them whether they drank much or little. Then all the time they were afflicted with insomnia and the desperate feeling of not being able to keep still.

In the period when the disease was at its height, the body, so far from wasting away, showed surprising powers of resistance to all the agony, so that there was still some strength left on the seventh or eighth day, which was the time when, in most cases, death came from the internal fever. But if people survived this critical period, then the disease descended to the bowels, producing violent ulceration and uncontrollable diarrhoea, so that most of them died later as a result of the weakness caused by this. For the disease, first settling in the head, went on to affect every part of the body in turn, and even when people escaped its worst effects, it still left its traces on them by fastening upon the extremities of the body. It affected the genitals, the fingers, and the toes, and many of those who recovered lost the use of these members; some, too, went blind. There were some also who, when they first began to get better, suffered from a total loss of memory, not knowing who they were themselves and being unable to recognize their friends.

Words indeed fail one when one tries to give a general picture of this disease; and as for the suffering of individuals, they seemed almost beyond the capacity of human nature to endure. Here in particular is a point where the plague showed itself to be something quite different from ordinary diseases: though there were many dead bodies lying about unburied, the birds and animals that eat human flesh either did not come near them or, if they did taste the flesh, died of it afterwards. Evidence for this may be found in the fact that there was a complete disappearance of all birds of prey: they were not to be seen either around the bodies or anywhere else. But dogs, being domestic animals, provided the best opportunity of observing this effect of the plague.

These, then, were the general features of the disease, though I have omitted all kinds of peculiarities which occurred in various individual cases. Meanwhile, during all this time there was no serious outbreak of any of the usual kinds of illness; if any such cases did occur, they ended in the plague. Some died in neglect, some in spite of every possible care being taken of them. As for a recognized method of treatment, it would be true to say that no such thing existed; what did good in some cases did harm in others. Those with naturally strong constitutions were no better able than the weak to resist the disease, which carried away all alike, even those who were treated and dieted with the greatest care. The

planning temples and other buildings to honor Athena, the patron goddess of the city, and to display to all Greeks the glory of the Athenian polis. To build support, Pericles also pointed out that his program would employ many Athenians and bring economic prosperity to the city. Construction of the Parthenon began in 447 B.C.E., followed by the Propylaea, the temple of Athena Nike (Athena the Victorious), and the Erechtheum (Map 3.5).

The Acropolis was the site of religious festivals, the most important of which was the Great Panathenae. Every four years all Athenians and legal residents formed a huge pro-

Chapter 3
The Development of Classical
Greece • ca. 2000–338 B.C.E.

70

CHAPTER LOCATOR | How did geography shape the early history of the Greeks?

The god Asclepius, represented by a snake, putting an end to urban plague. (Bibliothèque nationale de France)

most terrible thing of all was the despair into which people fell when they realized that they had caught the plague. Terrible, too, was the sight of people dying like sheep through having caught the disease as a result of nursing others. This indeed caused more deaths than anything else. For when people were afraid to visit the sick, then they died with no one to look after them. Indeed, there were many houses in which all the inhabitants perished through lack of attention. When, on the other hand, they did visit the sick, they lost their own lives, and this was particularly true of those who made it a point of honor to act properly. Such people felt ashamed to think of their own safety and went into their friends' houses at times when even the members of the household were so overwhelmed by the weight of their calamities that they had actually given up the usual practice of making laments for the dead. Yet still the ones who felt most pity for the sick and the dying were those who had had the plague themselves and had recovered from it. They knew what it was like and at the same time felt themselves to be safe, for no one

caught the disease twice, or, if he did, the second attack was never fatal. . . .

A factor that made matters much worse than they were already was the removal of people from the country into the city, and this particularly affected the newcomers. There were no houses for them, and, living as they did during the hot season in badly ventilated huts, they died like flies. The bodies of the dying were heaped one on top of the other, and half-dead creatures could be seen staggering about in the streets or flocking around the fountains in their desire for water.

The catastrophe was so overwhelming that people, not knowing what would happen next to them, became indifferent to every rule of religion and law. Athens owed to the plague the beginnings of a state of unprecedented lawlessness. People now began openly to venture on acts of self-indulgence which before then they used to keep in the dark. Thus they resolved to spend their money quickly and to spend it on pleasure, since money and life alike seemed equally ephemeral. As for what is called honor, no one showed himself willing to abide by its laws, so doubtful was it whether one would survive to enjoy the name for it. It was generally agreed that what was both honorable and valuable was the pleasure of the moment and everything that might conceivably contribute to that pleasure. No fear of god or law of man had a restraining influence. As for the gods, it seemed to be the same thing whether one worshiped them or not, when one saw the good and the bad dying indiscriminately. As for offenses against human law, no one expected to be punished. Instead, everyone felt that already a far heavier sentence had been passed on him and was hanging over him, and that before the time for its execution arrived, it was only natural to get some pleasure out of life.

This, then, was the calamity that fell upon Athens, and the times were hard indeed, with people dying inside the city and the land outside being laid waste. 〞

Source: Rex Warner, trans., *Thucydides, History of the Peloponnesian War* (Penguin Classics, 1954; rev. ed., 1972), pp. 152–156. Translation copyright © Rex Warner, 1954. Introduction and Appendices copyright © M. I. Finley, 1972. Reproduced by permission of Penguin Books Ltd.

QUESTIONS FOR ANALYSIS

1. What does this account of the plague say about human nature when in an extreme crisis?
2. Does popular religion offer any solace during such a catastrophe?
3. How did public laws and customs cope with such a disaster?

cession to bring the statue of Athena in the Parthenon an exquisite robe. After the religious ceremonies, all the people joined in a feast to honor Athena.

Once the procession began, they first saw the Propylaea, the ceremonial gateway, a building of complicated layout and grand design. On the right is the small temple of Athena Nike, built to commemorate the victory over the Persians. The Ionic frieze (a broad band of sculpture) above its columns depicts the struggle between the Greeks and the Persians. Here for all the world to see is a tribute to Athenian and Greek valor — and a reminder of Athens's part in the victory.

What was the polis and what was its role in Greek society?   What were the major developments of the Greek Archaic Age?   **How did war affect Greek civilization?**   How did Macedonia come to dominate Greece?

71

The Acropolis of Athens These buildings embody the noblest spirit of Greek architecture. From the entrance visitors walk through the Propylaea and its pillars (lower center). Ahead opens the grand view of the Parthenon, still noble in ruins (center). To the left stands the Erechtheum, the whole a monument to Athens itself. (Courtesy, Sotiris Toumbis Editions)

To the left of the visitors, as they pass through the Propylaea, stands the Erechtheum, an Ionic temple that housed several ancient shrines. On its southern side is the Portico of the Caryatids, a porch whose roof is supported by statues of Athenian maidens.

As visitors walk on, they obtain a full view of the Parthenon. The Parthenon is the chief monument to Athena and her city. The sculptures that adorn the temple portray the greatness of Athens and its goddess. The figures on the eastern pediment depict Athena's birth, those on the west the victory of Athena over the god Poseidon in their struggle for the possession of Attica. Inside the Parthenon stood a huge statue of Athena, the masterpiece of the great sculptor Phidias.

On the Acropolis the Athenians had built a magnificent monument to their goddesses and themselves, one that still moves people today. Even the pollution of modern Athens, while it is destroying these ancient buildings, cannot rob them of their splendor and charm.

The development of drama was tied to the religious festivals of the city and was as rooted in the life of the polis as were the architecture and sculpture of the Acropolis.

Map 3.5 Ancient Athens, ca. 450 B.C.E. By modern standards, the city of Athens was hardly more than a town, not much larger than one square mile. Yet this small area reflects the concentration of ancient Greek life in the polis.

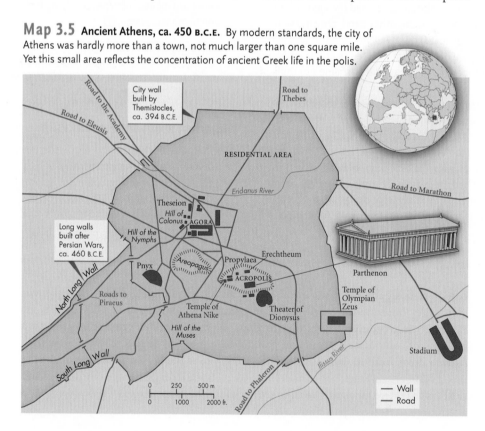

Chapter 3
The Development of Classical
Greece • ca. 2000–338 B.C.E.

72

CHAPTER LOCATOR | How did geography shape the early history of the Greeks?

The polis sponsored the production of plays and required wealthy citizens to pay the expenses of their production. At the beginning of the year, dramatists submitted their plays to the archon of the polis. He chose those he considered best and assigned a theatrical troupe to each playwright. Many plays were highly controversial, but the archons neither suppressed nor censored them.

The Athenian dramatists were the first artists in Western society to examine such basic questions as the rights of the individual, the demands of society on the individual, and the nature of good and evil. The dramatists used their art to portray, understand, and resolve life's basic conflicts.

Aeschylus (ES-kuh-luhs) (525–456 B.C.E.), the first of the great Athenian dramatists, was also the first to express the agony of the individual caught in conflict. In his trilogy of plays, *The Oresteia* (ohr-eh-STEE-uh), Aeschylus deals with the themes of betrayal, murder, and reconciliation, urging that reason and justice be applied to reconcile fundamental conflicts.

Sophocles (SOF-uh-kleez) (496–406 B.C.E.) also dealt with matters personal and political. Perhaps his most famous plays are *Oedipus* (EHD-uh-puhs) *the King* and its sequel, *Oedipus at Colonus*. *Oedipus the King* is the tragic story of a man doomed by the gods to kill his father and marry his mother. Try as he might to avoid his fate, his every action brings him closer to its fulfillment. When at last he realizes that he has carried out the decree of the gods, Oedipus blinds himself and flees into exile. In *Oedipus at Colonus* Sophocles dramatizes the last days of the broken king, whose patient suffering and uncomplaining piety win him an exalted position. In the end the gods honor him for his virtue.

With Euripides (yoo-RIP-uh-deez) (ca. 480–406 B.C.E.) drama entered a new, and in many ways more personal, phase. To him the gods were far less important than human beings. The essence of Euripides' tragedy is the flawed character—men and women who bring disaster on themselves and their loved ones because their passions overwhelm reason.

▪ Art and Philosophy in the Hellenic Period

PERIOD	SIGNIFICANT EVENTS	MAJOR WRITERS AND PHILOSOPHERS
Bronze Age 2000–1100 B.C.E.	Arrival of the Greeks in Greece	
Dark Age 1100–800 B.C.E.	Evolution of the polis Rebirth of literacy	Homer Hesiod
Archaic Age 800–500 B.C.E.	Rise of Sparta and Athens Colonization of the Mediterranean basin Flowering of lyric poetry Development of philosophy and science in Ionia	Anaximander Heraclitus Sappho Solon Thales
Classical Period 500–338 B.C.E.	Persian wars Peloponnesian War Rise of drama and historical writing Flowering of Greek philosophy Conquest of Greece by Philip of Macedonia	Aeschylus Aristophanes Aristotle Euripides Herodotus Plato Socrates Sophocles Thucydides

What was the polis and what was its role in Greek society?

What were the major developments of the Greek Archaic Age?

How did war affect Greek civilization?

How did Macedonia come to dominate Greece?

Writers of comedy treated the affairs of the polis and its politicians bawdily and often coarsely. Even so, their plays also were performed at religious festivals. Best known are the comedies of Aristophanes (eh-ruh-STAH-fuh-neez) (ca. 445–386 B.C.E.), an ardent lover of his city and a merciless critic of cranks and quacks. Like Aeschylus, Sophocles, and Euripides, Aristophanes used his art to dramatize his ideas on the right conduct of the citizen and the value of the polis.

Daily Life in Periclean Athens

In sharp contrast with the rich intellectual and cultural life of Periclean Athens stands the simplicity of its material life. The Athenian house was rather simple. It consisted of a series of rooms opening onto a central courtyard. Many houses had bedrooms on an upper floor. Artisans often set aside a room to use as a shop or work area. Larger houses often had a room at the front where the men of the family ate and entertained guests, and a *gynaikon* (women's quarter) at the back where women worked, ate, and slept. Other

▪ PICTURING THE PAST

Blacksmith's Shop
In the winter the blacksmith's shop, kept warm by a constant fire, was a favorite place for the men to chat and to come in from the cold while the smiths worked.

(The Plousios Painter, two-handled jar [amphora]. Greek, Late Archaic Period, about 500–490 B.C. Place of Manufacture: Greece, Attica, Athens. Ceramic, Black Figure. Height: 36.1 cm [14³⁄₁₆ in.]; diameter: 25.9 cm [10³⁄₁₆ in.]. Museum of Fine Arts, Boston, Henry Lillie Pierce Fund, 01.8035. Photograph © Museum of Fine Arts, Boston)

ANALYZING THE IMAGE What is happening in this scene? What tools and objects are depicted? What are the different men doing?

CONNECTIONS This vase shows the activities of men engaged in a trade. How much do you think the scene shown here differs from the activity of tradespeople today? Consider the people shown, the nature of the work, the clothing, and the objects in use.

To complete this activity online, go to the Online Study Guide at **bedfordstmartins.com/ mckaywestunderstanding**.

Chapter 3
The Development of Classical
74   **Greece • ca. 2000–338 B.C.E.**

CHAPTER LOCATOR   How did geography shape the early history of the Greeks?

rooms included the kitchen and bathroom. By modern standards there was not much furniture. In the men's dining room were couches, a sideboard, and small tables. Cups and other pottery were often hung from pegs on the wall. In the courtyard were the well, a small altar, and a washbasin. If the family lived in the country, the stalls of the animals faced the courtyard.

Cooking, done over a hearth in the house, provided warmth in the winter. Baking and roasting were done in ovens. Food consisted primarily of various grains, especially wheat and barley, as well as lentils, olives, figs, and grapes. Garlic and onion were popular garnishes, and wine was always on hand. The Greeks used olive oil for cooking, as an ointment, and as lamp fuel. The only Greeks who consistently ate meat were the Spartan warriors.

In the city a man might support himself as a craftsman or he could contract with the polis to work on public buildings, such as the Parthenon and Erechtheum. Certain crafts, including spinning and weaving, were generally done by women. Men and women without skills worked as paid laborers but competed with slaves for work. Slaves were usually foreigners and often "barbarians," people whose native language was not Greek.

Slavery was commonplace in Greece, as it was throughout the ancient world. Greek slavery resembled Mesopotamian slavery. Slaves received some protection under the law and could buy their freedom. On the other hand, masters could mistreat or neglect their slaves, although killing them was illegal. Most slaves in Athens served as domestics and performed light labor around the house. Nurses for children, teachers of reading and writing, and guardians for young men were often slaves. Other slaves were skilled workers who could be found working on public buildings or in small workshops.

Gender and Sexuality

The social condition of Athenian women has been the subject of much debate. Women appear frequently in literature and art, but rarely in historical accounts, which mostly record military and political events in which women seldom played a notable part. Yet that does not mean that women were totally invisible in the life of the polis.

Citizen women never appeared in court or in the public political assemblies that were the heart of Athenian democracy, though they did attend public festivals, ceremonies, and funerals. In a few cases, women were priestesses in the cults of various goddesses. Priestesses prayed in public on behalf of the city and, like priests, were paid for their services. The most prominent priestess was at Delphi, near Athens, where the Pythia, a priestess for life, passed on messages about the future from the god Apollo to priests for interpretation.

The law protected the status of free women of the citizen class. Only her children, not those of foreigners or slaves, could be citizens. Women in Athens and elsewhere in Greece received a certain amount of social and legal protection from their bridal gift of money or property. Upon marriage the bride's father gave the couple a gift of land or money that the husband administered. It was, however, never his; and in the rare case of divorce, it was returned to the wife.

A citizen woman's main functions were to bear and raise children. Childbirth could be dangerous for both mother and infant, so pregnant women usually made sacrifices or visited temples to ask help from the gods. Women relied on their relatives, on friends, and on midwives to assist in the delivery. Greek physicians did not usually concern themselves with obstetrical care.

Existing information shows that women actually lived much freer and more visible lives than Babylonian or Jewish women. Husbands and wives had different duties but shared the goal of building a happy and prosperous home for each other and their children. The wife ran every aspect of the house. She kept the family's accounts and drew up

Greek Courtship Here two young lovers embrace. With one arm around his girl and the other holding a wine vessel, he draws his girl nearer. With a smile she seems more interested in her music, for with her right thumb she turns the boy down. (Erich Lessing/Art Resource, NY)

the budget. She saw to the organization of the family's possessions and inspected everything that entered the house. The wife supervised the household slaves in their duties and personally cared for slaves who became ill. When the crops came in, she directed their storage.

Greek sexuality often remains misunderstood today. Some people derive their idea of it from the philosophers Plato and Aristotle, who praised love that was intellectual and nonsexual—platonic love—and were suspicious of the power of sexual passion. While they intellectualized sex, the soldier-poet Archilochus (d. 652 B.C.E.) preferred "to light upon the flesh of a maid and ram belly to belly and thigh to thigh."[1] Some few, but revealing, glimpses from the ancient sources indicate that women, too, enjoyed sex for its own sake.

Homosexuality was generally accepted in ancient Greece. In classical Athens, part of an adolescent citizen's training in adulthood was supposed to entail a hierarchical sexual and tutorial relationship with an older man, who most likely was married and may have had other female sexual partners as well. These relationships between adolescents and men were often celebrated in literature and art, in part because Athenians regarded perfection as possible only in the male. The perfect body was that of the young male, and perfect love was that between an adolescent and an older man. This love was supposed to become intellectualized and platonic once the adolescent became an adult.

A small number of sources refer to female-female sexual desire, the most famous of which are the poems of Sappho, a female poet who lived on the island of Lesbos in the sixth century B.C.E. Today the English word *lesbian* is derived from Sappho's home island of Lesbos. In one of her poems she recalled the words of her lover:

Sappho, if you do not come out,
I swear, I will love you no more.
O rise and free your lovely strength
From the bed and shine upon us.
Lifting off your Chian nightgown, and
Like a pure lily by a spring,
Bathe in the water.[2]

A younger man who was not troubled by these affairs proposed to Sappho, but she refused him because she was past childbearing age. This and the earlier examples indicate that sex was as complicated in ancient Greece as it is now.

Prostitution, both male and female, was another feature of Greek sexuality. It was both common and legal, but it was socially tainted. A male prostitute was generally despised, and Athenian men would lose their citizenship if they were convicted of prostitution. Society treated female prostitutes differently. Beautiful, articulate, and accomplished prostitutes were known as *hetairai*, "companions." (See "Individuals in Society: Aspasia," at right.) Lower-class ordinary prostitutes who only sold sex were called *pornoi*, "whores."

Chapter 3
The Development of Classical Greece • ca. 2000–338 B.C.E.

76

CHAPTER LOCATOR | How did geography shape the early history of the Greeks?

Roman portrait of Aspasia based on a Greek statue.
(Vatican Museums/Art Resource, NY)

"IF IT IS NECESSARY for me indeed to speak of female virtues, to those of you who have now become widows, I shall explain the entire situation briefly. It is in your hands whether you will not fall below your nature. The greatest glory to you is to be least talked about by men, either for excellence or blame" (Thucydides 2.46.1). These words were reportedly uttered by Pericles to the widows at a public funeral honoring those killed during the first year of the Peloponnesian War. At the same time he was enjoying a long-standing affair with Aspasia, who was very much talked about by men and women. Whether Pericles actually said these words is for the most part irrelevant. Their significance lies in their expression of the Athenian ideal of the proper Athenian lady. In short, she should stay at home and limit her talents to her household. This ideal became the reality for most Athenian women, whose names and actions were not recorded and thus did not become part of history. Aspasia was a notable exception.

Aspasia (as-PAY-zhuh) was born in the Greek city of Miletus and came to Athens in about 445 B.C.E. Little is known about her life, but she played a role in Athenian society that was far more renowned than, and far different from, that allegedly proposed by Pericles. The irony of her life is that she became his mistress and enjoyed a very public career, exactly the opposite of the call for women to stay anonymous attributed to Pericles in the Funeral Oration cited above.

Once in Athens, Aspasia may have become a hetaira (hih-TIGH-ruh), as the comic poet Aristophanes testifies. As such she accompanied men at dinner parties, where their wives would not have been welcome, and also served as a sexual partner. Yet she did more than drink and have sex with her clients. She also provided witty, intellectual conversation and publicly acted with perfect decorum. She thereby filled an intellectual role not usually expected of a proper wife. A successful hetaira could easily become the mistress of a wealthy and prominent man.

Aspasia fits into the category of a lovely and very intelligent companion. Legend reports that she taught rhetoric, an essential tool for Athenian politicians. That meant that her pupils were necessarily men. She thus enjoyed a rare opportunity to influence the men who shaped the political life of Athens. The Roman biographer Plutarch reports that Aspasia enjoyed the company of the foremost men in Athens. Their conversations included philosophy, and she is reputed to have taught Socrates the art of public speaking. While the claim is undoubtedly false, it points to her reputation as a very accomplished woman.

The great change in Aspasia's life came with her introduction to Pericles, who was especially taken with her rare political wisdom. After Pericles divorced his wife, he took Aspasia as his mistress. She and Pericles produced a son, also named Pericles. Aspasia was not an Athenian citizen, and it was illegal for the son of a foreign parent to be granted citizenship. Yet when Pericles' sons by his wife died in the plague, the Athenians made an exception and granted the young Pericles citizenship. That remarkable fact testifies to the respect that many Athenians felt not only for the great statesman but also for Aspasia. Others ridiculed the connection and felt that Pericles was making a fool of himself. The majority thought otherwise, or the son would not have been granted citizenship.

Aspasia's achievements are clear. She lifted herself from a vulnerable to a respected position in Athenian society. It is not enough to ascribe this to her beauty. Her intelligence and her sense of culture were equally, if not more, important. Social mobility in classical Athens was rare, but Aspasia proves that it was possible.

QUESTIONS FOR ANALYSIS

1. What talents enabled Aspasia to rise from the status of companion or courtesan to that of a generally respected person in society?
2. What made Aspasia's position in Athens precarious despite her obvious talents?

What was the polis and what was its role in Greek society?   What were the major developments of the Greek Archaic Age?   **How did war affect Greek civilization?**   How did Macedonia come to dominate Greece?

77

Greek Religion

Greek religion is extremely difficult for modern people to understand, largely because of the great differences between Greek and modern cultures. In the first place, the Greeks had no uniform faith or creed. Although they usually worshiped the same deities— Zeus, Hera, Apollo, Athena, and others—the cults of these gods and goddesses varied from polis to polis. The Greeks had no sacred books such as the Bible, and Greek religion was often more a matter of ritual than of belief. Nor did cults impose an ethical code of conduct. Greeks did not have to follow any particular rule of life, practice certain virtues, or even live decent lives in order to participate. Unlike the Egyptians and Hebrews, the Greeks lacked a priesthood as the modern world understands the term. In Greece priests and priestesses existed to care for temples and sacred property and to conduct the proper rituals, but not to make or enforce religious rules or doctrines.

Although temples to the gods were common, they were not normally places where a congregation met to worship as a spiritual community. Instead, the individual Greek man or woman either visited the temple occasionally on matters of private concern or walked in a procession to a particular temple to celebrate a particular festival. When the Greeks sought the favor of the gods, they offered sacrifices, usually of goats or chickens. By offering the gods parts of the sacrifice while consuming the rest themselves, worshipers forged a bond with the gods. Some deities were particularly worshiped by men and some by women.

The most important members of the Greek pantheon were Zeus, the king of the gods, and his wife, Hera. Although they were the mightiest and most honored of the deities who lived on Mount Olympus, their divine children were closer to ordinary people. Apollo was especially popular. He represented the epitome of youth, beauty, benevolence, and athletic skill. He was also the god of music and culture and in many ways symbolized the best of Greek culture. His sister Athena, who patronized women's crafts such as weaving, was also a warrior-goddess. Other divinities watched over other aspects of human life.

The Greeks also honored some heroes. A hero was born of a union of a god or goddess and a mortal and was considered an intermediate between the divine and the human. Herakles (or Hercules, as the Romans called him) was the most popular of the Greek heroes. According to belief, he successfully fulfilled twelve labors, all of which pitted him against mythical opponents or tasks. Worshipers believed that he, like other heroes, protected mortals from supernatural dangers and provided an ideal of vigorous masculinity.

Besides the Olympian gods, each polis had its own minor deities, and each deity had his or her own local cult. In many instances Greek religion involved the official gods and goddesses of the polis and their cults. The polis administered the cults and festivals, and everyone was expected to participate in this civic religion. Participating unbelievers, who seem to have been a small minority, were not considered hypocrites. Rather, they were seen as patriotic, loyal citizens who in honoring the gods, regardless of their personal views, also honored the polis.

Some Greeks turned to mystery cults, the most famous being the Eleusinian (el-YOO-seh-nee-uhn) mysteries in Attica. These cults promised life after death to those initiated into them. Once people had successfully undergone initiation, they were forbidden to reveal the secrets of the cult. Mystery cults like Eleusis inspired many similar cults in the Hellenistic period and foreshadowed many aspects of early Christianity.

Much religion was local and domestic. Each village possessed its own cults and rituals, and individual families honored various deities privately in their homes. The celebrations included all elements of society, women and slaves included. Many people also believed that magic rituals and spells were effective and sought the assistance of individuals reputed to have special knowledge or powers to cure disease, drive away ghosts, bring good weather, or influence the actions of others.

78

Chapter 3
The Development of Classical Greece • ca. 2000–338 B.C.E.

CHAPTER LOCATOR | How did geography shape the early history of the Greeks?

Sacrificial Scene Much of Greek religion was festive, as this scene demonstrates. The participants include women and boys dressed in their finest clothes and crowned with garlands. Musicians add to the festivities. Only the sheep will not enjoy the ceremony. (Scala/Art Resource, NY)

Though Greek religion in general was individual or related to the polis, the Greeks also shared some Pan-Hellenic festivals, the chief of which were held at Olympia in honor of Zeus and at Delphi in honor of Apollo. The festivities at Olympia included athletic contests that have inspired the modern Olympic games. Held every four years, these games attracted visitors from all over the Greek world and lasted well into Christian times. The Pythian games at Delphi were also held every four years, but they included musical and literary contests. Both the Olympic and the Pythian games were unifying factors in Greek life, bringing Greeks together culturally as well as religiously.

The Flowering of Philosophy

The myths and epics of the Mesopotamians are ample testimony that speculation about the origin of the universe and of humans did not begin with the Greeks. The signal achievement of the Greeks was the willingness of some to treat these questions in rational rather than mythological terms. Although Greek philosophy did not fully flower until the classical period, Ionian thinkers in the Archaic period had already begun to ask what the universe was made of. These men are called the Pre-Socratics, for their work preceded the philosophical revolution begun by the Athenian Socrates. Though they were keen observers, the Pre-Socratics rarely undertook deliberate experimentation. Instead, they took individual facts and wove them into general theories. They believed the universe was simple and was subject to natural laws. Drawing on their observations, they speculated about the basic building blocks of the universe and took the first steps toward the development of the scientific method. The culmination of Pre-Socratic thought was the theory that four simple substances made up the universe: fire, air, earth, and water.

With this impressive heritage behind them, the philosophers of the classical period ventured into new areas of speculation. This development was partly due to the work of Hippocrates (hih-PAH-kruh-teez) (ca. 430 B.C.E.), the father of medicine. Like Thales (THAY-leez), Hippocrates sought natural explanations for phenomena. Basing his opinions on empirical knowledge, he taught that natural means could be employed to fight disease. But Hippocrates broke away from the mainstream of Ionian speculation by declaring that medicine was a separate craft that had its own set of principles.

The distinction between natural science and philosophy on which Hippocrates insisted was also promoted by the Sophists, who traveled the Greek world teaching young men. Despite differences of opinion on philosophical matters, the Sophists all agreed that human beings were the proper subject of study. They also believed that excellence could be taught, and they used philosophy and rhetoric to prepare young men for life in the polis. The Sophists put great emphasis on logic and the meanings of words. They criticized traditional beliefs, religion, rituals, and myths and even questioned the laws of the polis. In essence, they argued that nothing is absolute, that everything is relative.

Socrates (ca. 470–399 B.C.E.) shared the Sophists' belief that human beings and their environment were the essential subjects of philosophical inquiry. His approach when posing ethical questions and defining concepts was to start with a general topic or problem and to narrow the matter to its essentials. He did so by continuous questioning rather than lecturing, a process known as the Socratic dialogue. Socrates thought that by constantly pursuing excellence, an essential part of which was knowledge, human beings could approach the supreme good and thus find true happiness. Yet in 399 B.C.E. Socrates was brought to trial, convicted, and executed on charges of corrupting the youth of the city and introducing new gods.

Socrates' student Plato (427–347 B.C.E.) carried on his master's search for truth, founding a philosophical school, the Academy. Plato believed that the ideal polis could exist only when its citizens were well educated. From education came the possibility of determining all of the virtues of life and combining them into a system that would lead to an intelligent, moral, and ethical life. He further concluded that only divine providence could guide people to virtue. In short, he equated god with the concept of good.

Plato developed the theory that there are two worlds: the impermanent, changing world of appearance that we know through our senses, and the eternal, unchanging realm of "forms" that constitute the essence of true reality. Only the mind can perceive eternal forms. The intellectual journey consists of moving from the realm of appearances to the realm of forms. His perfect polis was utopian and could exist only if its rulers were philosophers.

Aristotle (384–322 B.C.E.) carried on the philosophical tradition of Socrates and Plato. A student of Plato, Aristotle founded his own school at the Lyceum, an Athenian gymnasium. The range of Aristotle's thought is staggering. He approached the topic of the ideal polis more realistically than had Plato. He stressed moderation, concluding that the balance of his ideal state depended on people of talent and education who could avoid extremes.

Aristotle tried to understand the changes of nature—what caused them and where they led. His interests embraced logic, ethics, natural science, politics, poetry, and art. His method was the syllogism, whereby he reasoned from a general statement to a particular conclusion. Aristotle also tried to bridge the gap that Plato had created between abstract truth and concrete perception. He argued that the universe is finite, spherical, and eternal. In the process, he discussed an immaterial being that is his conception of god that neither created the universe nor guided it. His god, then, is without purpose. Yet for him scientific endeavor, the highest attainable form of living, reaches the divine.

Aristotle expressed the heart of his philosophy in two works, *Physics* and *Metaphysics*. In them he combined empiricism, or observation, and speculative method. In *Physics* he tried to explain all nature by describing how natural phenomena work on one another and how these actions lead to the results that people see around them daily. Although Aristotle considered nature impersonal, he also felt that it had its own purposes. In a sense, this is a rudimentary ancestor of the concept of evolution.

In *On the Heaven* Aristotle added ether (the sky) to air, fire, water, and earth as building blocks of the universe. He wrongly thought that the earth was the center of the universe, with the stars and planets revolving around it. The Hellenistic scientist Aristarchus

80

Chapter 3
**The Development of Classical
Greece • ca. 2000–338 B.C.E.**

CHAPTER LOCATOR   How did geography
shape the early history
of the Greeks?

of Samos later realized that the earth revolves around the sun, but this did not replace Aristotle's view. Not until the sixteenth century C.E. did Nicolaus Copernicus prove that the sun, not the earth, stood at the center of our solar system.

Athenian philosophers thus reflected their own society in their thought, but they also called for a broader examination of the universe and the place of humans in it than had earlier thinkers. Both the breadth of their vision and its limitations are important legacies to Western civilization.

▼ How did Macedonia come to dominate Greece?

The turbulent period from 404 to 338 B.C.E. is sometimes mistakenly seen as a time of failure and decline. It was instead a vibrant era in which Plato and Aristotle thought and wrote, one in which architecture, literature, oratory, and historical writing flourished. If the fourth century was a period of decline, this was so only in politics. The Peloponnesian War and its aftermath proved that the polis had reached the limits of its success as an effective political institution. The attempts of various city-states to dominate the others led only to incessant warfare.

The Greeks of the fourth century B.C.E. experimented seriously with two political concepts in the hope of preventing war. First was the Common Peace, the idea that the states of Greece, whether large or small, should live together in peace and freedom, each enjoying its own laws and customs. In 386 B.C.E. this concept was a vital part of a peace treaty with the Persian Empire in which the Greeks and Persians pledged themselves to live in harmony.

The second concept to become prominent was federalism. The new impetus toward federalism was intended more to gain security through numbers than to prevent war. Greek leagues had usually developed in regions where geography shaped a well-defined area and where people shared a broad kinship. By banding together, the people of these leagues could marshal their resources, both human and material, to defend themselves from outside interference. In the fourth century B.C.E. at least ten other federations of states came into being or were revitalized.

Common Peace A political concept created in the fourth century B.C.E. to prevent war based on the idea that the states of Greece should live together in peace and freedom, each enjoying its own laws and customs.

The Struggle for Hegemony

The chief states — Sparta, Athens, and Thebes — each tried to create a hegemony (hih-JEH-muh-nee), that is, political domination over other states, even though they sometimes paid lip service to the ideals of the Common Peace. In every instance, each major power wanted to be the leader, and the ambition, jealousy, pride, and fear of the major powers doomed the effort to achieve genuine peace.

When the Spartan commander Lysander defeated Athens in 404 B.C.E., the Spartans used their victory to build an empire instead of ensuring the freedom of all Greeks. Their decision brought them into conflict with Persia, which now demanded the return of Ionia to its control (see page 67). From 400 to 386 B.C.E. the Spartans fought the Persians for Ionia, a conflict that eventually engulfed Greece itself. After years of stalemate the Spartans made peace with Persia and their Greek enemies. The result was the first formal Common Peace, the King's Peace of 386 B.C.E., which cost Sparta its empire but not its position of dominance in Greece.

Not content with Sparta's hegemony of Greece, the Spartan king Agesilaos (ah-jeh-sih-LAY-uhs) betrayed the very concept of the Common Peace to punish cities that had opposed Sparta during the war. He used naked force against old enemies, especially the

hegemony Political domination over other states.

Statue of Eirene The Athenians erected this statue of Eirene (Peace) holding Ploutos (Wealth) in her left arm. Athens had seen only war for some fifty-six years, and the statue celebrated the Common Peace of 375 B.C.E. The bitter irony of this poignant scene is that the treaty lasted scarcely a year. (Glyptothek, Munich/Studio Koppermann)

Thebans, even though they had made peace. Agesilaos's imperialism was soon to lead to Sparta's downfall at the hands of the Thebans, the people he sought to tyrannize.

The first sign of Spartan failure came in 378 B.C.E. after the unprovoked attack on Athens. The enraged Athenians created the Second Athenian Confederacy, a federation of states to guarantee the Greeks their rights under the Common Peace. Thebes joined Athens, and the two fought Sparta until 371 B.C.E. Owing to its growing fear of Theban might, Athens made a separate peace with Sparta. Left alone, Thebes defended itself until later that year, when the brilliant Theban general Epaminondas (ih-pah-muh-NAHN-duhs) routed the Spartan army on the small plain of Leuctra.

The defeat of the once-invincible Spartans stunned the Greeks, who wondered how Thebes would use its victory. Epaminondas, also a gifted statesman, immediately grappled with the problem of how to translate military success into political reality. First, in a series of invasions, he eliminated Sparta as a major power and liberated Messenia. He concluded alliances with many Peloponnesian states but made no effort to dominate them. Steadfastly refusing to create a Theban empire, he instead sponsored federalism in Greece and threw his support behind the Common Peace. Although he made Thebes the leader of Greece from 371 to 362 B.C.E., other city-states and leagues were bound to Thebes only by voluntary alliances. By his insistence on the liberty of the Greeks, Epaminondas, more than any other person in Greek history, successfully blended the three concepts of hegemony, federalism, and the Common Peace. His premature death at the Battle of Mantinea in 362 B.C.E. put an end to his efforts, but not to these three political ideals. The question was whether anyone or any state could realize them all.

Philip II and Macedonian Supremacy

While the Greek states exhausted themselves in endless conflicts, the new power of Macedonia rose in the north. The Macedonians were Greeks, but their life on the fringe of the Hellenic world made them seem alien and almost non-Greek. Nevertheless, under a strong king Macedonia was a power to be reckoned with, and in 359 B.C.E. such a king ascended to the throne. Philip II was brilliant and cultured, and he fully understood the strengths and needs of the Macedonians.

The young Philip, already a master of diplomacy and warfare after years spent in Thebes, quickly saw Athens as the principal threat to Macedonia. Once he had secured the borders of Macedonia against barbarian invaders, he launched a series of military operations in the northwestern Aegean. Not only did he win rich territory, but he also slowly pushed the Athenians out of the region. Yet the Greeks themselves opened the road to his ultimate victory in Greece. The opportunity came from still another internal Greek conflict, the Sacred War of 356 to 346 B.C.E. The war broke out when the Phocians, a Greek people in whose land stood the sanctuary of Apollo at Delphi, seized and plundered the sacred temple. Their sacrilege was openly condoned by Athens and Sparta. When the Thebans and other Greeks failed to liberate Delphi, they invited Philip to intervene. He quickly crushed the Phocians in 346 B.C.E., intimidating Athens and Sparta with his fierceness.

In 338 B.C.E. the armies of Thebes and Athens met Philip's forces at the Boeotian city of Chaeronea (kayr-uh-NEE-uh). There Philip's army won a hard-fought victory that

Chapter 3
The Development of Classical Greece • ca. 2000–338 B.C.E.

82

CHAPTER LOCATOR | How did geography shape the early history of the Greeks?

gave him command of Greece and put an end to classical Greek freedom. Because the Greeks could not put aside their quarrels, they fell to an invader. Yet Philip was wise enough to retain much of what the fourth-century Greeks had achieved. Not opposed to the concepts of peace and federalism, he sponsored a new Common Peace in which all of Greece except Sparta, which refused to participate, was united in one political body under his leadership. Philip thus used the concepts of hegemony, the Common Peace, and federalism as tools of Macedonian domination. The ironic result was the end of the age of classical Greece.

←LOOKING BACK LOOKING AHEAD→

ONCE the Persians had established peace and stability throughout the Near East, they turned to Europe. Cyrus the Great first encountered Greek settlers in Anatolia. His successors unsuccessfully tried to conquer Greece, but by then these Indo-European peoples had turned the peninsula of Greece into one of the most vital beds of culture in Western history. They created governments that relied on popular participation, especially democracy and oligarchy. They also created history, in the modern sense of the word, and philosophy, and they made impressive contributions to art, architecture, and literature. Yet the Greeks nearly destroyed themselves in two centuries of warfare. Nonetheless, they overcame this ordeal to hand their precious heritage on to the West.

The heritage of the Greeks and Macedonians proved essential to the evolution of the Hellenistic period, but the older cultures of the East made the era unique in Western civilization. Although the Greeks failed to establish their beloved polis in the East, they and the Macedonians built monarchies that better governed both themselves and the native peoples with whom they lived. A major aspect of their success was the enormous expansion of trade and commerce, making the Hellenistic period far richer than its predecessor. The wealth of the East combined with the creativity of the Greeks led to new advances in science and medicine. When Alexander conquered much of the East, the Greeks and Macedonians thought themselves superior. Only in time did they appreciate the culture of their neighbors. When they did, they created a sophisticated culture of their own with broader horizons than ever before. ■

- **For a list of suggested readings for this chapter, visit** *bedfordstmartins.com/mckaywestunderstanding*.

- **For primary sources from this period, see** *Sources of Western Society,* Second Edition.

- **For Web sites, images, and documents related to topics in this chapter, see Make History at** *bedfordstmartins.com/mckaywestunderstanding*.

What was the polis and what was its role in Greek society?   What were the major developments of the Greek Archaic Age?   How did war affect Greek civilization?   How did Macedonia come to dominate Greece?

Step 1

GETTING STARTED Below are basic terms about this period in the history of Western civilization. Can you identify each term below and explain why it matters? To do this exercise online, go to bedfordstmartins.com/mckaywestunderstanding.

TERMS	WHO (OR WHAT) AND WHEN	WHY IT MATTERS
Minoan, p. 56		
Mycenaean, p. 56		
polis, p. 59		
acropolis, p. 59		
agora, p. 59		
hoplites, p. 59		
monarchy, p. 60		
tyranny, p. 60		
democracy, p. 60		
oligarchy, p. 60		
federalism, p. 60		
helots, p. 63		
Delian League, p. 67		
Common Peace, p. 81		
hegemony, p. 81		

Step 2

MOVING BEYOND THE BASICS The exercise below requires a more advanced understanding of the chapter material. Compare and contrast political and economic conditions in Greece during the Archaic and classical periods. Begin by filling in the chart below with descriptions of the political, economic, and material conditions in the Archaic and classical periods. When you are finished, consider the following questions: What were the sources of Greek unity in the Archaic Age? Why did that unity break down during the classical period? To do this exercise online, go to bedfordstmartins.com/mckaywestunderstanding.

PHASE	POLITICS	ECONOMICS	EXTERNAL THREATS AND INTERNAL DIVISIONS
Archaic Age			
Classical Period			

PUTTING IT ALL TOGETHER
Now that you've reviewed key elements of the chapter, take a step back and try to see the big picture. Remember to use specific examples from the chapter in your answers. **To do this exercise online, go to** bedfordstmartins.com/mckaywestunderstanding.

THE ORIGINS OF GREEK CIVILIZATION

- How did geography shape the early history of Greece?

- Compare and contrast the Minoans and the Mycenaeans. What elements of Minoan civilization did the Mycenaeans find attractive? Why?

- How did the polis embody key aspects of Greek society and culture? Is it fair to say that, in a sense, the polis was the essence of Greek civilization? Why or why not?

THE ARCHAIC AGE, 800–500 B.C.E.

- What sparked Greek expansion in the aftermath of the Dark Age? How did the process of colonization change Greek society and politics?

- Compare and contrast Sparta and Athens. To what extent do these two city-states represent different solutions to the same basic challenges?

THE CLASSICAL PERIOD, 500–338 B.C.E.

- Classical Greece was a period of almost constant warfare. With this in mind, compare and contrast classical Greece with earlier periods of endemic warfare in the Near East. What factors seem to have been conducive to peace in the ancient world? What conditions tended to produce war?

- How did the place of religion in Greek life compare to the role religion played in Near Eastern societies?

THE MACEDONIAN CONQUEST

- What efforts did the Greeks make to put an end to internal conflict among the Greek city-states? Why did these efforts fail?

- Is it fair to say that Greek civilization come to an end with the Macedonian conquest? Why or why not?

▪ In Your Own Words Imagine that you must explain Chapter 3 to someone who hasn't read it. What would be the most important points to include and why?

4

The Hellenistic World

336–30 B.C.E.

Two years after his conquest of Greece, Philip II of Macedonia fell victim to an assassin's dagger. Philip's twenty-year-old son, historically known as Alexander the Great (r. 336–323 B.C.E.), assumed the Macedonian throne. This young man, one of the most remarkable personalities of Western civilization, was to have a profound impact on history.

In 336 B.C.E. Alexander inherited not only Philip's crown but also his policies. After his victory at Chaeronea (kayr-uh-NEE-uh), Philip had organized the states of Greece into a huge league under his leadership and announced to the Greeks his plan to lead them and his Macedonians against the Persian Empire. After his father's death, Alexander made his father's plan his life's work. By overthrowing the Persian Empire and by spreading Hellenism—Greek culture, language, thought, and way of life— as far as India, Alexander was instrumental in creating a new Hellenistic era. As a result of Alexander's exploits, the individualistic and energetic culture of the Greeks came into intimate contact with the venerable older cultures of the Near East. The Hellenistic period would last until the Roman conquest of Egypt in 30 B.C.E., though Hellenistic thought and culture would endure. ∎

Life in the Hellenistic World. Hellenistic cities were centers of culture and the arts. In this first-center B.C.E. mosaic from Pompeii, masked street musicians perform for passersby. (Museo Archeologico Nazionale, Naples, Italy/The Bridgeman Art Library)

Chapter Preview

▶ How and why did Alexander the Great create an empire?

▶ How did Alexander's conquests change the world?

▶ How did Greek culture shape the Hellenistic kingdoms?

▶ What new economic connections were created in this period?

▶ What was the lasting impact of Hellenism?

▼ How and why did Alexander the Great create an empire?

Alexander proclaimed to the Greek world that the invasion of Persia was to be a great crusade, a mighty act of revenge for the Persian invasion of Greece in 480 B.C.E. (see Chapter 3). It would also be the means by which Alexander would create an empire of his own in the East.

In 334 B.C.E. Alexander led an army of Macedonians and Greeks into Persian territory in Asia Minor. With him went a staff of philosophers and poets, scientists whose job it was to map the country and study strange animals and plants, and a historian to write an account of the campaign. Alexander intended not only a military campaign but also an expedition of discovery.

In the next three years Alexander moved east into the Persian Empire, winning three major battles at the Granicus River, Issus, and Gaugamela (Map 4.1). When he reached Egypt, he seized the land without a battle, and he was proclaimed pharaoh, the legitimate ruler of the country. Next he marched into western Asia, where at Gaugamela he defeated the Persian army. After this victory the principal Persian capital of Persepolis easily fell to him. There he performed a symbolic act of retribution by burning the

Map 4.1 **Alexander's Conquests, 336–324 B.C.E.** This map shows the course of Alexander's invasion of the Persian Empire and the speed of his progress. More important than the great success of his military campaigns was his founding of Hellenistic cities in the East.

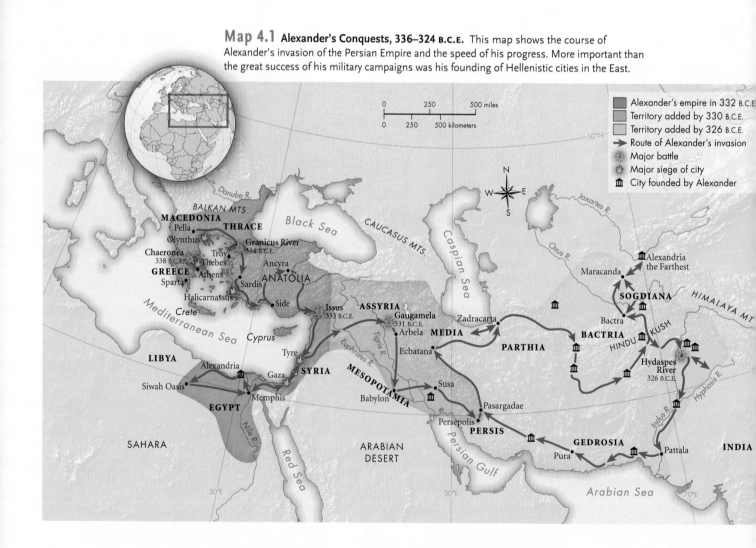

88

Chapter 4
The Hellenistic World
336–30 B.C.E.

CHAPTER LOCATOR

How and why did
Alexander the Great
create an empire?

buildings of Xerxes, the invader of Greece during the Persian War fifty years earlier. In 330 B.C.E. he took Ecbatana (ehk-BUH-tuh-nuh), the last Persian capital, and pursued the Persian king to his death.

The Persian Empire had fallen, but Alexander had no intention of stopping. With his Macedonian soldiers and Greek mercenaries, he set out to conquer the rest of Asia. He plunged deeper into the East, into lands completely unknown to the Greek world. It took his soldiers four additional years to conquer Bactria and the easternmost parts of the now-defunct Persian Empire, but still Alexander was determined to continue his march.

In 326 B.C.E. Alexander crossed the Indus River and entered India. There, too, he saw hard fighting, and finally at the Hyphasis (HIH-fuh-sihs) River his troops refused to go farther. Still eager to explore the limits of the world, Alexander turned south to the Arabian Sea. Though the tribes in the area did not oppose him, he waged a bloody, ruthless, and unnecessary war against them. After reaching the Arabian Sea and turning west, he led his army through the grim Gedrosian Desert. The army suffered fearfully, and many soldiers died along the way. Nonetheless, in 324 B.C.E. Alexander returned to his camp at Susa in the Greek-controlled region of Assyria. The great crusade was over, but Alexander never returned to his homeland of Macedonia. He died the next year in Babylon from fever, wounds, and excessive drinking. He was only thirty-two, but in just thirteen years he had created an empire that stretched from his homeland of Macedonia to India.

Chapter Chronology

340–262 B.C.E.	Rise of Epicurean and Stoic philosophies
336 B.C.E.	Alexander becomes king of Macedonia
334–324 B.C.E.	Alexander's Great Crusade
330 B.C.E.	Fall of Persian Empire
ca. 330–200 B.C.E.	Establishment of new Hellenistic cities
326 B.C.E.	Alexander reaches India; troops mutiny
323 B.C.E.	Alexander dies at age thirty-two
323–263 B.C.E.	War of succession leads to the establishment of Antigonid, Ptolemaic, and Seleucid dynasties
ca. 310–212 B.C.E.	Scientific developments in mathematics, astrology, and physics
ca. 200 B.C.E.	Mystery religions start flourishing
30 B.C.E.	Roman conquest of Egypt

Alexander at the Battle of Issus At left, Alexander the Great, bareheaded and wearing a breastplate, charges King Darius, who is standing in a chariot. The moment marks the turning point of the battle, as Darius turns to flee from the attack. (National Museum, Naples/Alinari/Art Resource, NY)

How did Alexander's conquests change the world?

How did Greek culture shape the Hellenistic kingdoms?

What new economic connections were created in this period?

What was the lasting impact of Hellenism?

▼ How did Alexander's conquests change the world?

Alexander so quickly became a legend during his lifetime that he still seems superhuman. That alone makes a reasoned interpretation of him very difficult. Some historians have seen him as a high-minded philosopher, and none can deny that he possessed genuine intellectual gifts. Others, however, have portrayed him as a bloody-minded autocrat, more interested in his own ambition than in the common good. Alexander is the perfect example of the need for historians to use care when interpreting known facts. (See "Listening to the Past: Alexander's Prayer to Establish a 'Brotherhood of Man,'" page 92.)

What is not disputed is that Alexander was instrumental in changing the face of politics in the eastern Mediterranean. In terms of this, his legacy is clear. His campaign swept away the Persian Empire, which had ruled the East for over two hundred years. In its place he established a Macedonian monarchy. More important in the long run was his founding of new cities and military colonies, which scattered Greeks and Macedonians throughout the East. Thus the practical result of Alexander's campaign was to open the East to the tide of Hellenism.

From Hellenic to Hellenistic

Hellenistic The new culture that arose when Alexander overthrew the Persian Empire and began spreading Hellenism—the Greek culture, language, thought, and way of life.

Without intending to do so Alexander changed the face of the world from Greece to India. He created the Hellenistic period, thereby ushering in a break with the Greek past. The Hellenic period discussed in Chapter 3 was marked by culture and ethnic unity. Greeks could travel from Thessaly to Sparta or from Corinth to Syracuse and find the same people speaking the same language. Political institutions were also largely the same, as were religious festivals. Life in the agora was fundamentally alike, as was family life. Greeks ate the same basic foods and enjoyed the same recreation. Nothing was strikingly different from region to region.

Alexander unknowingly changed that world. As Alexander pushed eastward, the Greeks came into contact with cultures very unlike theirs, many of them with old and venerable traditions. They found cities and kingdoms inhabited by peoples speaking incomprehensible languages. Peoples in the East worshiped their own gods, most of which bore no resemblance to the Olympian gods and goddesses. Easterners ate foods not found at home and lived in vast, open spaces unlike the Greeks' small Hellas. Greeks also did not find the polis. Instead, they confronted monarchy on a scale more pervasive than anything before seen. Whereas in the Hellenic period similarities largely marked Greek life, now difference became the rule. These were the challenges of the Hellenistic period.

The Political Legacy

The main question at Alexander's death was whether his vast empire could be held together. A major part of his legacy is what he had not done. Although he fathered a successor, the child was too young to assume the duties of kingship and was cruelly murdered by one of Alexander's generals, who viewed him as a future threat. That meant that Alexander's empire was a prize for the taking by the strongest of his generals. Within a week of Alexander's death, a round of fighting began that was to continue for forty years. No single Macedonian general was able to replace Alexander as emperor of his entire domain. In effect, the strongest divided it among themselves.

By 263 B.C.E. three officers had split the empire into large monarchies (Map 4.2). Antigonus Gonatas became king of Macedonia and established the Antigonid (an-

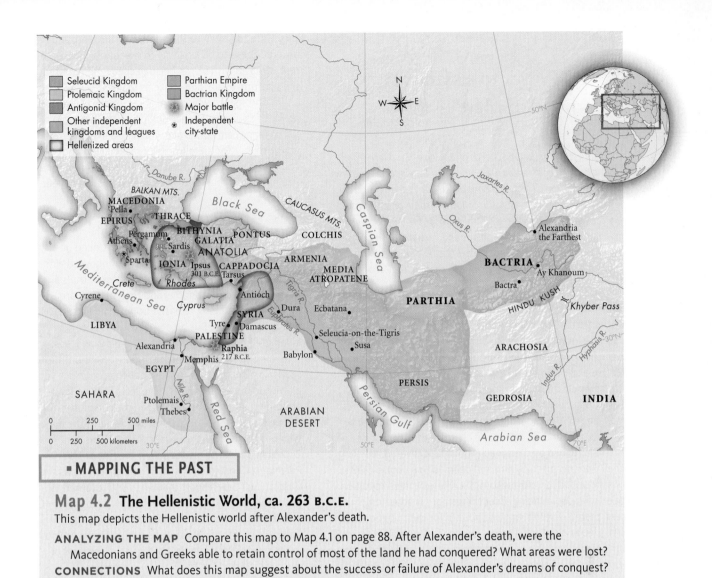

MAPPING THE PAST

Map 4.2 The Hellenistic World, ca. 263 B.C.E.

This map depicts the Hellenistic world after Alexander's death.

ANALYZING THE MAP Compare this map to Map 4.1 on page 88. After Alexander's death, were the Macedonians and Greeks able to retain control of most of the land he had conquered? What areas were lost?

CONNECTIONS What does this map suggest about the success or failure of Alexander's dreams of conquest?

To complete this activity online, go to the Online Study Guide at bedfordstmartins.com/mckaywestunderstanding.

TIH-guh-nuhd) dynasty. Ptolemy (TAH-luh-mee) made himself king of Egypt, and his descendants, the Ptolemies, assumed the powers and position of pharaohs. Seleucus (suh-LOO-kuhs), founder of the Seleucid (SUH-loo-suhd) dynasty, carved out a kingdom that stretched from the coast of Asia Minor to India.

The hold that these new monarchs had over their territories would prove fragile. In 263 B.C.E. Eumenes (yoo-MEHN-eez), the Greek ruler of Pergamum (PUHR-guh-muhm), a city in western Asia Minor, won his independence from the Seleucids and created the Pergamene monarchy. Though the Seleucid kings soon lost control of their easternmost provinces, Greek influence in this area did not wane. In modern Turkestan and Afghanistan another line of Greek kings established the kingdom of Bactria and even managed to spread their power and culture into northern India.

The political face of Greece itself changed during the Hellenistic period. The polis was replaced by leagues of city-states. The two most powerful and extensive

The Aetolian and Achaean Leagues, ca. 270–200 B.C.E.

Alexander's Prayer to Establish a "Brotherhood of Man"

In 324 B.C.E., after returning to Opis, north of Babylon in modern Iraq, Alexander found himself confronted with a huge and unexpected mutiny by his Macedonian veterans. He held a banquet to pacify them, including in the festivities Persians and other Asian followers, some nine thousand in all. During the festivities he offered a public prayer for harmony and partnership in rule between the Macedonians and Persians. Many modern scholars have interpreted this prayer as an expression of his desire to establish a "brotherhood of man." The following passage provides the evidence for this view

❝ 8. When [Alexander] arrived at Opis, he collected the Macedonians and announced that he intended to discharge from the army those who were useless for military service either from age or from being maimed in the limbs; and he said he would send them back to their own abodes. He also promised to give those who went back as much extra reward as would make them special objects of envy to those at home and arouse in the other Macedonians the wish to share similar dangers and labours. Alexander said this, no doubt, for the purpose of pleasing the Macedonians; but on the contrary they were, not without reason, offended by the speech which he delivered, thinking that now they were despised by him and deemed to be quite useless for military service. Indeed, throughout the whole of this expedition they had been offended at many other things; for his adoption of the Persian dress, thereby exhibiting his contempt for their opinion often caused them grief, as did also his accoutring the foreign soldiers called Epigoni in the Macedonian style, and the mixing of the alien horsemen among the ranks of the Companions. Therefore they could not remain silent and control themselves, but urged him to dismiss all of them from his army; and they advised him to prosecute the war in company with his father, deriding Ammon by this remark. When Alexander heard this . . . , he ordered the most conspicuous of the men who had tried to stir up the multitude to sedition to be arrested. He himself pointed out with his hand to the shield-bearing guards those whom they were to arrest, to the number of thirteen; and he ordered these to be led away to execution. When the rest, stricken with terror, became silent, he mounted the platform again, and spoke as follows:

9. "The speech which I am about to deliver will not be for the purpose of checking your start homeward, for, so far as I am concerned, you may depart wherever you wish; but for the purpose of making you understand when you take yourselves off, what kind of men you have been to us who have conferred such benefits upon you. . . .

10. . . . Most of you have golden crowns, the eternal memorials of your valour and of the honour you receive from me. Whoever has been killed has met with a glorious end and has been honoured with a splendid burial. Brazen statues of most of the slain have been erected at home, and their parents are held in honour, being released from all public service and from taxation. But no one of you has ever been killed in flight under my leadership. And now I was intending to send back those of you who are unfit for service, objects of envy to those at home; but since you all wish to depart, depart all of you! Go back and report at home that your king Alexander, the conqueror of the Persians, Medes, Bactrians, and Sacians; the man who has subjugated the Uxians, Arachotians, and Drangians; who has also acquired the rule of the Parthians, Chorasmians, and Hyrcanians, as far as the Caspian Sea . . . — report that when you returned to Susa you deserted him and went away, handing him over to the protection of conquered foreigners. Perhaps this report of yours will be both glorious to you in the eyes of men and devout I ween in the eyes of the gods. Depart!"

11. Having thus spoken, he leaped down quickly from the platform, and entered the palace, where he paid no attention to the decoration of his person, nor was any of his Companions admitted to see him. Not even on the morrow was any one of them admitted to an audience; but on the third day he summoned

were the Aetolian (ee-TOH-lee-uhn) League in western and central Greece and the Achaean (uh-KEE-uhn) League in the Peloponnesus. Once-powerful city-states like Athens and Sparta sank to the level of third-rate powers.

The political history of the Hellenistic period was dominated by the great monarchies and the Greek leagues. The political fragmentation and incessant warfare that marked the Hellenic period continued on an even wider and larger scale during the Hellenistic period. Never did the Hellenistic world achieve political stability or lasting peace. Just as the Greek states warred against one another until they fell to Macedonia, so the Hellenistic kingdoms repeated their example. After fighting among themselves, they confronted Rome from 146 to 30 B.C.E. They too finally fell to a power that brought the Mediterranean world unity and peace.

CHAPTER LOCATOR   How and why did Alexander the Great create an empire?

the select Persians within, and among them he distributed the commands of the brigades, and made the rule that only those whom he proclaimed his kinsmen should have the honour of saluting him with a kiss. But the Macedonians who heard the speech were thoroughly astonished at the moment, and remained there in silence near the platform; nor when he retired did any of them accompany the king, except his personal Companions and the confidential body-guards. Though they remained most of them had nothing to do or say; and yet they were unwilling to retire. But when the news was reported to them . . . they were no longer able to restrain themselves; but running in a body to the palace, they cast their weapons there in front of the gates as signs of supplication to the king. Standing in front of the gates, they shouted, beseeching to be allowed to enter, and saying that they were willing to surrender the men who had been the instigators of the disturbance on that occasion, and those who had begun the clamour. They also declared they would not retire from the gates either day or night, unless Alexander would take some pity upon them. When he was informed of this, he came out without delay; and seeing them lying on the ground in humble guise, and hearing most of them lamenting with loud voice, tears began to flow also from his own eyes. He made an effort to say something to them, but they continued their importunate entreaties. At length one of them, Callines by name, a man conspicuous both for his age and because he was a captain of the Companion cavalry, spoke as follows, "O king, what grieves the Macedonians is that you have already made some of the Persians kinsmen to yourself, and that Persians are called Alexander's kinsmen, and have the honour of saluting you with a kiss; whereas none of the Macedonians have as yet enjoyed this honour." Then Alexander, interrupting him, said, "But all of you without exception I consider my kinsmen, and so from this time I shall call you." When he had said this, Callines advanced and saluted him with a kiss, and so did all those who wished to salute him. Then they took up their weapons and returned to the camp, shouting and singing a song of thanksgiving. After this Alexander offered sacrifice to the gods to whom it was his custom to sacrifice, and gave a public banquet, over which he himself presided, with the Macedonians sitting around him; and next to them the Persians; after whom came the men of the other nations, preferred in honour for their personal rank or for some meritorious action. The king and his guests drew wine from the same bowl and poured out the same libations, both the Grecian prophets and the Magians commencing the ceremony. He prayed for other blessings, and especially that harmony and community of rule might exist between the Macedonians and Persians. 🔳

Source: Arrian, *Anabasis of Alexander* 7.8.1–11.9 in F. R. B. Godolphin, ed., *The Greek Historians*, vol. 2. Copyright © 1942 and renewed 1970 by Random House, Inc. Used by permission of Random House, Inc.

QUESTIONS FOR ANALYSIS

1. What was the purpose of the banquet at Opis?
2. Were all of the guests treated equally?
3. What did Alexander gain from bringing together the Macedonians and Persians?

This gilded bow and arrow case indicates that Alexander's success came at the price of blood. These vigorous scenes portray more military conflict than philosophical compassion. (Archaeological Museum Salonica/Dagli Orti/The Art Archive)

The Cultural Legacy

As Alexander moved farther east, distance alone presented him with a serious problem: how was he to retain contact with the Greek world behind him? Communications were vital, for he drew supplies and reinforcements from Greece and Macedonia. Alexander had to be sure that he was never cut off and stranded far from the Mediterranean world. His solution was to plant cities and military colonies in strategic places. Besides keeping the road open to the West, these settlements helped secure the countryside around them.

Alexander's cities and colonies became powerful instruments in the spread of Hellenism throughout the East. The Roman biographer Plutarch described Alexander's achievement in glowing terms: "Having founded over 70 cities among barbarian peoples and

How did Alexander's conquests change the world?

How did Greek culture shape the Hellenistic kingdoms?

What new economic connections were created in this period?

What was the lasting impact of Hellenism?

having planted Greek magistracies in Asia, Alexander overcame its wild and savage way of life."[1] Alexander opened the East to an enormous wave of immigration, and his successors continued his policy by inviting Greek colonists to settle in their realms. For seventy-five years after Alexander's death, Greek immigrants poured into the East. At least 250 new Hellenistic colonies were established. The Mediterranean world had seen no comparable movement of peoples since the Archaic Age, when wave after wave of Greeks had turned the Mediterranean basin into a Greek-speaking region (see Chapter 3).

The overall result of Alexander's settlements and those of his successors was the spread of Hellenism as far east as India. Throughout the Hellenistic period, Greeks and Easterners became familiar with and adapted themselves to each other's customs, religions, and ways of life. Although Greek culture did not completely conquer the East, it gave the East a vehicle of expression that linked it to the West. Hellenism became a common bond among the East, peninsular Greece, and the western Mediterranean.

▼ How did Greek culture shape the Hellenistic kingdoms?

When the Greeks entered Asia Minor, Egypt, and the more remote East, they encountered civilizations older than their own. In some ways the Eastern cultures were more advanced than the Greek, in other ways less so. Thus this great tide of Greek migration differed from preceding waves, which had spread over land that was uninhabited or inhabited by less-developed peoples.

Hellenistic monarchies offered Greeks economic and social opportunities. To encourage migration, cities were modeled on the polis with all of the familiar trappings of the homeland. In this way Easterners were introduced to Greek language, architecture, culture, and religion. While social mobility was generally greater for Greek men and women, Hellenistic kings ruled their cities tightly, and people had less political power than in classical Greece.

Cities and Kingdoms

One of the major developments of these new kingdoms was the resurgence of monarchy. Most of the new Hellenistic kingdoms embraced numerous different peoples who had little in common. Hellenistic kings thus needed a new political concept to unite them. One solution was the creation of a ruler cult that linked the king's authority with that of the gods. Thus, royal power had divine approval and was meant to create a political and religious bond between the kings and their subjects. These deified kings were not considered gods as mighty as Zeus or Apollo, and the new ruler cults probably had little religious impact on those ruled. Nonetheless, the ruler cult was an easily understandable symbol of unity within the kingdom.

Hellenistic kingship was hereditary, which gave women who were members of royal families more power than any women in democracies, in which citizenship was limited to men. Wives and mothers of kings had influence over their husbands and sons, and a few women ruled in their own right when there was no male heir.

Although Alexander's generals created huge kingdoms, the concept of monarchy, even when combined with the ruler cult, never replaced the ideal of the polis. Consequently, the monarchies never won the deep emotional loyalty that Greeks had once felt for the polis. Hellenistic kings needed large numbers of Greeks to run their kingdoms. Since Greek civilization was urban, the kings continued Alexander's policy of establishing cities throughout their kingdoms in order to entice Greeks to immigrate.

Royal Couple Cameo This Hellenistic cameo probably portrays King Ptolemy II and his sister Arsinoe II, rulers of the Ptolemaic kingdom of Egypt. During the Hellenistic period portraits of queens became more common because of their increased importance in governing the kingdom. (Erich Lessing/Art Resource, NY)

From 330 to 200 B.C.E. numerous Hellenistic cities were established. Yet the creation of these cities posed a serious political problem that the Hellenistic kings failed to solve.

To the Greeks civilized life was unthinkable without the polis, which was far more than a mere city. The Greek polis was by definition sovereign— an independent, autonomous state run by its citizens, free of any outside power or restraint. Hellenistic kings, however, refused to grant sovereignty to their cities. The Hellenistic monarch gave the city all the external trappings of a polis. Each had an assembly of citizens, a council to prepare legislation, and a board of magistrates to conduct political business. Yet, however similar to the Greek polis it appeared, such a city could not engage in diplomatic dealings, make treaties, pursue its own foreign policy, or wage its own wars. Nor could it govern its own affairs without interference from the king. In the eyes of the king, the city was an important part of the kingdom, but the welfare of the whole kingdom came first. The city had to follow royal orders, and the king often placed his own officials in it to see that his decrees were followed.

sovereign An independent, autonomous state run by its citizens and free of outside interference.

A Hellenistic city differed from a Greek polis in other ways as well. The Greek polis had one body of law and one set of customs. In the Hellenistic city Greeks represented an elite citizen class. Natives and non-Greek foreigners who lived in Hellenistic cities usually possessed lesser rights than Greeks and often had their own laws. In some instances this disparity spurred natives to assimilate Greek culture in order to rise politically and socially. The Hellenistic city was not homogeneous and could not spark the intensity of feeling that marked the polis.

An excellent example of this process comes from the city of Pergamum in northwestern Anatolia. Previously an important strategic site under Alexander, its new Greek rulers turned it into a magnificent city complete with all the typical buildings of the polis. They erected temples to the traditional deities, but they also built an imposing temple to the Egyptian gods. Furthermore, Jews established a synagogue in the city. Especially in the agora Greeks and indigenous people met to conduct business and to interact with each other. Greeks felt as though they were at home, and the evolving culture mixed Greek and local elements.

The old Greek cities of Asia Minor actually, if unintentionally, aided this development by maintaining and spreading traditions that went back for centuries. They served as models for the new foundations by providing a rich legacy of culture and tradition. In their very combination of physical beauty, refinement, and sophistication, they inspired imitation of the best in Greek culture.

In many respects the Hellenistic city resembled a modern city. It was a cultural center, a seat of learning, and a place where people could find amusement. The Hellenistic city was also an economic center that provided a ready market for grain and produce raised in the surrounding countryside. In short, the Hellenistic city offered cultural and economic opportunities.

Though Hellenistic kings never built a true polis, that does not mean that their urban policy failed. Rather, the Hellenistic city was to remain the basic social and political unit

The Great Altar of Pergamum A new Hellenistic city needed splendid art and architecture to prove its worth in Greek eyes. The king of Pergamum ordered the construction of this monumental altar, which is now in Berlin. The scenes depict the mythical victory of the Greek gods over the Giants, who symbolize barbarism. The altar served the propaganda purpose of celebrating the victory of Hellenism over the East. (Bildarchiv Preussischer Kulturbesitz/Art Resource, NY)

throughout the Hellenistic world until the sixth century C.E. Cities were the chief agents of Hellenization, and their influence spread far beyond their walls. They formed a broader cultural network in which Greek language, customs, and values flourished. Roman rule in the Hellenistic world would later be based on this urban culture, which facilitated the rise and spread of Christianity.

The Lives of the Greeks in the East

If the Hellenistic kings failed to satisfy the Greeks' political yearnings, they nonetheless succeeded in giving them unequaled economic and social opportunities. The ruling dynasties of the Hellenistic world were Macedonian, and Greeks filled all important political, military, and diplomatic positions. They constituted an upper class that sustained Hellenism in the East. Besides building Greek cities, Hellenistic kings offered Greeks land and money as lures to further immigration.

The opening of the East offered ambitious Greeks opportunities for success. The Hellenistic monarchy, unlike the Greek polis, did not depend solely on its citizens to fulfill its political needs. Talented Greek men had the opportunity to rise quickly in the government bureaucracy. Appointed by the king, these administrators did not have to stand for election each year, as had many officials of a Greek polis. Since they held their jobs year after year, they had time to evolve new administrative techniques. The needs of the Hellenistic monarchy and the opportunities it offered thus gave rise to a professional corps of Greek administrators.

Greeks also found employment in the armies and navies of the Hellenistic monarchies. Alexander had proved the Greco-Macedonian style of warfare to be far superior to that of other peoples, and Alexander's successors, themselves experienced officers, realized the importance of trained soldiers. Hellenistic kings were reluctant to arm the native populations or to allow them to serve in the army, fearing military rebellions among their conquered subjects. The result was the emergence of professional armies and navies consisting entirely of Greeks.

Chapter 4
The Hellenistic World
96   **336–30** B.C.E.

CHAPTER LOCATOR | How and why did Alexander the Great create an empire?

Marital Advice This small terra-cotta sculpture is generally seen as a mother advising her daughter, a new bride. Such intimate scenes of ordinary people were popular in the Hellenistic world, in contrast to the idealized statues of gods and goddesses of the classical period. (British Museum/ Michael Holford)

Greeks were able to dominate other professions as well. Eastern kingdoms and cities recruited Greek writers and artists to create Greek literature, art, and culture. Architects, engineers, and skilled craftsmen found their services in great demand to work on the Greek buildings commissioned by the Hellenistic monarchs.

Increased physical and social mobility benefited some women as well as men. More women learned to read than before, and they engaged in occupations in which literacy was beneficial, including care of the sick. During the Hellenistic period some women took part in commercial transactions. They still lived under legal handicaps; in Egypt, for example, a Greek woman needed a male guardian to buy, sell, or lease land; to borrow money; and to represent her in other transactions. Yet often such a guardian was present only to fulfill the letter of the law. The woman was the real agent and handled the business being transacted.

Because real power in the Hellenistic world was held by monarchs, the political benefits of citizenship were much less than they had been in the classical period. The diminished importance of citizenship meant that it was awarded more easily. Even women sometimes received honorary citizenship from foreign cities because of aid given in times of crisis.

Despite the opportunities they offered, the Hellenistic monarchies were hampered by their artificial origins. Their failure to win the political loyalty of their Greek subjects and their policy of wooing Greeks with lucrative positions encouraged feelings of uprootedness and self-serving individualism among Greek immigrants. Once a Greek man had left home to take service with, for instance, the army or the bureaucracy of the Ptolemies, he had no incentive beyond his pay and the comforts of life in Egypt to keep him there. If the Seleucid king offered him more money or a promotion, he might well accept it and take his talents to Asia Minor. Thus professional Greek soldiers and administrators were very mobile and were apt to look to their own interests, not their kingdom's.

One result of these developments was that the nature of warfare changed. Except in the areas of Greece, Hellenistic soldiers were professionals. Unlike the citizen hoplites of classical Greece, these men were trained, full-time soldiers. Hellenistic kings paid them well, often giving them land as an incentive to remain loyal. Only in Macedonia among the kingdoms of Greece was there a national army.

As long as Greeks continued to migrate east, the kingdoms remained stable and strong. However, the Hellenistic monarchies could not keep recruiting Greeks forever, in spite of their wealth and willingness to spend lavishly. In time the huge surge of immigration slowed greatly. Even then the Hellenistic monarchs were reluctant to recruit Easterners to fill posts normally held by Greeks. The result was at first the stagnation of the Hellenistic world and finally its collapse in the face of the young and vigorous Roman republic.

Greeks and Easterners

Because they understood themselves to be "the West," Greeks generally referred to Egypt and what we now call the Near East collectively as "the East." Many historians have continued that usage, seeing the Hellenistic period as a time when Greek and "Eastern" cultures blended to some degree. Hellenistic monarchies were remarkably successful in at least partially Hellenizing Easterners and spreading a uniform culture throughout the East, a culture to which Rome eventually fell heir. The prevailing institutions, laws, and language of the East became Greek. Indeed, the Near East had seen nothing comparable since the days when Mesopotamian culture had spread throughout the area.

Yet the spread of Greek culture was wider than it was deep. Hellenistic kingdoms were never entirely unified in language, customs, and thought. Greek culture took firmest hold along the shores of the Mediterranean, but farther east, in Persia and Bactria, it was less strong. The principal reason for this phenomenon is that Greek culture generally did not extend far beyond the reaches of the cities. Many urban residents adopted the aspects of Hellenism that they found useful, but others in the countryside generally did not embrace it wholly.

The Ptolemies in Egypt provide an excellent example of this situation. They made little effort to spread Greek culture, and unlike other Hellenistic kings they were not city builders, founding only the city of Ptolemais near Thebes. Initially untouched by Hellenism, the natives were nonetheless the foundation of the kingdom: they fed it by their labor in the fields and financed its operations with their taxes.

The Ptolemaic Kingdom, ca. 200 B.C.E.

Under the pharaohs talented Egyptians had been able to rise to high office, but during the third century B.C.E. the Ptolemies cut off this avenue of advancement. Instead of converting the natives to Hellenism, the Ptolemies tied them to the land even more tightly, making it nearly impossible for them to leave their villages. The bureaucracy of the Ptolemies was ruthlessly efficient, and the native population was viciously and cruelly exploited.

Throughout the third century B.C.E. the Greek upper class in Egypt had little to do with the native population, but in the second century B.C.E. Greeks and native Egyptians began to intermarry and mingle their cultures. The language of the native population influenced Greek, and many Greeks adopted the Egyptian religion and ways of life. Simultaneously, natives adopted Greek customs and language and began to play a role in the administration of the kingdom and even to serve in the army. The overall result was the evolution of a widespread Greco-Egyptian culture.

The Seleucids meanwhile became the great Hellenizers of this period. Continuing a policy similar to that of the Hittites and Persians before them, they linked western Asia Minor to Central Asia by maintaining a political and economic system that embraced all their subjects. At the same time they established Greek cities and military colonies throughout the region to nurture a vigorous and large Greek population.

The Seleucids had no elaborate plan for Hellenizing the native population, but the arrival of so many Greeks had a large impact. Seleucid military colonies were generally founded near native villages, thus exposing rural residents to all aspects of Greek life. Many Easterners found Greek political and cultural forms attractive and imitated them. In Asia Minor and Syria, for instance, numerous native villages and towns developed along Greek lines, and some of them grew into Hellenized cities. The Greek kings who replaced the Seleucids in the third century B.C.E. would spread Greek culture to their neighbors as far east as the Indian subcontinent.

Chapter 4
The Hellenistic World
98   336–30 B.C.E.

CHAPTER LOCATOR | How and why did Alexander the Great create an empire?

Cultural Blending Ptolemy V, a Macedonian by birth and the Hellenistic king of Egypt, dedicated this stone to the Egyptian sacred bull of the Egyptian god Ptah. Nothing here is Greek or Macedonian, a sign that the conquered had, in some religious and ceremonial ways, won over their conquerors. (Egyptian Museum, Cairo)

For non-Greeks the prime advantage of Greek culture was its very pervasiveness. The Greek language became the common speech of Egypt and the Near East. Greek became the speech of the royal court, bureaucracy, and army. It was also the speech of commerce: anyone who wanted to compete in business had to learn it. As early as the third century B.C.E. some Greek cities were giving citizenship to Hellenized natives.

The vast majority of Hellenized Easterners, however, took only the externals of Greek culture while retaining the essentials of their own ways of life. Though Greeks and Easterners adapted to each other's ways, there was never a true fusion of cultures. Nonetheless, each found useful things in the civilization of the other, and the two fertilized each other. This fertilization, this mingling of Greek and Eastern elements, is what makes Hellenistic culture unique and distinctive.

▼ What new economic connections were created in this period?

Alexander's conquest of the Persian Empire not only changed the political face of the ancient world but also brought the East fully into the sphere of Greek economics. East and West were linked in a broad commercial network. The spread of Greeks throughout the Near East and Egypt created new markets and stimulated trade.

Agriculture and Industry

Much of the revenue for the Hellenistic kingdoms was derived from agricultural products, rents paid by the tenants of royal land, and taxation of land. Trying to improve productivity, the rulers sponsored experiments on seed grain, selecting seeds that seemed the most hardy and productive. The Ptolemies made the greatest strides in agriculture, and the reason for their success was largely political. Egypt had a strong tradition of central authority dating back to the pharaohs, which the Ptolemies inherited and tightened. They could decree what crops Egyptian farmers would plant and what animals would be raised, and they had the power to mobilize native labor into the digging and maintenance of canals and ditches. But such progress was not possible in any other Hellenistic monarchy. Despite royal interest in agriculture and a more studied approach to it in the Hellenistic period, there is no evidence that agricultural productivity increased or influenced Eastern practices.

As with agriculture, although demand for goods increased during the Hellenistic period, no new techniques of production appear to have developed. Manual labor, not machinery, continued to turn out the raw materials and few manufactured goods the Hellenistic world used. Human labor was so cheap and so abundant that kings had no incentive to encourage the invention and manufacture of laborsaving machinery.

Apart from gold and silver, which were used primarily for coins and jewelry, iron was the most important metal and saw the most varied use. Even so, the method of its production never became very sophisticated. The Hellenistic Greeks did manage to produce a low-grade steel by adding carbon to iron.

Pottery remained an important commodity, and most of it was made locally. The coarse pottery used in the kitchen did not change at all. Fancier pots and bowls, decorated with a shiny black glaze, came into use during the Hellenistic period. This ware originated in Athens, but potters in other places began to imitate its style, heavily cutting into the Athenian market. In the second century B.C.E. a red-glazed ware, often called Samian, burst on the market and soon dominated it. Despite the change in pottery styles, the method of production of all pottery, whether plain or fine, remained essentially unchanged.

Commerce

Alexander's conquest of the Persian Empire had immediate effects on trade. In the conquered Persian capitals Alexander had found vast sums of gold, silver, and other treasure. This wealth financed the creation of new cities, the building of roads, and the development of harbors. Whole new fields lay open to Greek merchants, who eagerly took advantage of the new opportunities. Commerce itself was a leading area where Greeks and non-Greeks met on grounds of common interest. In bazaars, ports, and trading centers Greeks learned of Eastern customs and traditions while spreading knowledge of their own culture.

Trade was facilitated by the coining of money. Most of the great monarchies coined their money on the Attic standard, which meant that much of the money used in Hellenistic kingdoms had the same value. Traders were less in need of moneychangers than in the days when each major power coined money on a different standard.

The Seleucid and Ptolemaic dynasties traded as far afield as India, Arabia, and sub-Saharan Africa. Overland trade with India and Arabia was conducted by caravan and was largely in the hands of Easterners. Essential to the caravan trade from the Mediterranean to Afghanistan and India were the northern route to Dura on the Euphrates River and the southern route through Arabia. The desert of Arabia may seem at first unlikely terrain for a line of commerce, but to the east of it lies the plateau of Iran, from which trade routes stretched to the south and still farther east to China. Commerce from the East arrived at Egypt and the harbors of Palestine, Phoenicia, and Syria. From these ports goods flowed to Greece, Italy, and Spain. The backbone of this caravan trade was the camel — shaggy, ill-tempered, but durable and ideally suited to the harsh heart of the caravan routes.

Over the caravan routes traveled luxury goods that were light, rare, and expensive. In time these luxury items became more commonplace, in part the result of an increased volume of trade. In the prosperity of the period more people could afford to buy gold, silver, ivory, precious stones, spices, and a host of other easily transportable goods. Perhaps the most prominent goods in terms of volume were tea and silk, and the trade in silk later gave the major route east the name Great Silk Road. In return the Greeks and Macedonians sent east manufactured goods, especially metal weapons, cloth, wine, and olive oil. Although these caravan routes can trace their origins to earlier times, they became far more prominent in the Hellenistic period.

Numerous mercantile cities grew up along these caravan routes, places where native cultures combined with both Greek and Eastern cultures to create local but nonetheless

Great Silk Road The name of the major trading route to the east, so called because silk was one of the most prominent goods trafficked along it.

100

Chapter 4
The Hellenistic World
336–30 B.C.E.

CHAPTER LOCATOR | How and why did Alexander the Great create an empire?

cosmopolitan societies. The commercial contacts brought people together, even if sometimes indirectly. The merchants and the caravan cities were links in a chain that reached from the Mediterranean Sea to India and beyond to China. Ideas passed along these routes as easily as gold and ivory.

More economically important than the trade in luxury goods were commercial dealings in essential commodities like raw materials and grain and such industrial products as pottery. The Hellenistic monarchies usually raised enough grain for their own needs as well as a surplus for export. This trade in grain was essential for the cities of Greece and the Aegean, many of which could not grow enough grain. Fortunately for them, abundant wheat supplies were available nearby in Egypt and in the Crimea (crigh-MEE-uh) in southern Russia.

Most trade in bulk commodities was seaborne. Maritime trade provided opportunities for workers in other industries and trades: sailors, shipbuilders, dockworkers, accountants, teamsters, and pirates. Piracy was always a factor in the Hellenistic world and remained so until Rome extended its power throughout the East.

The Greek cities paid for their grain by exporting olive oil and wine. When agriculture and oil production developed in Syria, Greek products began to encounter competition from the Seleucid monarchy. Later in the Hellenistic period, Greek oil and wine found a lucrative market in Italy. Another significant commodity was fish, which for export was salted, pickled, or dried. This trade was doubly important because fish provided poor people with an essential element of their diet. Salt too was often imported, and there was some very slight trade in salted meat, which was a luxury item. Far more important was the trade in honey, dried fruit, nuts, and vegetables. Of raw materials, wood was high in demand, but little trade occurred in manufactured goods.

Slaves were a staple of Hellenistic trade. The wars provided prisoners for the slave market; to a lesser extent, so did kidnapping and capture by pirates. Both old Greek states and new Hellenistic kingdoms were ready slave markets, and throughout the Mediterranean world slaves were almost always in demand. Only the Ptolemies discouraged both the slave trade and slavery itself, and they did so only for economic reasons. Their system had no room for slaves, who would have competed with free labor. Otherwise slave labor was to be found in the cities and temples of the Hellenistic world, in the shops and fields, and in the homes of wealthier people.

Harbor and Warehouse at Delos During the Hellenistic period Delos became a thriving trading center. From Delos cargoes were shipped to virtually every part of the Mediterranean. (Rolf Richardson/age fotostock/SuperStock)

▼ What was the lasting impact of Hellenism?

The peoples of the Hellenistic era took the ideas and ideals of the classical Greeks and advanced them to new heights. Their achievements created the intellectual and religious atmosphere that deeply influenced Roman thinking and eventually the religious thought of liberal Judaism and early Christianity. Far from being stagnant, this was a period of vigorous growth. Its achievements included new religious ideas, startling innovations in philosophy, and remarkable advances in science and medicine.

Religion in the Hellenistic World

In religion the most significant new ideas were developed outside of Greece. At first the Hellenistic period saw the spread of Greek religious cults throughout the Near East and Egypt. When Hellenistic kings founded cities, they also built temples and established new cults for the old Olympian gods. The new cults enjoyed the prestige of being the religion of the conquerors, and they were supported by public money. The most attractive aspects of the Greek cults, at least to the Greeks, were their rituals and festivities. Greek cults sponsored literary, musical, and athletic contests, which were staged in beautiful surroundings among impressive Greek buildings. They fostered Greek culture and traditional sports and thus were a means of displaying Greek civilization outside of Greece.

Despite these advantages, Greek cults were primarily concerned with ritual, and participation did not require belief. The cults neither appealed to religious emotions nor embraced matters such as sin and redemption. Although the new cults were lavish in pomp and display, they could not satisfy deep religious feelings or spiritual yearnings.

Greeks increasingly sought solace from other sources. Educated and thoughtful people turned to philosophy as a guide to life, while others turned to superstition, magic, or astrology. Still others might shrug and speak of Tyche (TIGH-kee), a goddess related to fate or luck—an unpredictable and sometimes malevolent force.

Tyche The Greek goddess of fate or chance; an unpredictable and sometimes malicious force.

The Greeks always considered religion a matter best left to the individual, and Hellenistic kings made no effort to spread Greek religion among their Eastern subjects. Nor did native religions suffer from the arrival of the Greeks. Some Hellenistic kings limited the power of native priesthoods, but they also subsidized some indigenous cults with public money. Alexander the Great actually reinstated several cults that the Persians had suppressed.

Beginning in the second century B.C.E. some individuals were increasingly attracted to new mystery religions, so called because they featured a body of ritual not to be divulged to anyone not initiated into them. These new mystery cults incorporated aspects of both Greek and Eastern religions and had broad appeal for people who yearned for personal immortality.

mystery religions Cults that arose in the second century B.C.E., incorporating aspects of Greek and Eastern religions and involving secret rituals and the promise of life after death.

The mystery religions all claimed to save their adherents from the worst that fate could do and promised life for the soul after death. By the rites of initiation devotees were believed to be united with a god, usually male, who had himself died and risen from the dead. The sacrifice of the god and his victory over death saved the devotee from eternal death. Similarly, all mystery religions demanded a period of preparation in which the convert strove to become holy—that is, to live by the religion's precepts. Once aspirants had prepared themselves, they went through an initiation in which they learned the secrets of the religion. The initiation was usually a ritual of great emotional intensity symbolizing entry into a new life.

The most popular mystery religions were the Egyptian cults of Serapis (suh-RAY-puhs) and Isis. Serapis combined elements of the Egyptian god Osiris (god of the afterlife) with aspects of the Greek gods Zeus, Pluto (god of the underworld), and Asclepius (god of medicine). Serapis was believed to be the judge of souls, who rewarded virtuous and righteous people with eternal life. Like Asclepius, he was a god of healing. Cults devoted to Serapis were widespread, and many Hellenistic Greeks thought of him as Zeus.

The cult of Isis enjoyed even wider appeal than that of Serapis. Isis, wife of Osiris (see Chapter 1), claimed to have conquered Tyche and promised to save any mortal who came to her. She became the most important goddess of the Hellenistic world, and her worship was very popular among women. Her priests claimed that she had bestowed

Hellenistic Mystery Cult The scene depicts part of the ritual of initiation into the cult of Dionysus. The young woman has just completed the ritual and now dances in joy as the official with the sacred staff looks on. (Scala/Art Resource, NY)

on humanity the gift of civilization and founded law and literature. She was the goddess of marriage, conception, and childbirth, and like Serapis she promised to save the souls of her believers.

The new religions enjoyed one tremendous advantage over the old Greek mystery cults. Whereas old Greek mysteries were tied to particular places, such as Eleusis (ee-LOO-suhs), the new religions spread throughout the Hellenistic world. People did not have to undertake long and expensive pilgrimages to become members. In that sense the mystery religions came to the people, for temples of the new deities sprang up wherever Greeks lived.

Hellenism and the Jews

A prime illustration of cultural mingling is the impact of Greek culture on the Jews. At first Jews in Hellenistic cities were treated as resident aliens. As they grew more numerous, they received permission to form a political corporation, a *politeuma*, which gave them a great deal of autonomy. The Jewish politeuma, like the Hellenistic city, obeyed the king's commands, but there was virtually no royal interference with the Jewish religion. Indeed, the Greeks were always reluctant to tamper with anyone's religion. As a result, Hellenism and Judaism usually met on friendly terms.

Jews living in Hellenistic cities often embraced a good deal of Hellenism. So many learned Greek, especially in Alexandria, that the Old Testament was translated into Greek and services in the synagogue came to be conducted in Greek. Jews often took Greek names, used Greek political forms, adopted Greek practice by forming their own trade associations, put inscriptions on graves as the Greeks did, and much more. Yet no matter how much of Greek culture or its externals Jews borrowed, they normally remained attached to their religion.

Philosophy and the People

Philosophy during the Hellenic period was the exclusive province of the wealthy, for only they had leisure enough to pursue philosophical studies. During the Hellenistic period, however, philosophy reached out to touch the lives of more men and women than ever before. The reasons for this development were several. Since the ideal of the polis had declined, politics no longer offered people an intellectual outlet. Moreover, much of Hellenistic life, especially in the new cities of the East, seemed unstable and without venerable traditions. Greeks were far more mobile than they had ever been before, but their very mobility left them feeling uprooted. Many people in search of something permanent, something unchanging in a changing world, turned to philosophy. Another reason for the increased influence of philosophy was the decline of traditional religion and a growing belief in Tyche. To protect against the worst that Tyche could do, many Greeks looked to philosophy.

Philosophers themselves became much more numerous, and several new schools of philosophical thought emerged. In spite of their many differences, the major branches of philosophy agreed on the necessity of making people self-sufficient. They all recognized the need to equip men and women to deal successfully with Tyche. The major schools of Hellenistic philosophy all taught that people could be truly happy only when they had turned their backs on the world and focused full attention on one enduring thing. They differed chiefly on what that enduring thing was.

Two significant philosophies caught the minds and hearts of contemporary Greeks and some Easterners. The first was Epicureanism (eh-pih-kyoo-REE-uh-nih-zuhm). Epicurus (eh-pih-KYOOR-uhs) (340–270 B.C.E.) founded this school of philosophy on the belief that the principal good of human life is pleasure, which he defined as the absence of pain. By the pursuit of pleasure, he was not advocating drunken revels or sexual excess, which he thought caused pain. Instead, Epicurus concluded that any violent emotion is undesirable and advocated mild self-discipline. Even poverty he considered good, as long as people had enough food, clothing, and shelter. Epicurus also taught that individuals can most easily attain peace and serenity by ignoring the outside world and looking into their personal feelings and reactions. Although he did not deny the existence of the gods, he taught that they had no effect on human life.

Epicureanism taught its followers to ignore politics and issues, for politics led to tumult, which would disturb the soul. Although the Epicureans thought that the state originated through a social contract among individuals, they did not care about the political structure of the state. They were content to live under a democracy, oligarchy, monarchy, or any other form of government, and they never speculated about the ideal state.

Zeno (ZEE-noh) (335–262 B.C.E.), a philosopher from Cyprus, advanced a different concept of human beings and the universe. Zeno first came to Athens to form his own school, the Stoa, named after the building where he preferred to teach. His philosophy, called Stoicism, became the most popular Hellenistic philosophy. Zeno and

Epicureanism A practical philosophy founded by Epicurus, it argued that the principal good of human life is pleasure.

Stoicism The most popular of Hellenistic philosophies, it considered nature an expression of divine will; people could be happy only when living in accordance with nature.

Tyche This statue depicts Tyche as the city-goddess of Antioch, a new Hellenistic city founded by the Seleucid king Antiochus. Some Hellenistic Greeks worshiped Tyche in the hope that she would be kind to them. Philosophers tried to free people from her whimsies. Others tried to placate her. (Vatican Museums/Art Resource, NY)

Chapter 4
The Hellenistic World

104   336–30 B.C.E.

CHAPTER LOCATOR   How and why did Alexander the Great create an empire?

his followers considered nature an expression of divine will; in their view people could be happy only when living in accordance with nature. They stressed the unity of man and the universe, stating that all men were brothers and were obliged to help one another.

Unlike the Epicureans, the Stoics taught that people should participate in politics and worldly affairs. Yet this idea never led to the belief that individuals should try to change the order of things. The Stoics used the image of an actor in a play: the Stoic plays an assigned part but never tries to change the play. To the Stoics the important question was not whether they achieved anything, but whether they lived virtuous lives.

Though the Stoics evolved the concept of a world order, they thought of it strictly in terms of the individual. Like the Epicureans, they were indifferent to specific political forms. They believed that people should do their duty to the state in which they found themselves. The universal state they preached about was ethical, not political. The Stoics' most significant practical achievement was the creation of the concept of natural law. They concluded that as all men were brothers and were in harmony with the universe, one law—a part of the natural order of life—governed them all. The Stoic concept of a universal state governed by natural law would be one of the finest heirlooms the Hellenistic world passed on to Rome.

natural law A Stoic concept that a single law that was part of the natural order of life governed all people.

Hellenistic Science

The area in which Hellenistic culture achieved its greatest triumphs was science. The most notable of the Hellenistic astronomers was Aristarchus (ar-uh-STAHR-kuhs) of Samos (ca. 310–230 B.C.E.). Aristarchus concluded that the sun is far larger than the earth and that the stars are enormously distant from the earth. He argued against Aristotle's view that the earth was the center of the universe. Instead, Aristarchus developed the heliocentric theory—that the earth and planets revolve around the sun. His work is all the more impressive because he lacked even a rudimentary telescope.

heliocentric theory The theory of Aristarchus that the earth and planets revolve around the sun.

Unfortunately, Aristarchus's theories did not persuade the ancient world. In the second century C.E. Claudius Ptolemy, a mathematician, astronomer, and author of the influential *Geography* in Alexandria, accepted Aristotle's theory of the earth as the center of the universe, and this view prevailed for fourteen hundred years. Aristarchus's heliocentric (hee-lee-oh-SEHN-trik) theory lay dormant until resurrected in the sixteenth century by the brilliant Polish astronomer Nicolaus Copernicus (koh-PUHR-nih-kuhs).

In geometry Hellenistic thinkers discovered little that was new, but Euclid (YOO-kluhd) (ca. 300 B.C.E.), a mathematician who lived in Alexandria, compiled a valuable textbook of existing knowledge. His *The Elements of Geometry* has exerted immense influence on Western civilization, for it rapidly became the standard introduction to geometry.

The greatest thinker of the Hellenistic period was Archimedes (ca. 287–212 B.C.E.), a native of Syracuse. His mathematical research was his greatest contribution to Western thought. (See "Individuals in Society: Archimedes, Scientist and Inventor," page 106.)

Tower of the Winds Built in Athens in the mid-second century B.C.E., this forty-foot octagonal tower was used to tell time and predict the weather. The original tower contained eight sundials and an interior water clock that showed the hour, the day, and the phase of the moon. (Vladimir Khirman/Alamy)

Archimedes, Scientist and Inventor

ARCHIMEDES (ca. 287–212 B.C.E.) was born in the Greek city of Syracuse in Sicily, an intellectual center in which he pursued scientific interests. He was the most original thinker of his time and a practical inventor. In his book *On Plane Equilibriums* he dealt for the first time with the basic principles of mathematics, including the principle of the lever. He once said that if he were given a lever and a suitable place to stand, he could move the world. He also demonstrated how easily his compound pulley could move huge weights with little effort:

A three-masted merchant ship of the royal fleet had been hauled on land by hard work and many hands. Archimedes put aboard her many men and the usual freight. He sat far away from her; and without haste, but gently working a compound pulley with his hand, he drew her towards him smoothly and without faltering, just as though she were running on the surface.*

He likewise invented the Archimedian screw, a pump to bring subterranean water up to irrigate fields, which quickly came into common use. In his treatise *On Floating Bodies* Archimedes founded the science of hydrostatics. He concluded that whenever a solid floats in a liquid, the weight of the solid equals the weight of the liquid displaced. The way he made his discovery has become famous:

When he was devoting his attention to this problem, he happened to go to a public bath. When he climbed down into the bathtub there, he noticed that water in the tub equal to the bulk of his body flowed out. Thus, when he observed this method of solving the problem, he did not wait. Instead, moved with joy, he sprang out of the tub, and rushing home naked he kept indicating in a loud voice that he had indeed discovered what he was seeking. For while running he was shouting repeatedly in Greek, "Eureka, eureka" ("I have found it, I have found it").†

War between Rome and Syracuse unfortunately interrupted Archimedes' scientific life. In 213 B.C.E. during the Second Punic War, the Romans besieged the city. Hiero, its king and Archimedes' friend, asked the scientist for help in repulsing Roman attacks. Archimedes began to build remarkable devices that served as artillery. One shot missiles to break up infantry attacks. Others threw huge masses of stones that fell on the enemy with irresistible speed and noise. They tore gaping holes in the Roman lines and broke up attacks. Against Roman warships he built a machine consisting of huge beams that projected over the targets. Then the artillerymen dropped great weights onto the ships, like bombs. Even more complicated was an apparatus with beams from which large claws dropped onto the hulls of warships, hoisted them into the air, and dropped them back into the sea. In response, the Romans brought up an exceptionally large scaling ladder carried on ships. While it approached, Archimedes' artillery disabled it by hitting it repeatedly with stones weighing 500 pounds. At last the Romans became so fearful that whenever they saw a bit of rope or a stick of timber projecting over the wall they shouted, "There

Archimedes was willing to share his work with others, among them Eratosthenes (ehr-uh-TAHS-thuh-neez) (285–ca. 204 B.C.E.). From his native Cyrene in North Africa, Eratosthenes traveled to Athens, where he studied philosophy and mathematics. He refused to join any of the philosophical schools, for he was interested in too many things to follow any particular dogma. Around 245 B.C.E. King Ptolemy invited Eratosthenes to Alexandria. The Ptolemies had done much to make Alexandria an intellectual, cultural, and scientific center, and Eratosthenes became librarian of the royal library, a position of great prestige. The library was a huge collection of Greek writings, including such classic works as the poems of Homer, the histories of Herodotus and Thucydides, and the philosophical works of Plato and Aristotle. The library became one of the foremost intellectual centers of the ancient world.

Eratosthenes used mathematics to further the geographical studies for which he is most famous. He calculated the circumference of the earth geometrically, estimating it as about 24,675 miles. He was not wrong by much: the earth is actually 24,860 miles in circumference. Eratosthenes also concluded that the earth was a spherical globe, that the landmass was roughly four-sided, and that the land was surrounded by ocean. Using geographical information gained by Alexander the Great's scientists, Eratosthenes tried to fit the East into Greek geographical knowledge. He declared that a ship could sail from Spain either around Africa to India or directly westward to India. Not until the Age of Discovery did sailors actually prove Eratosthenes' theories.

Chapter 4
The Hellenistic World
336–30 B.C.E.

106

CHAPTER LOCATOR | How and why did Alexander the Great create an empire?

Archimedes' treatises were found on a palimpsest, a manuscript that was erased so that another text could be written over it. In about 1229 C.E. Christian monks erased the manuscript and used it for a prayer book. Scientists were able to read Archimedes' original text using digital processing of infrared light and X-rays. (Image by the Rochester Institute of Technology. Copyright resides with the owner of the Archimedes Palimpsest)

it is. Archimedes is trying some engine on us" and fled. When the Romans finally broke into Syracuse in 212 B.C.E., a Roman soldier came upon Archimedes in his study and killed him.

Much but not all of Archimedes' work survived him. In 1998 a new codex containing many of his treatises, some of them previously lost, turned up at a Christie's auction in New York. Someone had stolen it from a Greek Orthodox library in Constantinople after World War I, and it afterwards disappeared into the black market. Although the Greek government tried to prevent its sale, an anonymous buyer generously deposited it at the Walters Art Museum in Baltimore. Using X-rays and other modern techniques, specialists have painstakingly restored the manuscript, which had been painted over in the Middle Ages. Contemporary science is enabling classic scholars to read some of Archimedes' lost works.

QUESTIONS FOR ANALYSIS

1. How useful were Archimedes' inventions?
2. What effect did his weapons have on the Roman attackers?
3. What is the irony of Archimedes' death?

*Plutarch, *Life of Marcellus*.
†Vitruvius, *On Architecture*, 9 Preface, 10.

Hellenistic science also made an inestimable, if grim, contribution to practical life. The Greeks applied theories of mechanics to build siege machines, thus revolutionizing the art of warfare. Fully realizing the practical possibilities of the first effective artillery in Western history, Philip of Macedonia introduced the machines to the broader world. The catapult became the first and most widely used artillery piece. The earliest catapults could shoot only large arrows and small stones. By the time Alexander the Great besieged Tyre in 332 B.C.E., his catapults threw stones big enough to knock down city walls. Generals soon realized that they could also hurl burning bundles over the walls to start fires in the city. To approach enemy town walls safely, engineers built siege towers, large wooden structures that served as artillery platforms, and put them on wheels so that soldiers could roll them up to the wall. Once there archers stationed on top of them swept the enemy's ramparts with arrows, while other soldiers manning catapults added missile fire. Once the walls were cleared, soldiers from the siege towers swept over the enemy's ramparts and into the city. To aid the siege towers, generals added battering rams that consisted of long, stout shafts housed in reinforced shells. Inside the shell the crew pushed the ram up to the wall and then heaved the shaft against the wall. Rams proved even more effective than catapults in bringing down large portions of walls.

If these new engines made waging war more efficient, they also added to the misery of the people. War was no longer confined to the battlefield and fought between soldiers. Now the populations of whole cities feared for their lives. Many people were killed in

An Unsuccessful Delivery

This funeral monument depicts a mother who has perhaps lost her own life as well as her baby's. Childbirth was the leading cause of death for adult women in antiquity, though monuments showing this are quite rare. Another of the few that do show death in childbirth bears the heartbreaking words attributed to the mother by her grieving family: "All my labor could not bring the child forth; he lies in my womb, among the dead." (National Archaeological Museum, Athens/Archaeological Receipts Fund)

ANALYZING THE IMAGE Who might the various figures in this monument be? What do the expressions and gestures of these people tell us about what happened?

CONNECTIONS What were the main accomplishments of Hellenistic medicine? What did the different schools of Hellenistic medicine have to offer women in childbirth?

To complete this activity online, go to the Online Study Guide at bedfordstmartins.com/mckaywestunderstanding.

the slaughter and rape that generally came with the taking of the city. The survivors were often sold into slavery. Ironically, Hellenistic science, dedicated to improving human life, succeeded in making it more dangerous and horrible.

Hellenistic Medicine

The study of medicine flourished during the Hellenistic period. Herophilus, who lived in the first half of the third century B.C.E., worked at Alexandria and studied the writings of Hippocrates (see Chapter 3). He accepted Hippocrates' theory of the four humors and approached the study of medicine in a systematic, scientific fashion: he dissected dead bodies and measured what he observed. He discovered the nervous system and concluded that two types of nerves, motor and sensory, existed. Herophilus also studied the brain, which he considered the center of intelligence, and discerned the cerebrum (suh-REE-bruhm) and cerebellum (ser-uh-BEH-luhm). His other work dealt with the liver, lungs, and uterus. His younger contemporary Erasistratus also conducted research on the brain and nervous system and improved on Herophilus's work. Erasistratus too followed in the tradition of Hippocrates and believed that the best way for the body to heal itself was through diet and air.

Both Herophilus and Erasistratus were members of the Dogmatic school of medicine at Alexandria. In this school speculation played an important part in research, as did the study of anatomy. To learn more about human anatomy, Herophilus and Erasistratus dissected corpses and even vivisected criminals whom King Ptolemy contributed for the purpose. Better knowledge of anatomy led to improvements in surgery. These advances enabled the Dogmatists to invent new surgical instruments and techniques.

In about 280 B.C.E. Philinus and Serapion, pupils of Herophilus, led a reaction against the Dogmatists. Believing that the Dogmatists had become too speculative, they founded the Empiric school of medicine at Alexandria. Claiming that the Dogmatists' emphasis on anatomy and physiology was misplaced, they concentrated instead on the observation and cure of illnesses. They also laid heavier stress on the use of drugs and medicine to treat

Chapter 4
The Hellenistic World
108   336–30 B.C.E.

CHAPTER LOCATOR   How and why did Alexander the Great create an empire?

illnesses. Heraclides of Tarentum (perhaps first century B.C.E.) carried on the Empiric tradition and dedicated himself to the observation and use of medicines. He discovered the benefits of opium and worked with other drugs that relieved pain. He also steadfastly rejected the relevance of magic to drugs and medicines.

The Hellenistic world was also plagued by people who claimed to cure illnesses through incantations and magic. Their potions included such concoctions as blood from the ear of an ass mixed with water to cure fever, or the liver of a cat killed when the moon was waning and preserved in salt. These quacks even claimed that they could cure mental illness. The treatment for a person suffering from melancholy was calf dung boiled in wine. No doubt the patient became too sick to be depressed.

Quacks who prescribed such treatments were very popular but did untold harm to the sick and injured. They and greedy physicians also damaged the reputation of dedicated doctors who honestly and intelligently tried to heal and alleviate pain. Nonetheless, the work of men like Herophilus and Serapion made valuable contributions to the knowledge of medicine, and the fruits of their work were preserved and handed on to the West.

← LOOKING BACK LOOKING AHEAD →

IT CAN SAFELY BE SAID that Philip and Alexander broadened Greek and Macedonian horizons, but not in ways that they had intended. Although Alexander established Macedonian and Greek colonies across western and Central Asia for military reasons, they resulted in the spread of Hellenism.

The bond of Hellenism shared among the East, peninsular Greece, and the western Mediterranean was to prove supremely valuable to Rome in its efforts to impose a comparable political unity on the Western world. The economic unity of the Hellenistic world, like its cultural bonds, would likewise prove valuable to the Romans. They would also benefit from the Stoic concept of a universal state governed by natural law. The concept of one law for all people became a valuable tool when the Romans began to deal with many different peoples with different laws. The ideal of the universal state developed in Hellenistic Greece would be a rationale for extending the Roman Empire to the farthest reaches of the world. In the heart of the old Persian Empire, Hellenism was only a new influence that was absorbed by older ways of thought and life. Yet overall, in the exchange of ideas and the opportunity for different cultures to learn about one another, a new cosmopolitan society evolved. That society in turn made possible such diverse advances as a wider extent of trade and agriculture, the creation of religious and philosophical ideas that paved the way for Christianity, greater freedom for women, and remarkable advances in science and medicine. ■

- **For a list of suggested readings for this chapter, visit** *bedfordstmartins.com/mckaywestunderstanding.*

- **For primary sources from this period, see** *Sources of Western Society,* **Second Edition.**

- **For Web sites, images, and documents related to topics in this chapter, see Make History at** *bedfordstmartins.com/mckaywestunderstanding.*

How did Alexander's conquests change the world?

How did Greek culture shape the Hellenistic kingdoms?

What new economic connections were created in this period?

What was the lasting impact of Hellenism?

Chapter 4 Study Guide

Online Study Guide
bedfordstmartins.com/mckaywestunderstanding

Step 1

GETTING STARTED Below are basic terms about this period in the history of Western civilization. Can you identify each term below and explain why it matters? To do this exercise online, go to bedfordstmartins.com/mckaywestunderstanding.

TERMS	WHO (OR WHAT) AND WHEN	WHY IT MATTERS
Hellenistic, p. 90		
sovereign, p. 95		
Great Silk Road, p. 100		
Tyche, p. 102		
mystery religions, p. 102		
Epicureanism, p. 104		
Stoicism, p. 104		
natural law, p. 105		
heliocentric theory, p. 105		

Step 2

MOVING BEYOND THE BASICS The exercise below requires a more advanced understanding of the chapter material. Compare and contrast Greek identity in the Hellenic and Hellenistic worlds. You may want to review Chapter 3: The Development of Classical Greece as you complete this exercise. Begin by filling in the chart below with descriptions of key aspects of Hellenic Greece and the Hellenistic world. When you are finished, consider the following questions: How did the Greek sense of identity and political loyalty change after Alexander's conquests? For a Greek living and working in the larger Hellenistic world, what did it mean to be Greek? To do this exercise online, go to bedfordstmartins.com/mckaywestunderstanding.

PHASE	GOVERNMENT	ECONOMY	RELIGION AND PHILOSOPHY	CULTURAL DIVERSITY AND EXCHANGE
Hellenic Greece				
The Hellenistic World				

110

PUTTING IT ALL TOGETHER Now that you've reviewed key elements of the chapter, take a step back and try to see the big picture. Remember to use specific examples from the chapter in your answers. To do this exercise online, go to bedfordstmartins.com/mckaywestunderstanding.

ALEXANDER THE GREAT

- How did Alexander's campaign of conquest differ from previous Near Eastern efforts at empire building?

- Why did Alexander's empire split apart shortly after his death? What impact did this political fragmentation have on the development of the Hellenistic world?

POLITICAL, SOCIAL, AND ECONOMIC DEVELOPMENTS

- What role did new urban centers play in Hellenistic kingdoms? How did the Hellenistic city differ from the Hellenic polis?

- What characterized the relationship between Greeks and Easterners in the Hellenistic period? To what extent were Easterners "Hellenized"?

- What role did trade play in the diffusion of Greek culture?

RELIGION AND HELLENISTIC INTELLECTUAL ADVANCES

- What larger social and cultural trends were reflected in the increased popularity of mystery religions and philosophy during the Hellenistic period?

- Compare and contrast Hellenic and Hellenistic religion. What might explain the differences you note?

- How did Hellenistic philosophers and scientists build on the achievements of their Hellenic predecessors?

■ **In Your Own Words** Imagine that you must explain Chapter 4 to someone who hasn't read it. What would be the most important points to include and why?

5

The Rise of Rome

ca. 750–31 B.C.E.

"Who is so thoughtless and lazy that he does not want to know in what way and with what kind of government the Romans in less than 53 years conquered nearly the entire inhabited world and brought it under their rule—an achievement previously unheard of?"[1] This question was first asked by Polybius, a Greek historian who lived in the second century B.C.E.

What was that achievement? Was it simply the creation of a huge empire? Hardly. The Persians had done the same thing, and Alexander the Great had conquered vast territories in a shorter time. Was it the creation of a superior culture? Even the Romans admitted that in matters of art, literature, philosophy, and culture they learned from the Greeks. Rome's achievement lay in the ability of the Romans not only to conquer peoples but also to incorporate them into the Roman system. Unlike the Greeks, who refused to share citizenship, the Romans extended their citizenship first to the Italians and later to the peoples of the provinces. With that citizenship went Roman government and law. Rome created a world state that embraced the entire Mediterranean area and extended northward.

Nor was Rome's achievement limited to the ancient world. Rome's law, language, and administrative practices shaped later developments in Europe and beyond. London, Paris, Vienna, and many other modern European cities began as Roman colonies or military camps. When the Founding Fathers created the American republic, they looked to Rome as a model. On the darker side, Napoleon and Mussolini paid their own tribute to Rome by aping its forms. Whether Founding Fathers or modern dictators, all were acknowledging admiration for the Roman achievement. ■

Life in the Roman Republic. This fresco from Pompeii shows the wedding of the gods Venus and Mars. Although the event was not real, the dress and finery are typical of that seen at the weddings of Roman nobles. (Scala/Art Resource, NY)

Chapter Preview

▶ **How did the Romans become the dominant power in Italy?**

▶ **What were the key institutions of the Roman republic?**

▶ **How did the Romans build a Mediterranean empire?**

▶ **How did expansion affect Roman society and culture?**

▶ **What led to the fall of the Roman republic?**

▼ How did the Romans become the dominant power in Italy?

While the Greeks pursued their destiny in the East, other peoples in western Europe developed their own individual societies. The most historically important of them were the Etruscans (ih-TRUS-kuhns) and Romans who entered the peninsula of Italy and came into contact with the older cultures of the Mediterranean. The Etruscans were the first significant newcomers, followed by the Romans.

The Geography of Italy

West of Greece the boot-shaped peninsula of Italy, with Sicily at its toe, occupies the center of the Mediterranean basin (Map 5.1). To the south lies Africa; the distance between southwestern Sicily and the northern African coast is at one point only about a hundred

Map 5.1 Italy and the City of Rome, ca. 218 B.C.E. The geographical configuration of the Italian peninsula shows how Rome stood astride north-south communication routes and how the state that united Italy stood poised to move from Sicily into northern Africa.

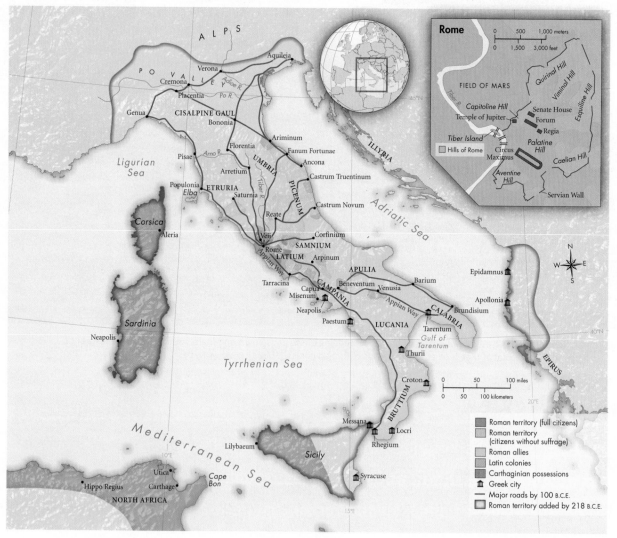

Chapter 5
The Rise of Rome
ca. 750–31 B.C.E.

114

CHAPTER LOCATOR | How did the Romans become the dominant power in Italy?

miles. Italy and Sicily literally divide the Mediterranean into two basins and form the focal point between the two halves.

Like Greece and other Mediterranean lands, Italy enjoys an almost subtropical climate. The winters are rainy, but the summer months are dry. Because of the climate the rivers of Italy usually carry little water during the summer, and some go entirely dry. Most of Italy's rivers are unsuitable for regular large-scale shipping. Thus, Italian rivers never became major thoroughfares for commerce and communications.

Geography discouraged maritime trade as well. Italy lacks the numerous good harbors that are such a feature of the Greek landscape. Only in the south are there good harbors, and Greek colonists had early claimed those ports for themselves. Yet geography gave rise to — and the rivers nourished — a bountiful agriculture that sustained a large population.

Geography encouraged Italy to look to the Mediterranean. In the north, Italy is protected by the Apennine Mountains, which break off from the Alps and form a natural barrier. The Apennines retarded but did not prevent peoples from penetrating Italy from the north. From the north the Apennines run southward for the entire length of the Italian boot, cutting off access to the Adriatic Sea. This barrier induced Italy to look west to Spain and Carthage rather than east to Greece. Even though most of the land is mountainous, the hill country is not as inhospitable as the Greek highlands. The fertility of the soil provided the basis for a large population. Nor did the mountains of Italy so carve up the land as to prevent the development of political unity, as was the case in Greece.

In their southward course the Apennines leave two broad and fertile plains, those of Latium and Campania. These plains attracted settlers and invaders from the time that peoples began to move into Italy. Among these peoples were the Romans, who established their city on the Tiber River in Latium.

The Etruscans and the Roman Settlement of Italy

The Etruscans arrived in Italy about 750 B.C.E., establishing permanent settlements that evolved into the first Italian cities. In political organization they resembled the Greek city-states, each governing itself while maintaining contact with its neighbors. The wealth of these cities, along with their political and military institutions, enabled them to form a loosely organized league of cities whose domination extended as far north as the Po Valley

Sarcophagus of Lartie Seianti
Although the sarcophagus is this noble Etruscan woman's place of burial, she is portrayed as in life, comfortable and at rest. The influence of Greek art on Etruscan is apparent in almost every feature of the sarcophagus. (Archaeological Museum, Florence/ Nimatallah/Art Resource, NY)

What were the key institutions of the Roman republic?

How did the Romans build a Mediterranean empire?

How did expansion affect Roman society and culture?

What led to the fall of the Roman republic?

and as far south as Latium and Campania (see Map 5.1). Their influence spread over the surrounding countryside, which they regularly cultivated. Having established a strong agricultural base, they mined the rich mineral resources of the land. Secure in their new home, they looked out to the wider world, especially to the East. The Mediterranean has always been a highway, and one of its major routes led to Greece. From an early period the Etruscans began to trade natural products, especially iron, for Greek luxury goods. They developed a rich cultural life that became the foundation of civilization throughout Italy. In the process they came in contact with a small collection of villages subsequently called Rome.

The Etruscans, ca. 500 B.C.E.

The Romans, to whom the Etruscans introduced the broader world, had settled in Italy by the eighth century B.C.E. According to one legend, Romulus and Remus founded the city in 753 B.C.E. (see inset of Map 5.1). They built Rome's first walls, reflecting the Etruscan concept of the pomerium, a sacred boundary intended to keep out anything evil or unclean. Under Etruscan influence the Romans prospered, spreading over all of Rome's seven hills.

The Etruscans soon drew the fledgling Rome into their orbit. From 753 to 509 B.C.E. a line of Etruscan kings ruled the city and introduced many customs. The Romans adopted the Etruscan alphabet, which the Etruscans themselves had adopted from the Greeks. The Romans also adopted symbols of political authority from the Etruscans. The symbol of the Etruscan king's right to execute or scourge his subjects was a bundle of rods and an ax, called the fasces, which the king's retainer carried before him on official occasions. When the Romans expelled the Etruscan kings, they continued using the fasces in this manner. In engineering and architecture the Romans adopted the vault and the arch from the Etruscans. Above all, it was thanks to the Etruscans that the Romans truly became urban dwellers.

Under the Etruscans Rome enjoyed contacts with the larger Mediterranean world, while the city continued to grow. In the years 575 to 550 B.C.E. temples and public buildings began to grace the city. The Capitoline Hill became its religious center when the temple of Jupiter Optimus Maximus (Jupiter the Best and Greatest) was built there. Rome's Forum ceased to be a cemetery and began its history as a public meeting place, a development parallel to that of the Greek agora. The Etruscans had found Rome a collection of villages and made it a city.

forum A public meeting place.

The Roman Conquest of Italy

The Romans expelled the Etruscan king Tarquin the Proud in 509 B.C.E., but, according to legend, not for political reasons. Tarquin had raped the noblewoman Lucretia (loo-KREE-shuh) when she refused his advances. She told her husband and father the whole story the next day. After they promised to avenge her, she committed suicide in shame. In avenging her death, legend has it, the family drove the Etruscans from Rome. In truth the Romans rebelled against Etruscan rule and founded the republic because they desired independence.

In the following years the Romans fought numerous wars with their neighbors on the Italian peninsula. They became soldiers, and the grim fighting bred tenacity, a prominent Roman trait. War also involved diplomacy, at which the Romans became masters. Alliances with the Latin towns around them provided a large reservoir of manpower.

CHAPTER LOCATOR   How did the Romans become the dominant power in Italy?

Their alliances also involved the Romans in other wars that took them farther afield in the peninsula.

One of the earliest wars involved the neighboring Aequi (EE-kwigh), who launched a serious invasion. The Romans called on Cincinnatus to assume the office of dictator. In this period the Roman dictator, unlike modern dictators, was a legitimate magistrate given ultimate powers for a specified period of time. The Roman officials found Cincinnatus working his farm. He listened to the appeal of his countrymen and accepted the office. Fifteen days later, after he had defeated the Aequi, he returned to his farm. Cincinnatus personified the ideal of the Roman citizen—a man of simplicity who put his duty to Rome before any consideration of personal interest or wealth.

Around 390 B.C.E. the Romans suffered a major setback when a new people, the Celts—or Gauls (gawls), as the Romans called them—swept aside a Roman army and sacked Rome. More intent on loot than on conquest, the Gauls agreed to abandon Rome in return for a thousand pounds of gold. Thereafter the Romans made it their policy never to accept peace, much less to surrender, so long as the enemy was still in the field.

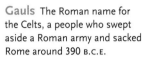

Gauls The Roman name for the Celts, a people who swept aside a Roman army and sacked Rome around 390 B.C.E.

From 390 to 290 B.C.E. the Romans rebuilt their city and recouped their losses. They also reorganized their army to create the mobile legion, a flexible unit capable of fighting on either broken or open terrain. The Romans finally brought Latium and their Latin allies fully under their control and conquered Etruria (see Map 5.1). In 343 B.C.E. they grappled with the Samnites in a series of bitter wars for the possession of Campania (kam-PAY-nyuh) and southern Italy. The Samnites were a formidable enemy, but the superior organization, institutions, and manpower of the Romans won out in the end. Although Rome had yet to subdue the whole peninsula, for the first time in history the city stood unchallenged in Italy.

The Romans spread their culture by sharing their religious cults, mythology, and drama. They, like the Greeks, liberally shared their religious beliefs with others, which in turn furthered the Romanization of Italy. Yet the spread of Roman culture was not part of a planned ideological onslaught by the Romans. Nor was it different from the ways in which the Romans extended their political, military, and legal systems. Even so, the process eventually created a common ground for all the peoples living in Italy and made Italy Roman. In later years the Romans continued this process until all these influences spread throughout the Mediterranean basin.

With many of their oldest allies, such as the Latin towns, the Romans shared full Roman citizenship. In other instances they granted citizenship without the franchise, that is, without the right to vote or hold Roman offices. Allies were subject to Roman taxes and calls for military service but ran their own local affairs. The Latin allies were able to acquire full Roman citizenship by moving to Rome.

franchise The right to vote or hold Roman office.

A very efficient means of keeping the Romans and their colonies together were the Roman roads. These roads provided an easy route of communication between the capital and outlying areas, allowed for the quick movement of armies, and offered an efficient means of trade.

By their willingness to extend their citizenship, the Romans took Italy into partnership. Here the political genius of Rome triumphed where Greece had failed. Rome proved itself superior to the Greek polis because it both conquered and shared the fruits of conquest with the conquered. The unwillingness of the Greek polis to share its citizenship condemned it to a limited horizon. Not so with Rome. The extension of Roman citizenship strengthened the state, gave it additional manpower and wealth, and laid the foundation of the Roman Empire.

The Gauls Sack Rome, ca. 390 B.C.E.

▼ What were the key institutions of the Roman republic?

Roman history is usually divided into two periods: the republic, the age in which Rome grew from a small city-state to ruler of an empire, and the empire, the period when the republican constitution gave way to constitutional monarchy.

The Roman republic consisted of a constitution and the people who made it. The Romans' first problem was to create the political institutions needed to govern effectively an ever-expanding and influential state. The second was the sharing of the obligations and privileges that came with that effort. The Romans struggled hard to meet these challenges. In the process they fashioned both a state and a society.

The Roman State

The Romans summed up their political existence in a single phrase, *senatus populusque Romanum*, "the Roman senate and people," which was often abbreviated as "SPQR." These words were a statement and a proclamation that epitomized the Roman people, their state, and their way of life. SPQR became a shorthand way of saying "Rome," just as "U.S.A." says "the United States of America."

The real genius of the Romans lay in the fields of politics and law. Unlike the Greeks, they did not often speculate on the ideal state or on political forms. Instead, they realistically met actual challenges and created institutions, magistracies, and legal concepts to deal with practical problems. Change was consequently commonplace in Roman political life, and the constitution evolved over time. Moreover, the Roman constitution, unlike the American, was not a single written document. Rather, it was a set of traditional beliefs, customs, and laws.

The Roman Forum The Roman Forum, adorned with stately buildings, formed the center of Roman political and social life. (age fotostock/SuperStock)

CHAPTER LOCATOR   How did the Romans become the dominant power in Italy?

In the early republic social divisions determined the shape of politics. Political power was in the hands of the aristocracy—the patricians, who were wealthy landowners. Patrician families formed clans, as did aristocrats in early Greece. Patrician men dominated the affairs of state, provided military leadership in time of war, and monopolized knowledge of law and legal procedure. The common people of Rome, the plebeians, had few of the patricians' political and social advantages. Many plebeian merchants increased their wealth in the course of Roman expansion, and some even formed powerful clans, but most plebeians were poor. They were the artisans, small farmers, and landless urban dwellers. All plebeians, rich and poor alike, were free citizens with a voice in politics. Nonetheless, they were overshadowed by the patricians.

Perhaps the greatest institution of the republic was the senate, which had originated under the Etruscans as a council of noble elders who advised the king. During the republic the senate advised the magistrates. Because the senate sat year after year, while magistrates changed annually, it provided stability and continuity. It also served as a reservoir of experience and knowledge. Technically, the senate could not pass legislation; it could only offer advice. But increasingly, because of the senate's prestige, its advice came to have the force of law.

The Romans created several assemblies through which men elected magistrates and passed legislation. The comitia centuriata (kuh-MEE-shee-uh sehn-tuhr-EE-ah-tuh) voted in centuries, or political blocs. The patricians possessed the majority of centuries because they shouldered most of the leadership and frontline infantry. Thus they could easily outvote the plebeians. In 471 B.C.E. plebeian men won the right to meet in an assembly of their own, the concilium plebis, and to pass ordinances. Later the bills passed in the concilium plebis were recognized as binding on the entire population.

The chief magistrates of the republic were the two consuls, who were elected for one-year terms. At first the consulship was open only to patrician men. The consuls commanded the army in battle, administered state business, convened the comitia centuriata, and supervised financial affairs. In effect, they and the senate ran the state. The consuls appointed quaestors (KWEH-stuhrs) to assist them in their duties, and in 421 B.C.E. the quaestorship became an elective office open to plebeian men. The quaestors took charge of the public treasury and prosecuted criminals in the popular courts.

In 366 B.C.E. the Romans created a new office, that of praetor (PREE-tuhr). When the consuls were away from Rome, the praetors could act in their place. The praetors dealt primarily with the administration of justice and the interpretation of the law.

Other officials included the powerful censors who had many responsibilities, the most important being supervision of public morals, the power to determine who lawfully could sit in the senate, the registration of citizens, and the leasing of public contracts. Later officials were the aediles (EE-dihls) who supervised the streets and markets and presided over public festivals.

One of the most important Roman achievements was the development of law. Roman law began as a set of rules that regulated the lives and relations of citizens. This civil law, or *ius civile*, consisted of statutes, customs, and forms of procedure. Roman assemblies added to the body of law, and praetors interpreted it.

As the Romans came into more frequent contact with foreigners, they had to devise laws to deal with disputes between Romans and foreigners. In these instances, where there was no precedent to guide the Romans, the legal decisions of the praetors proved of immense importance. The praetors resorted to the law of equity—what they thought was right and just to all parties. This situation illustrates the practicality and the genius of the Romans. By addressing specific, actual circumstances the praetors developed a body of law, the *ius gentium*, "the law of peoples," that applied to Romans and foreigners and that laid the foundation for a universal conception of law. By the time of the late republic, Roman jurists were reaching decisions on the basis of the Stoic concept of *ius naturale*, "natural law," a universal law that could be applied to all societies.

patricians The Roman aristocracy; wealthy landowners who held political power.

plebeians The common people of Rome.

senate Originating under the Etruscans as a council of noble elders who advised the king, the Roman senate advised the magistrates; over time its advice came to have the force of law.

consuls The two chief Roman magistrates; elected for one-year terms, consuls along with the senate ran the affairs of the state.

The Struggle of the Orders

A vital aspect of early Roman history was a conflict between patricians and plebeians usually known as the **Struggle of the Orders**. The plebeians wanted real political representation and safeguards against patrician domination. They also agitated for social reforms that would give them the right to intermarry with patricians and the ability to climb up the social scale. The plebeian effort to obtain recognition of these rights is the crux of the Struggle of the Orders.

Rome's early wars gave the plebeians the leverage they needed. Rome's survival depended on the army, and the army needed plebeians to fill the ranks of the infantry. To force the patricians to grant concessions, the plebeians seceded from the state in 494 B.C.E., literally walking out of Rome and refusing to serve in the army. The tactic worked and the patricians made important concessions. In 445 B.C.E. the patricians passed a law, the *lex Canuleia*, that for the first time allowed patricians and plebeians to marry one another. Furthermore, the patricians recognized the right of plebeians to elect their own officials, the **tribunes**. The tribunes had the right to protect the plebeians from the arbitrary conduct of patrician magistrates by bringing plebeian grievances to the senate for resolution.

The law itself was the plebeians' primary target. Only the patricians knew what the law was, and only they could argue cases in court. All too often they used the law for their own benefit. The plebeians wanted the law codified and published. The result of their agitation was the Law of the Twelve Tables. Later still, the plebeians forced the patricians to publish legal procedures as well. The plebeians had broken the patricians' legal monopoly and henceforth enjoyed full protection under the law.

The decisive plebeian victory came with the passage of the Licinian-Sextian laws in 367 B.C.E. Licinius and Sextus were plebeian tribunes who joined the poor to mount a sweeping assault on patrician privilege. The two tribunes won approval from the senate for a law that stipulated that one of the two annual consuls must be a plebeian. The Struggle of the Orders came to an end in 287 B.C.E. with the passage of a law, the *lex Hortensia*, that gave the resolutions of the concilium plebis the force of law for patricians and plebeians alike.

The results of the compromise between the patricians and the plebeians were far-reaching. Plebeians could now hold the consulship, which brought with it the consular title, places of honor in the senate, and such cosmetic privileges as wearing the purple toga, the symbol of aristocracy. Far more important, the compromise established a new nobility shared by the plebeians and the patricians. This would lead not to major political reform but to an extension of aristocratic rule. Nevertheless, the patricians were wise enough to give the plebeians wider political rights than they had previously enjoyed.

The Struggle of the Orders resulted in a Rome stronger and better united than before. It could have led to anarchy, but the values fostered by the social structure predisposed the Romans to compromise, especially in the face of common danger. The Struggle of the Orders produced a new concept of Roman citizenship. All male citizens shared equally under the law. Theoretically, all men could aspire to the highest political offices.

▼ How did the Romans build a Mediterranean empire?

Once the Romans had settled their internal affairs, they turned their attention outward. As seen earlier, they had already come to terms with the Italic peoples in Latium. Only later did Rome achieve primacy over its Latin allies, partly because of successful diplo-

Chapter 5
The Rise of Rome
ca. 750–31 B.C.E.

120

CHAPTER LOCATOR | How did the Romans become the dominant power in Italy?

Battle Between the Romans and the Germans

Rome's wars with the barbarians of western Europe comes to life in this relief from a Roman sarcophagus of 225 C.E. Even the bravery and strength of the Germans were no match for the steadiness and discipline of the Roman legions. (Vanni/Art Resource, NY)

ANALYZING THE IMAGE How would you describe this depiction of war? What does it suggest about the reality of Rome's wars with the barbarians?

CONNECTIONS What was the nature of Rome's overseas conquests? How did the Romans' treatment of the peoples in these unfamiliar territories differ from their conquest of Italy?

To complete this activity online, go to the Online Study Guide at bedfordstmartins.com/mckaywestunderstanding.

macy and partly because of overwhelming military power. In 238 B.C.E. Rome expanded even farther in Italy and extended its power across the sea to Sicily, Corsica, and Sardinia (sahr-DIHN-ee-uh).

Italy Becomes Roman

In only twenty years, from 282 to 262 B.C.E., the Romans established a string of colonies throughout Italy, some populated by Romans and others by Latins. The genius of the Romans lay in bringing these various peoples into one political system. First the Romans divided the Italians into two broad classes. Those living closest to Rome were incorporated into the Roman state. They enjoyed the full franchise and citizenship that the Romans themselves possessed. Italians who lived farther afield were considered allies. Although they received lesser rights of active citizenship, the allies retained their right of local self-government. The link between the allies and Rome was as much social as political, as both were ruled by aristocrats.

Contacts with their neighbors led the Romans to a better acquaintance with the heritage, customs, and laws of their fellow Italians. Rome and the rest of Italy began to share similar views of their common welfare. By including others in the Roman political and social system, Rome was making Italy Roman.

What were the key institutions of the Roman republic?　　**How did the Romans build a Mediterranean empire?**　　How did expansion affect Roman society and culture?　　What led to the fall of the Roman republic?

121

The Age of Conquest

In 282 B.C.E. the Romans embarked on a series of wars that left them rulers of the Mediterranean world. These wars were often unlike those against the Italians or Etruscans. As they moved south into Italy and later eastward against the Hellenistic kingdoms, the wars became fierce and were fought on a larger scale than those in Italy. Yet there was nothing ideological about them. The Romans did not map out grandiose strategies for world conquest. In many instances they did not even initiate action; they simply responded to situations as they arose.

The Samnite wars had drawn the Romans into the political world of southern Italy. In 282 B.C.E., alarmed by the powerful newcomer, the Greek city of Tarentum (tuh-REHN-tuhm) in southern Italy called for help from Pyrrhus (PIHR-uhs), king of Epirus (ih-PIGH-ruhs) in western Greece. Pyrrhus won two battles but suffered heavy casualties—thus the phrase "Pyrrhic victory" to describe a victory involving severe losses. Roman bravery and tenacity led Pyrrhus to comment: "If we win one more battle with the Romans, we'll be completely washed up."[2] The Romans threw new legions against Pyrrhus's army, and in 275 B.C.E. the Romans drove Pyrrhus from southern Italy and extended their sway over the area. They then needed to secure the island of Sicily (SIH-suh-lee) in order to block the expansion northward of Carthage.

The Punic Wars

By 264 B.C.E. Carthage (Map 5.2) was the unrivaled power of the western Mediterranean. Since the second half of the eighth century B.C.E., it had built its wealth on trade in tin and precious metals. It commanded one of the best harbors on the northern African coast and was supported by a fertile hinterland. By the fourth century B.C.E. they were fully integrated into the Hellenistic economy, which now spread from Gibraltar to the Parthian empire. Expansion led to war with the Etruscans and Greeks. At the end of a long string of wars, the Carthaginians had created and defended a mercantile empire that stretched from western Sicily to beyond Gibraltar.

First Punic War A war between Rome and Carthage in which Rome emerged the victor after twenty-three years of fighting.

The battle for Sicily set the stage for the **First Punic War** between Rome and Carthage, two powers expanding into the same area. The First Punic War lasted for twenty-three years (264–241 B.C.E.). The Romans quickly learned that they could not conquer Sicily unless they controlled the sea, so they built a navy. Of the seven major naval battles they fought with the Carthaginians, they won six and finally wore them down. In 241 B.C.E. the Romans took possession of Sicily, which became their first real province. Once again Rome's resources, manpower, and determination proved decisive.

The peace treaty between the two powers brought no peace, in part because in 238 B.C.E. the Romans took advantage of Carthaginian weakness to seize Sardinia and Corsica. The only way Carthage could recoup its fortune was by success in Spain, where the Carthaginians already enjoyed a firm foothold. In 237 B.C.E. Hamilcar Barca led an army to Spain in order to turn it into Carthaginian territory. In the following years Hamilcar and his son-in-law Hasdrubal (HAHZ-droo-buhl) subjugated much of southern Spain and in the process rebuilt Carthaginian power. Rome first made a treaty with Hasdrubal setting the boundary between Carthaginian and Roman interests at the Ebro River, and then began to extend its own influence in Spain.

Triumphal Column of Caius Duilius This monument celebrates Rome's first naval victory in the First Punic War. In the battle Caius Duilius destroyed fifty Carthaginian ships. He then celebrated his success by erecting this column. The prows of the enemy ships are shown projecting from the column. (Alinari/Art Resource, NY)

Chapter 5
The Rise of Rome
122   ca. 750–31 B.C.E.

CHAPTER LOCATOR   How did the Romans become the dominant power in Italy?

Map 5.2 Roman Expansion During the Republic, ca. 282–44 B.C.E.

Previous maps have shown that the Greeks and Macedonians concentrated their energies on opening the East. This map indicates that Rome for the first time looked to the West.

ANALYZING THE MAP Which years saw the greatest expansion of Roman power? How might the different geographic features have helped or hindered the expansion into certain areas?

CONNECTIONS What does this say about the expansion of Roman power in the Mediterranean? How did the Romans maintain their power across such a wide and diverse area?

To complete this activity online, go to the Online Study Guide at bedfordstmartins.com/mckaywestunderstanding.

In 221 B.C.E. Hamilcar's son Hannibal became Carthaginian commander in Spain. When Hannibal laid siege to Saguntum (suh-GUHN-tum), which lay within the sphere of Carthaginian interest, the Romans declared war, claiming that Carthage had attacked a friendly city. So began the Second Punic War. In 218 B.C.E. Hannibal struck first by marching more than a thousand miles over the Alps into Italy. Once there, he defeated one Roman army at the Battle of Trebia and later another at the Battle of Lake Trasimene. The following year Hannibal won his greatest victory at the Battle of Cannae (KAH-nee), in which he inflicted some forty thousand casualties on the Romans. He then spread devastation throughout Italy, and a number of cities in central and southern Italy rebelled against Rome. Syracuse, Rome's ally during the First Punic War, also went over to the Carthaginians. Yet Hannibal failed to crush Rome's iron circle of Latium, Etruria, and Samnium. The wisdom of Rome's political policy of extending rights and citizenship to its allies showed itself in these dark hours. And Rome fought back.

In 210 B.C.E. Rome found its answer to Hannibal in the young commander Scipio Africanus. Scipio copied Hannibal's methods of mobile warfare, streamlining the legions

Second Punic War A war fought between Carthage, led by Hannibal, and Rome; Roman victory meant that the western Mediterranean would henceforth be Roman.

by making their components capable of independent action and introducing new weapons. In the following years Scipio operated in Spain, which in 207 B.C.E. he wrested from the Carthaginians. That same year the Romans sealed Hannibal's fate in Italy. At the Battle of Metaurus the Romans destroyed a major Carthaginian army coming to reinforce Hannibal. Scipio then struck directly at Carthage itself, prompting the Carthaginians to recall Hannibal from Italy to defend the homeland.

In 202 B.C.E., near the town of Zama (see Map 5.2), Scipio defeated Hannibal in one of the world's truly decisive battles. Scipio's victory meant that the world of the western Mediterranean would henceforth be Roman. Roman language, law, and culture, fertilized by Greek influences, would in time permeate this entire region. The victory at Zama meant that Rome's heritage would be passed on to the Western world.

The Second Punic War contained the seeds of still other wars. Unabated fear of Carthage led to the Third Punic War. It was a needless, unjust, and savage conflict that ended in 146 B.C.E. when Scipio Aemilianus (AY-mihl-ee-ah-nuhs), grandson of Scipio Africanus, destroyed the hated rival.

During the war with Hannibal, the Romans had invaded Spain. When the Roman legions tried to reduce the Spanish tribes, they met with bloody and determined resistance. Not until 133 B.C.E., after years of brutal and ruthless warfare, did Scipio Aemilianus finally conquer Spain.

Rome Turns East

During the Second Punic War, King Philip V of Macedonia made an alliance with Hannibal against Rome. Despite the mortal struggle in the West, the Romans found the strength to turn eastward to settle accounts. Their first significant victory over the Macedonians came in 197 B.C.E. In defeat the Macedonians agreed to give full liberty to the Greeks. Two years later Rome defeated the Spartans. In 188 B.C.E. the Seleucid kingdom fell to the Romans, but decisive victory came in 146 B.C.E., when the Romans conquered the Achaean League, sacked Corinth, and finally defeated Macedonia, which they made a Roman province. In 133 B.C.E. the king of Pergamum bequeathed his kingdom to the Romans. The Ptolemies of Egypt wisely and safely kept on good terms with the Romans.

The Romans had used the discord and disunity of the Hellenistic world to divide and conquer it. Once they had done so, they faced the formidable challenge of governing it without further warfare, which they met by establishing the first Roman provinces in the East. They ultimately succeeded in fusing the culture and civilization of the Hellenistic world with the new and vibrant Roman civilization. Declaring the Mediterranean *mare nostrum*, "our sea," the Romans began to create political and administrative machinery to hold the Mediterranean together under a mutually shared cultural and political system.

▼ How did expansion affect Roman society and culture?

Rome had conquered the Mediterranean world, but some Romans considered that victory a misfortune. The historian Sallust (86–34 B.C.E.), writing from hindsight, complained that the acquisition of an empire was the beginning of Rome's troubles:

> *But when through labor and justice our Republic grew powerful, . . . then fortune began to be harsh and to throw everything into confusion. The Romans had easily borne labor, danger, uncertainty, and hardship. To them leisure, riches — otherwise desirable — proved*

Chapter 5
The Rise of Rome
ca. 750–31 B.C.E.

124

CHAPTER LOCATOR | How did the Romans become the dominant power in Italy?

to be burdens and torments. So at first money, then desire for power grew great. These things were a sort of cause of all evils.[3]

Sallust was not alone in his feelings. In the second century B.C.E. the Romans learned that they could not return to what they fondly considered a simple life. They were the most powerful nation in Europe. They had to change their institutions, social patterns, and way of thinking to meet the new era. In the end Rome triumphed here just as it had on the battlefield, for out of the turmoil would come the *pax Romana*—"Roman peace."

How did the Romans of the day meet these challenges? Obviously there are as many answers to these questions as there were Romans. Yet two men represent the major trends of the second century B.C.E. Cato the Elder shared the mentality of those who longed for the good old days and idealized the traditional agrarian way of life. Scipio Aemilianus led those who embraced the new urban life, with its eager acceptance of Greek culture. Their views exemplify the opposing sets of attitudes that marked Roman society and politics in the age of expansion.

Marcus Cato: The Traditional Ideal

Marcus Cato (234–149 B.C.E.) was born a plebeian, but his talent and energy carried him to Rome's highest offices. He created an image of himself as the bearer of "traditional" Roman virtues.

Like most Romans, Cato and his family began the day at sunrise. After a light breakfast Cato used the rest of his mornings to plead law cases. Because of his political aspirations, he often walked to the marketplace of the nearby town and defended anyone who wished his help. He received no fees for these services, but in return Cato's clients gave him their political support or their votes in repayment whenever he asked for them. This practice was known as clientage, a Roman custom whereby free men entrusted their lives to a more powerful man in exchange for support in public life and private matters.

Cato was the *paterfamilias*, the oldest male head of the family, a part of the patriarchal organization that included several related households (see Chapter 1). The paterfamilias held nearly absolute power over the lives of his wife and children as long as he lived. He could legally kill his wife for adultery or divorce her at will. Until the paterfamilias died, his sons could not legally own property. Along with his biological kin, the paterfamilias also had authority over slaves, servants, adopted children, and others who lived in his household.

Cato was married, as were almost all Roman citizens. Grooms were generally somewhat older than their brides, who often married in their early teens. Women could inherit property under Roman law, though they generally received a smaller portion of any family inheritance than their brothers did. A woman's inheritance usually came as a dowry on marriage. In the earliest Roman marriage laws, men could divorce their wives without any grounds while women could not divorce their husbands, but by Cato's time these laws had changed, and both men and women could initiate divorce.

Both Romans and Greeks felt that children should be raised in the lap by their mother, a woman who kept her house in good order and personally saw to the welfare of her children. In wealthy homes mothers employed slaves as wet nurses. According to Cato, his wife refused to delegate her maternal duties. Like most ordinary Roman women, she nursed her son herself and bathed and swaddled him daily.

Until the age of seven, children were under their mother's care. During this time the mother educated her daughters in the management of the household. After the age of seven, sons—and in many wealthy households daughters too—began to receive formal education. Formal education for wealthy children was generally by tutors, who were often Greek slaves, for parents wanted their children to learn Greek literature and

Roman School Seated between two students with scrolls in their hands, the teacher discusses a point with the student on his left. To his far left, a tardy student arrives, lunchbox in hand. Roman education, even in the provinces, lasted well into late antiquity, and was a cultural legacy to the medieval world. (Rheinisches Landesmuseum, Trier)

philosophy. By the late republic, there were also a few schools. Most children learned skills from their own parents or through apprenticeships with artisans.

In the country Romans like Cato took their main meal at midday. This meal included either coarse bread or porridge; it also included turnips, cabbage, olives, and beans. The family drank ordinary wine mixed with water.

The agricultural year followed the sun and the stars. The Roman farmer looked to the sky to determine when to plant, weed, shear sheep, and perform other chores. The main money crops were wheat and flax. Forage crops included clover, vetch, and alfalfa. Prosperous farmers like Cato raised olive trees chiefly for the oil. They also raised grapevines for the production of wine.

An influx of slaves from Rome's wars and conquests provided labor for the fields and elsewhere. To the Romans, slavery was a misfortune that befell some people, but it did not entail any racial theories. Races were not enslaved because the Romans thought them inferior. For the talented slave the Romans always held out the hope of eventual freedom. Manumission — the freeing of individual slaves by their masters — became so common that it was limited by law. Not even Christians questioned the institution of slavery. It was a fact of life.

For Cato and most other Romans, religion played an important part in life. Originally the Romans thought of the gods as invisible, shapeless natural forces. Only through Etruscan and Greek influence did Roman deities take on human form. Jupiter, the sky-god, and his wife Juno became equivalent to the Greek Zeus and Hera. The gods of the Romans were not loving and personal. They were stern, powerful, and aloof. The Romans honored the cults of their gods, hoping for divine favor.

Along with the great gods the Romans believed in spirits who haunted fields, forests, crossroads, and even the home itself. Some of these deities were hostile; only magic could ward them off. The spirits of the dead frequented places where they had lived. They too had to be placated but were ordinarily benign. As the Roman poet Ovid (43 B.C.E.– 17 C.E.) put it:

> *The spirits of the dead ask for little.*
> *They are more grateful for piety than for an expensive gift—*
> *Not greedy are the gods who haunt the Styx below.*
> *A rooftile covered with a sacrificial crown,*
> *Scattered kernels, a few grains of salt,*
> *Bread dipped in wine, and loose violets—*
> *These are enough.*[4]

Chapter 5
The Rise of Rome
126   ca. 750–31 B.C.E.

CHAPTER LOCATOR   How did the Romans become the dominant power in Italy?

A good deal of Roman religion consisted of rituals such as those Ovid describes. These practices lived on long after the Romans had lost interest in the great gods. Even Christianity could not entirely wipe them out. Instead, Christianity was to incorporate many of these rituals into its own style of worship.

Scipio Aemilianus: Greek Culture and Urban Life

The old-fashioned ideals that Cato represented came into conflict with a new urban culture that reflected Hellenistic influences. The conquest of the Mediterranean world and the spoils of war made Rome a great city. The spoils of war went to build baths, theaters, and other places of amusement. Romans and Italian townspeople began to spend more of their time in leisure pursuits. Simultaneously, the new responsibilities of governing the world produced in Rome a sophisticated society. Romans developed new tastes and a liking for Greek culture and literature. It became common for an educated Roman to speak both Latin and Greek. Hellenism dominated the cultural life of Rome.

One of the most avid devotees of Hellenism and the new was Scipio Aemilianus, the destroyer of Carthage. Scipio realized that broad and worldly views had to replace the old Roman narrowness. Rome was no longer a small city; it was the capital of the world, and Romans had to adapt themselves to that fact. Scipio became an innovator in both politics and culture. He developed a more personal style of politics that looked unflinchingly at the broader problems that the success of Rome brought to its people. He embraced Hellenism wholeheartedly. Perhaps more than anyone else of his day, Scipio represented the new Roman—imperial, cultured, and independent.

In his education and interests, too, Scipio broke with the past. As a boy he had received the traditional Roman training, learning to read and write Latin and becoming acquainted with the law. But as a young man he formed a lasting friendship with the historian Polybius, who actively encouraged him in his study of Greek language and culture and in his intellectual pursuits. In later life Scipio's love of Greek learning, rhetoric, and philosophy became legendary. Scipio also promoted the spread of Hellenism in Roman society.

The new Hellenism profoundly stimulated the growth and development of Roman art and literature. The Roman conquest of the Hellenistic East resulted in wholesale confiscation of Greek paintings and sculpture to grace Roman temples, public buildings, and private homes. Roman artists copied many aspects of Greek art, but their emphasis on realistic portraiture carried on a native tradition. The Greek influence on Roman literature was also strong.

The conquest of the Mediterranean world and the wealth it brought gave the Romans leisure, and Hellenism influenced how they spent their free time. Many rich urban dwellers changed their eating habits by consuming elaborate meals of exotic dishes. During the second century B.C.E. the Greek custom of bathing also became a Roman passion. Large buildings containing pools and exercise rooms went up in great numbers, and the baths became an essential part of the Roman city. Architects built intricate systems of aqueducts to supply the bathing establishments with water. The baths contained hot-air rooms to induce a good sweat and pools of hot and cold water to finish the actual bathing.

Conservatives railed at this Greek custom, calling it a waste of time and an encouragement to idleness. They were correct in that bathing establishments were more than just places to take a bath. They included gymnasia,

African Acrobat Conquest and prosperity brought exotic pleasure to Rome. This sculpture shows a young African woman in an attention-getting gymnastic pose. To add to the spice of her act, she uses a live crocodile as her platform. (Courtesy of the Trustees of the British Museum)

Roman Bath Once introduced into the Roman world, social bathing became a passion. These are the Roman baths at Bath, England, a city to which they gave their name. A triumph of sophisticated engineering, they also demonstrate how Roman culture and institutions influenced life on the perimeters of the Roman empire. In addition to hot water, bathers used oil for massage and metal scrapers to clean and renew their skin. (Horst Schafer/Photolibrary)

where men exercised and played ball. They also contained snack bars and halls, where people chatted and read, and even libraries and lecture halls. Women had opportunities to bathe, generally in separate facilities or at separate times.

The baths were socially important places where men and women went to see and be seen. Social climbers tried to talk to the right people and wangle invitations to dinner; politicians took advantage of the occasion to discuss the affairs of the day; marriages were negotiated by wealthy fathers. Prostitutes added to the attraction of many baths. Despite the protests of conservatives and moralists, the baths were enormously popular with both rich and poor Romans.

Did Hellenism and new social customs corrupt the Romans? Perhaps the best answer is this: the Roman state and the empire it ruled continued to exist for six more centuries. Rome did not collapse; the state continued to prosper. The high tide of its prosperity still lay in the future.

▼ What led to the fall of the Roman republic?

The wars of conquest created serious problems for the Romans, some of the most pressing of which were political. The republican constitution had suited the needs of a simple city-state but was inadequate to meet the requirements of Rome's new position in international affairs. A system of provincial administration had to be established to serve a state holding vast territory. Armies had to be provided for defense, and a system of tax collection had to be created. During the wars Roman generals commanded huge numbers of troops for long periods of time. These men of great power and prestige were becoming too mighty for the state to control. Although Rome's Italian allies had borne much of the burden of the fighting, they received fewer rewards than did Roman officers and soldiers. Italians began to agitate for full Roman citizenship, including the right to vote. These problems, complex and explosive, largely account for the turmoil of the closing years of the republic.

128

Chapter 5
The Rise of Rome
ca. 750–31 B.C.E.

CHAPTER LOCATOR | How did the Romans become the dominant power in Italy?

Unrest in Rome and Italy

Hannibal's operations and the warfare in Italy had left the countryside a shambles. The prolonged fighting had also drawn untold numbers of Roman and Italian men away from their farms for long periods. The families of these soldiers could not keep the land under full cultivation. When the legionaries returned to their farms in Italy, all too often their farms looked like the farms of people they had conquered. Two courses of action were open to them. They could rebuild, or they could sell their holdings. The wars of conquest had made some men astoundingly rich. These men wanted to invest their wealth in land. They bought up small farms to create huge estates, which the Romans called latifundia (lah-tuh-FUHN-dee-uh).

Selling their land appealed to the veterans for a variety of reasons. Many veterans had seen service in the East and had experienced the city life of the Hellenistic states. They were reluctant to settle down to a dull life on the farm. Often their farms were so badly damaged that rebuilding hardly seemed worthwhile. Besides, it was hard to make big profits from small farms. Nor could the veterans supplement their income by working on the latifundia. Although the owners of the latifundia occasionally hired free men as day laborers, they preferred to use slaves. Confronted by these conditions, veterans and their families opted to sell their land.

Most veterans migrated to the cities, especially to Rome. Although some found work, most did not. Industry and small manufacturing were generally in the hands of slaves. Even when work was available, slave labor kept the wages of free men low. Instead of a new start, veterans and their families encountered slum conditions.

This trend held ominous consequences for the strength of Rome's armies. The Romans had always believed that only landowners should serve in the army, for only they had something to fight for. Landless men, even if they were Romans and lived in Rome, could not be conscripted into the army. Once veterans sold their land, they became ineligible for further military service. The landless ex-legionaries wanted to be able to serve in the army again, and they were willing to support any leader who would allow them to.

One man who recognized the plight of Rome's peasant farmers and urban poor was an aristocrat, Tiberius Gracchus (tigh-BEER-ee-uhs GRAK-uhs) (163–133 B.C.E.). Appalled by what he saw, Tiberius warned his countrymen of the legionaries' plight:

> The wild beasts that roam over Italy have every one of them a cave or lair to lurk in. But the men who fight and die for Italy enjoy the common air and light, indeed, but nothing else. Houseless and homeless they wander about with their wives and children. . . . [T]hey fight and die to support others in luxury, and though they are styled masters of the world, they have not a single clod of earth that is their own.[5]

Tiberius Gracchus was dedicated to finding a solution to the problems of the veterans and the urban poor.

After his election as tribune of the people in 133 B.C.E., Tiberius proposed that public land be given to the poor in small lots. His reform proposal angered those who had usurped large tracts of public land for their own use. They had no desire to give any of it back, so they bitterly resisted Tiberius's efforts. This was to be expected, yet he unquestionably made additional problems for himself. He introduced his land bill in the concilium plebis without consulting the senate. When King Attalus III left the kingdom of Pergamum to the Romans in his will, Tiberius had the money appropriated to finance his reforms—another slap at the senate. As tribune he acted totally within his rights. Yet the way in which he proceeded was unprecedented.

Many powerful Romans became suspicious of Tiberius's growing influence with the people. Some considered his unparalleled methods tyranny. As a result, a large body of senators, led by the *pontifex maximus* (the chief priest), killed Tiberius in cold blood.

The death of Tiberius was the beginning of an era of political violence. In the end that violence would bring down the republic in 31 B.C.E.

Although Tiberius was dead, his land bill became law. Furthermore, Tiberius's brother Gaius Gracchus (153–121 B.C.E.) took up the cause of reform. Gaius (GAY-uhs) was a veteran soldier with an enviable record, and when he became tribune he demanded even more extensive reform than had his brother. To help the urban poor Gaius pushed legislation to provide them with cheap grain for bread. He defended his brother's land law and proposed that Rome send many of its poor and propertyless people out to form colonies in southern Italy. The prospect of new homes, land, and a fresh start gave the urban poor new hope and made Gaius popular among them.

Gaius went a step further and urged that all Italians be granted full rights of Roman citizenship. This measure provoked a storm of opposition, and it was not passed in Gaius's lifetime. In 91 B.C.E., however, many Italians revolted against Rome over the issue of full citizenship, thus triggering the Social War, so named from the Latin word *socium*, or "ally." After a brief but hard-fought war (91–88 B.C.E.), the senate gave Roman citizenship to all Italians. Had the senate listened to Gaius earlier, it could have prevented a great deal of bloodshed.

Like his brother Tiberius, Gaius aroused a great deal of personal and factional opposition. To many he seemed too radical and hasty to change things. When Gaius failed in 121 B.C.E. to win the tribunate for the third time, he feared for his life. In desperation he armed his staunchest supporters, whereupon the senate ordered the consul Opimius to restore order. He did so by having Gaius killed, along with three thousand of Gaius's supporters who opposed the senate's order. Once again the cause of reform had met with violence.

The death of Gaius brought little peace, and trouble came from two sources: the outbreak of new wars in the Mediterranean basin and further political unrest in Rome. In 112 B.C.E. Rome declared war against the rebellious Jugurtha (joo-GUHR-thuh), king of Numidia in North Africa. Numidia had been one of Rome's client kingdoms, a kingdom still ruled by its own king but subject to Rome. Client kingdoms followed Rome's lead in foreign affairs but conducted their own internal business according to their own laws and customs. In time many of these states became provinces of the Roman Empire.

The Roman legions made little headway against Jugurtha until 107 B.C.E., when Gaius Marius (MEHR-ee-uhs), an Italian new man (a politician not from the traditional Roman aristocracy), became consul. A man of fierce vigor and courage, Marius saw the army as the tool of his ambition. He took the unusual but not wholly unprecedented step of recruiting an army by permitting landless men to serve in the legions. Marius thus tapped Rome's vast reservoir of idle manpower. His volunteer army was a professional force, not a body of draftees. In 106 B.C.E. Marius and his new army handily defeated Jugurtha.

An unexpected war broke out in the following year when two German peoples, the Cimbri and Teutones, moved into Gaul and later into northern Italy. After the Germans had defeated Roman armies sent to repel them, Marius was again elected consul, even though he was legally ineligible. From 104 to 100 B.C.E. Marius annually held the consulship, putting unprecedented military power into a Roman commander's hands.

Before engaging the Germans, Marius encouraged enlistments by promising his volunteers land after the war. Poor and landless veterans flocked to him, and together they

Chapter 5
The Rise of Rome
130   ca. 750–31 B.C.E.

CHAPTER LOCATOR   How did the Romans become the dominant power in Italy?

conquered the Germans by 101 B.C.E. When Marius proposed a bill to grant land to his veterans, the senate refused to act, in effect turning its back on the soldiers of Rome. It was a disastrous mistake. Henceforth the legionaries expected the commanders—not the senate or the state—to protect their interests. By failing to reward the loyalty of Rome's troops, the senate set the stage for military rebellion and political anarchy.

Another strong general, Sulla (SUHL-uh), was elected to consul in 88 B.C.E. after putting down the Italian allies in the Social War. While Sulla was away from Rome fighting the last of the rebels, factions agitating on behalf of Marius had him deposed from his consulship. He immediately marched on Rome and restored order, but it was an ominous sign of the deterioration of Roman politics and political ideals. With some semblance of order restored, Sulla in 88 B.C.E. led an army to Asia Minor where Roman rule was being challenged. In Sulla's absence, rioting and political violence again exploded in Rome. Marius and his supporters marched on Rome and launched a reign of terror.

Although Marius died shortly after his return to power, his supporters continued to hold Rome. Sulla returned in 82 B.C.E. and after a brief but intense civil war, he entered Rome and ordered a ruthless butchery of his opponents. He also proclaimed himself dictator. He launched many political and judicial reforms, including strengthening the senate while weakening the tribunate, increasing the number of magistrates in order to administer Rome's provinces better, and restoring the courts.

In 79 B.C.E. Sulla voluntarily abdicated his dictatorship and permitted the republican constitution to function normally once again. Yet his dictatorship cast a long shadow over the late republic. Civil war was to be the constant lot of Rome for the next forty-eight years. One figure who stands apart from the struggles of the late republic is Cicero (106–43 B.C.E.), a practical politician whose greatest legacy to the Roman world and to Western civilization is his mass of political and oratorical writings. Yet Cicero commanded no legions, and only legions commanded respect. (See "Listening to the Past: Cicero and the Plot to Kill Caesar," page 132.)

Civil War

In the late republic Romans were grappling with the simple and inescapable fact that their old city-state constitution was unequal to the demands of overseas possessions and the governing of provinces. Once the senate and other institutions of the Roman state had failed to come to grips with the needs of the empire, once the authorities had lost control of their own generals and soldiers, and once the armies put their faith in commanders instead of in Rome, the republic was doomed.

Sulla's real political heirs were Pompey (PAHM-pee) and Julius Caesar. Pompey, a man of boundless ambition, began his career as one of Sulla's lieutenants. After his army put down a rebellion in Spain, he himself threatened to rebel unless the senate allowed him to run for consul. He and another ambitious politician, Crassus, pooled political resources, and both won the consulship. They dominated Roman politics until the rise of Julius Caesar, who became consul in 59 B.C.E. Together the three concluded a political alliance, the **First Triumvirate** (trigh-UHM-veh-ruht), in which they agreed to advance one another's interests.

The man who cast the longest shadow over these troubled years was Julius Caesar (100–44 B.C.E.). Born of a noble family, he had serious intellectual interests, and his literary ability was immense. Caesar was a superb orator, and his affable personality and wit made him popular. He was also a shrewd politician

First Triumvirate A political alliance among Caesar, Crassus, and Pompey in which they agreed to advance one another's interests.

Julius Caesar In this bust, the sculptor portrays Caesar as a man of power and intensity. The bust is a study of determination and an excellent example of Roman portraiture. (Museo Archeologico Nazionale Naples/Scala/Art Resource, NY)

LISTENING TO THE PAST

Cicero and the Plot to Kill Caesar

Marcus Tullius Cicero was born in January 106 B.C.E. After an excellent education, he settled in Rome to practice law. His meteoric career took him to the consulship in 63 B.C.E. By the time of Caesar's dictatorship in 44 B.C.E., Cicero was sixty-two years old and a senior statesman. Like many others, he was fully caught up in the events leading to Caesar's assassination and the resulting revolution. Shortly before the plot was carried out on March 15, 44 B.C.E. — the Ides of March — Caesar wrote Cicero a flattering letter telling him that "your approval of my actions elates me beyond words. . . . As for yourself, I hope I shall see you at Rome so that I can avail myself as usual of your advice and resources in all things."* By then, however, Cicero knew of and supported the plot to assassinate Caesar and prudently decided not to meet him. The following letters and speeches offer a personal account of Cicero's involvement in the plot and its aftermath.

Trebonius, one of the assassins, wrote to Cicero describing the murder, and on February 2, 43 B.C.E., Cicero gave this frank opinion of the events:

❝ Would to heaven you had invited me to that noble feast that you made on the ides of March: no remnants, most assuredly, should have been left behind. Whereas the part you unluckily spared gives us so much perplexity that we find something to regret, even in the godlike service that you and your illustrious associates have lately rendered to the republic. To say the truth, when I reflect that it was owing to the favor of so worthy a man as yourself that Antony now lives to be our general bane, I am sometimes inclined to be a little angry with you for taking him aside when Caesar fell as by this means you have occasioned more trouble to myself in particular than to all the rest of the whole community.† ❞

By the "part of the feast spared" he meant Marc Antony, Caesar's firm supporter and a fierce enemy of the assassins. But Cicero's joy and early triumph in the senate were short-lived, for Caesar's death led to a civil war. Two men led the cause for restoring the republic: Brutus, an aristocrat who had been raised by Cato, and Cassius, an unpopular but influential senator. Still undecided about what to do after the assassination, Cassius wrote to Cicero asking for advice. Cicero responded:

❝ Where to advise you to begin to restore order I must acknowledge myself at a loss. To say the truth, it is the tyrant alone, and not the tyranny, from which we seem to be delivered: for although the man [Caesar] is destroyed, we still serviley maintain all his despotic ordinances. We do more: and under the pretence of carrying his designs into execution, we approve of measures which even he himself would never have pursued. . . . This outrageous man [Antony] represents me as the principal advisor and promoter of your glorious efforts. Would to heaven the charge were true! For had I been a party in your councils, I should have put it out of his power thus to bother and embarrass our plans. But this was a point that depended on yourselves to decide; and since the opportunity is now over, I can only wish that I were capable of giving you any effective advice. But the truth is that I am utterly at a loss in how to act myself. For what is the purpose of resisting where one cannot oppose force by force?‡ ❞

At this stage the young Octavian, the future Augustus and Caesar's heir, appeared to claim his inheritance. He too sought Cicero's advice, and in a series of letters to his close friend Atticus, Cicero discussed the situation:

❝ On the second or third of November 44 B.C.E. a letter arrived from Octavian. He has great schemes afoot. He has won the veterans at Casilinum and Calatia over to his views, and no wonder since he gives them 500 denarii apiece. He plans to make a round of the other colonies. His object is plain: war with Antony and himself as commander-in-chief. So it looks to me as though in a few days' time we shall be in arms. But whom are we to follow? Consider his name; consider his age. . . . In short, he proffers himself as our leader and expects me to back him up. For my part I have recommended him to go to Rome. I imagine he will have the city rabble behind him, and the honest men too if he convinces them of his sincerity. Ah Brutus, where are you? What a golden opportunity you are losing! I could not foretell *this*, but I thought something of the kind would happen.§ ❞

of unbridled ambition. Since military service was an effective steppingstone to politics, Caesar launched his military career in Spain, where his courage won the respect and affection of his troops. Personally brave and tireless, Caesar was a military genius who knew how to win battles and turn victories into permanent gains.

In 58 B.C.E. Caesar became governor of Cisalpine Gaul (modern northern Italy). By 50 B.C.E. he had conquered all of Gaul (modern France). Caesar's account of his operations, his *Commentaries* on the Gallic wars, became a classic in Western literature. By

CHAPTER LOCATOR   How did the Romans become the dominant power in Italy?

Four days later Cicero records news of the following developments:

❝ Two letters for me from Octavian in one day! Now he wants me to return to Rome at once, says he wants to work through the senate. . . . In short, he presses and I play for time. I don't trust his age and I don't know what he's after. . . . I'm nervous of Antony's power and don't want to leave the coast. But I'm afraid of some star performance during my absence. Varro [an enemy of Antony] doesn't think much of the boy's plan, I take a different view. He has a strong force at his back and *can* have Brutus. And he's going to work quite openly, forming companies at Capua and paying out bounties. War is evidently coming any minute now."** **❞**

Bust of Cicero (Alinari/Art Resource, NY)

At last Cicero openly sided with Octavian. On April 21, 43 B.C.E., he denounced Antony in a speech to the senate. He reminded his fellow senators how they had earlier opposed Antony:

❝ Do you not remember, in the name of the immortal gods, what resolutions you have made against these men [Antony and his supporters]? You have repealed the acts of Antony. You have taken down his law. You have voted that they were carried by violence and with a disregard of the auspices. You have called out the troops throughout all Italy. You have pronounced that colleague and ally of all wickedness a public enemy. What peace can here be with this man? Even if he were a foreign enemy, still, after such actions as have taken place, it would be scarcely possible by any means whatever to have peace. Though seas and mountains and vast regions lay between you, still you would hate such a man without seeing him. But these men will stick to your eyes, and when they can to your very throats; for what fences will be strong enough for us to restrain savage beasts? Oh, but the result of war is uncertain. It is at all events in the power of brave men such as you ought to be to display your valor, for certainly brave men can do that, and not to fear the caprice of fortune.†† **❞**

When war broke out Cicero continued to speak out in the senate against Antony. Yet Cicero commanded no legions, and only legions commanded respect. At last Antony got his revenge when he had Cicero prosecuted as a public enemy. An ill and aging Cicero fled to the sea in a litter, but he was intercepted by Antony's men. With dignity Cicero stretched his hand out of the window of the litter, and a centurion cut it off together with the hand that had written the speeches against Antony. Years later Octavian, then the Roman emperor Augustus, said of Cicero: "A learned man, learned and a lover of his country."‡‡

QUESTIONS FOR ANALYSIS

1. What can you infer from these letters about how well prepared Brutus and Cassius were to take control of the government after Caesar's death?
2. What do these sources suggest about Cicero's importance?
3. What was Cicero's view of Octavian? Of Antony?

*To Atticus 9.16.2 in D. R. Shackleton-Bailey, *Cicero's Letters to Atticus*, vol. IV (Cambridge, U.K.: Cambridge University Press 1968), pp. 203–205.

†*To Trebonius* in T. de Quincy, *Cicero: Offices, Essays, and Letters* (New York: E. P. Dutton, 1942), pp. 328–329.

‡*To Cassius*, ibid., pp. 324–325.

§*To Atticus* 16.8.1–2. in D. R. Shackleton-Bailey, *Cicero's Letters to Atticus*, vol. VI (Cambridge, U.K.: Cambridge University Press, 1967), pp. 185–187.

**To Atticus 16.9. ibid., p. 189.

††*The Fourteenth Phillipic* in C. D. Yonge, *Cicero, Select Orations* (New York: Harper and Brothers, 1889), p. 499.

‡‡Plutarch, *Cicero* 49.15.

49 B.C.E. the First Triumvirate had fallen apart. Crassus had died in battle, and Caesar and Pompey, each suspecting the other of treachery, came to blows. The result was a long and bloody civil war that raged from Spain across northern Africa to Egypt.

Egypt, meanwhile, was embroiled in a battle for control between a brother and sister, Ptolemy XIII and Cleopatra VII (69–30 B.C.E.). Cleopatra first allied herself with Pompey but then switched her alliance to Caesar. The two became lovers as well as allies, and she bore him a son. She returned to Rome with Caesar, but she was hated by the Roman

INDIVIDUALS IN SOCIETY

Queen Cleopatra

CLEOPATRA III (69–30 B.C.E.) BECAME QUEEN of Egypt in 51 B.C.E. She was a lovely woman, clever and sophisticated. To her intellectual gifts she added a frank and often humorous sexuality that easily conquered men. She was passionately devoted to her Egyptian subjects. She was the first of the Hellenistic ruling family who could speak Egyptian in addition to Greek. During the Roman civil war then raging, Caesar visited Alexandria, the Egyptian capital. Charmed by Cleopatra, he declared her queen of Egypt, setting to rest a power struggle she was engaged in with her brother. Caesar and Cleopatra spent the winter together, and by the next year they produced a son. Cleopatra had chosen the winning side. She first saw Rome in 46 B.C.E., where she faced the dislike of the Romans, who considered her to be a decadent oriental queen. She never afterward trusted them. After Caesar's assassination, she returned to Alexandria.

There she witnessed the outbreak of another Roman civil war that pitted Octavian, Caesar's heir, against Marc Antony, who commanded the Roman army in the East. When Antony visited Alexandria in 41 B.C.E., he met Cleopatra, then at the height of her beauty. She dazzled him with her irresistible charm, casual sophistication, and vast wealth. The two soon spent weeks drinking, playing dice, and attending elaborate parties. They became passionate lovers and married in 37 B.C.E. Antony's wedding present to her was a huge grant of territory, much of it Roman, that greatly increased her power.

Octavian used Cleopatra's wedding gift as the reason to declare Antony a traitor. At the battle of Actium in 31 B.C.E., Octavian defeated Antony, who fled with Cleopatra. When they returned to Alexandria, they led a life of sumptuous dinners and drinking parties. They now lived only for each other. Cleopatra began experimenting with poisons and ordered her tomb built. In 30 B.C.E. Octavian besieged Alexandria. Cleopatra fled to her tomb, and Antony stabbed himself, but not fatally. He was carried to Cleopatra's tomb, where meeting for the last time, Antony died in Cleopatra's arms. Roman troops soon broke into Cleopatra's tomb and captured her alive. Octavian treated her kindly, allowing her to bury Antony in royal fashion. He afterward allowed her to visit the tomb and pour a libation at Antony's funeral urn. She kissed the urn and said her last good-bye. Upon returning to her private apartments, she took a poisonous asp from a bowl of figs and held the snake to her breast. She died quickly. Her last wish was to be buried with Antony.

Source: E. Fantham et al., *Women in the Classical World* (Oxford: Oxford University Press, 1994), p. 137.

QUESTIONS FOR ANALYSIS

1. How did Cleopatra benefit from her relationship with Caesar?
2. What real power did Cleopatra possess, and how did she use that power in the Roman world?

Bust of Cleopatra, probably from Alexandria. (Bildarchiv Preussischer Kulturbesitz/Art Resource, NY)

people as a symbol of the immoral East and a threat to what were viewed as traditional Roman values. (See "Individuals in Society: Queen Cleopatra," above.) Although Pompey enjoyed the official support of the Roman government, Caesar finally defeated Pompey's forces in 45 B.C.E. He had overthrown the republic and made himself dictator.

Julius Caesar was not merely another victorious general. Politically brilliant, he was determined to make basic reforms, even at the expense of the old constitution. He took the first long step to break down the barriers between Italy and the provinces, extending citizenship to many of the provincials who had supported him. Caesar also took measures to cope with Rome's burgeoning population. He drew up plans to send his veterans and some eighty thousand of the poor and unemployed to colonies throughout the Mediterranean. He founded at least twenty colonies, most of which were located in Gaul, Spain, and North Africa. These colonies were important agents in spreading Roman culture in the western Mediterranean. A Roman empire composed of citizens, not subjects, was the result.

In 44 B.C.E. a group of conspirators assassinated Caesar and set off another round of civil war. Caesar had named his eighteen-year-old grandnephew, Octavian (ahk-TAY-vee-uhn)—or Augustus, as he is better known to history—as his heir.

Chapter 5
The Rise of Rome
134 CA. 750–31 B.C.E.

CHAPTER LOCATOR | How did the Romans become the dominant power in Italy?

Augustus joined forces with two of Caesar's lieutenants, Marc Antony and Lepidus (LEH-puh-duhs), in a pact known as the Second Triumvirate, and together they hunted down and defeated Caesar's murderers. In the process, however, Augustus and Antony came into conflict.

Augustus and Antony in 41 B.C.E. divided the Roman world, with Augustus taking command of the West and Antony the East. Later that year Antony met Cleopatra, queen of Egypt. Becoming active in Roman power politics, she decided to support Antony, who became her ally and lover. In 33 B.C.E. Augustus branded Antony a traitor and a rebel, painting him as a romantic and foolish captive of the seductive Cleopatra. In 31 B.C.E., with the might of Rome at his back, Augustus defeated the fleet and army of Antony and Cleopatra at the battle of Actium in Greece, but the two escaped. Augustus pursued them to Egypt, and they committed suicide rather than fall into his hands. Augustus's victory at Actium put an end to an age of civil war that had lasted since the days of Sulla.

Second Triumvirate A pact between Augustus and two of Caesar's lieutenants, Marc Antony and Lepidus; together they hunted down and defeated Caesar's murderers.

← LOOKING BACK **LOOKING AHEAD** →

AS HELLENISTIC PEOPLES created and enjoyed an urbane culture, a new Indo-European people settled farther west in Italy. They were the Romans, who together with the Etruscans, introduced their own particular political and social contributions to the life of the Mediterranean. They spread their way of life throughout Italy through conquest and incorporation. After victorious wars with their Carthaginian neighbors, they expanded their way of life throughout the western Mediterranean basin. Coming next into intimate contact with the East, they both conquered and assimilated it until the entire Mediterranean became *mare nostrum*, our sea, one wide area of a generally accepted and rich culture. Yet their own successes brought war and civil unrest, for they had not yet learned how to govern their empire.

The final days of the republic, though filled with war and chaos, should not obscure the fact that much of the Roman achievement survived the march of armies. The Romans had conquered the Mediterranean world, only to find that conquest required them to change their life. Socially, they embraced Greek culture. Politically, their city-state constitution broke down and expired in the wars of the republic. Even so, men like Caesar and later Augustus sought new solutions to the problems confronting Rome. The result was a system of government capable of administering an empire with justice and fairness. Out of the failure arose the *pax Romana*—the Roman peace—of the empire. This period would witness the spread of Roman culture to northern Europe, indelibly leaving its mark on European culture. ▪

- ▪ **For a list of suggested readings for this chapter, visit** *bedfordstmartins.com/mckaywestunderstanding*.

- ▪ **For primary sources from this period, see** *Sources of Western Society*, Second Edition.

- ▪ **For Web sites, images, and documents related to topics in this chapter, see Make History at** *bedfordstmartins.com/mckaywestunderstanding*.

Chapter 5 Study Guide

Step 1

GETTING STARTED Below are basic terms about this period in the history of Western civilization. Can you identify each term below and explain why it matters? To do this exercise online, go to bedfordstmartins.com/mckaywestunderstanding.

TERMS	WHO (OR WHAT) AND WHEN	WHY IT MATTERS
forum, p. 116		
Gauls, p. 117		
franchise, p. 117		
patricians, p. 119		
plebeians, p. 119		
senate, p. 119		
consuls, p. 119		
Struggle of the Orders, p. 120		
tribunes, p. 120		
First Punic War, p. 122		
Second Punic War, p. 123		
First Triumvirate, p. 131		
Second Triumvirate, p. 135		

Step 2

MOVING BEYOND THE BASICS The exercise below requires a more advanced understanding of the chapter material. In this exercise you will examine the impact of Hellenism on Roman civilization. Fill in the chart below with descriptions of Marcus Cato and Scipio Aemilianus's careers and views on Greek culture and its effect on their society. When you are finished, consider the following questions: Why did Cato believe that Rome had been weakened by the new influences that accompanied expansion? Why did Scipio embrace all things Greek? To do this exercise online, go to bedfordstmartins.com/mckaywestunderstanding.

	CAREER	VIEWS ON GREEK CULTURE
Marcus Cato		
Scipio Aemilianus		

PUTTING IT ALL TOGETHER

Now that you've reviewed key elements of the chapter, take a step back and try to see the big picture. Remember to use specific examples from the chapter in your answers. To do this exercise online, go to bedfordstmartins.com/mckaywestunderstanding.

ITALY AND THE EARLY HISTORY OF THE ROMANS

- Compare and contrast the impact of geography on the early development of Greek and Roman civilization. In what ways was the geography of Italy more conducive to political unity than that of Greece?

- How did the Romans integrate conquered Italian territories into their state? How did their policies in this regard create a foundation for further expansion?

THE ROMAN REPUBLIC

- How did the evolution of Roman political institutions reflect the evolution of Roman society?

- How did the concept of Roman citizenship change over time? Why did it change?

ROMAN EXPANSION AND ITS CONSEQUENCES

- What motives underlay Roman expansion? What light do the Punic Wars shed on this question?

- What social and cultural tensions accompanied Roman expansion? How did the Romans adapt to the new conditions created by their conquest of the Mediterranean world?

THE LATE REPUBLIC

- What explains the instability that characterized Roman politics in the century following the Punic Wars? Why did republican institutions fail to produce the kinds of reforms and compromises that had resolved earlier political conflicts?

- What are the implications of the prevalence of violence and the increasing prominence of military leaders in the politics of the Late Republic? What do these trends tell us about the impact of expansion on the Roman state?

▪ **In Your Own Words** Imagine that you must explain Chapter 5 to someone who hasn't read it. What would be the most important points to include and why?

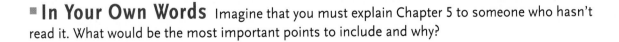

6

The Pax Romana

31 B.C.E.–284 C.E.

Had the Romans conquered the entire Mediterranean world only to destroy one another? At Julius Caesar's death in 44 B.C.E., it must have seemed so to many. Yet finally in 31 B.C.E, Augustus defeated Antony and his forces at the Battle of Actium, restoring peace after years of civil war. With peace came prosperity, new hope, and a new vision of Rome's destiny. The Roman poet Virgil expressed this vision most nobly:

> You, Roman, remember—these are your arts:
> To rule nations, and to impose the ways of peace,
> To spare the humble and to war down the proud.[1]

In place of the republic, Augustus established a constitutional monarchy. He attempted to achieve lasting cooperation in government and balance among the people, magistrates, senate, and army. His efforts were not always successful, and he did not permanently end civil war. Yet he carried on Caesar's reforms to create the structure that the modern world calls the Roman Empire. The first and second centuries C.E. were the time of the Roman peace—the pax Romana, a period of security, order, harmony, flourishing culture, and expanding economy. It was a period that saw the wilds of Gaul, Germany, eastern Europe, and western Africa introduced to Greco-Roman culture. By the third century C.E. Rome and its culture had left an indelible mark on the ages to come. ■

Life in Imperial Rome. Grocery stores like this one, where goods were sold and locals exchanged gossip, were common in imperial Rome. (Erich Lessing/Art Resource, NY)

Chapter Preview

▶ How did Augustus create a foundation for the Roman Empire?

▶ How did the Roman state develop after Augustus?

▶ What was life like in Rome during the golden age?

▶ How did Christianity grow into a major religious movement?

▶ What explains the chaos of the third century?

▼ How did Augustus create a foundation for the Roman Empire?

pax Romana A period of Roman security, order, harmony, flourishing culture, and expanding economy during the first and second centuries C.E.

principate Period from the reign of Augustus to the crisis of the third century with a government ruled by a princeps, or first citizen, who was in theory first among equals.

constitutional monarchy A monarchy in which the power of the ruler is restricted by the constitution and the laws of the nation.

When Augustus put an end to the civil wars that had raged since 88 B.C.E., he faced monumental problems of reconstruction. The first problem was to rebuild the republican constitution and the organs of government. Next he had to demobilize much of the army yet maintain enough soldiers in the provinces of the empire to meet the danger of barbarians at Rome's European frontiers. Augustus was highly successful in meeting these challenges. The pax Romana, his gift of peace to a war-torn world, sowed the seeds of a literary flowering that produced some of the finest fruits of the Roman mind.

The result of this work is commonly known as the "Augustan Settlement," a system of government that began in 31 B.C.E. and ended with Augustus's death in 14 C.E. Under this system, the emperor held all executive power in both the civil government and the military. The senate remained as a prestigious advisory body whose members also performed extraordinary functions at the desire and request of the emperor. The fledgling bureaucracy executed the ordinary functions of government under the emperor's authority.

The Principate and the Restored Republic

Augustus claimed that in restoring constitutional government he was also restoring the republic. Augustus planned for the senate to take on a serious burden of duty and responsibility. He expected it to administer some of the provinces, continue to be the chief deliberative body of the state, and act as a court of law. Yet he did not give the senate enough power to become his partner in government. As a result, the senate could not live up to the responsibilities that Augustus assigned to it.

Augustus could not simply surrender the reins of power, for someone else would have seized them, so he created his own position. He became *princeps civitatis* (prihn-SEHPS cih-vuh-TAY-tuhs), "first citizen of the state." The title itself carried no power; it indicated only that Augustus was the most distinguished of all Roman citizens. In an inscription known as the *Res Gestae* (the deeds of Augustus), Augustus described his constitutional position. (See "Listening to the Past: Augustus's *Res Gestae*," page 142.) In fact, much of the principate, as the period from the reign of Augustus to the crisis of the third century (see page 162) is known, was a legal fiction. Augustus claimed that the people had given him complete control of state affairs during the civil war. But with victory he transferred power to the Roman people and senate. Afterwards he was superior to all in rank, but he had no greater power than his colleagues in any magistracy.

Yet despite his claims, Augustus had not restored the republic. He had created a constitutional monarchy, something completely new in Roman history. This monarchy was one in which the emperor, while holding full executive power, was still bound to execute the laws of Rome. Augustus's power was limited constitutionally, but he held military and political powers well beyond those of his colleagues. As consul he had no more constitutional and legal power than his fellow consul (see page 119). Yet in addition to the

Augustus as Imperator Here Augustus, dressed in breastplate and uniform, emphasizes the imperial majesty of Rome and his role as imperator. The figures on his breastplate represent the restoration of peace, as seen by the powers of the sky at the top and Mother Earth with cornucopia below. (Scala/Art Resource, NY)

Chapter 6
The Pax Romana
140   31 B.C.E.–284 C.E.

CHAPTER LOCATOR | How did Augustus create a foundation for the Roman Empire?

consulship Augustus had many other magistracies, which his fellow consul did not. Constitutionally, his control within the state stemmed from the number of magistracies he held and the power granted him by the senate. Without specifically saying so, he had created the office of emperor, which included many traditional powers separated from their traditional offices.

The main source of Augustus's power was his position as commander of the Roman army. His title **imperator** (ihm-puh-RAH-tuhr), with which Rome customarily honored a general after a major victory, came to mean "emperor" in the modern sense of the term. Augustus governed the provinces where troops were needed for defense and guarded the frontiers from barbarian attack. He could declare war, he controlled deployment of the Roman army, and he paid its wages. Augustus never shared control of the army, and no Roman found it easy to defy him militarily.

Augustus made a momentous change in the army by making it a permanent professional force. Soldiers received regular and standard training under career officers who advanced in rank according to experience, ability, valor, and length of service. By making the army professional, Augustus forged a reliable tool for the defense of the empire. Yet the mere fact that men could make a career of the army meant that it became a recognized institution of government.

Chapter Chronology

31 B.C.E.–14 C.E.	Augustus's settlement
27 B.C.E.–68 C.E.	Julio-Claudian emperors; expansion into northern and western Europe; creation of the imperial bureaucracy
17 B.C.E.–17 C.E.	Golden age of Latin literature
ca. 3 B.C.E.–29 C.E.	Life of Jesus
69	Year of the four emperors; civil war; major breakdown of the concept of the principate
69–96	Flavian emperors; growing trend toward monarchy
70	Rebellion crushed in Judaea
ca. 70–90	Composition of the four canonical Gospels
96–180	Era of the five good emperors; golden age of prosperity; increased barbarian menace on the frontiers
235–284	Barracks emperors; civil war; breakdown of the empire; barbarian invasions; economic decline

The size of the army was a special problem for Augustus. Rome's legions numbered thousands of men, far more than were necessary to maintain peace. The same problem had constantly plagued the late republic, whose leaders never found a solution. Augustus solved the problem by founding some forty new colonies of ex-soldiers throughout the empire. Roman colonies were part of a system — the Roman Empire — that linked East with West in a mighty political, social, and economic network. Augustus's veterans took abroad with them their Latin language and culture, helping to spread Roman culture throughout the West.

imperator A title given to a general after a major victory that came to mean "emperor."

Augustus, however, failed to find a way to institutionalize his position with the army. The army was loyal to the princeps civitatis but not necessarily to the state. The Augustan principate worked well at first, but by the third century C.E. the army would make and break emperors at will. Nonetheless, it is a measure of Augustus's success that his settlement survived as long and as well as it did.

Administration of the Provinces

Augustus believed that the cities of the empire should look after their own affairs. He encouraged local self-government and urbanism. Augustus respected local customs and ordered his governors to do the same.

As a spiritual bond between the provinces and Rome, Augustus encouraged the cult of Roma, goddess and guardian of the state. In the Hellenistic East, where king worship was an established custom (see Chapter 4), the cult of Roma et [and] Augustus grew and spread rapidly. Augustus then introduced it in the West. By the time of his death in 14 C.E., nearly every province in the empire could boast an altar or a shrine to Roma et Augustus. In praying for the good health and welfare of the emperor, Romans and provincials were praying for the empire itself. The cult became a symbol of Roman unity.

How did the Roman state develop after Augustus?　　What was life like in Rome during the Golden Age?　　How did Christianity grow into a major religious movement?　　What explains the chaos of the third century?

141

LISTENING TO THE PAST

Augustus's *Res Gestae*

In 14 C.E. Augustus wrote for the Romans the Res Gestae, *an official account of his long career that began in 44 B.C.E., when he was nineteen years old. He had the original document engraved on two bronze columns erected in front of the Mausoleum of Augustus, a large tomb erected in Rome by Augustus that is still standing. Augustus offers his readers a firsthand account of his public life. He stresses that he had always acted according to the authority that the Romans bestowed upon him. He emphasizes his constant aim to seek genuine peace in order to further Rome's welfare and preserve its venerable traditions. Augustus in this document gives his account in simple terms that everyone could understand. It was his personal accounting to the people of Rome and to history.*

In the opening section Augustus lists his accomplishments and the honors bestowed upon him by the Roman senate and people.

❝ 1. At the age of nineteen, on my own initiative and at my own expense, I raised an army by means of which I restored liberty to the republic, which had been oppressed by the tyranny of a faction. . . .

2. Those who slew my father I drove into exile, punishing their deed by due process of law, and afterwards when they waged war upon the republic I twice defeated them in battle.

3. Wars, both civil and foreign, I undertook throughout the world, on sea and land, and when victorious I spared all citizens who sued for pardon. The foreign nations which could with safety be pardoned I preferred to save rather than to destroy. The number of Roman citizens who bound themselves to me by military oath was about 500,000. Of these I settled in colonies or sent back into their own towns, after their term of service, something more than 300,000, and to all I assigned lands, or gave money as a reward for military service. I captured six hundred ships, over and above those which were smaller than triremes.

4. . . . For successful operations on land and sea, conducted either by myself or by my lieutenants under my auspices, the senate on fifty-five occasions decreed that thanks should be rendered to the immortal gods. The days on which such thanks were rendered by decree of the senate numbered 890. . . .

6. . . . when the Senate and the Roman people unanimously agreed that I should be elected overseer of laws and morals, without a colleague and with the fullest power, I refused to accept any power offered me which was contrary to the traditions of our ancestors. ❞

In the next section Augustus tells of his personal donations to the republic.

❝ 20. The Capitolium and the theatre of Pompey, both works involving great expense, I rebuilt without any inscription of my own name. I restored the channels of the aqueducts which in several places were falling into disrepair through age, and doubled the capacity of the aqueduct called the Marcia by turning a new spring into its channel. . . . I rebuilt in the city eighty-two temples of the gods, omitting none which at that time stood in need of repair. . . .

22. Three times in my own name I gave a show of gladiators, and five times in the name of my sons or grandsons; in these shows there fought about ten thousand men. Twice in my own name I furnished for

Gold coin of Augustus portraying him as a law giver.
(Courtesy of the Trustees of the British Museum)

Roman Expansion into Northern and Western Europe

For the history of Western civilization, one of the most momentous aspects of Augustus's reign was Roman expansion into the wilderness of northern and western Europe (Map 6.1). Augustus began his work in the west and north by completing the conquest of Spain begun by Caesar. In Gaul he founded twelve new towns, and the Ro-

Chapter 6
The Pax Romana
142   31 B.C.E.–284 C.E.

CHAPTER LOCATOR   How did Augustus create a foundation for the Roman Empire?

the people an exhibition of athletes gathered from all parts of the world, and a third time in the name of my grandson. Four times I gave games in my own name; as representing other magistrates twenty-three times. . . . on twenty-six occasions I gave to the people, in the circus, in the forum, or in the amphitheatre, hunts of African wild beasts, in which about three thousand five hundred beasts were slain. 〞

Augustus concludes by recounting his deeds in peace and war.

〝 25. I freed the sea from pirates. About thirty thousand slaves, captured in that war, who had run away from their masters and had taken up arms against the republic, I delivered to their masters for punishment. The whole of Italy voluntarily took an oath of allegiance to me and demanded me as its leader in the war in which I was victorious at Actium. The provinces of the Spains, the Gauls, Africa, Sicily, and Sardinia took the same oath of allegiance. . . .

26. I extended the boundaries of all the provinces which were bordered by races not yet subject to our empire. The provinces of the Gauls, the Spains, and Germany, bounded by the ocean from Gades to the mouth of the Elbe, I reduced to a state of peace. The Alps, from the region such lies nearest to the Adriatic as far as the Tuscan Sea, I brought to a state of peace without waging on any tribe an unjust war. . . . On my order and under my auspices two armies were led, at almost the same time, into Ethiopia and into Arabia, which is called the "Happy," and very large forces of the enemy of both races were cut to pieces in battle and many towns were captured. . . .

28. I settled colonies of soldiers in Africa, Sicily, Macedonia, both Spains, Achaia, Asia, Syria, Gallia Narbonensis, Pisidia. Moreover, Italy has twenty-eight colonies founded under my auspices which have grown to be famous and populous during my lifetime. . . .

34. In my sixth and seventh consulships, when I had extinguished the flames of civil war, after receiving by universal consent the absolute control of affairs, I transferred the republic from my own control to the will of the senate and the Roman people. For this service on my part I was given the title of Augustus by decree of the senate, and the doorposts of my house were covered with laurels by public act, and a civic crown was fixed above my door, and a golden shield was placed in the Curia Julia whose inscription testified that the senate and the Roman people gave me this in recognition of my valour, my clemency, my justice, and my piety. . . .

35. While I was administering my thirteenth consulship the senate and the equestrian order and the entire Roman people gave me the title of Father of my Country, and decreed that this title should be inscribed upon the vestibule of my house and in the senate-house and in the Forum Augustum. . . . At the time of writing this I was in my seventy-sixth year. 〞

Source: Excerpts from *Velleius Paterculus*, Loeb Classical Library, vol. 152, trans. Frederick W. Shipley (Cambridge, Mass.: Harvard University Press), pp. 345, 349, 351, 355, 377, 379, 381, 383, 385, 387–389, 393, 399, 401. Copyright © 1924 by the President and Fellows of Harvard College. Reprinted by permission of the publishers and the Trustees of the Loeb Classical Library. The Loeb Classical Library® is a registered trademark of the President and Fellows of Harvard College.

QUESTIONS FOR ANALYSIS

1. What major themes does Augustus address in his account of his career?
2. How does Augustus portray himself in this document?
3. Does this account convince readers of Augustus's truth and sincerity?

man road system linked new settlements with one another and with Italy. In 12 B.C.E. Augustus ordered a major invasion of Germany beyond the Rhine. Roman legions advanced to the Elbe River, and the area north of the Main River and west of the Elbe was on the point of becoming Roman. But in 9 C.E. Augustus's general Varus lost some twenty thousand troops at the Battle of the Teutoburger (too-TOH-buhr-guhr) Forest. Thereafter the Rhine remained the Roman frontier.

How did the Roman state develop after Augustus?

What was life like in Rome during the Golden Age?

How did Christianity grow into a major religious movement?

What explains the chaos of the third century?

Map 6.1 Roman Expansion Under the Empire, 31 B.C.E.–138 C.E.
Following Roman expansion during the republic, Augustus added vast tracts of Europe to the Roman Empire, which the emperor Hadrian later enlarged by assuming control over parts of central Europe, the Near East, and North Africa.

Meanwhile Roman legions penetrated the area of modern Austria, southern Bavaria, and western Hungary. The regions of modern Serbia, Bulgaria, and Romania fell. Within this area the legionaries built fortified camps. Roads linked the camps with one another, and settlements grew up around the camps. Traders began to frequent the frontier and to traffic with the native people who lived there. Romans generally referred to such people as **barbarians**, a word derived from a Greek word for people who did not speak Greek. Thus Roman culture gradually spread into the northern wilderness.

Although this process is most clearly seen in the provincial towns and cities, people in the countryside likewise adopted aspects of Roman culture. All over the empire native peoples adopted those aspects that fit in with their own ways of life. Ambitious people throughout the empire also knew that the surest path to political advancement lay in embracing Roman civilization and culture. Nevertheless, they ran their local political and social lives as they had before, fitting them into the larger scheme of Roman government.

One excellent example of this process comes from the modern French city of Lyons. The site was originally the capital of a native tribe, and Caesar made it a Roman military settlement after his conquest of Gaul. In 12 B.C.E. Augustus took an important step toward Romanization and goodwill by making it a political and religious center, with responsibilities for administering the area and for honoring the gods of the Romans and Gauls. Physical symbols of this fusion of two cultures can still be seen today. An amphitheater and other buildings testify to the fact that the city was prosperous enough to afford

barbarians From the Greek word meaning people who don't speak Greek; Romans used the term to describe any tribes of people who were not Greco-Roman.

Chapter 6
The Pax Romana
144   **31 B.C.E.–284 C.E.**

CHAPTER LOCATOR   How did Augustus create a foundation for the Roman Empire?

Roman Legion Roof Plaque Roman soldiers practiced many crafts in addition to warfare. They often built roads, bridges, and buildings. They also quarried and made their own materials. The legionnaires of the Twentieth Legion stationed in Britain, whose symbol was a charging boar, made this clay plaque for a roof. (Grosvenor Museum, Chester, UK)

expensive Roman buildings and the style of life that they represented. In Lyons, as in many other of these new cities, a culture that was both Roman and native emerged. Although Lyons is typical of the success of Romanization in new areas, the arrival of the Romans often provoked resistance from tribes of peoples who were not Greco-Roman and who simply wanted to be left alone. The Romans maintained peaceful relations with the barbarians whenever possible, but Roman legions remained on the frontier to repel hostile barbarians.

The Flowering of Latin Literature

The Augustan settlement's gift of peace inspired a literary flowering unparalleled in Roman history. With good reason 17 B.C.E. to 17 C.E. is known as the golden age of Latin literature. Augustus and many of his friends actively encouraged poets and writers. Horace, one of Rome's finest poets, offered his own opinion of Augustus and his era:

> With Caesar [Augustus] the guardian of the state
> Not civil rage nor violence shall drive out peace,
> Nor wrath which forges swords
> And turns unhappy cities against each other.[2]

To a generation that had known only vicious civil war, Augustus's settlement was a blessing.

Roman poets and prose writers celebrated the dignity of humanity and the range of its accomplishments. They stressed the physical and emotional joys of a comfortable, peaceful life. Roman poets referred to the gods often and treated mythological themes, but the core of their work was always human, not divine.

Rome's greatest poet was Virgil (70–19 B.C.E.), a sensitive man who delighted in a simple life. Virgil wrote in his *Georgics* of the pleasures of farm life. The poems are vivid as well as pastoral, painting a charming picture of life in the Italian countryside during a period of peace. Virgil's masterpiece is the *Aeneid* (uh-NEE-ihd), an epic poem that is the Latin equivalent of the Greek *Iliad* and *Odyssey* (see Chapter 3). Virgil's account of the founding of Rome and the early years of the city gave final form to the legend of Aeneas (ih-NEE-uhs), a Trojan hero who escaped to Italy at the fall of Troy. As Virgil told it, Aeneas became the lover of Dido, the widowed queen of Carthage, but left her because his destiny called him to found Rome. Dido committed suicide, and their relationship eventually became the cause of the Punic Wars. In leaving Dido, an "Eastern" queen, Aeneas put the good of the state ahead of marriage or pleasure. The parallels between this story and the real events involving Antony and Cleopatra were not lost on Virgil's audience. This fit well with Augustus's aims; he had encouraged Virgil to write the *Aeneid* and made sure it was published immediately after Virgil died.

The poet Ovid (AH-vuhd) (43 B.C.E.–17 C.E.) shared Virgil's views of the simple pleasures of life and also celebrated the popular culture of the day. Ovid's most popular and probably greatest work is the epic poem *Metamorphoses*, in which he explored the boundaries between gods and mortals. Ovid told magical stories of changes drawn from Near Eastern and Greco-Roman myths. The poem is a tale of the hopes and efforts, the successes and failures of people through time.

Virgil and the *Aeneid* Virgil's great epic poem, the *Aeneid*, became a literary classic immediately on its appearance and has lost none of its power since. The Roman world honored Virgil for his poetic genius not only by treasuring his work but also by portraying him in art. Here two Muses flank the poet while he writes his epic poem. The Muses, nine in all, were minor Greek and Roman goddesses who were thought to inspire artists and writers. The female muses' role as inspiration, not authors, accurately reflects surviving Latin literature of the Augustan period, all of which is by male authors. (C. M. Dixon/Ancient Art & Architecture Collection)

The historian Livy was a friend of Augustus and a supporter of the principate. He especially approved of Augustus's efforts to restore what he saw as republican virtues. Livy's history of Rome, titled simply *Ab Urbe Condita* (*From the Founding of the City*), began with the legend of Aeneas and ended with the reign of Augustus. His theme of the republic's greatness fitted admirably with Augustus's program of restoring the republic.

The poet Horace (65–8 B.C.E.) rose from humble beginnings to friendship with Augustus. The son of an ex-slave and tax collector, Horace nonetheless received an excellent education, which he finished in Athens. After Augustus's victory he returned to Rome and became Virgil's friend. One of Horace's finest odes commemorates Augustus's victory over Antony and Cleopatra at Actium in 31 B.C.E. He depicted Cleopatra as a frenzied queen, drunk with desire to destroy Rome. Horace saw in Augustus's victory the triumph of West over East, of simplicity over oriental excess.

Social Changes

Concern with morality and with what were perceived as traditional Roman virtues was a matter not just for literature in Augustan Rome, but also for law. Augustus promoted marriage and childbearing through legal changes that released free women and freed-

Chapter 6
The Pax Romana
146   31 B.C.E.–284 C.E.

CHAPTER LOCATOR   How did Augustus create
a foundation for the
Roman Empire?

women (female slaves who had been freed) from male guardianship if they had given birth to a certain number of children. Men and women who were unmarried or had no children were restricted in the inheritance of property. Adultery, defined as sex with a married woman or with a woman under male guardianship, was made a crime, not simply the private family matter it had been. In imperial propaganda, Augustus had his own family depicted as a model of traditional morality, with his wife Livia at his side and dressed in conservative clothing.

In the late republic same-sex relationships were denounced as immoral for not producing children. Same-sex relationships among men in Rome had followed a pattern similar to that of Greece: often taking place between an older man and a younger, or between men who were different in social status, such as a slave and his owner. We do not know very much about same-sex relationships among women in Rome, though court gossip and criticism of powerful women sometimes included charges of such relationships, along with charges of heterosexual promiscuity and other sexual slander.

▪ PICTURING THE PAST

Ara Pacis

This scene from the Ara Pacis, the Altar of Peace erected in Rome by Augustus, celebrates Augustus's restoration of peace and imperial family values. On this side of the altar, Mother Earth is depicted with twin babies on her lap, framed by nymphs representing land and sea. Other sides of the altar show Romulus and Remus (another set of twins) and Augustus and his wife Livia in traditional Roman clothing. (Scala/Art Resource, NY)

ANALYZING THE IMAGE What elements are depicted, and how do they convey peace?

CONNECTIONS The Ara Pacis and the *Res Gestae* (see "Listening to the Past," page 142) commemorate the deeds of Augustus. What purpose might Augustus have had in commissioning these public works? Do you consider them a form of propaganda or a well-deserved celebration of his work on behalf of the republic? Why?

To complete this activity online, go to the Online Study Guide at bedfordstmartins.com/mckaywestunderstanding.

The Legacy of Augustus

Augustus put the empire on a new foundation. Constitutional monarchy was firmly established, and government was to all appearances a partnership between princeps and senate. Augustus's settlement was a delicate structure, and parts of it would in time be discarded. Nevertheless, it worked, and by building on it later emperors would carry on Augustus's work.

The solidity of Augustus's work became obvious at his death in 14 c.e. Since the principate was not technically an office, Augustus could not legally hand it to a successor. Augustus recognized this problem and long before his death had found a way to solve it. He shared his consular and tribunician powers with his adopted son, Tiberius, thus grooming him for the principate. In his will Augustus left most of his vast fortune to Tiberius, and the senate formally requested Tiberius to assume the burdens of the principate. Formalities apart, Augustus had succeeded in creating a dynasty.

▼ How did the Roman state develop after Augustus?

Augustus's success in creating solid political institutions was tested by the dynasty he created, the Julio-Claudians, whose members schemed against one another trying to win and hold power. This situation allowed a military commander, Vespasian (veh-SPAY-zhuhn), to claim the throne and establish a new dynasty, the Flavians. The Flavians were followed by the "five good emperors," who were successful militarily and politically.

The Julio-Claudians and the Flavians

For fifty years after Augustus's death the Julio-Claudian dynasty provided the emperors of Rome. Some of the Julio-Claudians, such as Tiberius and Claudius, were sound rulers and able administrators. Others, including Caligula and Nero, were weak and frivolous men who exercised their power poorly and to the detriment of the empire. Nonetheless, the Julio-Claudians were responsible for some notable achievements, and during their reigns the empire largely prospered. One of the most momentous achievements of the Julio-Claudians was Claudius's creation of an imperial bureaucracy composed of professional administrators. The effect of Claudius's innovations was to enable the emperor to rule the empire more easily and efficiently.

Praetorians Imperial bodyguard created by Augustus.

Augustus's creation of an imperial bodyguard known as the Praetorians had repercussions for his successors. In 41 c.e. the Praetorians murdered Caligula and forced the senate to ratify their choice of Claudius as emperor. The events were repeated frequently. During the first three centuries of the empire, the Praetorian Guard all too often murdered emperors they were supposed to protect and saluted emperors of their own choosing.

In 68 c.e. Nero's increasingly inept rule led to military rebellion and his death, thus opening the way to widespread disruption. In 69 c.e., the "year of the four emperors," four men claimed the position of emperor. Roman armies in Gaul, on the Rhine, and in the East marched on Rome to make their commanders emperor. The man who emerged triumphant was Vespasian, commander of the eastern armies.

Vespasian restored order to the Roman world and solved the problem of imperial succession by establishing the Flavian dynasty. Naming his

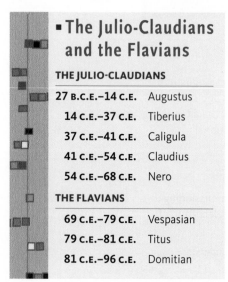

The Julio-Claudians and the Flavians

THE JULIO-CLAUDIANS

27 B.C.E.–14 C.E.	Augustus
14 C.E.–37 C.E.	Tiberius
37 C.E.–41 C.E.	Caligula
41 C.E.–54 C.E.	Claudius
54 C.E.–68 C.E.	Nero

THE FLAVIANS

69 C.E.–79 C.E.	Vespasian
79 C.E.–81 C.E.	Titus
81 C.E.–96 C.E.	Domitian

Chapter 6
The Pax Romana
148   31 B.C.E.–284 C.E.

CHAPTER LOCATOR | How did Augustus create a foundation for the Roman Empire?

sons Titus and Domitian as his successors, Vespasian turned the principate into an open and admitted monarchy. He also expanded the emperor's power by increasing the size of the bureaucracy Claudius had created. He restored the discipline of the armies, and he suppressed the rebellions that had erupted at the end of Nero's reign. The most famous had burst out in Judaea in 66 C.E., sparked by long-standing popular unrest and atrocities committed by Jews and Romans alike. The ensuing destruction of Jerusalem in 70 C.E. and the enslavement of the Jewish survivors was one of the few—and among the worst—failures of the Roman imperial system.

The Flavians carried on Augustus's work on the frontiers. Domitian won additional territory in Germany and consolidated it in two new provinces. He defeated barbarian tribes on the Danube frontier and strengthened that area as well. Despite his successful efforts to restore order, Domitian fell to an assassin's dagger. Nevertheless, the Flavians had given the Roman world peace and had kept the legions in line. Their work paved the way for the era of the "five good emperors," the golden age of the empire.

The Age of the Five Good Emperors

The Flavians gave way to a remarkable line of emperors known as the **five good emperors**—Nerva, Trajan, Hadrian, Antoninus Pius, and Marcus Aurelius—who created an almost unparalleled period of prosperity and peace. These emperors were among the noblest, most dedicated, and ablest men in Roman history. Yet the nature of their rule was considerably different from what it had been under Augustus.

Augustus had claimed that his influence arose from the collection of offices the senate had bestowed on him and that he was merely the first citizen. Under the Flavians the principate became a full-blown monarchy, and by the time of the five good emperors (also known as the Antonines) the principate was an office with definite rights, powers, and prerogatives. In the years between Augustus and the Antonines, the emperor had become an indispensable part of the imperial machinery.

The five good emperors were not power-hungry autocrats. The concentration of power was the result of empire, but they were absolute kings all the same. The easiest and most efficient way to run the Roman Empire was to invest the emperor with vast powers. As capable and efficient emperors took on new tasks and functions, the emperor's hand was felt in more areas of life and government. Increasingly the emperors became the source of all authority and guidance in the empire.

Typical of the five good emperors is the career of Hadrian, who became emperor in 117 C.E. Born in Spain, he caught the attention of his elder cousin Trajan, the future emperor, who started him on a military career. At age nineteen Hadrian served on the Danube frontier, where he learned the details of how the Roman army lived and fought and saw for himself the problems of defending the frontiers. When Trajan became emperor in 98 C.E., Hadrian was given important positions in which he learned how to defend and run the empire. At Trajan's death in 117 Hadrian assumed power.

five good emperors The name for the five emperors (Nerva, Trajan, Hadrian, Antoninus Pius, and Marcus Aurelius) who created an unparalleled period of peace and prosperity.

The Emperor Marcus Aurelius This equestrian statue, showing the emperor greeting his people, represents both the majesty and the peaceful intentions of this emperor and philosopher. Roman equestrian statues present an image of idealized masculinity, but most portray their subjects as fierce and warlike, not with a hand raised in peace as Marcus Aurelius's hand is here. (Tibor Bognar/Alamy)

One of the most significant changes since Augustus's day was the enormous growth of the imperial bureaucracy. Hadrian reformed this system by putting the bureaucracy on an organized, official basis. Hadrian also separated civil service from military service. These innovations made for more efficient running of the empire and increased the authority of the emperor.

The Roman army had also changed since Augustus's time. No longer a conquering force, the army was expected to defend what had already been won. Forts and watch stations guarded the borders. Outside the forts the Romans built a system of roads that allowed the forts to be quickly supplied and reinforced in times of trouble. The army had evolved into a garrison force, with legions guarding specific areas for long periods.

The personnel of the legions were changing, too. Italy could no longer supply all the recruits needed for the army. Increasingly only the officers came from Italy and from the more Romanized provinces. The legionaries were mostly drawn from the provinces closest to the frontiers. In the third century C.E. this shift would result in an army indifferent to Rome and its traditions. In the age of the five good emperors, however, the army was still a source of economic stability and a Romanizing agent. Men from the provinces and even barbarians joined the army to learn a trade and to gain Roman citizenship.

Roman Britain, ca. 130 C.E.

▼ What was life like in Rome during the golden age?

The years of peace and prosperity under the five good emperors are considered by many to represent the golden age of Rome. Life in the capital city was significantly different from that in the provinces of northern and western Europe, and the Romans went to no great lengths to spread their culture. Yet roads and secure sea-lanes linked the empire in one vast web, with men and women traveling and migrating more often than they had in earlier eras. Through this network of commerce and communication, greater Europe entered the economic and cultural life of the Mediterranean world.

Life in Imperial Rome

Rome was truly an extraordinary city, and with a population near a million it was one of the largest in the world. Although it boasted stately palaces and beautiful residential areas, most people lived in poorly built apartment houses. Fire and crime were perennial problems. Streets were narrow, drainage was inadequate, and sanitation was a common problem. Numerous inscriptions record prohibitions against dumping human refuse and even cadavers on the grounds of sanctuaries and cemeteries.

Engineers built an elaborate system that collected sewage from public baths, the ground floors of buildings, and public latrines. Private houses generally lacked toilets, so people emptied chamber pots onto the streets. Other cities in the empire used the same method of sanitation. Under the empire this situation improved. By comparison with medieval and early modern European cities, Rome was a healthy enough place to live.

Chapter 6
The Pax Romana
31 B.C.E.–284 C.E.

150

CHAPTER LOCATOR

How did Augustus create a foundation for the Roman Empire?

Rome was such a huge city that the surrounding countryside could not feed it. Because of the danger of starvation, the emperor, following republican practice, provided the citizen population with free grain for bread and, later, oil and wine. By feeding the citizenry the emperor prevented bread riots caused by shortages and high prices. For those who did not enjoy the rights of citizenship, the emperor provided grain at low prices. By maintaining the grain supply, the emperor kept the favor of the people and ensured that Rome's poor and idle did not starve.

A typical day for the Roman family began with a modest breakfast. Afterwards came a trip to the outdoor market for the day's provisions. Seafood was a favorite item, as the Romans normally ate meat only at festivals. Wine was the common drink. Ordinary men normally worked in small shops attached to their homes, and they sold their goods over the counters. Shoppers strolled along the streets, buying what they wanted or just chatting and enjoying the sights. Street musicians often added an air of festivity.

Children began their education at home. Mothers taught their daughters elementary reading, writing, and arithmetic. Daughters also learned how to manage the house and deport themselves like their mothers. Boys learned the basics of their future calling from their fathers, who also taught them the use of weapons for military service. Boys boxed, learned to ride when possible, and swam, all to increase their strength, while giving them basic skills. Ordinary boys then began plying their fathers' trade. Wealthy boys continued their formal training for a career. They usually mastered rhetoric and law for a political career. Others entered the army, usually as cadets on the staffs of prominent officers.

Roman Architecture These buildings demonstrate the beauty and utility of Roman architecture. The Coliseum in Rome (bottom) was the elegant sports arena in which gladiatorial games and mock naval battles were fought. The Pantheon in Rome (right) served as a temple of the deities of the seven planets. Its dome, 40 feet in diameter with a 30-foot opening in the center to admit light, was the greatest achievement in ancient cement construction. (Coliseum: Scala/Art Resource, NY; Pantheon: Gianni Dagli Orti/The Art Archive AA416527)

Gladiatorial Games Though hardly games, these contests were vastly popular among the Romans. Gladiators were usually slaves, but successful ones could gain their freedom. The fighting was hard but fair, and the gladiators shown here look equally matched. (Interphoto Press/Alamy)

Not many Romans pursued a medical career, which was considered beneath their dignity. While many physicians honestly sought to heal their patients and alleviate pain, many other incompetent and greedy practitioners claimed to cure illnesses through incantations and magic. The learned Pliny the Elder once railed against doctors: "Of all men only a physician can kill a man with total impunity. Oh no, on the contrary, censure goes to him who dies and *he* is guilty of excess, and furthermore *he* is blamed. . . . Let me not accuse their [physicians'] avarice, their greedy deals with those whose fate hangs in the balance, their setting a price on pain and their demands for down payment in case of death, and their secret doctrines."[3]

The emperor and other wealthy citizens also entertained the Roman populace, often at vast expense. The most popular forms of public entertainment were gladiatorial (gla-dee-uh-TAWR-ee-uhl) contests and chariot racing. Many **gladiators** were criminals who had been sentenced to death. They were given no defensive weapons and stood little real chance of surviving a fight with an armed man or wild animal. Other criminals were sentenced to fight in the arena as fully armed gladiators. Some gladiators were the slaves of gladiatorial trainers; others were prisoners of war. Still others were free men who volunteered for the arena. Even women at times engaged in gladiatorial combat. Some Romans protested gladiatorial fighting, but the emperors recognized the political value of such spectacles, and most Romans appear to have enjoyed them.

Roman spectacles such as gladiator fights and chariot racing were not everyday activities for Romans. As is evident on tombstone inscriptions, ordinary Romans were proud of their work and accomplishments. They were affectionate toward their families and friends. An impression of them can be gained from their epitaphs. Individual inscriptions and public laws testify to the increased manumission of slaves. One law actually restricted the freeing of slaves because this would allow them to receive public grain and gifts of money, both reserved for citizens. Some Romans complained that ex-slaves were debasing pure Roman citizenship. In fact most of those freed were house slaves who had virtually become members of the family.

Despite the increase in manumission, for many slaves, especially those who worked in the mines, life was hard. Those who failed in their escape attempts were returned to their masters and often branded on their foreheads. Others had metal collars fastened around their necks. One collar discovered near Rome read: "I have run away. Capture me. If you take me back to my master Zoninus, you will receive a gold coin."[4] Slavery was declining and manumission increasing, but slavery kept its dark side.

gladiators Criminals, slaves, and sometimes free men who fought each other or wild animals to the death in the arena as public entertainment.

Provincial Life

The rural population throughout the empire left few records, but the inscriptions that remain point to a melding of cultures. This melding can be seen in the evolution of Romance languages, which include Spanish, Italian, French, Portuguese, and Romanian. These languages evolved in the provinces, where people used Latin for legal and state religious purposes, eventually leading to a blending of Latin and their native tongues. The

CHAPTER LOCATOR   How did Augustus create a foundation for the Roman Empire?

process of cultural exchange was at first more urban than rural, but the importance of cities and towns to the life of the wider countryside ensured that its effects spread far afield.

A brief survey of the provinces illustrates the melding of culture. For instance in Gaul, country people retained their ancestral gods, and there was not much difference in many parts of the province between the original Celtic villages and their Roman successors. Along the Rhine River, Romans provided the capital for commerce, agricultural development of the land, and large-scale building. Roman merchants also became early bankers. The native inhabitants made up the labor force. They normally lived in villages and huts near the villas of successful merchants, whose wives bought Roman household items and clothing. Although Roman ideas spread and there was a good deal of cultural blending, native customs and religions continued to thrive. The Romans also learned about and began to respect native gods.

Roman soldiers were important agents in spreading Roman culture. (See "Individuals in Society: Bithus, a Typical Roman Soldier," page 154.) Soldiers had originally been prohibited from marrying, though they often formed permanent relationships with local women. In the late second century the emperor permitted them to marry, and mixed-ethnicity couples became common in border areas.

The situation on the eastern bank of the Rhine was also typical of life on the borders, but it demonstrates the rawer features of frontier life. The Romans brought peace and stability, first by building forts and roads, and then by opening the rivers to navigation. Around the forts grew native villages, and peace encouraged more intensive cultivation of the soil. The region became more prosperous than ever before, and prosperity attracted Roman settlers. Roman veterans mingled with the Celtic population and sometimes married into Celtic families. The **villa**, a country estate, was the primary unit of organized political life. This pattern of life differed from that of the Mediterranean, but it prefigured life in the early Middle Ages. In Britain, as well, the normal social and economic structures were farms and agricultural villages. Very few cities were to be found, and many native Britons were largely unacquainted with Greco-Roman culture.

villa A country estate that was the primary unit of organized political life in the provinces.

Across eastern Europe the pattern was much the same. In the Alpine provinces north of Italy, Romans and native Celts came into contact in the cities, but native cultures flourished in the countryside. In Illyria (ih-LIHR-ee-uh) and Dalmatia, regions of modern Albania, Croatia, and Montenegro, the native population never widely embraced either Roman culture or urban life. The Roman soldiers who increasingly settled parts of these lands made little effort to Romanize the natives, and there was less intermarriage than in Celtic areas. To a certain extent, however, Romanization occurred simply because the peoples lived in such close proximity.

In contrast with northern Europe, Asia Minor had long enjoyed the peace and stability of Roman rule. The lives of urban men and women reflected that benefit. In modern Turkey the well-preserved ruins of Aspendos give a full picture of life in this part of the provinces. The city sits among fertile fields, and the resources of the land provided raw materials for industry and trade. Manufactured goods and raw materials passed along a river next to the city that kept it in touch with the rest of the empire and brought in immigrants from elsewhere.

Life at a Roman Villa On the European borders of the Roman Empire, the villa was often as important as the town. The villa at Chedworth in Roman Britain was a typical villa that included a large courtyard with barns, gardens, storehouses, and buildings for processing agricultural products and manufacturing goods. The villa also included the living quarters of the owner and his family and quarters for servants and slaves set apart from the great houses. A small temple or shrine often provided a center for religious devotions. While self-contained, a villa was not necessarily isolated. The villa at Chedworth was connected by roads and rivers to similar neighboring villas. (Courtesy, John Buckler)

Bithus, a Typical Roman Soldier

FEW PEOPLE THINK OF SOLDIERS as missionaries of culture, but they often are. The culture that they spread is seldom of high intellectual or artistic merit, but they expose others to their own traditions, habits, and ways of thinking. A simple modern example may suffice. In World War II American GIs in Italy taught children there how to play baseball and many other things about the United States. The young Americans themselves learned a great deal about Italian life and values. Even today a stranger can wander around an Italian town and see the results of this meeting of two cultures.

The same was true of the armies of the Roman Empire. The empire was so vast even by modern standards that soldiers were recruited from all parts of it to serve in distant places. A soldier from the province of Syria might find himself keeping watch on Hadrian's Wall in Britain. He brought with him the ideas and habits of his birthplace and through his contact with people in other parts of the empire realized that others lived life differently. Despite their ethnic differences, they were united by many commonly shared beliefs and opinions. Although the Roman Empire never became totally Romanized, soldiers, like officials and merchants, played their part in disseminating Roman ideas of government, religion, and way of life.

One such person was the infantryman Bithus, who was born in Thrace in the northeastern region of modern Greece. His career was eventful but not particularly distinguished. He is, however, typical of many Roman soldiers. Bithus served in the auxiliaries, a secondary force comprised of noncitizens. Bithus's military life took him far from his native Thrace.

His career started with basic training during which he learned to march and to use standard weapons. His training over, Bithus was sent to Syria, where he spent most of his career. There he met others from as far west as Gaul and Spain, from West Africa, and from the modern Middle East. This experience gave him an idea of the size of the empire. It also taught him about life in other areas. Unlike many other cohorts that were shifted periodically, he saw service in one theater. While in the army, he raised a family, much like soldiers today. The children of soldiers like Bithus often themselves joined the army, which thereby became a fruitful source of its own recruitment. After twenty-five years of duty, Bithus received his discharge on November 7, 88. Upon mustering out of the army he received the grant of Roman citizenship for himself and his family.

In his civilian life the veteran enjoyed a social status that granted him honor and privileges accorded only to Roman citizens. From his military records there is no reason to conclude that Bithus had even seen Rome, but because of his service to it, he became as much a Roman as anyone born there.

The example of Bithus is important because he is typical of thousands of others who voluntarily supported the empire. In the process they learned about the nature of the empire and something about how it worked. They also exchanged experiences with other soldiers and the local population that helped shape a sense that the empire was a human as well as a political unit.

Source: *Corpus Inscriptionum Latinarum*, vol. 16, no. 35 (Berlin: G. Reimer, 1882).

QUESTIONS FOR ANALYSIS

1. What did Bithus gain from his twenty-five years of service in the Roman army?
2. What effect did soldiers such as Bithus have on the various parts of the Roman Empire where they served?

This veteran legionary wears body armor made of strips and plates of iron, an outer sheet of leather straps, and a crested helmet. (Courtesy of the Trustees of the British Museum)

Chapter 6
The Pax Romana

154   31 B.C.E.–284 C.E.

CHAPTER LOCATOR   How did Augustus create a foundation for the Roman Empire?

For the people of Aspendos the city was the focus of life. There the men handled their political affairs in the council house, and men and women frequented the marketplace for their ordinary needs. Temples and later a Christian basilica gave them ornate buildings in which to worship. In the theater men and women enjoyed the great plays of the past and those popular in their own day. Absent was a place for gladiatorial games. That too was typical of the eastern Roman Empire, where gladiatorial contests were far less popular than horse racing.

More than just places to live, cities like Aspendos were centers of the intellectual and cultural life that spread abroad. Taken together, the cities of the provinces united in a vibrant economic and cultural life that spanned the entire Mediterranean (Map 6.2). As long as the empire prospered and the revenues reached the imperial coffers, the Romans were willing to let the provinces live and let live. As a result, Europe fully entered into

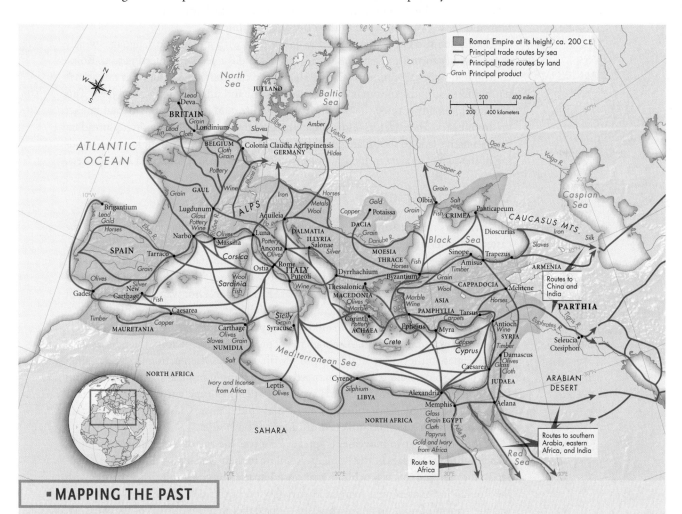

▪ MAPPING THE PAST

Map 6.2 The Economic Aspect of the Pax Romana, ca. 27–180 C.E.

This map gives a good idea of trade routes and the economic expansion of the Roman Empire at its height. Map 11.2 on page 294 is a similar map that shows trade in roughly the same area nearly a millennium later. Examine both maps and answer the following questions.

ANALYZING THE MAP What similarities and differences do you see in trade in the Mediterranean during these two periods?

CONNECTIONS To what extent did Roman trade routes influence later European trade routes?

To complete this activity online, go to the Online Study Guide at **bedfordstmartins.com/mckaywestunderstanding**.

the economic and cultural life of the Mediterranean world. The interconnectedness of the provinces would prove instrumental in facilitating the spread of a small native religion from Judaea.

▼ How did Christianity grow into a major religious movement?

During the reign of the emperor Tiberius (14–37 C.E.), Jesus preached in Judaea, attracted a following, and was executed on the order of the Roman prefect Pontius Pilate. At the time a minor event, it has become one of the best known moments in history. How did these two men come to their historic meeting?

The Hellenistic Greeks provided the entire East with a common language, widely shared literary forms, and a pervasive culture that had for years embraced Judaea. Rome contributed political administration to Hellenistic culture. The mixture was not always harmonious. In Judaea, Roman rule aroused hatred and unrest among some Jews. This climate of hostility formed the backdrop of Jesus' life, and it had a fundamental impact on his ministry. These factors also ultimately paved the way for Christianity to spread far from its native land to the broader world of the Roman Empire. Without an understanding of this age of anxiety in Judaea, one cannot fully appreciate Jesus and his followers.

Unrest in Judaea

The civil wars that destroyed the Roman republic had extended as far as Judaea in the eastern Mediterranean. Jewish leaders took sides in the conflict, and Judaea suffered its share of violence and looting. Although Augustus restored stability, his appointed king for Judaea, Herod (r. 37–4 B.C.E.), was hated by the Jews. At his death the Jews in Judaea broke out in revolt. For the next ten years Herod's successor waged almost constant war against the rebels. Added to the horrors of civil war were famine and plague.

To maintain order, Augustus made Judaea a province in 6 C.E., thus putting it fully under Roman administration. Although many prefects tried to perform their duties scrupulously, many others were indifferent to Jewish culture. Often acting from fear rather than cruelty, some prefects fiercely stamped out any signs of popular discontent. Pontius Pilate, prefect from 26 to 36 C.E., is typical of such incompetent officials. Especially hated were the Roman tax collectors, known as "publicans." Clashes between Roman troops and Jewish guerrillas inflamed the anger of both sides.

Among the Jews two movements spread. First was the rise of the Zealots, extremists who fought to rid Judaea of the Romans. Resolute in their worship of Yahweh (see Chapter 2), they refused to pay any but the tax levied by the Jewish temple. Their battles with the Roman legionaries were marked by savagery on both sides. The second movement was the growth of militant apocalypticism — the belief that the coming of the Messiah, the savior of Israel, was near. This belief was an old one among the Jews. But by the first century C.E. it had become more widespread and fervent than ever before. Apocalyptic predictions appeared in many texts, including the anonymous Apocalypse of Baruch, which foretold the destruction of the Roman Empire. First would come a period of great tribulation and misery. At the worst of the suffering, the Messiah would appear and destroy the Roman legions and all the kingdoms that had ruled Israel. Then the Messiah would inaugurate a period of happiness and plenty for the Jews.

As the ravages of war became widespread and conditions worsened, more and more people prophesied the imminent coming of the Messiah. According to Christian Scripture, one such was John the Baptist, "the voice of one crying in the wilderness, Prepare ye

Judaea in the Time of Jesus, ca. 30 C.E.

Messiah The savior of Israel, who according to apocalyptic predictions would destroy the Roman Empire and usher in a period of peace and plenty for the Jews; Christians believed that Jesus was the Messiah but that he would establish a spiritual kingdom, not an earthly one.

the way of the lord" (Matthew 3:3). Many Jews did just that. The sect described in the Dead Sea Scrolls (documents dealing with Jewish religious matters found in 1947 in caves near the Dead Sea) readied itself for the end of the world. Its members were probably Essenes, an ascetic group whose social organization closely resembled that of early Christians. Members of this group shared possessions, precisely as John the Baptist urged people to do. Yet this sect, unlike the Christians, also made military preparations for the day of the Messiah.

The pagan world of Rome is also part of the story of early Christianity. The term **pagans** (PAY-guhnz) refers to all those who believed in the Greco-Roman gods. Paganism at the time of Jesus' birth can be broadly divided into three spheres: the official state religion of Rome, the traditional Roman cults of hearth and countryside, and the new mystery religions that flowed from the Hellenistic East. The official state religion and its cults honored the traditional deities. Most Romans felt that the official cults had to be maintained for the welfare of the state, and Augustus was careful to link them to himself.

For emotional and spiritual satisfaction, many Romans turned to cults of home and countryside. These traditional cults brought the Romans back in touch with nature. Particularly popular was the rustic shrine—often a small building or a sacred tree in an enclosure—honoring the native spirit of the locality. Others found spiritual security and an emotional outlet in the various Hellenistic mystery cults. Mystery religions gave their adherents what neither the traditional cults nor philosophy could—the promise of immortality. Yet the mystery religions were by nature exclusive, and none was truly international, open to everyone.

The Life and Teachings of Jesus

Into this climate of Jewish Messianic hope and Roman religious yearning came Jesus of Nazareth (ca. 3 B.C.E.–29 C.E.). He was raised in Galilee, stronghold of the Zealots. A Jewish town, Galilee had come under Roman political rule. Roman culture remained a veneer, deeper among those who had political and business dealings with the Greeks and Romans than among ordinary folk. Through Galilee passed major trade routes on which ideas moved as easily as merchandise.

Much contemporary scholarship has attempted to understand who Jesus was and what he meant by his teachings. No agreement on these matters has been reached, and perhaps ultimately no final answers are possible. Historians can only try to understand these events using available sources, knowing that much ultimately remains unknown. The search for the historical Jesus is complicated by many factors. One is the difference between history and faith. History relies on proof for its conclusions; faith depends on belief. Thus whether Jesus is divine is not an issue to be decided by historians. Their role is to understand him in his religious, cultural, social, and historical context.

To sort out the various and often conflicting interpretations, historians must begin with the sources. The principal evidence for the life and deeds of Jesus comes from the four Gospels of the New Testament. The Gospels are records of Jesus' life and teachings. Writing after Jesus' death, the authors sought to use the Gospels to build a community of faith centered on Jesus as the Messiah.

Scholars debate when the Gospels were published, but many historians think that the earliest Gospel, that of Mark, appeared around 70 C.E. and the books of Luke, Matthew, and John early in the second century (ca. 90 C.E.). Biblical scholars have detected a number of discrepancies among the four Gospels. Perhaps the discrepancies came in part from the authors' having heard varying earlier accounts of Jesus' life and mission. Furthermore, the writers gave their own theological interpretations to further their goal of seeking converts. The Gospels were among the most widely circulated early accounts of Jesus' life, and by the fourth century officials in the Christian church decided that they,

pagans All those who believed in the Greco-Roman gods; non-Christians.

Earliest Known Depiction of Jesus This mural may be the earliest picture of Jesus. Found in the Roman camp at Dura-Europos on the Euphrates River and dating to 235 C.E., it depicts Jesus healing the paralytic. Early Christians used art to spread the message of the Gospels. (Yale University Art Gallery, Dura-Europos Collection)

heresy A religious practice or belief judged unacceptable by church officials.

along with other types of writings such as letters and prophesies, would form Christian Scripture.

These Gospels were not, however, the earliest accounts of Jesus' career. The first followers of Jesus lived by the sayings attributed to him. Their writings about Jesus circulated in slightly different versions before the creation of the Christian church. The early followers were not actually Christian in the strictest sense. They did not see Jesus as the Messiah, nor as the founder of a church. They considered him a teacher whose moral teachings on ethical behavior were appealing in troubled times. Only later did Mark and Luke incorporate their sayings into the Gospels. Other early documents also circulated in the first century C.E., most notably a group of so-called Lost Gospels. Early Christians attributed these writings to various apostles and other followers of Jesus. Prominent among them are the Gospels of Peter, Thomas, and Mary Magdalene. In 2006 a group of scholars published the so-called Lost Gospel of Judas Iscariot, the apostle who in the New Testament betrayed Jesus. Dating to the second century C.E. and discovered in a cave in Egypt in the 1970s, the new Gospel depicts Judas's betrayal as essential for Jesus to ascend to heaven. The often contradictory accounts in the various Gospels indicate that early Christianity had a number of diverse beliefs about Jesus' nature and purpose. Only slowly as the Christian church evolved into an institution did Christians draw the line between what they considered accurate teaching and what they considered false, or heresy.

Despite this diversity, there were certain things about Jesus' teachings that almost all the sources agree on: he preached of eternal happiness in a life after death. His teachings were essentially Jewish. Jesus was Jewish by birth, and his major deviation from orthodoxy was his insistence that he taught in his own name, not in the name of Yahweh. Was he the Messiah? A small band of followers thought so, and Jesus claimed that he was. Yet Jesus had his own conception of the Messiah. Unlike the Messiah of the Apocalypse of Baruch, Jesus would not destroy the Roman Empire. Jesus believed in a spiritual kingdom, not an earthly one. Shortly before his death, Jesus told the apostles that through his sacrifice he would wipe away all sins. He would save all who came to him. That was his mission.

Of Jesus' life and teachings the prefect Pontius Pilate knew little and cared even less. All that concerned him was the maintenance of peace and order. The crowds of ordinary, usually poor people following Jesus at the time of the Passover holiday—a highly emotional time in the Jewish year—alarmed Pilate. To avert riot and bloodshed, Pilate condemned Jesus to death. According to Christian Scripture, after being tortured, he was hung from a cross until he died.

On the third day after Jesus' crucifixion, an odd rumor began to circulate in Jerusalem. Some of Jesus' followers said he had risen from the dead, while others accused the followers of having stolen his body. For the earliest Christians and for generations to come, the resurrection of Jesus became a central element of faith—and, more than that, a promise: Jesus had triumphed over death, and his resurrection promised all Christians immortality. In Jerusalem, meanwhile, the tumult subsided and Jesus' followers lived quietly and peacefully.

Chapter 6
The Pax Romana
158   31 B.C.E.–284 C.E.

CHAPTER LOCATOR | How did Augustus create a foundation for the Roman Empire?

The Spread of Christianity

The memory of Jesus and his teachings survived and flourished. Believers in his divinity met in small assemblies or congregations, often in one another's homes, to discuss the meaning of his message. These earliest Christians defined their faith to fit the life of Jesus into an orthodox Jewish context. Only later did these congregations evolve into what can be called a church with a formal organization and set of beliefs.

The catalyst in the spread of Jesus' teachings and the formation of the Christian church was Paul of Tarsus, a Hellenized Jew who was comfortable in both the Roman and Jewish worlds. He had begun by persecuting the new sect, but on the road to Damascus he was converted to belief in Jesus. He was the single most important figure responsible for changing Christianity from a Jewish sect into a separate religion. Paul was familiar with Greek philosophy, and one of his seminal ideas may have stemmed from the Stoic concept of the unity of mankind. He proclaimed that the mission of Christianity was "to make one of all the folk of men" (Acts 17:26). He urged the Jews to include Gentiles (non-Jews) in the faith. His was the first universal message of Christianity.

Paul's vision proved both bold and successful. When he traveled abroad, he first met with the leaders of the local synagogue before going out among the people. He said that there was no difference between Jews and Gentiles, which in orthodox Jewish thought was not only revolutionary but also heresy. Paul found a ready audience among the Gentiles, who converted to the new religion with surprising enthusiasm.

Many early Christian converts were women. Paul greeted male and female converts by name in his letters, and he noted that women provided financial support for his activities. Missionaries and others spreading the Christian message worked through families and friendship networks. The growing Christian communities had different ideas about many things, including the proper gender roles for believers. Some communities favored giving women a larger role, while others were more restrictive. Contrary to modern notions, the early Christians were generally tolerated.

Christianity might have remained just another sect had it not reached Rome, the capital of the Western world. Events in Rome proved to be a dramatic step in the spread of Christianity for various reasons. First, Jesus had told his followers to spread his word throughout the world, thus making his teachings universal. The pagan Romans also considered their secular empire universal, and early Christians there combined these two concepts of universalism. Secular Rome provided another advantage to Christianity. If all roads led to Rome, they also led outward to the provinces of central and western Europe. The very stability and extent of the Roman Empire enabled early Christians easily to spread their faith southward to Africa and northward into Europe and across the channel to Britain (see Map 6.2).

Decorations in the catacombs of Rome testify to the vitality of the new religion and the pagan toleration of it. The catacombs were huge underground public structures where people were buried. In the early years of persecution, Christians sometimes took refuge in the catacombs. More generally, however, they used them as a meeting place to remember their dead and celebrate their rituals. The development of Christian art can be traced on their walls, with pagan and Christian motifs on early tombs and biblical scenes on later ones.

catacombs Huge public underground cemeteries; the Roman catacombs offered refuge in times of persecution and include early pagan and Christian art.

The Appeal of Christianity

In its doctrine of salvation and forgiveness, Christianity had a powerful ability to give solace and strength to believers. Christians believed that Jesus on the cross had defeated evil and that he would reward his followers with eternal life after death. Christianity also offered the possibility of forgiveness. Human nature was weak, and even the best Christians would fall into sin. But Jesus loved sinners and forgave those who repented.

The Catacombs of Rome The early Christians used underground crypts and rock chambers to bury their dead. The bodies were placed stacked in these galleries and then sealed up. The catacombs became places of pilgrimage, and in this way the dead continued to be united with the living. (Catacombe di Priscilla, Rome/Scala/Art Resource, NY)

Christianity was attractive because it gave the Roman world a cause. Instead of passivity, Christianity stressed the ideal of striving for a goal. Christians believed that they should spread the word of God. The Christian was not discouraged by temporary setbacks, believing Christianity to be invincible.

Christianity also gave its devotees a sense of community. Believers met regularly to celebrate the Eucharist (YOO-kuh-rist), a ritual commemorating the Last Supper, Jesus' last meal with his disciples before his arrest. Each individual community was in turn a member of a greater community. And that community, according to Christian Scripture, was indestructible, for Jesus had promised that "the gates of hell shall not prevail against it" (Matthew 16:18).

Christians and Pagans

Early Christians developed their beliefs amid the classical culture of their own past. As Christianity gained converts, several influential Christian thinkers taught Christians to coexist with the pagans around them. The apostle Peter advised:

> *For the sake of the Lord, accept the authority of every social institution. . . . God wants you to be good citizens. . . . Have respect for everyone and love for your community; fear God and honor the emperor.* (Peter 2:11–20)

Peter taught that God sanctioned the emperor as the rightful ruler of the people and his officials who governed them. After all, Jesus had commanded his follower "to render unto Caesar the things that are Caesar's" (Matthew 22:21).

Two Christian thinkers taught the early Christians how to combine pagan culture with Christian ethics. Justin Martyr (100–165 C.E.), born in Samaria, established a Christian school in Rome. Originally an adherent of Plato's philosophy, he believed that the pagan philosophers had foreshadowed Christianity. He sought in his works to note the similarities, not the differences, among Christians, pagans, and Jews. He thereby played an important role in creating Christian theology, the rational analysis of religious faith. Despite his efforts to find common ground for Greek philosophy and Christian religion, he never compromised his beliefs. In a local dispute at Rome in 165 C.E. he died defending Christianity, and his fellow believers gave him the name "Martyr" from the Greek word meaning "witness."

Justin was followed by Tertullian of Carthage (ca. 160–240 C.E.), an even more influential thinker. Tertullian also symbolized some of the contradictions in early Christian beliefs. He called philosophers such as Aristotle "hucksters of eloquence" and asked, "What has Athens to do with Jerusalem?" or "the Academy with the Church?" Yet Tertullian used the teachings of the Stoics to discuss Christian ethical problems. To that extent he combined pagan philosophy with Christian theology. Both Justin and Tertullian gave western Christianity an intellectual as well as a religious foundation.

At first many pagans genuinely misunderstood Christian rites and practices. As a rule, early Christians kept to themselves. Romans distrusted and feared their exclusiveness,

Chapter 6
The Pax Romana
160   31 B.C.E.–284 C.E.

CHAPTER LOCATOR   How did Augustus create a foundation for the Roman Empire?

Christian Oil Lamp When Christianity spread among the Romans, many of them decorated their household goods with Christian symbols. This lamp for an ordinary home includes the cross of Jesus on its neck. *X* (the + when tipped would read "x") and *P* are the first two Greek letters of *Christos*, Christ. (Zev Radovan/www.BibleLandPictures.com)

which seemed unsociable and even subversive. Pagans thought that such secret rites as the Eucharist, at which Christians said that they ate and drank the body and blood of Jesus, were acts of cannibalism. They considered Christianity one of the worst of the mystery cults, for one of the hallmarks of many of those cults was rituals that many Romans found unacceptable.

Christians themselves were partly responsible for the religious misunderstandings. They exaggerated the degree of pagan hostility to them, and most of the gory stories about the martyrs are fictitious. There were indeed some cases of pagan persecution of the Christians, but with few exceptions they were local and sporadic in nature. Overall, pagans and Christians alike enjoyed long periods of tolerance and even friendship. Nonetheless, some pagans thought that Christians were atheists because they denied the existence of pagan gods or called them evil spirits. Christians urged people not to worship pagan gods. In turn, pagans, who believed in their gods as fervently as the Christians in theirs, feared that the gods would withdraw their favor from the Roman Empire because of Christian blasphemy.

Another source of misunderstanding was that the pagans did not demand that the Christians believe in pagan gods. Official Roman religion was never a matter of belief or ethics but of publicly celebrated rituals linked to the good of the state. All the pagans expected was performance of a ritual sacrifice as a demonstration of patriotism and loyalty. Those Christians who participated were free to worship in peace, no matter what they personally believed.

As time went on, pagan hostility decreased. Pagans realized that Christians were not working to overthrow the state. After years of suspicion and distrust, Christians took their place as loyal Roman citizens. With fear of persecution disappearing, they freely shared their beliefs. The promise of a happy life after death to all believers increased the popularity of Christianity. By 284 C.E., though still an overall minority, Christianity had become the largest religious group in the empire.

▼ What explains the chaos of the third century?

The long years of peace and prosperity abruptly gave way to a period of domestic upheaval and foreign invasion. The last of the five good emperors was followed by a long series of able but ambitious military commanders who used their legions to make themselves emperors. Law yielded to the sword. Yet even during the worst of this ordeal, many people clung to the old Roman ideals. Only the political mechanisms of the empire — its sturdy civil service, its ordinary lower officials, and its loyal soldiers — staved off internal collapse and foreign invasion.

Civil Wars and Foreign Invasions

After the death of Marcus Aurelius, the last of the five good emperors, misrule by his successors led to a long and intense spasm of fighting. More than twenty different emperors ascended the throne in the forty-nine years between 235 and 284. At various times parts of the empire were lost to mutinous generals. So many military commanders

How did the Roman state develop after Augustus?　　How did the Roman state develop after Augustus?　　How did Christianity grow into a major religious movement?　　**What explains the chaos of the third century?**

161

Maximinus Thrax The first of the barracks emperors, Maximinus Thrax ruled Rome from 235–238. During most of his reign he fought the Germans on the frontiers. His rebellious troops murdered him, but other generals followed his ambition to rule. (Capitoline Museums, Rome. Photo: Mary-Lan Nguyen)

ruled that the middle of the third century has become known as the age of the barracks emperors. The Augustan principate had become a military monarchy, and that monarchy was nakedly autocratic.

Barbarians on the frontiers took full advantage of the chaos to overrun vast areas. When they reached the Rhine and the Danube, they often found gaping holes in the Roman defenses. During much of the third century bands of Goths, a Germanic people, devastated the Balkans as far south as Greece and down into Asia Minor. The Alamanni (ah-luh-MAN-igh), another Germanic people, swept across the Danube. At one point they reached Milan in Italy before being beaten back. Meanwhile, the Franks, still another Germanic folk, hit the Rhine frontier. Once loose, they invaded eastern and central Gaul and northeastern Spain. Saxons from Scandinavia sailed into the English Channel in search of loot. In the east the Sassanids (suh-SAH-nihdz) overran Mesopotamia. If the army had guarded the borders instead of creating and destroying emperors, these onslaughts probably would not have been successful.

barracks emperors The name of the period in the middle of the third century when many military commanders ruled.

Turmoil in Farm and Village Life

This chaos also disrupted areas elsewhere in the empire, even when the local people remained distant from barbarian invaders. Renegade soldiers and corrupt imperial officials together with many greedy local agents preyed on local people. In many places in the countryside, farmers appealed to the government to protect them so that they could cultivate the land. Others encountered officials who requisitioned their livestock and compelled them to do forced labor. Facing ruin, many rural families deserted the land and fled. Although some of those in authority were unsympathetic and even violent to villagers, many others tried to maintain order. Yet even the best of them also suffered. If they could not meet their tax quotas, they had to pay the deficits from their own pockets. Because the local officials were themselves being so hard-pressed, they squeezed what they needed from rural families. By the end of the third century, the entire empire tottered on the brink of ruin.

The Crisis of the Third Century

By 284 C.E. the empire had reached a crisis that threatened its downfall. The position of emperor was no longer gained by lawful succession but rather by victory in civil war. The empire had failed at the top, and the repercussions of the disaster spread throughout the empire with dire effects. The bureaucracy that Claudius and the Flavians had so carefully built was caught up in chaos. Though it still functioned, its efficiency was impaired. The ravages of civil war had greatly damaged the economy. High taxes added enormously to the economic problems. Unable to pay them, many farmers were driven off their land, and those remaining faced ruin. Agricultural productivity accordingly declined. Added to the economic woe was the decline in the value of the currency. Inflation wiped out savings and sent prices soaring. These calamities had reduced the empire to a shambles, and many wondered whether it had a future.

Chapter 6
The Pax Romana
162   **31 B.C.E.–284 C.E.**

CHAPTER LOCATOR | How did Augustus create a foundation for the Roman Empire?

Though the picture looked bleak, there were many reasons to hope for better days. The basic organization of the empire remained intact. By their determined efforts, the legions restored order on the frontiers. Despite temporary damage to agriculture, the economic strength of the empire remained essentially sound. The Romans still controlled the Mediterranean, which nurtured commerce. Together with the road system, the lines of communication held the empire together. In short, the Roman infrastructure was intact. Other aspects of life also looked promising. If later Latin literature never quite reached the golden age of Augustus, it nonetheless produced gifted writers. Roman artists continued to produce outstanding portraits, paintings, and mosaics. Roman architects built temples and theaters that were as beautiful as those of their predecessors. So the real challenge facing the Romans in 284 was to rebuild their empire on its solid foundation while there was still time.

←LOOKING BACK **LOOKING AHEAD**→

THE PERIOD OF THE ROMAN EMPIRE was an amazingly rich era in both economic and cultural terms. Roman emperors developed a system of government that efficiently ruled over vast areas of diverse people. The resulting stability and peace encouraged progress in intellectual matters and writing, leading to a golden age of Latin literature. Religion likewise took an entirely new course with the rise and spread of Christianity. All the while, the Romans incorporated new peoples into their way of life as the empire expanded into northern and western Europe. Yet during a long period of internal crisis and civil war, many barbarians swept over the frontiers to disrupt Roman rule and its life.

Rome saw a new period of transition, late antiquity, during which the old and the new came to terms. People still lived under the authority of the emperors, and the guidance of Roman law and culture continued relatively unchanged. Yet a gentle breeze of change also blew. Government evolved from the SPQR (see page 118) of the past to a new monarchy. Whereas in the past the pagan gods had overseen the welfare of the state, now the Christian God with the earthly aid of the emperor and church officials protected the realm. The empire itself split from the unified principate of Augustus into two tenuously linked empires dividing the Western world. That in the west became the home of barbarians who absorbed much of the prevailing Roman culture while altering it with their own ideas, customs, and even languages.

Through all these changes the lives of ordinary men and women did not change dramatically. They farmed, worked in cities, and hoped for the best for their families. As they took new ideas, blended them with old, and created new cultural forms and ways of meeting life's challenges, they would lay the foundations of the medieval world. ∎

- **For a list of suggested readings for this chapter, visit** *bedfordstmartins.com/mckaywestunderstanding*.

- **For primary sources from this period, see** *Sources of Western Society, Second Edition*.

- **For Web sites, images, and documents related to topics in this chapter, see Make History at** *bedfordstmartins.com/mckaywestunderstanding*.

Chapter 6 Study Guide

Step 1

GETTING STARTED Below are basic terms about this period in the history of Western civilization. Can you identify each term below and explain why it matters? To do this exercise online, go to bedfordstmartins.com/mckaywestunderstanding.

TERMS	WHO (OR WHAT) AND WHEN	WHY IT MATTERS
pax Romana, p. 140		
principate, p. 140		
constitutional monarchy, p. 140		
imperator, p. 141		
barbarians, p. 144		
Praetorians, p. 148		
five good emperors, p. 149		
gladiators, p. 152		
villa, p. 153		
Messiah, p. 156		
pagans, p. 157		
heresy, p. 158		
Gentiles, p. 159		
catacombs, p. 159		
barracks emperors, p. 162		

Step 2

MOVING BEYOND THE BASICS The exercise below requires a more advanced understanding of the chapter material. In this exercise, trace the evolution of imperial power in Rome by filling in the chart below with descriptions of the political, military, and economic developments under Augustus, the Julio-Claudians, the Flavians, the five good emperors, and the barracks emperors. When you are finished, consider the following questions: What challenges did all Roman emperors face? How did the imperial response to these challenges change over time? To do this exercise online, go to bedfordstmartins.com/mckaywestunderstanding.

PHASE	POLITICAL DEVELOPMENTS	MILITARY DEVELOPMENTS	ECONOMIC DEVELOPMENTS
Augustus			
Julio-Claudians			
Flavians			
The five good emperors			
The barracks emperors			

PUTTING IT ALL TOGETHER Now that you've reviewed key elements of the chapter, take a step back and try to see the big picture. Remember to use specific examples from the chapter in your answers. To do this exercise online, go to bedfordstmartins.com/mckaywestunderstanding.

AUGUSTUS AND HIS SUCCESSORS

- Compare and contrast Roman government under the republic and the principate. What were the most important reforms carried out under Augustus? How did they increase the stability of the Roman state?

- How and why did Rome move from the principate to an overt constitutional monarchy? What did Augustus's successors do to try to reinforce Augustus's reforms?

ROME IN THE GOLDEN AGE

- Describe a typical day for the average Roman citizen living in the city of Rome during the golden age. How did it compare to the experience of living in Athens during Greece's classical period?

- How did Rome help connect greater Europe to the economic and cultural life of the Mediterranean world?

THE COMING OF CHRISTIANITY

- How did political unrest in Judaea create the context for the emergence of Christianity?

- What factors facilitated the spread of Christianity throughout the Roman Empire? Why did many Romans initially fear Christianity? Why did such fears diminish over time?

IMPERIAL DECLINE

- What were the key components of Rome's third-century crisis? What was Roman government like in the decades following the death of Marcus Aurelius?

- Were the roots of the crisis of the third century fundamentally political or economic? What evidence can you present to support your position?

■ **In Your Own Words** Imagine that you must explain Chapter 6 to someone who hasn't read it. What would be the most important points to include and why?

7

Late Antiquity

250–600

The Roman Empire, with its powerful—and sometimes bizarre—leaders, magnificent buildings, luxurious clothing, and bloody amusements, has long fascinated people. Politicians and historians have closely studied the reasons for its successes and have even more closely analyzed the weaknesses that led to its eventual collapse. From the third century onward, the Western Roman Empire slowly disintegrated. Scholars have long seen this era as one of the great turning points in Western history, a time when the ancient world was transformed into the very different medieval world. During the past several decades, however, focus has shifted to continuities as well as changes, and what is now usually termed "late antiquity" has been recognized as a period of creativity and adaptation, not simply of decline and fall.

The two main agents of continuity in late antiquity were the Christian church and the Byzantine or Eastern Roman Empire. Missionaries and church officials spread Christianity within and far beyond the borders of the Roman Empire, bringing with them the Latin language and institutions based on Roman models. The Byzantine Empire lasted until 1453, a thousand years longer than the Western Roman Empire, and it preserved and transmitted much of ancient Greco-Roman law, philosophy, and institutions. The main agents of change in late antiquity were the barbarian groups migrating into the Roman Empire. They brought different social, political, and economic structures with them, but as they encountered Roman culture and became Christian, their own ways of doing things were also transformed. ■

Life in Late Antiquity. In this sixth-century ivory carving, a procession of people carry relics of a saint to a Christian church under construction. New churches often received holy items when they were dedicated, and processions were common ways in which people expressed community devotion. (Cathedral Treasury Trier. Photo: Ann Muenchow)

Chapter Preview

▸ How did Diocletian and Constantine try to reform the empire?

▸ How did the Christian church become a major force in Europe?

▸ What were the key characteristics of barbarian society?

▸ What were the consequences of the barbarian migrations?

▸ How did the church Christianize barbarian societies?

▸ How did the Byzantine Empire preserve the legacy of Rome?

▼ How did Diocletian and Constantine try to reform the empire?

In the middle of the third century, the Roman Empire faced internal turmoil and external attacks. But in the early fourth century, the emperor Diocletian (r. 284–305), who had risen through the ranks of the military to become emperor, restored order. His successor, Constantine (r. 306–337), continued his efforts to confront the empire's myriad problems.

Political Measures

Under Diocletian, Augustus's fiction of the emperor as first among equals gave way to the emperor as absolute autocrat. The emperor claimed that he was "the elect of god" — that he ruled because of divine favor. To underline the emperor's exalted position, Diocletian and Constantine adopted the court ceremonies and trappings of the Persian Empire. People entering the emperor's presence prostrated themselves before him and kissed the hem of his robes.

Diocletian recognized that the empire had become too great for one man to handle and divided it into a western half and an eastern half (Map 7.1). Diocletian assumed direct control of the eastern part; he gave the rule of the western part to a colleague, along with the title augustus. Around 293 Diocletian further delegated power by appointing two men to assist the augustus and him, each given the title of caesar. Although this system is known as the tetrarchy (TEE-trahr-kee) because four men ruled the empire, Diocletian was clearly the senior partner and final source of authority.

tetrarchy Diocletian's four-part division of the Roman Empire.

Diocletian's political reforms were a momentous step. The reorganization made the empire easier to administer and placed each of the four central military commands much closer to borders or other trouble spots, so that troops could be sent more quickly when needed. The tetrarchy soon failed because of succession problems, but much of Diocletian's reorganization remained.

Like Diocletian, Constantine came up through the army and ruled from the east, though he had authority over the entire empire. He established a new capital for the empire at Byzantium, a Greek city on the Bosporus, naming it "New Rome," though it was soon called Constantinople. He built defensive works along the borders of the empire, trying hard to keep it together, as did his successors. Despite their efforts, however, throughout the fourth century, the eastern and the western halves drifted apart.

Economic Issues

Diocletian inherited an empire that was less capable of recovery than in earlier times. Wars and invasions had disrupted normal commerce and the means of production. Mines were exhausted in the attempt to supply much-needed ores. In the cities, markets ceased to function, and

Diocletian's Tetrarchy This sculpture represents the possibilities and problems of the tetrarchy established by the emperor Diocletian to rule the Roman Empire. Each of the four men has one hand on another's shoulder, a symbol of solidarity, but the other on his sword, a gesture that proved prophetic when the tetrarchy failed soon after Diocletian's death and another struggle for power began. (Alinari/Art Resource, NY)

168

Chapter 7
Late Antiquity
250–600

CHAPTER LOCATOR | How did Diocletian and Constantine try to reform the empire?

travel became dangerous. The barracks emperors who preceded Diocletian had dealt with economic hardship by cutting the silver content of coins. The result was crippling inflation throughout the empire.

In an attempt to curb inflation, Diocletian issued an edict that fixed maximum prices and wages throughout the empire. Moreover, taxes became payable in kind, that is, in goods or produce instead of money. Constantine continued these measures, and also made occupations more rigid: all people involved in the growing, preparation, and transportation of food and other essentials were locked into their professions. In this period of severe depression many individuals and communities could not pay their taxes. In such cases local tax collectors, who were also locked into service, had to make up the difference from their own funds. This system soon wiped out a whole class of moderately wealthy people.

The emperors' measures did nothing to address central economic problems. Because of worsening conditions during the third and fourth centuries, many free tenant farmers and their families were killed, fled the land to escape the barbarians, or abandoned farms ravaged in the fighting. Consequently, large tracts of land lay deserted. Great landlords with ample resources began at once to reclaim as much of this land as they could. The huge villas that resulted were self sufficient. They often produced more than they consumed and sold their surplus in the countryside. They became islands of stability in an unsettled world.

The rural residents who remained on the land were exposed to the raids of barbarians or robbers and to the tyranny of imperial officials. In return for the protection and security landlords could offer, small landholders gave over their lands and their freedom. To guarantee a supply of labor, landlords denied them freedom to move elsewhere. Free men and women were becoming tenant farmers bound to the land, what would later be called serfs.

The Acceptance of Christianity

The turmoil of the third century seemed to some emperors, including Diocletian, to be the punishment of the gods. They stepped up persecution of Christians who would not sacrifice to Rome's traditional deities and were thus portrayed as disloyal to the empire. These persecutions were never very widespread or long-lived. Constantine made toleration official, legalizing

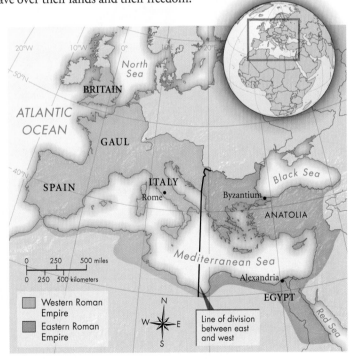

Map 7.1 The Division of the Roman World, 293 Under Diocletian, the Roman Empire was first divided into a western and an eastern half, a development that foreshadowed the medieval division between the Latin West and the Byzantine East.

How did the Christian church become a major force in Europe?

What were the key characteristics of barbarian society?

What were the consequences of the barbarian migrations?

How did the church Christianize barbarian societies?

How did the Byzantine Empire preserve the legacy of Rome?

the practice of Christianity throughout the empire in 312 and later being baptized as a Christian. He supported the church throughout his reign, expecting in return the support of church officials in maintaining order. Constantine also declared Sunday a public holiday, a day of rest for the service of God. Because of its favored position in the empire, Christianity slowly became the leading religion (Map 7.2).

In the fourth century theological disputes having to do with the nature of Christ divided the Christian community. For example, Arianism (AY-ree-uh-nih-zuhm), developed by Arius (ca. 250–336), a priest of Alexandria, held that Jesus was created by the will of God the Father and thus was not co-eternal with him. Many theologians branded Arius's position a heresy, that is, a belief that contradicted what was becoming the more widely accepted position on this issue.

Arianism enjoyed such popularity and provoked such controversy that Constantine interceded. In 325 he summoned church leaders to a council in Nicaea (nigh-SEE-uh) in Asia Minor and presided over it personally. The council produced the Nicene (nigh-SEEN) Creed, which defined the position that Christ is "eternally begotten of the Father" and of the same substance as the Father. Arius and those who refused to accept Nicene Christianity were banished. This did not end Arianism, however. Several later emperors

Arianism A theological belief that originated with Arius, a priest of Alexandria, denying that Christ was divine and co-eternal with God the Father.

Map 7.2 The Spread of Christianity to 600 Originating in Judaea, the southern part of modern Israel and Jordan, Christianity first spread throughout the Roman world and then beyond it in all directions.

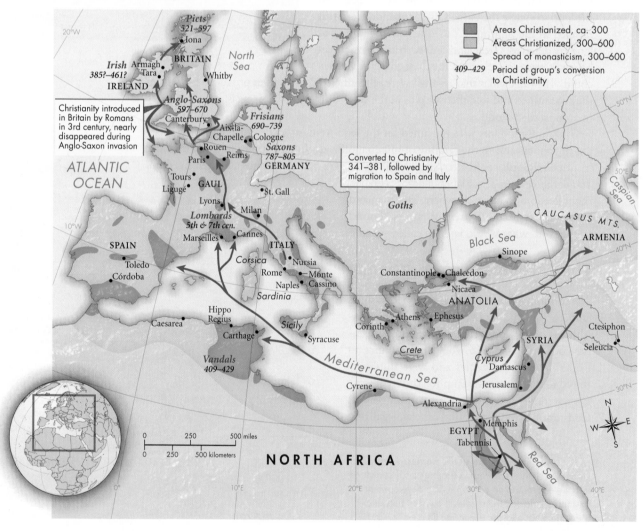

Chapter 7
Late Antiquity
170   250–600

CHAPTER LOCATOR   How did Diocletian and Constantine try to reform the empire?

were Arian, and Arian missionaries converted many barbarian tribes. The Nicene Creed says little specifically about the Holy Spirit, but in the following centuries the idea that the Father, Son, and Holy Spirit are "one substance in three persons"—the Trinity—became a central doctrine in Christianity, though again there were dissenters.

In 380 the emperor Theodosius (thee-uh-DOH-shee-uhs) made Nicene Christianity the official religion of the empire. Theodosius stripped Roman pagan temples of statues, made the practice of the old Roman state religion a treasonable offense, and persecuted Christians who dissented from orthodox doctrine. Most significant, he allowed the church to establish its own courts and to use its own body of law, called "canon law." The church courts, not the Roman government, had jurisdiction over the clergy and ecclesiastical disputes. At the death of Theodosius, the Christian church was considerably independent of the Roman state. The foundation for later growth in church power had been laid.

Later emperors continued the pattern of active involvement in church affairs. They appointed the highest officials of the church hierarchy; the emperors or their representatives presided at ecumenical councils; and the emperors controlled some of the material resources of the church. On the other hand, emperors after Theodosius rarely tried to impose their views in theological disputes.

▼ How did the Christian church become a major force in Europe?

As the emperors changed their policies about Christianity from persecution to promotion, the church grew, gradually becoming the most important institution in Europe. The able administrators and highly creative thinkers of the church developed permanent institutions and complex philosophical concepts that drew on the Greco-Roman tradition.

The Church and Its Leaders

The early Christian church benefited from the brilliant administrative abilities of some church leaders. With the empire in decay, educated people joined and worked for the church in the belief that it was the one institution able to provide leadership. Bishop Ambrose of Milan (339–397) is typical of the Roman aristocrats who held high public office, were converted to Christianity, and subsequently became bishops. Like many bishops, Ambrose had a solid education in classical law and rhetoric. He had a strong sense of his authority and even stood up to Emperor Theodosius, who had ordered Ambrose to hand over his major church—called a basilica—to the emperor:

Saint Jerome and Saint Ambrose A later woodcarving shows Saint Ambrose and Saint Jerome, two of the most important early church fathers, hard at work writing. Divine inspiration appears in the form of an angel and a dove. (Alinari/Art Resource, NY)

How did the Christian church become a major force in Europe?

What were the key characteristics of barbarian society?

What were the consequences of the barbarian migrations?

How did the church Christianize barbarian societies?

How did the Byzantine Empire preserve the legacy of Rome?

171

[D]o not burden your conscience with the thought that you have any right as Emperor over sacred things. . . . It is written, God's to God and Caesar's to Caesar. The palace is the Emperor's, the churches are the Bishop's. To you is committed jurisdiction over public, not over sacred buildings.[1]

The emperor relented. Ambrose's assertion that the church was supreme in spiritual matters and the state in secular issues was to serve as the cornerstone of the church's position on church-state relations for centuries. Ambrose came to be regarded as one of the fathers of the church, early Christian thinkers whose authority was regarded as second only to the Bible in later centuries.

Gradually the church adapted the organizational structure begun during the reign of Diocletian. The territory under the authority of a bishop was also called a diocese, with its center a cathedral, the church that contained the bishop's official seat of power. A bishop's jurisdiction extended throughout the diocese, and he came to control a large amount of land that was given to or purchased by the church. Bishops generally came from prominent families and had both spiritual and political power. They claimed to trace their spiritual ancestry back to Jesus' apostles, a doctrine called apostolic succession. Because of the special importance of their dioceses, five bishops—those of Antioch, Alexandria, Jerusalem, Constantinople, and Rome—gained the title of patriarch.

After the removal of the capital and the emperor to Constantinople, the power of the bishop of Rome grew because he was the only patriarch in the Western Roman Empire. The bishops of Rome stressed that Rome had special significance because of its history as the capital of a worldwide empire. More significantly, they asserted, Rome had a special place in Christian history. According to tradition, Saint Peter, chief of Jesus' disciples, had lived in Rome and been its first bishop. Thus as successors of Peter, the bishops of Rome—known as "popes," from the Latin word *papa*, meaning "father"—claimed a privileged position in the church hierarchy, an idea called the Petrine Doctrine. They stressed their supremacy over other Christian communities and urged other churches to appeal to Rome for the resolution of disputed doctrinal issues.

In the fifth century the popes also expanded the church's secular authority. Pope Leo I (pontificate 440–461) made treaties with several barbarian leaders who threatened the city of Rome. Gregory I (pontificate 590–604), later called "the Great," made an agreement with the barbarian groups who had cut off Rome's food supply, and he reorganized church lands to increase production, which he distributed to the poor. He had been an official for the city of Rome before he became a church official, and his administrative and diplomatic talents helped the church expand. He sent missionaries to the British Isles (see page 186) and wrote letters and guides instructing bishops on practical and spiritual matters. He promoted the ideas of Augustine (see page 175), particularly those that defined church rituals as essential for salvation.

The Development of Christian Monasticism

Christianity began and spread as a city religion. Since the first century, however, some especially pious Christians had felt that the only alternative to the decadence of urban life was complete separation from the world. They believed that the Christian life as set forth in the Gospel could not be lived in the midst of the immorality of Roman society.

This desire to withdraw from ordinary life led to the development of the monastic life. Monasticism began in Egypt in the third century. At first individuals like Saint Anthony of Egypt (251?–356) and small groups withdrew from cities and from organized society to seek God through prayer in desert or mountain caves and shelters. Gradually large colonies of monks gathered in the deserts of Upper Egypt. These monks were called hermits, from the Greek word *eremos*, meaning "desert." Many devout women also were attracted to this eremitical (ehr-uh-MIH-tihk-uhl) type of monasticism.

apostolic succession The doctrine that all bishops can trace their spiritual ancestry back to Jesus' apostles.

Petrine Doctrine A doctrine stating that the popes (the bishops of Rome) were the successors of Saint Peter and therefore heirs to his highest level of authority as chief of the apostles.

172

Chapter 7
Late Antiquity
250–600

CHAPTER LOCATOR   How did Diocletian and Constantine try to reform the empire?

The Egyptian ascetic Pachomius (puh-KOH-mee-uhs) (290–346?) drew thousands of men and women to the monastic life at Tabennisi on the Upper Nile. There were too many for them to live as hermits, so Pachomius organized communities of men and women, creating a new type of monasticism, known as coenobitic (seh-nuh-BIH-tik), that emphasized communal living. Saint Basil (329?–379), an influential bishop from Asia Minor and another of the fathers of the church, encouraged coenobitic monasticism. He and much of the church hierarchy thought that communal living provided an environment for training the aspirant in the virtues of charity, poverty, and freedom from self-deception.

Starting in the fourth century, information about Egyptian monasticism came to the West, and both men and women sought the monastic life. Most of the monasticism that developed in Gaul, Italy, Spain, England, and Ireland was coenobitic.

Monastery Life

In 529 Benedict of Nursia (480–543), who had experimented with both eremitical and communal forms of monastic life, wrote a brief set of regulations for the monks who had gathered around him at Monte Cassino between Rome and Naples. Benedict's guide for monastic life, known as *The Rule of Saint Benedict*, came to influence all forms of organized religious life in the Western Christian church. Men and women who lived in monastic houses all followed sets of rules, first those of Benedict and later those written by other individuals. Because of this, men who lived a communal monastic life came to be called **regular clergy**, from the Latin word *regulus* (rule). Priests and bishops who staffed churches in which people worshiped were called **secular clergy**. According to official church doctrine, women were not members of the clergy, but this distinction was not clear to most people.

The Rule of Saint Benedict outlined a monastic life of regularity, discipline, and moderation in an atmosphere of silence. Each monk had ample food and adequate sleep. The monk spent part of each day in formal prayer. This consisted of chanting psalms and other prayers from the Bible in the part of the monastery church called the "choir." The rest of the day was passed in manual labor, study, and private prayer. The monastic life as conceived by Saint Benedict was appealing because it struck a balance between asceticism and activity. It thus provided opportunities for men of entirely different abilities and talents—from mechanics to gardeners to literary scholars. The Benedictine form of religious life also proved congenial to women. Benedict's twin sister Scholastica (480–543) adapted the *Rule* for use by her community of nuns.

Benedictine monasticism also succeeded partly because it was so materially successful. In the seventh and eighth centuries monasteries pushed back forests and wastelands, drained swamps, and experimented with crop rotation. Benedictine houses made a significant contribution to the agricultural development of Europe. The communal nature of their organization, whereby property was held in common and profits were pooled and reinvested, made this contribution possible.

regular clergy Men and women who lived in monastic houses and followed sets of rules, first those of Benedict and later those written by other individuals.

secular clergy Priests and bishops who staffed churches where people worshiped and were not cut off from the world.

Saint Benedict Holding his *Rule* in his left hand, the seated and hooded patriarch of Western monasticism blesses a monk with his right hand. His monastery, Monte Cassino, is in the background. (Biblioteca Apostolica Vaticana)

How did the Christian church become a major force in Europe?

What were the key characteristics of barbarian society?

What were the consequences of the barbarian migrations?

How did the church Christianize barbarian societies?

How did the Byzantine Empire preserve the legacy of Rome?

173

Finally, monasteries conducted schools for local young people. Local and royal governments drew on the services of the literate men and able administrators the monasteries produced. This was not what Saint Benedict had intended, but perhaps the effectiveness of the institution he designed made it inevitable.

Christianity and Classical Culture

The growth of Christianity was not simply a matter of institutions such as the papacy and monasteries, but also of ideas. The earliest Christian thinkers sometimes rejected Greco-Roman culture, but as Christianity grew from a tiny persecuted group to the official religion of the Roman Empire, its leaders and thinkers gradually came to terms with classical culture (see Chapter 6). They incorporated elements of Greek and Roman philosophy and learning into Christian teachings, modifying them to fit with Christian notions.

Christian Teachings about Gender and Sexuality

Early Christians both adopted and adapted the then contemporary views of women, marriage, and sexuality. In his plan of salvation, Jesus considered women the equal of men. Women were among the earliest converts to Christianity and took an active role in its spread, preaching, acting as missionaries, being martyred alongside men, and perhaps even baptizing believers. Early Christians often met in people's homes and called one another brother and sister, a metaphorical use of family terms that was new to the Roman Empire. Women and men accepted the ascetic life, renouncing marriage and procreation to use their bodies for a higher calling. Some women, either singly or in monastic communities, declared themselves "virgins in the service of Christ." All this initially made Christianity seem dangerous to many Romans, who viewed marriage as the foundation of society and the proper patriarchal order.

Not all Christian teachings about gender were radical, however. In the first century C.E. male church leaders began to place restrictions on female believers. Women were forbidden to preach and were gradually excluded from holding official positions in Christianity other than in women's monasteries. Women who chose lives of virginity were to be praised, but even such women were not to be too independent. Both Jewish and classical Mediterranean culture viewed women's subordination as natural and proper, so in limiting the activities of female believers the Christian church was following well-established patterns, just as it modeled its official hierarchy after that of the Roman Empire.

Christian teachings about sexuality built on and challenged classical models. The rejection of sexual activity involved an affirmation of the importance of a spiritual life, but it also incorporated hostility toward the body found in some Hellenistic philosophies. Just as spirit was superior to matter, the mind was superior to the body. Though Christian teachings affirmed that God had created the material world and sanctioned marriage,

The Marys at Jesus' Tomb This late-fourth-century ivory panel tells the biblical story of Mary Magdalene and another Mary who went to Jesus' tomb to anoint the body (Matthew 28:1–7). At the top guards collapse when an angel descends from Heaven, and at the bottom the Marys listen to the angel telling them that Jesus had risen. Here the artist uses Roman artistic styles to convey Christian subject matter, an example of the assimilation of classical form and Christian teaching. (Castello Sforzesco/Scala/Art Resource, NY)

CHAPTER LOCATOR   How did Diocletian and Constantine try to reform the empire?

most Christian thinkers also taught that celibacy was the better life, and that anything that took one's attention from the spiritual world performed an evil function. For most clerical writers (who themselves were male), this temptation came from women, and in some of their writings, women themselves are evil. Thus the writings of the church fathers contain a strong streak of misogyny (hatred of women), which was passed down to later Christian thinkers. The church fathers also condemned same-sex relations, especially if they were between socially unequal individuals.

Saint Augustine on Human Nature, Will, and Sin

The most influential church father in the West was Saint Augustine of Hippo (354–430). Saint Augustine was born into an urban family in North Africa. His father, a minor civil servant, was a pagan; his mother, Monica, a devout Christian. Because his family was poor, the only avenue to success in a highly competitive world was a classical education. He excelled at rhetoric and, as was normal for young Roman men, began relations with a concubine, who later had his son.

Augustine took teaching positions first in Rome and then in Milan, where he had frequent conversations with Bishop Ambrose. Through his discussions with Ambrose and his own reading, Augustine became a Christian. He returned to Africa, where his mother and son soon died, and later became bishop of the seacoast city of Hippo Regius.

Augustine's autobiography, *The Confessions*, is a literary masterpiece and one of the most influential books in the history of Europe. It marks the synthesis of Greco-Roman forms and Christian thought. *The Confessions* describes Augustine's moral struggle, the conflict between his spiritual and intellectual aspirations and his sensual and material self. Augustine's ideas on sin, grace, and redemption became the foundation of all subsequent Western Christian theology. He wrote that the basic force in any individual is the will, which he defined as "the power of the soul to hold on to or to obtain an object without constraint." The end or goal of the will determines the moral character of the individual. When Adam ate the fruit forbidden by God in the Garden of Eden (Genesis 3:6), he committed the "original sin" and corrupted the will. Adam's sin was not simply his own, but it was passed on to all later humans through sexual intercourse; even infants were tainted. Original sin thus became a common social stain, in Augustine's opinion, transmitted by concupiscence, or sexual desire. Coitus was theoretically good since it was created by God, but it had been corrupted by sin, so every act of intercourse was evil and every child was conceived through a sinful act. By viewing sexual desire as the result of Adam and Eve's disobedience to divine instructions, Augustine linked sexuality even more clearly with sin than had earlier church fathers. Because Adam disobeyed God and fell, all human beings have an innate tendency to sin: their will is weak. But according to Augustine, God

Heaven in Augustine's *City of God* Augustine's writings were copied and recopied for many centuries in all parts of Europe, and they remained extremely influential. In this copy from a twelfth-century Czech illuminated manuscript of Augustine's *City of God*, the Czech king Wenzeslas and his grandmother are portrayed in the lower right corner; they probably paid for the manuscript. (Erich Lessing/Art Resource, NY)

How did the Christian church become a major force in Europe?

What were the key characteristics of barbarian society?

What were the consequences of the barbarian migrations?

How did the church Christianize barbarian societies?

How did the Byzantine Empire preserve the legacy of Rome?

175

sacraments Certain rituals defined by the church in which God bestows benefits on the believer through grace.

restores the strength of the will through grace, which is transmitted in certain rituals that the church defined as sacraments. Grace results from God's decisions, not from any merit on the part of the individual.

When barbarian forces captured the city of Rome in 410, pagans blamed the disaster on the Christians. In response, Augustine wrote *City of God*. This original work contrasts Christianity with the secular society in which it existed. According to Augustine, history is the account of God acting in time. Human history reveals that there are two kinds of people: those who live the life of the flesh, and those who live the life of the spirit in what Augustine called the City of God. The former will endure eternal hellfire; the latter will enjoy eternal bliss.

Augustine maintained that states came into existence as the result of Adam's fall and people's inclination to sin. He believed that the state was a necessary evil with the power to do good by providing the peace, justice, and order that Christians need in order to pursue their pilgrimage to the City of God. The church is responsible for the salvation of all—including Christian rulers. Church leaders later used Augustine's theory to defend their belief in the ultimate superiority of the spiritual power over the temporal. This remained the dominant political theory until the late thirteenth century.

▼ What were the key characteristics of barbarian society?

Augustine's *City of God* was written in response to the sack of Rome by an army of Visigoths, one of the many peoples the Romans labeled "barbarians." The word *barbarian* comes from the Greek *barbaro*, meaning someone who did not speak Greek. (To the Greeks, others seemed to be speaking nonsense syllables; "barbar" is the Greek equivalent of "blah-blah" or "yada-yada.") The Greeks used this word to include people such as the Egyptians, whom the Greeks respected. As it was used in Latin, however, *barbarian* also

Whalebone Chest This eighth-century chest made of whalebone, depicting warriors, other human figures, and a horse, tells a story in both pictures and words. The runes along the border are one of the varieties from the British Isles. Contact with the Romans led to the increasing use of the Latin alphabet, though runes and Latin letters were used side-by-side in some parts of northern Europe for centuries. (Erich Lessing/Art Resource, NY)

Chapter 7
Late Antiquity
176   **250–600**

CHAPTER LOCATOR

How did Diocletian and Constantine try to reform the empire?

came to imply unruly, savage, and primitive, the Romans' judgments of the people who lived beyond the northeastern boundary of Roman territory.

Scholars have long understood the importance of barbarian society, but they have been hampered in investigating it because most barbarian groups did not write and thus kept no written records before Christian missionaries introduced writing. Greek and Roman authors did describe barbarian society, but they were not always objective observers, instead using barbarians to highlight what they thought was right or wrong about their own cultures. Thus written records must be combined with archaeological evidence to gain a more accurate picture.

Barbarians included many different ethnic groups with social and political structures, languages, laws, and beliefs developed in central and northern Europe over many centuries. Among the largest barbarian groups were Celts (whom the Romans called Gauls) and Germans; Germans were further subdivided into various tribes, such as Ostrogoths, Visigoths, Burgundians, and Franks. Celts, Germans, and other barbarians brought their customs and traditions with them when they moved southward, and these gradually combined with classical and Christian patterns to form a new type of society.

Social and Economic Structures

Barbarian groups usually resided in small villages, and climate and geography determined the basic patterns of how they lived off the land. Many groups lived in small settlements on the edges of clearings where they used simple wooden plows to raise barley, wheat, oats, peas, and beans. The vast majority of people's caloric intake came from grain in some form.

Within the villages, there were great differences in wealth and status. Free men and their families constituted the largest class. The number of cattle a man possessed indicated his wealth and determined his social status. Free men also shared in tribal warfare. Slaves acquired through warfare worked as farm laborers, herdsmen, and household servants.

Ironworking represented the most advanced craft. The typical village had an oven and smiths who produced agricultural tools and instruments of war—one-edged swords, arrowheads, and shields. By the second century C.E. the swords produced by barbarian smiths were superior to the weapons of Roman troops.

In the first two centuries C.E. the quantity and quality of barbarian goods increased dramatically. Goods were used locally and for gift giving, a major social custom. Gift giving conferred status on

Visigothic Work and Play This page comes from one of the very few manuscripts from late antiquity to have survived, a copy of the first five books of the Old Testament—the Pentateuch—made around 600, perhaps in Visigothic Spain or North Africa. The top shows biblical scenes, while the bottom shows people engaged in everyday activities— building a wall, drawing water from a well, and trading punches. (Bibliothèque nationale de France)

How did the Christian church become a major force in Europe?

What were the key characteristics of barbarian society?

What were the consequences of the barbarian migrations?

How did the church Christianize barbarian societies?

How did the Byzantine Empire preserve the legacy of Rome?

177

the giver, whose giving showed his higher (economic) status, cemented friendship, and placed the receiver in his debt. Goods were also traded, though commercial exchange was less important in the barbarian world than in the Roman Empire.

Barbarian tribes were made up of kin groups comprised of families, the basic social unit in barbarian society. Families were responsible for the debts and actions of their members and for keeping the peace in general. Barbarian law codes set strict rules of inheritance based on position in the family and often set aside a portion of land that could not be sold or given away by any family member so that the family always retained some land.

Barbarian society was patriarchal: within each household the father had authority over his wife, children, and slaves. A woman was considered to be under the legal guardianship of a man, and she had fewer rights to own property than did Roman women. However, once women were widowed, they sometimes assumed their husbands' rights over family property and held the guardianship of their children.

Chiefs and Warriors

Barbarians generally had no notion of the state as we use the term today; they thought in social, not political, terms. The basic social unit was the tribe, a group whose members believed that they were all descended from a common ancestor. Blood united the tribe; kinship protected the members. Every tribe had its customs, and every member knew what they were.

Barbarian tribes were led by tribal chieftains. The chief was elected from among the male members of the most powerful family. He led the tribe in war, settled disputes among its members, conducted negotiations with outside powers, and offered sacrifices to the gods. The period of migrations and conquests of the Western Roman Empire witnessed the strengthening of the power of chiefs, who often adopted the title of king, though this title implies broader power than they actually had.

Closely associated with the chief in some tribes was the comitatus, or "war band." These warriors swore loyalty to the chief and fought with him in battle. A social egalitarianism existed among members of the war band. The comitatus had importance for the later development of feudalism.

During the migrations and warfare of the third and fourth centuries, the war band was transformed into a system of stratified ranks. Among the Ostrogoths, for example, a warrior nobility evolved. Contact with the Romans stimulated demand for goods such as metal armbands, which the Romans produced for trade with barbarian groups. Thus armbands promoted the development of hierarchical ranks within war bands. During the Ostrogothic conquest of Italy, warrior-nobles also began to acquire land as both a mark of prestige and a means to power. As land and wealth came into the hands of a small elite class, social inequalities within the tribe emerged and gradually grew stronger. These inequalities help explain the origins of the European noble class.

Barbarian Law

Early barbarian tribes had no written laws. Law was custom, but certain individuals were often given special training in remembering and retelling laws from generation to generation. Beginning in the late sixth century, however, some tribal chieftains began to collect, write, and publish lists of their customs and laws at the urging of Christian missionaries. The churchmen wanted to understand barbarian ways in order to assimilate the tribes into Christianity. Moreover, by the sixth century many barbarian kings needed written regulations for the Romans under their jurisdiction as well as for their own people.

The law code of the Salian Franks, one of the barbarian tribes, includes a feature common to many barbarian codes. Any crime that involved a personal injury, such as assault,

comitatus A war band of young men in a barbarian tribe who were closely associated with the king, swore loyalty to him, and fought with him in battle.

rape, and murder, was given a particular monetary value, called the wergeld (VEHR-gehld) (literally "man-money" or "money to buy off the spear"), that was to be paid by the perpetrator to the victim or the family. The wergeld varied according to the severity of the crime and also the social status of the victim.

wergeld Compensatory payment for death or injury set in many barbarian law codes.

If a person accused of a crime agreed to pay the wergeld and if the victim and his or her family accepted the payment, there was peace. If the accused refused to pay the wergeld or if the victim's family refused to accept it, a blood feud ensued. In this way barbarian law aimed to prevent or reduce violence.

At first, Romans had been subject to Roman law and barbarians to barbarian custom. As barbarian kings accepted Christianity and as Romans and barbarians increasingly intermarried, the distinction between the two sets of law blurred and, in the course of the seventh and eighth centuries, disappeared. The result would be the new feudal law, to which all who lived in certain areas were subject.

Barbarian Religion

Like Greeks and Romans, barbarians worshiped hundreds of gods and goddesses with specialized functions. They regarded certain mountains, lakes, rivers, or groves of trees as sacred because these were linked to deities. Rituals to honor the gods were held outdoors rather than in temples or churches, often at certain points in the yearly agricultural cycle. Presided over by a priest or priestess understood to have special abilities to call on the gods' powers, rituals sometimes involved animal (and perhaps human) sacrifice. Among the Celts, religious leaders called druids had legal and educational as well as religious functions, orally passing down laws and traditions from generation to generation. Bards singing poems and ballads also passed down myths and stories of heroes and gods.

The first written records of barbarian religion came from Greeks and Romans who encountered barbarians or spoke with those who had. They understood barbarian traditions through their own belief systems, often equating barbarian gods with Greco-Roman ones and adapting stories and rituals to blend the two. This assimilation appears to have gone both ways, at least judging by the names of the days of the week. In the Roman Empire, the days took their names from Roman deities or astronomical bodies, and they acquired those of corresponding barbarian gods in the Germanic languages of central and northern Europe. Jupiter's day, for example, became Thor's day (Thursday); both of these powerful gods were associated with thunder.

▼ What were the consequences of the barbarian migrations?

Migrating groups that the Romans labeled barbarians had pressed along the Rhine-Danube frontier of the Roman Empire off and on since about 100 B.C.E. (see Chapter 6). As this threat grew in the third and fourth centuries C.E., Roman armies sought to defend the border, but with troop levels low due to illness and a low birthrate, generals were forced to recruit barbarians to fill the ranks of the Roman army. Some barbarian leaders rose to the highest ranks of the Roman army and often assimilated into Roman culture, incorporating their own traditions and intermarrying with Roman families. Toward the end of the fifth century this barbarian assumption of authority stretched all the way to the top, and the last person with the title of emperor in the Western Roman Empire was deposed by a barbarian general.

Why did the barbarians migrate? In part, they were searching for more regular supplies of food, better farmland, and a warmer climate. In part they were pushed by groups

How did the Christian church become a major force in Europe?

What were the key characteristics of barbarian society?

What were the consequences of the barbarian migrations?

How did the church Christianize barbarian societies?

How did the Byzantine Empire preserve the legacy of Rome?

179

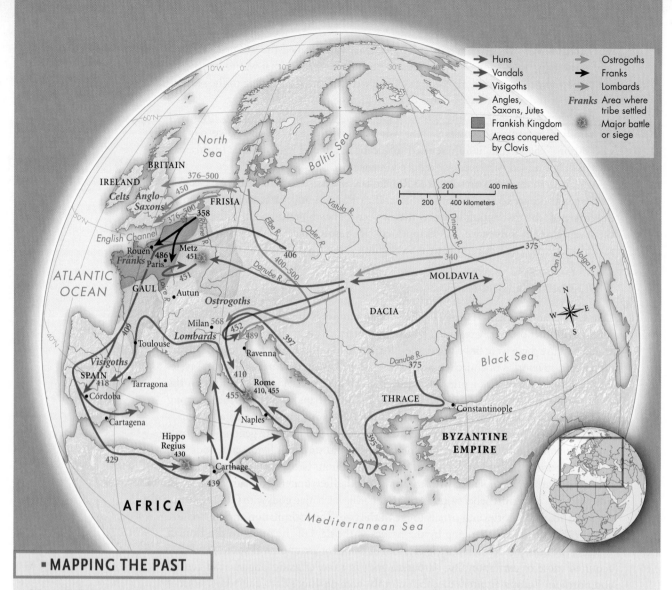

Map 7.3 The Barbarian Migrations, ca. 340–500

This map shows the migrations of various barbarian groups in late antiquity and can be used to answer the following questions.

ANALYZING THE MAP The movements of barbarian peoples used to be labeled "invasions" and are now usually described as "migrations." How do the dates on the map support the newer understanding of these movements?

CONNECTIONS Human migration is caused by a combination of push factors — circumstances that lead people to leave a place — and pull factors — things that attract people to a new location. Based on the information in this and earlier chapters, what push and pull factors might have shaped the migration patterns you see on the map?

To complete this activity online, go to the Online Study Guide at bedfordstmartins.com/mckaywestunderstanding.

living farther eastward, especially by the Huns from Central Asia in the fourth and fifth centuries. Conflicts within and among barbarian groups also led to war and disruption, which motivated groups to move (Map 7.3).

Celtic and Germanic People in Gaul and Britain

The Celts present a good example of both assimilation and conflict. Celtic-speaking peoples had lived in central Europe since at least the fifth century B.C.E. and spread out from there to the Iberian peninsula in the west, Hungary in the east, and the British Isles

Chapter 7
Late Antiquity
180   250–600

CHAPTER LOCATOR   How did Diocletian and
Constantine try to reform
the empire?

in the north. As Julius Caesar advanced northward into what he termed Gaul (present-day France) between 58 and 50 B.C.E. (see Chapter 5), he defeated many Celtic tribes. Celtic peoples conquered by the Romans often assimilated to Roman ways, adapting the Latin language and other aspects of Roman culture. In Roman Gaul and then in Roman Britain, towns were planned in the Roman fashion, with temples, public baths, theaters, and amphitheaters. In the countryside large manors controlled the surrounding lands. Roman merchants brought Eastern luxury goods and Eastern religions—including Christianity. The Romans suppressed the Celtic chieftains, and a military aristocracy made up of Romans—some of whom intermarried with Celtic families—governed. In the course of the second and third centuries, many Celts became Roman citizens and joined the Roman army.

By the fourth century C.E. Gaul and Britain were under pressure from Germanic groups moving westward, and Rome itself was threatened (see Map 7.3). Imperial troops withdrew from Britain in order to defend Rome, and the Picts from Scotland and the Scots from Ireland (both Celtic-speaking peoples) invaded territory held by the Britons. According to the eighth-century historian Bede (beed), the Briton king Vortigern invited the Saxons from Denmark to help him against his rivals. Saxons and other Germanic tribes from the area of modern-day Norway, Sweden, and Denmark turned from assistance to conquest. Their goal was plunder, and at first their invasions led to no permanent settlements. As more Germanic peoples arrived, however, they took over the best lands and eventually conquered most of Britain.

Historians have labeled the years 500 to 1066 (the year of the Norman Conquest) the Anglo-Saxon period of English history, after the two largest Germanic tribes, the Angles and the Saxons. The Germanic tribes destroyed Roman culture in Britain. Christianity disappeared, large urban buildings were allowed to fall apart, and tribal custom superseded Roman law.

Anglo-Saxon England was divided along ethnic and political lines. The Germanic kingdoms in the south, east, and center were opposed by the Britons in the west, who wanted to get rid of the invaders. The Anglo-Saxon kingdoms also fought among themselves, causing boundaries to shift constantly. Finally, in the ninth century, under pressure from the Viking invasions, the Celtic Britons and the Germanic Anglo-Saxons were molded together under the leadership of King Alfred of Wessex (r. 871–899).

Celtic Brooch This magnificent silver and gold brooch, used to hold a heavy wool cape in place, is decorated with red garnets and complex patterns of interlace. Made in Ireland, its patterns are similar to those found on Irish manuscripts from this era. (National Museum of Ireland, Dublin/Photo © Boltin Picture Library/The Bridgeman Art Library)

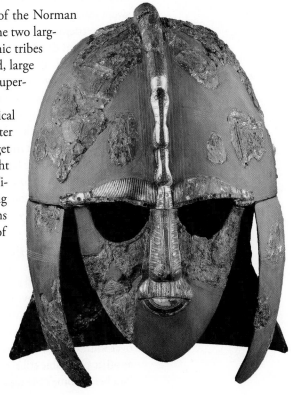

Anglo-Saxon Helmet This ceremonial bronze helmet from seventh-century England was found inside a ship buried at Sutton Hoo. The nearly 100-foot-long ship was dragged overland before being buried completely. It held one body and many grave goods, including swords, gold buckles, and silver bowls made in Byzantium. The unidentified person who was buried here was clearly wealthy and powerful. (Courtesy of the Trustees of the British Museum)

How did the Christian church become a major force in Europe?

What were the key characteristics of barbarian society?

What were the consequences of the barbarian migrations?

How did the church Christianize barbarian societies?

How did the Byzantine Empire preserve the legacy of Rome?

181

Visigoths and Huns

Germanic peoples included a number of groups with very different cultural traditions. The largest Germanic tribe, the Goths, was a polyethnic group consisting of perhaps one hundred thousand people. The tribe was supplemented by slaves and poor farmers who, because of their desperate situation under Roman rule, joined the Goths during their migrations. Based on their migration patterns, Goths have been further subdivided into Ostrogoths (eastern Goths) and Visigoths (western Goths), both of which played important roles in the political developments of late antiquity.

Pressured by defeat in battle, starvation, and the movement of other groups, the Visigoths moved westward from their homeland north of the Black Sea, and in 376 they petitioned the Roman emperor Valens to admit them to the empire. They offered to fight for Rome in exchange for the province of Thrace in what is now Greece and Bulgaria. Valens agreed, but the deal fell apart when crop failures led to famine and Roman authorities exploited the Visigoths' hunger by forcing them to sell their own people as slaves in exchange for dog flesh. The Visigoths revolted, joined with other barbarian enemies of Rome, and defeated the Roman army at the battle of Adrianople in 378, killing Valens in the process. This left a large barbarian army within the borders of the Roman Empire, and not that far from Constantinople.

Valens's successor made peace with the Visigoths, but relations worsened as the Visigoths continued migrating westward (see Map 7.3). Roman soldiers massacred thousands of their Visigothic allies and their families, and in response the Visigothic king Alaric I invaded Italy and sacked Rome in 410. Seeking to stabilize the situation at home, the imperial government pulled its troops from the British Isles and many areas north of the Alps, leaving these northern areas vulnerable to other migrating groups. A year later Alaric died, and his successor led his people into southwestern Gaul, where they established the Visigothic kingdom.

One significant factor in the migration of the Visigoths and other Germanic peoples was pressure from nomadic steppe peoples from Central Asia. Most prominent among these peoples were the Huns. Under the leadership of their warrior-king Attila, the Huns swept into central Europe in 451, attacking Roman settlements in the Balkans and Germanic settlements along the Danube and Rhine Rivers. Several Germanic groups allied with them, as did the sister of the Roman emperor, who hoped to take over power from her brother. Their troops combined with those of the Huns, and a huge army took the city of Metz, now in eastern France. After Attila turned his army southward and crossed the Alps into Italy, a papal delegation, including Pope Leo I himself, asked him not to attack Rome. Though papal diplomacy was later credited with stopping the advance of the Huns, a plague that spread among Hunnic troops and their dwindling food supplies were probably much more important. The Huns retreated from Italy, and within a year Attila was dead. Later leaders were not as effective, and the Huns were never again an important factor in European history. Their conquests had pushed many Germanic groups together, however, which transformed smaller bands into larger, more unified peoples that could more easily pick the Roman Empire apart.

Barbarian Kingdoms and the End of the Roman Empire

After they conquered an area, barbarians generally established states ruled by kings. The kingdoms did not have definite geographical borders, and their locations shifted as tribes moved. In the fifth century the Burgundians (buhr-GUHN-dee-uhns) ruled over lands in central France and western Switzerland. The Visigoths exercised a weak domination over southern France and much of the Iberian peninsula (modern Spain). The Vandals, another Germanic tribe, swept across Spain into North Africa in 429, and took over what had been Rome's breadbasket.

Barbarian states eventually came to include Italy itself. The Western Roman emperors were generally chosen by the more powerful successors of Constantine in the East, and they increasingly relied on barbarian commanders and their troops to maintain order. In the 470s a series of these commanders took over authority in name as well as in reality, deposing several Roman emperors. In 476 the barbarian chieftain Odoacer (oh-duh-WAY-suhr) deposed Romulus Augustus, the last person to have the title of Roman emperor in the West. Odoacer did not take on the title of emperor, thus this date marks the official end of the Roman Empire in the West. Emperor Zeno, the Roman emperor in the East ruling from Constantinople, worried about Odoacer's growing power, and promised Theoderic (r. 471–526), the leader of the Ostrogoths who had recently settled in the Balkans, the right to rule Italy if he defeated Odoacer. Theoderic's forces were successful, and in 493 Theoderic established an Ostrogothic state in Italy, with his capital at Ravenna.

For centuries, the end of the Roman Empire in the West was seen as a major turning point in history, the fall of the sophisticated and educated classical world to uncouth and illiterate tribes. Over the last several decades, however, many historians have put greater stress on continuities. The Ostrogoths, for example, maintained many Roman ways. Old Roman families continued to run the law courts and the city governments, and well-educated Italians continued to study the Greek classics.

In other barbarian states, as well, aspects of classical culture continued. Barbarian kings relied on officials trained in Roman law, and Latin remained the language of scholarly communication. Greco-Roman art and architecture still adorned the land, and people continued to use Roman roads, aqueducts, and buildings. The Christian church in barbarian states modeled its organization on that of Rome, and many bishops were from upper-class families that had governed the empire.

Very recently some historians and archaeologists have returned to an emphasis on change. They note that people may have traveled on Roman roads, but the roads were rarely maintained, and travel itself was much less secure than during the Roman Empire. Merchants no longer traded over long distances, so people's access to goods produced outside their local area plummeted. Knowledge about technological processes such as the making of glass and roof tiles declined or disappeared. There was intermarriage and cultural assimilation among Romans and barbarians, but there was also violence and great physical destruction.

The kingdom established by the Franks is a good example of this combination of peaceful assimilation and violent conflict. The Franks were a confederation of Germanic peoples who, in the fourth and fifth centuries, settled within the empire and allied with the Romans. The Franks believed that Merovech, a man of supernatural origins, founded their ruling dynasty, which was thus called Merovingian (mehr-uh-VIHN-jee-uhn).

The reign of Clovis (ca. 481–511) marks the decisive period in the development of the Franks as a unified people. Through military campaigns, Clovis acquired the central provinces of Roman Gaul and began to conquer southern Gaul from the Burgundians and Visigoths. Clovis's conversion to Roman Christianity brought him the crucial support of the bishops of Gaul in his campaigns against tribes that were still pagan or had accepted the Arian version of Christianity. (See "Listening to the Past: Gregory of Tours on the Conversion of Clovis," page 184.) Along with brutal violence, however, the next two centuries witnessed the steady assimilation of Franks and Romans, as many Franks adopted the Latin language and Roman ways, and Romans copied Frankish customs and Frankish personal names.

The Reign of Clovis, ca. 481–511

- Frankish lands, 481
- Territory gained under Clovis, 482–511

How did the Christian church become a major force in Europe?   What were the key characteristics of barbarian society?   **What were the consequences of the barbarian migrations?**   How did the church Christianize barbarian societies?   How did the Byzantine Empire preserve the legacy of Rome?

183

LISTENING TO THE PAST

Gregory of Tours on the Conversion of Clovis

Modern Christian doctrine holds that conversion is a process, the gradual turning toward Jesus and the teachings of the Christian Gospels. But in the early medieval world, conversion was perceived more as a one-time event determined by the tribal chieftain. If he accepted baptism, the mass conversion of his people followed. This selection about the Frankish king Clovis is from The History of the Franks *by Gregory, bishop of Tours (ca. 504–594), written about a century after the events it describes.*

❝ The first child which Clotild bore for Clovis was a son. She wanted to have her baby baptized, and she kept urging her husband to agree to this. "The gods whom you worship are no good," she would say. "They haven't even been able to help themselves, let alone others.... Take your Saturn, for example, who ran away from his own son to avoid being exiled from his kingdom, or so they say; and Jupiter, that obscene perpetrator of all sorts of mucky deeds, who couldn't keep his hands off other men, who had his fun with all his female relatives and couldn't even refrain from intercourse with his own sister....

"You ought instead to worship Him who created at a word and out of nothing heaven, and earth, the sea and all that therein is, who made the sun to shine, who lit the sky with stars, who peopled the water with fish, the earth with beasts, the sky with flying creatures, by whose hand the race of man was made, by whose gift all creation is constrained to serve in deference and devotion the man He made." However often the Queen said this, the King came no nearer to belief.... The Queen, who was true to her faith, brought her son to be baptized.... The child was baptized; he was given the name Ingomer; but no sooner had he received baptism than he died in his white robes. Clovis was extremely angry. He began immediately to reproach his Queen. "If he had been dedicated in the name of my gods," he said, "he would have lived without question; but now that he has been baptized in the name of your God he has not been able to live a single day!"

"I give thanks to Almighty God," replied Clotild, "the Creator of all things who has not found me completely unworthy, for He has deigned to welcome into his Kingdom a child conceived in my womb...."

Some time later Clotild bore a second son. He was baptized Chlodomer. He began to ail and Clovis said, "What else do you expect? It will happen to him as it happened to his brother: no sooner is he baptized in the name of your Christ than he will die!" Clotild prayed to the Lord and at His commands the baby recovered.

Queen Clotild continued to pray that her husband might recognize the true God and give up his idol-worship. Nothing could persuade him to accept Christianity. Finally war broke out against the Alamanni and in this conflict he was forced by necessity to accept what he had refused of his own free will. It so turned out that when the two armies met on the battlefield there was a great slaughter and the troops of Clovis were rapidly being annihilated. He raised his eyes to Heaven when he saw this, felt compunction in his heart and was moved to tears. "Jesus Christ," he said, "you who Clotild maintains to be the Son of the living God, you who deign to give help to those in travail and victory to those who trust in you, in faith I beg the glory of your help. If you will give me victory over my enemies, and if I may have evidence to that miraculous power which the people dedicated to your name say that they have experienced, then I will believe in you and I will be baptized in your name. I have called upon my own gods, but, as I see only too clearly, they have no intention of helping me. I therefore cannot believe that they possess any power for they do not come to the assistance of those who trust them. I now call upon you. I want to believe in you, but I must first be saved from my enemies." Even as he said this the Alamanni turned their backs and began to run away. As soon as they saw that their King was killed, they submitted to Clovis. "We beg you," they said, "to put an end to this slaughter. We are prepared to obey you." Clovis stopped the war. He made a speech in which he called for peace. Then he went home. He told the Queen how he had won a victory by calling on the name of Christ. This happened in the fifteenth year of his reign (496).

From Constantinople, Eastern Roman emperors worked to hold the empire together and to reconquer at least some of the West from barbarian tribes. The emperor Justinian (r. 527–565) waged long and hard-fought wars against the Ostrogoths and temporarily regained Italy and North Africa, but his conquests had disastrous consequences. Justinian's wars exhausted the resources of the state, destroyed Italy's economy, and killed a large part of Italy's population. The wars also paved the way for the easy conquest of Italy by another Germanic tribe, the Lombards, shortly after Justinian's death. In the late sixth century the territory of the Western Roman Empire came once again under barbarian sway.

Chapter 7
Late Antiquity
184   250–600

CHAPTER LOCATOR   How did Diocletian and Constantine try to reform the empire?

Ninth-century ivory carving showing Clovis being baptized by Saint Remigius. (Laurie Platt Winfrey/The Granger Collection, NY)

The Queen then ordered Saint Remigius, Bishop of the town of Rheims (reemz), to be summoned in secret. She begged him to impart the word of salvation to the King. The Bishop asked Clovis to meet him in private and began to urge him to believe in the true God, Maker of Heaven and earth, and to forsake his idols, which were powerless to help him or anyone else. The King replied: "I have listened to you willingly, holy father. There remains one obstacle. The people under my command will not agree to forsake their gods. I will go and put to them what you have just said to me." He arranged a meeting with his people, but God in his power had preceded him, and before he could say a word all those present shouted in unison: "We will give up worshipping our mortal gods, pious King, and we are prepared to follow the immortal God about whom Remigius preaches." This news was reported to the Bishop. He was greatly pleased and he ordered the baptismal pool to be made ready. . . . The baptistry was prepared, sticks of incense gave off clouds of perfume, sweet-smelling candles gleamed bright and the holy place of baptism was filled with divine fragrance. God filled the hearts of all present with such grace that they imagined themselves to have been transported to some perfumed paradise. King Clovis asked that he might be baptized first by the Bishop. Like some new Constantine he stepped forward to the baptismal pool, ready to wash away the sores of his old leprosy and to be cleansed in flowing water from the sordid stains which he had borne so long.

King Clovis confessed his belief in God Almighty, three in one. He was baptized in the name of the Father, the Son and the Holy Ghost, and marked in holy chrism [an anointing oil] with the sign of the Cross of Christ. More than three thousand of his army were baptized at the same time. 》

Source: *The History of the Franks by Gregory of Tours*, translated with an Introduction by Lewis Thorpe (Penguin Classics, 1974), pp. 141–144. Copyright © the Estate of Lewis Thorpe, 1974. Reproduced by permission of Penguin Books Ltd.

QUESTIONS FOR ANALYSIS

1. Who took the initiative in urging Clovis's conversion? What can we deduce from that?
2. According to this account, why did Clovis ultimately accept Christianity?
3. For the Salian Franks, what was the best proof of divine power?
4. On the basis of this selection, do you consider *The History of the Franks* reliable history? Why?

▼ How did the church Christianize barbarian societies?

Christian teachings were initially carried by all types of converts, but they were often spread into the countryside and into areas beyond the borders of the empire by those who had decided to dedicate their lives to the church, such as monks. Such missionaries

How did the Christian church become a major force in Europe?

What were the key characteristics of barbarian society?

What were the consequences of the barbarian migrations?

How did the church Christianize barbarian societies?

How did the Byzantine Empire preserve the legacy of Rome?

Staffordshire Hoard Artifact with Biblical Inscription This strip of gold bears a biblical inscription in somewhat misspelled Latin asking God for help against enemies. Made in the seventh century, it was buried sometime later along with hundreds of garnet-inlaid gold and silver weapon parts, and was discovered in 2009 in Staffordshire, England, as part of the largest hoard of Anglo-Saxon gold ever found. Who made it, who owned it, and who buried it will no doubt be a source of debate for decades, as the hoard modifies scholarly opinion about Anglo-Saxon England. (Birmingham Museum and Art Gallery)

were often sent by popes specifically to convert certain groups. As they preached to barbarian peoples, the missionaries developed new techniques to convert them.

Throughout barbarian Europe, religion was not a private or individual matter; it was a social affair; and the religion of the chieftain or king determined the religion of the people. Thus missionaries concentrated their initial efforts not on ordinary people, but on kings or tribal chieftains and the members of their families. Germanic kings sometimes accepted Christianity because they came to believe that the Christian God was more powerful than pagan gods and that the Christian God would deliver victory in battle. They also appreciated that Christianity taught obedience to kingly as well as divine authority. Christian missionaries were generally literate, and they taught reading and writing to young men who became priests or officials in the royal household, a service that kings appreciated.

Missionaries' Actions

The effective beginnings of Christianity in Gaul can be traced to Saint Martin of Tours (ca. 316–397), a Roman soldier who, after giving away half his cloak to a naked beggar, had a vision of Christ and was baptized. Martin founded the monastery of Ligugé, the first in Gaul, which became a center for the evangelization of the region. In 372 he became bishop of Tours.

Martin supported Nicene Christianity (see page 170), but many barbarian groups were converted by Arian missionaries, who also founded dioceses. The Ostrogoths, Visigoths, Lombards, and Vandals were all originally Arians, though over the sixth and seventh centuries most of them converted to Roman Christianity, sometimes peacefully and sometimes as a result of conquest.

Tradition identifies the conversion of Ireland with Saint Patrick (ca. 385–461). Born in England to a Christian family of Roman citizenship, Patrick was captured and enslaved by Irish raiders and taken to Ireland, where he worked as a herdsman for six years. He escaped and returned to England, where a vision urged him to Christianize Ireland. In preparation, Patrick studied in Gaul and was consecrated a bishop in 432.

Chapter 7
Late Antiquity
186 **250–600**

CHAPTER LOCATOR | How did Diocletian and Constantine try to reform the empire?

He returned to Ireland, where he converted the Irish tribe by tribe, first baptizing the king.

In his missionary work, Patrick had the strong support of Bridget of Kildare (kihl-DAIR) (ca. 450–528), daughter of a wealthy chieftain. Bridget defied parental pressure to marry and became a nun. She and the other nuns at Kildare instructed relatives and friends in basic Christian doctrine, made religious vestments (clothing) for churches, copied books, taught children, and above all set a religious example by their lives of prayer. In this way, in Ireland and later in continental Europe, women like the nuns at Kildare shared in the process of conversion.

The Christianization of the English began in earnest in 597, when Pope Gregory I sent a delegation of monks under a missionary named Augustine to Britain. When Augustine succeeded in converting Ethelbert, king of Kent, the baptism of Ethelbert's people took place as a matter of course. Augustine established his headquarters, or see, at Canterbury in southern England and is usually called "Augustine of Canterbury" to distinguish him from the more famous Augustine of Hippo.

In the course of the seventh century, two Christian forces competed for the conversion of the pagan Anglo-Saxons: Roman-oriented missionaries traveling north from Canterbury, and Celtic monks from Ireland and northwestern Britain. The Roman and Celtic church organizations, types of monastic life, and methods of arriving at the date of the central feast of the Christian calendar, Easter, differed completely. Through the influence of King Oswiu (OHS-wih) of Northumbria and the energetic abbess Hilda of Whitby, the Synod (ecclesiastical council) held at Hilda's convent of Whitby in 664 opted to follow the Roman practices. The conversion of the English and the close attachment of the English church to Rome had far-reaching consequences because Britain later served as a base for the Christianization of the continent (see Map 7.2), spreading Roman Christian teachings among both pagans and Arians.

The Process of Conversion

When a ruler marched his people to the waters of baptism, the work of Christianization had only begun. Christian kings could order their subjects to be baptized, married, and buried in Christian ceremonies, which they did increasingly across Europe. Churches could be built, and people could be required to attend services and belong to parishes, but the church could not compel people to accept Christian beliefs.

How did missionaries and priests get masses of pagan and illiterate peoples to understand Christian ideals and teachings? They did so through preaching, assimilation, the ritual of penance, and the veneration of saints. Missionaries preached the basic teachings of Christianity in simplified Latin or translated them into the local language. In monasteries and cathedrals, men—and a few women—wrote hymns, prayers, and stories about the lives of Christ and the saints. People heard these and slowly came to be familiar with Christian notions.

Deeply ingrained pagan customs and practices could not, however, be stamped out by words alone. Christian missionaries often pursued a policy of assimilation, easing the conversion of pagan men and women by stressing similarities between their customs and beliefs and those of Christianity. Missionaries and converts mixed pagan ideas and practices with Christian ones. Bogs and lakes sacred to Germanic gods became associated with saints. Aspects of existing midwinter celebrations, which often centered on the return of the sun as the days became longer, were incorporated into celebrations of Christmas. Spring rituals involving eggs and rabbits (both symbols of fertility) were added to Easter.

The ritual of penance was also instrumental in teaching people Christian ideas. Christianity taught that certain actions and thoughts were sins, that is, against God's

How did the Christian church become a major force in Europe?

What were the key characteristics of barbarian society?

What were the consequences of the barbarian migrations?

How did the church Christianize barbarian societies?

How did the Byzantine Empire preserve the legacy of Rome?

187

commands. Only by confessing these sins and asking forgiveness could a sinning believer be reconciled with God. Confession was initially a public ritual, but by the fifth century individual confession to a parish priest was more common. The person knelt before the priest, who questioned him or her about sins he or she might have committed. The priest then set a penance such as fasting or saying specific prayers to allow the person to atone for the sin. Penance gave new Christians a sense of expected behavior, encouraged the private examination of conscience, and offered relief from the burden of sinful deeds.

Most religious observances continued to be community matters, as they had been in the ancient world. People joined with family members, friends, and neighbors at their parish church to attend baptisms, weddings, and funerals presided over by a priest. The parish church often housed the relics of a saint, that is, bones, articles of clothing, or other objects associated with a person who had lived (or died) in a way that was spiritually heroic or noteworthy. This patron saint was understood to provide protection and assistance for those who came to worship, and the relics served as a link between the material world and the spiritual. Miracle stories about saints and their relics were an important part of Christian preaching and writing.

Christians came to venerate the saints as powerful and holy. They prayed to saints or to the Virgin Mary to intercede with God, or they simply asked the saints to assist and bless them. The entire village participated in processions marking saints' days or points in the agricultural year, often carrying images of saints or their relics around the houses and fields. The decision to become Christian was often made first by an emperor or king, but actual conversion was a local matter, as people came to feel that the parish priest and the patron saint provided them with benefits in this world and the world to come.

relics Bones, articles of clothing, or other objects associated with the life of a saint.

▼ How did the Byzantine Empire preserve the legacy of Rome?

Barbarian migrations and Christian conversions occurred throughout all of Europe in late antiquity, but their impact was not the same in the Western and Eastern halves of the Roman Empire. The Western Roman Empire gradually disintegrated, but the Roman Empire continued in the East. The Byzantine or Eastern Roman Empire (see Map 7.1) preserved the forms, institutions, and traditions of the old Roman Empire. Byzantine emperors traced their lines back past Constantine to Augustus, and the senate in Constantinople carried on the traditions of the old Roman senate. Most important, however, is how Byzantium protected the intellectual heritage of Greco-Roman civilization and then passed it on to the rest of Europe.

Sources of Byzantine Strength

While the Western parts of the Roman Empire gradually succumbed to barbarian invaders, the Byzantine Empire survived attacks by Central Asian steppe peoples such as the Huns and Avars, Germanic tribes, Persians, and Arabs (Map 7.4). Why didn't one or a combination of these enemies capture Constantinople as the Ostrogoths had taken Rome? The answer lies in strong military leadership and even more in the city's location and its excellent fortifications. Justinian's generals were able to reconquer much of Italy and North Africa from barbarian groups, making them part of the Byzantine Empire. Under the skillful command of General Priskos (d. 612), Byzantine armies inflicted a severe defeat on the Avars in 601, and under emperor Heraclius I (hehr-uh-KLIGHuhs) (r. 610–641) they crushed the Persians at Nineveh in Iraq. Massive triple walls, built by the emperors Constantine and Theodosius II (408–450) and kept in good repair, protected Constantinople from sea invasion. Attacking Constantinople by land posed greater geographical and logistical problems than a seventh- or eighth-century government could solve. The site was not absolutely impregnable—as the Venetians demonstrated in 1204 and the Ottoman Turks in 1453—but it was almost so. For centuries, the Byzantine Empire served as a bulwark for the West, protecting it against invasions from the East.

The Law Code of Justinian

One of the most splendid achievements of the Byzantine emperors was the preservation of Roman law for the medieval and modern worlds. Roman law had developed from many sources—decisions by judges, edicts of the emperors, legislation passed by the senate, and the opinions of jurists. By the fourth century it had become a huge, bewildering mass, and its sheer bulk made it almost unusable.

Sweeping and systematic codification took place under the emperor Justinian. He appointed a committee of eminent jurists to sort through and organize the laws. The result was the *Code*, which distilled Roman law into a coherent whole, eliminated outmoded laws and contradictions, and clarified the law itself. Not content with the *Code*, Justinian set about bringing order to the equally huge body of Roman jurisprudence, the science or philosophy of law.

During the second and third centuries, the foremost Roman jurists had expressed varied learned opinions on complex legal problems. To harmonize this body of knowledge,

Map 7.4 The Byzantine Empire, ca. 600 The strategic position of Constantinople on the waterway between the Black Sea and the Mediterranean was clear to Constantine when he chose the city as the capital of the Eastern Roman Empire. Byzantine territories in Italy were acquired in Emperor Justinian's sixth-century wars and were held for several centuries.

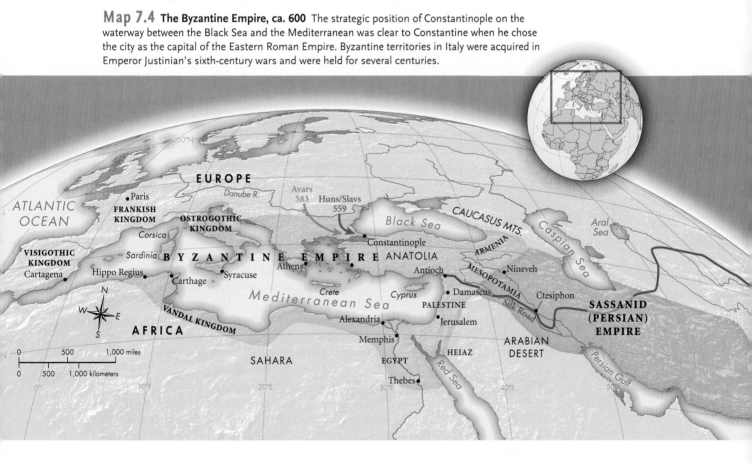

How did the Christian church become a major force in Europe?

What were the key characteristics of barbarian society?

What were the consequences of the barbarian migrations?

How did the church Christianize barbarian societies?

How did the Byzantine Empire preserve the legacy of Rome?

189

Justinian and His Attendants

This mosaic indicates the uniting of religious and secular authority in the person of the emperor. It is composed of thousands of tiny cubes of colored glass or stone called *tessarae*, which are set in plaster against a blazing golden background. (Scala/Art Resource, NY)

ANALYZING THE IMAGE Which figure is Justinian, and how did you identify him as such? What types of subjects are shown with him?

CONNECTIONS This representation of Justinian's rule is infused with order and respect. How did Justinian's accomplishments measure up to this depiction?

To complete this activity online, go to the Online Study Guide at bedfordstmartins.com/mckaywestunderstanding.

Justinian directed his jurists to clear up disputed points and to issue definitive rulings. Accordingly, in 533 his lawyers published the *Digest*, which codified Roman legal thought.

Finally, Justinian's lawyers compiled a handbook of civil law, the *Institutes*. These three works—the *Code*, the *Digest*, and the *Institutes*—are the backbone of the *corpus juris civilis* (KAWR-puhs JOOR-uhs sih-VIH-luhs), the "body of civil law," which is the foundation of law for nearly every modern European nation.

Byzantine Intellectual Life

The Byzantines prized education; because of them many masterpieces of ancient Greek literature have survived to influence the intellectual life of the modern world. The literature of the Byzantine Empire was predominately Greek, although politicians, scholars,

Chapter 7
Late Antiquity
190   250–600

CHAPTER LOCATOR   How did Diocletian and Constantine try to reform the empire?

and lawyers also spoke and used Latin. More people could read in Byzantium than anywhere else in Christian Europe at the time, and, history was a favorite topic.

The most remarkable Byzantine historian was Procopius (ca. 500–562), who left an approving account of Justinian's reconquest of North Africa and Italy, but he also wrote the *Secret History*, a vicious and uproarious attack on Justinian and his wife, the empress Theodora. (See "Individuals in Society: Theodora of Constantinople," page 192.)

Although the Byzantines discovered little that was new in mathematics and geometry, they passed Greco-Roman learning on to the Arabs, who made remarkable advances with it. In science the Byzantines made advances only in terms of military applications. For example, the best-known Byzantine scientific discovery was an explosive compound known as "Greek fire" that was heated and propelled by a pump through a bronze tube. As the liquid jet left the tube, it was ignited—somewhat like a modern flamethrower. In mechanics Byzantine scientists improved and modified artillery and siege machinery.

The Byzantines devoted a great deal of attention to medicine, and the general level of medical competence was far higher in the Byzantine Empire than in western Europe. Yet their physicians could not cope with a disease similar to bubonic plague, often called the "Justinian plague," that swept through the Byzantine Empire and parts of western Europe between 542 and about 560. The epidemic had profound political as well as social consequences: it weakened Justinian's military resources, thus hampering his efforts to restore unity to the Mediterranean world.

By the ninth or tenth century, most major Greek cities had hospitals for the care of the sick. The hospitals might be divided into wards for different illnesses, and hospital staff had surgeons, practitioners, and aides with specialized responsibilities. The imperial Byzantine government bore the costs of these medical facilities.

The Orthodox Church

The continuity of the Roman Empire in the East meant that Christianity developed differently there than it did in the West. The emperors in Constantinople were understood to be Christ's representatives on earth. Emperors called councils, appointed church officials, and regulated the income of the church. As in Rome, there was a patriarch in Constantinople, but he did not develop the same powers that the pope did in the West because there was never a similar power vacuum into which he needed to step. The Orthodox church, the name generally given to the Eastern Christian church, was less independent of secular control than the Western Christian church.

Monasticism in the Orthodox world differed in fundamental ways from the monasticism that evolved in western Europe. First, while *The Rule of Saint Benedict* gradually became the universal guide for all western European monasteries, each individual house in the Byzantine world developed its own set of rules for organization and behavior. Second, education never became a central feature of Orthodox monasteries. Monks and nuns had to be literate to perform the appropriate rituals, but no Orthodox monastery assumed responsibility for the general training of the local young.

There were also similarities between Western and Eastern monasticism. As in the West, Eastern monasteries became wealthy property owners, with fields, pastures, livestock, and buildings. Since bishops and patriarchs of the Orthodox church were recruited only from the monasteries, these also exercised cultural influence.

Like their counterparts in the West, Byzantine missionaries traveled far beyond the boundaries of the empire seeking converts. In 863 the emperor Michael III sent the brothers Cyril (826–869) and Methodius (muh-THOH-dee-uhs) (815–885) to preach Christianity in Moravia (the region of modern central Czech Republic). Other missionaries succeeded in converting the Russians in the tenth century. Cyril invented a Slavic alphabet using Greek characters, later termed the "Cyrillic (suh-RIH-lihk) alphabet" in his

Orthodox church Eastern Christian church in the Byzantine Empire.

How did the Christian church become a major force in Europe?

What were the key characteristics of barbarian society?

What were the consequences of the barbarian migrations?

How did the church Christianize barbarian societies?

How did the Byzantine Empire preserve the legacy of Rome?

191

INDIVIDUALS IN SOCIETY

Theodora of Constantinople

The empress Theodora shown with a halo, a symbol of power. Like Justinian, she had power over secular and religious institutions, much to the dismay of many at Justinian's court. (Scala/Art Resource, NY)

THE MOST POWERFUL WOMAN IN BYZANTINE
history was the daughter of a bear trainer for the circus. Theodora (ca. 497–548) grew up in what her contemporaries regarded as an undignified and morally suspect atmosphere, and she worked as a dancer and burlesque actress, both dishonorable occupations in the Roman world. Despite her background, she caught the eye of Justinian, who was then a military leader and whose uncle (and adoptive father) Justin had himself risen from obscurity to become the emperor of the Byzantine Empire. Under Justinian's influence, Justin changed the law to allow an actress who had left her disreputable life to marry whom she liked, and Justinian and Theodora married in 525. When Justinian was proclaimed co-emperor with his uncle Justin on April 1, 527, Theodora received the rare title of *augusta*, empress. Thereafter her name was linked with Justinian's in the exercise of imperial power.

Most of our knowledge of Theodora's early life comes from the *Secret History*, a tell-all description of the vices of Justinian and his court written by Procopius (pruh-KOH-pee-uhs) (ca. 550), who was the official court historian and thus spent his days praising those same people. In the *Secret History* he portrays Theodora and Justinian as demonic, greedy, and vicious, killing courtiers to steal their property. In scene after detailed scene, Procopius portrays Theodora as particularly evil, sexually insatiable, depraved, and cruel, a temptress who used sorcery to attract men, including the hapless Justinian.

In one of his official histories, *The History of the Wars of Justinian*, Procopius presents a very different Theodora. Riots between the supporters of two teams in chariot races — who formed associations somewhat like both street gangs and political parties — had turned deadly, and Justinian wavered in his handling of the perpetrators. Both sides turned against the emperor, besieging the palace while Justinian was inside it. Shouting N-I-K-A (victory), the rioters swept through the city, burning and looting, and destroyed half of Constantinople. Justinian's counselors urged flight, but, according to Procopius, Theodora rose and declared:

> For one who has reigned, it is intolerable to be an exile. . . . If you wish, O Emperor, to save yourself, there is no difficulty: we have ample funds and there are the ships. Yet reflect whether, when you have once escaped to a place of security, you will not prefer death to safety. I agree with an old saying that the purple [that is, the color worn only by emperors] is a fair winding sheet [to be buried in].

Justinian rallied, had the rioters driven into the hippodrome, and ordered between thirty and thirty-five thousand men and women executed. The revolt was crushed and Justinian's authority restored, an outcome approved by Procopius.

Other sources describe or suggest Theodora's influence on imperial policy. Justinian passed a number of laws that improved the legal status of women, such as allowing women to own property the same way that men could and to be guardians over their own children. Justinian is reputed to have consulted her every day about all aspects of state policy, including religious policy regarding the doctrinal disputes that continued throughout his reign. Theodora's influence over her husband and her power in the Byzantine state continued until she died, perhaps of cancer, twenty years before Justinian. Her influence may have even continued after death, for Justinian continued to pass reforms favoring women and, at the end of his life, accepted her interpretation of Christian doctrine. Institutions that she established, including hospitals, orphanages, houses for the rehabilitation of prostitutes, and churches, continued to be reminders of her charity and piety.

Theodora has been viewed as a symbol of the manipulation of beauty and cleverness to attain position and power, and also as a strong and capable co-ruler who held the empire together during riots, revolts, and deadly epidemics. Just as Procopius expressed both views, the debate has continued to today among writers of science fiction and fantasy as well as biographers and historians.

QUESTIONS FOR ANALYSIS

1. How would you assess the complex legacy of Theodora?
2. Since the public and private views of Procopius are so different regarding the empress, should he be trusted at all as a historical source?

Chapter 7
Late Antiquity

192   250–600

CHAPTER LOCATOR | How did Diocletian and Constantine try to reform the empire?

honor. In the tenth century other missionaries spread Christianity, the Cyrillic alphabet, and Byzantine art and architecture to Russia. The Byzantines were so successful that the Russians would later claim to be the successors of the Byzantine Empire. For a time Moscow was even known as the "Third Rome" (the second Rome being Constantinople).

← LOOKING BACK **LOOKING AHEAD** →

THE CHRISTIAN CHURCH and the barbarian states absorbed many aspects of Roman culture, and the Roman Empire continued to thrive in the east as the Byzantine Empire, but western Europe in 600 was very different than it had been in 250. The Western Roman Empire had slowly disintegrated under pressure from barbarian groups. Barbarian kings ruled small states from Italy to Norway, while churches and monasteries rather than emperors and wealthy individuals took on the role of building new buildings and providing education. The city of Rome no longer attracted a steady stream of aspiring immigrants and it had shrunk significantly, as had many other cities, which were no longer centers of innovation. As the vast network of Roman colonies dissolved, economies everywhere became more localized. Commentators such as Augustine advised people to put their faith in the eternal City of God rather than in worldly cities, for human history would always bring great change. People who lived with Augustine in Hippo would have certainly understood such counsel, for they watched the Vandals move swiftly across North Africa and bring an end to Roman rule there. Although Justinian's Byzantine forces retook the area a little over a century later, the culture that survived was as much barbarian as Roman, with smaller cities, less trade, and fewer schools.

Two hundred years after the Vandal attack, the residents of Byzantine North Africa confronted another fast-moving army of conquest, Arabian forces carrying a new religion, Islam. This Arabic expansion dramatically shaped the development of Western civilization. Though the end of the Roman Empire in 476 has long been seen as a dramatic break in European history, the expansion of Islam two centuries later may have been even more significant. Many of the patterns set in late antiquity continued, however. Warrior values such as physical prowess, bravery in battle, and loyalty to one's lord remained central and shaped the development of the political system known as feudalism. The Frankish kingdom established by Clovis continued to expand, becoming the most important state in Europe. The economic and political power of the Christian church expanded as well, with monasteries and convents providing education for their residents. The vast majority of people continued to live in small villages, trying to raise enough grain to feed themselves and their families, and asking the help of the saints to overcome life's difficulties. ■

- **For a list of suggested readings for this chapter, visit** *bedfordstmartins.com/mckaywestunderstanding.*

- **For primary sources from this period, see** *Sources of Western Society,* Second Edition.

- **For Web sites, images, and documents related to topics in this chapter, see Make History at** *bedfordstmartins.com/mckaywestunderstanding.*

■ Chapter 7 Study Guide

| Step 1 | **GETTING STARTED** Below are basic terms about this period in the history of Western civilization. Can you identify each term below and explain why it matters? To do this exercise online, go to bedfordstmartins.com/mckaywestunderstanding. |

TERMS	WHO (OR WHAT) AND WHEN	WHY IT MATTERS
tetrarchy, p. 168		
Arianism, p. 170		
apostolic succession, p. 172		
Petrine Doctrine, p. 172		
regular clergy, p. 173		
secular clergy, p. 173		
sacraments, p. 176		
comitatus, p. 178		
wergeld, p. 179		
relics, p. 188		
Orthodox church, p. 191		

| Step 2 | **MOVING BEYOND THE BASICS** The exercise below requires a more advanced understanding of the chapter material. Consider the changes in the Greco-Roman world between 250 and 600. Then fill in the chart with descriptions of key aspects of life. When you are finished, consider the following questions: What changed between 250 and 600? What were the important continuities? To do this exercise online, go to bedfordstmartins.com/mckaywestunderstanding. |

YEAR	SOCIAL AND ECONOMIC RELATIONS	POLITICS AND WARFARE	RELIGION AND CULTURE
250			
600			

PUTTING IT ALL TOGETHER Now that you've reviewed key elements of the chapter, take a step back and try to see the big picture. Remember to use specific examples from the chapter in your answers. To do this exercise online, go to bedfordstmartins.com/mckaywestunderstanding.

RECONSTRUCTION UNDER DIOCLETIAN AND CONSTANTINE

- What were the most important political and economic problems facing the empire during the reign of Diocletian? Why did Diocletian and his successors have only limited success in solving these problems?

- Compare and contrast Diocletian's and Constantine's attitudes toward Christianity. How might you explain the differences you note?

THE GROWTH OF THE CHRISTIAN CHURCH AND THE SPREAD OF CHRISTIANITY

- Is it more accurate to say that Rome was Christianized or that the Christian church was Romanized? What evidence can you present to support your position?

- Why did so many barbarian elites aid in the spread of Christianity in Europe? What does the receptivity of such elites to Christianity tell us about barbarian society and culture?

THE BARBARIANS

- Compare and contrast the role of family in barbarian and Roman society. What key features did the two societies have in common?

- What explains the barbarian migrations of late antiquity? What does their success in overcoming Roman defenses in the West tell us about their strengths and the Romans' weaknesses?

THE BYZANTINE EMPIRE

- Compare and contrast the Western Roman Empire and the Eastern Roman Empire in the period just prior to the fall of the Western Roman Empire. Why was the Eastern Roman Empire able to withstand the pressure of barbarian migrations, while the Western Roman Empire was not?

- In what ways did the Byzantines preserve the culture and institutions of the Roman Empire? Why was this so important for the future development of Western civilization?

■ **In Your Own Words** Imagine that you must explain Chapter 7 to someone who hasn't read it. What would be the most important points to include and why?

8

Europe in the Early Middle Ages

600–1000

By the fifteenth century scholars in the growing cities of northern Italy began to think that they were living in a new era, one in which the glories of ancient Greece and Rome were being reborn. What separated their time from classical antiquity, in their opinion, was a long period of darkness, to which a seventeenth-century professor gave the name "Middle Ages." In this conceptualization, Western history was divided into three periods—ancient, medieval, and modern—an organization that is still in use today.

For a long time the end of the Roman Empire in the West was seen as the division between the ancient period and the Middle Ages, but, as we saw in the last chapter, there was continuity as well as change, and the transition from ancient to medieval was a slow process, not a single event. The agents in this process included not only the barbarian migrations that broke the Roman Empire apart but also the new religion of Islam, Slavic and steppe peoples in eastern Europe, and Christian officials and missionaries. The period from the end of antiquity (ca. 600–1000), conventionally known as the "early Middle Ages," was a time of disorder and destruction, but it also marked the creation of a new type of society. While agrarian life continued to dominate Europe, leaders formed political structures that would influence later European history, and Christianity became a powerful institution. People at the time did not know that they were living in an era that would later be labeled "middle" or sometimes even "dark," and we can wonder whether they would have shared this negative view of their own times. ∎

Life in the Early Middle Ages. In this manuscript illumination from Spain, Muslim fishermen take a rich harvest from the sea. Fish were an important part of the diet of all coastal peoples in medieval Europe and were often salted and dried to preserve them for later use. (The Granger Collection, NY)

Chapter Preview

- ▶ **What were the origins of Islam and how did it spread?**

- ▶ **How did the Franks build and govern a European empire?**

- ▶ **What were the accomplishments of the Carolingian Renaissance?**

- ▶ **What were the consequences of the ninth-century invasions?**

- ▶ **How did conflict shape European development during this period?**

▼ What were the origins of Islam and how did it spread?

In the seventh century c.e. two empires dominated the area today called the Middle East: the Byzantine-Greek-Christian empire and the Sassanid-Persian-Zoroastrian empire. Between the two lay the Arabian peninsula, where a merchant called Muhammad began to have religious visions around 610. By the time he died in 632, all Arabia had accepted his creed of Islam. A century later his followers controlled what is now Syria, Palestine, Egypt, North Africa, Spain, and part of France. This Arabic expansion profoundly affected the development of Western civilization as well as the history of Africa and Asia.

The Arabs

In Muhammad's time Arabia was inhabited by various tribes, many of them Bedouins (BEH-duh-wihnz). These nomadic peoples grazed goats and sheep. The power of the Bedouins came from their fighting skills, and they used horses and camels to travel long distances. Other Arabs lived more settled lives in the southern valleys and coastal towns along the Red Sea, supporting themselves by agriculture and trade. Caravan routes crisscrossed Arabia and carried goods to Byzantium, Persia, and Syria.

For all Arabs, the basic social unit was the clan—a group of blood relations connected through the male line. Clans expected loyalty from their members and in turn provided support and protection. Arabs of all types respected one another's customs, which included observance of family obligations and avoidance of socially unacceptable behavior. In addition, they had certain religious rules and rituals in common. For example, all Arabs kept three months of the year as sacred; during that time fighting stopped so that everyone could attend holy ceremonies in peace. The city of Mecca was the religious center of the Arab world, and fighting was never tolerated there. All Arabs prayed at the Ka'ba (KAH-buh), the sanctuary in Mecca. Within the Ka'ba was a sacred black stone that Arabs believed had fallen from Heaven and was thus the dwelling place of a god. Strong economic links connected all Arab peoples, but what eventually molded the diverse Arab tribes into a powerful political and social unity was the religion based on the teachings of Muhammad.

The Prophet Muhammad

Qur'an The sacred book of Islam.

Except for a few vague remarks in the **Qur'an** (kuh-RAHN), the sacred book of Islam, Muhammad (ca. 571–632) left no account of his life. Arab tradition accepts some of the sacred stories that developed about him as historically true, but those accounts were not written down until about a century after his death. Orphaned at the age of six, Muhammad was raised by his grandfather. As a young man he became a merchant in the caravan trade. Later he entered the service of a wealthy widow, and their subsequent marriage brought him financial independence.

The Qur'an reveals Muhammad to be an extremely devout man, ascetic, self-disciplined, and literate, but not formally educated. He prayed regularly, and when he was about forty, he began to experience religious visions. Unsure for a time about what he should do, Muhammad discovered his mission after a vision in which the angel Gabriel instructed him to preach.

Muhammad's revelations were written down by his followers during his lifetime and organized into chapters, called *sura*, shortly after his death. In 651 Muhammad's third successor arranged to have an official version published. The Qur'an is regarded by Muslims as the direct words of God to his Prophet Muhammad and is therefore especially

Chapter 8
Europe in the Early Middle Ages
198 600–1000

CHAPTER LOCATOR | What were the origins of Islam and how did it spread?

revered. At the same time, other sayings and accounts of Muhammad, which gave advice on matters that went beyond the Qur'an, were collected into books termed *hadith* (huh-DEETH). Muslim tradition (*Sunna*) consists of both the Qur'an and the hadith.

Muhammad's visions ordered him to preach a message of a single God and to become God's prophet, which he began to do in his hometown of Mecca. He gathered followers slowly but he also provoked a great deal of resistance. In 622 he migrated with his followers to Medina, an event termed the *hijra* (hih-JIGH-ruh) that marks the beginning of the Muslim calendar. At Medina, Muhammad was much more successful, gaining converts and working out the basic principles of the faith. That same year, through the Charter of Medina, the first *umma*, or religious and political community, was formed, and it included the local Jewish community. This umma established a precedent for the later protection of Jews under Islam.

In 630 Muhammad returned to Mecca at the head of a large army, and he soon united the nomads of the desert and the merchants of the cities into an umma of *Muslims*, a word meaning those who comply with God's will. The religion itself came to be called Islam, which means "submission to God." The Ka'ba was re-dedicated as a Muslim holy place, and Mecca became the most holy city in Islam.

By the time Muhammad died in 632, Islam prevailed throughout the Arabian peninsula. During the next century one rich province of the old Roman Empire after another

Chapter Chronology

ca. 571–632	Life of the Prophet Muhammad
651	Official version of the Qur'an published
711	Muslim forces defeat Visigothic kingdom
711–720	Muslim conquest of Spain
ca. 760–840	Carolingian Renaissance
768–814	Reign of Charlemagne
800	Imperial coronation of Charlemagne
800–900	Free peasants in western Europe increasingly tied to the land as serfs
843	Treaty of Verdun divides Carolingian kingdom
850–1000	Most extensive Viking voyages and conquests
ca. 900	Establishment of Kievan Rus
911	Vikings establish Normandy
950	Muslim Córdoba is Europe's largest and most prosperous city
1000	Stephen crowned first king of Hungary

Muhammad and the Earlier Prophets Muhammad (center), with his head surrounded by fire representing religious fervor, leads Abraham, Moses, and Jesus in prayer (left). Islamic tradition holds that Judaism, Christianity, and Islam all derive from the religion of Abraham, but humankind had strayed from that faith. Therefore, Muhammad, as "the seal [last] of the prophets," had to transmit God's revelations to humankind. (Bibliothèque nationale de France)

How did the Franks build and govern a European empire?

What were the accomplishments of the Carolingian Renaissance?

What were the consequences of the ninth-century invasions?

How did conflict shape European development during this period?

came under Muslim domination—first Syria, then Egypt, and then all of North Africa (Map 8.1). Long and bitter wars (572–591, 606–630) between the Byzantine and Persian Empires left both so weak and exhausted that they easily fell to Muslim attack.

The Teachings and Expansion of Islam

Muhammad's religion eventually attracted great numbers of people, partly because of the straightforward nature of its doctrines. The strictly monotheistic theology outlined in the Qur'an has only a few central tenets: Allah, the Arabic word for God, is all-powerful and all-knowing. Muhammad, Allah's prophet, preached his word and carried his message. Muhammad described himself as the successor both of the Jewish patriarch Abraham and of Christ, and he claimed that his teachings replaced theirs. He invited and won converts from Judaism and Christianity.

Because Allah is all-powerful, believers must submit themselves to him. All Muslims have the obligation of the *jihad* (jee-HAHD), to strive or struggle to lead a virtuous life and to spread God's rule and law. In some cases, jihad, which literally means "self-exertion," is individual against sin; in others it is social and communal and could involve armed conflict, though this is not an essential part of jihad. Jihad is closely related to the central feature of Muslim doctrine, the coming Day of Judgment. Muslims believe that the Day of Judgment will come; consequently, all of a Muslim's thoughts and actions should be oriented toward the Last Judgment and the rewards of Heaven.

To merit the rewards of Heaven, a person must follow the strict code of moral behavior that Muhammad prescribed. The Muslim must recite a profession of faith in God and in Muhammad as God's prophet. The believer must pray five times a day, fast and pray

Map 8.1 **The Spread of Islam, 622–900** The rapid expansion of Islam in a relatively short span of time testifies to the Arabs' superior fighting skills, religious zeal, and economic organization as well as to their enemies' weaknesses.

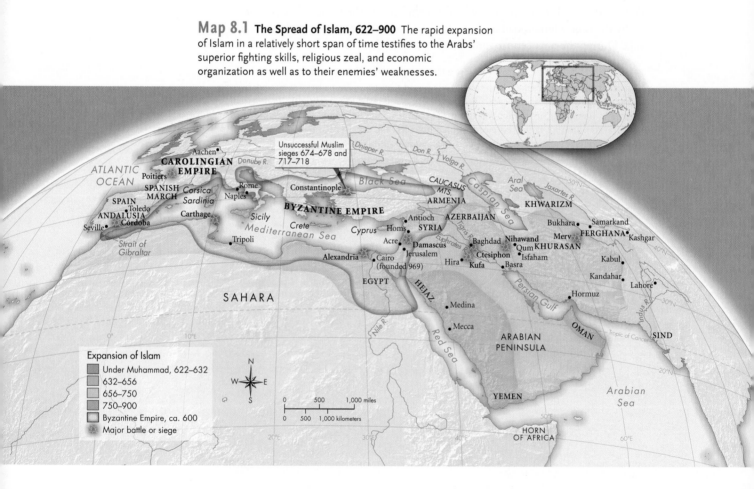

Chapter 8
Europe in the Early Middle Ages
200   **600–1000**

CHAPTER LOCATOR   What were the origins of Islam and how did it spread?

during the sacred month of Ramadan, and contribute alms to the poor and needy. If possible, the believer must make a pilgrimage to Mecca once during his or her lifetime. According to the Muslim shari'a (shuh-REE-uh), or sacred law, these five practices—the profession of faith, prayer, fasting, giving alms to the poor, and pilgrimage to Mecca—constitute the Five Pillars of Islam.

The Qur'an forbids alcoholic beverages and gambling. It condemns business usury—that is, lending money at interest rates or taking advantage of market demand for products by charging high prices for them. A number of foods, such as pork, are also forbidden, a dietary regulation adopted from the Mosaic law of the Hebrews.

Polygyny, the practice of men having more than one wife, was common in Arab society before Muhammad, though for economic reasons the custom was limited to the well-to-do. The Qur'an limited the number of wives a man could have. The Qur'an also sets forth a strict sexual morality and condemns immoral behavior on the part of men as well as women.

With respect to matters of property, Muslim women of the early Middle Ages had more rights than Western women. For example, a Muslim woman retained complete jurisdiction over one-third of her property when she married and could dispose of it in any way she wished. Women in most European countries and the United States did not gain these rights until the nineteenth century.

It was the tenets of Islam preached by Muhammad that bound all Arabs together. Despite the clarity and unifying force of Muslim doctrine, however, divisions developed within the Islamic faith within decades of Muhammad's death. Neither the Qur'an nor the hadith gave clear guidance about how successors to Muhammad were to be chosen, but a group of Muhammad's closest followers chose Abu Bakr (uh-BOO BAH-kuhr), who was a close friend of the Prophet and a member of a clan affiliated with the Prophet's clan, as caliph, a word meaning "successor." Another faction backed Ali, Muhammad's cousin and son-in-law, who, they stated, the Prophet had designated as imam, or leader. Ali was chosen as the fourth caliph in 656, but he was assassinated only five years later. His supporters began to assert that he should rightly have been the first caliph and that any caliph who was not a descendant of Ali was a usurper. These supporters of Ali—termed *Shi'ites*—saw Ali and subsequent imams as the divinely inspired leaders of the community. The larger body of Muslims who accepted the first elections—termed *Sunnis*—saw the caliphs as political leaders. Since Islam did not have an organized church and priesthood, the caliphs had an additional function of safeguarding and enforcing the religious law (*shari'a*) with the advice of scholars (*ulama*), particularly the jurists, judges, and scholastics who were knowledgeable about the Qur'an and hadith. After the assassination of Ali, the caliphate passed to members of the Umayyad (oo-MIGH-uhd) clan, who asserted control and brought stability to the growing Muslim empire. They established their capital at Damascus in Syria, and the Muslim faith continued to expand eastward to India and westward across North Africa.

Life in Muslim Spain

In Europe, Muslim political and cultural influence was felt most strongly in the Iberian Peninsula. In 711 a Muslim force crossed the Strait of Gibraltar and easily defeated the weak Visigothic kingdom; by 720 the Muslims controlled most of Spain. A member of the Umayyad dynasty, Abd al-Rahman (AHB-dal-ruh-MAHN) (r. 756–788), established a kingdom in Spain with its capital at Córdoba (KAWR-doh-buh).

Throughout the Islamic world, Muslims used the term al-Andalus to describe the part of the Iberian Peninsula under Muslim control. In the eighth century al-Andalus included the entire peninsula from Gibraltar in the south to the Cantabrian Mountains in the north (see Map 8.1, left). Today we often use the word *Andalusia* (an-duh-LOO-zhuh) to refer especially to southern Spain, but eighth-century Christians throughout

Five Pillars of Islam The five practices Muslims must fulfill according to the shari'a, or sacred law, including the profession of faith, prayer, fasting, giving alms to the poor, and pilgrimage to Mecca.

caliph A successor to Muhammad and a title later used for certain Muslim rulers

al-Andalus The part of the Iberian Peninsula under Muslim control in the eighth century, encompassing most of modern-day Spain.

Muslim Garden in Spain Tranquil gardens such as this one built by Muslim rulers in Granada represented paradise in Islamic culture, perhaps because of the religion's desert origins. Muslim architectural styles shaped those of Christian Spain, and they were later taken to the New World by Spanish conquerors. (Adam Woolfitt/Corbis)

Europe called the peninsula "Moorish Spain" because the Muslims who invaded and conquered it were Moors—Berbers from northwest Africa.

The ethnic term *Moorish* can be misleading, however, because the peninsula was home to sizable numbers of Jews and Christians as well as Muslim Moors. With Muslims, Christians, and Jews trading with and learning from one another and occasionally intermarrying, Moorish Spain and Norman Sicily (see Chapter 9) were the only distinctly pluralistic societies in medieval Europe.

Some scholars believe that the eighth and ninth centuries in Andalusia were an era of remarkable interfaith harmony. Jews in Muslim Spain were generally treated well, and Córdoba became a center of Jewish as well as Muslim learning. Many Christians adopted Arabic patterns of speech and dress and developed an appreciation for Arabic music and poetry. Some Christian women of elite status chose the Muslim practice of veiling their faces in public. Records describe Muslim and Christian youths joining in celebrations and merrymaking.

By 950 Córdoba had a population of about a half million, making it Europe's largest and most prosperous city. Many residents lived in large houses, streets were well-paved and well-lighted, and there was an abundance of fresh water for drinking and bathing. The largest library contained 400,000 volumes, a vast collection, particularly when compared with the largest library in northern Europe at the Benedictine abbey of St. Gall in Switzerland, which had only 600 books.

In Spain, as elsewhere in the Arab world, the Muslims had an enormous impact on agricultural development. They began the cultivation of rice, sugar cane, citrus fruits, dates, figs, eggplants, carrots, and, after the eleventh century, cotton. These crops, together with new methods of field irrigation, provided the population with food products unknown in the rest of Europe. Muslims also brought technological innovations westward, including new kinds of sails and navigational instruments, as well as paper.

Muslim-Christian Relations

What did early Muslims think of Jesus? Jesus is mentioned many times in the Qur'an. He is described as a righteous prophet chosen by God who performed miracles and continued the work of Abraham and Moses, and he was a sign of the coming Day of Judgment. But Muslims held that Jesus was an apostle only, not God, and that people (that is, Christians) who called Jesus divine committed blasphemy (showing contempt for God). Muslims esteemed the Judeo-Christian Scriptures as part of God's revelation, although they believed that the Qur'an superseded them.

Chapter 8
Europe in the Early Middle Ages
202   600–1000

CHAPTER LOCATOR | What were the origins of Islam and how did it spread?

Harvesting Dates This detail from an ivory casket given to a Córdoban prince reflects the importance of fruit cultivation in the Muslim-inspired agricultural expansion in southern Europe in the ninth and tenth centuries. (Louvre/Réunion des Musées Nationaux/Art Resource, NY)

Muslims called Jews and Christians *dhimmis*, or "protected people," because they were "people of the book," that is, the Hebrew Scriptures. Christians and Jews in the areas Muslims conquered were allowed to continue practicing their faith, although they did have to pay a special tax. This toleration was sometimes accompanied by suspicion, however. In Spain, Muslim teachers increasingly feared that close contact with Christians and Jews would lead to Muslim contamination and threaten the Islamic faith. Thus, beginning in the late tenth century, Muslim regulations began to officially prescribe what Christians, Jews, and Muslims could do. A Christian, however much assimilated, remained an infidel. An infidel was an unbeliever, and the word carried a pejorative or disparaging connotation.

infidel A disparaging term used for a person who does not believe in a particular religion.

By about 950 Caliph Abd al-Rahman III (912–961) of the Umayyad Dynasty of Córdoba ruled most of the Iberian Peninsula from the Mediterranean in the south to the Ebro River in the north. Christian Spain consisted of the tiny kingdoms of Castile, León, Catalonia, Aragon, Navarre, and Portugal. Civil wars among al-Rahman's descendants weakened the caliphate, and the small northern Christian kingdoms began to expand southward, sometimes working together. When Christian forces conquered Muslim territory, Christian rulers regarded their Muslim and Jewish subjects as infidels and enacted restrictive measures similar to those in Muslim lands. Christian bishops worried that even a knowledge of Islam would lead to ignorance of essential Christian doctrines, and interfaith contacts declined.

Science and Medicine

Despite growing suspicions on both sides, the Islamic world profoundly shaped Christian European culture in Spain and elsewhere. Toledo, for example, became an important center of learning through which Arab intellectual achievements entered and influenced western Europe. Arabic knowledge of science and mathematics, derived from the Chinese, Greeks, and Hindus, was highly sophisticated. The Muslim mathematician al-Khwarizmi (al-KHWAHR-uhz-mee) (d. 830) wrote the first work in which the word *algebra* is used mathematically. Al-Khwarizmi adopted the Hindu system of numbers (1, 2, 3, 4)

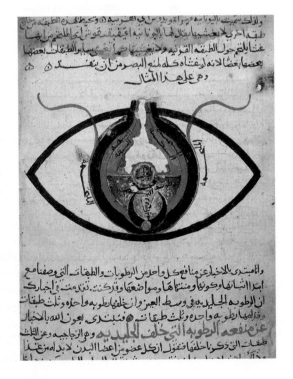

Eye in Muslim Medical Text This illustration of the eye comes from a book on eye diseases written about 1200 in Arabic. The author draws on a long tradition of research into eye diseases in the Muslim world to provide advice to physicians about treatment, including the removal of cataracts. Muslim and Jewish medical practitioners were particularly known for their skills in healing ailments of the eyes, which were common in medieval Europe. (Egyptian Museum Cairo/Gianni Dagli Orti/The Art Archive)

and applied mathematics to problems of physics and astronomy. Scholars in Baghdad translated Euclid's *Elements*, the basic text for plane and solid geometry (see Chapter 4). Muslims also instructed Westerners in the use of the zero, which permitted the execution of complicated problems of multiplication and long division.

Middle Eastern Arabs translated and codified the scientific and philosophical learning of Greek and Persian antiquity. In the ninth and tenth centuries that knowledge was brought to Spain, where between 1150 and 1250 it was translated into Latin. Europeans' knowledge of Aristotle (see Chapter 3) changed the entire direction of European philosophy and theology.

Muslim medical knowledge far surpassed that of the West. By the ninth century Arab physicians had translated most of the treatises of Hippocrates and produced a number of important works of their own. Arabic science reached its peak in the physician, philologist, philosopher, poet, and scientist ibn-Sina of Bukhara (980–1037), known in the West as Avicenna (ah-vuh-SEH-nuh). His *Canon of Medicine* codified all Greco-Arabic medical thought, described the contagious nature of tuberculosis and the spreading of diseases, and listed 760 pharmaceutical drugs.

Unfortunately, many of these treatises came to the West as translations from Greek to Arabic and then to Latin; they inevitably lost a great deal in translation. Nevertheless, in the ninth and tenth centuries Arabic knowledge and experience in anatomy and pharmaceutical prescriptions much enriched Western knowledge.

▼ How did the Franks build and govern a European empire?

Several centuries before the Muslim conquest of Spain, the Frankish king Clovis converted to Roman Christianity and established a large kingdom in what had been Roman Gaul (see Chapter 7). Though at that time the Frankish kingdom was simply one barbarian kingdom among many, it grew to become the most important state in Europe, expanding to become an empire.

The Merovingians

Clovis established the Merovingian dynasty in the late fifth century (see Chapter 7), and under Clovis the Frankish kingdom included much of what is now France and a large section of southwestern Germany. At his death, the kingdom was divided among his four sons. In the centuries that followed, Merovingian Gaul was wracked by civil wars, chronic violence, and political instability as Clovis's descendants fought among themselves. So brutal and destructive were these wars that the term *Dark Ages* was at one time used to designate the entire Merovingian period. Now historians point to creativity in this era as well as violence, and note that even the civil wars did not threaten the Merovingian royal family, as the conflicts were led by family members rather than outsiders trying to gain the throne.

Merovingian rulers had multiple sources of income. These included revenues from the royal estates and the "gifts" of subject peoples. New lands might be conquered and confiscated, and they served to replace lands donated as monastic or religious endowments. All free landowners paid a land tax, although some landowners gradually gained immunity from doing so. Tolls and customs duties on roads, bridges, and waterways (and the goods transported over them) and fines imposed for criminal offenses also yielded income. As with the Romans, the minting of coins was a royal monopoly, with drastic penalties for counterfeiting.

Chapter 8
Europe in the Early Middle Ages
204   **600–1000**

CHAPTER LOCATOR   What were the origins of Islam and how did it spread?

Merovingian Army This sixth- or seventh-century ivory depicts a nobleman in civilian dress followed by seven warriors. The power of the Frankish aristocracy rested on such private armies. Here the soldiers carry spears and bows and arrows, but iron swords were also common weapons. (Rheinisches Landesmuseum, Trier)

The Franks also adapted some of their offices and units of government from the Romans. For example, the basis of the administrative system in the Frankish kingdom was the civitas — Latin for a city and surrounding territory — similar to the political organization of the Roman Empire. A comites (KOH-mih-tehs) — senior official or royal companion, later called a count — presided over the civitas, as had governors in Rome. Many comites came from families that had been administrators in Roman Gaul. They were usually native to the regions they administered and knew their areas well. Frankish royal administration involved another official, the *dux* (dooks) or duke. He was a military leader, commanding troops in the territory of several civitas, and thus responsible for all defensive and offensive strategies. Clovis and his descendants also issued capitularies — Roman-style administrative and legislative orders — in an attempt to maintain order in Merovingian society.

Within the royal household, Merovingian politics provided women with opportunities, and some queens not only influenced but occasionally also dominated events. Because the finances of the kingdom were merged with those of the royal family, queens often had control of the royal treasury just as more ordinary women controlled household expenditures. The status of a princess or queen also rested on her diplomatic importance, with her marriage sealing, or divorce breaking, an alliance; on her personal relationship with her husband and her ability to give him sons and heirs; and on her role as the mother and guardian of princes who had not reached legal adulthood.

Merovingian rulers and their successors led peripatetic lives, traveling constantly to check up on local administrators and peoples. Merovingian kings also relied on the comites and bishops to gather and send local information to them. The court or household of Merovingian kings included scribes who kept records, legal officials who advised the king on matters of law, and treasury agents responsible for aspects of royal finance. These officials could all read and write Latin. Over them all presided the mayor of the palace, the most important secular figure after the king, who governed the palace and the kingdom in the king's absence. Mayors were usually from one of the great aristocratic families, which increasingly through intermarriage blended Frankish and Roman elites. These families possessed landed wealth and they often had rich and lavish lifestyles.

civitas The city and surrounding territory that served as a basis of the administrative system in the Frankish kingdoms, based on Roman models.

comites A senior official or royal companion, later called a count, who presided over the civitas.

How did the Franks build and govern a European empire?   What were the accomplishments of the Carolingian Renaissance?   What were the consequences of the ninth-century invasions?   How did conflict shape European development during this period?

205

The Rise of the Carolingians

From this aristocracy one family gradually emerged to replace the Merovingian dynasty. The rise of the Carolingians—whose name comes from the Latin *Carolus*, or Charles, the name of several important members of the family—rests on several factors. First, the Carolingian Pippin I (d. 640) acquired the powerful position of mayor of the palace and passed the title on to his heirs. Although the mayor of the palace was technically employed by the ruling family, the Carolingians would use their influential position to win support for themselves and eventually subvert Merovingian authority. Second, a series of advantageous marriage alliances brought the family estates and influence in different parts of the Frankish world. This provided the Carolingians with landed wealth and treasure with which to reward their allies and followers. Third, military victories over supporters of the Merovingians gave the Carolingians a reputation for strength and ensured their dominance. Pippin I's great-grandson, Charles Martel (r. 714–741) waged war successfully against the Saxons, Frisians, Alamanni, and Bavarians, which further enhanced the family's prestige. In 732 Charles Martel defeated a Muslim force near Poitiers (pwah-tee-AY) in central France. Charles Martel and later Carolingians used this victory to enhance their reputation, portraying themselves as defenders of Christendom against the Muslims.

Saint Boniface The top of this illustration from an early eleventh-century Fulda Mass book shows St. Boniface baptizing. The bottom panel shows his death scene, with the saint protecting himself with a Gospel book. The fluttering robes are similar to those in earlier Anglo-Saxon books, probably modeled on illustrations in books that Boniface brought to Fulda Abbey from England. (Stadtsbibliothek Bamberg, Ms. Lit. I, fol. 126v)

The battle of Poitiers helped the Carolingians acquire the support of the church, perhaps their most important asset. Charles Martel and his son Pippin III (r. 751–768) further strengthened their ties to the church by supporting the work of Christian missionaries. The most important of these missionaries was the Englishman Boniface (BAH-nuh-fays) (680–754), who had close ties to the Roman pope. As they preached, baptized, and established churches, missionaries like Boniface included the Christian duty to obey secular authorities as part of their message, thus extending to Frankish rulers the church's support of secular power that had begun with Constantine (see Chapter 7).

As mayor of the palace, Charles Martel had exercised the power of king of the Franks. His son Pippin III aspired to the title as well as the powers. Pippin's diplomats were able to convince an embattled Pope Zacharias to declare that Pippin should be king in exchange for military support against the Lombards, who were threatening the papacy. Chilperic, the last Merovingian ruler, was consigned to a monastery. An assembly of Frankish magnates elected Pippin king, and Boniface anointed him. When in 754 Lombard expansion again threatened the papacy, Pope Stephen II journeyed to the Frankish kingdom seeking help. On this occasion, he personally anointed Pippin with the sacred oils and gave him the title "Patrician of the Romans." Pippin promised restitution of the papal lands and later made a gift of estates in central Italy.

Chapter 8
Europe in the Early Middle Ages
206   600–1000

CHAPTER LOCATOR   What were the origins of Islam and how did it spread?

Because of his anointment, Pippin's kingship took on a special spiritual and moral character. Prior to Pippin only priests and bishops had received anointment. Pippin became the first to be anointed with the sacred oils and acknowledged as *rex et sacerdos* (reks et SAHK-ehr-dohs), meaning king and priest. By having himself anointed, Pippin cleverly eliminated possible threats to the Frankish throne by other claimants, and the pope promised him support in the future. An important alliance had been struck between the papacy and the Frankish monarchs. When Pippin died, his son Charles the Great (r. 768–814), generally known as Charlemagne, succeeded him.

The Warrior-Ruler Charlemagne

Charlemagne's adviser and friend Alcuin (ca. 735–804; see page 212) wrote that "a king should be strong against his enemies, humble to Christians, feared by pagans, loved by the poor and judicious in counsel and maintaining justice."[1] Charlemagne worked to realize that ideal in all its aspects. Through brutal military expeditions that brought wealth and by peaceful travel, personal appearances, and the sheer force of his personality, Charlemagne sought to awe newly conquered peoples and rebellious domestic enemies.

If an ideal king was "strong against his enemies" and "feared by pagans," Charlemagne more than met the standard. His reign was characterized by constant warfare; according to the chroniclers of the time, only seven years between 714 and 814 were peaceful. In continuing the expansionist policies of his ancestors, Charlemagne fought more than fifty campaigns and became the greatest warrior of the early Middle Ages. He subdued all of the north of modern France, but his greatest successes were in today's Germany, battles he justified as spreading Christianity to pagan peoples. In the course of a bloody thirty-year war against the Saxons, he added most of the northwestern German peoples to the Frankish kingdom. Charlemagne's secretary and biographer Einhard reported that Charlemagne ordered more than four thousand Saxons killed on one day and deported thousands more. Those who surrendered were forced to become Christian, often in mass baptisms. He established bishoprics in areas he had conquered so that church officials and church institutions became important means of imposing Frankish rule.

Charlemagne also achieved spectacular results in the south, incorporating Lombardy into the Frankish kingdom. He ended Bavarian independence and defeated the nomadic Avars, opening eastern Germany for later settlement by Franks. He successfully fought the Byzantine Empire for Venetia, Istria, and Dalmatia and temporarily annexed those areas to his kingdom. Charlemagne's only defeat came at the hands of the Basques of northwestern Spain.

By around 805 the Frankish kingdom included all of northwestern Europe except Scandinavia and Britain (Map 8.2). Not since the Roman emperors of the third century C.E. had any ruler controlled so much of the Western

Map 8.2 Charlemagne's Conquests, ca. 768–814 Though Charlemagne's hold on much of his territory was relatively weak, the size of his empire was not equaled again until the nineteenth-century conquests of Napoleon.

Frankish Kingdom, 768
Areas conquered by Charlemagne
Tributary peoples
Byzantine Empire
811 Date of conquest

world. Other than brief periods under Napoleon and Hitler, Europe would never again see as large a unified state as it had under Charlemagne.

Carolingian Government and Society

Charlemagne's empire was not a state as people today understand that term; it was a collection of peoples and clans. For administrative purposes, Charlemagne divided his entire kingdom into counties based closely on the old Merovingian civitas. Each of the approximately six hundred counties was governed by a count (or in his absence by a viscount) who published royal orders, held courts and resolved legal cases, collected taxes and tolls, raised troops for the army, and supervised maintenance of roads and bridges. As a link between local authorities and the central government, Charlemagne appointed officials called *missi dominici* (mih-see doh-MEH-nee-chee), "agents of the lord king," who checked up on the counts and held courts to handle judicial and financial issues.

▪ PICTURING THE PAST

Charlemagne and His Wife

This illumination from a ninth-century manuscript portrays Charlemagne with one of his wives. Marriage was an important tool of diplomacy for Charlemagne, and he had a number of wives and concubines. (Erich Lessing/Art Resource, NY)

ANALYZING THE IMAGE What does Charlemagne appear to be doing? How would you characterize his wife's reaction?

CONNECTIONS Does this depiction of a Frankish queen match what you've read about Frankish queens? On what accomplishments did a queen's status rest?

To complete this activity online, go to the Online Study Guide at bedfordstmartins.com/mckaywestunderstanding.

Chapter 8
Europe in the Early Middle Ages
208   600–1000

CHAPTER LOCATOR   What were the origins of Islam and how did it spread?

Medieval Plowing Peasants work heavy soil with a hoe and a simple wooden plow pulled by two oxen, from an illustrated encyclopedia written by a Carolingian scholar who had studied under Alcuin at Charlemagne's palace school. Some medieval manuscripts present idealized depictions of rural life, but here the artist captures the hard physical labor involved. (Bildarchiv Preussischer Kulturbesitz/Art Resource, NY)

Considering the size of Charlemagne's empire, the counts and royal agents were few and far between, and the authority of the central government was weak. The abbots and bishops who served as Charlemagne's advisers envisioned a unified Christian society presided over by a king who was responsible for maintaining peace, law, and order and doing justice. This remained a vision, however, not reality. Instead, society was held together by alliances among powerful families, along with dependent relationships cemented by oaths promising faith and loyalty. These were the seeds from which medieval feudalism was to develop.

Family alliances were often cemented by sexual relations, including those of Charlemagne himself. Charlemagne had a total of four legal wives, most from other Frankish tribes, and six concubines. Charlemagne's personal desires certainly shaped his complicated relationships, but the security and continuation of his dynasty and the need for diplomatic alliances were also important motives. Despite all the women, only three of Charlemagne's sons reached adulthood, and only one outlived him. Four surviving grandsons did ensure perpetuation of the family, however, and the marriages themselves linked Charlemagne with other powerful families even in the absence of sons.

In terms of social changes, the Carolingian period witnessed moderate population growth. The highest aristocrats and church officials lived well, with fine clothing and at least a few rooms heated by firewood. Male nobles hunted and managed their estates, while female nobles generally oversaw the education of their children and sometimes inherited and controlled land on their own. Craftsmen and craftswomen on manorial estates manufactured textiles, weapons, glass, and pottery, primarily for local consumption. Sometimes abbeys and manors served as markets; goods were shipped away to towns and fairs for sale; and a good deal of interregional commerce existed. In the towns, artisans and merchants produced and traded luxury goods for noble and clerical patrons. When compared with earlier Roman cities or with Muslim cities of the time, however, Carolingian cities were small; few north of the Alps had more than seven thousand people.

The modest economic expansion benefited townspeople and nobles, but it did not significantly alter the lives of most people, who continued to live in isolated estates and small villages. Here life was precarious. Crops could easily be wiped out by hail, cold, or rain, and transporting food from other areas was impossible. People's diets centered on grain, which was baked into bread, brewed into beer, and especially cooked into gruel. To this were added seasonal vegetables such as peas, cabbage, and onions, and tiny amounts of animal protein, mostly cheese. Clothing and household goods were just as simple, and houses were drafty, smoky, and often shared with animals. Work varied by the season, but at all times of the year it was physically demanding and yielded relatively little. What little there was had to be shared with landowners, who demanded their taxes and rents in the form of crops, animals, or labor.

The Imperial Coronation of Charlemagne

In autumn of the year 800, Charlemagne paid a momentous visit to Rome. Einhard gives this account of what happened:

> *His last journey there [to Rome] was due to another factor, namely that the Romans, having inflicted many injuries on Pope Leo—plucking out his eyes and tearing out his tongue, he had been compelled to beg the assistance of the king. Accordingly, coming to Rome in order that he might set in order those things which had exceedingly disturbed the condition of the Church, he remained there the whole winter. It was at the time that he accepted the name of Emperor and Augustus. At first he was so much opposed to this that he insisted that although that day was a great [Christian] feast, he would not have entered the Church if he had known beforehand the pope's intention.*[2]

For centuries scholars have debated the reasons for the imperial coronation of Charlemagne. Did Charlemagne plan the ceremony in Saint Peter's on Christmas Day, or did he merely accept the title of emperor? What did he have to gain from it? If, as Einhard implies, the coronation displeased Charlemagne, was that because it put the pope in the superior position of conferring power on the emperor? What were Pope Leo's motives in arranging the coronation?

Though final answers will probably never be found, several things seem certain. First, after the coronation Charlemagne considered himself an emperor ruling a Christian people. Through his motto, *Renovatio romani imperi* (Revival of the Roman Empire), Charlemagne was consciously perpetuating old Roman imperial notions while at the same time identifying with the new Rome of the Christian church. Second, Leo's ideas about gender and rule undoubtedly influenced his decision to crown Charlemagne. In 800 the ruler of the Byzantine Empire was the Empress Irene, the first woman to rule Byzantium in her own name, but Leo did not regard her authority as legitimate because she was female. He thus claimed to be placing Charlemagne on a vacant throne. Third, both parties gained: the Carolingian family received official recognition from the leading spiritual power in Europe, and the papacy gained a military protector. Not surprisingly, the Byzantines regarded the papal acts as rebellious and Charlemagne as a usurper. The imperial coronation thus marks a decisive break between Rome and Constantinople.

The coronation of Charlemagne, whether planned by the Carolingian court or by the papacy, was to have a profound effect on the course of German history and on the later history of Europe. In the centuries that followed, German rulers were eager to gain the imperial title and to associate themselves with the legends of Charlemagne and ancient Rome. Ecclesiastical authorities, on the other hand, continually cited the event as proof that the dignity of the imperial crown could be granted only by the pope.

Chapter 8
Europe in the Early Middle Ages

210   600–1000

CHAPTER LOCATOR   What were the origins of Islam and how did it spread?

▼ What were the accomplishments of the Carolingian Renaissance?

As he built an empire through conquest and strategic alliances, Charlemagne also set in motion a cultural revival that had long-lasting consequences. The stimulus he gave to scholarship and learning may, in fact, be his most enduring legacy, although at the time most people continued to live in a world where knowledge was transmitted orally.

The Carolingian Renaissance

In Roman Gaul through the fifth century, the general culture rested on an education that stressed grammar, Greco-Roman works of literature and history, and the legal and medical treatises of the Roman world. Beginning in the seventh and eighth centuries, a new cultural tradition common to Gaul, Italy, the British Isles, and to some extent Spain emerged. This culture was based primarily on Christian sources. Scholars have called the new Christian and ecclesiastical culture of the period from about 760 to 840, and the educational foundation on which it was based, the "Carolingian Renaissance" because Charlemagne was its major patron.

Charlemagne directed that every monastery in his kingdom should cultivate learning and educate the monks and secular clergy so that they would have a better understanding of the Christian writings. He also urged the establishment of cathedral and monastic schools where boys might learn to read and to pray properly. Thus the main purpose of this rebirth of learning was to promote an understanding of the Scriptures and of Christian writers and to instruct people to pray and praise God in the correct manner.

Women shared with men the work of evangelization and the new Christian learning. Rulers, noblemen, and noble-women founded monasteries for nuns, each governed by an abbess. Women's monasteries housed women who were unmarried, and also often widows; children being taught to read and recite prayers and chants; elderly people seeking a safe place to live; and travelers needing hospitality. Some female houses were, in fact, double monasteries in which the abbess governed two adjoining establishments, one for women and one for men.

In monasteries and cathedral schools, monks, nuns, and scribes copied books and manuscripts and built up libraries. They developed the beautifully clear handwriting known as "Carolingian minuscule," with both uppercase and lowercase letters, from which modern Roman type is derived. Scribes primarily copied Christian works, but also ancient secular literature. Almost all of the works of Roman authors that we are now able to read were preserved by the efforts

Saint Matthew This manuscript illumination shows Saint Matthew hard at work writing the Gospel that bears his name. He is holding a horn with ink in one hand and a quill in the other. Produced around 800 for Ebbo, the archbishop of the Frankish city of Reims, the illustrations in these Gospels seem strikingly modern in their portrayal of human emotion. (Erich Lessing/Art Resource, NY)

of Carolingian scribes. Some scholars went beyond copying to develop their own ideas, and by the middle years of the ninth century there was an outpouring of more sophisticated original works. Ecclesiastical writers imbued with the legal ideas of ancient Rome and the theocratic ideals of Saint Augustine instructed the semi-barbaric rulers of the West.

The most important scholar at Charlemagne's court was Alcuin (al-KYOO-ihn), who came from Northumbria, one of the kingdoms in England. He was the leader of a palace school at Aachen (AH-kehn), where Charlemagne assembled learned men from all over Europe. From 781 until his death, Alcuin was the emperor's chief adviser on religious and educational matters. Alcuin's letters to Charlemagne set forth political theories on the authority, power, and responsibilities of a Christian ruler.

Carolingian Miniscule In the Carolingian period, books played a large role in the spread of Christianity and in the promotion of learning. The development of the clearer script known as Carolingian miniscule shown here made books more legible and more efficient because more words could fit on the page. (The Schoyen Collection MS 076, Schoyen Bede de Tabernaculo, Oslo and London)

Through monastic and cathedral schools, basic literacy in Latin was established among some of the clergy and even among some of the nobility. By the tenth century the patterns of thought and the lifestyles of educated western Europeans were those of Rome and Latin Christianity. Most people, however, continued to live in an oral and visual world. They spoke local languages, which did not have a written form. Christian services continued to be conducted in Latin, but not all village priests were able to attend a school, and many simply learned the service by rote. Thus, the Carolingian Renaissance did not trickle down to ordinary people.

This division between a learned culture of Latin that built on the knowledge of the ancient world and a vernacular culture of local traditions can also be seen in medicine. Christian teaching supported concern for the poor, sick, and downtrodden. Churchmen taught that all knowledge came from God, who had supplied it for people to use for their own benefit. The foundation of a school at Salerno in southern Italy in the ninth century gave a tremendous impetus to medical study. The school's location attracted Arabic, Greek, and Jewish physicians from all over the Mediterranean region.

Despite the advances at Salerno, however, physicians were few in the early Middle Ages, and only the rich could afford them. Local folk medicine practiced by nonprofessionals provided help for commoners, with treatments made from herbs, bark, and other natural ingredients. Infants and children were especially susceptible to a range of illnesses, and about half of the children born died before age five. Although a few people lived into their seventies, most did not, and a person of forty was considered old.

Scholarship and Religious Life in Northumbria

Charlemagne's court at Aachen was not the only center of learning in early medieval Christian Europe. Another was the Anglo-Saxon kingdom of Northumbria. Northumbrian creativity owes a great deal to the intellectual curiosity and collecting zeal of Saint Benet Biscop (ca. 628–689), who brought manuscripts and other treasures back from Italy. These formed the library on which much later study rested.

Northumbrian monasteries produced scores of books: missals (used for the celebration of the Mass); psalters (SAL-tuhrs), which contained the 150 psalms and other prayers used

Chapter 8
Europe in the Early Middle Ages
212   600–1000

CHAPTER LOCATOR | What were the origins of Islam and how did it spread?

THE FINEST REPRESENTATIVE OF NORTHUMBRIAN, and indeed all Anglo-Saxon, scholarship is Bede (ca. 673–735). He was born into a noble family, and when he was seven his parents gave him to Benet Biscop's monastery at Wearmouth to become a monk (see page 269). Later he was sent to the new monastery at Jarrow five miles away. Surrounded by the hundreds of pagan and Christian books Benet Biscop had brought from Italy, Bede spent the rest of his life there, studying and writing. He wrote textbooks on grammar and writing designed to help students master the intricacies of Latin, commentaries on the Old and New Testaments, historical works relating the lives of abbots and the development of the church, and scientific works on time. His biblical commentaries survive in hundreds of manuscripts, indicating that they were widely studied throughout the Middle Ages. His doctrinal works led him to be honored after his death with the title "Venerable," and centuries after his death to be named a "doctor of the church" by the pope.

Bede's religious writings were actually not that innovative, but his historical writings were, particularly his best-known work, the *Ecclesiastical History of the English People*, written about 720. The book is just what its title says it is: an *ecclesiastical* history, in which Bede's main topic is the growth of Christianity in England. It begins with a short discussion of Christianity in Roman Britain, then skips to Augustine of Canterbury's mission to the Anglo-Saxons (see page 187). Most of the book tells the story of Christianity's spread from one small kingdom in England to another, with missionaries and the kings who converted to Christianity as its heroes, and ends with Bede's own day. Bede searched far and wide for his information, discussed the validity of his evidence, compared various sources, and exercised critical judgment. He includes accounts of miracles, but, like the stories of valiant missionaries, these are primarily related to provide moral lessons, which all medieval writers thought was the chief purpose of history.

One of the lessons that Bede sought to tell with history is that Christianity should be unified, and one feature of the *Ecclesiastical History of the English People* inadvertently provided a powerful model for this. In his history, Bede adopted a way of reckoning time proposed by an earlier monk that would eventually provide a uniform chronology for all Christians. He dated events from the incarnation of Christ, rather than from the foundation of the city of Rome, as the Romans had done, or the years of kings' reigns, as the Germans did. His history was recopied by monks in many parts of Europe, who used this dating method, *anno Domini*, "in the year of the Lord" (later abbreviated A.D.), for their own histories as well. (Though Bede does talk about "before the time of the incarnation of our Lord," the reverse dating system of B.C., "before Christ," does not seem to have been widely used before 1700.) Disputes about whether the year began with the incarnation

A manuscript portrait of Bede, with the Holy Spirit in the form of a dove whispering in his ear, a symbol of divine inspiration. There are no contemporary descriptions of Bede, so this later medieval artist was free to imagine what he looked like. (Bodleian Library, University of Oxford, Ms Digby 20, folio 194r)

(that is, the conception) of Christ or his birth, and whether these occurred in 1 B.C. or 1 A.D. (the Christian calendar does not have a year zero) continued after Bede, but his method triumphed.

QUESTIONS FOR ANALYSIS

1. How do the career and accomplishments of Bede fit with the notion of an early medieval "renaissance" of learning?
2. Does Bede's notion that history has a moral purpose still shape the writing of history? Do you agree with him?
3. The Christian calendar dates from a midpoint rather than from a starting point the way many of the world's calendars do. What advantages does this create in reckoning time? What would you see as the primary reason the Christian calendar has now been widely adopted worldwide?

by the monks in their devotions; commentaries on the Scriptures; illuminated manuscripts; law codes; and collections of letters and sermons. (See "Individuals in Society: The Venerable Bede," page 213.) The finest product of Northumbrian art is probably the Gospel book produced at Lindisfarne (LIHN-duhs-fahrn) monastery around 700. The book was produced by a single scribe working steadily over a period of several years, with the expenses involved in the production of such a book probably supplied by the monastery's aristocratic patrons.

As in Charlemagne's empire, women were important participants in Northumbrian Christian culture. Perhaps the most important abbess of the early medieval period anywhere in Europe was Saint Hilda (d. 680). A noblewoman of considerable learning and

Nuns and Learning In this tenth-century manuscript, the scholar Saint Aldhelm offers his book *In Praise of Holy Virgins* to a group of nuns, one of whom already holds a book. Early medieval nuns and monks spent much of their time copying manuscripts, preserving much of the learning of the classical world as well as Christian texts. (His Grace the Archbishop of Canterbury and the Trustees of Lambeth Palace Library. MS 200, fol. 68v)

administrative ability, she ruled the double monastery of Whitby on the Northumbrian coast, advised kings and princes, and encouraged scholars and poets. As was discussed in Chapter 7, Hilda played a key role in the adoption of Roman practices by Anglo-Saxon churches.

At about the time the monks at Lindisfarne were producing their Gospel book, another author was probably at work on a nonreligious epic poem, *Beowulf* (BAY-uh-woolf). The poem tells the story of the hero Beowulf's progress from valiant warrior to wise ruler: first he fights and kills the monster Grendel and Grendel's mother, and later in life he slays a dragon that was threatening his people, dying in the process. In contrast to most writings of this era, which were in Latin, *Beowulf* was written in the vernacular Anglo-Saxon. The identity of its author (or authors) is unknown, but it was written in Christian England, and the author might have been a Northumbrian monk. All the events of the tale take place in (an imagined) pagan Denmark and Sweden, however, suggesting the close relationship between England and the northern European continent in the early Middle Ages.

▼ What were the consequences of the ninth-century invasions?

Charlemagne left his vast empire to his sole surviving son, Louis the Pious (r. 814–840), who attempted to keep the empire intact. This proved to be impossible. Members of the nobility engaged in plots and open warfare against the emperor, often allying themselves with one of Louis's three sons. In 843, shortly after Louis's death, those sons agreed to the Treaty of Verdun (vehr-DUHN), which divided the empire into three parts: Charles the Bald received the western part; Lothar the middle and the title of emperor; and Louis the eastern part, from which he acquired the title "the German." Though no one knew it at the time, this treaty set the pattern for political boundaries in Europe that has been maintained until today.

After the Treaty of Verdun, continental Europe was fractured politically. All three kingdoms controlled by the sons of Louis the Pious were torn by domestic dissension and disorder. The frontier and coastal defenses erected by Charlemagne and maintained by Louis the Pious were neglected. No European political power was strong enough to put up effective resistance to external attacks. Beginning around 850 three main groups began relentless attacks on Europe: Vikings from Scandinavia, representing the final wave of Germanic migrants; Muslims from the Mediterranean; and Magyars forced westward by other peoples (Map 8.3).

Treaty of Verdun Treaty signed in 843 by Charlemagne's grandsons dividing the Carolingian empire into three parts and setting the pattern for political boundaries in Europe still in use today.

The Treaty of Verdun, 843

Vikings in Western Europe

From Scotland to Sicily, there arose in the ninth century the prayer, "Save us, O God, from the violence of the Northmen." The Northmen, also known as Vikings, were Germanic peoples from the area of modern-day Norway, Sweden, and Denmark who had remained beyond the sway of the Christianizing influences of the Carolingian Empire.

Propelled either by oars or by sails, deckless, and about sixty-five-feet long, a Viking ship could carry between forty and sixty men—enough to harass an isolated monastery or village. Using such ships, the Vikings moved swiftly,

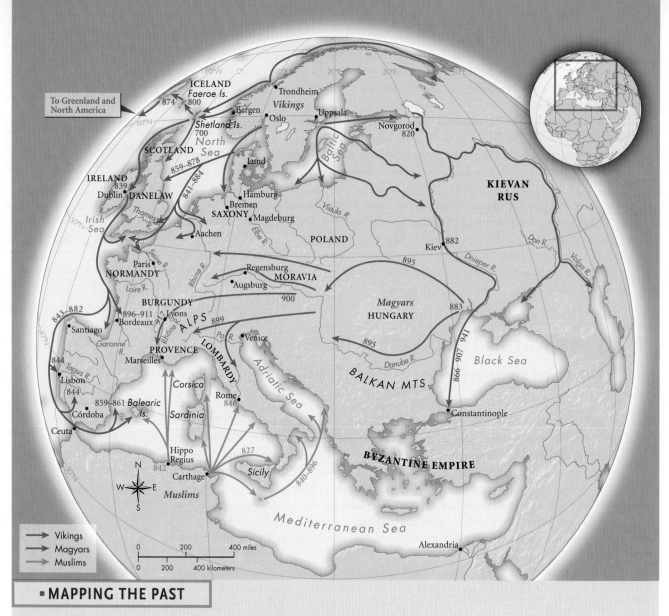

Map 8.3 Invasions and Migrations of the Ninth Century
This map shows the Viking, Magyar, and Arab invasions and migrations in the ninth century. Compare it with Map 7.3 (page 180) on the barbarian migrations of late antiquity to answer the following questions.

ANALYZING THE MAP What similarities do you see in the patterns of migration in these two periods? What significant differences?

CONNECTIONS How did Viking expertise in shipbuilding and sailing make their migrations different from those of earlier Germanic tribes? How did this set them apart from the Magyar and Muslim invaders of the ninth century?

To complete this activity online, go to the Online Study Guide at bedfordstmartins.com/mckaywestunderstanding.

attacked, and escaped to return again. The Carolingian Empire, with no navy, was helpless.

Scholars disagree about the reasons for Viking attacks and migrations. A very unstable Danish kingship and disputes over the succession led to civil war and disorder, which may have driven warriors abroad in search of booty and supporters. The population of Scandinavia may have grown too large for the available land to support. Cities on the coasts of northern Europe offered targets for plunder. Goods plundered could

Animal Head Post from Viking Ship Skilled woodcarvers produced ornamental heads for posts on ships, sledges, wagons, and bedsteads. The fearsome quality of many carvings suggests that they were intended to ward off evil spirits and to terrify. (© Museum of Cultural History—University of Oslo, Norway)

then be sold, and looting raids turned into trading ventures. Some scholars assert that the Vikings were looking for trade and new commercial contacts from the beginning.

Whatever the motivations, Viking attacks were savage. The Vikings burned, looted, and did extensive property damage. They seized magnates and high churchmen and held them for ransom; they also demanded tribute from kings. In 844–845 Charles the Bald had to raise seven thousand pounds of silver. Across the English Channel Anglo-Saxon rulers collected a land tax, the Danegeld, to buy off the Vikings. In the Seine and Loire Valleys the frequent presence of Viking war bands seems to have had economic consequences, stimulating the production of food and wine and possibly the manufacture (for sale) of weapons and the breeding of horses.

The slave trade represented an important part of Viking plunder and commerce. Slaves, known as *thralls*, were common in Scandinavian society, and Vikings took people from the British Isles and territories along the Baltic Sea as part of their booty. They sold them as slaves in the markets of Dublin and Magdeburg, at the fairs of Lyons, and in seaports of the Muslim world.

In the early tenth century Danish Vikings besieged Paris with fleets of more than a hundred highly maneuverable ships, and the Frankish king Charles the Simple bought them off in 911 by giving them a large part of northern France. There the Vikings established the province of "Northmanland," or Normandy as it was later known, intermarrying with the local population and creating a distinctive Norman culture. From there they sailed around Spain and into the Mediterranean, eventually conquering Sicily from the Muslim Arabs in 1060–1090, while other Normans crossed the English Channel, defeating Anglo-Saxon forces in 1066. Between 850 and 1000 Viking control of northern Europe reached its zenith. Norwegian Vikings moved farther west than any Europeans had before, establishing permanent settlements on Iceland and short-lived settlements in Greenland and Newfoundland in what is now Canada. (See "Listening to the Past: Eirik's Saga," page 218.)

The Vikings made positive contributions to the areas they settled. They carried their unrivaled knowledge of shipbuilding and seamanship everywhere. The northeastern and central parts of England where the Vikings settled became known as the *Danelaw* because Danish, not English, law and customs prevailed there. Scholars believe that some legal institutions, such as the ancestor of the modern grand jury, originated in the Danelaw. Exports from Ireland included iron tools and weapons manufactured there by Viking metalsmiths.

Slavs and Vikings in Eastern Europe

Vikings also brought change in eastern Europe, which was largely populated by Slavs. In antiquity the Slavs lived in central Europe. With the start of the mass migrations of the late Roman Empire, the Slavs moved in different directions and split into what later historians identified as three groups: West, South, and East Slavs.

LISTENING TO THE PAST

Eirik's Saga

Sturdy Viking ships sailed throughout the seas of northern Europe in the ninth century, and in 860 reached Iceland, where a few Irish monks who had crossed the sea in skin boats lived in isolated huts. Thousands of settlers followed, and by 930 Iceland had a population of about thirty thousand. It had few natural resources and depended on trade, exporting wool and sheepskins in exchange for grain, timber, and many other products. It also exported poetry, for the Icelanders developed a rich oral tradition of stories about kings, heroes, and ordinary people, known as sagas, which were written down in the twelfth to fourteenth centuries.

The sagas — full of violence, jealousy, sex, and ambition — relate events that happened in the first generations after Iceland was settled. These include the settlement of Greenland in the 980s by Eirik the Red and the establishment of two villages on its west coast. Here the Vikings came into contact with indigenous Inuit people, who they called Skraelings. Further westward sailing brought them to the coast of Canada, which they named Vinland because of wild grapes or grapelike vines growing there. They established a village at what is now l'Anse aux Meadows on Newfoundland, and perhaps in other places along the Canadian coast. These North American settlements were inhabited for only a short time, however, and in the fourteenth century, with worsening climate, the Greenland settlements were abandoned as well.

The voyages to Vinland are described in two sagas, but for centuries these were discounted as myth, one of the many legends contained in sagas. Archaeological finds in the 1960s proved that the Vikings really were in Newfoundland, although debates continue about the location of various landscape features mentioned in the sagas. There is no debate that the sagas present a vivid picture of the men and women who sailed and settled the northern seas, as well as brief glimpses of the people they encountered.

❝ There was a man called Thorvald, who was the father of Eirik the Red. He and Eirik left their home [in Norway] because of some killings and went to Iceland. . . . Eirik's slaves started a landslide that destroyed the farm of a man called Valthjof, so Eyjolf Saur, one of Valthjof's kinsmen, killed the slaves. . . . For this Eirik killed Eyjolf Saur . . . Eyjolf's kinsmen took action over his killing, and Eirik was banished.

[After killing several more people in disagreements over property, Eirik was sentenced to outlawry, and set out from Iceland in search of land he had heard about.] He put out to sea past Snaefells Glacier . . . and in the spring went to Eiriksfjord [in Greenland], where he decided to make his home. That summer he explored the wilderness to the west and gave names to many landmarks there. [The next] summer Eirik set off to colonize the country he had discovered; he named it *Greenland*, for he said that people would be much more tempted to go there if it had an attractive name. . . .

Eirik was married to a woman called Thjodhild, and had two sons, Thorstein and Leif; they were both promising young men. . . . Leif sailed to Norway, [and on sailing back to Greenland] ran into prolonged difficulties at sea, and finally came upon lands whose existence he had never suspected. There were fields of wild wheat growing there, and vines, and among the trees there were maples. They took some samples of all these things. . . .

[The next year] there was great discussion at Brattahild [Eirik's farm in Greenland] about going in search of Vinland, where, it was said, there was excellent land to be had. The outcome was that Thorfinn Karlsefni [Leif's brother-in-law] and Snorri Thorbrandsson prepared their ship and made ready to search for Vinland that summer. . . . Altogether there were 160 people taking part in this expedition. [They sailed west and after sighting land] unloaded their ships and settled down [in this place], which they named Straumfjord. They had brought with them livestock of all kinds and they looked around for natural produce. . . . They stayed there that winter, which turned out to be a very severe one. . . . [In the spring] they sailed south for a long time and eventually came to a river that flowed down into a lake and from the lake into the sea. . . . [H]ere they found wild wheat growing in fields on all the low ground and grape vines on all the higher ground. . . . They stayed there for a fortnight, enjoying themselves and noticing nothing untoward. They had their livestock with them. But early one morning as they looked around they caught sight of nine skin-boats. The men in them were waving sticks which made a noise like flails . . . then they rowed away south round the headland. . . .

They stayed there that winter. There was no snow at all, and all the livestock were able to fend for themselves. Then early one morning in spring, they saw a great horde of skin-boats approaching from the south, so dense it looked as if the estuary were strewn with charcoal; and the sticks were being waved from every boat. Karlsefni's men raised their shields and the two parties began to trade. What the natives wanted most to buy was red cloth; they also wanted to buy swords and spears, but Karlsefni and Snorri forbade that. In exchange for the cloth they traded grey fur pelts. [Several weeks later] Karlsefni's men saw a huge number of boats coming in from the south, pouring in like a torrent. There was a fierce battle and a hail of missiles came flying over, for the Skraelings were using catapults. This terrified Karlsefni and his men so much that their only thought was to flee, and they retreated farther up the river. They did not halt

Chapter 8
Europe in the Early Middle Ages

218   600–1000

CHAPTER LOCATOR | What were the origins of Islam and how did it spread?

A reconstruction of a Viking ship sails in the English Channel. (© Reuters/Corbis)

until they reached some cliffs, where they prepared to make a resolute stand.

Freydis [the daughter of Eirik the Red, who was on the expedition with her husband] came out and saw the retreat. She shouted, "Why do you flee from such pitiful wretches, brave men like you? You should be able to slaughter them like cattle. If I had weapons, I am sure I could fight better than any of you."

The men paid no attention to what she was saying. Freydis tried to join them but could not keep up because she was pregnant. She was following them into the woods when the Skraelings closed in on her. In front of her lay a dead man, Thorbrand Snorrason, with a flintstone buried in his head, and his sword beside him. She snatched up the sword and prepared to defend herself. When the Skraelings came rushing toward her she pulled one of her breasts out of her bodice and slapped it with the sword. The Skraelings were terrified at the sight of this and fled back to their boats and hastened away. Karlsefni and his men came over to her and praised her for her courage. . . .

Karlsefni and his men had realized by now that although the land was excellent they could never live there in safety or freedom from fear, because of the native inhabitants. So they made ready to leave the place and return home. . . . They returned to Straumfjord and spent the third winter there. But now quarrels broke out frequently; those who were unmarried kept pestering the married men. . . .

They set sail before a southerly wind and reached Markland, where they came upon five Skraelings — a bearded man, two women, and two children. Karlsefni and his men captured the two boys, but the others got away. . . . They took the boys with them and taught them the language, and baptized them. . . . Finally they reached Greenland, and spent the winter with Eirik the Red. ❯❯

Source: *The Vinland Sagas: The Norse Discovery of America*, translated with an Introduction by Magnus Magnusson and Hermann Pálsson (Penguin Classics, 1965), pp. 76, 77–78, 84, 85–86, 93, 94, 95, 98, 99–100, 102, 103. Copyright © Magnus Magnusson and Hermann Pálsson, 1965. Reproduced by permission of Penguin Books Ltd.

QUESTIONS FOR ANALYSIS

1. As related in the sagas, what factors motivated Eirik the Red and others to travel to new lands?
2. What indication do you find that the Vinland voyages were for settlement rather than simply conquest? What obstacles arose as they proceeded?
3. How does the author of the saga make the Viking encounters with indigenous peoples into a compelling story?

The group labeled the West Slavs included the Poles, Czechs, Slovaks, and Wends. The South Slavs—comprising peoples who became the Serbs, Croats, Slovenes, Macedonians, and Bosnians—migrated southward into the Balkans. In the seventh century Slavic peoples of the west and south created the state of Moravia along the banks of the Danube River. By the tenth century Moravia's residents were Roman Christian, along with most of the other West and South Slavs. The pattern was similar to that of the Germanic tribes: first the ruler was baptized, and then missionaries preached, built churches, and spread Christian teachings among the common people. The ruler of Poland was able to convince the pope to establish an independent archbishopric there in 1000, the beginning of a long-lasting connection between Poland and the Roman church. In the Balkans the Serbs accepted Orthodox Christianity, while the Croats became Roman Christian, a division with a long impact; it was one of the factors in the civil war in this area in the late twentieth century.

Between the fifth and ninth centuries the eastern Slavs moved into the vast areas of present-day European Russia and Ukraine. This enormous area consisted of an immense virgin forest to the north, where most of the eastern Slavs settled, and an endless prairie grassland to the south. In the ninth century the Vikings appeared in the lands of the eastern Slavs. Called "Varangians" (va-RAN-gee-uhnz) in the old Russian chronicles, the Vikings were interested primarily in gaining wealth through plunder and trade. Moving up and down the rivers, they soon linked Scandinavia and northern Europe to the Black Sea and to the Byzantine Empire's capital at Constantinople. They raided and looted the cities along the Caspian Sea several times in the tenth century, taking booty and slaves, which they then sold elsewhere; thus raiding turned into trading, and the Scandinavians later established settlements, intermarried, and assimilated with Slavic peoples.

In order to increase and protect their international commerce and growing wealth, the Vikings declared themselves the rulers of the eastern Slavs. The Varangian ruler Oleg (r. 878–912) established his residence at Kiev in modern-day Ukraine. He and his successors ruled over a loosely united confederation of Slavic territories known as Rus, with its capital at Kiev, until 1054.

Oleg and his clansmen quickly became assimilated into the Slavic population, taking local wives and emerging as the noble class. Missionaries of the Byzantine Empire converted the Vikings and local Slavs to Eastern Orthodox Christianity, accelerating the unification of the two groups. Thus the rapidly Slavified Vikings left two important legacies for the future: in about 900 they created a loose unification of Slavic territories, Kievan Rus, under a single ruling prince and dynasty, and they imposed a basic religious unity by accepting Orthodox Christianity, as opposed to Roman Catholicism, for themselves and the eastern Slavs.

Kievan Rus A confederation of Slavic territories, with its capital at Kiev, ruled by descendants of the Vikings.

Even at its height under Great Prince Iaroslav (YAHR-uh-slahv) the Wise (r. 1019–1054), the unity of Kievan Rus was extremely tenuous. Trade, not government, was the main concern of the rulers. Moreover, the Slavified Vikings failed to find a way to peacefully transfer power from one generation to the next. In early Rus there were apparently no fixed rules, and much strife accompanied each succession. Possibly to avoid such chaos, Great Prince Iaroslav, before his death in 1054, divided Kievan Rus among his five sons, who in turn divided their properties when they died. Between 1054 and 1237, Kievan Rus disintegrated into more and more competing units. The princes divided their land like private property because they thought of it as private property. A prince

Kievan Rus, ca. 1050

owned a certain number of farms or landed estates and had them worked directly by his people, mainly slaves. Outside of these estates, which constituted the princely domain, the prince exercised only limited authority in his principality. Excluding the clergy, two kinds of people lived there: the noble boyars (BOY-ahrz) and the commoner peasants.

The boyars were descendants of the original Viking warriors, and they also held their lands as free and clear private property. Although the boyars normally fought in princely armies, the customary law declared that they could serve any prince they wished. The ordinary peasants were also truly free. They could move at will wherever opportunities were greatest. In a touching phrase of the times, theirs was "a clean road, without boundaries."[3] In short, fragmented princely power, private property, and personal freedom all went together.

boyars Nobles in Russia who were descendants of Viking warriors and held their lands as free and clear private property.

Magyars and Muslims

Groups of central European steppe peoples known as Magyars also raided villages in the late ninth century, taking plunder and captives, and forcing leaders to pay tribute in an effort to prevent further looting and destruction. Moving westward, small bands of Magyars on horseback reached as far as Spain and the Atlantic coast. They subdued northern Italy, compelled Bavaria and Saxony to pay tribute, and even penetrated into the Rhineland and Burgundy.

Magyar forces were defeated by a combined army of Frankish and other Germanic troops at the Battle of Lechfeld near Augsburg in southern Germany in 955, and the Magyars settled in the area that is now Hungary in eastern Europe. Much as Clovis had centuries earlier, the Magyar ruler Géza (GEE-zuh) (r. 970–997), who had been a pagan, became a Roman Christian. This gave him the support of the papacy and offered prospects for alliances with other Roman Christian rulers against the Byzantine Empire, Hungary's southern neighbor. Géza's son Stephen I (r. 997–1038) was officially crowned the king of Hungary by a papal representative on Christmas Day of 1000. Hungary's alliance with the papacy shaped the later history of eastern Europe just as Charlemagne's alliance with the papacy shaped western European history. The Hungarians adopted settled agriculture, wrote law codes, and built towns, and Hungary became an important crossroads of trade for German and Muslim merchants.

The ninth century also saw invasions into Europe from the south. In many ways these were a continuation of the earlier Muslim conquests in the Iberian Peninsula, but now they focused on Sicily and mainland Italy. Muslim attacks on Sicily began in the seventh century, and by the end of the ninth century they controlled most of the island. The Muslims drove northward, sacked Rome in 846, and captured towns along the Adriatic coast almost all the way to Venice. They attacked Mediterranean settlements along the coast of Provence and advanced on land as far as the Alps. In the tenth century Frankish, papal, and Byzantine forces were able to retake much territory, though the Muslims continued to hold Sicily well into the eleventh century.

What was the impact of these invasions? From the perspective of those living in what had been Charlemagne's empire, Viking, Magyar, and Muslim attacks contributed to increasing disorder and violence. Italian, French, and English sources often describe this period as one of terror and chaos. People in other parts of Europe might have had a different opinion, however. In Muslim Spain scholars worked in thriving cities, and new crops such as rice enhanced ordinary people's lives. In eastern Europe states such as Moravia and Hungary became strong kingdoms. A Viking point of view might be the most positive, for by 1100 descendants of the Vikings not only ruled their homelands in Denmark, Norway, and Sweden but they also ruled Normandy, England, Sicily, Iceland, and Kievan Rus, with an outpost in Greenland and occasional voyages to North America.

▼ How did conflict shape European development during this period?

The large-scale division of Charlemagne's empire into three parts in the ninth century led to a decentralization of power at the local level. Civil wars weakened the power and prestige of kings. Likewise, the great invasions, especially those of the Vikings, weakened royal authority. The western Frankish kings were unable to halt the invaders, and the local aristocracy had to assume responsibility for defense. Thus, the great aristocratic families increased their authority in the regions of their vested interests, governing virtually independent territories in which distant and weak kings could not interfere. Common people turned for protection to the strongest power, the local counts, whom they considered their rightful rulers, and free peasants sank to the level of serfs.

Decentralization and the Origins of "Feudalism"

The political power of the Carolingian rulers had long rested on the cooperation of the dominant social class, the Frankish aristocracy. Charlemagne and his predecessors relied on the nobles to help wage wars of expansion and suppress rebellions, and in return these families were given a share of the lands and riches confiscated by the rulers. The most powerful nobles were those able to gain the allegiance of warriors, often symbolized in

Homage and Fealty In this manuscript illumination, a vassal kneels before the lord, places his clasped hands between those of the lord, and declares, "I become your man." Although the rites of entering a feudal relationship varied widely across Europe and sometimes were entirely verbal, we have a few illustrations of them. Sometimes the lord handed over a clump of earth, representing the fief, and the ceremony concluded with a kiss, symbolizing the peace between them. (ONB/Vienna, Picture Archive, Cod. 2262, fol. 174 v.)

Chapter 8
Europe in the Early Middle Ages
222   600–1000

CHAPTER LOCATOR   What were the origins of Islam and how did it spread?

an oath-swearing ceremony that grew out of earlier Germanic oaths of loyalty. In this ceremony a warrior (knight) swore his loyalty as a vassal to the more powerful individual, who became his lord. In return for the vassal's loyalty, aid, and military assistance, the lord promised him protection and material support. This support might be a place in the lord's household but was more likely land that the vassal controlled called a *feudum* or fief (feef). The fief might contain forests, churches, and towns. The fief theoretically still belonged to the lord, and the vassal only had the use of it. Peasants living on a fief produced the food and other goods necessary to maintain the knight.

Though historians debate this, fiefs appear to have been granted extensively first by Charles Martel and then by his successors, including Charlemagne and his grandsons. These fiefs went to their most powerful nobles. As the Carolingians' control of their territories weakened, the practice of granting fiefs moved to the local level, with lay lords, bishops, and abbots as well as kings granting fiefs. This system, later named feudalism, was based on personal ties of loyalty cemented by grants of land rather than on allegiance to an abstract state or governmental system. In some parts of Europe, such as Ireland and the Baltic area, warrior-aristocrats or clan chieftains were the ultimate political authorities; they generally did not grant fiefs to secure loyalty but relied on strictly personal ties. Thus the word *feudal* does not properly apply to these areas.

Feudalism provided some degree of cohesiveness in a society that lacked an adequate government bureaucracy, a sophisticated method of taxation, or even the beginnings of a national consciousness. In fact, because vassals owed administrative as well as military service to their lords, feudalism actually functioned as a way to organize political authority.

Along with granting fiefs to knights, lords gave fiefs to the clergy for spiritual services or promises of allegiance. In addition, the church held pieces of land on its own and granted fiefs to its own knightly vassals. Abbots and abbesses of monasteries, bishops, and archbishops were either lords or vassals in many feudal arrangements.

Women other than abbesses were generally not granted fiefs, but in most parts of Europe daughters could inherit them if their fathers had no sons. Occasionally, women did go through ceremonies swearing homage and fealty and to send fighters when the lord demanded them. More commonly, women acted as surrogates when their husbands were away, defending the territory from attack and carrying out administrative duties.

Feudalism existed at two social levels: at the higher level were the lords of great feudal principalities; below them were their knights, holding fiefs that may have been no larger than a small village with its surrounding land. A wide and deep gap in social standing and political function separated these levels. Far below both of these social levels, and not really part of the system of feudalism at all, were the peasants, who made up the vast majority of the population in medieval Europe.

Manorialism, Serfdom, and the Slave Trade

Most European people in the early Middle Ages were peasants who lived in family groups in villages or small towns. They made their living predominantly by raising crops and animals. The village and the land surrounding it were called a *manor*. Some fiefs might include only one manor, while great lords or kings might have hundreds of manors under their direct control. Residents of manors worked for their lord in exchange for protection, a system that was later referred to as manorialism. Free peasants surrendered themselves and their lands to the lord's jurisdiction. The land was given back, but the peasants became tied to it by various kinds of payments and services. Like feudalism, manorialism involved an exchange. Because the economic power of the warring class rested on landed estates worked by peasants, feudalism and manorialism were inextricably linked.

vassal A warrior who swore loyalty and service to a noble in exchange for land, protection, and support.

fief A piece of land granted by a feudal lord to a vassal in return for service and loyalty.

feudalism A political system in which a vassal was promised protection and material support by a lord in return for his loyalty, aid, and military assistance.

manorialism A system in which residents of manors, or farming villages, provided work and goods for their lord in exchange for protection.

Local custom determined precisely what services villagers would provide to their lord, but certain practices became common throughout Europe. The peasant was obliged to give the lord a percentage of the annual harvest. The peasant paid a fee to marry someone from outside the lord's estate, and another fee to inherit property. Above all, the peasant became part of the lord's permanent labor force.

serfs Peasants bound to the land by a relationship with a feudal lord.

In entering into a relationship with a feudal lord, free farmers lost status. Their position became servile, and they became **serfs**. That is, they were bound to the land and could not leave it without the lord's permission. Serfdom was not the same as slavery in that lords did not own the person of the serf, but serfs were subject to the jurisdiction of the lord's court in any dispute over property and in any case of suspected criminal behavior.

The transition from freedom to serfdom was slow. In the late eighth century there were still many free peasants. And within the legal category of serfdom there were many economic levels, ranging from the highly prosperous to the desperately poor. Nevertheless, a social and legal revolution was taking place. By the year 800 perhaps 60 percent of the population of western Europe had been reduced to serfdom. The ninth-century Viking assaults on Europe created extremely unstable conditions and individual insecurity, increasing the need for protection, accelerating the transition to serfdom, and leading to additional loss of personal freedom.

Though serfdom was not slavery, the Carolingian trade in actual slaves was extensive, generally involving persons captured in war or raids. Many of these were people from eastern Europe who spoke Slavic languages—hence the origin of our word *slave*. Merchants in early medieval towns used slaves to pay the suppliers of the luxury goods their noble and clerical customers desired, most of which came into Europe from the East. Slaves sold across the Mediterranean fetched three or four times the amounts brought within the Carolingian Empire, so most slaves were sold to Muslims. For Europeans and Arabs alike, selling captives and other slaves was standard procedure. Christian moralists sometimes complained about the sale of Christians to non-Christians, but they did not object to slavery itself.

CHAPTER LOCATOR   What were the origins of Islam and how did it spread?

← LOOKING BACK LOOKING AHEAD →

THE CULTURE THAT EMERGED IN EUROPE in the early Middle Ages has justifiably been called the first "European" civilization. While it was by no means civilized by modern standards, it had definite characteristics that were shared across a wide region. Other than in Muslim Spain and the pagan areas of northern and eastern Europe, almost all people were baptized Christians. Everywhere—including Muslim and pagan areas—most people lived in small villages, supporting themselves and paying their obligations to their superiors by raising crops and animals. These villages, increasingly granted to knights in exchange for loyalty and service to a noble lord, were at the core of a feudal society that had little concept of abstract political ideals. The educated elite was infused with Latin ideas and models, for Latin was the common language—written as well as spoken—of educated people in most of Europe.

In the several centuries after 1000, these characteristics—Christianity, village-based agriculture, feudalism, and Latin culture—would not disappear. Historians conventionally term the era from 1000 to about 1300 the "High Middle Ages," but this era was built on a foundation that had already been established. The soaring Gothic cathedrals that were the most glorious architectural feature of the High Middle Ages were often constructed on the footings of early medieval churches, and their walls were built of stones that had once been part of Carolingian walls and castles. Similarly, political structures grew out of the institutions established in the Carolingian period, and later literary and cultural flowerings followed the model of the Carolingian Renaissance in looking to the classical past. Less positive developments also had their roots in the early Middle Ages, including hostilities between Christians and Muslims that would motivate the Crusades and the continued expansion of serfdom and other forms of unfree labor. ■

- **For a list of suggested readings for this chapter, visit** *bedfordstmartins.com/mckaywestunderstanding*.

- **For primary sources from this period, see** *Sources of Western Society,* Second Edition.

- **For Web sites, images, and documents related to topics in this chapter, see Make History at** *bedfordstmartins.com/mckaywestunderstanding*.

How did the Franks build and govern a European empire?

What were the accomplishments of the Carolingian Renaissance?

What were the consequences of the ninth-century invasions?

How did conflict shape European development during this period?

Step 1

GETTING STARTED Below are basic terms about this period in the history of Western civilization. Can you identify each term below and explain why it matters? To do this exercise online, go to bedfordstmartins.com/mckaywestunderstanding.

TERMS	WHO (OR WHAT) AND WHEN	WHY IT MATTERS
Qur'an, p. 198		
Five Pillars of Islam, p. 201		
caliph, p. 201		
al-Andalus, p. 201		
infidel, p. 203		
civitas, p. 205		
comites, p. 205		
Treaty of Verdun, p. 215		
Kievan Rus, p. 220		
boyars, p. 221		
vassal, p. 223		
fief, p. 223		
feudalism, p. 223		
manorialism, p. 223		
serfs, p. 224		

Step 2

MOVING BEYOND THE BASICS The exercise below requires a more advanced understanding of the chapter material. Examine the transition from the ancient period to the Middle Ages by filling in the chart below with descriptions of the most important social, economic, and political developments of the early Middle Ages, dividing the developments you describe between those that are indicative of continuity with the ancient period and those that are indicative of a substantial break with the past. When you are finished, consider the following questions: In what aspects of medieval life do you see the most continuity with the past? In what aspects do you see the most dramatic change? To do this exercise online, go to bedfordstmartins.com/mckaywestunderstanding.

	SOCIAL	ECONOMIC	POLITICAL
Continuity			
Change			

PUTTING IT ALL TOGETHER Now that you've reviewed key elements of the chapter, take a step back and try to see the big picture. Remember to use specific examples from the chapter in your answers. To do this exercise online, go to bedfordstmartins.com/mckaywestunderstanding.

ISLAM

- What are the core teachings of Islam? How do they compare to the core teachings of Christianity and Judaism?
- What kind of society developed in Muslim Spain? How did religious toleration contribute to Muslim Spain's cultural and economic accomplishments?

THE FRANKS

- How did the Franks combine Germanic and Roman institutions in the government of their territories?
- What explains Charlemagne's military and political success? In your opinion, what were the Carolingians' most important long-term contributions to European civilization?

INVASIONS AND MIGRATIONS

- Compare and contrast the invasions and migrations that threatened Europe in the early Middle Ages with those that led to the fall of the Western Roman Empire. What similarities and differences do you note?
- What positive consequences, if any, were there of the ninth-century invasions? What groups and peoples may have benefited from them?

POLITICAL AND ECONOMIC DECENTRALIZATION

- Define feudalism. What circumstances explain its development? Whose interests did it serve?

- What explains the trend in the ninth and tenth centuries toward reduced freedom for Europe's agricultural population? Why did European peasants accept serfdom? What choices did they have?

■ **In Your Own Words** Imagine that you must explain Chapter 8 to someone who hasn't read it. What would be the most important points to include and why?

9

State and Church in the High Middle Ages

1000–1300

The concept of the state had been one of Rome's great legacies to Western civilization, but for almost five hundred years after the disintegration of the Roman Empire in the West, the state as a reality did not exist. Political authority was completely decentralized, with power spread among many feudal lords. The deeply fragmented fiefdoms, kingdoms, and territories that covered the early medieval European continent did not have the characteristics or provide the services of a modern state.

Beginning in the last half of the tenth century, the invasions that had contributed to European fragmentation gradually ended, and domestic disorder slowly subsided. Feudal rulers began to develop new institutions of law and government that enabled them to assert their power over lesser lords and the general population. Centralized states slowly crystallized, first in western Europe, and then in eastern and northern Europe. At the same time, energetic popes built their power within the Western Christian church and asserted their superiority over kings and emperors. A papal call to retake the holy city of Jerusalem led to nearly two centuries of warfare between Christians and Muslims. Christian warriors, clergy, and settlers moved out from western and central Europe in all directions, so that through conquest and colonization border regions were gradually incorporated into a more uniform European culture. ∎

Life in the High Middle Ages. In this thirteenth-century manuscript, knights of King Henry II stab Archbishop Thomas Becket in Canterbury Cathedral in 1170, a dramatic example of church-state conflict. Becket was soon made a saint, and the spot where the murder occurred became a pilgrimage site. (British Library/HIP/Art Resource, NY)

Chapter Preview

▶ How did monarchs try to centralize political power?

▶ How did the administration of law evolve in this period?

▶ What led to conflict between the papacy and secular leaders?

▶ What were the causes and consequences of the Crusades?

▶ How did Christianity spread during the High Middle Ages?

▼ How did monarchs try to centralize political power?

The modern state is an organized territory with definite geographical boundaries, a body of law, and institutions of government. The modern national state counts on the loyalty of the majority of its citizens; in return it provides citizens with order and protection. It supplies a currency or medium of exchange that permits financial and commercial transactions, and it conducts relations with foreign governments. To accomplish these minimal functions, the state must have officials, bureaucracies, laws, courts of law, soldiers, information, and money. This modern concept of state could not exist during the political instability of the early Middle Ages. Boundaries and loyalties were in constant flux. Civil unrest was rampant. Rulers did not have jurisdiction over many people or the income to support a bureaucracy, and their laws affected a relative few. There existed many, frequently overlapping layers of authority—earls, counts, barons, knights—between a king and the ordinary people.

Beginning in the eleventh century medieval rulers worked to promote domestic order, reducing private warfare and civil anarchy. In some parts of Europe lords in control of large territories began to manipulate feudal institutions to build up their power even further, becoming kings over growing and slowly centralizing states. As rulers expanded their territories and extended their authority, they developed larger bureaucracies, armies, judicial systems, and other institutions of state to maintain control. Because these institutions cost money, rulers in various countries initiated systems for generating revenue and handling financial matters. Although some rulers were more successful than others, the solutions they found to these problems laid the foundations for modern national states.

The Bayeux Tapestry Many events in the battles of the eleventh century over who would rule England were recorded in an embroidery panel measuring 231 feet by 19 inches. In this scene, two nobles (center left) and a bishop (center right) acclaim Harold Godwinson as king of England (center). Harold holds a scepter and an orb with a cross on top, symbolizing his secular and religious authority. The embroidery provides an important historical source for the clothing, armor, and lifestyles of the Norman and Anglo-Saxon warrior classes. It is now on display in Bayeux (bay-YUH), France, and it is incorrectly called a "tapestry," a different kind of needlework. (Tapisserie de Bayeux et avec autorisation spéciale de la Ville de Bayeux)

Chapter 9
State and Church in the High

230   **Middle Ages • 1000–1300**

CHAPTER LOCATOR | How did monarchs try to centralize political power?

The Norman Conquest, 1066

England

Throughout the ninth century the Vikings had made a concerted effort to conquer and rule all of Anglo-Saxon England. Because of its proximity to Scandinavia and its lack of unity under a single ruler, England probably suffered more from Viking invasions than any other part of Europe. In 878 Alfred, king of the West Saxons (or Wessex), defeated the Vikings, inaugurating a period of recovery and stability in England. Alfred and his immediate successors built a system of local defenses and slowly extended royal rule beyond Wessex to other Anglo-Saxon peoples until one law, royal law, took precedence over local custom. England was divided into local units called "shires," or counties, each under the jurisdiction of a shire-reeve (a word that soon evolved into "sheriff") appointed by the king. Sheriffs were unpaid officials from well-off families responsible for collecting taxes, law enforcement, and raising infantry.

The Viking invasions of England did not end, however, and the island eventually came under Viking rule. The Viking Canute (kuh-NOOT) (r. 1016–1035) made England the center of his empire while promoting a policy of assimilation and reconciliation between Anglo-Saxons and Vikings. When Canute's heir Edward died childless, there were a number of claimants to the throne of England—the Anglo-Saxon noble Harold Godwinson (ca. 1022–1066), the Norwegian king Harald III (r. 1045–1066), and Duke William of Normandy.

In 1066 the forces of Harold Godwinson crushed an invading Norwegian army in northern England, then quickly marched south when they heard that William had invaded England with his Norman vassals. Harold was decisively defeated by William at the Battle of Hastings—an event now known as the Norman conquest. In both

How did the administration of law evolve in this period? | What led to conflict between the papacy and secular leaders? | What were the causes and consequences of the Crusades? | How did Christianity spread during the High Middle Ages?

231

England and Normandy, William the Conqueror limited the power of his noble vassals and church officials, and he transformed the feudal system into a unified monarchy. In England he replaced Anglo-Saxon sheriffs with Normans. He retained another Anglo-Saxon device, the writ, through which the central government communicated with people at the local level, using the local tongue.

In addition to retaining Anglo-Saxon institutions that served his purposes, William also introduced a major innovation, the Norman inquest or general inquiry. William wanted to determine how much wealth there was in his new kingdom, who held what land, and what land had been disputed among his vassals since the conquest of 1066. Groups of royal officials were sent to every part of the country to gather this information. The resulting record, called the *Domesday Book* from the Anglo-Saxon word *doom*, meaning "judgment," still survives. It is an invaluable source of social and economic information about medieval England.

The *Domesday Book* provided William and his descendants with information vital for the exploitation and government of the country. Knowing the amount of wealth every area possessed, the king could tax accordingly. Knowing the amount of land his vassals had, he could allot knight service fairly. The book helped William and future English kings regard their country as one unit.

William's son Henry I (r. 1100–1135) established a bureau of finance called the Exchequer that became the first institution of the government bureaucracy of England. In addition to various taxes and annual gifts, Henry's income came from money paid to the Crown for settling disputes and as penalties for crimes, as well as money due to him in his private position as feudal lord. Henry, like other medieval kings, made no distinction between his private income and state revenues, though the officials of the Exchequer began to keep careful records of the monies paid into and out of the royal treasury.

Domesday Book A general inquiry about the wealth of his lands ordered by William of Normandy; it is a valuable source of social and economic information about medieval England.

Exchequer The bureau of finance established by Henry I; the first institution of the governmental bureaucracy of England.

Domesday Book William the Conqueror's thorough survey of medieval England, recorded in the massive *Domesday Book*, is an invaluable source of social and economic information. To assess the value of his land, William's officials took note of many forms of economic activity, including beekeeping as shown in the manuscript illumination. (book: The National Archives, UK; beekeeping: © British Library Board)

Chapter 9
State and Church in the High
232   **Middle Ages • 1000–1300**

CHAPTER LOCATOR | How did monarchs try to centralize political power?

In 1128 Henry's daughter Matilda was married to Geoffrey of Anjou; their son became Henry II of England and inaugurated the Angevin (AN-juh-vuhn) dynasty. Henry II inherited the French provinces of Anjou, Normandy, Maine, and Touraine in northwestern France. Then in 1152 he claimed lordship over Aquitaine, Poitou (pwah-TOO), and Gascony in southwestern France through his marriage to the great heiress Eleanor of Aquitaine (Map 9.1). Each of the provinces in Henry's Angevin empire was separate and was only loosely linked to the others by dynastic law and personal oaths. The histories of England and France became closely intertwined, however, leading to disputes and conflicts down to the fifteenth century.

France

France also became increasingly unified in this era. Following the death of the last Carolingian ruler in 987, an assembly of nobles selected Hugh Capet (kah-PAY) as his successor. Soon after his own coronation, Hugh crowned his oldest surviving son Robert as king to ensure the succession and prevent disputes after his death. This broke with the earlier practices of elective kingship or dividing a kingdom among one's sons, establishing instead the principle of primogeniture (pry-muh-JEH-nuh-choor), in which the king's eldest son received the Crown as his rightful inheritance. Primogeniture became the standard pattern of succession in medieval western Europe, and it also became an increasingly common pattern of inheritance for noble titles as well as land and other forms of wealth among all social classes.

The Capetian kings were weak, but they laid the foundation for later political stability. This stability came slowly. In the early twelfth century France still consisted of a number of virtually independent provinces. Unlike the king of England, who reigned supreme over a unified kingdom, the king of France maintained clear jurisdiction over a relatively small area (see Map 9.1). Over time medieval French kings worked to increase the royal domain and extend their authority over the provinces.

The work of unifying France began under Louis VI's grandson Philip II (r. 1180–1223), also known as Philip Augustus. When King John of England, who was Philip's vassal for the rich province of Normandy, defaulted on his feudal obligation to come to the French court, Philip declared Normandy forfeit to the French crown. He enforced his declaration militarily, and in 1204 Normandy fell to the French. He gained other northern provinces as well, and by the end of his reign Philip was effectively master of northern France. In the thirteenth century Philip Augustus's descendants acquired important holdings in the south. By the end of the thirteenth century most of the provinces of modern France had been added to the royal domain through diplomacy, marriage, war, and inheritance.

In addition to expanding the royal territory, Philip Augustus devised a method of governing the provinces and providing for communication between the central government

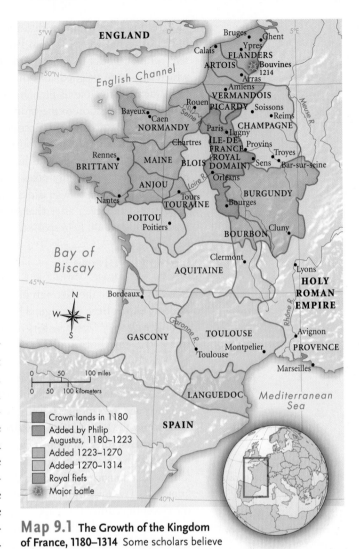

Map 9.1 The Growth of the Kingdom of France, 1180–1314 Some scholars believe that Philip II received the title "Augustus" (from a Latin word meaning "to increase") because he vastly expanded the territories of the kingdom of France. The province of Toulouse (too-LOOZ) in the south became part of France as a result of the crusade against the Albigensians (see page 251).

primogeniture An inheritance system in which the oldest son inherits all land and noble titles.

How did the administration of law evolve in this period?   What led to conflict between the papacy and secular leaders?   What were the causes and consequences of the Crusades?   How did Christianity spread during the High Middle Ages?

233

in Paris and local communities. Each province retained its own institutions and laws, but royal agents were sent from Paris into the provinces as the king's official representatives with authority to act for him. These agents were never natives of the provinces to which they were assigned, and they could not own land there. This policy reflected the fundamental principle of French administration that officials should gain their power from their connection to the monarchy, not from their own wealth or local alliances.

Philip Augustus and his successors were slower and less effective than were English kings at setting up an efficient bureau of finance. There was no national survey of property like the *Domesday Book* to help determine equitable levels of taxation, and French nobles resisted paying any taxes or fees. Not until the fourteenth century, as a result of the Hundred Years' War, did a national financial bureau emerge—the Chamber of Accounts—and even after that French nobles continued to pay little or no taxes, a problem that would help spark the French Revolution.

Central Europe

In central Europe the German king Otto I (r. 936–973) defeated many other lords to build his power from his original base in Saxony. Some of our knowledge of Otto derives from *The Deeds of Otto*, a history of his reign in heroic verse written by a nun, Hroswitha (rahs-WEE-thuh) of Gandersheim (ca. 935–ca. 1003). Hroswitha saw Otto's victories as part of God's plan: "As often as he set out for war, there was not a people, though haughty because of its strength, that could harm or conquer him, supported as he was by the consolation of the heavenly King."[1]

Otto had God's money as well as God's favor, garnering financial support from church leaders and the bulk of his army from ecclesiastical lands. He also asserted the right to control ecclesiastical appointments. Before receiving religious consecration and being invested with the staff and ring symbolic of their offices, bishops and abbots had to perform feudal homage for the lands that accompanied the church office. This practice, later known as "lay investiture," created a grave crisis between the church and monarchy in the eleventh century (see page 242).

In 955 Otto I inflicted a crushing defeat on the Magyars in the battle of Lechfeld (see Chapter 8), which made Otto a great hero to the Germans. In 962 he used this victory to have himself crowned emperor by the pope in Aachen, which had been the capital of the Carolingian Empire. He chose this site to symbolize his intention to continue the tradition of Charlemagne and to demonstrate papal support for his rule. It was not exactly clear what Otto was the emperor of, however, though by the eleventh century people were increasingly using the term Holy Roman Empire to refer to a loose confederation of principalities, duchies (DUH-cheez), cities, bishoprics, and other types of regional governments stretching from Denmark to Rome and from Burgundy to Poland (Map 9.2).

Holy Roman Empire The loose confederation of principalities, duchies, cities, bishoprics, and other types of regional governments stretching from Denmark to Rome and from Burgundy to Poland.

Seal of Frederick Barbarossa Rulers and other figures of authority signed proclamations, laws, and documents to make them official, but they also attached wax seals that often bore their likenesses. Like the portrait of Harold Godwinson on the Bayeux tapestry, this seal of Frederick Barbarossa shows him seated on a throne, wearing a crown, and holding an orb and a scepter, all of which were symbols of power. (Bildarchiv Preussischer Kulturbesitz/ Art Resource, NY)

Chapter 9
State and Church in the High Middle Ages • 1000–1300

234

CHAPTER LOCATOR   How did monarchs try to centralize political power?

In this large area of central Europe, unified nation-states did not come into existence until the nineteenth century. Before that time the Holy Roman emperors shared power with princes, dukes, archbishops, counts, bishops, abbots, and cities. The office of emperor remained an elected one, though the electors included only seven men—four secular rulers of large territories within the empire and three archbishops.

Through most of the first half of the twelfth century, civil war wracked Germany. When Conrad III died in 1152, the resulting anarchy was so terrible that the electors decided the only alternative to continued chaos was the selection of a strong ruler. They chose Frederick Barbarossa of the house of Hohenstaufen (HOH-uhn-shtow-fuhn) (r. 1152–1190).

Like William the Conqueror in England and Philip in France, Frederick required vassals to take an oath of allegiance to him as emperor and appointed officials to exercise full imperial authority over local communities. He forbade private warfare and established sworn peace associations with the princes of various regions. These peace associations punished criminals and those who breached the peace.

Between 1154 and 1188 Frederick made six military expeditions into Italy in an effort to assert his imperial rights over the increasingly wealthy towns of northern Italy. While he initially made significant conquests in the north, the Italian cities formed leagues to oppose him, and they also allied with the papacy. In 1176 Frederick suffered a crushing defeat at Legnano (see Map 9.2). This battle marked the first time a feudal cavalry of armed knights was decisively defeated by an army largely made of infantrymen from the cities. Frederick was forced to recognize the municipal autonomy of the northern Italian cities and the pope's sovereignty in central Italy.

Map 9.2 **The Holy Roman Empire, ca. 1200** Frederick Barbarossa greatly expanded the size of the Holy Roman Empire, but it remained a loose collection of various types of governments.

Sicily

The kingdom of Sicily is a good example of how a strong government could be built on a feudal base by determined rulers. Between 1061 and 1091 a Norman knight, Roger de Hauteville, with papal support and a small band of mercenaries, defeated the Muslims and Byzantines who controlled Sicily. Roger then faced the problem of governing Sicily's heterogeneous population of native Sicilians, Italians, Greeks, Jews, Arabs, and Normans. Roger distributed scattered fiefs to his followers so no vassal would have a centralized power base. He took an inquest of royal property and rights, and he forbade private warfare. To these Norman practices, Roger fused Arabic and Greek governmental devices. For example, he retained the main financial agency of the previous Muslim rulers, the diwān (dee-WAHN), a sophisticated bureau for record keeping and administration.

How did the administration of law evolve in this period?

What led to conflict between the papacy and secular leaders?

What were the causes and consequences of the Crusades?

How did Christianity spread during the High Middle Ages?

235

Palatine Chapel at Palermo Muslim craftsmen from Egypt painted the wooden ceiling of the royal chapel for King Roger of Sicily. This section shows the diverse peoples—Jews, Christians, and Muslims—who lived in Palermo. (Burgerbibliothek Bern Cod. 120 II, fol. 98r)

In 1137 Roger's son and heir, Count Roger II, took the city of Naples and much of the surrounding territory in southern Italy. The entire area came to be known as the kingdom of Sicily (or sometimes the kingdom of the Two Sicilies), and was often caught up in conflicts between the pope, the Holy Roman emperor, and the kings of France and Spain over control of Italy.

Roger II's grandson Frederick II (r. 1212–1250) was crowned king of the Germans at Aachen (1216) and Holy Roman emperor at Rome (1220). He concentrated his attention on Sicily, however, and showed little interest in the northern part of the Holy Roman Empire. Frederick repeated Roger's ban on private warfare and placed all castles and towers under royal administration. He also replaced town officials with royal governors and subordinated feudal and ecclesiastical courts to the king's courts.

Frederick had grown up in multicultural Sicily, knew six languages, wrote poetry, and supported scientists, scholars, and artists, whatever their religion or background. In 1224 he founded the University of Naples to train officials for his bureaucracy. He too continued the use of Muslim institutions such as the diwān, and he tried to administer justice fairly to all his subjects, declaring, "We cannot in the least permit Jews and Saracens [Muslims] to be defrauded of the power of our protection and to be deprived of all other help, just because the difference of their religious practices makes them hateful to Christians," implying a degree of toleration exceedingly rare at the time.[2]

Frederick transformed the kingdom of Sicily. But Sicily required constant attention, and Frederick's absences on crusades and on campaigns in mainland Italy took their toll. Shortly after he died, the unsupervised bureaucracy fell to pieces. The pope, as feudal overlord of Sicily, called in a French prince to rule. Frederick's reign had also weakened imperial power in the German parts of the empire, and in the later Middle Ages lay and ecclesiastical princes held sway in the Holy Roman Empire. This was one of the reasons that Germany and Italy did not become unified states until the nineteenth century.

Kingdom of Sicily, 1137

The Iberian Peninsula

From the eleventh to the thirteenth centuries, power in the Iberian peninsula shifted from Muslim to Christian rulers. In the eleventh century divisions and civil war in the caliphate of Córdoba allowed Christian armies to conquer an increasingly large part of the

Chapter 9
State and Church in the High Middle Ages • 1000–1300
236

CHAPTER LOCATOR | How did monarchs try to centralize political power?

Córdoba Mosque and Cathedral The huge arches of the Great Mosque at Córdoba dwarf the cathedral built in the center after the city was conquered by Christian armies in 1236. During the reconquista, Christian kings often transformed mosques into churches, often by simply adding Christian elements such as crosses and altars to the existing structures. (dbimages/Alamy)

Iberian Peninsula. Castile, in the north-central part of the peninsula, became the strongest of the growing Christian kingdoms, and Aragon, in the northeast, the second most powerful. In 1085 King Alfonso VI of Castile and León captured Toledo in central Spain. The following year forces of the Almoravid dynasty that ruled much of northwestern Africa defeated Christian armies, and halted Christian advances southward, though they did not retake Toledo. The Almoravids reunified the Muslim state for several generations, but the Christians regrouped, and in their North African homeland the Almoravids were overthrown by a rival dynasty, the Almohads, who then lay claim to the remaining Muslim territories in southern Spain.

Alfonso VIII (1158–1214), aided by the kings of Aragon, Navarre, and Portugal, crushed the Almohad-led Muslims at Las Navas de Tolosa in 1212, accelerating the Christian push southward. James the Conqueror of Aragon (r. 1213–1276) captured Valencia on the Mediterranean coast in 1233, and three years later Ferdinand of Castile and León captured Córdoba. With the fall of Seville in 1248, Christians controlled the entire Iberian Peninsula, save for the small state of Granada (Map 9.3).

Muslim Spain had had more cities than any other country in Europe, and Christian Spain became highly urbanized. Victorious Christian rulers expelled the Muslims and recruited immigrants from many places. This period thus witnessed a huge migration of peoples from the north to cities from which the Muslims had been pushed out in the central and southern parts of the peninsula. The chief mosques in these cities became cathedrals, and Muslim art was destroyed.

Map 9.3 The Reconquista, ca. 750–1492 The Christian conquest of Muslim Spain was followed by ecclesiastical reorganization, with the establishment of dioceses, monasteries, and the Latin liturgy, which gradually tied the peninsula to the heartland of Christian Europe and to the Roman papacy.

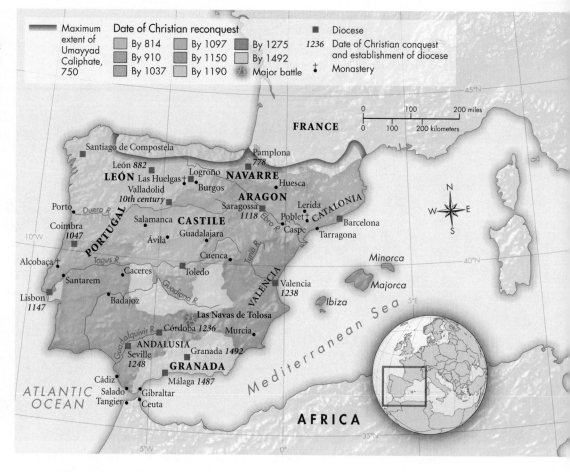

reconquista The Christian term for the conquest of Muslim territories in the Iberian Peninsula by Christian forces.

Fourteenth-century clerical propagandists would call the movement to expel the Muslims the reconquista (reconquest)—a sacred and patriotic crusade to wrest the country from "alien" Muslim hands. This religious myth became part of Spanish political culture and of the national psychology.

▼ How did the administration of law evolve in this period?

Throughout Europe the form and application of laws depended on local and provincial custom and practice. In the twelfth and thirteenth centuries the law was a hodgepodge of customs, feudal rights, and provincial practices. Rulers wanted to blend these elements into a uniform system of rules acceptable and applicable to all their peoples, though their success at doing so varied.

Local Laws and Royal Courts

The French king Louis IX (r. 1226–1270) was famous in his time for his concern about justice. Each French province retained its unique laws and procedures, but Louis IX created a royal judicial system. He established the Parlement of Paris, a kind of supreme court that welcomed appeals from local administrators and from the courts of feudal

Chapter 9
State and Church in the High
238   Middle Ages • 1000–1300

CHAPTER LOCATOR   How did monarchs try to centralize political power?

lords throughout France. By the very act of appealing the decisions of feudal courts to the Parlement of Paris, French people in far-flung provinces were recognizing the superiority of royal justice. Louis was also the first French monarch to publish laws for the entire kingdom, and he sent royal judges to hear complaints of injustice. The Parlement of Paris registered (or announced) these laws. Louis sought to identify justice with the kingship, and gradually royal justice touched all parts of the kingdom.

In the Holy Roman Empire, justice was administered at two levels. The manorial or seigneurial court, presided over by the local lay or ecclesiastical lord, dealt with such matters as damage to crops and fields, trespass, boundary disputes, and debt. Dukes, counts, margraves (another high noble), bishops, and abbots possessed authority over larger regions, and they dispensed justice in serious criminal cases. Regional magistrates held powers of high justice, that is, the right to execute a criminal. The Holy Roman emperors established a court of appeal similar to that of the French kings, but in their disunited empire it had little power.

England also had a variety of local laws with procedures and penalties that varied from one part of the country to another. Henry I occasionally sent out circuit judges, royal officials who traveled a given circuit or district, to hear civil and criminal cases. Henry II (r. 1154–1189) made this way of extending royal justice an annual practice. Every year royal judges left London and set up court in the counties. These courts regularized procedures in civil cases, gradually developing the idea of a common law, or law that applied throughout the whole country. Over the next two or three centuries common law became a reality as well as a legal theory. The common law relied on precedent: a decision in an important case served as an authority for deciding similar cases. Thus written codes of law played a less important role in England than they did elsewhere.

common law A body of English law established by King Henry II's court that in the next two or three centuries became common to the entire country.

Henry also improved procedure in criminal justice. In 1166 he instructed the sheriffs to summon local juries to conduct inquests and draw up lists of known or suspected criminals. These lists, or indictments, sworn to by the juries, were to be presented to the royal judges when they arrived in the community. Gradually, in the course of the thirteenth century, the king's judges adopted the practice of calling on twelve people (other than the accusing jury) to consider the question of innocence or guilt. This became the trial jury.

King Versus Archbishop

One aspect of Henry's judicial reforms encountered stiff resistance. In 1164 Henry II insisted that everyone, including clerics, be subject to the royal courts. The archbishop of Canterbury, Thomas Becket, vigorously protested that church law required clerics to be subject to church courts. Becket's opposition grew out of the conflict between temporal and spiritual powers. The disagreement between Henry II and Becket dragged on for years. Late in December 1170, in a fit of rage, Henry expressed the wish that Becket be destroyed, although he had earlier been his close friend. Four knights took the king at his word. They rode to Canterbury Cathedral and, as the archbishop was leaving evening services, murdered him.

The assassination of an archbishop turned public opinion in England and throughout western Europe against the king, and Henry had to back down. He did public penance for the murder and gave up his attempts to bring clerics under the authority of the royal court.

The Magna Carta

In the later years of Henry II's reign, his sons, spurred on by their mother Eleanor of Aquitaine, fought against their father and against one another for power and land. Richard I, known as the Lion-Hearted (r. 1189–1199), won this civil war and acceded to

How did the administration of law evolve in this period?

What led to conflict between the papacy and secular leaders?

What were the causes and consequences of the Crusades?

How did Christianity spread during the High Middle Ages?

239

the throne on Henry's death. Soon after, however, he departed on a crusade to the Holy Land and during his reign he spent only six months in England. Richard was captured on his way back from the crusades and held by the Holy Roman Emperor for a very high ransom, paid primarily through loans and high taxes on the English people.

John (r. 1199–1216) inherited his father's and brother's heavy debts, and his efforts to squeeze money out of his subjects created an atmosphere of resentment. In July 1214 John's cavalry suffered a defeat at the hands of Philip Augustus of France at Bouvines in Flanders. This battle ended English hopes for the recovery of territories from France and also strengthened the opposition to John. Rebellion begun by northern barons eventually grew to involve many key members of the English nobility. After lengthy negotiations, John met the barons in 1215 at Runnymede and was forced to approve the peace treaty called the Magna Carta.

To contemporaries, the Magna Carta was intended to redress the grievances that particular groups—the barons, the clergy, the merchants of London—had against King John. In time, however, it came to signify the principle that everyone, including the king and the government, must obey the law. In the later Middle Ages references to the Magna Carta underlined the Augustinian theory that a government, to be legitimate, must promote law, order, and justice (see Chapter 6). The Magna Carta also contains the germ of the idea of "due process of law," meaning that a person has the right to be heard and defended in court and is entitled to the protection of the law. Because later generations referred to the Magna Carta as a written statement of English liberties, it gradually came to have an almost sacred importance as a guarantee of law and justice.

Magna Carta A peace treaty intended to redress the grievances that particular groups had against King John, later viewed as the source of English rights and liberty more generally.

Law in Everyday Life

Statements of legal principles such as the Magna Carta were not how most people experienced the law in medieval Europe. Instead they were involved in or witnessed something judged to be a crime, and then experienced or watched the determination of

Punishment of Adulterers A man and a woman found guilty of adultery are led naked through the streets in this thirteenth-century French manuscript, preceded by heralds blowing horns and followed by men carrying sticks. This procession may be driving the couple out of town; banishment was a very common punishment for a number of crimes, including theft and assault. (Visual Arts Library/Art Resource, NY)

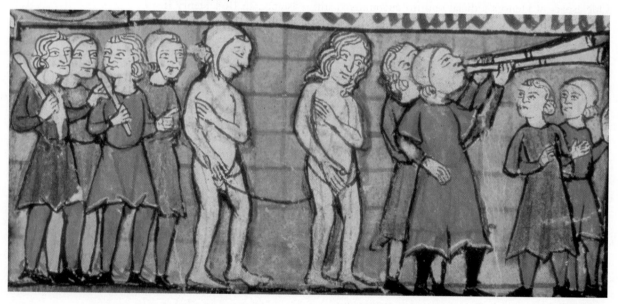

Chapter 9
State and Church in the High
240   Middle Ages • 1000–1300

CHAPTER LOCATOR   How did monarchs try to centralize political power?

guilt and the punishment. Judges determined guilt or innocence in a number of ways. In some cases, particularly those in which there was little clear evidence, they ordered a trial by ordeal. For example, the accused might be tied hand and foot and dropped in a lake or river. People believed that water was a pure substance and would reject anything foul or unclean. Thus a person who sank was considered innocent; a person who floated was found guilty. Trial by ordeal was a ritual that appealed to the supernatural for judgment.

Trials by ordeal were relatively rare, and their use declined during the High Middle Ages as judges and courts increasingly favored more rational procedures. Instead judges heard testimony, sought witnesses, and read written evidence if it was available. A London case in 1277 provides a good example of how law worked on the ground. Around Easter, the owner of a house in the city in which the tenant had disappeared sent a man to clean it, "but when he came to a dark and narrow place where coals were usually kept, he there found [a] headless body; upon seeing which, he sent word to the chamberlain and sheriffs." These officials went to the house and interviewed the neighbors. The men who lived nearby said that the headless body belonged to Symon de Winten, a tavern owner, whom they had seen quarrelling with his servant Roger in early December. That night Roger "seized a knife, and with it cut the throat of Symon quite through, so that the head was entirely severed from the body." He had stuffed the body in the coal room, stolen clothes and a silver cup, and disappeared.[3] The surviving records don't indicate whether Roger was ever caught, but they do indicate that the sheriffs took something from the neighbors who testified as "surety," that is, cash or goods as a pledge that their testimony was true. Taking sureties from witnesses was a common practice, which may be why the neighbors had not come forward on their own. People were supposed to report crimes, and they could be fined for not doing so, but it is clear from this case that such community involvement in crime fighting did not always happen.

Had Roger been caught and found guilty, his punishment would have been as public as the investigation. Murder was a capital crime and executions took place outdoors on a scaffold. Hanging was the most common method of execution, although nobles might be beheaded.

▼ What led to conflict between the papacy and secular leaders?

During the High Middle Ages, the papacy sought to make the church more independent of secular control. In the ninth and tenth centuries feudal lords controlled the appointment of church officials. Priests and bishops were appointed to advance the political ambitions of their own families rather than for special spiritual qualifications. A combination of political machinations and sexual immorality ensued, damaging the church's moral prestige. Under the leadership of a series of reforming popes in the eleventh century, the church tried to correct some of these problems, but the popes' efforts were sometimes challenged by medieval kings and emperors.

The Gregorian Reforms

During the ninth and tenth centuries the church had come under the control of kings and feudal lords, who chose priests and bishops in their territories, granting them fiefs and expecting loyalty and service in return. Church offices were sometimes sold outright—a practice called simony (SIGH-muh-nee). Not surprisingly, clergy at all

simony The buying and selling of church offices, officially prohibited but often practiced.

levels who had bought their positions, or had been granted them for political reasons, provided little spiritual guidance, and their personal lives were rarely models of high moral standards.

Popes were chosen by wealthy Roman families from among their members, and after gaining the papal office they paid more attention to their families' political fortunes than to the institutional or spiritual health of the church. For example, Pope John XII (pontificate 955–963) was appointed pope by his powerful father when he was only eighteen, and lacking interest in spiritual matters he concentrated on expanding papal territories.

At the local parish level, there were many married priests. The Roman church had always encouraged clerical celibacy, and celibacy had been an obligation for ordination since the fourth century. But in the tenth and eleventh centuries probably a majority of European priests were married or living with women.

Serious efforts to change all this began under Pope Leo IX (pontificate 1049–1054). Leo ordered clergy in Rome to dismiss their wives and invalidated the ordination of church officials who had purchased their offices. Pope Leo and his successors believed that secular or lay control over the church was largely responsible for the its lack of moral leadership, so they proclaimed the church independent from secular rulers. The Lateran Council of 1059 decreed that the authority and power to elect the pope rested solely in the **college of cardinals**, a special group of priests from the major churches in and around Rome. When the office of pope was vacant, the cardinals were responsible for governing the church.

Leo's successor Pope Gregory VII (pontificate 1073–1085) was even more vigorous in his championing of reform and expansion of papal power; for that reason, the eleventh-century movement is frequently called the "Gregorian reform movement." He denounced clerical marriage and simony, and he ordered those who disagreed excommunicated (cut off from the sacraments and all Christian worship). He believed that the pope, as the successor of Saint Peter, was the vicar of God on earth and that papal orders were the orders of God. Thus he was the first pope to emphasize the political authority of the papacy. Gregory was particularly opposed to **lay investiture**—the selection and appointment of church officials by secular authority. In February 1075 Pope Gregory held a council at Rome that decreed that clerics who accepted investiture from laymen were to be deposed, and laymen who invested clerics were to be excommunicated.

The church's penalty of **excommunication** relied for its effectiveness on public opinion. Gregory believed that the strong support he enjoyed for his moral reforms would carry over to his political ones; he thought that excommunication would compel rulers to abide by his changes. Immediately, however, Henry IV in the Holy Roman Empire, William the Conqueror in England, and Philip I in France protested. Gregory's reforms would deprive them not only of church income but also of the right to choose which monks and clerics would help them administer their kingdoms. The tension between the papacy and the monarchy would have a major impact on both institutions and on society.

Meanwhile, the Gregorian reform movement built a strict hierarchical church structure with bishops and ordained priests higher in status than nuns, who could not be ordained. The double monasteries of the early Middle Ages were placed under the authority of male abbots. Church councils in the eleventh and twelfth centuries forbade monks and nuns to sing church services together and ordered priests to limit their visits to convents, heightening the sense that contact with nuns should be viewed with suspicion and avoided when possible. The reformers' emphasis on clerical celibacy and chastity led them to portray women as impure and lustful. Thus in 1298 in the papal decree *Periculoso*, Pope Boniface VIII ordered all nuns to be strictly cloistered, that is, to remain permanently inside the walls of the convent, and for visits with those from outside the house to be limited. *Periculoso* was not enforced everywhere, but it did mean that convents became more cut off from medieval society.

college of cardinals A special group of high clergy with the authority and power to elect the pope and the responsibility to govern the church when the office of the pope is vacant.

lay investiture The selection and appointment of church officials by secular authority.

excommunication A penalty used by the Christian church that meant being cut off from the sacraments and all Christian worship.

Chapter 9
State and Church in the High
242   **Middle Ages • 1000–1300**

CHAPTER LOCATOR | How did monarchs try to centralize political power?

Emperor Versus Pope

The strongest reaction to Gregory's moves came from the Holy Roman Empire. Pope Gregory accused Henry of lack of respect for the papacy and insisted that disobedience to the pope was disobedience to God. Henry argued that Gregory's type of reform undermined royal authority. Within the empire, those who had the most to gain from the dispute quickly took advantage of it. In January 1076 many of the German bishops who had been invested by Henry withdrew their allegiance from the pope. Gregory replied by excommunicating them and suspending Henry. The pope "absolve[d] all Christians from the oath which they have made to [Henry]," which delighted the lay nobility, for they could now advance their own interests without interference from the king. Powerful nobles invited the pope to come to Germany to settle their dispute with Henry, and Gregory hastened to support them. The Christmas season of 1076 witnessed an ironic situation in Germany: the clergy supported the emperor, while the great nobility favored the pope.

Henry managed to outwit the pope temporarily. Crossing the Alps in January 1077, he approached the castle of Countess Matilda of Tuscany (ca. 1046–1115) at Canossa in the Apennines (AH-puh-nighnz), where the pope was staying. According to a letter later sent by the pope to his German noble allies, Henry stood for three days in the snow, imploring the pope to lift the excommunication. Henry's pleas for forgiveness won him public sympathy, and the pope readmitted the emperor to the Christian community, though he warned "that the whole question at issue is as yet little cleared up."[4]

Gregory was right. When the sentence of excommunication was lifted, Henry regained the emperorship and authority over his rebellious subjects, but continued his moves against papal power. In 1080 Gregory again excommunicated and deposed the emperor. In return, when Gregory died in 1085, Henry invaded Italy, captured Rome, and controlled the city. But Henry won no lasting victory. Gregory's successors encouraged Henry's sons to revolt against their father.

Finally, in 1122 at a conference held at Worms, the issue was settled by compromise. Bishops were to be chosen according to canon law—that is, by the clergy. But since lay rulers were permitted to be present at ecclesiastical elections and to accept or refuse feudal homage from the new prelates, they still

Countess Matilda A staunch supporter of the reforming ideals of the papacy, Countess Matilda planned this dramatic meeting at her castle. The arrangement of the figures—King Henry kneeling, Abbot Hugh of Cluny lecturing, and Matilda persuading—suggests contemporary understanding of the scene in which Henry received absolution. Matilda's vast estates in northern Italy and her political contacts in Rome made her a person of considerable influence in the late eleventh century. (Biblioteca Apostolica Vaticana)

possessed an effective veto over ecclesiastical appointments. Papal power was enhanced, but neither side won a clear victory.

The long controversy over lay investiture had tremendous social and political consequences in Germany. The lengthy struggle between papacy and emperor allowed emerging noble dynasties to enhance their position. To control their lands, the great lords built castles, symbolizing their increased power and growing independence. The German high aristocracy subordinated the knights, enhanced restrictions on peasants, and compelled Henry IV and Henry V to surrender certain rights and privileges. When the papal-imperial conflict ended in 1122, the nobility held the balance of power in Germany. Thus, particularism, localism, and feudal independence characterized the Holy Roman Empire in the High Middle Ages.

The Popes and Church Law

In the late eleventh century and throughout the twelfth and thirteenth, the papacy pressed Gregory's campaign for reform of the church. The popes held a series of councils, known as the Lateran councils, that ratified decisions ending lay investiture, ordered bishops to live less extravagantly, and passed other measures designed to make procedures more uniform. They also passed a series of measures against clerical marriage, ordering married priests to give up their wives and children or face dismissal. The councils declared marriage a sacrament—a ceremony that provided visible evidence of God's grace—and forbade divorce.

Pope Urban II laid the foundations for the papal monarchy by reorganizing the central government of the Roman church, the papal writing office (the chancery), and papal finances. He recognized the college of cardinals as a definite consultative body. These agencies, together with the papal chapel, constituted the *curia Romana* (Roman curia).

canon law Church law, which had its own courts and procedures.

The Roman curia had its greatest impact as a court of law. As the highest ecclesiastical tribunal, it formulated church law, termed canon law. The church developed a system of courts separate from those of secular rulers that handled disputes over church property and ecclesiastical elections, and especially questions of marriage and annulment. Most of the popes in the twelfth and thirteenth centuries were canon lawyers who expanded the authority of church courts.

The most famous of the lawyer-popes was Innocent III (pontificate 1198–1216), who became the most powerful pope in history. During his pontificate the church in Rome declared itself to be supreme, united, and "catholic" (worldwide), responsible for the earthly well-being as well as the eternal salvation of Christians everywhere. Innocent pushed the kings of France, Portugal, and England to do his will, compelling King Philip Augustus of France to take back his wife, Ingeborg of Denmark. He forced King John of England to accept as archbishop of Canterbury a man John did not want.

Innocent called the fourth Lateran Council in 1215, which affirmed the idea that ordained priests had the power to transform bread and wine during church ceremonies into the body and blood of Christ (a change termed "transubstantiation"). According to papal doctrine, priests now had the power to mediate for everyone with God, which set the spiritual hierarchy of the church above the secular hierarchies of kings and other rulers. The council affirmed that Christians should confess their sins to a priest at least once a year. It also ordered Jews and Muslims to wear special clothing that set them apart from Christians.

By the early thirteenth century papal efforts at reform begun more than a century earlier had attained phenomenal success. Some of Innocent III's successors, however, abused their prerogatives, even using secular weapons, including military force, to maintain their leadership. The conflict between the papacy and secular powers was not over, and it emerged again in the late thirteenth century (see Chapter 11).

Chapter 9
State and Church in the High
244 **Middle Ages • 1000–1300**

CHAPTER LOCATOR | How did monarchs try to centralize political power?

▼ What were the causes and consequences of the Crusades?

The Crusades of the eleventh and twelfth centuries were the most obvious manifestation of the papal claim to the leadership of Christian society. The Crusades were wars sponsored by the papacy for the recovery of the holy city of Jerusalem from the Muslims. The enormous popular response to papal calls for crusading reveals the influence of the reformed papacy and the depth of religious fervor among many different types of people. The Crusades also reflected the church's new understanding of the noble warrior class, for whom war against the church's enemies was understood as a religious duty.

Crusades Holy wars sponsored by the papacy for the recovery of the Holy Land from the Muslims from the late eleventh to the late thirteenth centuries.

Background and Motives

The medieval church's attitude toward violence was contradictory. On the one hand, church councils threatened excommunication for anyone who attacked peasants, clerics, or merchants or destroyed crops and unfortified places. This movement was termed the Peace of God. They tried to limit the number of days on which fighting was permitted—prohibiting it on Sundays, on special feast days, and in the seasons of Lent and Advent. On the other hand, popes supported armed conflict against kings and emperors if this worked to their advantage. After a serious theological disagreement in 1054 split the Orthodox church of Byzantium and the Roman church of the West, Pope Leo IX also contemplated invading the Byzantine Empire. In the years that followed, various popes believed that military campaigns might increase Roman influence in Byzantine territories and eventually lead to the reunion of the two churches, with Rome at the head.

Although conflicts in which Christians fought Christians were troubling to many thinkers, war against non-Christians was another matter. By the ninth century popes and other church officials encouraged war in defense of Christianity, promising spiritual benefits to those who died fighting. By the eleventh century these benefits were extended to all those who joined a campaign. Christian thinkers were also developing the concept of purgatory, a place where those on their way to heaven stayed for a while to do any penance they had not completed while alive. Engaging in holy war could shorten one's time in purgatory, or, as many people understood the promise, allow one to head straight to paradise. Popes signified this by providing indulgences, grants with the pope's name on them that lessened earthly penance and postmortem purgatory.

indulgences Grants by the pope that lessened or eliminated the penance that sinners had to pay on earth and in purgatory before ascending to Heaven.

Preachers communicated these ideas widely and told stories about warrior-saints. Saint James, for example, whose shrine in the northwest corner of Spain at Compostela was a popular place for Christian pilgrims to visit, was known as *Matamoros*, the Killer of Moors (that is, of Muslims). The support of the papacy for Christian armies in the reconquista in Spain was not just spiritual, but also financial and legal, as was papal support in the Norman campaign against the Muslims in Sicily. In both campaigns Pope Gregory VII asserted that any land conquered from the Muslims belonged to the papacy because it had been a territory held by infidels.

Along with increasing Christian hatred of Muslims, the ideology of holy war also escalated Christian hostility toward Jews. Between the sixth and tenth centuries Jews had settled along the trade routes of western Europe. In the eleventh century they played a major role in the international trade between the Muslim Middle East and the West. Jews also lent money to peasants, townspeople, and nobles, and debt bred resentment.

Religious devotion had long been expressed through pilgrimages to holy places, and these were increasingly described in military terms, as battles against the hardships along the way and the enemies of Christ. Pilgrims to Jerusalem were often armed, so the line between pilgrimage and holy war on this particular route was becoming blurred.

How did the administration of law evolve in this period?

What led to conflict between the papacy and secular leaders?

What were the causes and consequences of the Crusades?

How did Christianity spread during the High Middle Ages?

245

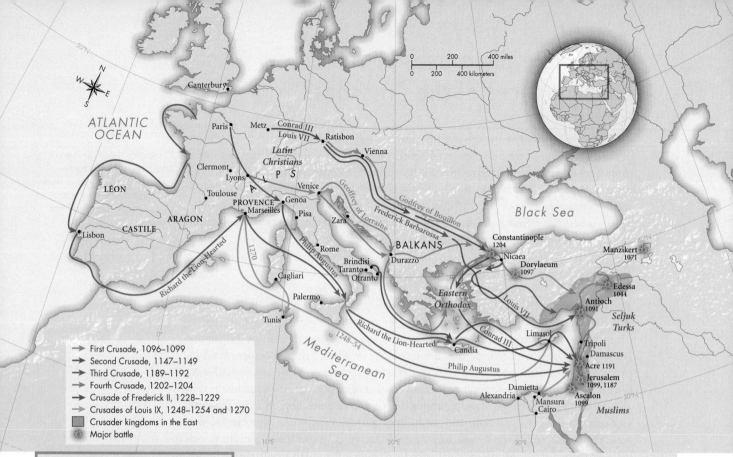

Map 9.4 The Crusades

This map shows the many different routes that Western Christians took over the centuries to reach Jerusalem.

ANALYZING THE MAP How were the results of the various Crusades shaped by the routes that the Crusaders took?

CONNECTIONS How did the routes and Crusader kingdoms offer opportunities for profit?

To complete this activity online, go to the Online Study Guide at bedfordstmartins.com/mckaywestunderstanding.

The Arabic Muslims who had ruled Jerusalem and the surrounding territory for centuries allowed Christian pilgrims to travel freely, but in the late eleventh century the Seljuk (SEHL-jook) Turks took over Palestine, defeating both Arabic and Byzantine armies (Map 9.4). The emperor at Constantinople appealed to the West for support, asserting that the Turks would make pilgrimages to holy places more dangerous, and that the holy city of Jerusalem should be in Christian hands. The emperor's appeal fit well with papal aims, and in 1095 Pope Urban II called for a great Christian holy war against the infidels. Urban offered indulgences to those who would fight for and regain the holy city of Jerusalem.

The Course of the Crusades

Thousands of western Christians of all classes joined the First Crusade in 1096. Of all of the developments of the High Middle Ages, none better reveals Europeans' religious and emotional fervor and the influence of the reformed papacy than the extraordinary outpouring of support for the First Crusade.

Chapter 9
State and Church in the High
246 Middle Ages • 1000–1300

CHAPTER LOCATOR

How did monarchs try
to centralize political
power?

The First Crusade was successful, mostly because of the dynamic enthusiasm of the participants. The Crusaders had little more than religious zeal. They knew nothing about the geography or climate of the Middle East. Although there were several high nobles with military experience among them, the Crusaders could never agree on a leader, and the entire expedition was marked by disputes among the great lords. Lines of supply were never set up. Starvation and disease wracked the army, and the Turks slaughtered hundreds of noncombatants. The army pressed on, defeating the Turks in several land battles and besieging a few larger towns. (See "Listening to the Past: An Arab View of the Crusades," page 248.) Finally in 1099, they reached Jerusalem, and after a monthlong siege they got inside the city, where they slaughtered the Muslim defenders. Fulcher of Chartres, a chaplain on the First Crusade, described the scene:

> Amid the sound of trumpets and with everything in an uproar they attacked boldly, shouting "God help us!" . . . They ran with the greatest exultation as fast as they could into the city and joined their companions in pursuing and slaying their wicked enemies without cessation. . . . If you had been there your feet would have been stained to the ankles in the blood of the slain. What shall I say? None of them were left alive. Neither women nor children were spared.[5]

In the aftermath of the First Crusade, four small "Crusader states"—Jerusalem, Edessa, Tripoli, and Antioch, each centered on a city—were established (see Map 9.4). Castles and fortified towns were built to defend against Muslim reconquest. Between 1096 and 1270 the crusading ideal was expressed in eight papally approved expeditions, though none after the First Crusade accomplished very much. Despite this lack of success, for roughly two hundred years members of noble families in Europe went nearly every generation.

The Crusades inspired the establishment of new religious orders, particularly military orders dedicated to protecting the Christian kingdoms. The most important was the Knights Templars, founded in 1119 with the strong backing of Saint Bernard of Clairvaux (klehr-VOH). Speaking both of the Templars and the Crusades in general, Saint Bernard commented, "If the cause of the fighting is good, the consequence of the fighting cannot be evil."[6]

Women from all walks of life participated in the Crusades. After her husband, King Fulk, died, Queen Melisande ruled the Latin kingdom of Jerusalem. When King Louis IX of France was captured on the Seventh Crusade (1248–1254), his wife Queen Marguerite negotiated the surrender of the Egyptian city of Damietta to the Muslims. In war zones some women concealed their sex by donning chain mail and helmets, and they fought with the knights. Others joined in the besieging of towns and castles. More typically, women provided water to fighting men, a service not to be underestimated in the hot, dry climate of the Middle East. They worked as washerwomen, foraged for food, and provided sexual services. There were many more European men than women, however, so marriage and sexual relations between Christian men and Muslim women were not unheard of, although marriages between Western Christian men and Orthodox Christian women who lived in the area were more common.

The Muslim states in the Middle East were politically fragmented when the Crusaders first came, and it took about a century for them to reorganize. They did so dramatically under Saladin (Salah al-Din), who unified Egypt and Syria, and in 1187 the Muslims retook Jerusalem. Christians immediately attempted to take it back in what was later called the Third Crusade (1189–1192). Frederick Barbarossa of the Holy Roman Empire, Richard the Lion-Hearted of England, and Philip Augustus of France participated. The Third Crusade was better financed than previous ones. But disputes among the leaders and strategic problems prevented any lasting results. The Crusaders were not successful in retaking

How did the administration of law evolve in this period?   What led to conflict between the papacy and secular leaders?   **What were the causes and consequences of the Crusades?**   How did Christianity spread during the High Middle Ages?

247

LISTENING TO THE PAST

An Arab View of the Crusades

The Crusades helped shape the understanding that Arabs and Europeans had of each other and all subsequent relations between the Christian West and the Arab world. To medieval Christians the Crusades were papally approved military expeditions for the recovery of holy places in Palestine; to the Arabs these campaigns were "Frankish wars" or "Frankish invasions" for the acquisition of territory. Early in the thirteenth century Ibn Al-Athir (1160–1223), a native of Mosul, an important economic and cultural center in northern Mesopotamia (modern Iraq), wrote a history of the First Crusade. He relied on Arab sources for the events he described. Here is his account of the Crusaders' capture of Antioch.

❝ The power of the Franks first became apparent when in the year 478/1085–86* they invaded the territories of Islam and took Toledo and other parts of Andalusia. Then in 484/1091 they attacked and conquered the island of Sicily and turned their attention to the African coast. Certain of their conquests there were won back again but they had other successes, as you will see. In 490/1097 the Franks attacked Syria. This is how it all began: Baldwin, their King, a kinsman of Roger the Frank who had conquered Sicily, assembled a great army and sent word to Roger saying: "I have assembled a great army and now I am on my way to you, to use your bases for my conquest of the African coast. Thus you and I shall become neighbors."

Roger called together his companions and consulted them about these proposals. "This will be a fine thing for them and for us!" they declared, "for by this means these lands will be converted to the Faith!" At this Roger raised one leg and farted loudly, and swore that it was of more use than their advice. "Why?" "Because if this army comes here it will need quantities of provisions and fleets of ships to transport it to Africa, as well as reinforcements from my own troops. Then, if the Franks succeed in conquering this territory they will take it over and will need provisioning from Sicily. This will cost me my annual profit from the harvest. If they fail they will return here and be an embarrassment to me here in my own domain." . . .

He summoned Baldwin's messenger and said to him: "If you have decided to make war on the Mus-

In this vivid battle scene from a chronicle written in 1218 by an English monk, Christians and Muslims, both wearing chain mail, fight at close quarters. Slain warriors and a dead horse, common sights on the battlefield, lie underneath them. (© Corpus Christi College, Oxford, UK/The Bridgeman Art Library)

Jerusalem, but they did keep their hold on port towns, and Saladin allowed pilgrims safe passage to Jerusalem. He also made an agreement with Christian rulers for keeping the peace. From that point on, the Crusader states were more important economically than politically or religiously, giving Italian and French merchants direct access to Eastern products.

In 1202 Innocent III sent out preachers who called on Christian knights to retake Jerusalem. Those who responded—in what would become the Fourth Crusade—

lims your best course will be to free Jerusalem from their rule and thereby win great honor. I am bound by certain promises and treaties of allegiance with the ruler of Africa." So the Franks made ready to set out to attack Syria. Another story is that the Fatimids of Egypt were afraid when they saw the Seljuqids extending their empire through Syria as far as Gaza, until they reached the Egyptian border and Atsiz invaded Egypt itself. They therefore sent to invite the Franks to invade Syria and so protect Egypt from the Muslims.† But God knows best. When the Franks decided to attack Syria they marched east to Constantinople, so that they could cross the straits and advance into Muslim territory by the easier, land route. When they reached Constantinople, the Emperor of the East refused them permission to pass through his domains. He said: "Unless you first promise me Antioch, I shall not allow you to cross into the Muslim empire." His real intention was to incite them to attack the Muslims, for he was convinced that the Turks, whose invincible control over Asia Minor he had observed, would exterminate every one of them. They accepted his conditions and in 490/1097 they crossed the Bosphorus at Constantinople. . . . They . . . reached Antioch, which they besieged.

When Yaghi Siyan, the ruler of Antioch, heard of their approach, he was not sure how the Christian people of the city would react, so he made the Muslims go outside the city on their own to dig trenches, and the next day sent the Christians out alone to continue the task. When they were ready to return home at the end of the day he refused to allow them. "Antioch is yours," he said, "but you will have to leave it to me until I see what happens between us and the Franks." "Who will protect our children and our wives?" they said. "I shall look after them for you." So they resigned themselves to their fate, and lived in the Frankish camp for nine months, while the city was under siege.

Yaghi Siyan showed unparalleled courage and wisdom, strength and judgment. If all the Franks who died had survived they would have overrun all the lands of Islam. He protected the families of the Christians in Antioch and would not allow a hair of their heads to be touched. After the siege had been going on for a long time the Franks made a deal with . . . a cuirassmaker called Ruzbih whom they bribed with a fortune in money and lands. He worked in the tower that stood over the riverbed, where the river flowed out of the city into the valley. The Franks sealed their pact with the cuirassmaker, God damn him! and made their way to the watergate. They opened it and entered the city. Another gang of them climbed the tower with their ropes. At dawn, when more than 500 of them were in the city and the defenders were worn out after the night watch, they sounded their trumpets. . . . Panic seized Yaghi Siyan and he opened the city gates and fled in terror, with an escort of thirty pages. His army commander arrived, but when he discovered on enquiry that Yaghi Siyan had fled, he made his escape by another gate. This was of great help to the Franks, for if he had stood firm for an hour, they would have been wiped out. They entered the city by the gates and sacked it, slaughtering all the Muslims they found there. This happened in jumada I (491/April/May 1098). . . .

It was the discord between the Muslim princes . . . that enabled the Franks to overrun the country. 〞

Source: Excerpt from pp. 3–6 in *Arab Historians of the Crusades*, edited and translated by Francesco Gabrieli. © 1969 by Routledge & Kegan Paul Ltd. Published by the University of California Press. Used with permission of the University of California Press.

QUESTIONS FOR ANALYSIS

1. Most Christian histories of the Crusades begin with Pope Urban II's call in 1095. What does Ibn Al-Athir see as the beginning? How would this make his view of the Crusades different from that of Christian chroniclers?
2. How does Ibn Al-Athir characterize the Christian leaders Roger and Baldwin? How does this compare with his characterization of Yaghi Siyan, the Muslim ruler of Antioch?
3. To what does Ibn Al-Athir attribute the fall of Antioch? To what does he attribute Christian defeats of the Muslims more generally? What does this suggest about his view of Christian military capabilities?

*Muslims traditionally date events from Muhammad's *hijra*, or migration, to Medina, which occurred in 622 according to the Christian calendar.

†Although Muslims, Fatimids were related doctrinally to the Shi'ites, and the dominant Sunni Muslims considered the Fatimids heretics.

negotiated with the Venetians to take them by boat to Cairo. Venetian interests combined with a succession struggle over the Byzantine throne led the fleet to instead go to Constantinople. Once there, the Crusaders decided to capture and sack Constantinople. The Crusaders installed one of their own as emperor, but in reality the Byzantine Empire was divided among the Crusaders, the Venetians, and the Byzantine imperial family. The Byzantines reasserted their control over the empire in 1261, but it was much smaller and weaker. It soon consisted of little more than the city of Constantinople.

| How did the administration of law evolve in this period? | What led to conflict between the papacy and secular leaders? | **What were the causes and consequences of the Crusades?** | How did Christianity spread during the High Middle Ages? |

249

The Capture of Jerusalem in 1099

As engines hurl stones to breach the walls, Crusaders enter on scaling ladders. Scenes from Christ's passion in the top half of the piece identify the city as Jerusalem. (Bibliothèque nationale de France)

READING THE IMAGE What do you think the author's point of view is about the events shown? Would you characterize the painting as a positive or negative depiction of war? What does this suggest about the artist's motives in creating this work?

CONNECTIONS How might the images shown be different if this had been drawn by a Muslim artist living in Jerusalem?

To complete this activity online, go to the Online Study Guide at bedfordstmartins.com/mckaywestunderstanding.

Chapter 9
State and Church in the High
250   Middle Ages • 1000–1300

CHAPTER LOCATOR   How did monarchs try to centralize political power?

Moreover, the assault by one Christian people on another—even though one of the original goals of the Crusades had been to reunite the Greek and Latin churches—made the split between the churches permanent. It also helped discredit the entire crusading movement and obviously had no effect on Muslim control of Jerusalem and other areas.

Nonetheless, there were a few more efforts. The Seventh Crusade in 1248, led by King Louis IX of France (r. 1223–1270), tried to come in through Egypt. Louis also sent monks to the court of the Mongols in Central Asia to make a treaty that would encircle the Muslims. The monks were unsuccessful, but they brought back geographical knowledge of Asia and the peoples they had encountered. Louis himself was captured in the crusade, but he ransomed himself and then led another crusade, on which he was killed. Though Louis was made a saint shortly after his death, his crusades had accomplished nothing. In the end, it was the Mamluk rulers of Egypt who conquered the Crusader states. In 1291 the Crusaders' last stronghold, the port of Acre, fell. Some knights continued their crusading efforts in Spain, where the rulers of Aragon and Castile continued fighting Muslims until 1492.

Crusades Within Europe

Crusades were also mounted against groups within Europe that were perceived as threats. The Teutonic Knights, a military order, waged a crusade against pagans in the Baltic region and eventually formed a state there. The popes declared several campaigns against German emperors to be crusades. In 1208 Pope Innocent III proclaimed a crusade against a group in southern France known as the Albigensians (al-buh-JEHN-see-uhns). The Albigensians asserted that a good God had created spiritual things, and an evil God had created material things. In this dualistic understanding, the soul was good and the body evil. Forces of good and evil battled constantly, and the best life was one of extreme asceticism with as few physical and material things as possible. They used the teachings of Jesus about the evils of material goods to call for the church to give up its property. They rejected the authority of the pope and the sacraments of the church, and they began setting up their own bishoprics.

The Albigensians won many adherents in southern France, especially in the towns and cities. Fearing that religious division would lead to civil disorder, the French monarchy joined Pope Innocent III's crusade, inflicting a savage defeat on the Albigensians in 1213. After more years of fighting, the leaders agreed to terms of peace, which left the French monarchy the primary beneficiary.

The end of the war did not mean an end to Albigensianism, but henceforth the papacy decided to combat heresy through education and individual punishment. In the 1230s the papacy established the papal Inquisition, sending out inquisitors with the power to seek suspected heretics, question them in private without revealing who had denounced them, and sentence them to punishments ranging from penance to life imprisonment. (For more on the Inquisition, see Chapter 11.) Heretics who did not repent were handed over to the secular government to be burned, and their property was confiscated.

Inquisition Court established by the papacy with power to investigate and try Albigensians and other individuals for heresy and other religious crimes.

Consequences of the Crusades

The Crusades testified to the religious enthusiasm of the High Middle Ages and gave kings and the pope opportunities to expand their bureaucracies. They also provided kings with the perfect opportunity to get rid of troublemaking knights, particularly restless younger sons for whom the practice of primogeniture meant few prospects.

How did the administration of law evolve in this period?

What led to conflict between the papacy and secular leaders?

What were the causes and consequences of the Crusades?

How did Christianity spread during the High Middle Ages?

251

INDIVIDUALS IN SOCIETY

The Jews of Speyer

IN THE WINTER OF 1095–1096 news of Pope Urban II's call for a crusade spread. In spring 1096 the Jews of northern France, fearing that a crusade would arouse anti-Semitic hostility, sent a circular letter to the Rhineland's Jewish community seeking its prayers. Jewish leaders in Mainz responded, "All the [Jewish] communities have decreed a fast. . . . May God save us and save you from all distress and hardship. We are deeply fearful for you. We, however, have less reason to fear (for ourselves), for we have heard not even a rumor of the crusade."* Ironically, French Jewry survived almost unscathed, while the Rhenish Jewry suffered frightfully.

Beginning in the late tenth century Jews trickled into Speyer (SHPY-uhr) — partly through Jewish perception of opportunity and partly because of the direct invitation of the bishop of Speyer. The bishop's charter meant that Jews could openly practice their religion, could not be assaulted, and could buy and sell goods. But they could not proselytize their faith, as Christians could. Jews also extended credit on a small scale and, in an expanding economy with many coins circulating, determined the relative value of currencies. Unlike their Christian counterparts, many Jewish women were literate and acted as moneylenders. Jews also worked as skilled masons, carpenters, and jewelers. As the bishop had promised, the Jews of Speyer lived apart from Christians in a walled enclave where they exercised autonomy: they maintained law and order, raised taxes, and provided religious, social, and educational services for their community. (This organization lasted in Germany until the nineteenth century.) Jewish immigration to Speyer accelerated; everyday relations between Jews and Christians were peaceful.

But Christians resented Jews as newcomers, outsiders, and aliens; for enjoying the special protection of the bishop; and for providing economic competition. Anti-Semitic ideology had received enormous impetus from the virulent anti-Semitic writings of Christian apologists in the first six centuries C.E. Jews, they argued, were *deicides* (DEE-uh-sighdz) (Christ killers). Worse, Jews could understand the truth of Christianity but deliberately rejected it; thus they were inhuman. By the late eleventh century anti-Semitism was an old and deeply rooted element in Western society.

Late in April 1096 Emich of Leisingen, a petty lord from the Rhineland who had the reputation of being a lawless thug, approached Speyer with a large band of Crusaders. Joined by a mob of burghers, they planned to surprise the Jews in their synagogue on Saturday morning, May 3, but the Jews prayed early and left before the attackers arrived. Furious, the mob randomly murdered eleven Jews. The bishop took the entire Jewish community into his castle, arrested some of the burghers, and cut off their hands. News of these events raced up the Rhine to Worms, creating confusion in the Jewish community. Some took refuge with Christian friends; others sought the bishop's protection.

A combination of Crusaders and burghers killed a large number of Jews, looted and burned synagogues, and desecrated the Torah (see Chapter 2) and other books in Speyer. Proceeding to the old and prosperous city of Mainz, Crusaders continued attacking Jews. Facing overwhelming odds, eleven hundred Jews killed their families and themselves. Crusaders and burghers vented their hatred by inflicting bar-

The Crusades introduced some Europeans to Eastern luxury goods, but their immediate cultural impact on the West remains debatable. Strong economic and intellectual ties with the East had already been developed by the late eleventh century. The Crusades did provide great commercial profits for Italian merchants, who profited from outfitting military expeditions, the opening of new trade routes, and the establishment of trading communities in the Crusader states. Since commerce with the West benefited both Muslims and Europeans, it continued to flourish even after the Crusader states collapsed.

The Crusades proved to be a disaster for Jewish-Christian relations. Inspired by the ideology of holy war and resentment of Jewish economic activities, Christian armies on their way to Jerusalem on the First Crusade joined with local mobs to attack Jewish families and sometimes entire Jewish communities. (See "Individuals in Society: The Jews of Speyer," above.) Later Crusades brought similar violence, enhanced by accusations that

Chapter 9
State and Church in the High
252   **Middle Ages • 1000–1300**

CHAPTER LOCATOR   How did monarchs try to centralize political power?

This illustration from the margins of a thirteenth-century chronicle written by an English monk shows Jews — identified by the tablets they were required to wear on their clothing — being beaten. Such violence sometimes escalated into mass murder. (© British Library Board)

baric tortures on the wounded and dying. The Jews were never passive; everywhere they resisted.

If the Crusades had begun as opposition to Islam, after 1096 that hostility extended to all those whom Christians saw as enemies of society, including heretics such as the Albigensians and Jews. But Jews continued to move to the Rhineland and to make important economic and intellectual contributions. Crusader-burgher attacks served as harbingers of events to come in the later Middle Ages and well into modern times.

QUESTIONS FOR ANALYSIS

1. What were the roots of the anti-Semitic ideology of the Middle Ages, and how did the ideology contribute to the attacks on the Jews of Speyer?
2. Modern scholars would agree that the attackers had "dehumanized" the Jews of Speyer. What is meant by this term, and can you give other examples?

*Quoted in R. Chazan, *In the Year 1096: The First Crusade and the Jews* (Philadelphia: Jewish Publication Society, 1996), p. 28.

Jews engaged in the ritual murder of Christians to use their blood in religious rites. Legal restrictions on Jews gradually increased throughout Europe. In 1290 King Edward I of England expelled the Jews from England in return for a large parliamentary grant; it would be four centuries before they would be allowed back in. King Philip the Fair of France followed Edward's example in 1306, and many Jews went to the area of southern France known as Provence, which was not yet part of the French kingdom. In July 1315 the king's need for revenue led him to readmit the Jews to France in return for a huge lump sum and for an annual financial subsidy, but the returning Jews faced hostility and increasing pressure to convert, as did Jews in Aragon and Castile.

The Crusades also left an inheritance of deep bitterness in Christian-Muslim relations. Each side dehumanized the other, viewing those who followed the other religion as infidels. Whereas Europeans perceived the Crusades as sacred religious movements, Muslims saw them as expansionist and imperialistic.

How did the administration of law evolve in this period?

What led to conflict between the papacy and secular leaders?

What were the causes and consequences of the Crusades?

How did Christianity spread during the High Middle Ages?

253

The European Crusades shaped the identity of the West. They represent the first great colonizing movement beyond the geographical boundaries of the European continent. The ideal of a sacred mission to conquer or convert Muslim peoples entered Europeans' consciousness and became a continuing goal.

▼ How did Christianity spread during the High Middle Ages?

The Crusades had a profound impact on both Europe and the Middle East, but they were not the only example of Christian expansion in the High Middle Ages. After 1000, people and ideas moved from western France and western Germany into Ireland, Scandinavia, the Baltic lands, and eastern Europe, with significant cultural consequences for those territories. Wars of expansion, the establishment of new Christian bishoprics, and the vast migration of colonists, together with the papal emphasis on a unified Christian world, brought about the gradual Christianization of a larger area (Map 9.5).

Map 9.5 The Baltic Region, ca. 1300 By 1300 most of the Baltic area had been Christianized through the efforts of bishops, monks, the military order of the Teutonic Knights, and German settlers.

Chapter 9
State and Church in the High
254   Middle Ages • 1000–1300

CHAPTER LOCATOR   How did monarchs try to centralize political power?

Northern Europe

Ireland had been Christian since the days of Saint Patrick (see Chapter 7), but in the twelfth century Norman knights crossed from England, defeated Irish lords, and established fiefs with the kings of England as the ultimate authority. Following the Roman ecclesiastical structure, they also established bishoprics with defined territorial dioceses. Similarly, Anglo-Norman knights poured into Scotland in the twelfth century, bringing the fief and the diocese.

Latin Christian influences entered the Scandinavian and Baltic regions also primarily through the erection of dioceses. As an easily identifiable religious figure, as judge, and as the only person who could ordain priests, the bishop was the essential instrument in the spread of Christianity. Otto I established the first Scandinavian dioceses in Denmark. In Norway Christianity spread in coastal areas beginning in the tenth century, and King Olaf II (r. 1015–1028) brought in clergy and bishops from England and Germany to establish the church more firmly. From Norway Christianity spread to Iceland. In all of these areas, royal power advanced institutional Christianity.

Christianity progressed more slowly in Sweden and Finland, in part because royal power was weaker. In 1164, however, Uppsala in Sweden, long a center of the pagan cults of Thor and Odin, became a diocese. Sweden took over much of modern-day Finland in the thirteenth century, and Swedish-speaking settlers moved into islands and coastal areas. Christian missionaries preached, baptized, and built churches, working among both the Swedish-speaking and Finnish-speaking populations.

Eastern Europe

The German emperor Otto I planted a string of dioceses along his northern and eastern frontiers, hoping to pacify the newly conquered Slavs in eastern Europe. Frequent Slavic revolts illustrate the people's resentment of German lords and clerics, and they indicate that the church did not easily penetrate the region. In the same way that French knights had been used to crush the Albigensians, German nobles built castles and ruthlessly crushed revolts. Albert the Bear, for example, a German noble, proclaimed a crusade against the Slavs and invited German knights to colonize conquered territories. A military order of German knights founded in Palestine, the Teutonic (too-TAH-nihk) Knights, moved their operations to eastern Europe and waged wars against the pagan Prussians in the Baltic region. After 1230, from a base in Poland, they established a new territory,

Hedwig of Bavaria Married to the duke of Silesia, Hedwig (1174–1243) worked to expand both Christianity and German influence in eastern Europe, inviting German clergy into her duchy and founding several monasteries. In this manuscript commissioned by her fourteenth-century descendants (shown kneeling), Hedwig carries a book, a rosary, and a tiny statue of the Virgin Mary, references to her devout character. (The John Paul Getty Museum, Los Angeles, Court Atelier of Duke Ludwig I of Liegnitz and Brieg [illuminator], *Vita beatae Hedwigis*, 1353. Tempera colors, colored washes and ink bound between wood boards covered with red-stained pigskin, 34.1 × 24.8 cm)

How did the administration of law evolve in this period?

What led to conflict between the papacy and secular leaders?

What were the causes and consequences of the Crusades?

How did Christianity spread during the High Middle Ages?

255

Christian Prussia, and gradually the entire eastern shore of the Baltic came under their hegemony.

The church also moved into central Europe, first in Bohemia in the tenth century and from there into Poland and Hungary in the eleventh. In the twelfth and thirteenth centuries, thousands of settlers poured into eastern Europe. New immigrants were German in descent, name, language, and law. Hundreds of small market towns populated by these newcomers supplied the needs of the rural countryside. Larger towns such as Kraków and Riga engaged in long-distance trade and gradually grew into large urban centers.

Christendom

Christendom The term used by early medieval writers to refer to the realm of Christianity.

Through the actions of the Roman emperors Constantine and Theodosius (see Chapter 7), Christianity became in some ways a state as well as a religion. Early medieval writers began to use the word Christendom to refer to this realm of Christianity. Sometimes notions of Christendom were linked directly to specific states, such as Charlemagne's empire and the Holy Roman Empire. More often Christendom was vague, a sort of loose sense of the body of all people who were Christian. When the pope called for Crusades, for example, he spoke not only of the retaking of Jerusalem, but also of the defense of Christendom. When missionaries, officials, and soldiers took Christianity into the Iberian Peninsula, Scandinavia, or the Baltic region, they understood what they were doing as the expansion of Christendom.

From the point of view of popes such as Gregory VII and Innocent III, Christendom was a unified hierarchy with the papacy at the top. They pushed for uniformity of religious worship and campaigned continually for the same pattern of religious service, the Roman liturgy in Latin, in all countries and places. They forbade vernacular Christian rituals or those that differed in their pattern of worship. Under Innocent III papal directives and papal legates flowed to all parts of Europe. Twelve hundred church officials obediently came to Rome from the borderlands as well as the heartland for the Fourth Lateran Council of 1215. Christians celebrated the same religious service everywhere.

As we have seen in this chapter, however, not everyone had the same view. Kings and emperors may have accepted the Roman liturgy in the areas under their control, but they had their own ideas of the way power should operate in Christendom, even if this brought them into conflict with the papacy. This did not mean that they had any less loyalty to Christendom as a concept, however, but simply a different idea about how it should be structured and who could best defend it. The battles in the High Middle Ages between popes and kings and between Christians and Muslims were signs of how deeply religion had replaced tribal, political, and ethnic structures as the essence of Western culture.

Chapter 9
State and Church in the High
256   **Middle Ages • 1000–1300**

CHAPTER LOCATOR   How did monarchs try to centralize political power?

←LOOKING BACK LOOKING AHEAD→

THE HIGH MIDDLE AGES were a time when kings, emperors, and popes expanded their powers and created financial and legal bureaucracies to support those powers. As monarchs developed these new institutions, their kingdoms began to function more like modern states than disorganized territories. With political expansion and stability came better communication of information, more uniform legal systems, and early financial institutions. Popes made the church more independent of lay control, established the papal curia and a separate system of canon law, and developed new ways of raising revenue. They supported the expansion of Christianity in southern, northern, and eastern Europe, and they proclaimed a series of Crusades against Muslims to extend still further the boundaries of a Christendom under their control.

Many of the systems of the High Middle Ages expanded in later centuries and are still in existence today: the financial department of the British government remains the Exchequer; the pope is still elected by the college of cardinals and is assisted by the papal curia; the legal systems of Britain and many former British colonies (including the United States) are based on common law; the Roman Catholic, Eastern Orthodox, and Anglican Churches still operate law courts that make rulings based on canon law. These systems also contained the seeds of future problems, however, for wealthier nations could sustain longer wars, independent popes more easily abuse their power, and crusading ideology justify the enslavement, expulsion, or extermination of whole peoples.

Despite the long-lived impact of the growth of centralized political and ecclesiastical power—for good or ill—most people who lived during the high medieval period witnessed changes much closer to home that had a far greater impact on their own lives, families, and local communities. Kings and popes sent tax collectors, judges, and sometimes soldiers, but they were far away. For most people, what went on in their families and local communities was far more important. ■

- **For a list of suggested readings for this chapter, visit** *bedfordstmartins.com/mckaywestunderstanding*.

- **For primary sources from this period, see** *Sources of Western Society*, Second Edition.

- **For Web sites, images, and documents related to topics in this chapter, see Make History at** *bedfordstmartins.com/mckaywestunderstanding*.

How did the administration of law evolve in this period?	What led to conflict between the papacy and secular leaders?	What were the causes and consequences of the Crusades?	**How did Christianity spread during the High Middle Ages?**

Step 1

GETTING STARTED Below are basic terms about this period in the history of Western civilization. Can you identify each term below and explain why it matters? To do this exercise online, go to bedfordstmartins.com/mckaywestunderstanding.

TERMS	WHO (OR WHAT) AND WHEN	WHY IT MATTERS
Domesday Book, p. 232		
Exchequer, p. 232		
primogeniture, p. 233		
Holy Roman Empire, p. 234		
reconquista, p. 238		
common law, p. 239		
Magna Carta, p. 240		
simony, p. 241		
college of cardinals, p. 242		
lay investiture, p. 242		
excommunication, p. 242		
canon law, p. 244		
Crusades, p. 245		
indulgences, p. 245		
Inquisition, p. 251		
Christendom, p. 256		

Step 2

MOVING BEYOND THE BASICS The exercise below requires a more advanced understanding of the chapter material. Examine the process of political centralization in England, France, the Iberian Peninsula, central Europe, and Sicily by filling in the chart below with descriptions of developments in each region in three key areas: administration and bureaucracy, armies and warfare, and judicial systems. When you are finished, consider the following questions: What policies and tactics were common to centralizing efforts across Europe? What obstacles to political centralization remained at the end of the High Middle Ages? To do this exercise online, go to bedfordstmartins.com/mckaywestunderstanding.

REGION	ADMINISTRATION AND BUREAUCRACY	ARMIES AND WARFARE	JUDICIAL SYSTEMS
England			
France			
The Iberian Peninsula			
Central Europe			
Sicily			

PUTTING IT ALL TOGETHER Now that you've reviewed key elements of the chapter, take a step back and try to see the big picture. Remember to use specific examples from the chapter in your answers. To do this exercise online, go to bedfordstmartins.com/mckaywestunderstanding.

POLITICAL AND LEGAL CENTRALIZATION

- What are the key characteristics of modern national states? What steps did medieval monarchs take toward the creation of such states?

- Why did medieval monarchs try to expand the scope of royal judicial systems? How might the expansion of royal law be connected to the expansion of royal power?

CHURCH AND STATE

- What were the key components of papal reform efforts? What problems were the reforms meant to address? How successful were they?

- In what areas did the power of the church and of secular leaders overlap in the High Middle Ages? How did such overlaps lead to conflicts between the papacy and Europe's monarchs?

THE CRUSADES

- Compare and contrast the Crusades and the Spanish reconquista. What important similarities do you note?

- How did the Crusades help forge closer connections between Europe and the Muslim world? How did they help drive a wedge between the two civilizations?

THE CONTINUING CHRISTIANIZATION OF EUROPE

- What explains the key role monarchs often played in Christianization? What benefits did monarchs hope to gain from the expansion of the church and its teachings?

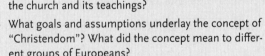

- What goals and assumptions underlay the concept of "Christendom"? What did the concept mean to different groups of Europeans?

■ **In Your Own Words** Imagine that you must explain Chapter 9 to someone who hasn't read it. What would be the most important points to include and why?

10

The Life of the People in the High Middle Ages

1000–1300

In a text produced at the court of Anglo-Saxon king Alfred, Christian society is described as composed of three orders: those who pray, those who fight, and those who work. This image of society became popular in the High Middle Ages, especially among people who worried that the social organization might be breaking down. Such people asserted that the three orders had been established by God and that every person had been assigned a fixed place in the social order.

This three-part model does not fully describe medieval society, however. There were degrees of wealth and status within each group. The model does not take townspeople and the emerging commercial classes (see Chapter 11) into consideration. Its categorization of "those who pray" disregards people who were not Christian, such as Jews, Muslims, and pagans. Those who used the model, generally bishops and other church officials, ignored the fact that each of these groups was made up of both women and men; they spoke only of warriors, monks, and farmers. Despite—or perhaps because of—these limitations, the model of the three orders was a powerful mental construct. We can use it to organize our investigation of life in the High Middle Ages, though we can broaden our categories to include groups and issues that medieval authors did not. ■

Life in the High Middle Ages. In this scene from a German manuscript, the artist shows men and women of different ages sowing seed and harvesting grain. All residents in a village, including children, engaged in agricultural tasks. (Rheinisches Landesmuseum, Bonn/ The Bridgeman Art Library)

Chapter Preview

▶ **What was village life like in medieval Europe?**

▶ **How did religion shape everyday life in medieval Europe?**

▶ **What roles did nobles play in medieval society?**

▶ **What roles did monks and nuns play in medieval life?**

▼ What was village life like in medieval Europe?

Since villagers did not perform what were considered "noble" deeds, the aristocratic monks and clerics who wrote the records that serve as historical sources did not spend time or precious writing materials on the peasantry. When common people were mentioned, it was usually with contempt or in terms of the services and obligations they owed. There were exceptions. In the early twelfth century Honorius (huh-NAWR-ee-uhs), a monk and teacher at the monastery of Autun, wrote: "What do you say about the agricultural classes? Most of them will be saved because they live simply and feed God's people by means of their sweat."[1]

Slavery, Serfdom, and Upward Mobility

the three orders Model of the divisions of society in the High Middle Ages into those who pray, those who fight, and those who work.

When discussing the three orders, medieval theologians lumped everyone who worked the land into the category of "those who work," but in fact there were many levels of peasants ranging from outright slaves to free and very rich farmers. The High Middle Ages was a period of considerable fluidity with significant social mobility, particularly because people's legal status was based on memory and traditions, not on written documents.

The number of slaves who worked the land declined steadily in the High Middle Ages. Those who remained tended to live with wealthier peasant families or with lords, doing whatever work their masters ordered. Most rural people in western Europe during this period were serfs rather than slaves, though the

---

▪ PICTURING THE PAST

The Three Orders of Society

This fourteenth-century book illustration shows the most common image of medieval society: those who fight, those who pray, and those who work. The nun shown in the center panel was not technically a member of the clergy, but most people considered nuns as such. (Bibliothèque royale, Brussels)

ANALYZING THE IMAGE Who is included in the depiction of each category of society? Who is not?

CONNECTIONS Are the categories of those who fight, those who pray, and those who work useful for understanding life in the High Middle Ages? If not, what additional categories do you think need to be added?

To complete this activity online, go to the Online Study Guide at bedfordstmartins.com/mckaywestunderstanding.

distinction between slave and serf was not always clear. Both lacked freedom and both were subject to the arbitrary will of one person, the lord. Unlike a slave, however, a serf could not be bought and sold like an animal.

Most serfs lived in their own families, not with others, and worked small plots of land; in addition, all serfs were required to perform labor services on a lord's land, usually three days a week except during the planting or harvest seasons, when it was more. Serfs frequently had to pay arbitrary levies on common occurrences. When a man married, he had to pay his lord a fee. When he died, his son or heir had to pay an inheritance tax to inherit his parcels of land. The precise amounts of tax paid to the lord on these important family occasions depended on local custom and tradition.

Serfdom was a hereditary condition. A person born a serf was likely to die a serf, though many serfs did secure their freedom. The development of a money economy that began in the eleventh century (see Chapter 11) advanced the cause of freedom for serfs more than any other factor. With the advent of a money economy, serfs could save money and use it to buy their freedom.

Another opportunity for increased personal freedom came when lords organized groups of villagers to cut down forests or fill in swamps and marshes between villages to make more land available for farming. Free and serf peasants migrated to these new farmlands, and some went much farther, such as German peasants who migrated eastward into Slavic lands. This type of agricultural advancement frequently improved the peasants' social and legal condition. A serf could clear a patch of fen or forestland, make it productive, and, through prudent saving, buy more land and eventually purchase freedom. In addition to serfs who migrated to find new opportunities, peasants who remained in the villages of their birth often benefited because landlords, threatened with the loss of serfs, relaxed ancient obligations and duties. While it would be unwise to exaggerate the social impact of the settling of new territories, frontier lands in the High Middle Ages did provide opportunities for upward mobility.

The Manor

Most European peasants, free and serf, lived in family groups in small villages. One or more villages and the land surrounding them made up a manor controlled by a noble lord or a church official such as a bishop, abbot, or abbess. Peasant dwellings were usually clumped together, with the fields stretching out beyond the group of houses. Most villages had a church. In some the lord's large residence was right next to the small peasant houses, while in others the lord lived in a castle separate from the village (Figure 10.1). Manors controlled by a single lord varied greatly in size;

Chapter Chronology

909	Abbey of Cluny established
1050–1300	Steady rise in population; period of milder climate
1098	Cistercian Order established
1100s	Production of iron increases; hospitals and other homes for the sick begin appearing; knights begin claiming noble status
1200s	Expansion of noble territories increases migration of serfs; notion of chivalry develops
1215	Fourth Lateran Council accepts seven sacraments

Figure 10.1 **A Medieval Manor** The basic unit of rural organization and the center of life for most people, the manor constituted the medieval peasants' world.

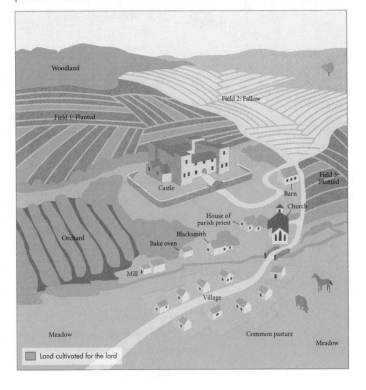

Woodland

Field 2: Fallow

Field 1: Planted

Castle

Field 3: Planted

Barn

Church

House of parish priest

Orchard

Blacksmith

Bake oven

Mill

Village

Meadow

Common pasture

Meadow

Land cultivated for the lord

CHAPTER LOCATOR | **What was village life like in medieval Europe?** | How did religion shape everyday life in medieval Europe? | What roles did nobles play in medieval society? | What roles did monks and nuns play in medieval life?

263

Boarstall Manor, Buckinghamshire In 1440 Edmund Rede, lord of this estate, had a map made showing his ancestor receiving the title from King Edward I (bottom). Note the manor house, church, and peasants' cottages along the central road. In the common fields, divided by hedges, peasants cultivated on a three-year rotation cycle: winter wheat, spring oats, a year fallow. We don't know whether peasants were allowed to hunt the deer shown in the forest. (Buckinghamshire Record Office, Aylesbury)

some contained a number of villages, and some were very small. Regardless of size, the manor was the basic unit of medieval rural organization and the center of rural life.

The arable land of the manor was divided between the lord and the peasantry, with the lord's portion known as the demesne (dih-MAYN), or home farm. A manor usually held pasture or meadowland for the grazing of cattle, sheep, and sometimes goats. Often the manor had some forestland as well. Forests were valuable resources, providing wood, ash, and resin for a variety of purposes. Forests were also used for feeding pigs, cattle, and domestic animals on nuts, roots, and wild berries. If the manor was intersected by a river, it had a welcome source of fish and eels.

Lords generally appointed officials— termed "bailiffs" in England—from outside the village to oversee the legal and business operations of their manors, collect taxes and fees, and handle disputes. Villages in many parts of Europe also developed institutions of self-government to handle issues such as crop rotation, and they chose additional officials such as constables and ale-tasters without the lord's interference. Women had no official voice in running the village, but they did buy, sell, and hold land independently and, especially as widows, head households. In areas of Europe where men were gone fishing or foresting for long periods of time, or where men left seasonally or more permanently in search of work elsewhere, women made decisions about the way village affairs were to be run, though they did not set up formal institutions to do this.

Manors do not represent the only form of medieval rural economy. In parts of Germany and the Netherlands and in much of southern France, free independent farmers owned land outright, free of rents and services. Their farms tended to be small and were surrounded by large estates that gradually swallowed them up. In Scandinavia the soil was so poor and the climate so harsh that people tended to live on widely scattered farms rather than in villages, but they still lived in relatively small family groups.

Work

The peasants' work was typically divided according to gender. Men were responsible for clearing new land, plowing, and caring for large animals, and women were responsible for caring for small animals, spinning, and preparing food. Both sexes planted and harvested, though often there were gender-specific tasks within each of these major undertakings.

Once children were able to walk, they helped their parents with the hundreds of chores that had to be done. Small children were set to collecting eggs if the family had chickens, or gathering twigs and sticks for firewood. As they grew older, children had more responsible tasks, such as weeding the family's vegetable garden, milking the cows, shearing the sheep, cutting wood for fires, and helping with the planting or harvesting.

Medieval farmers employed the open-field system, a pattern that differs sharply from modern farming practices. In the open-field system, the arable land of a manor was divided into two or three fields without hedges or fences to mark the individual holdings of the lord, serfs, and freemen. The village as a whole decided what would be planted in each field, rotating the crops according to tradition and need. Some fields would be planted in crops such as wheat, rye, peas, or barley for human consumption, some in oats or other crops for both animals and humans, and some would be left unworked or fallow to allow the soil to rejuvenate. In most areas with open-field agriculture the holdings farmed by any one family did not consist of a whole field but, instead, of strips in many fields. If one strip held by a family yielded little, strips in a different field might be more bountiful. Families worked their own land and the lord's, but they also cooperated with other families if they needed help, particularly during harvest time. This meant that all shared in any disaster as well as in any large harvest.

Meteorologists think that a slow but steady retreat of polar ice occurred between the ninth and eleventh centuries, and Europe experienced a significant warming trend during the period from 1050 to 1300. The mild winters and dry summers associated with this warming trend helped to increase agricultural output throughout Europe.

The tenth and eleventh centuries also witnessed a number of agricultural improvements, especially in the development of mechanisms that replaced or aided human labor. Mills driven by wind and water power represented significant engineering advancements, dramatically reducing the time and labor required to grind grain. Water mills were also well suited to the process known as fulling—cleansing and beating woven cloth so that tiny fibers filled in the holes between the threads, making the cloth more wind- and waterproof—enabling men and women to full cloth at a much faster rate. In the flat areas of northern Europe, such as Holland, where fast-flowing streams were rare, windmills were more common than water mills.

Women's productivity in medieval Europe grew because of water and wind power. In the ancient world, slaves had been responsible for grinding the grain for bread; as slavery was replaced by serfdom, grinding became a woman's task. When water- and wind-driven mills were introduced into an area, women were freed from the task of grinding grain and could turn to other tasks, such as raising animals, working in gardens or vineyards, and raising and preparing flax to make linen. Women could also devote more time to spinning yarn, which was the bottleneck in cloth production, as each weaver needed at least six spinners. Thus wind and water power contributed to the increase in cloth production in medieval Europe.

In the early twelfth century the production of iron increased significantly. Much of this was used for weapons and armor, but it also filled a growing demand in agriculture. Iron was first used for plowshares, and then for pitchforks, spades, and axes. Harrows—cultivating instruments with heavy teeth that broke up and smoothed the soil—began to have iron instead of wooden teeth, making them more effective and less likely to break.

Plows and harrows were increasingly drawn by horses rather than oxen. The development of the padded horse collar led to dramatic improvements. The horse collar meant that the animal could put its entire weight into the task of pulling. The use of horses spread in the twelfth century because their greater speed brought greater efficiency to farming and reduced the amount of human labor involved.

The thirteenth century witnessed a tremendous spurt in the use of horses to haul carts to market. Consequently, goods reached market faster, and peasants had access to more markets. Peasants not only sold vegetables, grain, and animals but they also bought metal

open-field system System in which the arable land of a manor was divided into two or three fields without hedges or fences to mark individual holdings.

CHAPTER LOCATOR | **What was village life like in medieval Europe?** | How did religion shape everyday life in medieval Europe? | What roles did nobles play in medieval society? | What roles did monks and nuns play in medieval life?

265

Ox Team Plowing From an eleventh-century calendar showing manorial occupations, this illustration for January—the time for sowing winter wheat—shows two pair of oxen pulling a wheeled plow. Wheeled plows allowed for faster work and deeper tillage, but they still required large inputs of human labor. Here one man prods the animals, a second directs the plow blade, and a third drops seed in the ground. (© British Library Board, Cott. Tib. B.V.3, Min. Pt 1)

tools, leather shoes, and other goods. Their opportunities for spending on at least a few nonagricultural goods multiplied.

Increased agricultural output had a profound impact on society, improving Europeans' health, commerce, industry, and general lifestyle. More food meant that fewer people suffered from hunger and malnourishment on a daily basis, and that devastating famines were rarer. Higher yields brought more food for animals as well as people, and the amount of meat that people ate increased slightly. A better diet had an enormous impact on women's lives in particular. More food meant increased body fat, which increased fertility, and more meat—which provided iron—meant that women were less anemic and less subject to opportunistic diseases. Improved opportunities also encouraged people to marry somewhat earlier, which meant larger families and further population growth.

Home Life and Diet

Life for most people in medieval Europe meant country life. Most people rarely traveled more than twenty-five miles beyond their villages. This way of life did not have entirely unfortunate results. People were closely connected with their family, certain of its support and help in time of trouble. The relative peace and political stabilization allowed people to develop a strong sense of place and a pride in their community.

In western and central Europe, villages were generally made up of small houses for individual families. Households consisted of one married couple, their children (including stepchildren), and perhaps one or two other relatives. The household thus contained primarily a nuclear family. In southern and eastern Europe, extended families were more likely to live in the same household or very near one another.

The size and quality of peasants' houses varied according to their relative prosperity, and that prosperity usually depended on the amount of land held. Poorer peasants lived in windowless cottages built of wood and clay or wattle (poles interwoven with branches or reeds) and thatched with straw. Such a cottage consisted of one large room that served as the kitchen and living quarters for all. A shed attached to the house provided storage for tools and shelter for animals. Prosperous peasants added rooms, and some wealthy peasants in the early fourteenth century had two-story houses with separate bedrooms for parents and children. For most people, however, living space was cramped, dark, smoky, and smelly, with animals and people both sharing tight quarters, sometimes with each other.

Every house had a small garden and an outbuilding. Onions, garlic, turnips, and carrots were grown and were stored through the winter in the main room of the dwelling or in the shed attached to it. Preserving and storing foods were the basic responsibilities of the women and children.

The mainstay of the diet for peasants everywhere—and for all other classes—was bread. It was a hard, black substance made of barley, millet, and oats, rarely of expensive wheat flour. Most households did not have ovens, which were expensive to build and posed a fire danger. Thus bread was baked in communal ovens or purchased from households that specialized in bread baking. The main meal was often bread and a thick soup of vegetables and grains eaten around noon. Animals were too valuable to be used for food on a regular basis, but weaker animals were often slaughtered in the fall so that they did not need to be fed through the winter, and their meat was salted and eaten on feast days such as Christmas and Easter.

The diet of people living in an area with access to a river, lake, or stream would be supplemented with fish, which could be preserved by salting. People living close to the sea could gather shellfish. Many places had severe laws against hunting and trapping in the

Making Cloth In this household scene, women in the foreground prepare cloth while men in the background eat a meal. The woman on the left is trimming small threads off with a one-bladed shear, and the one on the right is boiling the cloth to clean and bleach it. Women usually made the clothing for themselves and their families, although the more elaborate clothing worn by nobles was made by professional tailors and seamstresses. (Austrian National Library, Vienna/The Bridgeman Art Library)

Baking Bread Bread and beer or ale were the main manorial products for local consumption. While women dominated the making of ale and beer, men and women cooperated in the making and baking of bread. Most people did not have ovens in their own homes because of the danger of fire, but instead used the communal manorial oven, which, like a modern pizza oven, could bake several loaves at once. (Bibliothèque nationale de France)

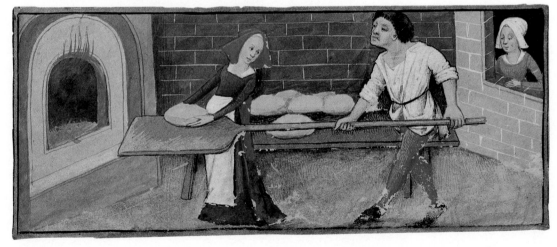

CHAPTER LOCATOR | **What was village life like in medieval Europe?** · How did religion shape everyday life in medieval Europe? · What roles did nobles play in medieval society? · What roles did monks and nuns play in medieval life?

267

forests. Deer, wild boars, and other game were strictly reserved for the king and nobility. These laws were flagrantly violated, however, and stolen rabbits and wild game often found their way to peasants' tables.

Medieval households were not self-sufficient: they bought cloth, metal, leather goods, and even some food from village market stalls. They also bought and drank large quantities of ale, the universal drink of the common people in northern Europe. Women dominated in the production of ale for the community market.

Health Care

Scholars are only beginning to explore questions of medieval health care, and there are still many aspects of public health that we know little about. The steady rise in population between the mid-eleventh and fourteenth centuries, usually attributed to warmer climate, increased food supply, and a reduction of violence with growing political stability, may also be ascribed partly to better health care.

What care existed for the sick? As in the past, the sick everywhere depended above all on the private nursing care of relatives and friends. Beginning in the twelfth century in the British Isles, however, the royal family, the clergy, noble men and women, and newly rich merchants also established institutions to care for the sick or for those who for some reason could not take care of themselves. Within city walls they built hospitals, which were not hospitals in the modern sense, but rather places where those with chronic diseases that were not contagious, poor expectant mothers, the handicapped, people recovering from injuries, foundling children, and mentally retarded or psychologically disturbed children or adults went for care. Outside city walls they built leprosariums or small hospices for people with leprosy and other contagious diseases.

In the twelfth century medical personnel at hospitals were trained on the job, but by the thirteenth century some had studied with the faculties of medicine at Europe's new universities (see Chapter 11). Outside of hospitals, people suffering from wounds, skin diseases, or broken bones turned to barber-surgeons who were trained in an apprenticeship system. For other internal ailments people used apothecaries—also trained through an apprenticeship system—to suggest and mix drugs. People also relied on men and women who had no official training at all, but who had learned healing techniques from their parents or other older people.

Treatments were often mixtures of herbal remedies, sayings, specific foods, prayers, amulets, and ritual healing activities. Such combinations were also what people prescribed for themselves, for most treatment of illness was handled by home remedies handed down orally or perhaps through a cherished handwritten family herbal, cookbook, or household guide.

Childbirth and Child Abandonment

The most dangerous period of life for any person, peasant or noble, was infancy and early childhood. In normal years perhaps as many as one-third of all children died before age five, and this share climbed to more than half in years with plagues, droughts, or famines. Reaching adulthood meant that people had survived the most dangerous part of their lives, and many lived well into their fifties and sixties.

Childbirth was dangerous for mothers as well as for infants. Women developed prayers, rituals, and special sayings to ensure safe and speedy childbirth. Village women helped one another through childbirth, and women who were more capable acquired specialized midwifery skills. In larger towns and cities, such women gradually developed into professional midwives who were paid for their services and who trained younger women as apprentices, just as barber-surgeons and apothecaries trained their male apprentices.

For most women, however, childbirth was handled by female friends and family, not by professionals.

The abandonment of infants and young children was widely practiced throughout the Middle Ages. Parents or guardians left children at a monastery or church, sold them, or legally gave the authority for their upbringing to some other person or institution. Sometimes parents believed that someone of greater means or status might find the child and bring it up in better circumstances than the natal parents could provide. Christian parents gave their children to monasteries as religious acts, donating them to the service of God in the same way they might donate money.

Recent research suggests that abandonment was very common among the poor until about the year 1000. The next three hundred years, which saw great agricultural change and relative prosperity, witnessed a low point in the abandonment of poor children. On the other hand, in the twelfth and thirteenth centuries the incidence of noble parents giving their younger sons and daughters to religious houses increased dramatically. This resulted from and also reinforced the system of primogeniture, in which estates were passed intact to the eldest son instead of being divided among heirs (Chapter 9). Monasteries provided noble younger sons and daughters with career opportunities, and this also removed them as contenders for family land.

Child Donated to a Monastery In this twelfth-century manuscript, an abbot receives a small boy from a man who is probably his father. The man also gives the abbot money, which further enhanced the value of this offering of his son. The boy does not look enthusiastic at the prospects of his life in the monastery. (The J. Paul Getty Museum, Los Angeles. Unknown illuminator, Initial Q: An Abbot Receiving a Child Decretum, ca. 1170–1180 [83.MQ.163.fol.63])

▼ How did religion shape everyday life in medieval Europe?

Apart from the land, the weather, and local legal and social conditions, religion had the greatest impact on the daily lives of ordinary people in the High Middle Ages. Most people in medieval Europe were Christian, but there were small Jewish communities scattered in many parts of Europe and Muslims in the Iberian Peninsula, Sicily, other Mediterranean islands, and southeastern Europe.

Christian Life in Medieval Villages

For Christians the village church was the center of community life — social, political, and economic, as well as religious — with the parish priest in charge of a host of activities. Standing at the side door of the church, the priest read orders and messages from royal and ecclesiastical authorities to his parishioners gathered outside. The front of the church, with its scenes of the Last Judgment, was the background against which royal judges traveling on circuit disposed of civil and criminal cases. In busy cities, business agreements and commercial exchanges were made in the square in front of the church or even inside the church itself.

CHAPTER LOCATOR | What was village life like in medieval Europe? | **How did religion shape everyday life in medieval Europe?** | What roles did nobles play in medieval society? | What roles did monks and nuns play in medieval life?

269

Although church law placed the priest under the bishop's authority, the manorial lord appointed the priest. Parish priests were peasants and often were poor. Since they often worked in the fields with the people, they understood the people's labor, needs, and frustrations. The parish priest was also responsible for the upkeep of the church and for taking the lead in providing aid to the poorest of the village.

The center of the Christian religious life was the Mass in which a priest consecrated bread and wine and distributed it to believers, in a re-enactment of Jesus' actions in the Bible. Every Sunday and on holy days, villagers watched and listened to Mass, which was recited in Latin—a language that few commoners could speak or understand. At least once a year they were expected to take part in the ceremony and eat the consecrated bread. This usually happened at Easter, after they had confessed their sins to a priest and been assigned a penance in compensation for them. The feasts that accompanied baptisms, weddings, funerals, and other celebrations were commonly held in the churchyard. Medieval drama originated in the church. Mystery plays, based on biblical episodes, were performed originally in the sanctuary, later in the churchyard, and eventually at stations around the town.

The scripted portions of the Mass were said in Latin, but the priest delivered his weekly sermons in the vernacular. A common complaint was that priests did a poor job of explaining basic Christian teachings to their parishioners. Nevertheless, people grasped the meaning of biblical stories and church doctrines from the paintings on the church walls or, in wealthy parishes, the scenes on stained-glass windows.

Along with attending Mass and confessing their sins, people engaged in rituals heavy with religious symbolism. Scriptural references and proverbs dotted everyone's language. The English *good-bye*, the French *adieu*, and the Spanish *adios* all derive from words meaning "God be with you." Everyone participated in village processions to honor the saints and ask their protection. The entire calendar was filled with reference to events in the life of Jesus and his disciples, such as Christmas, Easter, and Pentecost. The signs and symbols of Christianity were everywhere, but so, people believed, was the Devil, who lured them to evil deeds.

Saints and Sacraments

Along with days marking events in the life of Jesus, the Christian calendar was filled with saints' days. Veneration of the saints had been an important tool of Christian conversion since late antiquity (see Chapter 7), and the cult of the saints was a central feature of popular culture in the Middle Ages. People believed that the saints possessed supernatural powers that enabled them to perform miracles, and the saint became the special property of the locality in which his or her relics rested. Relics such as bones, tears, saliva, articles of clothing, and even the dust from the saint's tomb were enclosed in the church altar. In return for the saint's healing and support, peasants would offer the saint prayers, loyalty, and gifts. (See "Listening to the Past: The Pilgrim's Guide to Santiago de Compostela," page 272.)

In the later Middle Ages popular hagiographies (ha-gee-AH-gruh-fees)—biographies of saints based on myths, legends, and popular stories—attributed specialized functions to the saints. Saint Elmo (ca. 300), who supposedly had preached unharmed during a thunder and lightning storm, became the patron of sailors. Saint Agatha (third century), whose breasts were torn with shears because she rejected the attentions of a powerful suitor, became the patron of wet nurses, women with breast difficulties, and bell ringers (because of the resemblance of breasts to bells).

How were saints chosen? Since the early days of Christianity, individuals whose exemplary virtue was proved by miracles at their tombs had been venerated by laypeople. Roman authorities insisted that they had the exclusive right to examine the lives and activities of candidates for sainthood in a formal "trial," but ordinary people continued to

Statue of St. Anne, the Virgin Mary, and the Christ Child Nearly every church had at least one image of the Virgin Mary, the most important figure of Christian devotion in medieval Europe. In this thirteenth-century wooden sculpture, she is shown holding the infant Jesus and is herself sitting on the lap of her mother Anne. Statues such as this reinforced people's sense that the heavenly family was much like theirs, with grandparents who sometimes played important roles. (Scala/Art Resource, NY)

declare people saints. Between 1185 and 1431 only seventy official investigations were held at Rome, but hundreds of new persons across Europe were venerated as saints. Some clergy preached against the veneration of saints' relics and called it idolatry, but their appeals had little effect.

The Virgin Mary, Christ's mother, was the most important saint. In the eleventh century theologians began to emphasize Mary's spiritual motherhood of all Christians. Masses specially commemorated her, churches were built in her honor, and hymns and prayers to her multiplied. Villagers listened intently to sermons telling stories about her life and miracles.

Along with the veneration of saints, sacraments were an important part of religious practice in the High Middle Ages. Twelfth-century theologians expanded on Saint Augustine's understanding of sacraments (see Chapter 7) and created an entire sacramental system. The list of seven sacraments (baptism, penance, the Eucharist, confirmation, marriage, priestly ordination, anointment of the dying) was formally accepted by the Fourth Lateran Council in 1215. Most sacraments had to be dispensed by a priest, although spouses officially administered the sacrament of marriage to each other, and laypeople could baptize a dying infant or anoint a dying person if no priest could be found. Medieval Christians believed that these seven sacraments brought God's grace, the divine assistance or help needed to lead a good Christian life and to merit salvation. The sacramental system enhanced the authority of priests over people's lives, but it did not replace strong personal devotion to the saints.

Muslims and Jews

The centrality of Christian ceremonies to daily life for most Europeans meant that those who did not participate were clearly marked as outsiders. This included Muslims in the Iberian Peninsula, where Christian rulers were establishing kingdoms in territory won through the reconquista (see Chapter 9). Islam was outlawed in their territories, and some of the Muslims left Spain or were forced out, leaving room for new settlers from elsewhere in Christian Europe. Other Muslims converted. In more isolated villages, people simply continued their Muslim rituals and practices, though they might hide this from the local priest or visiting church or government officials.

Islam was geographically limited in medieval Europe, but by the late tenth century Jews could be found in many areas, often brought in from other parts of Europe as clients of rulers because of their skills as merchants. There were Jewish communities in

CHAPTER LOCATOR | What was village life like in medieval Europe? | **How did religion shape everyday life in medieval Europe?** | What roles did nobles play in medieval society? | What roles did monks and nuns play in medieval life?

271

The Pilgrim's Guide to Santiago de Compostela

Making pilgrimages to the shrines of holy persons is a common practice in many religions. A pilgrimage to Mecca, for example, is obligatory for all Muslims. Many Christian shrines contained a body understood to be that of a saint or objects that had been in physical contact with the saint; thus believers perceived shrines as places where Heaven and earth met. A visit to a shrine and veneration of the saint's relics, Christians believed, would lead to the saint's intercession with God. Medieval Christians of all social classes made pilgrimages; even serfs were supposed to be allowed to leave their manor if they wanted to go on a pilgrimage. After Jerusalem and Rome, the shrine of Santiago de Compostela (Saint James at Compostela) in the Iberian Peninsula became the most famous in the Christian world. The shrine was situated in the kingdom of Navarre (nuh-VAHR), a small state in what is now northwestern Spain.

The apostle James is said to have carried Christianity to Spain, then returned to Palestine where he was beheaded, the first apostle martyred. Somehow James's bones were miraculously taken back to Compostela, where they were later discovered, and the first of a series of churches was built on the site. In 1075 Alfonso VI of Castile, one of the most important leaders of the reconquista, began construction of a huge shrine-cathedral at the site of James's tomb. In the 1300s James himself was linked to the reconquista, as church and state officials promoted the legend that James had begun the expulsion of Muslims from Spain. The fact that the Prophet Muhammad, the founder of Islam, lived six centuries after James did not bother those telling the story, and images of "St. James the Moor-slayer" became common.

Pilgrims streamed to the site from all over Europe, particularly as roads were improved and hostels and inns opened along the routes. Once at the shrine, pilgrims were expected to make contributions as large as their means allowed, lest the saint be offended and retaliate with some sort of affliction. Pilgrims' donations financed the superb Romanesque sculpture at Santiago. In the twelfth century an unknown French author gathered many of the pilgrims' experiences, along with accounts of the life and martyrdom of Saint James and the miracles attributed to him after his death. He put these together in a sort of guidebook, which

was frequently recopied for interested readers. This Pilgrim's Guide describes the scene at the cathedral itself and also details the characteristics of people one would meet on the way.

❝ The church, however, was begun in the year 1116 of the Spanish era [1078 C.E.]. . . . From the time when it was begun up to the present day, this church is renewed by the light of the miracles of the blessed James. In it, indeed, health is given to the sick, sight restored to the blind, the tongue of the mute is loosened, hearing is given to the deaf, soundness of limb is granted to cripples, the possessed are delivered, and what is more, the prayers of the faithful are heard, their vows are accepted, the bonds of sin are broken, heaven is opened to those who knock, consolation is given to the grieving, and all the people of foreign nations, flocking from all parts of the world, come together here in crowds bearing with them gifts of praise to the Lord. . . .

After this valley is found the land of Navarre which abounds in bread and wine, milk and cattle.

Map 10.1 **Medieval Pilgrims' Routes** Monasteries in Cluny, Vézelay, Saint-Gilles, and Moissac served as inns for pilgrims.

Italian and French cities and in the cities along the Rhine such as Cologne, Worms, Speyer, and Mainz. Jewish dietary laws require meat to be handled in a specific way, so Jews had their own butchers; there were Jewish artisans in many other trades as well. Jews held weekly religious services on Saturday, the Sabbath holy day of rest, and celebrated an annual cycle of holidays, including the High Holidays of Rosh Hashanah and Yom Kippur in the fall and Passover in the spring. Each of these holidays involved special prayers,

The Navarrese and Basques [BASKZ; another group that lived in Navarre] are held to be exactly alike in their food, their clothing and their language, but the Basques are held to be of whiter complexion than the Navarrese. The Navarrese wear short black garments extending just down to the knee, like the Scots, and they wear sandals which they call *lavarcas* made of raw hide with the hair on and are bound around the foot with thongs, covering only the soles of the feet and leaving the upper foot bare. In truth, they wear black woollen hooded and fringed capes, reaching to their elbows, which they call *saias*. These people, in truth, are repulsively dressed, and they eat and drink repulsively. For in fact all those who dwell in the household of a Navarrese, servant as well as master, maid as well as mistress, are accustomed to eat all their food mixed together from one pot, not with spoons but with their own hands, and they drink with one cup. If you saw them eat you would think them dogs or pigs. If you heard them speak, you would be reminded of the barking of dogs. For their speech is utterly barbarous. . . .

This is a barbarous race unlike all other races in customs and in character, full of malice, swarthy in color, evil of face, depraved, perverse, perfidious, empty of faith and corrupt, libidinous, drunken, experienced in all violence, ferocious and wild, dishonest and reprobate, impious and harsh, cruel and contentious, unversed in anything good, well-trained in all vices and iniquities, like the Geats and Saracens in malice. . . .

However, they are considered good on the battlefield, bad at assaulting fortresses, regular in giving tithes, accustomed to making offerings for altars. For, each day, when the Navarrese goes to church, he makes God an offering of bread or wine or wheat or some other substance. . . . Then comes Galicia [guh-LIH-shee-uh] . . . this is wooded and has rivers

and is well-provided with meadows and excellent orchards, with equally good fruits and very clear springs; there are few cities, towns or cornfields. It is short of wheaten bread and wine, bountiful in rye bread and cider, well-stocked with cattle and horses, milk and honey, ocean fish both gigantic and small, and wealthy in gold, silver, fabrics, and furs of forest animals and other riches, as well as Saracen treasures. The Galicians, in truth, more than all the other uncultivated Spanish peoples, are those who most closely resemble our French race by their manners, but they are alleged to be irascible and very litigious. 》

Pilgrim's badge from Santiago de Compostela. Enterprising smiths made metal badges for pilgrims to buy as proof of their journey and piety. The scallop-shell shape shown here became associated with Saint James and eventually with pilgrimages in general. Pilgrims who had visited many shrines would clink from the many badges worn on their hats or capes, sometimes becoming objects of satire just as tourists laden with souvenirs are today. (Institut Amatller d'Art Hispànic)

Source: *The Pilgrim's Guide to Santiago de Compostela*, critical edition and annotated translation by Paula Gerson, Jeanne Krochalis, Annie Shaver-Crandell, and Alison Stones. Copyright © 1997. Reprinted by permission of the authors. Data for map from Jonathan Sumption, *Pilgrimage: An Image of Medieval Religion* (Totowa, N.J.: Rowman and Littlefield, 1975).

QUESTIONS FOR ANALYSIS

1. What sorts of miracles does the author describe as happening at the church? How would you compare his description of the miracles with the descriptions of the people?
2. How would you evaluate the author's opinion of the people of Navarre? of Galicia? How does he compare these people to his own countrymen, the French?
3. Pilgrimages were in many ways the precursors of modern tourism. How would you compare the two in terms of economic effects and the expectations of the travelers?

services, and often foods, and many of them commemorated specific events from Jewish history, including various times when Jews had been rescued from captivity.

Jews could supply other Jews with goods and services, but rulers and city leaders increasingly restricted their trade with Christians to banking and moneylending. This enhanced Christian resentment, as did the ideology of holy war that accompanied the Crusades (see Chapter 9). Violence against Jews and restrictions on their activities increased

CHAPTER LOCATOR | What was village life like in medieval Europe? | **How did religion shape everyday life in medieval Europe?** | What roles did nobles play in medieval society? | What roles did monks and nuns play in medieval life?

273

further in much of Europe. Jews were expelled from England and later from France, and many of them went to Muslim and Christian areas of the Iberian Peninsula. The rulers of both faiths initially welcomed them, though restrictions and violence gradually became more common there as well. Jews continued to live in the independent cities of the Holy Roman Empire and Italy, and some migrated eastward into new towns that were being established in Slavic areas.

Rituals of Marriage and Birth

Increasing suspicion and hostility marked relations between religious groups throughout the Middle Ages, but there were also important similarities in the ways Christians, Jews, and Muslims in Europe understood and experienced their religions. In all three traditions, every major life transition was marked by a ceremony that included religious elements.

Christian weddings might be held in the village church or at the church door. A priest's blessing was often sought, though it was not essential to the marriage, for Christian doctrine defined marriage as an agreement between a man and a woman. Muslim weddings were also finalized by a contract between the bride and groom and were often overseen by a wedding official. Jewish weddings were guided by statements in Talmudic law that weddings were complete when the bride had entered the "chuppah," which medieval Jewish authorities interpreted to mean a room in the groom's house.

Wedding Door of the Cathedral in Strasbourg Medieval cathedrals, such as this one from the thirteenth century, sometimes had a side door depicting a biblical story of ten young women who went to meet a bridegroom. Five of them wisely took extra oil for their lamps, while five foolishly did not (Matthew 25:1–13). In the story, which is a parable about being prepared for the end of the world, the foolish maidens were out of oil when the bridegroom arrived and they missed the wedding feast. The "maidens' door" became a popular site for weddings, which were held right in front of it. (Erich Lessing/Art Resource, NY)

For spouses of all faiths, the wedding ceremony was followed by a wedding party that often included secular rituals. Some rituals symbolized the "proper" hierarchical relations between the spouses—such as placing the husband's shoe on the bedstead over the couple, symbolizing his authority—or worked to ensure the couple's fertility—such as untying all the knots in the household, for tying knots was one way that people reputed to have magical powers bound up the reproductive power of a man. All this came together in what was often the final event of a wedding, the religious official blessing the couple in their marriage bed, often with family and friends standing around or banging on pans, yelling, or otherwise making as much noise as possible.

The friends and family members had generally been part of the discussions, negotiations, and activities leading up to the marriage. Among serfs the lord's permission was often required, with a special fee paid to obtain this. The involvement of family and friends in choosing one's spouse might lead to conflict, but more often the wishes of the young people and their parents, kin, and community were quite similar: all hoped for marriages that provided economic security, honorable standing, and a good number of healthy children. The best marriages offered companionship, emotional support, and even love, but these were understood to grow out of the marriage, not necessarily precede it. Breaking up a marriage meant breaking up the basic production and consumption unit, which was a very serious matter, so marital dissolution by any means other than the death of one spouse was rare.

Most brides hoped to be pregnant soon after the wedding. Christian women hoping for children said special prayers to the Virgin Mary or her mother Anne. Some wore amulets of amber, bone, or mistletoe, thought to increase fertility. Others repeated charms and verses they had learned from other women, or in desperate cases, went on pilgrimages to make special supplications. Muslim and Jewish women wore small cases with sacred verses or asked for blessings from religious leaders. Women continued these prayers and rituals through pregnancy and childbirth, often combining religious traditions with folk beliefs handed down orally.

Judaism, Christianity, and Islam all required women to remain separate from the community for a short time after childbirth and often had special ceremonies welcoming them back once this period was over. These rituals often included prayers, such as this one from the Christian ritual of thanksgiving and purification, called churching, which a woman celebrated six weeks after giving birth: "Almighty and everlasting God, who has freed this woman from the danger of bearing a child, consider her to be strengthened from every pollution of the flesh so that with a clean heart and pure mind she may deserve to enter into the bosom of our mother, the church, and make her devoted to Your service."[2]

Religious ceremonies also welcomed children into the community. Among Christian families, infants were baptized soon after they were born, for without the sacrament of baptism they could not enter Heaven. Thus midwives who delivered children who looked especially weak and sickly often baptized them in an emergency service. In normal baptisms, the women who had assisted the mother in the birth often carried the baby to church, where carefully chosen godparents vowed their support. Godparents were often close friends or relatives, but parents might also choose prominent villagers or even the local lord in the hope that he might later look favorably on the child and provide for him or her in some way.

Within Judaism, a boy was circumcised by a religious official and given his name in a ceremony when he was in his eighth day of life. This *brit milah*, or "covenant of circumcision," was viewed as a reminder of the covenant between God and Abraham described in Hebrew Scripture. Muslims also circumcised boys in a special ritual, though the timing varied from a few days after birth to adolescence.

Death and the Afterlife

Death was similarly marked by religious ceremonies. Christians called for a priest to perform the sacrament of extreme unction when they thought the hour of death was near. The priest brought a number of objects and substances regarded as having power over death and the sin related to it. Holy water, holy oil, and a censer with incense all connected to rites that purified and blessed the dying. A crucifix served to remind the dying of Christ's own agony and the promise of salvation. Most important, the priest gave the dying person a last communion host.

Once the person had died, the body was buried within a day or two. Family and friends joined in a funeral procession; sometimes extra women were hired so that the mourning and wailing were especially loud and intense, a sign of the family's devotion. The procession carried the body into the church, where there were psalms, prayers, and a funeral Mass, and then to a consecrated space for burial. The wealthy were sometimes buried inside the church — in the walls, under the floor, or under the building itself in a crypt — but most people were buried in the churchyard or a cemetery close by. Priests were hired to say memorial masses on anniversaries of family deaths, especially one week, one month, and one year afterward; large churches had a number of side altars so that many masses could be going on at one time.

Learned theologians increasingly emphasized the idea of purgatory, the place where souls on their way to Heaven went after death to make amends for their earthly sins. Memorial masses, prayers, and donations made in the names of the dead could shorten

CHAPTER LOCATOR | What was village life like in medieval Europe? | **How did religion shape everyday life in medieval Europe?** | What roles did nobles play in medieval society? | What roles did monks and nuns play in medieval life?

275

their time in purgatory and hasten their way to Heaven. So could indulgences, those papal grants that relieved a person from earthly penance. Indulgences were initially granted for performing meritorious acts, such as going on a pilgrimage or crusade, but gradually they could be acquired for a small fee. With this, their spiritual benefits became transferable, so they could be purchased to shorten the stay in purgatory of one's deceased relatives, as well as lessen one's own penance or time in purgatory. Thus death did not sever family obligations and connections.

The living also had obligations to the dead among Muslims and Jews. In both groups, deceased people were to be buried quickly, and special prayers were to be said by mourners and family members. Muslims fasted on behalf of the dead and maintained a brief period of official mourning. The Qur'an promises an eternal paradise with flowing rivers to "those who believe and do good deeds" (Qur'an, 4:57) and a Hell of eternal torment to those who do not.

Jews observed specified periods of mourning during which the normal activities of daily life were curtailed. Every day for eleven months after a death and every year after that on the anniversary of the death, a son of the deceased was to recite Kaddish, a special prayer of praise and glorification of God. Judaism emphasized life on earth more than an afterlife, so beliefs about what happens to the soul after death were more varied; the very righteous might go directly to a place of spiritual reward, but most souls went first to a place of punishment and purification generally referred to as *Gehinnom*. After a period that did not exceed twelve months, the soul ascended to the world to come. Those who were completely wicked during their lifetimes might simply go out of existence or continue in an eternal state of remorse.

▼ What roles did nobles play in medieval society?

nobility A small group of people at the top of the medieval social structure who held most of the social and political power.

The **nobility**, though a small fraction of the total population, strongly influenced all aspects of medieval culture—political and religious (Chapter 9) and economic, educational, and artistic (Chapter 11). Despite political, scientific, and industrial revolutions, the nobility continued to hold real political and social power in Europe into the nineteenth century. In order to account for this continuing influence, it is important to understand the development of the nobility in the High Middle Ages.

Origins and Status of the Nobility

In the early Middle Ages noble status was generally limited to a very few families who either were descended from officials at the Carolingian court or were leading families among Germanic tribes. Beginning in the eleventh century, knights in the service of higher nobles or kings began to claim noble status. The noble class grew larger and more diverse, ranging from poor knights who held tiny pieces of land (or sometimes none at all) to dukes and counts with vast territories.

chivalry Code of conduct originally devised by the clergy to transform the crude and brutal behavior of the knightly class.

Originally, most knights focused solely on military skills, but around 1200 a different ideal of knighthood emerged, usually termed **chivalry** (SHIH-vuhl-ree). Chivalry was a code of conduct originally devised by the clergy to transform the crude and brutal behavior of the knightly class. It may have originated in oaths administered to Crusaders in which fighting was declared to have a sacred purpose. Other qualities gradually became part of chivalry: bravery, generosity, honor, graciousness, mercy, and eventually gallantry toward women, what came to be called "courtly love." (See "Listening to the Past: Courtly Love Poetry," page 310.) The chivalric ideal created a new standard of masculinity for

Saint Maurice Some of the individuals who were held up to young men as models of ideal chivalry were probably real, but their lives were embellished with many stories. One of these was Saint Maurice (d. 287), a soldier apparently executed by the Romans for refusing to renounce his Christian faith. He first emerges in the Carolingian period, and later he was held up as a model knight and declared a patron of the Holy Roman Empire and protector of the imperial army in wars against the pagan Slavs. His image was used on coins, and his cult was promoted by the archbishops of Magdeburg, who moved his relics to their cathedral. Until 1240 he was portrayed as a white man, but after that he was usually represented as a black man, as in this sandstone statue from Magdeburg Cathedral (ca. 1250). We have no idea why this change happened. (Courtesy, The Menil Foundation, Houston)

nobles, in which loyalty and honor remained the most important qualities, but graceful dancing and intelligent conversation were not considered unmanly.

Childhood

For children of aristocratic birth, the years from infancy to around the age of seven or eight were primarily years of play. At about the age of seven, a boy of the noble class who was not intended for the church was placed in the household of one of his father's friends or relatives. There he became a servant to the lord and received formal training in arms. He was expected to serve the lord at the table, to assist him as a private valet, and, as he gained experience, to care for the lord's horses and equipment.

Training was in the arts of war. The boy learned to ride and to manage a horse. He had to be able to wield a sword, hurl a lance, shoot with a bow and arrow, and care for armor and other equipment. Increasingly, in the eleventh and twelfth centuries, noble youths learned to read and write some Latin. Still, literacy among the nobility did not become more common until the thirteenth century. Formal training was concluded around the age of twenty-one with the ceremony of knighthood. The custom of knighting, though never universal, seems to have been widespread in France and England but not in Germany.

Noble girls were also trained in preparation for their future tasks. They were often taught to read the local language and perhaps some Latin. They learned to write and to do enough arithmetic to keep household accounts. They also learned music, dancing, and embroidery and how to ride and hunt, both common noble pursuits. Much of this took place in the girl's own home, but, like boys, noble girls were often sent to the homes of relatives or higher nobles to act as servants or ladies in waiting and to learn how to run a household.

Youth and Marriage

The ceremony of knighthood was one of the most important in a man's life, but knighthood did not necessarily mean adulthood, power, and responsibility. Sons were completely dependent on their fathers for support. A young man remained a youth until he was in a financial position to marry—that is, until his father died. That might not happen until he was in his late thirties, and marriage at forty was not uncommon. Increasingly, families adopted primogeniture, with property passing to the oldest son. Younger sons might be forced into the clergy or simply forbidden to marry.

Once knighted, the young man traveled for two to three years. His father selected a group of friends to accompany, guide, and protect him. The band's chief pursuit was fighting. They meddled in local conflicts, sometimes departed on crusades, hunted, and did the

CHAPTER LOCATOR | What was village life like in medieval Europe? | How did religion shape everyday life in medieval Europe? | **What roles did nobles play in medieval society?** | What roles did monks and nuns play in medieval life?

277

tournament circuit. The tournament, in which a number of men competed from horseback (in contrast to the joust, which involved only two competitors), gave the young knight experience in pitched battle and a way to show off his masculinity before an audience. Since the horses and equipment of the vanquished were forfeited to the victors, the knight could also gain a reputation and a profit.

Parents often wanted to settle daughters' futures as soon as possible. Men tended to prefer young brides. A woman in her late twenties or thirties would have fewer years of married fertility, limiting the number of children she could produce and thus threatening the family's continuation. Therefore, aristocratic girls in the High Middle Ages were married at around the age of sixteen, often to much older men. In the early Middle Ages the custom was for the groom to present a dowry to the bride and her family, but by the late twelfth century the process was reversed because men were in greater demand. Thereafter, the sizes of dowries offered by brides and their families rose higher and higher.

Power and Responsibility

A male member of the nobility became an adult when he came into the possession of his property. He then acquired authority over lands and people. With it went responsibility. In the words of Honorius of Autun:

> *Soldiers: You are the arm of the Church, because you should defend it against its enemies. Your duty is to aid the oppressed, to restrain yourself from rapine and fornication, to repress those who impugn the Church with evil acts, and to resist those who are rebels against priests. Performing such a service, you will obtain the most splendid of benefices from the greatest of Kings.*[3]

Nobles rarely lived up to this ideal, however, and there are countless examples of nobles stealing church lands instead of defending them, tyrannizing the oppressed rather than aiding them, and regularly engaging in "rapine and fornication" rather than resisting them.

The responsibilities of a nobleman in the High Middle Ages depended on the size and extent of his estates, the number of dependents, and his position in his territory relative to others of his class and to the king. As a vassal, he was required to fight for his lord or for the king when called on to do so. By the mid-twelfth century this service was limited to forty days a year in most parts of western Europe. The noble was obliged to attend his lord's court on important religious or family occasions.

Until the late thirteenth century, when royal authority intervened, a noble in France or England had great power over the people on his estates. He maintained order among them and dispensed justice to them. Holding the manorial court, which punished criminal acts and settled disputes, was one of his gravest obligations. The quality of justice varied widely: some lords were vicious tyrants who exploited and persecuted their peasants and vassals; others were reasonable and evenhanded.

Women played a large and important role in the functioning of the estate. They were responsible for the practical management of the household's "inner economy"—cooking, brewing, spinning, weaving, caring for yard animals. When the lord was away for long periods, the women frequently managed the herds, barns, granaries, and outlying fields as well. Often the responsibilities of the estate fell to them permanently, as the number of men slain in medieval warfare ran high.

Throughout the High Middle Ages, fighting remained the dominant feature of the noble lifestyle. The church's preaching and condemnations reduced, but did not stop, violence. Lateness of inheritance, depriving nobles of constructive outlets for their energy, together with the military ethos of their culture, encouraged petty warfare and disorder.

The Lady and the Unicorn Tapestry This tapestry, woven in Flanders for a nobleman at the French court, expresses many of the ideals of noble life. A beautiful young woman stands in front of a tent with battle flags. On her right is a lion, symbol of earthly power. On her left is a unicorn, a beast that could only be captured by a virgin. Medieval people viewed the unicorn both as an allegory of Christ (who was "captured" by the Virgin Mary when he was born) and of an earthly lover tamed by his beloved. The enigmatic words "to my only desire" on the top of the tent may refer to either spiritual or romantic love, for both were viewed as appropriate motivations for noble action. (Erich Lessing/Art Resource, NY)

The nobility thus represented a constant source of trouble for the monarchy. In the thirteenth century kings drew on the financial support of the middle classes—that is, urban professionals, small landholders, and merchants—to build the administrative machinery that gradually laid the foundations of strong royal government. The Crusades relieved the rulers of France, England, and the German Empire of some of their most dangerous elements. Complete royal control of the nobility, however, came only in modern times.

▼ What roles did monks and nuns play in medieval life?

Priests, bishops, monks, and nuns played significant roles in medieval society, both as individuals and as members of institutions. Medieval people believed that monks and nuns performed an important social service when they prayed. Just as the knights protected and defended society with the sword and the peasants provided sustenance through their toil, so the monks and nuns worked to secure God's blessing for society with their prayers and chants.

CHAPTER LOCATOR | What was village life like in medieval Europe? | How did religion shape everyday life in medieval Europe? | What roles did nobles play in medieval society? | **What roles did monks and nuns play in medieval life?**

279

Monastic Revival

In the early Middle Ages many religious houses followed the Benedictine *Rule*, while others developed their own patterns (see Chapter 7). In the High Middle Ages this diversity became more formalized, and religious orders, groups of monastic houses following a particular rule, were established. Historians term the foundation, strengthening, and reform of religious orders in the High Middle Ages the "monastic revival." They link it with the simultaneous expansion of papal power (see Chapter 9) because many of the same individuals were important in both.

The best Benedictine monasteries had been centers of learning, copying and preserving manuscripts, maintaining schools, and setting high standards of monastic observance. Charlemagne had encouraged and supported these monastic activities, and the collapse of the Carolingian Empire had disastrous effects.

The Viking, Magyar, and Muslim invaders attacked and ransacked many monasteries across Europe, causing some religious communities to flee and disperse. In the period of political disorder that followed the disintegration of the Carolingian Empire, many religious houses fell under the control and domination of local lords. Powerful laymen appointed themselves or their relatives as abbots, took the lands and goods of monasteries, and spent monastic revenues. The level of spiritual observance and intellectual activity in monasteries and convents declined.

The secular powers who selected church officials compelled them to become vassals. Abbots, bishops, and archbishops thus had military responsibilities. As feudal lords themselves, ecclesiastical officials also had judicial authority over knights and peasants on their lands. The conflict between a church official's religious duties on the one hand and his judicial and military obligations on the other posed a serious dilemma.

The first sign of reform came in 909, when William the Pious, duke of Aquitaine, established the abbey of Cluny in Burgundy. Duke William declared that the monastery was to be free from any feudal responsibilities to him or any other lord, its members subordinate only to the pope. The monastery at Cluny came to exert vast religious influence and initially held high standards of religious behavior. In the eleventh century Cluny was fortunate in having a series of highly able abbots who ruled for a long time. In a disorderly world, Cluny gradually came to represent stability. Therefore, laypersons placed lands under its custody and monastic priories under its jurisdiction for reform (a priory is a religious house, with generally a smaller number of residents than an abbey, governed by a prior or prioress). In this way, hundreds of monasteries, primarily in France and Spain, came under Cluny's authority.

Deeply impressed laypeople showered gifts on monasteries with good reputations, such as Cluny and its many daughter houses. But as the monasteries became richer, the lifestyle of the monks grew increasingly luxurious. Monastic observance and spiritual fervor declined. Soon fresh demands for reform were heard, and the result was the founding of new religious orders in the late eleventh and early twelfth centuries.

The Cistercians (sihs-TUHR-shuhnz)—because of their phenomenal expansion and the great economic, political, and spiritual influence they exerted—are the best representatives of the new reforming spirit. In 1098 a group of monks left the rich abbey of Molesmes in Burgundy because, in the words of the twelfth-century chronicler-monk William of Malmesbury, "purity could not be preserved in a place where riches and gluttony warred against even the heart that was well inclined." They founded a new house in the swampy forest of Cîteaux (si-TOH). They planned to avoid all involvement with secular feudal society, and they decided to accept only uncultivated lands far from regular habitation. The early Cistercians determined to keep their services simple and their lives austere.

The first monks at Cîteaux experienced sickness, a dearth of recruits, and terrible privations. But their high ideals made them, in William's words, "a model for all monks, a mirror for the diligent, and a spur for the indolent."[4] In 1112 a twenty-three-year-old

Chapter 10
The Life of the People in the
280   High Middle Ages • 1000–1300

nobleman called Bernard joined the community at Cîteaux. Three years later Bernard was appointed founding abbot of Clairvaux (klahr-VOH) in Champagne. From this position he conducted a vast correspondence, attacked the theological views of Peter Abelard (see Chapter 11), and intervened in the disputed papal election of 1130. He also drafted a constitution for the Knights Templars and urged Christians to go on the Second Crusade. This reforming movement gained impetus. Cîteaux founded 525 new monasteries in the course of the twelfth century, and its influence on European society was profound (Map 10.2).

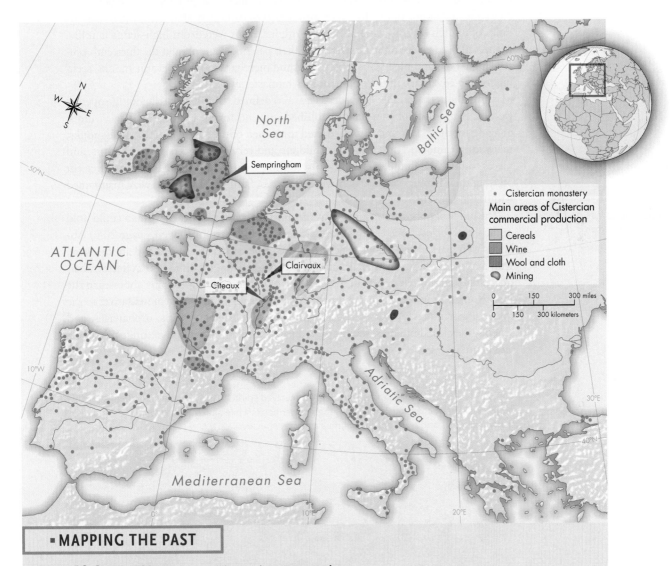

▪ MAPPING THE PAST

Map 10.2 Twelfth-Century Cistercian Expansion

The rapid expansion of the Cistercian order in the twelfth century reflects the spiritual piety of the age and its enormous economic vitality.

ANALYZING THE MAP The Cistercians originally intended to live far from existing towns and villages and to not be involved in traditional feudal-manorial society. Does this map suggest they were successful in their aims? (To answer this, you may also want to look at the maps in Chapter 11.)

CONNECTIONS Compare the main areas of Cistercian commercial production to the trade and manufacturing routes shown on Map 11.2 (page 294). How might the original goals of the Cistercians have been compromised by their economic activities?

To complete this activity online, go to the Online Study Guide at bedfordstmartins.com/mckaywestunderstanding.

CHAPTER LOCATOR | What was village life like in medieval Europe? | How did religion shape everyday life in medieval Europe? | What roles did nobles play in medieval society? | **What roles did monks and nuns play in medieval life?**

281

Unavoidably, Cistercian success brought wealth, and wealth brought power. By the later twelfth century economic prosperity and political power had begun to compromise the original Cistercian ideals.

Life in Convents and Monasteries

Medieval monasteries were religious institutions whose organization and structure fulfilled the social needs of the feudal nobility. The monasteries provided noble boys with education and opportunities for ecclesiastical careers. Although a few men who rose in the ranks of church officials were of humble origins, most were from high-status families. Many had been given to the monastery by their parents. Beginning in the thirteenth century more boys and men from professional and merchant families became monks, seeking to take advantage of the opportunities monasteries offered.

Throughout the Middle Ages social class also defined the kinds of religious life open to women. Kings and nobles usually established convents for their daughters, sisters, aunts, or aging mothers. Entrance was restricted to women of the founder's class. Like monks, many nuns came into the convent as children, and very often sisters, cousins, aunts, and nieces could all be found in the same place. Thus, though nuns were to some degree cut off from their families because they were cloistered, family relationships were maintained within the convent.

abbess/prioress Head of a convent for women.

The office of abbess or prioress was the most powerful position a woman could hold in medieval society. (See "Individuals in Society: Hildegard of Bingen," page 284.) Abbesses were part of the feudal structure in the same way that bishops and abbots were, with manors under their financial and legal control. They appointed tax collectors, bailiffs, judges, and often priests in the territory under their control. Some abbesses in the Holy Roman Empire even had the right to name bishops and send representatives to the imperial assemblies. Abbesses also opened and supported hospitals, orphanages, and schools; they hired builders, sculptors, and painters to construct and decorate residences and churches.

Convent Life Life in monasteries and convents involved spiritual and physical labor. In this English prayer book, nuns chant the liturgy from their prayer books while sitting in the wooden choir, a task that both monks and nuns did seven times a day. (HIP/Art Resource, NY)

Monk and Nun in Stocks Monks and nuns were sometimes criticized for immorality, luxurious living, and inattention to their vows. Such criticism was expressed in plays, songs, and also in pictures. This painting shows a monk and nun in stocks, heavy wooden frames with holes for restraining the ankles and sometimes the wrists, used as punishment. A person confined in stocks endured great physical discomfort as well as the shame of public disgrace. The painting is most likely not a realistic scene, but rather part of a satirical criticism of monastic life. (© British Library Board, Roy. 10. f. IV. 187)

Monasteries for men were headed by an **abbot** or **prior**, who was generally a member of a noble family, often a younger brother in a family with several sons. The main body of monks, known as "choir monks," were largely of noble or middle-class background, and they did not till the land themselves. Men from peasant families who had been given to the monastery as children or entered through some other means occasionally took vows and became choir monks, but more often they served as lay brothers. They had simpler religious obligations than did the choir monks and did the manual labor essential to running the monastery. In each house one monk, the cellarer—or general financial manager—was responsible for supervising the lay brothers and other peasants who did agricultural labor. In women's houses, a nun acted as cellarer and was in charge of lay sisters who did the actual physical work. The novice master or novice mistress was responsible for the training of recruits. The efficient operation of a monastic house also required the services of cooks, laundresses, gardeners, seamstresses, mechanics, blacksmiths, pharmacists, and others whose essential work has left, unfortunately, little written trace.

> **abbot/prior** Head of a monastery for men.

The pattern of life within individual monasteries varied widely from house to house and from region to region. One central activity, however, was performed everywhere. Daily life centered on the liturgy or Divine Office, psalms and other prayers prescribed by Saint Benedict that monks and nuns prayed seven times a day and once during the night. Prayers were offered for peace, rain, good harvests, the civil authorities, and the monks' families and benefactors. Monastic patrons in turn lavished gifts on the monasteries, which often became very wealthy. Everything connected with prayer was understood as praise of God, so abbeys spent a large percentage of their income on splendid objects to enhance the service, including sacred vessels of embossed silver or gold, altar cloths of the finest silks or velvets, embroideries, and beautiful reliquaries to house the relics of the patron saint.

In some abbeys monks and nuns spent much of their time copying books and manuscripts and then illuminating them, decorating them with human and animal figures or elaborate designs, often painted in bright colors or gold. A few monasteries and convents became centers of learning where talented residents wrote their own works as well as copying those of others.

Monks and nuns also performed social services. Monasteries often ran schools that gave primary education to young boys, while convents took in girls. Abbeys like Saint

CHAPTER LOCATOR | What was village life like in medieval Europe? | How did religion shape everyday life in medieval Europe? | What roles did nobles play in medieval society? | **What roles did monks and nuns play in medieval life?**

283

THE TENTH CHILD OF A LESSER NOBLE FAMILY, Hildegard (HIHL-duh-gahrd) (1098–1179) was given as a child to an abbey in the Rhineland when she was eight years old; there she learned Latin and received a good education. She spent most of her life in various women's religious communities, two of which she founded herself. When she was a child, she began having mystical visions, often of light in the sky, but told few people about them. In middle age, however, her visions became more dramatic: "And it came to pass . . . when I was 42 years and 7 months old, that the heavens were opened and a blinding light of exceptional brilliance flowed through my entire brain. And so it kindled my whole heart and breast like a flame, not burning but warming . . . and suddenly I understood of the meaning of expositions of the books."* She wanted the church to approve of her visions and wrote first to Saint Bernard of Clairvaux, who answered her briefly and dismissively, and then to Pope Eugenius, who encouraged her to write them down. Her first work was *Scivias (Know the Ways of the Lord)*, a record of her mystical visions that incorporates vast theological learning.

Possessed of leadership and administrative talents, Hildegard left her abbey in 1147 to found the convent of Rupertsberg near Bingen. There she produced *Physica (On the Physical Elements)* and *Causa et Curae (Causes and Cures)*, scientific works on the curative properties of natural elements, poems, a mystery play, and several more works of mysticism. She carried on a huge correspondence with scholars, prelates, and ordinary people. When she was over fifty, she left her community to preach to audiences of clergy and laity. She was the only woman of her time whose opinions on religious matters were considered authoritative by the church.

Hildegard's visions have been explored by theologians and also by neurologists, who judge that they may have originated in migraine headaches, as she reports many of the same phenomena that migraine sufferers do: auras of light around objects, areas of blindness, feelings of intense doubt and intense euphoria. The interpretations that she develops come from her theological insight and learning, however, not illness. That same insight also

emerges in her music, which is what she is best known for today. Eighty of her compositions survive — a huge number for a medieval composer — most of them written to be sung by the nuns in her convent, so they have strong lines for female voices. Many of her songs and chants have been recorded recently by various artists and are available on compact disk, as downloads, and on several Web sites.

QUESTIONS FOR ANALYSIS

1. Why do you think Hildegard sought church approval for her visions after keeping them secret for so many years?
2. In what ways is Hildegard's life representative of nuns' lives in the High Middle Ages? In what ways were her accomplishments extraordinary?

*From *Scivias*, trans. Mother Columba Hart and Jane Bishop, *The Classics of Western Spirituality* (New York/Mahwah: Paulist Press, 1990), p. 65.

Inspired by heavenly fire, Hildegard begins to dictate her visions to her scribe. The original of this elaborately illustrated twelfth-century copy of *Scivias* disappeared from Hildegard's convent during World War II, but fortunately a facsimile had already been made. (Private Collection/The Bridgeman Art Library)

Albans, situated north of London on a busy thoroughfare, served as hotels and resting places for travelers. Monasteries frequently operated "hospitals" and leprosariums, which provided care and attention to the sick, the aged, and the afflicted—primitive care, it is true, but often all that was available. Monasteries and convents also fed the poor. At the French abbey of Saint-Requier in the eleventh century, for example, 110 persons were given food daily. In short, monasteries and convents performed a variety of social services in an age when there was no "state" and no conception of social welfare as a public responsibility.

← LOOKING BACK LOOKING AHEAD →

THE IMAGE OF EUROPEAN SOCIETY as divided into three orders—those who fight, those who pray, those who work—was overly simplistic when it was first developed in the ninth century, but it did encompass most of the European population. Movement between those groups was possible. Both noble and peasant children given to monasteries by their parents could become monks and nuns. Members of noble families became abbots and abbesses. Sometimes through service to a lord, a few peasants rose to the rank of knight. It was also true that younger sons of knights could sink to the peasantry if they had too many brothers and were unlucky in war or marriage.

By the eleventh century, though the three-part social model still encompassed most people, growing towns housed increasing numbers of men and women who fit into none of the groups. Townspeople were recruited from all three orders, and the opportunities offered by towns eventually speeded up social and economic change. As they grew, towns replaced monasteries as the primary centers of culture in medieval Europe, with their walls and cathedrals dominating the landscape. ■

- **For a list of suggested readings for this chapter, visit** *bedfordstmartins.com/mckaywestunderstanding*.

- **For primary sources from this period, see** *Sources of Western Society*, Second Edition**.**

- **For Web sites, images, and documents related to topics in this chapter, see Make History at** *bedfordstmartins.com/mckaywestunderstanding*.

CHAPTER LOCATOR | What was village life like in medieval Europe? | How did religion shape everyday life in medieval Europe? | What roles did nobles play in medieval society? | **What roles did monks and nuns play in medieval life?**

285

Step 1

GETTING STARTED Below are basic terms about this period in the history of Western civilization. Can you identify each term below and explain why it matters? To do this exercise online, go to bedfordstmartins.com/mckaywestunderstanding.

TERMS	WHO (OR WHAT) AND WHEN	WHY IT MATTERS
the three orders, p. 262		
open-field system, p. 265		
nobility, p. 276		
chivalry, p. 276		
tournament, p. 278		
religious orders, p. 280		
Cistercians, p. 280		
abbess/prioress, p. 282		
abbot/prior, p. 283		

Step 2

MOVING BEYOND THE BASICS The exercise below requires a more advanced understanding of the chapter material. Examine the social structure of medieval Europe by filling in the chart below with descriptions of the medieval peasantry, nobility, and clergy. Describe each group's characteristics and lifestyle, as well as important developments and trends affecting the group's composition and status. When you are finished, consider the following questions: How accurate was the medieval model that divided society into those who work, those who fight, and those who pray? How might you modify this model to create a better picture of the reality of medieval life? To do this exercise online, go to bedfordstmartins.com/mckaywestunderstanding.

GROUP	CHARACTERISTICS	LIFESTYLE	DEVELOPMENTS AND TRENDS
Peasants			
Nobility			
Clergy			

PUTTING IT ALL TOGETHER Now that you've reviewed key elements of the chapter, take a step back and try to see the big picture. Remember to use specific examples from the chapter in your answers. To do this exercise online, go to bedfordstmartins.com/mckaywestunderstanding.

VILLAGE LIFE

- How did isolation shape rural life in medieval Europe? What connections did European peasants have to the world beyond the manor?

- How much social mobility was there in medieval Europe? Did social mobility increase or decrease over the course of the High Middle Ages? Why?

POPULAR RELIGION

- What might explain the popularity of the saints in medieval Europe? In this context, how might social and economic conditions have shaped religious beliefs and practices?

- What role did religious rituals play in major life transitions, such as birth, marriage, and death? What light do such rituals shed on popular religion in medieval Europe?

THE NOBILITY

- What role did warfare play in the lifestyle and self-image of the European nobility? What changes in European society might explain the emergence of chivalry in the High Middle Ages?

- What explains the enduring power of the nobility in European society? How did the nobility justify their status?

MONASTERIES AND CONVENTS

- Compare and contrast the monastic revival and papal reform movements of the High Middle Ages (see Chapter 9 for a discussion of papal reform). What common problems prompted both movements? What goals did the movements share?

- What was the medieval ideal of the monastic life? Why was this ideal so hard for monasteries to achieve and sustain?

■ **In Your Own Words** Imagine that you must explain Chapter 10 to someone who hasn't read it. What would be the most important points to include and why?

11

The Creativity and Challenges of Medieval Cities

1100–1300

The High Middle Ages witnessed some of the most remarkable achievements in the entire history of Western society. Europeans displayed tremendous creativity and vitality in many facets of culture. Relative security and an increasing food supply allowed for the growth and development of towns and a revival of long-distance trade. City dwellers thus had a greater variety of material goods than did villagers, and they also interacted with a greater variety of people. Some urban merchants and bankers became as wealthy as great nobles, though cities were also home to large numbers of poor people. Trade brought in new ideas as well as merchandise, and cities developed into intellectual and cultural centers. The university, a new—and very long-lasting—type of educational institution came into being, providing advanced training in theology, medicine, and law. Traditions and values were spread orally through stories and songs, as people gathered to hear about the exploits of great kings or the affairs of famous lovers. Some of these stories were written down as part of the development of vernacular literature, for more people could read in cities than in rural areas. Gothic cathedrals, where people saw beautiful stained-glass windows and listened to complex music, manifested medieval people's deep Christian faith and their pride in their own cities. Many urban residents were increasingly dissatisfied with the Christian church, however, and turned to heretical movements that challenged church power. ■

Life in a Medieval City. This detail from a manuscript illumination shows a street scene of a medieval town, with a barber, cloth merchants, and an apothecary all offering their wares and services on the ground floors of their household-workshops.
(Snark/Art Resource, NY)

Chapter Preview

▶ What led to Europe's economic growth and reurbanization?

▶ What was life like in a medieval city?

▶ How did universities serve the needs of medieval society?

▶ How did literature and architecture express medieval values?

▶ How did urban growth shape European religious life?

▼ What led to Europe's economic growth and reurbanization?

The rise of towns and the growth of a new business and commercial class was a central part of Europe's recovery after the disorders of the ninth and tenth centuries. The growth of towns was made possible by some of the changes we have already traced: a rise in population; increased agricultural output, which provided an adequate food supply for new town dwellers; and a small amount of peace and political stability, which allowed merchants to transport and sell goods. As towns gained legal and political rights, merchant and craft guilds grew more powerful, and towns became centers of production as well as trading centers.

The Rise of Towns

Early medieval society was agricultural and rural. The emergence of a new class that was neither of these constituted a social revolution. Most of the members of the new class — artisans and merchants — came from the peasantry. As well, the landless younger sons of

Emperor Frederick II Granting Privileges A young and handsome Frederick II, with a laurel wreath symbolizing his position as emperor, signs a grant of privileges for a merchant of the Italian city of Asti in this thirteenth-century manuscript. Frederick wears the flamboyant and fashionable clothing of a high noble — long-toed shoes, slit sleeves, and a cape of ermine tails — while the merchant seeking his favor is dressed in more sober and less expensive garb. (Scala/Art Resource, NY)

290

Chapter 11
The Creativity and Challenges
of Medieval Cities • 1100–1300

CHAPTER LOCATOR

What led to Europe's economic growth and reurbanization?

large families were driven away by land shortage. Some were forced by war and famine to seek new possibilities. Others were immigrants colonizing newly conquered lands, as in central Europe and Spain after the reconquista (see Chapter 9). And some were unusually enterprising, adventurous, and curious; they were simply willing to take a chance.

Medieval towns began in many different ways. Some were fortifications erected as a response to the ninth-century Viking invasions, into which farmers from the surrounding countryside moved when their area was attacked. Later, merchants were attracted to the fortifications because they had something to sell and wanted to be where the customers were. Other towns grew up around great cathedrals (see page 308) and monasteries whose schools drew students—potential customers—from far and wide. Many other towns grew from the sites of earlier Roman army camps.

Regardless of their origins, medieval towns had a few common characteristics. Each town had a marketplace, and most had a mint for the coining of money. The town also had a court to settle disputes. In addition, medieval towns were enclosed by walls. As population increased, towns rebuilt their walls, expanding the living space to accommodate growing numbers.

No matter where groups of traders congregated, they settled on someone's land and had to secure permission to live and trade from king, count, abbot, or bishop. Aristocratic nobles and churchmen were initially hostile to the new middle class. They soon realized, however, that profits and benefits flowed to them and their territories from the towns set up on their land.

The growing towns of medieval Europe slowly gained legal and political rights, including the right to hold municipal courts that alone could judge members of the town, the right to select the mayor and other municipal officials, and the right to tax residents. Feudal lords were often reluctant to grant towns self-government, fearing loss of authority and revenue if they gave the merchants full independence. When merchants bargained for a town's political independence, however, they offered sizable amounts of ready cash and sometimes promised payments for years to come. Consequently, feudal lords ultimately agreed to self-government.

In addition to working for the political independence of the towns, merchants and townspeople tried to acquire liberties for themselves. In the Middle Ages *liberties* meant special privileges. Town liberties included the privilege of living and trading on the lord's land. The most important privilege a medieval townsperson could gain was personal freedom. It gradually developed that a serf who fled his or her manor and lived in a town for a year and a day was free of servile obligations and status. Thus the growth of towns contributed to a slow decline of serfdom in western Europe, although this would take centuries.

Towns developed throughout much of Europe, but the concentration of the textile industry in the Low Countries (present-day Holland, Belgium, and French Flanders) brought into being the most populous cluster of cities in western Europe: Ghent (gehnt) with about 56,000 people, Bruges (broozh) with 27,000, and Tournai and Brussels with perhaps 20,000 each. Venice, Florence, and Paris, each with about 110,000 people, and Milan with possibly 200,000 led all Europe in population (Map 11.1).

Chapter Chronology

ca. 1100	Merchant guilds become rich and powerful in many cities; artisans begin to found craft guilds
1100–1300	Height of construction of cathedrals in Europe
1143	Founding of Lübeck, first city in the Hanseatic League
ca. 1200	Founding of first universities
1216	Papal recognition of Dominican order
1221	Papal recognition of Franciscan order
1225–1274	Life of Thomas Aquinas; *Summa Theologica*
1233	Papacy begins to use friars to staff the Inquisition
ca. 1300	Bill of exchange becomes most common method of commercial payment in western Europe
1300s	Clocks in general use throughout Europe
1302	Pope Boniface VIII declares all Christians subject to the pope in *Unam Sanctam*

What was life like in a medieval city?   How did universities serve the needs of medieval society?   How did literature and architecture express medieval values?   How did urban growth shape European religious life?

291

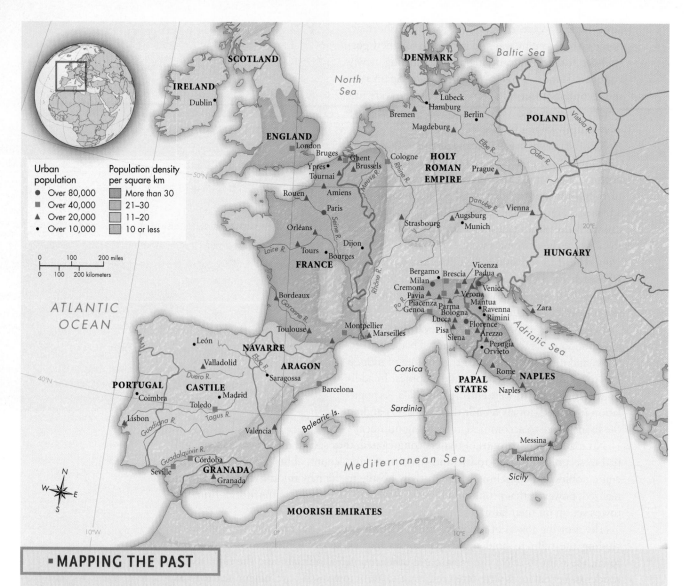

Urban population
- ● Over 80,000
- ■ Over 40,000
- ▲ Over 20,000
- • Over 10,000

Population density per square km
- More than 30
- 21–30
- 11–20
- 10 or less

▪ MAPPING THE PAST

Map 11.1 European Population Density, ca. 1300

The development of towns and the reinvigoration of trade were directly related in medieval Europe. Using all three maps in this chapter and the information in your text, answer the following questions.

ANALYZING THE MAP What were the four largest cities in Europe? What part of Europe had the highest density of towns?

CONNECTIONS What role did textile and other sorts of manufacturing play in the growth of towns? How was the development of towns related to that of universities, monastery schools, and cathedral schools?

To complete this activity online, go to the Online Study Guide at bedfordstmartins.com/mckaywestunderstanding.

Merchant and Craft Guilds

The merchants, who were influential in winning towns' independence from feudal lords, also used their power and wealth to control life within the city walls. The merchants of a

merchant guild A band of merchants that prohibited nonmembers from trading in the town.

town joined together to form a merchant guild that prohibited nonmembers from trading in the town. Guild members often made up the earliest town government, so that a town's economic policies were determined by its merchants' self-interest. By the beginning of the twelfth century, especially in the towns of the Low Countries and northern

292

Chapter 11
**The Creativity and Challenges
of Medieval Cities** • 1100–1300

CHAPTER LOCATOR | What led to Europe's economic growth and reurbanization?

Italy, the leaders of the merchant guilds were rich and powerful. They constituted an oligarchy in their towns, controlling economic life and bargaining with kings and lords for political independence.

While most towns were initially established as trading centers, they quickly became centers of production as well. Peasants looking for better opportunities left their villages and moved to towns, providing both workers and mouths to feed. Some began to specialize in certain types of food and clothing production. Over time certain cities became known for their fine fabrics, their reliable arms and armor, or their elegant gold and silver work.

Like merchants, producers recognized that organizing would bring benefits, and beginning in the twelfth century in many cities they developed **craft guilds** that regulated most aspects of production. In most cities individual guilds achieved a monopoly in the production of one particular product, forbidding nonmembers to work. The craft guild then chose some of its members to act as inspectors and set up a court to hear disputes between members, though the city court remained the final arbiter.

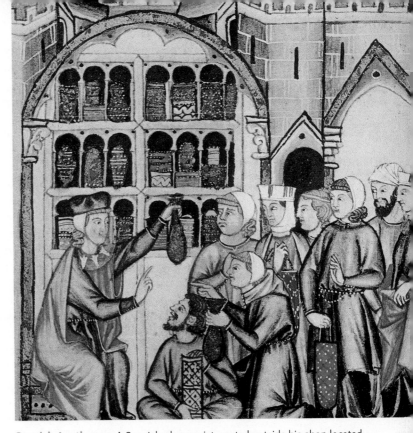

Spanish Apothecary A Spanish pharmacist, seated outside his shop located within the town walls, describes the merits of his goods to a crowd of Christians and Muslims. This thirteenth-century painting captures the variety of people and products that could be found in cities, particularly those in Spain, where urban residents included Christians, Muslims, and Jews. (Laurie Platt Winfrey/The Granger Collection, NY)

Each guild set the pattern by which members were trained. A boy who wanted to become a weaver, for instance, or whose parents wanted him to, spent four to seven years as an apprentice. When the apprenticeship was finished, a young artisan spent several years as journeyman, working in the shop of a master artisan. He then could make his "masterpiece" — in the case of weavers, a long piece of cloth. If the other masters judged the cloth acceptable, and if they thought the market in their town was large enough to support another weaver, the journeyman could then become a master and start a shop.

craft guild A band of producers that regulated most aspects of production.

Many guilds required masters to be married, as they recognized the vital role of the master's wife. She assisted in running the shop, often selling the goods her husband had produced. Most guilds allowed a master's widow to continue operating a shop for a set period of time after her husband's death, for they recognized that she had the necessary skills and experience. Such widows paid all guild dues, but they were not considered full members and could not vote or hold office in the guild. The fact that women were not formally guild members did not mean that they did not work in guild shops, however; for alongside the master's wife and daughters, female domestic servants often performed such less-skilled tasks as preparing raw materials and cleaning finished products. In addition, in a handful of cities with highly-developed economies there were a few all-female guilds, especially in spinning gold thread or weaving silk ribbons for luxury clothing, in which girls were formally apprenticed in the same way boys were in regular craft guilds.

Both craft and merchant guilds were not only economic organizations but also systems of social support. They took care of elderly masters who could no longer work, and they often supported masters' widows and orphans. They maintained an altar at a city church and provided for the funerals of members and the baptisms of their children.

What was life like in a medieval city?　　How did universities serve the needs of medieval society?　　How did literature and architecture express medieval values?　　How did urban growth shape European religious life?

293

Guild members marched together in city parades. They reinforced their feelings of solidarity with one another by special ceremonies and distinctive dress.

The Revival of Long-Distance Trade

The growth of towns went hand in hand with a remarkable revival of trade as artisans and craftsmen manufactured goods for both local and foreign consumption (Map 11.2). Most trade centered in towns and was controlled by professional traders. Long-distance trade was risky and required large investments of capital. Robbers and thieves roamed virtually all of the overland trade routes. Pirates infested the sea-lanes, and shipwrecks were common. Since the risks were so great, merchants preferred to share them. A group of people would thus pool their capital to finance an expedition to a distant place. When the ship or caravan returned and the goods brought back were sold, the investors would share the profits. If disaster struck the caravan, an investor's loss was limited to the amount of that individual's investment.

In the late eleventh century the Italian cities, especially Venice, led the West in trade in general and completely dominated trade with the East. At the same time, the towns of Bruges, Ghent, and Ypres (EE-pruh) in Flanders built a vast industry in the manufacture of cloth, becoming leaders in the trade of textiles.

Map 11.2 Trade and Manufacturing in Thirteenth-Century Europe
Note the overland and ocean lines of trade and the sources of silver, iron, copper, lead, paper, wool, carpets and rugs, and slaves.

294

Chapter 11
The Creativity and Challenges
of Medieval Cities • 1100–1300

CHAPTER LOCATOR | What led to Europe's economic growth and reurbanization?

Two circumstances help explain the lead Venice and the Flemish towns gained in long-distance trade. Both areas enjoyed a high degree of peace and political stability. Geographical factors were equally, if not more, important. Venice was ideally located at the northwestern end of the Adriatic Sea, with easy access to the trans-alpine land routes as well as the Adriatic and Mediterranean sea-lanes. The markets of North Africa, Byzantium, and Russia and the great fairs (large periodic gatherings that attracted buyers, sellers, and goods) of Ghent in Flanders and Champagne in France provided commercial opportunities that Venetian merchants quickly seized. The geographical situation of Flanders also offered unusual possibilities: just across the Channel from England, Flanders had easy access to English wool. With this wool, cloth makers could produce high-quality cloth, one of the few European products for which there was a market in the East.

From the late eleventh through the thirteenth centuries, Europe enjoyed a steadily expanding volume of international trade. Trade surged markedly with demand for sugar and Asian spices to season a bland diet and for fine wines from the Rhineland, Burgundy, and Bordeaux. Other items were highly sought after like luxury woolens from Flanders and Tuscany, furs from Ireland and Russia, brocades and tapestries from Flanders and silks from Constantinople—and even China. Household furnishings such as silver plate were also in demand. The military aristocracy sought swords and armor for their battles. As the trade volume expanded, the use of cash became more widespread. Beginning in the 1160s the opening of new silver mines in Germany, Bohemia, northern Italy, northern France, and western England led to the minting and circulation of vast quantities of silver coins.

Business Procedures

The economic surge of the High Middle Ages caused business procedures to change radically. To meet the greater volume of goods being exchanged, the work of merchants became specialized. Three separate types of merchants emerged. The sedentary merchant ran the "home office," financing and organizing the firm's entire export-import trade. The carriers transported goods by land and sea. And the company agents lived abroad and, on the advice of the home office, looked after sales and procurements.

Commercial correspondence proliferated, and regular courier service among commercial cities began. Commercial accounting became more complex when firms had to deal with shareholders, manufacturers, customers, branch offices, employees, and competing firms. Tolls on roads became high enough to finance what has been called a "road revolution" involving new surfaces, bridges, new passes through the Alps, and new inns and hospices for travelers. The growth of mutual confidence among merchants facilitated the growth of sales on credit.

In all these business transformations, merchants of the Italian cities led the way. (See "Individuals in Society: Francesco Datini," page 296.) They formalized their agreements with new types of contracts, including permanent partnerships termed *compagnie* (kahm-pah-NYEE). Compagnie meant literally "bread together," that is, sharing bread; this is the root of the word *company*. Many of these compagnies began as agreements between brothers or other relatives and in-laws, but they quickly grew to include people who were not family members.

The ventures of the German Hanseatic League also illustrate these new business procedures. The **Hanseatic** (han-see-AT-ik) **League** was a mercantile association of towns. Initially the towns of Lübeck and Hamburg wanted mutual security, exclusive trading rights, and, where possible, a monopoly. During the next century, perhaps two hundred cities from Holland to Poland joined the league. From the thirteenth to the sixteenth centuries, the Hanseatic League controlled the trade of northern Europe. In the fourteenth century the Hanseatics branched out into southern Germany and Italy by land and into French, Spanish, and Portuguese ports by sea.

Hanseatic League A mercantile association of towns begun in northern Europe that allowed for mutual protection and security.

INDIVIDUALS IN SOCIETY

Francesco Datini

IN 1348, WHEN HE WAS A YOUNG TEENAGER, Francesco Datini (1335–1410) lost his father, his mother, a brother, and a sister to the Black Death epidemic that swept through Europe (see Chapter 12). Leaving his hometown of Prato in northern Italy, he apprenticed himself to merchants in nearby Florence for several years to learn accounting and other business skills. At fifteen, he moved to the city of Avignon (ah-veen-YOHN) in southern France. The popes were at this point living in Avignon instead of Rome, and the city offered many opportunities for an energetic and enterprising young man. Datini first became involved in the weapons trade, which offered steady profits. Then he became a merchant of spices, wool and silk cloth, and jewels. He was very successful, and when he was thirty-one he married the young daughter of another merchant in an elaborate wedding that was the talk of Avignon.

In 1378 the papacy returned to Italy, and Datini soon followed, setting up trading companies in Prato, Pisa, Florence, and eventually other cities. He focused on cloth and leather. He sought to control the trade in products used for preparation as well, especially the rare dyes that created the brilliant colors favored by wealthy noblemen and townspeople. He eventually had offices all over Europe and became one of the richest men of his day, opening a mercantile bank with many branch offices and a company that produced cloth.

Statue of Francesco Datini located outside the city hall in Prato. (Peter Horree/Alamy)

Datini was more successful than most, but what makes him particularly stand out was his record keeping. He kept careful account books and ledgers, all of them headed by the phrase "in the name of God and profit." He wrote to the managers of each of his offices every week, providing them with careful advice and blunt criticism: "You cannot see a crow in a bowl of milk." Taking on the son of a friend as an employee, he wrote to the young man: "Do your duty well, and you will acquire honor and profit, and you can count on me as if I were your own father. But if you do not, then do not count on me; it will be as if I had never known you."

When Datini was away from home, which was often, he wrote to his wife every day, and she sometimes responded in ways that were less deferential than we might expect of a woman who was many years younger. "I think it is not necessary," she wrote at one point, "to send me a message every Wednesday to say that you will be here on Sunday, for it seems to me that on every Friday you change your mind."

Datini's obsessive record keeping lasted beyond his death, for someone saved all of his records — hundreds of ledgers and contracts, eleven thousand business letters, and over a hundred thousand personal letters — in sacks in his opulent house in Prato, where they were found in the nineteenth century. They provide a detailed picture of medieval business practices and also reveal much about Datini as a person. Ambitious, calculating, luxury-loving, and a workaholic, Datini seems similar to a modern CEO. Like many of today's self-made billionaires, at the end of his life Datini began to think a bit more about God and less about profit. In his will, he set up a foundation for the poor in Prato and a home for orphans in Florence, both of which are still in operation. In 1967 scholars established an institute for economic history in Prato, naming it in Datini's honor; the institute now manages the collection of Datini documents and gathers other relevant materials in its archives.

Source: Iris Origo, *The Merchant of Prato: Francesco di Marco Datini, 1335–1410* (New York: Alfred A. Knopf, Inc., 1957).

QUESTIONS FOR ANALYSIS

1. How would you evaluate Datini's motto, "In the name of God and profit"? Is it an honest statement of his aims, a hypocritical justification of greed, a blend of both, or something else?
2. Changes in business procedures in the Middle Ages have been described as a "commercial revolution." Do Datini's business ventures support this assessment? How?

296

Chapter 11
The Creativity and Challenges
of Medieval Cities • 1100–1300

CHAPTER LOCATOR | What led to Europe's economic growth and reurbanization?

The Hanseatic League, ca. 1300–1400

• Principal Hanseatic town
▲ Hanseatic trading partner

At cities such as Bruges and London, Hanseatic merchants secured special trading concessions, exempting them from all tolls and allowing them to trade at local fairs. Hanseatic merchants established foreign trading centers, called "factories" because the commercial agents in them were called "factors." By the late thirteenth century, Hanseatic merchants had developed an important business technique, the business register. Merchants publicly recorded their debts and contracts and received a league guarantee for them.

The dramatic increase in trade ran into two serious difficulties in medieval Europe. One was the problem of minting money. Despite investment in mining operations to increase the production of metals, the amount of precious metal available for coins was not adequate for the increased flow of commerce. Merchants developed paper letters of exchange, in which coins or goods in one location were exchanged for a sealed letter, which could be used in place of metal coinage elsewhere. Developed in the late twelfth century, the bill of exchange became the normal method of making commercial payments by the early fourteenth century among the cities of western Europe, and it proved to be a decisive factor in the later development of credit and commerce in northern Europe.

The second problem was a moral and theological one. Church doctrine frowned on lending money at interest, termed *usury*. This doctrine was developed in the early Middle Ages when loans were mainly for consumption, to tide someone over, for instance, until the next harvest. Theologians reasoned that it was wrong for Christians to take advantage of the bad luck or need of another Christian. As moneylending became more important to commercial ventures, the church relaxed its position. It declared that some interest was legitimate as a payment for the risk the investor was taking, and that only interest above a certain level would be considered usury.

Lübeck The dominant city in the Hanseatic League, Lübeck is portrayed in this woodcut as densely packed within its walls, with church steeples and the city hall dominating the skyline, and boats carrying goods and people moving swiftly along the river. Even in this stylized scene, the artist captures the key features of the "Queen of the Hanse": crowded, proud, and centered on commerce. (Private Collection/The Stapleton Collection/The Bridgeman Art Library)

LVBECA VRBS IMPERIALIS LIBERA, CIVITATVM WAN-DALICARVM, ET INCLYTÆ HANSEATICÆ SOCIETATIS CAPVT.

What was life like in a medieval city?

How did universities serve the needs of medieval society?

How did literature and architecture express medieval values?

How did urban growth shape European religious life?

The stigma attached to lending money was in many ways attached to all the activities of a medieval merchant. Medieval people were uneasy about a person making a profit merely from the investment of money rather than labor, skill, and time. Merchants themselves shared these ideas to some degree, so they gave generous donations to the church and to charities. They also took pains not to flaunt their wealth. By the end of the Middle Ages, however, society had begun to accept the role of the merchant.

The Commercial Revolution

commercial revolution The transformation of the European economy as a result of changes in business procedures and growth in trade.

Changes in business procedures, combined with the growth in trade, led to a transformation of the European economy often called the commercial revolution by historians, who see it as the beginning of the modern capitalist economy. In calling this transformation the "commercial revolution," historians point not only to increases in the sheer volume of trade and in the complexity and sophistication of business procedures but also to the development of a new "capitalist spirit" in which making a profit is regarded as a good thing in itself. Because capitalism in the Middle Ages primarily involved trade rather than production, it is referred to as *mercantile capitalism*.

Part of this capitalist spirit was a new attitude toward time. Country people needed only approximate times—dawn, noon, sunset—for their work. Monasteries needed much more precise times to call monks together for the recitation of the Divine Office. In the early Middle Ages monks used a combination of hourglasses, sundials, and water-clocks to determine the time, and then rang bells by hand. About 1280 new types of mechanical mechanisms seem to have been devised in which weights replaced falling water and bells were rung automatically. The merchants who ran city councils quickly saw such clocks as both useful and a symbol of their prosperity. Mechanical clocks, usually installed on the cathedral or town church, were in general use in Italy by the 1320s, in Germany by the 1330s, in England by the 1370s, and in France by the 1380s. Buying and selling goods had initiated city people into the practice of quantification, and clocks contributed to the development of a mentality that conceived of the universe in quantitative terms.

The commercial revolution created a great deal of new wealth, which did not escape the attention of kings and other rulers. Wealth could be taxed, and through taxation kings could create strong and centralized states. In the years to come, alliances with the middle classes enabled kings to defeat feudal powers and aristocratic interests and to build the states that came to be called "modern." The commercial revolution also provided the opportunity for thousands of serfs to improve their social position. The slow but steady transformation of European society from almost completely rural and isolated to relatively more sophisticated constituted the greatest effect of the commercial revolution that began in the eleventh century.

Even so, merchants and business people did not run medieval communities other than in central and northern Italy and in the county of Flanders. Kings and nobles maintained ultimate control over most European cities. Most towns remained small, and urban residents never amounted to more than 10 percent of the total European population. The commercial changes of the eleventh through thirteenth centuries did, however, lay the economic foundations for the development of urban life and culture.

▼ What was life like in a medieval city?

In their backgrounds and abilities, townspeople represented diversity and change. Their occupations and their preoccupations were different from those of the feudal nobility and the laboring peasantry. Cities were crowded and polluted, though people flocked

Chapter 11
The Creativity and Challenges of Medieval Cities • 1100–1300

298

CHAPTER LOCATOR | What led to Europe's economic growth and reurbanization?

into them because they offered the possibility of economic advancement, social mobility, and improvement in legal status.

City Life

Walls surrounded almost all medieval towns and cities, and constant repair of the walls was usually the town's greatest expense. Peasants and merchants set up their carts as stalls just inside the gates of city walls or at a central marketplace. Most streets in a medieval town were marketplaces as much as passages for transit. Because there was no way to preserve food easily, people had to shop every day, and the market was where they met their neighbors, exchanged information, and talked over recent events.

In some respects the entire city was a marketplace. A window or door in a craftsman's home opened onto the street and displayed the finished product made within to attract passersby. The family lived above the business on the second or third floor. As the business and the family expanded, additional stories were added. Initially, houses were made of wood and thatched with straw. Fire was a constant danger, and because houses were built so close to one another, fires spread rapidly. Municipal governments consequently urged construction in stone or brick.

Most medieval cities developed with little town planning. As the population increased, space became more and more limited. Air and water pollution presented serious problems. Many families raised pigs for household consumption in sties next to the house. Horses and oxen, the chief means of transportation and power, dropped tons of dung on the streets every year. It was universal practice in the early towns to dump household waste, both animal and human, into the road in front of one's house.

People of all sorts, from beggars to fabulously wealthy merchants, regularly rubbed shoulders in the narrow streets and alleys of crowded medieval cities. This interaction did not mean that people were unaware of social differences, however, for clothing was a clear marker of social standing and sometimes of occupation. Wealthier urban residents wore bright colors, imported silk or fine woolen fabrics, and fancy headgear, while poorer ones wore darker clothing made of rough linen or linen and wool blends.

Astronomical Clock This astronomical clock, made in 1410 and still in use, sits above the marketplace in Prague, now the capital of the Czech Republic. The main central dial represents the position of the sun and the moon in the sky. Large public clocks became common features of medieval cities. With gears that regulated the striking of bells, these machines marked time for urban people. (François Punet/Sygma/Corbis)

In the later Middle Ages many cities attempted to make clothing distinctions a matter of law as well as of habit. City councils passed **sumptuary laws** that regulated the value of clothing and jewelry that people of different social groups could wear. Only members of high social groups could wear velvet, satin, pearls, or fur, for example, or have clothing embroidered with gold thread or dyed in colors that were especially expensive to produce. Along with enforcing social differences, sumptuary laws also attempted to impose moral standards by prohibiting plunging necklines on women or doublets (fitted buttoned jackets) that were too short on men. The laws also protected local industries by restricting the use of imported fabrics or other materials.

Some of these laws marked certain individuals as members of groups not fully acceptable in urban society. Prostitutes might be required to wear red or yellow bands on

sumptuary laws Laws that regulated the value and style of clothing and jewelry that various social groups could wear, as well as the amount they could spend on celebrations.

What was life like in a medieval city? | How did universities serve the needs of medieval society? | How did literature and architecture express medieval values? | How did urban growth shape European religious life?

299

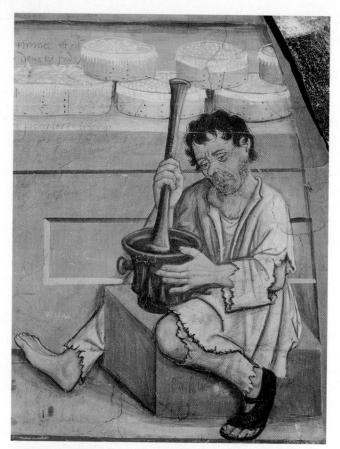

Poor Man at Work In this Italian fresco, a poor man grinds ingredients for medicine outside an apothecary's shop. The urban poor often survived by a combination of begging, picking up odd jobs when they could, and illegal activities. (Scala/Art Resource, NY)

their clothes, and Jews yellow circles or stars to distinguish them from their Christian neighbors. In some cities, sumptuary laws were expanded to include restrictions on expenditures for parties and family celebrations, again set by social class. Sumptuary laws were frequently broken and were difficult to enforce, but they provide evidence of the many material goods available to urban dwellers as well as the concern of city leaders about the social mobility and extravagance they saw all around them.

Servants and the Poor

Many urban houses took in domestic servants. A less wealthy household employed one woman who assisted in all aspects of running the household. A wealthier one employed a large staff of male and female servants with specific duties. When there was only one servant, she generally lived and ate with the family, for there was rarely enough space for separate quarters. Even in wealthier households that had many rooms, servants were rarely separated from their employers the way they would be in the nineteenth century, but instead lived on intimate terms with them. In Italian cities, household servants included slaves, usually young women brought in from areas outside of western Christianity, such as the Balkans.

Along with live-in servants, many households hired outside workers to do specific tasks. Urban workers laundered clothing and household linens, cared for children or invalids, carried goods around the city, and repaired houses and walls. In contrast to rural peasants who raised most of their own food, urban workers bought all their food, so they felt any increase in food prices immediately. Their wages were generally low, and children from such families sought work at very young ages. In cities with extensive cloth production, such as Florence or the towns of Flanders, the urban poor included workers who were at the mercy of the ups and downs of the market for cloth.

Illegal activities offered another way for people to support themselves. They stole from houses and people's pockets, fencing the goods for cash with local pawnbrokers or selling them in another town. Cities also drew in orphans, blind and handicapped people, and the elderly, who resorted to begging for money and food.

Popular Entertainment

Games and sports were common forms of entertainment and relaxation. There were games akin to modern football, rugby, stickball, and soccer in which balls were kicked, hit, and thrown. Wrestling matches and dog fights were also popular. People played cards, dice, and board games of all types. They trained dogs to fight each other or put them in an enclosure to fight a captured bear. All these sports and games were occasions for wagering and gambling, which preachers sometimes condemned (especially when the games were attached to a holiday or saint's day celebration) but had little power to control.

Chapter 11
The Creativity and Challenges
300   **of Medieval Cities • 1100–1300**

CHAPTER LOCATOR   What led to Europe's economic growth and reurbanization?

Young Men Playing Stickball With their tunics hitched up in their belts so that they could move around more easily, young men play a game involving hitting a ball with a stick. Games involving bats and balls were popular, for the equipment needed was made from simple, inexpensive materials. (The Granger Collection/The Art Archive)

Religious and family celebrations also meant dancing, which the church also attempted to ban or at least regulate, again with little success. Dancers were accompanied by a variety of instruments: reed pipes such as the chalumeau (shal-yuh-MOH) (an ancestor of the clarinet) and shawm (predecessor to the oboe); woodwinds such as flutes, panpipes, and recorders; stringed instruments including dulcimers, harps, lyres, lutes, zithers, and mandolins; brass instruments such as horns and trumpets; and percussion instruments like drums and tambourines. Musicians playing string or percussion instruments often sang as well, and people sang without instrumental accompaniment on festive occasions or while working.

▼ How did universities serve the needs of medieval society?

Just as the first strong secular states emerged in the thirteenth century, so did the first universities. This was no coincidence. The new bureaucratic states and the church needed educated administrators, and universities were a response to this need.

Origins

In the early Middle Ages, outside of the aristocratic court or the monastery, anyone who received an education got it from a priest. Priests instructed boys on the manor in the

Latin words of the Mass and taught them the rudiments of reading and writing. Few boys acquired elementary literacy, however, and peasant girls did not obtain even that.

Since the time of the Carolingian Empire, monasteries and cathedral schools had offered most of the available formal instruction. Schools attached to cathedrals and run by the bishop and his clergy were frequently situated in cities, and in the eleventh century in Italian cities like Bologna (boh-LOH-nyuh), wealthy businessmen established municipal schools. In the course of the twelfth century, cathedral schools in France and municipal schools in Italy developed into universities that attracted students from a wide area (Map 11.3). The first European universities appeared in Italy in Bologna, where the specialty was law, and Salerno, where the specialty was medicine.

Map 11.3 Intellectual Centers of Medieval Europe Universities provided more-sophisticated instruction than did monastery and cathedral schools, but all served to educate European males who had the money to attend.

Chapter 11
The Creativity and Challenges
302 **of Medieval Cities • 1100–1300**

CHAPTER LOCATOR   What led to Europe's
economic growth and
reurbanization?

Legal Curriculum

The growth of the University of Bologna coincided with a revival of interest in Roman law during the investiture controversy. The study of Roman law as embodied in the Justinian *Code* had never completely died out in the West, but in the late eleventh century a complete manuscript of the *Code* was discovered in a library in Pisa. This discovery led scholars in nearby Bologna, beginning with Irnerius (ehr-NEH-ree-uhs) (ca. 1055–ca. 1130), to study and teach Roman law intently.

Irnerius and other teachers at Bologna taught law not as a group of discrete bits of legislation, but as an organic whole related to the society it regulated, an all-inclusive system based on logical principles that could be applied to difficult practical situations. Thus, as social and economic structures changed, law would change with them. Jurists educated at Bologna and later at other universities were hired by rulers and city councils to systematize their law codes and write legal treatises. In the 1260s the English jurist

▪ PICTURING THE PAST

Law Lecture at Bologna
This beautifully carved marble sculpture, with the fluid lines of clothing characteristic of late Gothic style, suggests the students' intellectual intensity. (Museo Civico, Bologna/Scala/Art Resource, NY)

ANALYZING THE IMAGE Medieval students often varied widely in age. Does this image reflect that reality? Can the students pictured be classified in other ways, such as by class, sex, or race?

CONNECTIONS In what ways does this image resemble a typical university classroom today? In what ways does it differ?

To complete this activity online, go to the Online Study Guide at **bedfordstmartins.com/mckaywestunderstanding**.

Henry Bracton wrote a comprehensive treatise bringing together the laws and customs of England. About the same time King Alfonso X of Castile issued the *Siete Partidas (Book in Seven Parts)* that set out a detailed plan for administering his whole kingdom according to Roman legal principles.

Canon law (see Chapter 9) was also shaped by the reinvigoration of Roman law, and canon lawyers in ever greater numbers were hired by church officials or became prominent church officials themselves. In about 1140 the Benedictine monk Gratian put together a collection of nearly 3,800 texts covering all areas of canon law. His collection, known as the *Decretum*, became the standard text on which teachers of canon law lectured and commented.

Jewish scholars as well as Christian ones produced elaborate commentaries on law and religious tradition. Medieval universities were closed to Jews, but in some cities in the eleventh century special rabbinic academies opened that concentrated on the study of the Talmud, a compilation of legal arguments, proverbs, sayings, and folklore that had been produced in the fifth century in Babylon (present-day Iraq). Men seeking to become rabbis—highly respected figures within the Jewish community, with authority over economic and social as well as religious matters—spent long periods of time studying the Talmud, which served as the basis for their legal decisions in all areas of life.

Medical Training

At Salerno in southern Italy interest in medicine had persisted for centuries. Medical practitioners received training first through apprenticeship and then in an organized medical school. Individuals associated with Salerno, such as Constantine the African (1020?–1087)—who was a convert from Islam and later a Benedictine monk—began to translate medical works out of Arabic. These translations included writings by the ancient Greek physicians and Muslim medical writers.

Medical studies at Salerno were based on classical ideas, particularly those of Hippocrates and Aristotle (see Chapter 3). For the ancient Greeks, ideas about the human body were very closely linked to philosophy and to ideas about the natural world in general. Prime among these was the notion of the four bodily humors—blood, phlegm, black bile, and yellow bile. These fluids were contained in the body and were believed to influence bodily health. Disease was generally regarded as an imbalance of bodily humors, which could be diagnosed by taking a patient's pulse or examining his or her urine. Treatment was thus an attempt to bring the humors back into balance, which might be accomplished through diet or drugs, or more directly by vomiting, emptying one's bowels, or bloodletting.

The ideas of this medical literature spread throughout Europe from Salerno and became the basis of train-

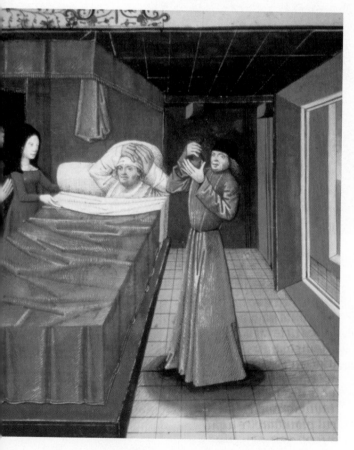

Physician's Diagnosis University-trained physicians rarely touched patients, but instead diagnosed illness by looking at patients' urine. This illustration appeared in a French translation of *De Proprietatibus Rerum (The Properties of Things)*, a medieval encyclopedia by Bartholomaeus Anglicus, an English Franciscan who taught at the universities of Paris and Magdeburg in Germany. This encyclopedia, which was widely copied, includes material from Greek, Arabic, and Jewish medical writers. (Snark/Art Resource, NY)

Chapter 11
The Creativity and Challenges of Medieval Cities • 1100–1300

304

CHAPTER LOCATOR | What led to Europe's economic growth and reurbanization?

ing for physicians at other medieval universities. University training gave physicians high social status and allowed them to charge high fees. They were generally hired directly by patients as needed, though some had more permanent positions as members of the household staffs of especially wealthy nobles or rulers.

Theology and Philosophy

Law and medicine were important academic disciplines in the Middle Ages, but theology was "the queen of sciences," so termed because it involved the study of God, who made all knowledge possible. Paris became the place to study theology. In the first decades of the twelfth century, students from all over Europe crowded into the cathedral school of Notre Dame in Paris.

University professors were known as "schoolmen" or Scholastics. They developed a method of thinking, reasoning, and writing in which questions were raised and authorities cited on both sides of a question. The goal of the Scholastic method was to arrive at definitive answers and to provide rational explanations for what was believed on faith. Schoolmen held that reason and faith constituted two harmonious realms whose truths complemented each other.

The Scholastic approach rested on the recovery of classical philosophical texts. Ancient Greek and Arabic texts entered Europe in the early twelfth century by way of Islamic intellectual centers at Baghdad, Córdoba, and Toledo (see Chapter 8). The major contribution of Arabic culture to the new currents of Western thought rested in the stimulus Arabic philosophers and commentators gave to Europeans' reflection on ancient Greek texts and the ways these texts fit with Christian teachings.

Scholastics University professors who developed a method of thinking, reasoning, and writing in which questions were raised and authorities cited on both sides of a question.

Abelard and Heloise

One of the young men drawn to Paris was Peter Abelard (A-buh-lahrd) (1079–1142), the son of a minor Breton knight. Abelard was fascinated by logic, which he believed could be used to solve most problems. He had a brilliant mind and, though orthodox in his philosophical teaching, appeared to challenge ecclesiastical authorities. His book *Sic et Non (Yes and No)* was a list of apparently contradictory propositions drawn from the Bible and the writings of the church fathers. Abelard used a method of systematic doubting in his writing and teaching. As he put it in the preface to *Sic et Non*, "By doubting we come to questioning, and by questioning we perceive the truth." While other scholars merely asserted theological principles, Abelard discussed and analyzed them. Abelard was severely censured by a church council, but his cleverness, boldness, and imagination made him a highly popular figure among students.

Abelard's reputation for brilliance drew the attention of one of the cathedral canons, Fulbert, who hired Abelard to tutor his intellectual niece Heloise. The relationship between teacher and pupil passed beyond the intellectual. Heloise became pregnant, and Canon Fulbert pressured the couple to marry. The couple agreed, but they wanted the marriage kept secret for the sake of Abelard's career. Distrusting Abelard, Canon Fulbert hired men to castrate him. Wounded in spirit as well as body, Abelard persuaded Heloise to enter a convent. He became a monk; and their baby, baptized Astrolabe (AS-truh-layb) for a recent Muslim navigational invention, was given to Heloise's family for adoption. Abelard spent his later years as abbot of an obscure monastery in Brittany, where he supposedly wrote an autobiographical statement, *A History of My Calamities*, describing his rise and fall.

Heloise secured a copy of Abelard's *History* and took great exception to his statement that their relationship had been based solely on physical desire. She felt that she gained no spiritual reward from her life in the convent, because she had not entered out of religious convictions. Despite her unhappiness, she became a competent prioress who looked after the nuns in her care, and she succeeded in convincing Abelard to provide letters of spiritual direction for her community. The two were united in death and later buried together in a cemetery in Paris. Both *A History of My Calamities* and the letters of Abelard and Heloise are examples of the new self-awareness of the period, grounded in the rebirth of learning of which the development of universities was an important part.

Thomas Aquinas

Thirteenth-century Scholastics devoted an enormous amount of time to collecting and organizing knowledge on all topics. Such a collection was published as a *summa*, or reference book. Saint Thomas Aquinas (1225–1274), a professor at Paris, produced the most famous collection, the *Summa Theologica*, which deals with a vast number of theological questions.

Prime among these questions was the relationship between reason and faith, a central issue for all Scholastic philosophers. Aquinas drew an important distinction between them. He maintained that, although reason can demonstrate many basic Christian principles such as the existence of God, other fundamental teachings such as the Trinity and original sin cannot be proved by logic. That reason cannot establish them does not mean they are contrary to reason. Rather, people understand such doctrines through revelation embodied in Scripture. Scripture cannot contradict reason, nor reason Scripture:

> *The light of faith that is freely infused into us does not destroy the light of natural knowledge [reason] implanted in us naturally. For although the natural light of the human mind is insufficient to show us these things made manifest by faith, it is nevertheless impossible that these things which the divine principle gives us by faith are contrary to these implanted in us by nature [reason]. Indeed, were that the case, one or the other would have to be false, and, since both are given to us by God, God would have to be the author of untruth, which is impossible. . . .*[1]

Aquinas also investigated the branch of philosophy called *epistemology* (ih-pihs-tuh-MAH-luh-jee), which is concerned with how a person knows something. Aquinas stated that one knows, first, through sensory perception of the physical world—seeing, hearing, touching, and so on. He maintained that there can be nothing in the mind that is not first in the senses. Second, knowledge comes through reason, the mind exercising its natural abilities. Aquinas stressed the power of human reason to know, even to know God. His five proofs for God's existence exemplify the Scholastic method of knowing. His work later became the fundamental text of Roman Catholic doctrine.

Life at a University

The influx of students eager for learning, together with dedicated and imaginative teachers, created the atmosphere in which universities grew. In northern Europe—at Paris and later at Oxford and Cambridge in England—associations or guilds of professors organized universities. They established the curriculum, set the length of time for study, and determined the form and content of examinations. By the end of the fifteenth century there were at least eighty universities in Europe.

Students at universities were generally considered to be lower-level members of the clergy—this was termed being in "minor orders"—so that any students accused of legal infractions were tried in church, rather than in city, courts. This clerical status, along with widely held ideas about women's lesser intellectual capabilities, meant that university education was restricted to men, a situation that did not change until after World War I.

Though university classes were not especially expensive, the many years that university required meant that the sons of peasants or artisans could rarely attend, unless they

Chapter 11
The Creativity and Challenges
306   **of Medieval Cities • 1100–1300**

CHAPTER LOCATOR   What led to Europe's economic growth and reurbanization?

could find wealthy patrons who would pay their expenses while they studied. Most students were the sons of urban merchants or lower-level nobles, especially the younger sons who would not inherit family lands.

At all universities the standard method of teaching was the lecture—that is, a reading. The professor read a passage from the Bible, the Justinian *Code*, or one of Aristotle's treatises. He then explained and interpreted the passage; his interpretation was called a *gloss*. Texts and glosses were sometimes collected and reproduced as textbooks. Because books had to be copied by hand, they were extremely expensive, and few students could afford them. Students therefore depended on their own or friends' notes accumulated over a period of years. The choice of subjects was narrow. The syllabus at all universities consisted of a core of ancient texts that all students studied and attempted to master.

Examinations were given after three, four, or five years of study, when the student applied for a degree. Examinations were oral and very difficult. If the candidate passed, he was awarded a license to teach, which was the earliest form of academic degree. Most students, however, did not become teachers. They staffed the expanding diocesan, royal, and papal administrations.

Students did not spend all their time listening to lectures or debating. Much information about medieval students concerns what we might call "extracurricular" activities: university regulations forbidding them to throw rocks at professors; sermons about breaking and entering, raping local women, attacking town residents, and disturbing church services; and court records discussing their drunken brawls, riots, fights, and duels. Students lived in rented rooms or by the late thirteenth century in residential colleges, both of which could be costly. The money sent by parents or patrons was often not sufficient for all expenses, so students augmented it by begging, thieving, or doing odd jobs. They also delayed finishing their studies because life as a student could be pleasant, without the responsibilities that came with becoming fully adult.

▼ How did literature and architecture express medieval values?

The High Middle Ages saw the creation of new types of literature, architecture, and music. Technological advances in such areas as papermaking and stone masonry made innovations possible, as did the growing wealth and sophistication of patrons. Artists and artisans flourished in the more secure environment of the High Middle Ages, producing works that celebrated the glories of love, war, and God.

Vernacular Literature and Drama

Latin was the language used in university education, scholarly writing, and works of literature. In contrast to Roman times, however, by the High Middle Ages no one spoke Latin as his or her original mother tongue. The barbarian invasions, the mixture of peoples, and evolution over time had resulted in a variety of local dialects that blended words and linguistic forms in various ways. These dialects were regionally specific, and as kings increased the size of their holdings they often ruled people who spoke many different dialects.

In the early Middle Ages almost all written works continued to be in Latin, but in the High Middle Ages some authors began to write in their local dialect, that is, in the everyday language of their region, which linguistic historians call the vernacular. This new vernacular literature gradually transformed some local dialects into literary languages, such as French, German, Italian, and English, while other dialects, such as Breton and

vernacular literature
Writings in the author's local dialect, that is, in the everyday language of the region.

What was life like in a medieval city?   How did universities serve the needs of medieval society?   **How did literature and architecture express medieval values?**   How did urban growth shape European religious life?

307

Bavarian, remained (and remain to this day) largely means of oral communication. Most people in the High Middle Ages could no more read vernacular literature than they could read Latin, however, so oral transmission continued to be the most important way information was conveyed and traditions passed down.

By the thirteenth century, techniques of making paper from old linen cloth and rags began to spread from Spain, where they had been developed by the Arabs, providing a much cheaper material on which to write (see Chapter 8). People started to write down things that were more mundane and less serious in various vernacular dialects, using spellings that were often personal and idiosyncratic. The writings included fables, legends, stories, and myths that had circulated orally for generations, and slowly a body of written vernacular literature developed.

Stories and songs in the vernacular were performed and composed at the courts of nobles and rulers. In Germany and most of northern Europe, the audiences favored stories and songs recounting the great deeds of warrior heroes. These epics, known as *chansons de geste* (SHAN-suhn duh JEHST; songs of great deeds), celebrate violence, slaughter, revenge, and physical power. In southern Europe, especially in the area of southern France known as Provence, poets who called themselves **troubadours** (TROO-buh-dorz) wrote and sang lyric verses celebrating love, desire, beauty, and gallantry. (See "Listening to the Past: Courtly Love Poetry," page 310.) Troubadours included a few women, called *trobairitz*, most of whose exact identities are not known.

Since the songs of the troubadours were widely imitated in Italy, England, and Germany, they spurred the development of vernacular literature there as well. The romantic motifs of the troubadours also influenced the northern French *trouvères* (troo-VEHRZ), who wrote adventure-romances in the form of epic poems in a language we call Old French, the ancestor of modern French. At the court of his patron, Marie of Champagne, Chrétien de Troyes (KREH-tyen deh TWAH) (ca. 1135–ca. 1190) used the legends of the fifth-century British king Arthur and his knights as the basis for innovative tales of battle and forbidden love. Most of the troubadours and trouvères came from and wrote for the aristocratic classes, and their poetry suggests the interests and values of noble culture. Their influence eventually extended to all social groups, however, for people who could not read heard the poems and stories from people who could, so that what had originally come from oral culture was recycled back into it every generation.

Drama, derived from the church's liturgy, emerged as a distinct art form during the High Middle Ages. Plays based on biblical themes and on the lives of the saints were performed in the towns, first in churches and then at the town marketplace. Mystery plays were financed and performed by "misteries," members of the craft guilds, and miracle plays were acted by amateurs or professional actors, not guild members. By combining comical farce based on ordinary life with serious religious scenes, plays gave ordinary people an opportunity to identify with religious figures and think about the mysteries of their faith.

troubadours Poets who wrote and sang lyric verses celebrating love, desire, beauty, and gallantry.

Churches and Cathedrals

The development of secular vernacular literature focusing on human concerns did not mean any lessening of the importance of religion in medieval people's lives. As we have seen, religious devotion was expressed through daily rituals, holiday ceremonies, and the creation of new institutions such as universities and religious orders. People also wanted permanent visible representations of their piety, and both church and city leaders wanted physical symbols of their wealth and power. These aims found their outlet in the building of tens of thousands of churches, chapels, abbeys, and, most spectacularly, **cathedrals** in the twelfth and thirteenth centuries. A cathedral is the church of a bishop and the administrative headquarters of a diocese. The word comes from the Greek word *kathe-*

cathedral The church of a bishop and the administrative headquarters of a diocese.

Notre Dame Cathedral, Paris This view offers a fine example of the twin towers (left), the spire and great rose window over the south portal (center), and the flying buttresses that support the walls and the vaults. Like hundreds of other churches in medieval Europe, it was dedicated to the Virgin Mary. With a spire rising more than 300 feet, Notre Dame was the tallest building in Europe. (David R. Frazier/Photo Researchers)

dra, meaning seat, because the bishop's throne, a symbol of the office, is located in the cathedral.

Most of the churches in the early Middle Ages had been built primarily of wood, which meant they were susceptible to fire. They were often small, with a flat roof, in a rectangular or slightly cross-shaped form called a *basilica*, based on earlier Roman public buildings. With the end of the Viking and Magyar invasions and the increasing political stability of the eleventh century, bishops and abbots supported the construction of larger and more fire-resistant churches made almost completely out of stone. These were based on the basilican style, but features were added that made the cross shape more pronounced. As the size of the church grew horizontally, it also grew vertically. Builders adapted Roman-style rounded barrel vaults made of stone for the ceiling; this use of Roman forms led the style to be labeled **Romanesque**.

The next architectural style was **Gothic** so named by later Renaissance architects who thought that only the uncouth Goths could have invented so disunified a style. In Gothic churches the solid stone barrel-vaulted roof was replaced by a roof made of stone ribs with plaster in between. This made the ceiling much lighter, so that the side pillars and walls did not need to carry so much weight. Exterior arched stone supports called *flying buttresses* also carried some of the weight of the roof, so solid walls could be replaced by windows, which let in great amounts of light.

Begun in the Île-de-France in the twelfth century, Gothic architecture spread throughout France with the expansion of royal power. From France the new style spread to England, Germany, Italy, Spain, and eastern Europe. In those countries, the Gothic style

Romanesque An architectural style with rounded arches and small windows.

Gothic An architectural style typified by pointed arches and large stained-glass windows.

What was life like in a medieval city? How did universities serve the needs of medieval society? **How did literature and architecture express medieval values?** How did urban growth shape European religious life?

309

LISTENING TO THE PAST

Courtly Love Poetry

Whether female or male, the troubadour poets celebrated fin'amor, *a Provençal word for the pure or perfect love a knight was supposed to feel for his lady, which has in English come to be called "courtly love." In courtly love poetry, the writer praises his or her love object, idealizing the beloved and promising loyalty and great deeds. Most of these songs are written by, or from the perspective of, a male lover who is socially beneath his female beloved; her higher status makes her unattainable, so the lover's devotion can remain chaste and pure, rewarded by her handkerchief, or perhaps a kiss, but nothing more. The noblemen and noblewomen who listened to these songs viewed such love as ennobling, and some authors even wrote courtly love poetry directed to the Virgin Mary, the ultimate unattainable woman.*

Scholars generally agree that poetry praising pure and perfect love originated in the Muslim culture of the Iberian Peninsula, where heterosexual romantic love had long been the subject of poems and songs. Southern France was a border area where Christian and Muslim cultures mixed; Spanish Muslim poets sang at the courts of Christian nobles, and Provençal poets picked up their romantic themes.

Other aspects of courtly love are hotly debated. Was it simply a literary convention, or did it shape actual behavior? Did it celebrate adultery, or was true courtly love pure (and unrequited)? How should we interpret medieval physicians' reports of people (mostly young men) becoming gravely ill from "lovesickness"? Did the doctors really believe in the physical power of love? Were there actually "courts of love" in which women judged lovers based on a system of rules? Did courtly love lead to greater respect for women or toward greater misogyny, as desire for a beloved so often ended in frustration?

It is very difficult to know whether courtly love literature influenced the treatment of real women to any great extent — peasant women were certainly no less in danger of rape from knightly armies in the thirteenth century than they had been in the tenth — but it did introduce an ideal of heterosexual romance into Western literature that had not been there in the classical or early medieval period. People who study contemporary popular culture note how much courtly love ideals still shape romantic conventions. Countless movies, songs, and novels explore love between people of different social groups, though now the love generally remains pure by having either the lover or the beloved tragically die young.

The following poem was written by Arnaut Daniel, a thirteenth-century troubadour praised by writers from Dante in the thirteenth century to Ezra Pound in the twentieth. Not much is known about him, but the songs that have survived capture courtly love conventions perfectly.

> I only know the grief that comes to me,
> to my love-ridden heart, out of over-loving,
> since my will is so firm and whole
> that it never parted or grew distant from her
> whom I craved at first sight, and afterwards:
> and now, in her absence, I tell her burning words;
> then, when I see her, I don't know, so much I have to,
>   what to say.
>
> To the sight of other women I am blind, deaf to
>   hearing them
> since her only I see, and hear and heed,
> and in that I am surely not a false slanderer,
> since heart desires her more than mouth may say;
> wherever I may roam through fields and valleys,
>   plains and mountains
> I shan't find in a single person all those qualities
> which God wanted to select and place in her.
>
> I have been in many a good court,
> but here by her I find much more to praise:
> measure and wit and other good virtues,
> beauty and youth, worthy deeds and fair disport;
> so well kindness taught and instructed her
> that it has rooted every ill manner out of her:
> I don't think she lacks anything good.
>
> No joy would be brief or short
> coming from her whom I endear to guess [my
>   intentions],
> otherwise she won't know them from me,
> if my heart cannot reveal itself without words,
> since even the Rhone [River], when rain swells it,
> has no such rush that my heart doesn't stir
> a stronger one, weary of love, when I behold her.
>
> Joy and merriment from another woman seems false
>   and ill to me,
> since no worthy one can compare with her,
> and her company is above the others'.
> Ah me, if I don't have her, alas, so badly she has
>   taken me!
> But this grief is amusement, laughter and joy,
> since in thinking of her, of her am I gluttonous and
>   greedy:
> ah me, God, could I ever enjoy her otherwise!

competed with strong indigenous architectural traditions and thus underwent transformations that changed it to fit local usage.

The economic growth of the period meant that merchants, nobles, and the church could afford the costs of this unparalleled building boom. Extraordinary amounts of

Chapter 11
The Creativity and Challenges of Medieval Cities • 1100–1300

310

CHAPTER LOCATOR | What led to Europe's economic growth and reurbanization?

And never, I swear, I have liked game or ball so much,
or anything has given my heart so much joy
as did the one thing that no false slanderer
made public, which is a treasure for me only.
Do I tell too much? Not I, unless she is displeased:
beautiful one, by God, speech and voice
I'd lose ere I say something to annoy you.

And I pray my song does not displease you
since, if you like the music and lyrics,
little cares Arnaut whether the unpleasant ones like
   them as well. 🙶

*Far fewer poems by female troubadours (trobairitz)
have survived than by male troubadours, but those that
have express strong physical and emotional feelings.
The following song was written in the twelfth century
by the Countess of Dia. She was purportedly the wife
of a Provençal nobleman, though biographies of both
troubadours and trobairitz were often made up to fit
the conventions of courtly love, so we don't know for
sure. The words to at least four of her songs have survived,
one of them with the melody, which is very rare.*

🙶 I've suffered great distress
From a knight whom I once owned.
Now, for all time, be it known:
I loved him — yes, to excess. His jilting I've regretted,
Yet his love I never really returned. Now for my sin I
   can only burn:
Dressed, or in my bed.

O if I had that knight to caress
Naked all night in my arms,
He'd be ravished by the charm
Of using, for cushion, my breast. His love I more
   deeply prize
Than Floris did Blancheor's
Take that love, my core, My sense, my life, my eyes!

Lovely lover, gracious, kind,
When will I overcome your fight?
O if I could lie with you one night!
Feel those loving lips on mine! Listen, one thing sets
   me afire:
Here in my husband's place I want you,
If you'll just keep your promise true: Give me
   everything I desire. 🙶

In this fourteenth-century painting, a lady puts the helmet on her beloved
knight. (akg-images)

Sources: First poem: Used by permission of Leonardo Malcovati, editor and
translator of *Prosody in England and Elsewhere: A Comparative Approach* (London:
Gival Press, 2006), and online at http://www.trobar.org/troubadours/; second
poem: quoted in J. J. Wilhelm, ed., *Lyrics of the Middle Ages: An Anthology* (New
York: Garland Publishers, 1993), pp. 83–84. Reprinted with permission.

QUESTIONS FOR ANALYSIS

1. Both of these songs focus on a beloved who does not return the
   lover's affection. What similarities and differences do you see
   in them?
2. How does courtly love reinforce other aspects of medieval society?
   Are there aspects of medieval society it contradicts?
3. Can you find examples from current popular music that parallel
   the sentiments expressed in these two songs?

money were needed to build these houses of worship. Moreover, money was not the
only need. A great number of artisans had to be assembled: quarrymen, sculptors, stone-
cutters, masons, mortar makers, carpenters, blacksmiths, glassmakers, roofers. Each master craftsman had apprentices, and unskilled laborers had to be recruited for the heavy

What was life like in a
medieval city?

How did universities
serve the needs of
medieval society?

How did literature and
architecture express
medieval values?

How did urban growth
shape European
religious life?

work. Bishops and abbots sketched out what they wanted and set general guidelines, but they left practical needs and aesthetic considerations to the master mason. He held overall responsibility for supervision of the project.

Since cathedrals were symbols of civic pride, towns competed to build the largest and most splendid church. In northern France in the late twelfth and early thirteenth centuries, cathedrals grew progressively taller. In 1163 the citizens of Paris began Notre Dame Cathedral, planning it to reach the height of 114 feet from the floor to the ceiling at the highest point inside. When reconstruction of Chartres Cathedral was begun in 1194, it was to be 119 feet high. The construction of a large cathedral was rarely completed in a lifetime; many were never finished at all. Because generation after generation added to the buildings, many Gothic churches show the architectural influences of two or even three centuries.

Stained glass beautifully reflects the creative energy of the High Middle Ages. It is both an integral part of Gothic architecture and a distinct form of painting. As Gothic churches became more skeletal and had more windows, stained glass replaced manuscript illumination as the leading form of painting. From large sheets of colored glass made by glassblowers, artisans cut small pieces, linked them together with narrow strips of lead, and set them in an iron frame prepared to fit the window opening. Windows showed scenes from the Old and New Testaments and the lives of the saints, designed to teach people doctrines of the Christian faith through visual images. They also showed scenes from the lives of the ordinary merchants and artisans who paid for them.

Stained-Glass Window in Chartres Cathedral In this thirteenth-century window, Noah is building his ark while a workman brings him lumber. Like many stained-glass windows, this depicts both a biblical scene and medieval urban life. Workers carrying lumber and stone would have been a common sight around any cathedral. (Erich Lessing/Art Resource, NY)

Tapestry making also came into its own in the fourteenth century. Heavy woolen tapestries were first made in the monasteries and convents as wall hangings for churches. Because they could be moved and lent an atmosphere of warmth, they replaced mural paintings. Early tapestries depicted religious scenes, but later hangings, produced for use in knightly houses and noble castles, bore secular designs, especially romantic forests and hunting spectacles.

Once at least part of a Gothic cathedral had been built, the building began to be used for religious services. Although town residents attended weekly services in their local churches, they gathered in cathedrals for baptisms, funerals, and saint's day services. They also used them for guild meetings and other secular purposes. Services became increasingly complex to fit with their new surroundings.

The frenzy to create the most magnificent Gothic cathedrals eventually came to an end. Begun in 1247, the cathedral in Beauvais reached a height of 157 feet in the interior, exceeding all others. Unfortunately, the weight imposed on the vaults was too great, and the building collapsed in 1284. The collapse was viewed as an aber-

Chapter 11
The Creativity and Challenges of Medieval Cities • 1100–1300
312

CHAPTER LOCATOR | What led to Europe's economic growth and reurbanization?

ration, for countless other cathedrals were in various stages of completion at the same time, and none of them fell. Seen in hindsight, however, it can be viewed as a harbinger. Very few cathedrals not finished at the time of the collapse were ever finished, and even fewer were started. In the fourteenth century the church itself splintered, and the cities that had so proudly built cathedrals were decimated by famine and disease.

▼ How did urban growth shape European religious life?

The soaring towers of Gothic cathedrals were visible symbols of the Christian faith and civic pride of medieval urban residents, but many city people also felt that the church did not meet their spiritual needs. The bishops, usually drawn from the feudal nobility, did not understand urban culture and were suspicious of it. The new monastic orders of the twelfth century, such as the Cistercians, situated in remote, isolated areas had little relevance to the towns. Townspeople wanted a pious clergy capable of preaching the Gospel, and they disapproved of clerical ignorance and luxurious living, particularly when they contrasted the easy life of many churchmen with the grim lives of the urban poor.

Heretical Groups

Ironically, the Gregorian reform movement (see Chapter 9), which had worked to purify the church of disorder and enhance papal power, contributed to townspeople's dissatisfaction with the church. Papal moves against simony, for example, led to widespread concern about the role of money in the church just as papal tax collectors were becoming more efficient and sophisticated. Papal efforts to improve the sexual morality of the clergy led some laypersons to assume they could, and indeed should, remove priests for any type of immorality or for not living according to standards that the parishioners judged appropriate.

Criticism of the church emerged in many places but found its largest audience in the cities, where the contrast between wealth and poverty could be seen more acutely and where people could more easily find others who agreed with them. In northern Italian towns, the monk Arnold of Brescia (BREH-shah) (ca. 1090–1155), a vigorous advocate of strict clerical poverty, denounced clerical wealth. In France, Peter Waldo (ca. 1140–ca. 1218), a rich merchant of the city of Lyons, gave his money to the poor and preached that only prayers, not sacraments, were needed for salvation. The Waldensians (wahl-DEHN-shuhnz)—as Peter's followers were called—bitterly attacked the sacraments and church hierarchy, and they carried these ideas across Europe. Critical of the clergy and spiritually unfulfilled, townspeople joined the Waldensians. As we saw in Chapter 9, the Albigensians, whose supporters were most numerous in highly urbanized southern France, asserted that the material world was evil and that people who rejected worldly things, not wealthy bishops or the papacy, should be the religious leaders. The papacy denounced Arnold of Brescia and both the Waldensians and Albigensians as heretics, that is, as people who held to doctrines that the church defined as incorrect. Arnold led a revolt against the pope and was hanged for rebellion, and the papacy began extensive campaigns to wipe out the Waldensians and the Albigensians.

The Friars

In its struggle against heresy, the church gained the support of two remarkable men, Saint Dominic and Saint Francis, and of the orders they founded. Born in Castile, a province of Spain, Domingo de Gúzman (1170?–1221) received a sound education and was

What was life like in a medieval city?   How did universities serve the needs of medieval society?   How did literature and architecture express medieval values?   **How did urban growth shape European religious life?**

313

ordained a priest. In 1206 he accompanied his bishop on an unsuccessful mission to win back the Albigensians in southern France. Determined to succeed through ardent preaching, Domingo ("Dominic") subsequently returned to France with a few followers. In 1216 the group—officially known as the Preaching Friars, though often called Dominicans—won papal recognition as a new religious order.

Dominicans The followers of Dominic, officially known as the Preaching Friars.

Francesco di Bernardone (1181–1226), son of a wealthy Italian cloth merchant in the city of Assisi, had a religious conversion and decided to live and preach the Gospel in absolute poverty. He was particularly inspired by two biblical texts: "If you seek perfection, go, sell your possessions, and give to the poor. You will have treasure in heaven. Afterward, come back and follow me" (Matthew 19:21); and Jesus' advice to his disciples as they went out to preach, "Take nothing for the journey, neither walking staff nor travelling bag, nor bread, nor money" (Luke 9:3). Francis's asceticism did not emphasize withdrawal from the world, but joyful devotion in it. In contrast to the Albigensians, who saw the material world as evil, Francis saw all creation as God-given and good. He was widely reported to perform miracles involving animals and birds, and wrote hymns to natural objects. "Be praised, my Lord, through our sister Mother Earth" went one, "who feeds us and rules us and produces various fruits with colored flowers and herbs."

The simplicity, humility, and joyful devotion with which Francis carried out his mission soon attracted companions. Although he resisted pressure to establish an order, his followers became so numerous that he was obliged to develop some formal structure. In 1221 the papacy approved the Rule of the Little Brothers of Saint Francis, as the Franciscans were known.

Franciscans The followers of Francis and his mission of simplicity, humility, and devotion.

The new Dominican and Franciscan orders differed significantly from older monastic orders such as the Benedictines and the Cistercians. First, the Dominicans and Franciscans were friars, not monks. Their lives and work focused on the cities and university towns, the busy centers of commercial and intellectual life, not the secluded and cloistered world of monks. They thought that more contact with ordinary Christians, not less, was a better spiritual path.

friars Men belonging to certain religious orders who did not live in monasteries but out in the world.

Second, the friars stressed apostolic poverty, a life based on the teaching of the Gospels in which they would own no property and depend on Christian people for their material needs. Hence they were called *mendicants*, from the Latin word for begging. The friars' emphasis on clerical poverty was very close to that of Arnold of Brescia and Peter Waldo, but most Franciscans and Dominicans did not extend this into a criticism of the church as an institution, so they received papal support rather than opposition.

The friars' mission to the towns and the poor, their ideal of poverty, and their compassion for the human condition made them vastly popular. They interpreted Christian doctrine for the new urban classes. By living Christianity as well as preaching it, they won the respect of medieval city residents.

They also addressed the spiritual and intellectual needs of the middle classes and the wealthy. The Dominicans preferred that their friars be university graduates in order to better preach to a sophisticated urban society. Dominicans soon held professorial chairs at leading universities, and they counted Thomas Aquinas, probably the greatest medieval philosopher in Europe, as their most famous member. The Franciscans followed suit at the universities and also produced intellectual leaders.

Women sought to develop similar orders devoted to active service out in the world. Clare of Assisi (1193–1253) sought to live in poverty and became a follower of Francis, who established a place for her to live in a church in Assisi. She was joined by other women, and they attempted to establish a rule for life in their community that would follow Francis's ideals of absolute poverty and allow them to serve the poor. Her rule was accepted by the papacy only after many decades, and then only because she agreed that the order, called the Poor Clares, would be cloistered.

Beguines Groups of laywomen seeking to live religious lives in the growing cities of Europe.

In the growing cities of Europe, especially in the Netherlands, groups of laywomen seeking to live religious lives came together as what later came to be known as Beguines

Saint Francis Gives Up His Worldly Possessions When Francis's wealthy father ordered Francis to give him back the money he had given to a church, Francis instead took off all his clothes and returned them to his father, signifying his dependence on his father in Heaven rather than on his earthly father. The fresco of this event, painted seventy years after Francis's death for the church erected in his honor in Assisi, captures the consternation of Francis's father and the confusion of the local bishop (holding the cloth in front of the naked Francis), who had told the young man to obey his earthly father. By the time the church was built, members of the Franciscan order were in violent disagreement over what Francis would have thought about a huge church built in his honor and other issues of clerical wealth. (Scala/Art Resource, NY)

(bay-GEENS). They lived communally in small houses called *beguinages*, combining lives of prayer with service to the needy. Beguine spirituality emphasized direct personal communication with God, sometimes through mystical experiences, rather than through the intercession of a saint or official church rituals. Many Beguines were also devoted to the church's sacraments, especially the Eucharist, and initially some church officials gave guarded approval of the movement. By the fourteenth century, however, they were declared heretical, and much of their property was confiscated, for church officials were clearly uncomfortable with women who were neither married nor cloistered nuns.

What was life like in a medieval city?

How did universities serve the needs of medieval society?

How did literature and architecture express medieval values?

How did urban growth shape European religious life?

The Friars and Papal Power

Beginning in 1233 the papacy used the friars to staff its new ecclesiastical court, the Inquisition. *Inquisition* means "investigation," and the Franciscans and Dominicans developed expert methods of rooting out unorthodox thought. It is ironic that groups whose teachings were similar in so many ways to those of heretics were charged with rooting them out. This irony was probably most pronounced in the case of the Spiritual Franciscans, a group that broke away from the main body of the Franciscan order to follow Francis's original ideals of absolute poverty. When they denied the pope's right to countermand that ideal, he ordered them tried by the Inquisition.

Modern Americans consider the procedures of the Inquisition exceedingly unjust, and there was substantial criticism of it in the Middle Ages. People who were accused did not learn the evidence against them or see their accusers; they were subjected to lengthy interrogations often designed to trap them; and torture could be used to extract confessions. Medieval people, however, believed that heretics destroyed the souls of their neighbors and destroyed the very bonds of society. By the mid-thirteenth century secular governments as well as the church steadily pressed for social conformity, and they had the resources to search out and punish heretics. So successful was the Inquisition as a tool of royal and papal power that within a century heresy had been virtually extinguished in the cities, although heretical groups continued to survive in the more isolated mountain areas of Spain, France, Switzerland, and Italy.

Popes and kings jointly supported the Inquisition, but in the late thirteenth century the papacy came into a violent dispute with several of Europe's leading rulers that had echoes of the earlier controversy over lay investiture (see Chapter 9). Pope Boniface VIII (pontificate 1294–1303), arguing from precedent, insisted that King Edward I of England and Philip the Fair of France obtain his consent for taxes they had imposed on the clergy. Edward immediately denied the clergy the protection of the law, and Philip halted the shipment of all ecclesiastical revenue to Rome. Boniface had to back down.

The battle for power between the papacy and the French monarchy became a bitter war of propaganda, with Philip at one point calling the pope a heretic. Finally, in 1302, in a letter titled *Unam Sanctam*, Boniface insisted that all Christians—including kings—were subject to the pope. Philip maintained that he was completely sovereign in his kingdom and responsible to God alone. French mercenary troops assaulted and arrested the aged pope at Anagni in Italy. Although Boniface was soon freed, he died shortly afterward. The confrontation at Anagni foreshadowed serious difficulties in the Christian church, but religious struggle was only one of the crises that would face Western society in the fourteenth century.

Unam Sanctam An official letter issued by Pope Boniface VIII claiming that all Christians were subject to the pope.

316

Chapter 11
The Creativity and Challenges
of Medieval Cities • 1100–1300

CHAPTER LOCATOR   What led to Europe's economic growth and reurbanization?

←LOOKING BACK **LOOKING AHEAD**→

THE HIGH MIDDLE AGES represent one of the most creative periods in the history of Western society. Institutions that are important parts of the modern world, including universities, jury trials, and investment banks, were all developed in this era. Advances were made in urban life, trade, architectural design, and education. Through the activities of merchants, Europeans again saw products from Africa and Asia in city marketplaces, as they had in Roman times, and wealthier urban residents bought them. Individuals and groups such as craft guilds provided money for building and decorating magnificent Gothic cathedrals, where people heard increasingly complex music and watched plays that celebrated both the lives of the saints and their own daily struggles.

Toward the end of the thirteenth century, however, there were increasing signs of impending problems. The ships and caravans bringing exotic goods also brought new pests, including rodents, insects, and disease pathogens. The new vernacular literature created a stronger sense of national identity, which increased hostility toward others. The numbers of poor continued to grow, and the efforts of the friars to aid their suffering were never enough. As the century ended, some urban residents continued to wear the fine clothes that marked their status, but others exchanged these for the sackcloth or rough robes of penitents. They gathered for worship not to honor God and his saints, but to ask them why they were punishing humans. ▪

- **For a list of suggested readings for this chapter, visit** *bedfordstmartins.com/mckaywestunderstanding*.

- **For primary sources from this period, see** *Sources of Western Society,* Second Edition.

- **For Web sites, images, and documents related to topics in this chapter, see Make History at** *bedfordstmartins.com/mckaywestunderstanding*.

What was life like in a medieval city?   How did universities serve the needs of medieval society?   How did literature and architecture express medieval values?   **How did urban growth shape European religious life?**

Chapter 11 Study Guide

Step 1

GETTING STARTED Below are basic terms about this period in the history of Western civilization. Can you identify each term below and explain why it matters? To do this exercise online, go to bedfordstmartins.com/mckaywestunderstanding.

TERMS	WHO (OR WHAT) AND WHEN	WHY IT MATTERS
merchant guild, p. 292		
craft guild, p. 293		
Hanseatic League, p. 295		
commercial revolution, p. 298		
sumptuary laws, p. 299		
Scholastics, p. 305		
vernacular literature, p. 307		
troubadours, p. 308		
cathedral, p. 308		
Romanesque, p. 309		
Gothic, p. 309		
Dominicans, p. 314		
Franciscans, p. 314		
friars, p. 314		
Beguines, p. 314		
Unam Sanctam, p. 316		

Step 2

MOVING BEYOND THE BASICS The exercise below requires a more advanced understanding of the chapter material. Compare and contrast urban and rural life during the High Middle Ages by filling in the chart below with descriptions of economic, social, and cultural conditions in medieval towns and in the medieval countryside. You may want to review Chapter 10 and its account of rural village life before you begin this exercise. When you are finished, consider the following questions: In what ways did urban and rural life differ? What accounts for the differences you note? To do this exercise online, go to bedfordstmartins.com/mckaywestunderstanding.

	ECONOMY	SOCIETY	CULTURE
Urban Life			
Rural Life			

ECONOMIC GROWTH AND TOWN LIFE

• Compare and contrast the European economy in the Early and High Middle Ages. What important differences do you note? What new conditions made economic growth and urban revitalization in the High Middle Ages possible?

• What were the most important conse-quences of the economic surge of the High Middle Ages? In what ways did Euro-pean society change during this period? In what ways did it stay the same?

MEDIEVAL UNIVERSITIES

• What was the connec-tion between the cen-tralization of political power and the emer-gence of the university in the High Middle Ages? What institutions and individuals promoted, and benefited from, the rise of the university?

• What characterized the intellectual life of the High Middle Ages? How did medieval scholars and thinkers integrate Greco-Roman ideas into their own work?

LITERATURE AND ARCHITECTURE

• What does the increasing use of the vernacular in European literature tell us about the changing nature of European culture in the High Middle Ages? What groups might be interested in such literature? Why?

• What does the construction of Gothic cathedrals tell us about the society, economy, and culture of the High Middle Ages? What conditions were necessary for the completion of such ambitious structures?

CITIES AND THE CHURCH

• What made medieval towns and cities centers of religious independence and heterodoxy? Why might new religious ideas find a more receptive audience in urban, as opposed to rural, society?

• In what ways were the mendicant orders particularly suited for urban religious life? What role did such orders play in the Roman church?

■ **In Your Own Words** Imagine that you must explain Chapter 11 to someone who hasn't read it. What would be the most important points to include and why?

12

The Crisis of the Late Middle Ages

1300–1450

During the late Middle Ages the last book of the New Testament, the Book of Revelation, inspired thousands of sermons and hundreds of religious tracts. The Book of Revelation deals with visions of the end of the world, with disease, war, famine, and death—often called the "Four Horsemen of the Apocalypse"—triumphing everywhere. It is no wonder this part of the Bible was so popular, for between 1300 and 1450 Europeans experienced a frightful series of shocks. The climate turned colder, leading to poor harvests and famine. People weakened by hunger were more susceptible to disease, and in the middle of the fourteenth century a new disease, probably the bubonic plague, spread throughout Europe. Over several years the plague killed millions of people, and there was no effective treatment. War devastated the countryside, especially in France, leading to widespread discontent and peasant revolts. Workers in cities also revolted against dismal working conditions, and violent crime and ethnic tensions increased. Death and preoccupation with death make the fourteenth century one of the most wrenching periods of Western civilization. Yet, in spite of the pessimism and crises, important institutions and cultural forms, including representative assemblies and national literatures, emerged. Even institutions that experienced severe crisis, such as the Christian church, saw new types of vitality. ■

Life in the Late Middle Ages. Peasants and urban workers rose up in revolt across Europe in the fourteenth century. In this French illustration, Wat Tyler, the leader of the English Peasant's Revolt, is stabbed during a meeting with the king. Tyler died soon afterward, and the revolt was ruthlessly crushed. (Bibliothèque nationale de France)

Chapter Preview

▶ How did climate change shape the late Middle Ages?

▶ How did the Black Death reshape European society?

▶ What were the consequences of the Hundred Years' War?

▶ Why did the church come under increasing attack?

▶ What explains the social unrest of the late Middle Ages?

▼ How did climate change shape the late Middle Ages?

In the first half of the fourteenth century, Europe experienced a series of climate changes that led to lower levels of food production, which had dramatic and disastrous ripple effects. Political leaders attempted to find solutions but were unable to deal with the economic and social problems that resulted.

Climate Change and Famine

The period from about 1000 to about 1300 saw a warmer than usual climate in Europe, which underlay all the changes and vitality of the High Middle Ages. About 1300 the climate changed, becoming colder and wetter. Historical geographers refer to the period from 1300 to 1450 as a "little ice age." An unusual number of storms brought torrential rains, ruining the wheat, oat, and hay crops on which people and animals almost everywhere depended. Poor harvests—and one in four was likely to be poor—led to scarcity and starvation. Almost all of northern Europe suffered a Great Famine in the years 1315 to 1322, which contemporaries interpreted as a recurrence of the biblical "seven lean years" (Genesis 42).

Even in non-famine years, the cost of grain, livestock, and dairy products rose sharply, in part because diseases hit cattle and sheep. Increasing prices meant that fewer people could afford to eat. Reduced caloric intake meant increased susceptibility to disease, especially for infants, children, and the elderly. Workers on reduced diets had less energy, which in turn meant lower productivity, lower output, and higher grain prices.

Great Famine A terrible famine from 1315 to 1322 that hit much of Europe after a period of climate change.

Death from Famine In this fifteenth-century painting, dead bodies lie in the middle of a path, while a funeral procession at the right includes a man with an adult's coffin and a woman with the coffin of an infant under her arm. People did not simply allow the dead to lie in the street in medieval Europe, though during famines and epidemics it was sometimes difficult to maintain normal burial procedures. (Erich Lessing/Art Resource, NY)

Chapter 12
The Crisis of the Late
322   Middle Ages • 1300–1450

CHAPTER LOCATOR | How did climate change shape the late Middle Ages?

Social Consequences

The changing climate and resulting agrarian crisis of the fourteenth century had grave social consequences. Poor harvests and famine led to the abandonment of homesteads. In parts of the Low Countries and in the Scottish-English borderlands, entire villages were abandoned, and many people became vagabonds, wandering in search of food and work. In Flanders and East Anglia (eastern England), some peasants were forced to mortgage, sublease, or sell their holdings to richer farmers in order to buy food. Throughout the affected areas, young men and women sought work in the towns, postponing marriage. Overall, the population declined because of the deaths caused by famine and disease, though the postponement of marriages and the resulting decline in offspring may have also played a part.

As the subsistence crisis deepened, starving people focused their anger on the rich, speculators, and the Jews, who were often associated with moneylending, because Christian authorities restricted their ownership of land and opportunities to engage in other trades. Rumors spread of a plot by Jews and their agents, the lepers, to kill Christians by poisoning the wells. Based on "evidence" collected by torture, many lepers and Jews were killed, beaten, or heavily fined.

Meanwhile, the international character of trade and commerce meant that a disaster in one country had serious implications elsewhere. For example, the infection that attacked English sheep in 1318 caused a sharp decline in wool exports in the following years. Without wool, Flemish weavers could not work, and thousands were laid off. Without woolen cloth, the businesses of Flemish, Hanseatic, and Italian merchants suffered. Unemployment encouraged people to turn to crime.

Government responses to these crises were ineffectual. The three sons of Philip the Fair who sat on the French throne between 1314 and 1328 condemned speculators who held stocks of grain back until conditions were desperate and prices high, and they forbade the sale of grain abroad. These measures had few actual results.

In England, Edward I's son, Edward II (r. 1307–1327), also condemned speculators after his attempts to set price controls on livestock and ale proved futile. He did try to buy grain abroad, but little was available. Such grain as reached southern English ports was stolen by looters and sold on the black market. The Crown's efforts at famine relief failed.

Chapter Chronology

1300–1450	Little ice age
1309–1376	Babylonian Captivity; papacy in Avignon
1310–1320	Dante writes *Divine Comedy*
1315–1322	Great Famine in northern Europe
1320s	First large-scale peasant rebellion in Flanders
1337–1453	Hundred Years' War
1347	Black Death arrives in Europe
1358	Jacquerie peasant uprising in France
1366	Statute of Kilkenny
1378–1417	Great Schism
1381	English Peasants' Revolt
1387–1400	Chaucer writes *Canterbury Tales*

▼ How did the Black Death reshape European society?

Around 1300 improvements in ship design allowed year-round shipping for the first time. European merchants took advantage of these advances, and ships continually at sea carried all types of cargo. They also carried vermin of all types, especially insects and rats, which often harbored disease pathogens. Rats, fleas, and cockroaches could live for months on the cargo carried along the coasts, disembarking at ports with the grain, cloth, or other merchandise. Thus, medieval shipping facilitated the spread of diseases over very long distances. The most frightful of these diseases, carried on Genoese ships, first emerged in western Europe in 1347, a disease that was later called the **Black Death**.

Black Death Plague that first struck Europe in 1347 and killed perhaps one-third of the population.

Pathology

Most historians and microbiologists identify the disease that spread in the fourteenth century as the bubonic plague. The disease normally afflicts rats. Fleas living on the infected rats drink their blood and then pass the bacteria that cause the plague on to the next rat they bite. Usually the disease is limited to rats and other rodents, but at certain points in history—perhaps when most rats have been killed off—the fleas have jumped from their rodent hosts to humans and other animals.

Differences between the fourteenth-century pandemic and other outbreaks of bubonic plague have led some historians to conclude that the fourteenth-century outbreak was actually not the bubonic plague, but a different disease, perhaps something like the Ebola virus. Efforts to establish the precise nature of the disease fuel continued study of medical aspects of the plague, with scientists using innovative techniques such as studying the tooth pulp of bodies in medieval cemeteries to see if it contains DNA from plague-causing agents.

Though there is some disagreement about exactly what kind of disease the plague was, there is no dispute about its dreadful effects on the body. The classic symptom of the bubonic plague was a growth the size of a nut or an apple in the armpit, in the groin, or on the neck. This was the boil, or bubo, that gave the disease its name and caused agonizing pain. The next stage was the appearance of spots or blotches caused by bleeding under the skin. Finally, the victim began to cough violently and spit blood. This stage, indicating the presence of millions of bacilli in the bloodstream, signaled the end, and death followed in two or three days.

Spread of the Disease

Plague symptoms were first described in 1331 in southwestern China, part of the Mongol Empire. Plague-infested rats accompanied Mongol armies and merchant caravans as they crossed central Asia in the 1330s. The rats then stowed away on ships, carrying the disease to the ports of the Black Sea by the 1340s.

In October 1347 Genoese ships brought the plague from Black Sea ports to Messina, from which it spread across Sicily. Venice and Genoa were hit in January 1348, and from the port of Pisa (PEE-zuh) the disease spread south to Rome and east to Florence and all of Tuscany. By late spring southern Germany was attacked. After the plague infected the French port of Marseilles, it spread to southern France and Spain. In June 1348 it was introduced into England, and from there the disease traveled north into Scandinavia. The plague seems to have entered Poland through the Baltic seaports and spread eastward from there (Map 12.1).

Medieval urban conditions were ideal for the spread of disease. Narrow streets were filled with refuse, human excrement, and dead animals. Houses whose upper stories projected over the lower ones blocked light and air, and extreme overcrowding was commonplace.

People were already weakened by famine, and standards of personal hygiene remained frightfully low. Fleas and body lice were universal afflictions: everyone from peasants to archbishops had them. One more bite did not cause much alarm, and the association among rats, fleas, and the plague was as yet unknown.

Mortality rates can be only educated guesses because population figures for the period before the arrival of the plague do not exist for most countries and cities. Of a total English population of perhaps 4.2 million, probably 1.4 million died of the Black Death. Densely populated Italian cities endured incredible losses. Florence lost between one-half and two-thirds of its population when the plague visited in 1348. Islamic parts of Europe were not spared, nor was the rest of the Muslim world. The most widely accepted estimate for western Europe and the Mediterranean is that the plague killed about one-third of the population in the first wave of infection.

Chapter 12
The Crisis of the Late
324   **Middle Ages • 1300–1450**

CHAPTER LOCATOR   How did climate change shape the late Middle Ages?

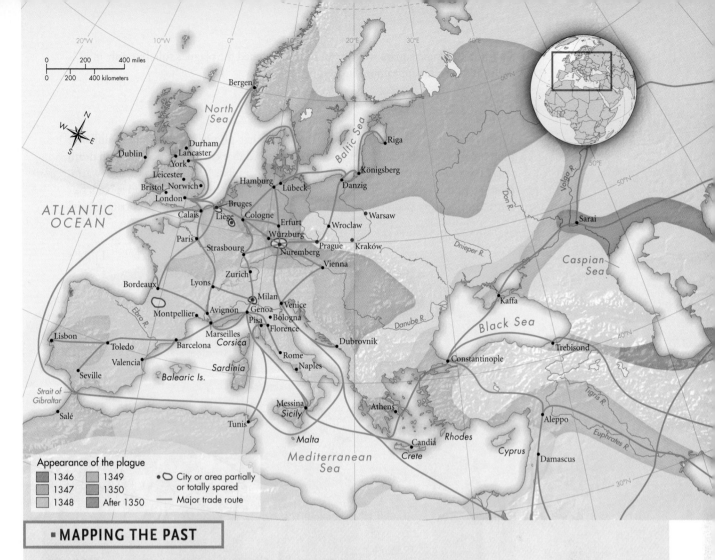

Appearance of the plague

■ 1346	■ 1349	● ○ City or area partially or totally spared
■ 1347	■ 1350	
■ 1348	■ After 1350	— Major trade route

▪ MAPPING THE PAST

Map 12.1 The Course of the Black Death in Fourteenth-Century Europe

The bubonic plague spread northward across Europe, beginning in the late 1340s with the first cases of disease reported in the ports of the Black Sea.

ANALYZING THE MAP When did the plague reach Paris? How much time passed before it spread to the rest of northern France and southern Germany? Which cities and regions were spared?

CONNECTIONS How did the expansion of trade that resulted from the commercial revolution contribute to the spread of the Black Death?

To complete this activity online, go to the Online Study Guide at bedfordstmartins.com/mckaywestunderstanding.

Nor did central and eastern Europe escape the ravages of the disease. As the Black Death took its toll on the Holy Roman Empire, waves of emigrants fled to Poland, Bohemia, and Hungary, sometimes taking plague with them. In the Byzantine Empire the plague ravaged the population. The youngest son of Emperor John VI Kantakouzenos died just as his father took over the throne in 1347. "So incurable was the evil," wrote John later in his history of the Byzantine Empire, "that neither any regularity of life, nor any bodily strength could resist it. Strong and weak bodies were all similarly carried away, and those best cared for died in the same manner as the poor."[1]

Across Europe the Black Death recurred intermittently from the 1360s to 1400. It reappeared from time to time over the following centuries, though never with the same virulence because Europeans now had some resistance. Improved standards of hygiene

How did the Black Death reshape European society?

What were the consequences of the Hundred Years' War?

Why did the church come under increasing attack?

What explains the social unrest of the late Middle Ages?

and strictly enforced quarantine measures also lessened the plague's toll, but only in 1721 did it make its last appearance in Europe.

Care of the Sick

Fourteenth-century medical literature indicates that physicians tried many different things to prevent and treat the plague. They observed that crowded cities had high death rates, especially when the weather was warm and moist. We understand that warm, moist conditions make it easier for germs, viruses, and bacteria to grow and spread, but fourteenth-century people thought in terms of "poisons" in the air or "corrupted air"

▪ PICTURING THE PAST

Patients in a Hospital

Most victims of the plague died at home, but some went to special plague hospitals. This fifteenth-century painting shows what would have been a common scene, with female members of religious orders or Beguines caring for patients in a hospital. Here the women are also allegorical figures, judging the patients' worth as they take their pulse. At the right stands Justice holding scales, and at the left Prudence holding a rod. (Giraudon/The Bridgeman Art Library)

ANALYZING THE IMAGE What does this image suggest about the care for plague victims? Do the conditions shown at this hospital suggest that there is hope for these patients?

CONNECTIONS How does the allegorical depiction of the nuns shown here explain how medieval people understood the plague?

To complete this activity online, go to the Online Study Guide at bedfordstmartins.com/mckaywestunderstanding.

Chapter 12
The Crisis of the Late
326   **Middle Ages • 1300–1450**

CHAPTER LOCATOR   How did climate change shape the late Middle Ages?

coming from swamps, unburied animals, or the positions of the stars, rather than germs. Their treatments thus focused on ridding the air and the body of these poisons, and on rebalancing bodily fluids to bring people back to health.

It is noteworthy that, in an age of mounting criticism of clerical wealth (see page 336), the behavior of the clergy during the plague was often exemplary. Priests, monks, and nuns cared for the sick and buried the dead. In places like Venice, from which even physicians fled, priests remained to give what ministrations they could. Consequently, their mortality rate was phenomenally high. The German clergy especially suffered a severe decline in personnel in the years after 1350.

There were limits to care, however. Many realized that the plague was spread from person to person. Thus, to avoid contagion, wealthier people often fled cities for the countryside, though sometimes this simply spread the plague faster. Some cities tried shutting their gates to prevent infected people and animals from coming in, which worked in a few cities. They also walled up houses in which there was plague, trying to isolate those who were sick from those who were still healthy. In the words of the Italian writer Giovanni Boccaccio (1313–1375), "almost no one cared for his neighbor . . . brother abandoned brother . . . and—even worse, almost unbelievable—fathers and mothers neglected to tend and care for their children."[2]

Economic, Religious, and Cultural Effects

Economic historians and demographers sharply dispute the impact of the plague on the economy in the late fourteenth century. The traditional view that the plague had a disastrous effect has been greatly modified. The clearest evidence comes from England, where by the early fifteenth century most landlords enjoyed the highest revenues of the medieval period. Why? The answer appears to lie in the fact that England and many parts of Europe suffered from overpopulation in the early fourteenth century. Population losses caused by famines and the Black Death led to increased productivity by restoring a more efficient balance between labor, land, and capital.

The Black Death brought on a general European inflation. High mortality produced a fall in production, shortages of goods, and a general rise in prices. The price of wheat in most of Europe increased, as did the costs of meat, sausage, and cheese. This inflation continued to the end of the fourteenth century. But labor shortages meant that workers could demand better wages, and the broad mass of people enjoyed a higher standard of living. The greater demand for labor also meant greater mobility for peasants in rural areas and for industrial workers in the towns and cities.

The plague also had effects on religious practices. It is not surprising that some people sought release from the devastating affliction in wild living, but more became more deeply pious. Rather than seeing the plague as a medical issue, they instead interpreted it as the result of an evil within themselves. Thus, the best remedies were religious ones: asking for forgiveness, prayer, trust in God, making donations to churches, and trying to live better lives.

Some Christians turned to the severest forms of asceticism and frenzied religious fervor, joining groups of flagellants, who whipped and scourged themselves as penance for their and society's sins in the belief that the Black Death was God's punishment for humanity's wickedness. Groups of flagellants traveled from town to town, often growing into unruly mobs. Officials worried that they would provoke violence and riots, and ordered groups to disband or forbade them to enter cities.

flagellants People who believed that the plague was God's punishment for sin and sought to do penance by flagellating (whipping) themselves.

Along with seeing the plague as a call to reform their own behavior, however, people also searched for scapegoats, and savage cruelty sometimes resulted. Just as in the decades before the plague, many people believed that the Jews had poisoned the wells of Christian communities and thereby infected the drinking water. This charge led to the murder of thousands of Jews across Europe.

How did the Black Death reshape European society?   What were the consequences of the Hundred Years' War?   Why did the church come under increasing attack?   What explains the social unrest of the late Middle Ages?

327

The literature and art of the late Middle Ages reveal a terribly morbid concern with death. One highly popular literary and artistic motif, the Dance of Death, depicted a dancing skeleton leading away living people, often in order of their rank. In the words of one early fifteenth-century English poem:

> *Death spareth not low nor high degree. . . .*
> *Sir Emperor, lord of all the ground,*
> *Sovereign Prince, and highest of nobles*
> *You must forsake your round apples of gold*
> *Leave behind your treasure and riches*
> *And with others to my dance obey.*[3]

Dance of Death In this fifteenth-century fresco from a tiny church in Croatia, skeletons lead people from all social classes to their death. No one is spared, for the procession includes a king and queen, a pope, a bishop, and a little child. (Vladimir Bugarin, photographer)

Chapter 12
The Crisis of the Late
328 **Middle Ages • 1300–1450**

CHAPTER LOCATOR | How did climate change shape the late Middle Ages?

Popular endowments of educational institutions multiplied. The years of the Black Death witnessed the foundation of new colleges at old universities and of entirely new universities. The foundation charters specifically mention the shortage of priests and the decay of learning. Whereas universities such as those at Bologna and Paris had international student bodies, new institutions established in the wake of the Black Death had more national or local constituencies. Thus the international character of medieval culture weakened, paving the way for schism (SKIH-zuhm) in the Catholic Church even before the Reformation.

▼ What were the consequences of the Hundred Years' War?

The plague ravaged populations in Asia, North Africa, and Europe; in western Europe a long international war added further misery to the frightful disasters of the plague. England and France had engaged in sporadic military hostilities from the time of the Norman Conquest in 1066, and in the middle of the fourteenth century these became more intense. From 1337 to 1453, the two countries intermittently fought one another in what was the longest war in European history.

Causes

The Hundred Years' War had both distant and immediate causes, including disagreements over rights to land, a dispute over the succession to the French throne, and economic conflicts. A distant cause was the duchy of Aquitaine, which became part of the holdings of the English crown when Eleanor of Aquitaine married King Henry II of England in 1152 (see Chapter 9; a duchy is a territory ruled by a duke). In 1259 Henry III of England had signed the Treaty of Paris with Louis IX of France, affirming English claims to Aquitaine in return for becoming a vassal of the French crown. French policy in the fourteenth century was strongly expansionist, however, and the French kings resolved to absorb the duchy into the kingdom of France. Aquitaine therefore became a disputed territory.

The immediate political cause of the war was a dispute over who would inherit the French throne after Charles IV of France, the last surviving son of Philip the Fair, died childless in 1328. With him ended the Capetian dynasty of France. Charles IV did have a sister — Isabella — and her son was Edward III, king of England. An assembly of French high nobles, meaning to exclude Isabella and Edward from the French throne, proclaimed that "no woman nor her son could succeed to the [French] monarchy." French lawyers defended the position with the invented tradition that the exclusion of women from ruling or passing down the right to rule was part of Salic Law, a sixth-century law code of the Franks (see Chapter 7), and that Salic Law itself was part of the fundamental law of France. The nobles passed the crown to Philip VI of Valois (r. 1328–1350), a nephew of Philip the Fair.

In 1329 Edward III paid homage to Philip VI for Aquitaine. In 1337 Philip, eager to exercise full French jurisdiction in Aquitaine, confiscated the duchy. Edward III interpreted this action as a violation of the treaty of 1259 and as a cause for war. Moreover, Edward argued, as the eldest directly surviving male descendant of Philip the Fair, he deserved the title of king of France. Edward III's dynastic argument upset the feudal order in France: to increase their independent power, French vassals of Philip VI used the excuse that they had to transfer their loyalty to a different overlord, Edward III. One reason the war lasted so long was that it became a French civil war, with some French

▪ The Hundred Years' War

1337	Philip VI of France confiscates Aquitaine
1346	English longbowmen defeat French knights at Crécy
1356	English defeat French at Poitiers
1370s–1380s	French recover some territory
1415	English defeat the French at Agincourt
1429	French victory at Orléans; Charles VII crowned king
1431	Joan of Arc declared a heretic and burned at the stake
1440s	French reconquer Normandy and Aquitaine
1453	War ends
1456	Joan cleared of charges of heresy and declared a martyr

nobles, most importantly the dukes of Burgundy, supporting English monarchs in order to thwart the centralizing goals of the French crown.

The governments of both England and France manipulated public opinion to support the war. The English public was convinced that the war was waged for one reason: to secure for King Edward the French crown he had been unjustly denied. Edward III issued letters to the sheriffs describing the evil deeds of the French in graphic terms. Kings in both countries instructed the clergy to deliver sermons filled with patriotic sentiment. Philip VI sent agents to warn communities about the dangers of invasion. Royal propaganda on both sides fostered a kind of early nationalism, and both sides developed a deep hatred of the other.

Economic factors involving the wool trade and the control of Flemish towns were linked to these long-term and immediate political issues. The wool trade between England and Flanders served as the cornerstone of both countries' economies. Flanders was a fief of the French crown, and the Flemish aristocracy was highly sympathetic to the monarchy in Paris. But the wealth of Flemish merchants and cloth manufacturers depended on English wool, and Flemish burghers strongly supported the claims of Edward III. The disruption of commerce with England threatened their prosperity.

English Successes

The war began with a series of French sea raids on English coastal towns in 1337, but the French fleet was almost completely destroyed when it attempted to land soldiers on English soil, and from that point on the war was fought almost entirely in France and the Low Countries (Map 12.2). It consisted mainly of a series of sieges and cavalry raids, fought in fits and starts, with treaties along the way to halt hostilities.

During the war's early stages, England was highly successful. At Crécy in northern France in 1346, English longbowmen scored a great victory over French knights and crossbowmen. Although the aim of the longbow was not very accurate, it allowed for rapid reloading, and an English archer could send off three arrows to the French crossbowman's one. The result was a blinding shower of arrows that unhorsed the French knights and caused mass confusion. The ring of cannon — probably the first use of artillery in the West — created further panic. Edward III's son, Edward the Black Prince, used the same tactics ten years later to smash the French at Poitiers, where he captured the French king and held him for ransom. Edward was not able to take all of France, but the English held Aquitaine and other provinces, and they allied themselves with many of France's feudal vassals. After a brief peace, the French fought back and recovered some territory,

Chapter 12
The Crisis of the Late
330 **Middle Ages • 1300–1450**

CHAPTER LOCATOR | How did climate change shape the late Middle Ages?

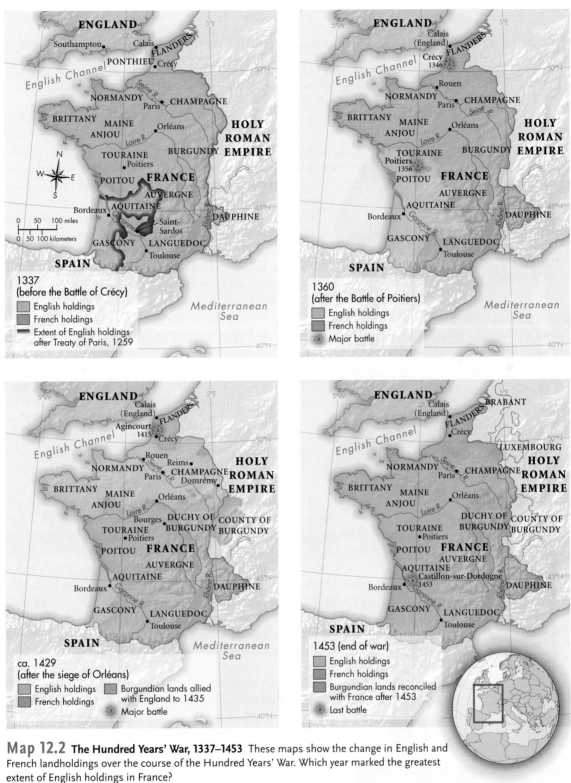

Map 12.2 The Hundred Years' War, 1337–1453 These maps show the change in English and French landholdings over the course of the Hundred Years' War. Which year marked the greatest extent of English holdings in France?

and a treaty again halted hostilities as both sides concentrated on conflicts over power at home.

War began again in 1415 when Henry V of England (r. 1413–1422) invaded. At Agincourt (AH-jihn-kort), Henry's army defeated a much larger French force, again primarily through the skill of English longbowmen. Henry followed up his triumph at

Agincourt The location near Arras in Flanders where an English victory in 1415 led to the reconquest of Normandy.

Suit of Armor This fifteenth-century suit of Italian armor protected its wearer, but its weight made movement difficult. Both English and French mounted knights wore full armor at the beginning of the Hundred Years' War, but by the end they wore only breastplates and helmets, which protected their vital organs but allowed greater mobility. This particular suit has been so well preserved that it was most likely never used in battle; it may have been made for ceremonial purposes. (Image copyright © The Metropolitan Museum of Art/Art Resource, NY)

Agincourt with the reconquest of Normandy, and by 1419 the English had advanced to the walls of Paris. Henry married the daughter of the French king, and a treaty made Henry and any sons the couple would have heir to the French throne. It appeared as if Henry would indeed rule both England and France, but he died unexpectedly in 1422, leaving an infant son as heir. The English continued their military victories, however, and besieged the city of Orléans (or-lay-AHN), the only major city in northern France not under their control. But the French cause was not lost.

Joan of Arc and France's Victory

The ultimate French success rests heavily on the actions of Joan, an obscure French peasant girl whose vision and military leadership revived French fortunes and led to victory. (Over the centuries, she acquired the name "of Arc"— *d'Arc* in French—based on her father's name; she never used this name for herself, but called herself "the maiden"— *la Pucelle* in French.) Born in 1412 in the village of Domrémy in Champagne, Joan grew up in a religious household. During adolescence she began to hear voices, which she later said belonged to Saint Michael, Saint Catherine, and Saint Margaret. In 1428 these voices spoke to her with great urgency, telling her that the dauphin (DOH-fuhn), the uncrowned King Charles VII, had to be crowned and the English expelled from France. Joan traveled to the French court where she was granted an audience with Charles, who had her questioned about her angelic visions and examined to make sure she was the virgin she said she was. She secured his support to travel with the French army to Orléans dressed as a knight and dictated a letter to the English ordering them to surrender:

King of England . . . , do right in the King of Heaven's sight. Surrender to The Maid sent hither by God the King of Heaven. . . . She comes in God's name to establish the Blood Royal, ready to make peace if you agree to abandon France and repay what you have taken.[4]

Such words coming from a teenage girl were laughable given the recent course of the conflict, but Joan was amazingly successful. She inspired and led French attacks, and the English retreated from Orléans. The king made Joan co-commander of the entire army, and she led it to a string of military victories; other cities simply surrendered without a fight and returned their allegiance to France. In July 1429, two months after Orléans, Charles VII was crowned king at Reims.

Siege of the Castle of Mortagne Medieval warfare usually consisted of small skirmishes and attacks on castles. This miniature shows the French besieging an English-held castle near Bordeaux in 1377 that held out for six months. Most of the soldiers use longbows, although at the left two men shoot primitive muskets above a pair of cannon. Painted in the late fifteenth century, the scene reflects military technology available at the time it was painted, not at the time of the actual siege. (© British Library Board, MS Royal 14 e. IV f. 23)

Joan and the French army continued their fight against the English and their Burgundian allies. In 1430 the Burgundians captured Joan. Charles refused to ransom her, and she was sold to the English, who tried and condemned her for heresy. In 1431 she was burned at the stake in the marketplace at Rouen.

The French army continued its victories without her. The Burgundians switched their allegiance to the French, who reconquered Normandy and, finally, ejected the English from Aquitaine. As the war dragged on, and the human and financial costs mounted, demands for an end increased in England. Parliamentary opposition to additional war grants stiffened, fewer soldiers were sent, and more territory passed into French hands. At the war's end in 1453, only the town of Calais (KA-lay) remained in English hands.

What of Joan? A new trial in 1456 — requested by Charles VII, who either had second thoughts about his abandonment of Joan or did not wish to be associated with a condemned heretic — was held by the pope. This cleared her of all charges and declared her a martyr. She became a political symbol of France from that point on, and sometimes also a symbol of the Catholic Church in opposition to the government of France. In 1920, for example, she was canonized as a saint shortly after the French government declared separation of church and state in France.

Aftermath

In France thousands of soldiers and civilians had been slaughtered and hundreds of thousands of acres of rich farmland were ruined, leaving the rural economy of many parts of France a shambles. The war had disrupted trade and the great fairs, resulting in the drastic reduction of French participation in international commerce. Defeat in battle and heavy taxation contributed to widespread dissatisfaction and aggravated peasant grievances.

The war had wreaked havoc in England as well, even though only the southern coastal ports saw battle. England spent the huge sum of over £5 million on the war effort, and despite the money raised by some victories, the net result was an enormous financial loss. The government attempted to finance the war by raising taxes on the wool crop, which priced wool out of the export market.

In both England and France, men of all social classes had volunteered to serve in the war in the hope of acquiring booty and becoming rich, and some were successful in the early years of the war. As time went on, however, most fortunes seem to have been squandered as fast as they were made. In addition, the social order was disrupted as the knights who ordinarily served as sheriffs, coroners, jurymen, and justices of the peace were abroad.

The war stimulated technological experimentation, especially with artillery. Cannon revolutionized warfare, making the stone castle no longer impregnable. Because only central governments, not private nobles, could afford cannon, they strengthened the military power of national states.

representative assemblies Deliberative meetings of lords and wealthy urban residents that flourished in many European countries between 1250 and 1450 and were the precursors to the English Parliament, German diets, and Spanish cortes.

The long war also had a profound impact on the political and cultural lives of the two countries. Most notably, it stimulated the development of the English Parliament. Between 1250 and 1450, representative assemblies flourished in many European countries. In the English Parliament, German diets, and Spanish *cortes*, deliberative practices developed that laid the foundations for the representative institutions of modern democratic nations. While representative assemblies declined in most countries after the fifteenth century, the English Parliament endured. Edward III's constant need for money to pay for the war compelled him to summon not only the great barons and bishops, but knights of the shires and burgesses from the towns as well. Parliament met in thirty-seven of the fifty years of Edward's reign.

The frequency of the meetings is significant. Representative assemblies were becoming a habit. Knights and wealthy urban residents—or the "Commons," as they came to be called—recognized their mutual interests and began to meet apart from the great lords. The Commons gradually realized that they held the country's purse strings, and a parliamentary statute of 1341 required parliamentary approval of all nonfeudal levies. By signing the law, Edward III acknowledged that the king of England could not tax without Parliament's consent.

In England, theoretical consent to taxation and legislation was given in one assembly for the entire country. France had no such single assembly; instead, there were many regional or provincial assemblies. Why did a national representative assembly fail to develop in France? Linguistic, geographical, economic, legal, and political differences were very strong. People tended to think of themselves as Breton, Norman, Burgundian, and so on, rather than French. Provincial assemblies, highly jealous of their independence, did not want a national assembly. In addition, the initiative for convening assemblies rested with the king. But some monarchs lacked the power to call such assemblies, and others, including Charles VI, found the idea of representative assemblies distasteful.

In both countries, however, the war did promote the growth of nationalism—the feeling of unity and identity that binds together a people. After victories, each country experienced a surge of pride in its military strength. Just as English patriotism ran strong after Crécy and Poitiers, so French national confidence rose after Orléans. French national feeling demanded the expulsion of the enemy not merely from Normandy and Aquitaine but from all French soil. Perhaps no one expressed this national consciousness better than Joan when she exulted that the enemy had been "driven out of *France.*"

Chapter 12
The Crisis of the Late
334   Middle Ages • 1300–1450

CHAPTER LOCATOR | How did climate change shape the late Middle Ages?

▼ Why did the church come under increasing attack?

In times of crisis or disaster, people of all faiths have sought the consolation of religion. In the fourteenth century, however, the official Christian church offered little solace. In fact, the leaders of the church added to the sorrow and misery of the times. In response to this lack of leadership, members of the clergy challenged the power of the pope, and laypeople challenged the authority of the church itself. Women and men increasingly relied on direct approaches to God, often through mystical encounters, rather than on the institutional church.

The Babylonian Captivity and the Great Schism

Conflicts between the secular rulers of Europe and the popes were common throughout the High Middle Ages, and in the early fourteenth century the dispute between King Philip the Fair of France and Pope Boniface VIII became particularly bitter (see Chapter 11). With Boniface's death, in order to control the church and its policies, Philip pressured the new pope, Clement V, to settle in Avignon in southeastern France. The popes lived in Avignon from 1309 to 1376, a period in church history often called the **Babylonian Captivity**.

The Babylonian Captivity badly damaged papal prestige. The seven popes at Avignon concentrated on bureaucratic matters to the exclusion of spiritual objectives. Though some of the popes led austere lives, the general atmosphere was one of luxury and extravagance. The leadership of the church was cut off from its historic roots and the source of its ancient authority, the city of Rome. In 1377 Pope Gregory XI brought the papal court back to Rome. Unfortunately, he died shortly after the return. Between the time of Gregory's death and the opening of the conclave, Roman citizens put great pressure on the cardinals to elect an Italian. The cardinals chose a distinguished administrator, the archbishop of Bari, Bartolomeo Prignano, who took the name Urban VI.

Urban VI (pontificate 1378–1389) had excellent intentions for church reform, but he went about it in a tactless manner. He attacked clerical luxury, denouncing individual cardinals by name, and even threatened to excommunicate certain of them. The cardinals slipped away from Rome and met at Anagni. They declared Urban's election invalid because it had come about under threats from the Roman mob, and they asserted that Urban himself was excommunicated. The cardinals then elected Cardinal Robert of Geneva, the cousin of King Charles V of France, as pope. Cardinal Robert took the name Clement VII. There were thus two popes in 1378 — Urban at Rome and Clement VII (pontificate 1378–1394), who set himself up at Avignon. So began the **Great Schism**, which divided Western Christendom until 1417.

The powers of Europe aligned themselves with Urban or Clement along strictly political lines. France naturally recognized the French pope, Clement. England, France's longtime enemy, recognized the Italian pope, Urban. Scotland, an ally of France, supported Clement. Aragon, Castile, and Portugal hesitated before deciding for Clement at Avignon. The German emperor, who bore ancient hostility to France, recognized Urban. At first the Italian city-states recognized Urban; later, they opted for Clement.

Babylonian Captivity The period from 1309 to 1376 when the popes resided in Avignon rather than in Rome. The phrase refers to the seventy years when the Hebrews were held captive in Babylon.

Great Schism The division, or split, in church leadership from 1378 to 1417 when there were two, then three, popes.

The Great Schism, 1378–1417

- Allegiance to Rome
- Allegiance to Avignon
- Official allegiance to Rome but with shifting local allegiances

Avignon • Rome •

John of Spoleto, a professor at the law school at Bologna, eloquently summed up intellectual opinion of the schism: "The longer this schism lasts, the more it appears to be costing, and the more harm it does; scandal, massacres, ruination, agitations, troubles and disturbances."[5] The schism weakened the religious faith of many Christians and brought church leadership into serious disrepute.

Critiques, Divisions, and Councils

Criticism of the church during the Avignon papacy and the Great Schism often came from the ranks of highly learned clergy and lay professionals. One of these was William of Occam (1289?–1347?), a Franciscan friar and philosopher. Occam argued vigorously against the papacy and also wrote philosophical works in which he questioned the connection between reason and faith that had been developed by Thomas Aquinas (see Chapter 11). All governments should have limited powers and be accountable to those they govern, according to Occam, and church and state should be separate.

The Italian lawyer and university official Marsiglio of Padua (ca. 1275–1342) agreed with Occam. In his *Defensor Pacis (The Defender of the Peace)*, Marsiglio argued against the medieval idea of a society governed by both church and state, with church supreme. Instead, Marsiglio claimed, the state was the great unifying power in society, and the church should be subordinate to it. Church leadership should rest in a general council made up of laymen as well as priests, and superior to the pope. Marsiglio was excommunicated for these radical ideas, and his work was condemned as heresy—as was Occam's—but in the later fourteenth century many thinkers agreed with these two critics of the papacy. They believed that reform of the church could best be achieved through periodic assemblies, or councils, representing all the Christian people. Those who argued this position were called conciliarists.

The English scholar and theologian John Wyclif (ca. 1330–1384) went further than the conciliarists in his argument against medieval church structure. Wyclif wrote that Scripture alone should be the standard of Christian belief and practice, and papal claims of secular power had no foundation in the Scriptures. He urged that the church be stripped of its property. He wanted Christians to read the Bible for themselves and produced the first complete translation of the Bible into English.

conciliarists People who believed that the authority in the Roman church should rest in a general council composed of clergy, theologians, and laypeople, rather than in the pope alone.

Wyclif's followers, called Lollards by those who ridiculed them, from a Dutch word for "mumble," spread his ideas and made many copies of his Bible. Lollard teaching allowed women to preach, and women played a significant role in the movement. Lollards were persecuted in the fifteenth century; some were executed, some recanted, and others continued to meet secretly to read and discuss the Bible and other religious texts in English.

Decorative Spoon Taking as his text a contemporary proverb, "When the fox preaches, beware your geese," the artist shows, in the bowl of this spoon from the southern Netherlands, a fox dressed as a monk or friar, preaching with three dead geese in his hood, while another fox grabs one of the congregation. The preaching fox reads from a scroll bearing the word *pax* (peace), implying the perceived hypocrisy of the clergy. The object from about 1430 suggests the widespread criticism of churchmen in the late Middle Ages. (Painted enamel and gilding on silver; 17.6 cm [6⅞ in]. Museum of Fine Arts, Boston, Helen and Alice Coburn Fund, 51.2472)

Chapter 12
The Crisis of the Late
336   Middle Ages • 1300–1450

CHAPTER LOCATOR   How did climate change shape the late Middle Ages?

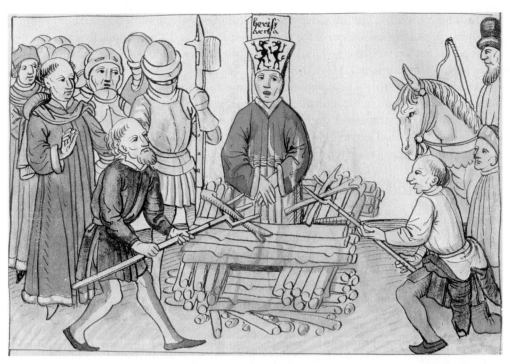

The Execution of Jan Hus This fifteenth-century manuscript illustration shows workers placing logs on Hus's funeral pyre at the Council of Constance, while soldiers, officials, a priest, and a cardinal look on. Hus became an important symbol of Czech independence, and in 1990 the Czech Republic declared July 6, the date of his execution in 1415, a national holiday. (University Library, Prague/ Gianni Dagli Orti/The Art Archive)

Students returning from study at the University of Oxford around 1400 brought Wyclif's ideas with them to Prague, the capital of what was then Bohemia and is now the Czech Republic. There another university theologian, Jan Hus (yahn huhs) (ca. 1372–1415), built on them. He also denied papal authority, called for translations of the Bible into the local Czech language, and declared indulgences—papal offers of remission of penance—useless. Hus gained many followers, who linked his theological ideas with their opposition to the church's wealth and power and with a growing sense of Czech nationalism in opposition to the international power of the pope. Hus's followers were successful at defeating the combined armies of the pope and the emperor many times. In the 1430s the emperor finally agreed to recognize the Hussite church in Bohemia, which later merged with other Protestant churches.

The Hussite Revolution, 1415–1436

Division of any type threatened the church, and in response to continued calls throughout Europe for a council, the cardinals of Rome and Avignon summoned a council at Pisa in 1409. That gathering of prelates and theologians deposed both popes and selected another. Neither the Avignon pope nor the Roman pope would resign, however, and the result was the creation of a threefold schism.

Finally, under pressure from the German emperor Sigismund (SIH-guhs-muhnd), a great council met at the imperial city of Constance (1414–1418). It had three objectives: to end the schism, to reform the church, and to wipe out heresy. The council moved first on the last point: despite being granted a safe-conduct to go to Constance by the emperor, Jan Hus was tried, condemned, and burned at the stake as a heretic in 1415. The council also eventually healed the schism. It deposed both the Roman pope and the successor of the pope chosen at Pisa, and it isolated the Avignon antipope. A conclave elected a new leader, the Roman cardinal Colonna, who took the name Martin V (pontificate 1417–1431).

Martin proceeded to dissolve the council. Nothing was done about reform, the third objective of the council. In the later fifteenth century the papacy concentrated on Italian problems to the exclusion of universal Christian interests. But the schism and the conciliar movement had exposed the crying need for ecclesiastical reform, thus laying the foundation for the great reform efforts of the sixteenth century.

Lay Piety and Mysticism

The moral failings of the monks and parish clergy and the scandal of the Great Schism did much to weaken the spiritual mystique of the clergy in the popular mind. Thus during the fourteenth and fifteenth centuries laypeople began to develop their own forms of piety. They also exercised increasing control over parish affairs.

Lay Christian men and women often formed confraternities, voluntary lay groups organized by occupation, devotional preference, neighborhood, or charitable activity. Confraternities expanded rapidly in larger cities and many villages with the growth of the mendicant orders in the thirteenth century. Some confraternities specialized in praying for souls in purgatory, either for specific individuals or for the anonymous mass of all souls. By the late Middle Ages they held dances, church festivals, and collections to raise money to clean and repair church buildings and to supply churches with candles and other liturgical objects. Like craft guilds, most confraternities were groups of men, but separate women's confraternities were formed in some towns, often to oversee the production of vestments, altar cloths, and other items made of fabric. All confraternities carried out special devotional practices such as prayers or processions, often without the leadership of a priest.

In Holland beginning in the late fourteenth century, a group of pious laypeople called the Brethren and Sisters of the Common Life lived in stark simplicity while daily carrying out the Gospel teaching of feeding the hungry, clothing the naked, and visiting the sick. They sought to make religion a personal inner experience. The spirituality of the Brethren and Sisters of the Common Life found its finest expression in the classic *The Imitation of Christ* by the Dutch monk Thomas à Kempis (1380?–1471), which gained wide appeal among laypeople. It urges Christians to take Christ as their model, seek perfection in a simple way of life, and look to the Scriptures for guidance in living a spiritual life. In the mid-fifteenth century the movement had founded houses in the Netherlands, in central Germany, and in the Rhineland.

For some individuals, both laypeople and clerics, religious devotion included mystical experiences. (See "Individuals in Society: Meister Eckhart," right.) Bridget of Sweden (1303–1373) was a noblewoman who journeyed to Rome after her husband's death. She began to see visions and gave advice based on these visions to both laypeople and church officials. At the end of her life Bridget made a pilgrimage to Jerusalem, where she saw visions of the Virgin Mary, who described to her exactly how she was standing "with my knees bent" when she gave birth to Jesus, and how she "showed to the shepherds the nature and male sex of the child."[6] Bridget's visions provide evidence of the ways in which laypeople used their own experiences to enhance their religious understanding; Bridget's own experiences of childbirth shaped the way she viewed the birth of Jesus, and she related to the Virgin Mary in part as one mother to another.

The confraternities and mystics were generally not considered heretical unless they began to challenge the authority of the papacy the way some conciliarists and Wyclif and Hus did. However, the movement of lay piety did alter many people's perceptions of their own spiritual power.

confraternities Voluntary lay groups organized by occupation, devotional preference, neighborhood, or charitable activity.

Chapter 12
The Crisis of the Late
338 **Middle Ages • 1300–1450**

CHAPTER LOCATOR | How did climate change shape the late Middle Ages?

MYSTICISM — THE DIRECT EXPERIENCE of the divine through sudden insight or intuition — is an aspect of many world religions and has been part of Christianity throughout its history. During the late Middle Ages, however, mysticism became an important part of the piety of many laypeople, especially in the Rhineland area of Germany, rather than a rare experience of only a few. In this they were guided by the sermons of the churchman generally known as Meister Eckhart. Born into a German noble family, Eckhart (1260–1329?) joined the Dominican order and studied theology at Paris and Cologne, attaining the academic title of "master" (*Meister* in German). The leaders of the Dominican order appointed him to a series of administrative and teaching positions, and he wrote learned treatises in Latin that reflected his scholastic training and deep understanding of classical philosophy.

He also began to preach in German, attracting many listeners through his beautiful language and mystical insights. God, he said, was "an oversoaring being and an overbeing nothingness," whose essence was beyond the ability of humans to express: "if the soul is to know God, it must know Him outside time and place, since God is neither in this or that, but One and above them." Only through "unknowing," emptying oneself, could one come to experience the divine. Yet God was also present in individual human souls, and to a degree in every creature, all of which God called into being before the beginning of time. Within each soul there was what Eckhart called a "little spark," an innermost essence that allows the soul — with God's grace and Christ's redemptive action — to come to God. "Our salvation depends upon our knowing and recognizing the Chief Good which is God Himself," preached Eckhart; "the Eye with which I see God is the same Eye with which God sees me." "I have a capacity in my soul for taking in God entirely," he went on, a capacity that was shared by all humans, not simply members of the clergy or those with special spiritual gifts. Although Eckhart did not reject church sacraments or the hierarchy, he frequently stressed that union with God was best accomplished through quiet detachment and simple prayer rather than pilgrimages, extensive fasts, or other activities: "If the only prayer you said in your whole life was 'thank you,' that would suffice."*

Eckhart's unusual teachings led to charges of heresy in 1327, which Eckhart denied. The pope — who was at this point in Avignon — presided over a trial condemning him, but Eckhart appears to have died during the course of the proceedings or shortly thereafter. His writings were ordered destroyed, but many survived, and his teachings continued to be spread by his followers.

In the last few decades, Meister Eckhart's ideas have been explored and utilized by philosophers and mystics in other religious traditions, including Buddhism, Hinduism, and neo-paganism, as well as by Christians. Books of his sermons sell widely for their spiritual insights, and quotations from them — including the one above about thank-you prayers — can be found on coffee mugs, tote bags, and T-shirts.

QUESTIONS FOR ANALYSIS

1. Why might Meister Eckhart's preaching have been viewed as threatening by the leaders of the church?
2. Given the situation of the church in the late Middle Ages, why might mysticism have been attractive to pious Christians?

Meister Eckhart's Sermons, trans. Claud Field (London: n.p., 1909).

A sixteenth-century woodcut of Meister Eckhart teaching.
(Visual Connection Archive)

▼ What explains the social unrest of the late Middle Ages?

At the beginning of the fourteenth century, famine and disease profoundly affected the lives of European peoples. As the century wore on, decades of slaughter and destruction added further woes. In many parts of France and the Low Countries, fields lay in ruin or untilled for lack of labor power. In England, as taxes increased, criticisms of government policy and mismanagement multiplied. Crime and new forms of business organization aggravated economic troubles, and throughout Europe the frustrations of the common people erupted into widespread revolts.

Peasant Revolts

While peasants had endured centuries of exploitation, the difficult conditions of the fourteenth and fifteenth centuries spurred a wave of peasant revolts across Europe. Peasants were sometimes joined by their urban counterparts on the social ladder, resulting in a wider revolution of poor against rich.

The first large-scale rebellion was in Flanders in the 1320s (Map 12.3). In order to satisfy peace agreements, Flemish peasants were forced to pay taxes to the French, who claimed fiscal rights over the county of Flanders. Monasteries also pressed peasants for additional money above their customary tithes. In retaliation, peasants burned and pillaged castles and aristocratic country houses. A French army crushed peasant forces. Savage repression and the confiscation of peasant property followed in the 1330s.

Jacquerie A massive uprising by French peasants in 1358 protesting heavy taxation.

In 1358, when French taxation for the Hundred Years' War fell heavily on the poor, the frustrations of the French peasantry exploded in a massive uprising called the Jacquerie (zhah-kuh-REE). Crowds swept through the countryside, slashing the throats of nobles, burning their castles, raping their wives and daughters, and killing or maiming their horses and cattle. Artisans, small merchants, and parish priests joined the peasants. Urban and rural groups committed terrible destruction, and for several weeks the nobles were on the defensive. Then the upper class united to repress the revolt with merciless ferocity. Thousands of peasants, innocent as well as guilty, were cut down. That forcible suppression of social rebellion, without any effort to alleviate its underlying causes, served to drive protest underground.

English Peasants' Revolt Revolt by English peasants in 1381 in response to changing economic conditions.

The 1381 English Peasants' Revolt involved thousands of people. Its causes were complex and varied from place to place. In general, though, the thirteenth century had witnessed the steady replacement of labor services by cash rents, and the Black Death had drastically cut the labor supply. As a result, peasants demanded higher wages and fewer manorial obligations. Their lords countered in 1351 with the Statute of Laborers, a law freezing wages and binding workers to their manors.

The statute could not be enforced, but a huge gap remained between peasants and their lords, and the peasants sought release for their economic frustrations in revolt. Economic grievances combined with other factors. The south of England, where the revolt broke out, had been subjected to destructive French raids during the Hundred Years' War. The English government did little to protect the south, and villagers grew increasingly frightened and insecure. Moreover, decades of aristocratic violence against the weak peasantry had bred hostility and bitterness. Social and religious agitation by the popular preacher John Ball fanned the embers of discontent. Ball's famous couplet calling for a return to the social equality that had existed in the Garden of Eden — "When Adam delved and Eve span; / Who was then the gentleman?" — reflected real revolutionary sentiment.

Chapter 12
The Crisis of the Late
340 Middle Ages • 1300–1450

CHAPTER LOCATOR | How did climate change shape the late Middle Ages?

The English revolt was ignited by the reimposition of a tax on all adult males. Despite widespread opposition to the tax in 1380, the royal council ordered the sheriffs to collect it again in 1381 on penalty of a huge fine. Beginning with assaults on the tax collectors, the uprising in England followed a course similar to that of the Jacquerie in France. Castles and manors were sacked. Manorial records were destroyed. Many nobles were murdered. The center of the revolt lay in the highly populated and economically advanced south and east, but sections of the north also witnessed rebellions (see Map 12.3).

The boy-king Richard II (r. 1377–1399) met the leaders of the revolt, agreed to charters ensuring peasants' freedom, tricked them with false promises, and then crushed the uprising with terrible ferocity. In the aftermath of the revolt, the nobility tried to restore the labor obligations of serfdom, but they were not successful, and the conversion to money rents continued. The English Peasants' Revolt did not bring social equality to England, but rural serfdom continued to decline, and it disappeared in England by 1550.

Map 12.3 **Fourteenth-Century Peasant Revolts** In the late Middle Ages, peasant and urban uprisings were endemic, as common as factory strikes in the industrial world. The threat of insurrection served to check unlimited exploitation.

How did the Black Death reshape European society?

What were the consequences of the Hundred Years' War?

Why did the church come under increasing attack?

What explains the social unrest of the late Middle Ages?

Christine de Pizan (1364?–1430) was the daughter and wife of highly educated men who held positions at the court of the king of France. She was widowed at twenty-five with young children and an elderly mother to support. Christine, who herself had received an excellent education, decided to support her family through writing, an unusual choice for anyone in this era and unheard of for a woman. She began to write prose works and poetry, sending them to wealthy individuals in the hope of receiving their support. Her works were well received, and Christine gained commissions to write specific works, including a biography of the French king Charles V, several histories, a long poem celebrating Joan of Arc's victory, and a book of military tactics. She became the first woman in Europe to make her living as a writer.

Among Christine's many works were several in which she considered women's nature and proper role in society, which had been a topic of debate since ancient times. The best known of these was The City of Ladies *(1404), in which she ponders why so many men have a negative view of women and provides examples of virtuous women to counter this view. A second book,* The Treasure of the City of Ladies *(1405, also called* The Book of Three Virtues*), provides moral suggestions and practical advice on behavior and household management for women of all social classes. Most of the book is directed toward princesses and court ladies (who would have been able to read it), but she also includes shorter sections for the wives of merchants and artisans, serving women, female peasants, and even prostitutes. This is her advice to the wives of artisans, whose husbands were generally members of urban craft guilds, such as blacksmiths, bakers, or shoemakers.*

❝ All wives of artisans should be very painstaking and diligent if they wish to have the necessities of life. They should encourage their husbands or their workmen to get to work early in the morning and work until late, for mark our words, there is no trade so good that if you neglect your work you will not have difficulty putting bread on the table. And besides encouraging the others, the wife herself should be involved in the work to the extent that she knows all about it, so that she may know how to oversee his workers if her husband is absent, and to reprove them if they do not do well. She ought to oversee them to keep them from idleness, for through careless workers the master is sometimes ruined. And when customers come to her husband and try to drive a hard bargain, she ought to warn him solicitously to take care that he does not make a bad deal. She should advise him to be chary of giving too much credit if he does not know precisely where and to whom it is going, for in this way many come to poverty, although sometimes the greed to earn more or to accept a tempting proposition makes them do it.

In addition, she ought to keep her husband's love as much as she can, to this end: that he will stay at home more willingly and that he may not have any reason to join the foolish crowds of other young men in taverns and indulge in unnecessary and extravagant expense, as many tradesmen do, especially in Paris. By treating him kindly she should protect him as well as she can from this. It is said that three things drive a man from his home: a quarrelsome wife, a smoking fireplace and a leaking roof. She too

Urban Conflicts

In Flanders, France, and England, peasant revolts often blended with conflicts involving workers in cities. Unrest also occurred in Italian, Spanish, and German cities. The revolts typically flared in urban centers, where the conditions of work were changing for many people. In the thirteenth century craft guilds had organized the production of most goods, with masters, journeymen, and apprentices working side-by-side. In the fourteenth century a new system evolved to make products on a larger scale. Capitalist investors hired many households, with each household performing only one step of the process. Initially these investors were wealthy bankers and merchants, but eventually shop masters themselves embraced the system. This promoted a greater division within guilds between wealthier masters and the poorer masters and journeymen they hired.

While capitalism provided opportunities for some artisans to become investors and entrepreneurs, especially in cloth production, for many it led to a decrease in income and status. Guilds sometimes responded to crises by opening up membership, but they more often responded to competition by limiting membership to existing guild families, which meant that journeymen who were not master's sons or who could not find a master's widow or daughter to marry could never become masters themselves. They remained

Chapter 12
The Crisis of the Late
342   Middle Ages • 1300–1450

CHAPTER LOCATOR   How did climate change shape the late Middle Ages?

Several manuscripts of Christine's works, such as this one, included illustrations showing her writing, which would have increased their appeal to the wealthy individuals who purchased them. (© British Library Board, Harl. 79487, fol. 3r Det.)

ought to remind her husband that they should live so frugally that their expenditure does not exceed their income, so that at the end of the year they do not find themselves in debt.

If she has children, she should have them instructed and taught first at school by educated people so that they may know how better to serve God. Afterwards they may be put to some trade by which they may earn a living, for whoever gives a trade or business training to her child gives a great possession. The children should be kept from wantonness and from voluptuousness above all else, for truly it is something that most shames the children of good towns and is a great sin of mothers and fathers, who ought to be the cause of the virtue and good behavior of their children, but they are sometimes the reason (because of bringing them up to be finicky and indulging them too much) for their wickedness and ruin. **"**

Source: Christine de Pizan, *The Treasure of the City of Ladies*, or *The Book of the Three Virtues*, translated with an introduction by Sarah Lawson (Penguin Classics, 1985). This translation copyright © 1985 by Sarah Lawson. Reprinted by permission of Penguin Books Ltd. For more on Christine, see C. C. Willard, *Christine de Pizan: Her Life and Works* (1984), and S. Bell, *The Lost Tapestries of the City of Ladies: Christine de Pizan's Renaissance Legacy* (2004).

ought to stay at home gladly and not go every day traipsing hither and yon gossiping with the neighbours and visiting her chums to find out what everyone is doing. That is done by slovenly housewives roaming about the town in groups. Nor should she go off on these pilgrimages got up for no good reason and involving a lot of needless expense. Furthermore, she

QUESTIONS FOR ANALYSIS

1. How would you describe Christine's view of the ideal artisan's wife?
2. The regulations of craft guilds often required that masters who ran workshops be married. What evidence does Christine's advice provide for why guilds would have stipulated this?
3. How are economic and moral virtues linked for Christine?

journeymen their entire lives, losing their sense of solidarity with the masters of their craft. Resentment led to rebellion over economic issues.

Urban uprisings were also sparked by issues involving honor, such as employers' requiring workers to do tasks they regarded as beneath them. As their actual status and economic prospects declined and their work became basically wage labor, journeymen and poorer masters emphasized skill and honor as qualities that set them apart from less-skilled workers.

Guilds increasingly came to view the honor of their work as tied to an all-male workplace. When urban economies were expanding in the High Middle Ages, the master's wife and daughters worked alongside him, and female domestic servants also carried out productive tasks. (See "Listening to the Past: Christine de Pizan, Advice to the Wives of Artisans," above.) Masters' widows ran shops after the death of their husbands. But in the fourteenth century a woman's right to work slowly eroded. First, masters' widows were limited in the amount of time they could keep operating a shop or were prohibited from hiring journeymen; then female domestic servants were excluded from any productive tasks; then the number of daughters a master craftsman could employ was limited. When women were allowed to work, it was viewed as a substitute for charity.

How did the Black Death reshape European society?

What were the consequences of the Hundred Years' War?

Why did the church come under increasing attack?

What explains the social unrest of the late Middle Ages?

Sex in the City

Peasant and urban revolts and riots had clear economic bases, but some historians have suggested that late medieval marital patterns may have also played a role in unrest. In northwestern Europe, people believed that couples should be economically independent before they married, so both spouses spent long periods saving money and learning skills, or they waited until their own parents had died and the family property was distributed.

The most unusual feature of this pattern was the late age of marriage for women. Unlike in earlier time periods and in most other parts of the world, a woman in late medieval northern and western Europe entered marriage as an adult and took charge of running a household immediately. She was thus not as dependent on her husband or mother-in-law as was a woman who married at a younger age.

Men of all social groups were older when they married. In general, men were in their middle or late twenties at first marriage. Journeymen, apprentices, and students at universities were often explicitly prohibited from marrying. The prohibitions on marriage for certain groups of men and the late age of marriage for most men meant that cities and villages were filled with large numbers of young adult men with no family responsibilities who often formed the core of riots and unrest. Not surprisingly, this situation also contributed to a steady market for sexual services outside of marriage, what in later centu-

City Brothel In this rather fanciful scene of a medieval brothel, two couples share baths and wine, while a third is in bed in the back, and two nobles peer in from a window across the street. Most brothels were not this elaborate, although some did have baths. Many cities also had commercial bath houses where people paid a small fee to take a hot bath, a luxury otherwise unavailable. Bath houses did sometimes offer sex, but their main attraction was hot water. (Bibliothèque nationale de France)

Chapter 12
The Crisis of the Late
344   **Middle Ages • 1300–1450**

⌐CHAPTER LOCATOR | How did climate change shape the late Middle Ages?

ries was termed prostitution. Research on the southern French province of Languedoc in the fourteenth and fifteenth centuries has revealed the establishment of legal houses of prostitution in many cities. The towns of Languedoc were not unique. Public authorities in Amiens, Dijon, Paris, Venice, Genoa, London, Florence, Rome, most of the larger German towns, and the English port of Sandwich set up brothels.

Young men associated visiting brothels with achieving manhood, though for the women themselves their activities were work. Some women had no choice, for they had been traded to the brothel manager by their parents or other people as payment for debt, or had quickly become indebted to the manager (most of whom were men) for the clothes and other finery regarded as essential to their occupation. Poor women—and men—also sold sex illegally outside of city brothels, combining this with other sorts of part-time work such as laundering or sewing. Prostitution was an urban phenomenon because only populous towns had large numbers of unmarried young men, communities of transient merchants, and a culture accustomed to a cash exchange.

Though selling sex for money was legal in the Middle Ages, the position of women who did so was always marginal. In the late fifteenth century cities began to limit brothel residents' freedom of movement and choice of clothing, requiring them to wear distinctive head coverings or bands on their clothing so that they would not be mistaken for "honorable" women. The cities also began to impose harsher penalties on women who did not live in the designated house or section of town.

Along with buying sex, young men also took it by force. Unmarried women often found it difficult to avoid sexual contact. Many of them worked as domestic servants, where their employers or employers' sons or male relatives could easily coerce them, or they worked in proximity to men. Rape was a capital crime in many parts of Europe, but the actual sentences handed out were more likely to be fines and brief imprisonment, with the severity of the sentence dependent on the social status of the victim and the perpetrator.

Same-sex relations were another feature of medieval life. Same-sex relations were of relatively little concern to church or state authorities in the early Middle Ages, but this attitude changed beginning in the late twelfth century. By 1300 most areas had defined such actions as "crimes against nature." Same-sex relations, usually termed "sodomy," became a capital crime in most of Europe, with adult offenders threatened with execution by fire. The Italian cities of Venice, Florence, and Lucca created special courts to deal with sodomy, which saw thousands of investigations.

Same-sex relations often developed within the context of all-male environments, such as the army, the craft shop, and the artistic workshop, and were part of the collective male experience. Homoerotic relationships played important roles in defining stages of life, expressing distinctions of status, and shaping masculine gender identity. Same-sex relations involving women almost never came to the attention of legal authorities, so it is difficult to find out how common they were. However, female-female desire was expressed in songs, plays, and stories, as was male-male desire, offering evidence of the way people understood same-sex relations.

Same-Sex Relations This illustration, from a thirteenth-century French book of morals, interprets female and male same-sex relations as the work of devils. The illustration was painted at the time that religious and political authorities were increasingly criminalizing same-sex relations. (ONB/Vienna, Picture Archives, Cod. 2554, fol. 2r)

Fur-Collar Crime

The Hundred Years' War had provided employment and opportunity for thousands of idle and fortune-seeking knights. But during periods of truce and after the war finally ended, many nobles once again had little to do. Inflation hurt them. Although many were living on fixed incomes, their chivalric code demanded lavish generosity and an aristocratic lifestyle. Many nobles turned to crime as a way of raising money. The fourteenth and fifteenth centuries witnessed a great deal of "fur-collar crime," so called for the miniver fur nobles alone were allowed to wear on their collars.

Groups of noble bandits roamed the English countryside, stealing from both rich and poor. When accused of wrongdoing, fur-collar criminals intimidated witnesses, threatened jurors, and bribed judges. Criminal activity by nobles continued decade after decade because governments were too weak to stop it.

The ballads of Robin Hood, a collection of folk legends from late medieval England, describe the adventures of the outlaw hero and his merry men as they avenge the common people against fur-collar criminals — grasping landlords, wicked sheriffs, and mercenary churchmen. Robin Hood was a popular figure because he symbolized the deep resentment of aristocratic corruption and abuse; he represented the struggle against tyranny and oppression.

Ethnic Tensions and Restrictions

Large numbers of people in the twelfth and thirteenth centuries migrated from one part of Europe to another in search of food, work, and peace: the English into Scotland and Ireland; Germans, French, and Flemings into Poland, Bohemia, and Hungary; the French into Spain. The colonization of frontier regions meant that peoples of different ethnic backgrounds lived side-by-side. Everywhere in Europe, towns recruited people from the countryside (see Chapter 11). In frontier regions, townspeople were usually long-distance immigrants and, in eastern Europe, Ireland, and Scotland, ethnically different from the surrounding rural population. In eastern Europe, German was the language of the towns; in Irish towns, French, the tongue of Norman or English settlers, predominated.

In the early periods of conquest and colonization, and in all regions with extensive migrations, a legal dualism existed: native peoples remained subject to their traditional laws; newcomers brought and were subject to the laws of the countries from which they came. The great exception to this broad pattern of legal pluralism was Ireland. From the start, the English practiced an extreme form of discrimination toward the native Irish that provoked great bitterness. The English distinguished between the free and the unfree, and the entire Irish population, simply by the fact of Irish birth, was unfree. When English legal structures were established beginning in 1210, the Irish were denied access to the common-law courts. In civil (property) disputes, an English defendant need not respond to his Irish plaintiff; no Irish person could make a will. In criminal procedures, the murder of an Irishman was not considered a felony.

Other than in Ireland, although native peoples commonly held humbler positions, both immigrant and native townspeople prospered during the expanding economy of the thirteenth century. But with the economic turmoil of the fourteenth century, ethnic tensions multiplied.

The late Middle Ages witnessed a movement away from legal pluralism or dualism and toward legal homogeneity and an emphasis on blood descent. The dominant ethnic group in an area tried to bar others from positions of church leadership and guild membership. Marriage laws were instituted that attempted to maintain ethnic purity by prohibiting intermarriage, and some church leaders actively promoted ethnic discrimination.

Chapter 12
The Crisis of the Late
346 **Middle Ages • 1300–1450**

CHAPTER LOCATOR | How did climate change shape the late Middle Ages?

The most extensive attempt to prevent intermarriage and protect ethnic purity is embodied in Ireland's Statute of Kilkenny (1366), which states that "there were to be no marriages between those of immigrant and native stock; that the English inhabitants of Ireland must employ the English language and bear English names; that they must ride in the English way [that is, with saddles] and have English apparel; that no Irishmen were to be granted ecclesiastical benefices or admitted to monasteries in the English parts of Ireland."[7]

Late medieval chroniclers used words such as *gens* (jehnz; race or clan) and *natio* (NAH-tee-oh; species, stock, or kind) to refer to different groups. They held that peoples differed according to language, traditions, customs, and laws. None of these were unchangeable, however, and commentators increasingly also described ethnic differences in terms of "blood" — "German blood," "English blood," and so on — which made ethnicity heritable. Religious beliefs also came to be conceptualized as blood, with people regarded as having Jewish blood, Muslim blood, or Christian blood. Blood was also used as a way to talk about social differences, especially for nobles. Persons of "noble blood" were prohibited from marrying commoners in many parts of Europe. As Europeans increasingly came into contact with people from Africa and Asia, and particularly as they developed colonial empires, these notions of blood also became a way of conceptualizing racial categories.

Literacy and Vernacular Literature

The development of ethnic identities had many negative consequences, but a more positive effect was the increasing use of the vernacular, that is, the local language that people actually spoke, rather than Latin. Two masterpieces of European culture, Dante's *Divine Comedy* (1310–1320) and Chaucer's *Canterbury Tales* (1387–1400), illustrate a sophisticated use of the rhythms and rhymes of the vernacular.

The *Divine Comedy* of Dante Alighieri (DAHN-tay ah-luh-GYER-ee) (1265–1321) is an epic poem of one hundred cantos (verses), each of whose three equal parts describes one of the realms of the next world: Hell, Purgatory, and Paradise. The Roman poet Virgil, representing reason, leads Dante through Hell, where Dante observes the torments of the damned and denounces the disorders of his own time. Passing up into Purgatory, Virgil shows the poet how souls are purified of their disordered inclinations. From Purgatory, Beatrice, a woman Dante once loved and the symbol of divine revelation in the poem, leads him to Paradise.

The *Divine Comedy* portrays contemporary and historical figures, comments on secular and ecclesiastical affairs, and draws on the Scholastic philosophy of uniting faith and reason. Within the framework of a symbolic pilgrimage, the *Divine Comedy* embodies the psychological tensions of the age. A profoundly Christian poem, it also contains bitter criticism of some church authorities. In its symmetrical structure and use of figures from the ancient world such as Virgil, the poem perpetuates the classical tradition, but as the first major work of literature in the Italian vernacular, it is distinctly modern.

Geoffrey Chaucer (1342–1400) was an official in the administrations of the English kings Edward III and Richard II and wrote poetry as an avocation. Chaucer's *Canterbury Tales* is a collection of stories in lengthy rhymed narrative. On a pilgrimage to the shrine of Saint Thomas Becket at Canterbury (see Chapter 9), thirty people of various social backgrounds tell tales. In depicting the interests and behavior of all types of people, Chaucer presents a rich panorama of English social life in the fourteenth century. Like the *Divine Comedy*, the *Canterbury Tales* reflects the cultural tensions of the times. Ostensibly Christian, many of the pilgrims are also materialistic, sensual, and worldly, suggesting the ambivalence of the broader society's concern for the next world and frank enjoyment of this one.

Statute of Kilkenny Laws issued in 1366 that discriminated against the Irish, forbidding marriage between the English and the Irish, requiring the use of the English language, and denying the Irish access to ecclesiastical offices.

How did the Black Death reshape European society?   What were the consequences of the Hundred Years' War?   Why did the church come under increasing attack?   **What explains the social unrest of the late Middle Ages?**

347

School Signboard Ambrosius Holbein, elder brother of the artist Hans Holbein, produced this signboard for the Swiss educator Myconius. It is an excellent example of what we would call commercial art—art used to advertise, in this case Myconius's profession. The German script above promised that all who enrolled, girls and boys, would learn to read and write. Most schools were for boys only, but a few offered instruction for girls as well. (Offentliche Kunstsammlung, Basel/ Giraudon/The Bridgeman Art Library)

Beginning in the fourteenth century, a variety of evidence attests to the increasing literacy of laypeople. Wills and inventories reveal that many people, not just nobles, possessed books—mainly devotional, but also romances, manuals on manners and etiquette, histories, and sometimes legal and philosophical texts. In England the number of schools in the diocese of York quadrupled between 1350 and 1500. Information from Flemish and German towns is similar: children were sent to schools and were taught the fundamentals of reading, writing, and arithmetic. Laymen increasingly served as managers or stewards of estates and as clerks to guilds and town governments; such positions obviously required the ability to keep administrative and financial records.

The penetration of laymen into the higher positions of governmental administration, long the preserve of clerics, also illustrates rising lay literacy. With growing frequency, the upper classes sent their daughters to convent schools, where, in addition to instruction in singing, religion, needlework, deportment, and household management, girls gained the rudiments of reading and sometimes writing.

The spread of literacy represents a response to the needs of an increasingly complex society. Trade, commerce, and expanding government bureaucracies required more and more literate people. Late medieval culture remained an oral culture in which most people received information by word of mouth. But by the fifteenth century the evolution toward a more literate culture was already perceptible, and craftsmen would develop the new technology of the printing press in response to the increased demand for reading materials.

Chapter 12
The Crisis of the Late
348   **Middle Ages • 1300–1450**

CHAPTER LOCATOR | How did climate change shape the late Middle Ages?

←LOOKING BACK LOOKING AHEAD→

THE FOURTEENTH AND EARLY FIFTEENTH CENTURIES were certainly times of crisis in western Europe, meriting the label "calamitous" given to them by one prominent historian. Famine, disease, and war decimated the European population, and traditional institutions, including secular governments and the church, did little or nothing or, in some cases, made things worse. Trading connections that had been reinvigorated in the High Middle Ages spread the most deadly epidemic ever experienced through western Asia, North Africa, and almost all of Europe. No wonder survivors experienced a sort of shell shock and a fascination with death.

The plague did not destroy the prosperity of the medieval population, however, and it may in fact have indirectly improved the European economy. Wealthy merchants had plenty of money to spend on luxuries and talent. In the century after the plague, Italian artists began to create new styles of painting, writers new literary forms, educators new types of schools, and philosophers new ideas about the purpose of human life. These cultural changes eventually spread to the rest of Europe, following the same paths that the plague had traveled. ▪

- **For a list of suggested readings for this chapter, visit** *bedfordstmartins.com/mckaywestunderstanding*.

- **For primary sources from this period, see** *Sources of Western Society*, Second Edition.

- **For Web sites, images, and documents related to topics in this chapter, see Make History at** *bedfordstmartins.com/mckaywestunderstanding*.

How did the Black Death reshape European society?

What were the consequences of the Hundred Years' War?

Why did the church come under increasing attack?

What explains the social unrest of the late Middle Ages?

Chapter 12 Study Guide

Step 1

GETTING STARTED Below are basic terms about this period in the history of Western civilization. Can you identify each term below and explain why it matters? To do this exercise online, go to bedfordstmartins.com/mckaywestunderstanding.

TERMS	WHO (OR WHAT) AND WHEN	WHY IT MATTERS
Great Famine, p. 322		
Black Death, p. 323		
flagellants, p. 327		
Agincourt, p. 331		
representative assemblies, p. 334		
Babylonian Captivity, p. 335		
Great Schism, p. 335		
conciliarists, p. 336		
confraternities, p. 338		
Jacquerie, p. 340		
English Peasants' Revolt, p. 340		
Statute of Kilkenny, p. 347		

Step 2

MOVING BEYOND THE BASICS The exercise below requires a more advanced understanding of the chapter material. Examine the consequences of the Black Death by filling in the chart below with descriptions of the disease's economic, social, political, and cultural and religious impact on the late Middle Ages. When you are finished, consider the following questions: What impact did the economic and social disruption associated with the Black Death have on medieval politics? How would such a cataclysmic event destabilize the status quo? To do this exercise online, go to bedfordstmartins.com/mckaywestunderstanding.

	ECONOMIC	SOCIAL	POLITICAL	CULTURAL AND RELIGIOUS
Consequences of the Black Death				

CLIMATE CHANGE AND THE BLACK DEATH

- What weaknesses in medieval society and government were revealed by the climate change of the Late Middle Ages? Why were governments and communities unable to produce effective responses to the problems climate change created?

- How did Europeans react to the devastation wreaked by the Black Death? How did the disease change the culture of medieval Europe?

THE HUNDRED YEARS' WAR

- Why did the Hundred Years' War drag on as long as it did? What explains the inability of French and English leaders to bring the conflict to a final resolution? Did they even want to?

- What were the most important political consequences of the Hundred Years' War? How did it contribute to the growth of nationalism in England and France?

CHALLENGES TO THE CHURCH

- In your opinion, is it fair to describe the fourteenth-century Roman church as a failed institution? Why or why not?

- What does the lay religious activity of the fourteenth century tell us about the values and beliefs of late medieval Europeans? What kind of religious life did fourteenth-century Europeans want? What religious ideals did they hold?

SOCIAL UNREST

- Compare and contrast fourteenth-century rebellions and uprisings in England and France. What common causes and conditions linked rebellions in both countries?

- Why did perceptions of ethnic difference and ethnic hierarchy sharpen in the fourteenth century? Can you think of any more recent parallels to this development?

■ **In Your Own Words** Imagine that you must explain Chapter 12 to someone who hasn't read it. What would be the most important points to include and why?

13

European Society in the Age of the Renaissance

1350–1550

While war gripped northern Europe, a new culture emerged in southern Europe. The fourteenth century witnessed remarkable changes in Italian intellectual, artistic, and cultural life. Artists and writers thought that they were living in a new golden age, but not until the sixteenth century was this change given the label we use today—the Renaissance, derived from the French word for "rebirth." That word was first used by art historian Giorgio Vasari (1511–1574) to describe the art of "rare men of genius" such as his contemporary Michelangelo. Through their works, Vasari judged, the glory of the classical past had been reborn after centuries of darkness. Over time, the word's meaning was broadened to include many aspects of life during that period throughout Europe. The new attitude had a slow diffusion out of Italy, with the result that the Renaissance "happened" at different times in different parts of Europe.

Later scholars increasingly saw the cultural and political changes of the Renaissance, along with the religious changes of the Reformation (see Chapter 14) and the European voyages of exploration (see Chapter 15), as ushering in the "modern" world. Some historians view the Renaissance as a bridge between the medieval and modern eras because it corresponded chronologically with the late medieval period and because there were many continuities along with the changes. Others have questioned whether the word *Renaissance* should be used at all to describe an era in which many social groups saw decline rather than advance. The debates remind us that these labels—medieval, Renaissance, modern—are intellectual constructs devised after the fact. They all contain value judgments, just as do other chronological designations, such as the "golden age" of Athens and the "Roaring Twenties." ∎

Life in the Renaissance. In this detail from a fresco, Italian painter Lorenzo Lotto captures the mixing of social groups in a Renaissance Italian city. Wealthy merchants, soldiers, and boys intermingle, while at the right women sell vegetables and bread, a common sight at any city marketplace. (Scala/Art Resource, NY)

Chapter Preview

▶ How did politics and economics shape the Renaissance?

▶ What new ideas were associated with the Renaissance?

▶ How did changes in art reflect new Renaissance ideals?

▶ What were the key social hierarchies in Renaissance Europe?

▶ How did nation-states evolve in this period?

▼ How did politics and economics shape the Renaissance?

Renaissance A French word meaning "rebirth," first used by art historian and critic Giorgio Vasari to refer to the rebirth of the culture of classical antiquity.

patronage Financial support of writers and artists by cities, groups, and individuals, often to produce specific works or works in specific styles.

The magnificent art and new ways of thinking in the Renaissance rest on economic and political developments in the city-states of northern Italy. Economic growth laid the material basis for the Italian Renaissance, and ambitious merchants gained political power to match their economic power. They then used their money and power to buy luxuries and hire talent in a system of patronage, through which cities, groups, and individuals commissioned writers and artists to produce specific works. Political leaders in Italian cities admired the traditions and power of ancient Rome, and this esteem shaped their commissions. Thus, economics, politics, and culture were interconnected.

Trade and Prosperity

Northern Italian cities led the way in the great commercial revival of the eleventh century. By the middle of the twelfth century Venice had grown enormously rich through overseas trade, as had Genoa and Milan. These cities made important strides in shipbuilding that allowed their ships to sail all year long at accelerated speeds and to carry ever more merchandise.

Another commercial leader, and the city where the Renaissance began, was Florence, situated on the Arno River. Its favorable location on the main road northward from Rome made Florence a commercial hub, and the city grew wealthy buying and selling all types of goods throughout Europe and the Mediterranean. Florentine merchants also loaned and invested money, and they acquired control of papal banking toward the end of the thirteenth century. Florentine mercantile families began to dominate European banking on both sides of the Alps, setting up offices in major European and North African cities. The banking profits that poured back to Florence were pumped into urban industries. By the early fourteenth century the city had about eighty thousand people, about twice the population of London at that time. Profits contributed to the city's economic vitality and allowed banking families to control the city's politics and culture.

By the first quarter of the fourteenth century, the economic foundations of Florence were so strong that even severe crises could not destroy the city. Florence suffered frightfully from the Black Death, losing at least half its population, and serious labor unrest shook the political establishment (see Chapter 12). Nevertheless, the basic Florentine economic structure remained stable.

In Florence and other cities, wealth allowed many people greater material pleasures, a more comfortable life, and the leisure time to appreciate and patronize the arts.

A Florentine Bank Scene Originally a "bank" was just a counter; moneychangers who sat behind the counter became "bankers," exchanging different currencies and holding deposits for merchants and businesspeople. In this scene from fifteenth-century Florence, the bank is covered with an imported Ottoman geometric rug, one of many imported luxury items handled by Florentine merchants. (Prato, San Francesco/Scala/Art Resource, NY)

Chapter 13
European Society in the Age of the Renaissance • 1350–1550

354

CHAPTER LOCATOR | How did politics and economics shape the Renaissance?

Merchants and bankers commissioned public and private buildings from architects, and they hired sculptors and painters to decorate their homes and churches. The rich, social-climbing residents of Venice, Florence, Genoa, and Rome came to see life more as an opportunity to be enjoyed than as a painful pilgrimage to the City of God.

Communes and Republics of Northern Italy

The northern Italian cities were communes, sworn associations of free men who, like other town residents, began in the twelfth century to seek political and economic independence from local nobles. The merchant guilds that formed the communes built and maintained the city walls, regulated trade, collected taxes, and kept civil order. The local nobles frequently moved into the cities, marrying into rich commercial families and starting their own businesses. This merger of the northern Italian feudal nobility and the commercial elite created a powerful oligarchy, a small group that ruled the city and surrounding countryside. Yet because of rivalries among different powerful families within the ruling oligarchy, Italian communes were often politically unstable.

Unrest coming from below exacerbated the instability. Merchant elites made citizenship in the communes dependent on a property qualification, years of residence within the city, and social connections. Only a tiny percentage of the male population possessed these qualifications. The common people, called the popolo, were disenfranchised and heavily taxed, and they bitterly resented their exclusion from power. Throughout most of the thirteenth century, in city after city, the popolo used armed force to take over the city governments. Republican governments—in which political power theoretically resides in the people and is exercised by their chosen representatives—were established in numerous cities, including Florence. The victory of the popolo proved temporary, however, because they could not establish civil order within their cities. Merchant oligarchies reasserted their power and sometimes brought in powerful military leaders to establish order.

Many cities in Italy became signori (seen-YOHR-ee), in which one man ruled and handed down the right to rule to his son. Some signori kept the institutions of communal government in place, but these had no actual power. As a practical matter, there wasn't much difference between oligarchic regimes and signori. Oligarchies maintained a façade of republican government, but the judicial, executive, and legislative functions of government were restricted to a small class of wealthy merchants.

In the fifteenth and sixteenth centuries the signori in many cities and the most powerful merchant oligarchs in others transformed their households into courts. Courtly culture afforded signori and oligarchs the opportunity to display and assert their wealth and power. They built magnificent palaces and required all political business to be done there. The rulers of Florence, Milan, and other northern Italian cities became patrons of the arts. They hired architects to design and build private palaces and public city halls, artists to fill them with paintings and sculptures, and musicians and composers to fill them with music. Ceremonies connected with family births, baptisms, marriages, and funerals offered occasions for pageantry and elaborate ritual. Cities welcomed rulers who

Chapter Chronology

ca. 1350	Petrarch develops ideas of humanism
1434–1737	Medici family in power in Florence
1440s	Invention of movable metal type
1447–1535	Sforza family dominates politics in Milan
1455–1471	Wars of the Roses in England
1469	Marriage of Isabella of Castile and Ferdinand of Aragon
1477	Louis XI conquers Burgundy
1478	Establishment of the Inquisition in Spain
1492	Spain conquers Granada, ending reconquista; practicing Jews expelled from Spain
1494	Invasion of Italy by Charles VIII of France
1508–1512	Michelangelo paints ceiling of Sistine Chapel
1513	Machiavelli, *The Prince*
1563	Establishment of first formal academy for artistic training in Florence

communes Sworn associations of free men in Italian cities led by merchant guilds that sought political and economic independence from local nobles.

popolo Disenfranchised common people in Italian cities who resented their exclusion from power.

signori Government by one-man rule in Italian cities such as Milan.

courts Magnificent households and palaces where the signori and the most powerful merchant oligarchs required political business to be conducted.

Battle of San Romano Fascinated by perspective—the representation of spatial depth or distance on a flat surface—the Florentine artist Paolo Uccello (1397–1475) celebrated the 1432 Florentine victory over Siena in this painting. Though a minor battle, it started Florence on the road to domination over smaller nearby states. The painting hung in Lorenzo de' Medici's bedroom. (National Gallery, London/Erich Lessing/Art Resource, NY)

were visiting with magnificent entrance parades. Rulers of nation-states later copied and adapted all these aspects of Italian courts.

City-States and the Balance of Power

Renaissance Italians had a passionate attachment to their individual city-states: political loyalty and feeling centered on the local city. This intensity of local feeling perpetuated the dozens of small states and hindered the development of one unified state.

In the fifteenth century five powers dominated the Italian peninsula: Venice, Milan, Florence, the Papal States, and the kingdom of Naples (Map 13.1). The major Italian city-states controlled the smaller ones, such as Siena, Mantua, Ferrara, and Modena, and competed furiously among themselves for territory. While the states of northern Europe were moving toward centralization and consolidation, the world of Italian politics resembled a jungle where the powerful dominated the weak. Venice, with its trade empire, ranked as an international power. Though Venice was a republic in name, an oligarchy of merchant-aristocrats actually ran the city. Milan was also called a republic, but the signori of the Sforza (SFORT-sah) family dominated Milan from 1447 to 1535. Likewise, in Florence the form of government was republican, but starting in 1434 the great Medici (MEH-duh-chee) banking family held power almost continually for centuries. The Medici family produced three popes, and most other Renaissance popes were also members of powerful Italian families, selected for their political skills, not their piety. Pope Alexander VI (pontificate 1492–1503) was the most ruthless; aided militarily and politically by his illegitimate son Cesare Borgia (CHE-zah-ray BAWR-zhuh), he reasserted papal authority in the papal lands. South of the Papal States, the kingdom of Naples was under the control of the king of Aragon.

In one significant respect, however, the Italian city-states anticipated future relations among competing European states after 1500. Whenever one Italian state appeared to

Map 13.1 The Italian City-States, ca. 1494 In the fifteenth century the Italian city-states represented great wealth and cultural sophistication, though their many political divisions throughout the peninsula invited foreign intervention.

gain a predominant position within the peninsula, other states combined to establish a balance of power against the major threat. In the formation of these alliances, Renaissance Italians invented the machinery of modern diplomacy: permanent embassies with resident ambassadors in capitals where political relations and commercial ties needed continual monitoring. The resident ambassador was one of the great political achievements of the Italian Renaissance.

At the end of the fifteenth century Venice, Florence, Milan, and the papacy possessed great wealth and represented high cultural achievement. Wealthy and divided, however, they were also an inviting target for invasion. When Florence and Naples entered into an agreement to acquire Milanese territories, Milan called on France for support, and the French king Charles VIII (r. 1483–1498) invaded Italy in 1494.

In Florence, the French invasion was interpreted as the fulfillment of a prophecy by the Dominican friar Girolamo Savonarola (1452–1498) that God would punish Italy for its moral vice and corrupt leadership. The Medici dynasty that ruled Florence fell after the French invasion, and Savonarola became the political and religious leader of the city. He reorganized the government and called on people to destroy anything that might lead them to sin: fancy clothing, cosmetics, pagan books, musical instruments, paintings or poetry that celebrated human beauty. For a time Savonarola was wildly popular, but eventually people tired of his moral denunciations, and he was excommunicated by the pope, tortured, and burned at the stake. The Medici returned as the rulers of Florence.

The French invasion inaugurated a new period in Italian and European power politics. Italy became the focus of international ambitions and the battleground of foreign armies, particularly those of France and the Holy Roman Empire in a series of conflicts called the Habsburg-Valois Wars (named for the German and French dynasties). The Italian cities suffered severely from continual warfare, especially in the frightful sack of Rome in 1527 by imperial forces under the emperor Charles V. Thus the failure of the city-states to form a federal system, to consolidate, or at least to establish a common foreign policy led to centuries of subjection by outside invaders. Italy was not to achieve unification until 1870.

▼ What new ideas were associated with the Renaissance?

The Renaissance was characterized by self-conscious awareness among educated Italians that they were living in a new era. Somewhat ironically, this idea rested on a deep interest in ancient Latin and Greek literature and philosophy. Through reflecting on the classics, Renaissance thinkers developed new notions of human nature, new plans for education, and new concepts of political rule. The advent of the printing press with movable type would greatly accelerate the spread of their ideas throughout Europe.

Humanism

Giorgio Vasari was the first to use the word *Renaissance* in print, but he was not the first to feel that something was being reborn. Two centuries earlier the Florentine poet and scholar Francesco Petrarch (1304–1374) became obsessed with the classical past. He felt that the writers and artists of ancient Rome had reached a level of perfection in their work that had never since been duplicated. Petrarch believed that writers of his own day should follow these ancient models and that the recovery of classical texts would bring about a new golden age of intellectual achievement, an idea that many others came to share.

Petrarch thought he was witnessing the dawning of a new era in which writers and artists would recapture the glory of the Roman republic. Around 1350 he proposed a new kind of education to help them do this, in which young men would study the works of ancient Latin and Greek authors, using them as models of how to write clearly, argue effectively, and speak persuasively. The study of Latin classics became known as the *studia humanitates* (STOO-dee-uh oo-mahn-ee-TAH-tayz), usually translated as "liberal studies" or the "liberal arts." People who advocated it were known as *humanists* and their program as

Saltcellar of Francis I In gold and enamel, Benvenuto Cellini depicts on this precursor of the saltshaker from about 1540 the Roman sea god, Neptune, sitting beside a small boat-shaped container holding salt from the sea. Opposite him, a female figure personifying Earth guards pepper. Portrayed on the base are the four seasons and the times of day, symbolizing seasonal festivities and daily meal schedules. Classical figures were common subjects in Renaissance art. (Kunsthistorisches Museum, Vienna/The Bridgeman Art Library)

Chapter 13
**European Society in the Age of
the Renaissance • 1350–1550**

358

CHAPTER LOCATOR | How did politics and economics shape the Renaissance?

humanism. Like all programs of study, humanism contained an implicit philosophy: that human nature and achievements, evident in the classics, were worthy of contemplation.

humanism A program of study designed by Italians that emphasized the critical study of Latin and Greek literature with the goal of understanding human nature.

The glory of Rome had been brightest, in the opinion of the humanists, in the works of the Roman author and statesman Cicero (106 B.C.E.–43 B.C.E.). Cicero had lived during the turbulent era when Julius Caesar and other powerful generals transformed the Roman republic into an empire (see Chapter 5). In forceful and elegantly worded speeches, letters, and treatises, Cicero supported a return to republican government. Petrarch and other humanists admired Cicero's use of language, literary style, and political ideas. Many humanists saw Caesar's transformation of Rome as a betrayal of the great society, marking the beginning of a long period of decay that the barbarian migrations had simply sped up.

In the fifteenth century Florentine humanists became increasingly interested in Greek philosophy as well as Roman literature, especially in the ideas of Plato. Under the patronage of Cosimo de' Medici (1389–1464), the most powerful man in Florence, the scholar Marsilio Ficino (1433–1499) began to lecture to an informal group of Florence's cultural elite. Ficino regarded Plato as a divinely inspired precursor to Christ, and he translated Plato's dialogues into Latin, attempting to synthesize Christian and Platonic teachings. Plato's emphasis on the spiritual and eternal over the material and transient fit well with Christian teachings about the immortality of the soul. Platonic ideas about love, that the highest form of love was spiritual desire for pure, perfect beauty uncorrupted by bodily desires, could easily be interpreted as Christian desire for the perfection of God.

For Ficino and his most brilliant student, Giovanni Pico della Mirandola (1463–1494), both Christian and classical texts taught that the universe was a hierarchy of beings from God down through spiritual beings to material beings, with humanity the crucial link right in the middle, both material and spiritual. In his essay, "On the Dignity of Man" (1486), Pico stressed that man possesses great dignity because he was made as Adam in the image of God before the Fall and as Christ after the Resurrection. According to Pico, man is the one part of the created world that has no fixed place, but he can freely choose whether to rise to the realm of the angels or descend to the realm of the animals; because of the divine image planted in him, he is truly a "miraculous creature."

Man's miraculous nature meant there are no limits to what he can accomplish and Renaissance thinkers increasingly stressed individual achievement. They were especially interested in individuals who had risen above their background to become brilliant, powerful, or unique. (See "Individuals in Society: Leonardo da Vinci," page 372.) Such individuals had the admirable quality of **virtù** (ver-TOO), which is not virtue in the sense of moral goodness, but the ability to shape the world around them according to their will. Renaissance historians included biographies of individuals with virtù in their histories of cities and nations, describing ways in which they had affected the course of history. Through the quality of their works and their influence on others, artists could also exhibit virtù, an idea that Vasari captures in the title of his major work, *The Lives of the Most Excellent Painters, Sculptors and Architects*. His subjects were not simply excellent: they had achieved the pinnacle of excellence.

virtù The quality of being able to shape the world according to one's own will.

The last artist included in Vasari's book is Vasari himself, for Renaissance thinkers did not exclude themselves when they searched for models of talent and achievement. Leon Battista Alberti (1404–1472) had similar views of his own achievements. He had much to be proud of, making contributions in a wide variety of fields. In his autobiography—written late in his life, and in the third person, so that he calls himself "he" instead of "I"—Alberti described his personal qualities and accomplishments:

Assiduous in the science and skill of dealing with arms and horses and musical instruments, as well as in the pursuit of letters and the fine arts, he was devoted to the knowledge of the most strange and difficult things. . . . He played ball, hurled the javelin, ran, leaped, wrestled. . . . He learned music without teachers . . . and then turned to physics and the mathematical arts. . . . Ambition was alien to him. . . . When his favorite dog died he wrote a funeral oration for him.[1]

His achievements in many fields did make Alberti a "Renaissance man," as we use the term, though it may be hard to believe his assertion that "ambition was alien to him."

Education

Humanists thought that their recommended course of study in the classics would provide essential skills for future diplomats, lawyers, military leaders, businessmen, and politicians, as well as writers and artists. It would provide a much broader and more practical type of training than that offered at universities, which at the time focused on theology and philosophy or on theoretical training for lawyers and physicians. Humanists poured out treatises on the structure and goals of education and the training of rulers and leaders. They taught that a life active in the world should be the aim of all educated individuals and that education was not simply for private or religious purposes, but it benefited the public good.

Humanists put their ideas into practice. Beginning in the early fifteenth century, they opened schools and academies in Italian cities and courts in which pupils began with Latin grammar and rhetoric, went on to study Roman history and political philosophy, and then learned Greek in order to study Greek literature and philosophy. Gradually, humanist education became the basis for intermediate and advanced education for well-to-do urban boys and men. Humanist schools were established in Florence, Venice, and other Italian cities, and by the early sixteenth century in Germany, France, and England.

Humanists disagreed about education for women. Many saw the value of exposing women to classical models of moral behavior and reasoning, but they also wondered whether a program of study that emphasized eloquence and action was proper for women, whose sphere was generally understood to be private and domestic. Women themselves were more bold in their claims about the value of the new learning. Although humanist academies were not open to women, through tutors or programs of self-study a few women did become educated in the classics. They argued in letters and published writings that reason was not limited to men and that learning was compatible with virtue for women as well as men. (See "Listening to the Past: Perspectives on Humanist Learning and Women," page 362.)

No book on education had broader influence than Baldassare Castiglione's *The Courtier* (1528). This treatise sought to train, discipline, and fashion the young man into the courtly ideal, the gentleman. According to Castiglione (kahs-teel-YOH-nay), who himself was a courtier serving several different rulers, the educated man should have a broad background in many academic subjects, and his spiritual and physical as

Portrait of Baldassare Castiglione In this portrait by Raphael, the most sought-after portrait painter of the Renaissance, Castiglione is shown dressed exactly as he advised courtiers to dress, in elegant but subdued clothing that would enhance the splendor of the court, but never outshine the ruler. (Scala/Art Resource, NY)

Chapter 13
European Society in the Age of
360   **the Renaissance • 1350–1550**

CHAPTER LOCATOR | How did politics and economics shape the Renaissance?

well as his intellectual capabilities should be trained. Above all, he should be able to speak and write eloquently. Castiglione also included discussion of the perfect court lady, who, like the courtier, was to be well educated and be able to sing, dance, and paint. Physical beauty, delicacy, affability, and modesty were also important qualities for court ladies.

In the sixteenth and seventeenth centuries, *The Courtier* was translated into every European language and widely read. It influenced the social mores and patterns of conduct of elite groups in Renaissance and early modern Europe. It became a how-to manual for people seeking to improve themselves and rise in the social hierarchy as well. Echoes of its ideal for women have perhaps had an even longer life.

Political Thought

Ideal courtiers should preferably serve an ideal ruler, and biographies written by humanists often describe rulers in glowing terms. For such flattering portraits of living rulers or their ancestors, authors sometimes received positions at court, or at least substantial payments. Particularly in Italian cities, however, which often were divided by political factions, taken over by homegrown or regional despots, and attacked by foreign armies, such ideal rulers were hard to find. Humanists thus looked to the classical past for their models. Some, such as the humanist historian and Florentine city official Leonardo Bruni (1374–1444), argued that republicanism was the best form of government. Others used the model of Plato's philosopher-king in the *Republic* to argue that rule by an enlightened single individual might be best. Both sides agreed that educated men should be active in the political affairs of their city, a position historians have since termed "civic humanism."

The most famous (or infamous) civic humanist, and ultimately the best-known political theorist of this era, was Niccolò Machiavelli (1469–1527). After the ouster of the Medici with the French invasion of 1494, Machiavelli was secretary to one of the governing bodies in the city of Florence, responsible for diplomatic missions and organizing a citizen army. Power struggles in Florence between rival factions brought the Medici family back to power, and Machiavelli was arrested, tortured, and imprisoned on suspicion of plotting against them. He was released but had no government position, and he spent the rest of his life writing and making fruitless attempts to regain employment.

Machiavelli's most famous work, *The Prince* (1513), uses the examples of classical and contemporary rulers to argue that the function of a ruler (or any government) is to preserve order and security. Weakness would only lead to disorder, civil war, or conquest by an outsider. To preserve the state a ruler should use whatever means he needs—brutality, lying, manipulation—but should not do anything that would make the populace turn against him. Stealing or cruel actions done for a ruler's own pleasure would lead to resentment and destroy the popular support needed for a strong, stable realm. "It is much safer for the prince to be feared than loved," Machiavelli advised, "but he ought to avoid making himself hated."[2]

Like the good humanist he was, Machiavelli knew that effective rulers exhibited the quality of virtù. He presented examples from the classical past of just the type of ruler he was describing, but he also wrote about contemporary leaders. Cesare Borgia (1475?–1507), Machiavelli's primary example, was the son of Rodrigo Borgia, a Spanish nobleman who later became Pope Alexander VI. Cesare Borgia combined his father's power and his own ruthlessness to build up a city-state in central Italy. Despite Borgia's efforts, his state fell apart after his father's death, which Machiavelli ascribed not to weakness, but to the operations of fate (*fortuna*, for-TOO-nah, in Italian), whose power even the best-prepared and most merciless ruler could not fully escape, though he should try. Fortuna was personified and portrayed as a goddess in ancient Rome and Renaissance Italy, and Machiavelli's last words about fortune are expressed in gendered terms: "It is

LISTENING TO THE PAST

Perspectives on Humanist Learning and Women

Italian humanists set out the type of education that they regarded as ideal and promoted its value to society and the individual. Several women from the bustling cities of northern Italy became excited by the new style of learning, and through tutors or programs of self-study became extremely well educated. Like male humanists, they wrote letters, orations, lectures, and dialogues demonstrating their learning on such topics as truth, virtue, knowledge, fame, and friendship. They circulated these to acquaintances and people whose good opinion they valued. Occasionally they presented orations and lectures orally in public settings or noble courts.

Some male humanists, including the influential Florentine official Leonardo Bruni, suggested that no woman who shared her ideas in public could possibly be virtuous, but by the middle of the fifteenth century other humanists celebrated the entrance of at least a few women into the largely male world of learning. The Venetian humanist nobleman Lauro Quirini (ca. 1420–ca. 1475), for example, had heard about the learned Isotta Nogarola (1418–1466) from her brother and from reading a collection of her letters. In this letter he praises her accomplishments and advises her on a plan of study.

Letter from Lauro Quirini to Isotta Nogarola, ca. 1450

❝ This letter asks of you nothing else than that you pursue in the most splendid way, until death, that same course of right living that you have followed since childhood. . . . Rightful therefore, should you also, famous Isotta, receive the highest praises, since you have, if I may so speak, overcome your own nature. For that true virtue that is proper to men you have pursued with remarkable zeal — not the mediocre virtue that many men seek, but that which would befit a man of the most flawless and perfect wisdom. . . . Therefore dissatisfied with the lesser studies, you have applied your noble mind to those highest disciplines, in which there is need for keenness of intelligence and mind. For you are engaged in the art of dialectic, which shows the way to learning the truth. Having mastered it, you may become engaged in a still more splendid and fertile field of philosophy [metaphysics]. . . .

Read studiously, then, the glorious works of Boethius Severnius, unquestionably a most intelligent and abundantly learned man.* Read all the treatises he learnedly composed on the dialectic art. . . . After you have mastered dialectic, which is the method of knowing, you should read diligently and carefully the moral books of Aristotle, which he writes divinely, in which you may unfailingly recognize the essence of true and solid virtue. . . . Then, after you have also digested this part of philosophy, which is concerned with human matters, equipped with your nobility of the soul you should also set out for that ample and vast other part [divine matters]. . . . Here you should begin especially with those disciplines that we call by the Greek term mathematics. . . .

Diligently and carefully follow the Arabs, who very nearly approach the Greeks. You should constantly and assiduously read Averroes, admittedly a barbarous and uncultivated man, but otherwise an exceptional philosopher and rare judge of things.† . . . Read Thomas Aquinas often, who provides as it were an entryway to the understanding of Aristotle and Averroes.‡ . . .

You should also make use of those studies, moreover, that you have splendidly embraced from your youth, and especially history, for history is as it were the teacher of life, which somehow makes the wisdom of the ancients ours and inflames us to imitate great men. . . .

Take care of yourself so that you may be well, and study so that you may be wise. . . . For nothing is more lovely than philosophy, nothing more beautiful, nothing more lovable, as our Cicero said, to which I add, perhaps more truly, that there is nothing among human things more divine than philosophy. ❞

The Venetian Cassandra Fedele (1465–1558) applied advice such as Quirini's to her own studies. She became the best-known female scholar in her time, corresponding with humanist writers, church officials, university professors, nobles, and even the rulers of Europe, including Isabella and Ferdinand of Spain. She became a positive example in the debate about women. She gave this oration in Latin at the University of Padua in honor of her (male) cousin's graduation.

better to be impetuous than cautious, for fortune is a woman, and if one wishes to keep her down, it is necessary to beat her and knock her down."[3]

The Prince is often seen as the first modern guide to politics, though Machiavelli was denounced for writing it, and people later came to use the word "Machiavellian" to mean cunning and ruthless. Medieval political philosophers regarded the standards by which all governments were to be judged as emanating from moral principles established by

Chapter 13
European Society in the Age of
362   the Renaissance • 1350–1550

CHAPTER LOCATOR   How did politics and economics shape the Renaissance?

Woodcut showing Isotta Nogarola with her books, from Jacopo Bergamo's *Of Many Renowned and Wicked Women* (1497), a listing of good and evil women. ([Ferrara: Laurentius de Rubeis de Valentia, 1497]. Photo: Visual Connection Archive)

In Praise of Letters

❝ I shall speak very briefly on the study of the liberal arts, which for humans is useful and honorable, pleasurable and enlightening since everyone, not only philosophers but also the most ignorant man, knows and admits that it is by reason that man is separated from beasts. For what is it that so greatly helps both the learned and the ignorant? What so enlarges and enlightens men's minds the way that an education in and knowledge of literature and the liberal arts do? . . . But erudite men who are filled with the knowledge of divine and human things turn all their thoughts and considerations toward reason as though toward a target, and free their minds from all pain, though plagued by many anxieties. These men are scarcely subjected to fortune's innumerable arrows and they prepare themselves to live well and in happiness. They follow reason as their leader in all things; nor do they consider themselves only, but they are also accustomed to assisting others with their energy and advice in matters public and private.

And so Plato, a man almost divine, wrote that those states would be fortunate in which the men who were heads of state were philosophers or in which philosophers took on the duty of administration. . . . The study of literature refines men's minds, forms and makes bright the power of reason, and washes away all stains from the mind, or at any rate, greatly cleanses it. It perfects the gifts and adds much beauty and elegance to the physical and material advantages that one has received by nature. States, however, and their princes who foster and cultivate these studies become more humane, more gracious, and more noble. For this reason, these studies have won for themselves the sweet appellation, "humanities." . . . Just as places that lie unused and uncultivated become fertile and rich in fruits and vegetables with men's labor and hard work and are always made beautiful, so are our natures cultivated, enhanced, and enlightened by the liberal arts. . . .

But enough on the utility of literature since it produces not only an outcome that is rich, precious, and sublime, but also provides one with advantages that are extremely pleasurable, fruitful, and lasting—benefits that I myself have enjoyed. And when I meditate on the idea of marching forth in life with the lowly and execrable weapons of the little woman—the needle and the distaff [the rod onto which yarn is wound after spinning]—even if the study of literature offers women no rewards or honors, I believe women must nonetheless pursue and embrace such studies alone for the pleasure and enjoyment they contain. ❞

Sources: Isotta Nogarola, *Complete Writings*, ed. and trans. Margaret L. King and Diana Robin, *The Other Voice in Early Modern Europe* (Chicago: University of Chicago Press, 2004), pp. 108–113 Copyright © 2004 by The University of Chicago Press. All rights reserved. Reproduced by permission. Cassandra Fedele, *Letters and Orations*, ed. and trans. Diana Robin, *The Other Voice in Early Modern Europe* (Chicago: University of Chicago Press, 2000), pp. 159–162. Copyright © 2000 by The University of Chicago Press. All rights reserved. Reproduced by permission.

QUESTIONS FOR ANALYSIS

1. What do Quirini and Fedele view as the best course of study?
2. What do they see as the purposes of such study? Are these purposes different for men and women?
3. Quirini is male and Fedele female. Does the gender of the authors shape their ideas about humanist learning in general, or about its appropriateness for women?

*Boethius (ca. 480–524) was a philosopher and adviser to King Theoderic (see page 183); he translated Aristotle's works on logic from Greek into Latin.

†Averroes (1126–1198) was an Islamic philosopher from Spain who wrote commentaries on Aristotle.

‡Thomas Aquinas (1225–1274) was a scholastic theologian and philosopher who brought together Aristotelian philosophy and Christian teachings (see page 306).

God. Machiavelli argued that governments should instead be judged by how well they provided security, order, and safety to their populace. A ruler's moral code in maintaining these was not the same as a private individual's, for a leader could—indeed, should—use any means necessary. This more pragmatic view of the purposes of government, and Machiavelli's discussion of the role of force and cruelty, was unacceptable to many.

What new ideas were associated with the Renaissance?   How did changes in art reflect new Renaissance ideals?   What were the key social hierarchies in Renaissance Europe?   How did nation-states evolve in this period?

363

Christian Humanism

In the last quarter of the fifteenth century, young men from the Low Countries, France, Germany, and England flocked to Italy, absorbed the "new learning," and carried it back to their own countries. Northern humanists shared the ideas of Ficino and Pico about the wisdom of ancient texts, but they went beyond Italian efforts to synthesize the Christian and classical traditions to see humanist learning as a way to bring about reform of the church and deepen people's spiritual lives. These **Christian humanists**, as they were later called, thought that the best elements of classical and Christian cultures should be combined.

> **Christian humanists** Northern humanists who interpreted Italian ideas about and attitudes toward classical antiquity and humanism in terms of their own religious traditions.

The English humanist Thomas More (1478–1535) began life as a lawyer, studied the classics, and entered government service. He was most famous, however, for his controversial dialogue *Utopia* (1516), a word More invented from the Greek words for "nowhere." *Utopia* describes a community on an island somewhere beyond Europe where all children receive a good education, primarily in the Greco-Roman classics, and adults divide their days between manual labor or business pursuits and intellectual activities. The problems that plagued More's fellow citizens, such as poverty and hunger, have been solved by a beneficent government. Because private property promoted inequality and greed, profits from business and property are held in common. There is religious toleration, and order and reason prevail. Because Utopian institutions are perfect, however, dissent and disagreement are not acceptable.

More's purposes in writing *Utopia* have been widely debated. Some view it as a revolutionary critique of More's own hierarchical and violent society, some as a call for an even firmer hierarchy, and others as part of the humanist tradition of satire. It was widely read by learned Europeans in the Latin in which More wrote it, and later in vernacular translations, and its title quickly became the standard word for any imaginary society.

Procession of the Magi This segment of a huge fresco covering three walls of a chapel in the Medici Palace in Florence shows members of the Medici family and other contemporary individuals in a procession accompanying the biblical three wise men (*magi* in Italian) as they brought gifts to the infant Jesus. The painting was ordered in 1459 by Cosimo and Piero de' Medici, who had just finished building the family palace in the center of the city. Reflecting the self-confidence of his patrons, artist Bennozzo Gozzoli places the elderly Cosimo and Piero at the head of the procession, accompanied by their grooms. The group behind them includes Pope Pius II (in the last row in a red hat that ties under the chin) and the artist (in the second to the last row in a red hat with gold lettering). (Scala/Art Resource, NY)

Chapter 13
European Society in the Age of the Renaissance • 1350–1550

364

CHAPTER LOCATOR   How did politics and economics shape the Renaissance?

Better known by contemporaries than Thomas More was the Dutch humanist Desiderius Erasmus (dez-ih-DAYR-ee-us ih-RAZ-muhs) (1466?–1536) of Rotterdam. Erasmus's long list of publications includes *The Education of a Christian Prince* (1504), a book combining idealistic and practical suggestions for the formation of a ruler's character through the careful study of Plutarch, Aristotle, Cicero, and Plato; *The Praise of Folly* (1509), a satire of worldly wisdom and a plea for the simple and spontaneous Christian faith of children; and, most important, a critical edition of the Greek New Testament (1516). In the preface to the New Testament, Erasmus explained the purpose of his great work: "I wish that even the weakest woman should read the Gospel—should read the epistles of Paul. And I wish these were translated into all languages, so that they might be read and understood, not only by Scots and Irishmen, but also by Turks and Saracens."[4]

Two fundamental themes run through all of Erasmus's work. First, education is the means to reform, the key to moral and intellectual improvement. The core of education ought to be study of the Bible and the classics. Second, the essence of Erasmus's thought is, in his own phrase, "the philosophy of Christ." By this Erasmus meant that Christianity is an inner attitude of the heart or spirit. Christianity is not formalism, special ceremonies, or law; Christianity is Christ—his life and what he said and did, not what theologians have written.

The Printed Word

The fourteenth-century humanist Petrarch and the sixteenth-century humanist Erasmus had similar ideas about many things, but the immediate impact of their ideas was very different because of one thing: the printing press with movable metal type. The ideas of Petrarch were spread slowly from person to person by hand copying. The ideas of Erasmus were spread quickly through print, in which hundreds or thousands of identical copies could be made in a short time.

Printing with movable metal type developed in Germany in the 1440s as a combination of existing technologies. Several metalsmiths, most prominently Johan Gutenberg, recognized that the metal stamps used to mark signs on jewelry could be covered with ink and used to mark symbols onto a surface, in the same way that other craftsmen were using carved wood stamps to print books. (This woodblock printing technique originated in China and Korea centuries earlier.) Gutenberg and his assistants made stamps—later called *type*—for every letter of the alphabet and built racks that held the type in rows. This type could be rearranged for every page and so used over and over.

The printing revolution was also enabled by the ready availability of paper, which was also made using techniques that had originated in China and were brought into Europe

Printing Press In this reproduction of Gutenberg's printing press, metal type sits in a frame ready to be placed in the bottom part of the press, with a leather-covered ink ball nearby for spreading ink on the type. Paper was then placed over the type, and a heavy metal plate brought down onto the paper with a firm pull of the large wooden handle, a technology adapted from wine presses. (Erich Lessing/Art Resource, NY)

through Muslim Spain. By the fifteenth century the increase in urban literacy, the development of primary schools, and the opening of more universities had created an expanding market for reading materials of all types (see Chapter 12). Even before the printing revolution, professional copyists writing by hand and block-book makers, along with monks and nuns in monasteries, were already churning out reading materials on paper as fast as they could for the growing number of people who could read.

Gutenberg's invention involved no special secret technology or materials, and he was not the only one to recognize the huge market for books and set up a press (Map 13.2).

■ MAPPING THE PAST

Map 13.2 The Growth of Printing in Europe, 1448–1551

The speed with which artisans spread printing technology across Europe provides strong evidence for the growing demand for reading material. Presses in the Ottoman Empire were first established by Jewish immigrants who printed works in Hebrew, Greek, and Spanish.

ANALYZING THE MAP What part of Europe had the greatest number of printing presses by 1550? What explains this?

CONNECTIONS Printing was developed in response to a market for reading materials. Use Maps 11.2 and 11.3 (pages 294 and 302) to help explain why printing spread the way it did.

To complete this activity online, go to the Online Study Guide at bedfordstmartins.com/mckaywestunderstanding.

Historians estimate that, within a half century of the publication of Gutenberg's Bible in 1456, somewhere between 8 million and 20 million books were printed in Europe. Whatever the actual figure, the number is far greater than the number of books produced in all of Western history up to that point.

The effects of the invention of movable-type printing were not felt overnight. Nevertheless, movable type brought about radical changes, transforming both the private and the public lives of Europeans. Print shops were gathering places for people interested in new ideas. Though printers were trained through apprenticeships just like blacksmiths or butchers, they had connections to the world of politics, art, and scholarship that other craftsmen did not.

Printing gave hundreds or even thousands of people identical books, so that they could more easily discuss the ideas that the books contained with one another in person or through letters. Printed materials reached an invisible public, allowing silent individuals to join causes and groups of individuals widely separated by geography to form a common identity. This new group consciousness could compete with older, localized loyalties.

Government and church leaders both used and worried about printing. They printed government documents, and they also attempted to censor books and authors whose ideas they thought were wrong. Such censorship was not, however, very effective and books were printed secretly and smuggled all over Europe.

Printing also stimulated the literacy of laypeople and eventually came to have a deep effect on their private lives. Printers produced anything that would sell. They printed professional reference sets for lawyers, doctors, and students, and historical romances, biographies, and how-to manuals for the general public. They discovered that illustrations increased a book's sales, so they published books on a wide range of topics—from history to pornography—full of woodcuts and engravings. Single-page broadsides and flysheets allowed great public events and "wonders" to be experienced vicariously by a stay-at-home readership. Since books and other printed materials were read aloud to illiterate listeners, print bridged the gap between the written and oral cultures.

▼ How did changes in art reflect new Renaissance ideals?

No feature of the Renaissance evokes greater admiration than its artistic masterpieces. In all the arts, the city of Florence led the way. But Florence was not the only artistic center, for Rome and Venice also became important, and northern Europeans perfected their own styles.

Patronage and Power

As we saw earlier in this chapter, powerful urban groups often commissioned works of art in early Renaissance Italy. The Florentine cloth merchants, for example, delegated Filippo Brunelleschi (fihl-EEP-oh broo-nayl-LAYS-kee) to build the magnificent dome on the cathedral of Florence and selected Lorenzo Ghiberti (law-REHN-tsoh gee-BEHR-tee) to design the bronze doors of the adjacent Baptistery, a separate building in which baptisms were performed. These works represented the merchants' dominant influence in the community.

Increasingly in the later fifteenth century, wealthy individuals and rulers, rather than corporate groups, sponsored works of art. Such men spent vast sums on the arts as a means of glorifying themselves and their families. Writing in about 1470, Florentine ruler Lorenzo de' Medici declared that his family had spent hundreds of thousands of

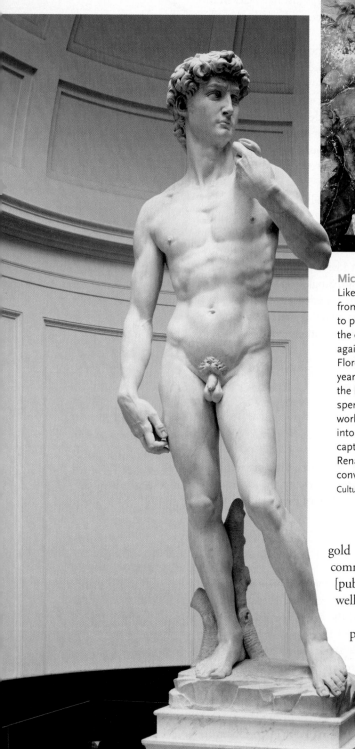

Michelangelo's *David* (1501–1504) and the *Last Judgment* (detail, 1537–1541) Like all Renaissance artists, Michelangelo worked largely on commissions from patrons. Officials of the city of Florence contracted the young sculptor to produce a statue of the Old Testament hero David (left) to be displayed on the city's main square. Michelangelo portrayed David anticipating his fight against the giant Goliath, and the statue came to symbolize the republic of Florence standing up to its larger and more powerful enemies. More than thirty years later, Michelangelo was commissioned by the pope to paint a scene of the Last Judgment on the altar wall of the Sistine Chapel, where he had earlier spent four years covering the ceiling with magnificent frescoes. The massive work shows a powerful Christ standing in judgment, with souls ascending into Heaven while others are dragged by demons into Hell (above). The *David* captures ideals of human perfection and has come to be an iconic symbol of Renaissance artistic brilliance, while the dramatic and violent *Last Judgment* conveys both terror and divine power. (sculpture: Scala/Ministero per i Beni e le Attività Culturali/Art Resource, NY; painting: Alinari/The Bridgeman Art Library)

gold florins for artistic and architectural commissions, but commented, "I think it casts a brilliant light on our estate [public reputation] and it seems to me that the monies were well spent and I am very pleased with this."[5]

Patrons varied in their level of involvement as a work progressed; some simply ordered a specific subject or scene, while others oversaw the work of the artist or architect very closely. For example, Pope Julius II (pontificate 1503–1513), who commissioned Michelangelo to paint the ceiling of the Vatican's Sistine Chapel in Rome in 1508, demanded that the artist work as fast as he could and frequently visited him at his work with suggestions and criticisms.

Chapter 13
European Society in the Age of
368   **the Renaissance • 1350–1550**

CHAPTER LOCATOR   How did politics and economics shape the Renaissance?

In addition to power, art reveals changing patterns of consumption among the nobility and wealthy merchants in Renaissance Italy. In the rural world of the Middle Ages, society had been organized for war, and men of wealth spent their money on military gear. As Italian nobles settled in towns (see Chapter 11), they adjusted to an urban culture. Rather than employing knights for warfare, cities hired mercenaries. Expenditure on military hardware declined. For the rich merchant or the noble recently arrived from the countryside, a grand urban palace, along with its furnishings and decorations, represented the greatest outlay of cash. By the late sixteenth century the Strozzi banking family of Florence spent even more on household goods than they did on clothing, jewelry, or food, though these were increasingly elaborate as well.

Changing Artistic Styles

The content and style of Renaissance art were often different from those of the Middle Ages. Religious topics remained popular among both patrons and artists, but frequently the patron had himself and his family portrayed in the scene. As the fifteenth century advanced and humanist ideas spread more widely, classical themes and motifs, such as the lives and loves of pagan gods and goddesses, figured increasingly in painting and sculpture, with the facial features of the gods sometimes modeled on living people.

The individual portrait emerged as a distinct artistic genre. Rather than reflecting a spiritual ideal, as medieval painting and sculpture tended to do, Renaissance portraits showed human ideals, often portrayed in a more realistic style. Florentine painters led the way in the use of realism and perspective, the linear representation of distance and space on a flat surface. The sculptor Donatello (1386–1466) revived the classical figure, with its balance and self-awareness. In architecture, Filippo Brunelleschi (1377–1446) looked to the classical past for inspiration, designing a hospital for orphans and foundlings in which all proportions were carefully thought out to achieve a sense of balance and harmony.

Art produced in northern Europe in the fourteenth and fifteenth centuries tended to be more religious in orientation than that produced in Italy. Some Flemish painters, notably Rogier van der Weyden (1399/1400–1464) and Jan van Eyck (1366–1441), were considered the artistic equals of Italian painters and were much admired in Italy. Northern architecture, however, was little influenced by the classical revival so obvious in Renaissance Italy.

Descent from the Cross, ca. 1435
Taking as his subject the suffering and death of Jesus, a popular theme of Netherlandish piety, Rogier van der Weyden shows Christ's descent from the cross, surrounded by nine sorrowing figures. An appreciation of human anatomy, the rich fabrics of the clothes, and the pierced and bloody hands of Jesus were all intended to touch the viewers' emotions. (Museo del Prado/Scala/Art Resource, NY)

In the early sixteenth century the center of the new art shifted from Florence to Rome, where wealthy cardinals and popes wanted visual expression of the church's and their own families' power and piety. Pope Julius II tore down the old Saint Peter's Basilica and began work on the present structure in 1506. Michelangelo went to Rome from Florence in about 1500 and began the series of statues, paintings, and architectural projects from which he gained an international reputation, most famously, the dome for Saint Peter's and the ceiling and altar wall of the nearby Sistine Chapel.

Raphael Sanzio (1483–1520), another Florentine, got the commission for frescoes in the papal apartments, and in his relatively short life he painted hundreds of portraits and devotional images. Raphael (RAF-ee-uhl) also oversaw a large workshop with many collaborators and apprentices and wrote treatises on his philosophy of art in which he emphasized the importance of imitating nature and developing an orderly sequence of design and proportion.

Venice became another artistic center in the sixteenth century. Titian (TIH-shuhn) (1490–1576) and other sixteenth-century painters developed an artistic style known in English as "mannerism" (from *maniera* or "style" in Italian) in which artists sometimes distorted figures, exaggerated musculature, and heightened color to express emotion and drama more intently. (Michelangelo's painting of the Last Judgment in the Sistine Chapel, shown on page 368, is painted in the mannerist style.)

The Renaissance Artist

Some patrons rewarded certain artists very well, and some artists gained great public acclaim. This adulation of the artist has led many historians to view the Renaissance as the beginning of the concept of the artist as having a special talent. In the Middle Ages people believed that only God created, albeit through individuals; the medieval conception recognized no particular value in artistic originality. Renaissance artists and humanists came to think that a work of art was the deliberate creation of a unique personality who transcended traditions, rules, and theories. Michelangelo and Leonardo da Vinci perhaps best embody the new concept of the Renaissance artist as genius. (See "Individuals in Society: Leonardo da Vinci," page 372.)

It is important not to overemphasize the Renaissance notion of genius. As certain artists became popular and well-known, they could assert their own artistic styles and pay less attention to the wishes of patrons, but even major artists generally worked according to the patron's specific guidelines. Whether in Italy or northern Europe, most Renaissance artists trained in the workshops of older artists. Though they might be men of genius, artists were still expected to be well trained in proper artistic techniques and stylistic conventions, for the notion that artistic genius could show up in the work of an untrained artist did not emerge until the twentieth century. Beginning artists spent years copying drawings and paintings, learning how to prepare paint and other artistic materials, and, by the sixteenth century, reading books about design and composition. Younger artists gathered together in the evenings for further drawing practice. By the later sixteenth century some of these informal groups had turned into more formal artistic "academies," the first of which was begun in 1563 in Florence by Vasari under the patronage of the Medicis.

All the most famous and most prolific Renaissance artists were male. The types of art in which more women were active, such as textiles, needlework, and painting on porcelain, were not regarded as "major arts," but only as "minor" or "decorative" arts. Nonetheless, several women did become well-known as painters in their day. Stylistically, their works are different from one another, but their careers show many similarities. The majority of female painters were the daughters of painters or of minor noblemen with ties to artistic circles. Many were eldest daughters or came from families in which there were no sons, so their fathers took unusual interest in their careers. Many women began their

Chapter 13
European Society in the Age of
370   the Renaissance • 1350–1550

CHAPTER LOCATOR | How did politics and economics shape the Renaissance?

Botticelli, *Primavera* (Spring), ca. 1482 Framed by a grove of orange trees, Venus, goddess of love, is flanked on her right by Flora, goddess of flowers and fertility, and on her left by the Three Graces, goddesses of banquets, dance, and social occasions. Above, Venus's son Cupid, the god of love, shoots darts of desire, while at the far right the wind god Zephyrus chases the nymph Chloris. The entire scene rests on classical mythology, though some art historians claim that Venus is an allegory for the Virgin Mary. Botticelli captured the ideal for female beauty in the Renaissance: slender, with pale skin, a high forehead, red-blond hair, and sloping shoulders. (Digital image © The Museum of Modern Art/Licensed by Scala/Art Resource, NY)

careers before they were twenty and produced far fewer paintings after they married, or stopped painting entirely. Women were not allowed to study the male nude, which was viewed as essential if one wanted to paint large history or biblical paintings with many figures. Women could also not learn the technique of fresco, in which colors are applied directly to wet plaster walls, because such works had to be done in public, which was judged inappropriate for women. Joining a group of male artists for informal practice was also seen as improper, and the artistic academies that were established were for men only. Like universities, humanist academies, and most craft guild shops, artistic workshops were male-only settings in which men of different ages came together for training and created bonds of friendship, influence, patronage, and sometimes intimacy.

Women were not alone in being excluded from the institutions of Renaissance culture. Though a few rare men of genius such as Leonardo and Michelangelo emerged from artisanal backgrounds, most scholars and artists came from families with at least some money. Renaissance culture did not influence the lives of most people in cities and did not affect life in the villages at all. A small, highly educated minority of literary humanists and artists created the culture of and for an exclusive elite. The Renaissance maintained, or indeed enhanced, a gulf between the learned minority and the uneducated multitude that has survived for many centuries.

What new ideas were associated with the Renaissance?

How did changes in art reflect new Renaissance ideals?

What were the key social hierarchies in Renaissance Europe?

How did nation-states evolve in this period?

Lady with an Ermine. The enigmatic smile and smoky quality of this portrait can be found in many of Leonardo's works.
(Czartoryski Museum, Kraków/The Bridgeman Art Library)

WHAT MAKES A GENIUS? A DEEP CURIOSITY
about an extensive variety of subjects? A divine spark that emerges in talents that far exceed the norm? Or is it just "one percent inspiration and ninety-nine percent perspiration," as Thomas Edison said. However it is defined, Leonardo da Vinci counts as a genius. In fact, Leonardo was one of the individuals whom the Renaissance label "genius" was designed to describe: a special kind of human being with exceptional creative powers. Leonardo (who, despite the title of a recent bestseller, is always called by his first name) was born in Vinci, near Florence, the illegitimate son of Caterina, a local peasant girl, and Ser Piero da Vinci, a notary public. Caterina later married another native of Vinci. When Ser Piero's marriage to Donna Albrussia produced no children, he and his wife took in Leonardo. Ser Piero secured Leonardo's apprenticeship with the painter and sculptor Andrea del Verrocchio in Florence. In 1472, when Leonardo was just twenty years old, he was listed as a master in Florence's "Company of Artists."

Leonardo's most famous portrait, *Mona Lisa*, shows a woman with an enigmatic smile that Giorgio Vasari described as "so pleasing that it seemed divine rather than human." The portrait, probably of the young wife of a rich Florentine merchant (her exact identity is hotly debated), may actually be the best known painting in the history of art. One of its competitors in that designation would be another work of Leonardo's, *The Last Supper*, which has been called "the most revered painting in the world."

Leonardo's reputation as a genius does not rest simply on his paintings, however, which are actually few in number, but rather on the breadth of his abilities and interests. He is often understood to be the first "Renaissance man," a phrase we still use for a multitalented individual. He wanted to reproduce what the eye can see, and he drew everything he saw around him, including executed criminals hanging on gallows as well as the beauties of nature. Trying to understand how the human body worked, Leonardo studied live and dead bodies, doing autopsies and dissections to investigate muscles and circulation. He carefully analyzed the effects of light, and he experimented with perspective.

Leonardo used his drawings as the basis for his paintings and also as a tool of scientific investigation. He drew plans for hundreds of inventions, many of which would become reality centuries later, such as the helicopter, tank, machine gun, and parachute. He was hired by one of the powerful new rulers in Italy, Duke Ludovico Sforza of Milan, to design weapons, fortresses, and water systems, as well as to produce works of art. Leonardo left Milan when Sforza was overthrown in war and spent the last years of his life painting, drawing, and designing for the pope and the French king.

Leonardo experimented with new materials for painting and sculpture, some of which worked and some of which did not. The experimental method he used to paint *The Last Supper* caused the picture to deteriorate rapidly, and it began to flake off the wall as soon as it was finished. Leonardo regarded it as never quite completed, for he could not find a model for the face of Christ who would evoke the spiritual depth he felt the figure deserved. His gigantic equestrian statue in honor of Ludovico's father, Duke Francesco Sforza, was never made, and the clay model collapsed. He planned to write books on many subjects but never finished any of them, leaving only notebooks. Leonardo once said that "a painter is not admirable unless he is universal." The patrons who supported him — and he was supported very well — perhaps wished that his inspirations would have been a bit less universal in scope, or at least accompanied by more perspiration.

Sources: Giorgio Vasari, *Lives of the Artists*, vol. 1, trans. G. Bull (London: Penguin Books, 1965); S. B. Nuland, *Leonardo da Vinci* (New York: Lipper/Viking, 2000).

QUESTIONS FOR ANALYSIS

1. In what ways do the notion of a "genius" and of a "Renaissance man" both support and contradict one another? Which better fits Leonardo?
2. Has the idea of artistic genius changed since the Renaissance? How?

Chapter 13
European Society in the Age of
372   **the Renaissance • 1350–1550**

CHAPTER LOCATOR | How did politics and economics shape the Renaissance?

Esther Before Ahasuerus, ca. 1630 In this oil painting, Artemisia Gentileschi shows an Old Testament scene of the Jewish woman Esther who saved her people from being killed by her husband, King Ahasuerus. This deliverance is celebrated in the Jewish holiday of Purim. The elaborate clothes shown are of the type worn in Renaissance courts. As was typical for female painters of her day, Gentileschi was trained by her father. She mastered the dramatic style favored in the early seventeenth century and became known especially for her portraits of strong biblical and mythological heroines. (Image copyright © The Metropolitan Museum of Art/Art Resource, NY)

▼ What were the key social hierarchies in Renaissance Europe?

The division between educated and uneducated people was only one of many social hierarchies evident in the Renaissance. Social hierarchies in the Renaissance built on the orders of the Middle Ages — those who fight, pray, and work — but they also developed new features that contributed to modern social hierarchies, such as those of race, class, and gender.

Race and Slavery

Renaissance people did not use the word *race* the way we do, but often used "race," "people," and "nation" interchangeably for ethnic, national, religious, or other groups. They did make distinctions based on skin color that provide some of the background for later conceptualizations of race, but these distinctions were interwoven with other characteristics when people thought about human differences.

Ever since the time of the Roman republic, a small number of black Africans had lived in western Europe. They had come, along with white slaves, as the spoils of war. Even after the collapse of the Roman Empire, Muslim and Christian merchants continued to

African Slaves in Europe, 1400–1550	
ca. 1400–1450	Portuguese sailors bring about a thousand Africans a year to Mediterranean ports.
ca. 1450–1500	Flow of African slaves increases to many thousands per year.
ca. 1530	Between four thousand and five thousand African slaves are sold to the Portuguese each year.
ca. 1550	Blacks, slave and free, constitute about 10 percent of the population of the Portuguese cities of Lisbon and Évora and roughly 3 percent of the Portuguese population overall.

import them. And, beginning in the fifteenth century, sizable numbers of black slaves entered Europe.

Although blacks were concentrated in the Iberian Peninsula, there must have been some Africans in northern Europe as well. In the 1580s, for example, Queen Elizabeth I of England complained that there were too many "blackamoores" competing with needy English people for places as domestic servants. Black servants were much sought after; the medieval interest in curiosities, the exotic, and the marvelous continued in the Renaissance. Italian aristocrats had their portraits painted with their black pageboys to indicate their wealth. Blacks were so greatly in demand at the Renaissance courts of northern Italy, in fact, that the Venetians defied papal threats of excommunication to secure them.

In Portugal, Spain, and Italy slaves supplemented the labor force in virtually all occupations—as servants, agricultural laborers, craftsmen, and seamen on ships going to Lisbon and Africa. Agriculture in Europe did not involve large plantations, so large-scale agricultural slavery did not develop there as it would in the late fifteenth century in the New World.

Until the voyages down the African coast in the late fifteenth century, Europeans had little concrete knowledge of Africans and their cultures. They perceived Africa as a remote place, the home of strange people isolated by heresy and Islam from superior European civilization. Africans' contact, even as slaves, with Christian Europeans could only "improve" the blacks, they thought. The expanding slave trade reinforced negative preconceptions about the inferiority of black Africans.

Wealth and the Nobility

The word *class*—working class, middle class, upper class—was not used in the Renaissance to describe social divisions, but by the thirteenth century, and even more so by the fifteenth, the idea of a hierarchy based on wealth was emerging alongside the medieval concept of orders (see Chapter 10). This was particularly true in towns. Most residents of towns were technically members of the "third order," that is "those who work." However, this group now included rich merchants whose wealth rivaled the richest nobles. As we saw earlier, in many cities these merchants had gained political power to match their economic might, becoming merchant oligarchs who ruled through city councils. This hierarchy of wealth was more

Laura de Dianti, 1523 The Venetian artist Titian shows a young Italian woman with a gorgeous blue dress and an elaborate pearl and feather headdress, accompanied by a young black page with a gold earring. Both the African page and the headdress connect the portrait's subject with the exotic, though slaves from Africa and the Ottoman Empire were actually common in wealthy Venetian households. (Courtesy, Heinz Kisters Collection)

374

Chapter 13
European Society in the Age of
the Renaissance • 1350–1550

CHAPTER LOCATOR | How did politics and economics shape the Renaissance?

changeable than the hierarchy of orders, allowing individuals and families to rise—and fall—within one generation.

The development of a hierarchy of wealth did not mean an end to the hierarchy of orders, however, and even poorer nobility still had higher status than wealthy commoners. Thus, wealthy Italian merchants bought noble titles and country villas, and wealthy English and Spanish merchants were eager to marry their daughters and sons into often-impoverished noble families. The nobility maintained its status in most parts of Europe not by maintaining rigid boundaries, but by taking in and integrating the new social elite of wealth.

Gender Roles

Renaissance people would not have understood the word *gender* to refer to categories of people, but they would have easily grasped the concept. Toward the end of the four-teenth century, learned men (and a few women) began what was termed the **debate about women**, a debate about women's character and nature that would last for centu-ries. Misogynist (muh-SAH-juh-nihst) critiques of women from both clerical and secular authors denounced females as devious, domineering, and demanding. In answer, sev-eral authors compiled lists of famous and praiseworthy women. Christine de Pizan was among the writers who were not only interested in defending women, but also in explor-ing the reasons behind women's secondary status. (See "Listening to the Past: Christine de Pizan, Advice to the Wives of Artisans," page 342, and "Listening to the Past: Perspec-tives on Humanist Learning and Women," page 362.)

Beginning in the sixteenth century, the debate about women also became a debate about female rulers, sparked primarily by dynastic accidents in many countries, including Spain, England, France, and Scotland, which led to women serving as advisers to child kings or ruling in their own right. The questions were vig-orously and at times viciously disputed. They di-rectly concerned the social construction of gender. Which was (or should be) the stronger determi-nant of character and social role, gender or rank? Despite a prevailing sentiment that women were not as fit to rule as men, there were no successful rebellions against female rulers simply because they were women, but in part this was because female rulers emphasized qualities regarded as masculine—physical bravery, stamina, wisdom, duty—whenever they appeared in public.

Ideas about women's and men's proper roles de-termined the actions of ordinary men and women even more forcefully. The dominant notion of the "true" man was that of the married head of

debate about women Debate among writers and thinkers in the Renaissance about women's qualities and proper role in society.

Phyllis Riding Aristotle Among the many scenes that expressed the debate about women visually were woodcuts, engravings, paintings, and even cups and plates that showed the classical philosopher Aristotle as an old man being ridden by the young beautiful Phyllis (shown here in a German woodcut). The origins of the story are uncertain, but in the Renaissance everyone knew the tale of how Aristotle's infatuation with Phyllis led to his ridicule. Male moralists used it as a warning about the power of women's sexual allure, though women may have interpreted it differently. (Réunion des Musées Nationaux/Art Resource, NY)

household, so men whose social status and age would have normally conferred political power but who remained unmarried did not participate to the same level as their married brothers. Unmarried men in Venice, for example, could not be part of the ruling council.

Women were also understood as either "married or to be married," even if the actual marriage patterns in Europe left many women (and men) unmarried until quite late in life (see Chapter 12). This meant that women's work was not viewed as supporting a family—even if it did—and was valued less than men's. If they worked for wages, and many women did, women earned about half to two-thirds of what men did even for the same work.

The maintenance of appropriate power relationships between men and women, with men dominant and women subordinate, served as a symbol of the proper functioning of society as a whole. Disorder in the proper gender hierarchy was linked with social upheaval and was viewed as threatening. Of all the ways in which Renaissance society was hierarchically arranged—social rank, age, level of education, race, occupation—gender was regarded as the most "natural" and therefore the most important to defend.

▼ How did nation-states evolve in this period?

The High Middle Ages had witnessed the origins of many of the basic institutions of the modern state. Sheriffs, inquests, juries, circuit judges, professional bureaucracies, and representative assemblies all trace their origins to the twelfth and thirteenth centuries. The linchpin for the development of states, however, was strong monarchy, and during the period of the Hundred Years' War, no ruler in western Europe was able to provide effective leadership. The resurgent power of feudal nobilities weakened the centralizing work begun earlier.

Beginning in the fifteenth century rulers utilized aggressive methods to rebuild their governments. First in the regional states of Italy, then in the expanding monarchies of France, England, and Spain, rulers began the work of reducing violence, curbing unruly nobles, and establishing domestic order.

France

The Black Death and the Hundred Years' War left France drastically depopulated, commercially ruined, and agriculturally weak. Nonetheless, Charles VII (r. 1422–1461), the ruler whom Joan of Arc had seen crowned at Reims, revived the monarchy and France. He seemed an unlikely person to do so. Frail and indecisive, Charles VII nevertheless began France's long recovery.

Charles reconciled the Burgundians and Armagnacs (ahr-muhn-YAKZ), who had been waging civil war for thirty years. By 1453 French armies had expelled the English from French soil except in Calais. Charles reorganized the royal council, giving increased influence to lawyers and bankers, and strengthened royal finances through the imposition of new taxes.

By establishing regular companies of cavalry and archers, Charles created the first permanent royal army. His son Louis XI (r. 1461–1483) improved upon Charles's army and

The Expansion of France, 1475–1500

HOLY ROMAN EMPIRE

• Paris

FRANCE

SPAIN

- ☐ Crown lands, ca. 1475
- ☐ Territory added by 1483
- ☐ Territory added by 1498
- ☐ Independent fiefs
- — Boundary of France, ca. 1500

Chapter 13
European Society in the Age of the Renaissance • 1350–1550

376

CHAPTER LOCATOR   How did politics and economics shape the Renaissance?

used it to control the nobles' separate militias and to curb urban independence. The army was also employed in 1477 when Louis conquered Burgundy upon the death of its ruler Charles the Bold. Three years later, the extinction of the house of Anjou (AN-joo) with the death of its last legitimate male heir brought Louis the counties of Anjou, Bar, Maine, and Provence.

Two further developments strengthened the French monarchy. The marriage of Louis XII (r. 1498–1515) and Anne of Brittany added the large western duchy of Brittany to the state. Then the French king Francis I and Pope Leo X reached a mutually satisfactory agreement about church and state powers in 1516. The new treaty, the Concordat of Bologna, approved the pope's right to receive the first year's income of new bishops and abbots. In return, Leo X recognized the French ruler's right to select French bishops and abbots. French kings thereafter effectively controlled the appointment and thus the policies of church officials in the kingdom.

England

English society also suffered severely from the disorders of the fifteenth century. The aristocracy dominated the government of Henry IV (r. 1399–1413) and indulged in disruptive violence at the local level. Population continued to decline. Between 1455 and 1471 adherents of the ducal houses of York and Lancaster waged civil war, commonly called the Wars of the Roses. The chronic disorder hurt trade, agriculture, and domestic industry. Under the pious but mentally disturbed Henry VI (r. 1422–1461), the authority of the monarchy sank lower than it had been in centuries.

The Yorkist Edward IV (r. 1461–1483) began establishing domestic tranquility. He succeeded in defeating the Lancastrian forces and after 1471 began to reconstruct the monarchy. Edward, his brother Richard III (r. 1483–1485), and Henry VII (r. 1485–1509) of the Welsh house of Tudor worked to restore royal prestige, to crush the power of the nobility, and to establish order and law at the local level.

Edward IV and subsequently the Tudors, excepting Henry VIII, conducted foreign policy on the basis of diplomacy, avoiding expensive wars. Thus the English monarchy did not depend on Parliament for money, and the Crown undercut that source of aristocratic influence.

Under Henry VII, the center of royal authority was the royal council, which governed at the national level. There Henry VII revealed his distrust of the nobility: though not completely excluded, very few great lords were among the king's closest advisers. Instead he chose men from among the smaller landowners and urban residents trained in law. The council conducted negotiations with foreign governments and secured international recognition of the Tudor dynasty through the marriage in 1501 of Henry VII's eldest son Arthur to Catherine of Aragon, the daughter of Ferdinand and Isabella of Spain. The council dealt with real or potential aristocratic threats through a judicial offshoot, the Court of Star Chamber. Persons brought before this court were not entitled to see evidence against them; sessions were secret; torture could be applied to extract confessions; and juries were not called. These procedures ran directly counter to English common-law precedents, but they effectively reduced aristocratic troublemaking.

When Henry VII died in 1509, he left a country at peace both domestically and internationally, a substantially augmented treasury, an expanding wool trade, and the dignity and role of the royal majesty much enhanced.

Spain

While England and France laid the foundations of unified nation-states during the Middle Ages, Spain remained a conglomerate of independent kingdoms. By the middle of the fifteenth century, the kingdoms of Castile and Aragon had become dominant; and the

Iberian Peninsula, with the exception of Granada, had been won for Christianity. But even the wedding in 1469 of Isabella of Castile and Ferdinand of Aragon did not bring about administrative unity. Rather, their marriage constituted a dynastic union of two royal houses, not the political union of two peoples. Although Ferdinand and Isabella (r. 1474–1516) pursued a common foreign policy, until about 1700 Spain existed as a loose confederation of separate kingdoms, each maintaining its own cortes (parliament), laws, courts, and systems of coinage and taxation (Map 13.3).

Ferdinand and Isabella were able to exert their authority in ways similar to the rulers of France and England, however. They curbed aristocratic power by excluding high nobles from the royal council, instead appointing lesser landowners. The council and various government boards recruited men trained in Roman law, which exalted the power

Map 13.3 The Unification of Spain and the Expulsion of the Jews, Fifteenth Century
The marriage of Ferdinand of Aragon and Isabella of Castile in 1469 brought most of the Iberian peninsula under one monarchy, although different parts of Spain retained distinct cultures, languages, and legal systems. In 1492 Ferdinand and Isabella conquered Granada, where most people were Muslim, and expelled the Jews from all of Spain. Spanish Jews resettled in cities of Europe and the Mediterranean that allowed them in, including many in Muslim states such as the Ottoman Empire. Muslims were also expelled from Spain over the course of the sixteenth and early seventeenth centuries.

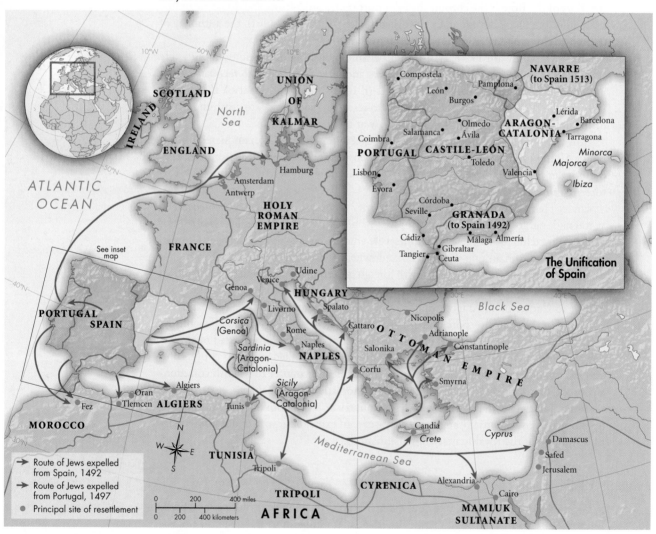

Chapter 13
European Society in the Age of the Renaissance • 1350–1550

378

CHAPTER LOCATOR   How did politics and economics shape the Renaissance?

■ **PICTURING THE PAST**

Tax Collectors

New types of taxes, and more effective methods of tax collection, were essential to the growth of Renaissance states, but they were often highly unpopular. In this painting from about 1540 the Dutch artist Marinus van Reymerswaele depicts two tax collectors as they count their take and record it in a ledger. Tax collectors were men of middling status, but here they are wearing clothing more appropriate for nobles.

ANALYZING THE IMAGE What elements of the men's clothing suggests wealth? How would you describe the expressions on their faces? What does the painting suggest about the artist's opinion of tax collectors?

CONNECTIONS In Spain converso tax collectors were widely resented. What were some of the reasons behind this resentment? What public event was an outgrowth of this hatred, and what were its aims?

To complete this activity online, go to the Online Study Guide at bedfordstmartins.com/mckaywestunderstanding.

What new ideas were associated with the Renaissance?

How did changes in art reflect new Renaissance ideals?

What were the key social hierarchies in Renaissance Europe?

How did nation-states evolve in this period?

of the Crown. They also secured from the Spanish Borgia pope Alexander VI the right to appoint bishops in Spain and in the Hispanic territories in America, enabling them to establish the equivalent of a national church. With the revenues from ecclesiastical estates, they were able to expand their territories to include the remaining land held by Arabs in southern Spain. The victorious entry of Ferdinand and Isabella into Granada on January 6, 1492, signaled the conclusion of the reconquista (see Map 9.3 on page 238).

There still remained a sizable and, in the view of the majority of the Spanish people, potentially dangerous minority, the Jews. When the kings of France and England had expelled the Jews from their kingdoms (see Chapter 9), many had sought refuge in Spain. During the long centuries of the reconquista, Christian kings had renewed Jewish rights and privileges; in fact, Jewish industry, intelligence, and money had supported royal power. While Christians borrowed from Jewish moneylenders and while all who could afford them sought Jewish physicians, a strong undercurrent of resentment of Jewish influence and wealth festered.

In the fourteenth century anti-Semitism in Spain was aggravated by anti-Jewish preaching, by economic dislocation, and by the search for a scapegoat during the Black Death. Anti-Semitic pogroms swept the towns of Spain, and perhaps 40 percent of the Jewish population was killed or forced to convert. Those converted were called *conversos* or New Christians. Conversos were often well educated and held prominent positions in government, the church, medicine, law, and business. Numbering perhaps two hundred thousand in a total Spanish population of about 7.5 million, New Christians and Jews in fifteenth-century Spain exercised influence disproportionate to their numbers.

Such successes bred resentment and many doubted the sincerity of the New Christians' conversions. Queen Isabella shared these suspicions, and she and Ferdinand had received permission from Pope Sixtus IV in 1478 to establish their own Inquisition. Investigations and trials began immediately, as officials of the Inquisition looked for conversos who showed any sign of incomplete conversion.

Officials of the Inquisition developed a new type of anti-Semitism. A person's status as a Jew, they argued, could not be changed by religious conversion, because it was in the person's blood and was heritable, so Jews could never be true Christians. In what were known as "purity of blood" laws, having pure Christian blood became a requirement for noble status. Ideas about Jews developed in Spain were important components in European concepts of race, and discussions of "Jewish blood" later expanded into notions of the "Jewish race."

In 1492, shortly after the conquest of Granada, Isabella and Ferdinand issued an edict expelling all practicing Jews from Spain. Many Muslims in Granada were forcibly baptized and became another type of New Christian investigated by the Inquisition. Absolute religious orthodoxy and purity of blood served as the theoretical foundation of the Spanish national state.

The Spanish national state rested on marital politics as well as military victories and religious courts. In 1496 Ferdinand and Isabella married their second daughter Joanna, heiress to Castile, to the archduke Philip, heir to the Burgundian Netherlands and the Holy Roman Empire. Philip and Joanna's son, Charles V (r. 1519–1556), thus succeeded to a vast inheritance. When Charles's son Philip II joined Portugal to the Spanish crown in 1580, the Iberian Peninsula was at last politically united.

New Christians A term applied to Jews and Muslims who accepted Christianity; in many cases they included Christians whose families had converted centuries earlier.

Chapter 13
European Society in the Age of
380   the Renaissance • 1350–1550

CHAPTER LOCATOR   How did politics and economics shape the Renaissance?

←LOOKING BACK LOOKING AHEAD →

THE ART HISTORIAN Giorgio Vasari, who first called this era the Renaissance, thought that his contemporaries had both revived the classical past and gone beyond it. Vasari's judgment was echoed for centuries, as the art, architecture, educational ideas, social structures, and attitude toward life of the Renaissance were set in sharp contrast with those of the Middle Ages: whereas the Middle Ages were corporate and religious, the Renaissance was individualistic and secular. More recently, historians and other scholars have stressed continuity as well as change. Families, kin networks, guilds, and other corporate groups remained important in the Renaissance, and religious belief remained firm. This reevaluation changes our view of the relationship between the Middle Ages and the Renaissance. It may also change our view of the relationship between the Renaissance and the dramatic changes in religion that occurred in Europe in the sixteenth century. Those religious changes, the Reformation, used to be viewed as a rejection of the values of the Renaissance and a return to the intense concern with religion of the Middle Ages. This idea of the Reformation as a sort of counter-Renaissance may be true to some degree, but there are powerful continuities as well. Both movements looked back to a time they regarded as purer and better than their own, and both offered opportunities for strong individuals to shape their world in unexpected ways. ■

- **For a list of suggested readings for this chapter, visit** *bedfordstmartins.com/mckaywestunderstanding*.

- **For primary sources from this period, see** *Sources of Western Society, Second Edition.*

- **For Web sites, images, and documents related to topics in this chapter, see Make History at** *bedfordstmartins.com/mckaywestunderstanding*.

What new ideas were associated with the Renaissance?

How did changes in art reflect new Renaissance ideals?

What were the key social hierarchies in Renaissance Europe?

How did nation-states evolve in this period?

▪ Chapter 13 Study Guide

Online Study Guide
bedfordstmartins.com/mckaywestunderstanding

Step 1 — GETTING STARTED

GETTING STARTED Below are basic terms about this period in Western civilization. Can you identify each term below and explain why it matters? To do this exercise online, go to bedfordstmartins.com/mckaywestunderstanding.

TERMS	WHO (OR WHAT) AND WHEN	WHY IT MATTERS
Renaissance, p. 354		
patronage, p. 354		
communes, p. 355		
popolo, p. 355		
signori, p. 355		
courts, p. 355		
humanism, p. 359		
virtù, p. 359		
Christian humanists, p. 364		
debate about women, p. 375		
New Christians, p. 380		

Step 2 — MOVING BEYOND THE BASICS

MOVING BEYOND THE BASICS The exercise below requires a more advanced understanding of the chapter material. Examine the broad historical context of the Italian Renaissance by filling in the chart below with descriptions of the social, economic, political, and cultural roots of the Renaissance. When you are finished, consider the following questions: What key differences between Italy and the rest of Europe explain the fact that the Renaissance began in the city-states of Italy, and not in one of the western monarchies? To do this exercise online, go to bedfordstmartins.com/mckaywestunderstanding.

	SOCIAL	ECONOMIC	POLITICAL	CULTURAL
The Roots of the Renaissance				

Step 3

PUTTING IT ALL TOGETHER

Now that you've reviewed key elements of the chapter, take a step back and try to see the big picture. Remember to use specific examples from the chapter in your answers. To do this exercise online, go to bedfordstmartins.com/mckaywestunderstanding.

RENAISSANCE ITALY

- How did the growth of international trade shape the political development of Italy? How might international connections have also helped foster the Renaissance?

- Compare and contrast the city-states of Renaissance Italy and ancient Greece. What similar patterns and challenges emerged in both contexts?

INTELLECTUAL AND ARTISTIC DEVELOPMENTS

- Compare and contrast the way medieval and Renaissance scholars viewed the classical world. What important differences do you note?

- What might explain the Renaissance interest in artistic "genius"? What does this interest tell you about the values and beliefs of Renaissance thinkers and writers?

SOCIAL HIERARCHY IN RENAISSANCE EUROPE

- What did Renaissance Europeans mean by the term *race*? How does their definition differ from your own understanding of the term?

- What might explain the increased interest in the differences between men and women during the Renaissance? Can you connect the "debate about women" to larger intellectual trends?

POLITICS AND THE STATE

- How did the monarchs of England, France, and Spain use royal councils to augment their own power? What does the use of such councils tell you about the common problems facing the rulers of all three countries?

- How were notions of race and religion used in the formation of Spanish national identity? Why might Spanish monarchs have found it advantageous to attack religious and ethnic minorities?

▪ In Your Own Words

Imagine that you must explain Chapter 13 to someone who hasn't read it. What would be the most important points to include and why?

14

Reformations and Religious Wars

1500–1600

Calls for reform of the Christian church began very early in its history. Throughout the centuries, men and women believed that the early Christian church represented a golden age, akin to the golden age of the classical past celebrated by Renaissance humanists. When Christianity became the official religion of the Roman Empire in the fourth century, many believers thought that the church had abandoned its original mission, and they called for a return to a church that was not linked to the state. Throughout the Middle Ages individuals and groups argued that the church had become too wealthy and powerful, and they urged monasteries, convents, bishoprics, and the papacy to give up their property and focus on service to the poor. Some asserted that basic teachings of the church were not truly Christian and that changes were needed in theology as well as in institutional structures and practices. The Christian humanists of the late fifteenth and early sixteenth centuries urged reform, primarily through educational and social change. What was new in the sixteenth century was the breadth of acceptance and the ultimate impact of the calls for reform. This acceptance was due not only to religious issues and problems within the church, but also to political and social factors. In 1500 there was one Christian church in western Europe to which all Christians at least nominally belonged. One hundred years later there were many, a situation that continues today. ■

Religious Violence in Urban Life. This 1590 painting shows Catholic military forces, including friars in their robes, processing through one of the many towns affected by the French religious wars that followed the Reformation. (Erich Lessing/Art Resource, NY)

Chapter Preview

▶ What were the central beliefs of Protestant reformers?

▶ How did politics shape the course of the Reformation?

▶ How did Protestantism spread beyond German-speaking lands?

▶ How did the Catholic Church respond to the new religious situation?

▶ Why did religious violence escalate in this period?

▼ What were the central beliefs of Protestant reformers?

In early sixteenth-century Europe a wide range of people had grievances with the church. Educated laypeople such as Christian humanists and urban residents, villagers and artisans, and church officials themselves called for reform. This widespread dissatisfaction helps explain why the ideas of Martin Luther found a ready audience. Within a decade of his first publishing his ideas (using the new technology of the printing press), much of central Europe and Scandinavia had broken with the Catholic Church, and even more radical concepts of the Christian message were being developed and linked to calls for social change.

The Christian Church in the Early Sixteenth Century

Europeans in the early sixteenth century were deeply pious. Despite—or perhaps because of—the depth of their piety, many people were also highly critical of the Roman Catholic Church and its clergy. The papal conflict with the German emperor Frederick II in the thirteenth century, followed by the Babylonian Captivity and the Great Schism, badly damaged the prestige of church leaders, and the fifteenth-century popes' inattention to spiritual issues did not help matters. Papal tax collection methods were attacked orally and in print. Some criticized the papacy itself as an institution, and even the great wealth and powerful courts of the entire church hierarchy. Some groups and individuals argued that certain doctrines taught by the church, such as the veneration of saints and the centrality of the sacraments, were incorrect. They suggested measures to reform institutions, improve clerical education and behavior, and alter basic doctrines.

anticlericalism Opposition to the clergy.

pluralism The clerical practice of holding more than one church benefice (or office) at the same time and enjoying the income from each.

In the early sixteenth century court records, bishops' visitations of parishes, and popular songs and printed images show widespread anticlericalism, or opposition to the clergy. The critics concentrated primarily on three problems: clerical immorality, clerical ignorance, and clerical pluralism (the practice of holding more than one church office at a time), with the related problem of absenteeism. Many priests, monks, and nuns lived pious lives of devotion, learning, and service and had strong support from the laypeople in their areas, but everyone also knew (and repeated) stories about lecherous monks, lustful nuns, and greedy and uneducated priests.

In regard to absenteeism and pluralism, many clerics held several benefices (BEH-nuh-fihs-ehz), or offices, simultaneously, but they seldom visited the benefices, let alone performed the spiritual responsibilities those offices entailed. Instead, they collected revenues from all of them and hired a poor priest to fulfill the spiritual duties of a particular local church. Many Italian officials in the papal curia, the pope's court in Rome, held benefices in England, Spain, and Germany. Revenues from those countries paid the Italian clerics' salaries, provoking not only charges of absenteeism but also nationalistic resentment aimed at the upper levels of the church hierarchy, which was increasingly viewed as foreign.

There was also local resentment of clerical privileges and immunities. Priests, monks, and nuns were exempt from civic responsibilities, such as defending the city and paying taxes. Yet religious orders frequently held large amounts of urban property, in some cities as much as one-third. City governments were increasingly determined to integrate the clergy into civic life by reducing their privileges and giving them public responsibilities. Urban leaders wanted some say in who would be appointed to high church offices, rather than having this decided far away in Rome. This brought city leaders into opposition with bishops and the papacy, which for centuries had stressed the independence of the church from lay control and the distinction between members of the clergy and laypeople.

Chapter 14
Reformations and Religious
386 Wars • 1500–1600

CHAPTER LOCATOR | What were the central beliefs of Protestant reformers?

Martin Luther

By itself, widespread criticism of the church did not lead to the dramatic changes of the sixteenth century. Those resulted from the personal religious struggle of a German university professor and priest, Martin Luther (1483–1546). Luther was born at Eisleben in Saxony. His father sent him to school and then to the University of Erfurt, where he earned a master's degree. Luther was to proceed to the study of law and a legal career. Instead, however, a sense of religious calling led him to join the Augustinian friars, a religious order whose members often preached to, taught, and assisted the poor. Luther was ordained a priest in 1507 and after additional study earned a doctorate of theology.

Martin Luther's scrupulous observance of religious routine, frequent confessions, and fasting gave him little spiritual peace. Through his study of Saint Paul's letters in the New Testament, he gradually arrived at a new understanding of Christian doctrine. He came to believe that salvation and justification come through faith. Faith is a free gift of God's grace, not the result of human effort. Moreover, God's word is revealed only in Scripture, not in the traditions of the church.

At the same time that Luther was engaged in scholarly reflections and professorial lecturing, Pope Leo X authorized the sale of a special Saint Peter's indulgence to finance his building plans in Rome. The archbishop who controlled the area in which Wittenberg was located, Albert of Mainz, was an enthusiastic promoter of this indulgence sale. For his efforts, he received a share of the profits in order to pay off a debt he had incurred in order to purchase a papal dispensation allowing him to become the bishop of several other territories as well.

What exactly was an **indulgence**? According to Catholic theology, individuals who sin could be reconciled to God by confessing their sins to a priest and by doing an assigned penance. But beginning in the twelfth century theologians increasingly emphasized the idea of purgatory, a place where souls on their way to Heaven went to make further amends for their earthly sins. Both earthly penance and time in purgatory could be shortened by drawing on what was termed the "treasury of merits." This was a collection of all the virtuous acts that Christ, the apostles, and the saints had done during their lives. An indulgence was a document, signed by the pope or another church official, that substituted a virtuous act from the treasury of merits for penance or time in purgatory.

Albert's indulgence sale promised that the purchase of indulgences would bring full forgiveness for one's own sins or release from purgatory for a loved one. One of the slogans — "As soon as coin in coffer rings, the soul from purgatory springs" — brought phenomenal success, and people traveled from miles around to buy indulgences.

Luther was severely troubled that many people believed they had no further need for repentance once they had purchased indulgences. In 1517 he wrote a letter to Archbishop Albert on the subject and enclosed his "Ninety-five Theses on the Power of Indulgences." His argument was that indulgences undermined the seriousness of the sacrament of penance, competed with the preaching of the Gospel, and downplayed the

Chapter Chronology

1517	Martin Luther, "Ninety-five Theses on the Power of Indulgences"
1521	Diet of Worms
1521–1559	Habsburg-Valois wars
1525	Peasants' War in Germany
1526	Turkish victory at Mohács, which allows spread of Protestantism in Hungary
1530s	Henry VIII ends the authority of the pope in England
1535	Angela Merici establishes the Ursulines as first women's teaching order
1536	John Calvin, *The Institutes of the Christian Religion*
1540	Papal approval of Society of Jesus (Jesuits)
1542	Pope Paul III establishes Supreme Sacred Congregation of the Roman and Universal Inquisition
1545–1563	Council of Trent
1553–1558	Reign of Mary Tudor and temporary restoration of Catholicism in England
1555	Peace of Augsburg, official recognition of Lutheranism
1558–1603	Reign of Elizabeth in England
1560–1660	Height of the European witch-hunt
1568–1578	Civil war in the Netherlands
1572	Saint Bartholomew's Day massacre
1588	England defeats Spanish Armada
1598	Edict of Nantes

indulgence A document issued by the Catholic Church lessening penance or time in purgatory, widely believed to bring forgiveness of all sins.

How did politics shape the course of the Reformation?

How did Protestantism spread beyond German-speaking lands?

How did the Catholic Church respond to the new religious situation?

Why did religious violence escalate in this period?

387

Selling Indulgences A German woodcut shows a monk offering an indulgence, with the official seals of the pope attached, as people run to put their money in the box. This woodcut is critical of the sale of indulgences, as it shows the monk riding on a donkey, an animal long viewed as a symbol of ignorance. Indulgences were often printed fill-in-the-blank forms. This one, purchased in 1521, has space for the indulgence seller's name at the top, the buyer's name in the middle, and the date at the bottom. (woodcut: akg-images; indulgence: Visual Connection Archive)

importance of charity in Christian life. After Luther's death, biographies reported that the theses were also nailed to the door of the church at Wittenberg Castle on October 31, 1517. Such an act would have been very strange—they were in Latin and written for those learned in theology, not for normal churchgoers—but it has become a standard part of Luther lore.

The theses were quickly printed, first in Latin and then in German translation. Luther was ordered to come to Rome, although because of the political situation in the empire, he was able instead to engage in formal scholarly debate with a representative of the church, Johann Eck, at Leipzig in 1519. He refused to take back his ideas and continued to develop his calls for reform, publicizing them in a series of printed pamphlets in which he moved further and further away from Catholic theology. Both popes and church councils could err, he wrote, and secular leaders should reform the church if the pope and clerical hierarchy did not. There was no distinction between clergy and laypeople, and requiring clergy to be celibate was a fruitless attempt to control a natural human drive.

Chapter 14
**Reformations and Religious
Wars • 1500–1600**

288

CHAPTER LOCATOR

What were the central
beliefs of Protestant
reformers?

The papacy responded with a letter condemning some of Luther's propositions, ordering that his books be burned, and ordering him to recant or be excommunicated. Luther retaliated by publicly burning the letter. By 1521, when the excommunication was supposed to become final, Luther's theological issues had become interwoven with public controversies about the church's wealth, power, and basic structure. The papal legate wrote of the growing furor, "All Germany is in revolution. Nine-tenths shout 'Luther' as their war cry; and the other tenth cares nothing about Luther, and cries 'Death to the court of Rome.'"[1] In this charged atmosphere, the twenty-one-year-old emperor Charles V held his first diet (assembly of the nobility, clergy, and cities of the Holy Roman Empire) in the German city of Worms, and he summoned Luther to appear. Luther refused to give in to demands that he take back his ideas. His appearance at the Diet of Worms in 1521 created an even broader audience for reform ideas, and throughout central Europe other individuals began to preach and publish against the existing doctrines and practices of the church.

Protestant Thought

The most important early reformer other than Luther was the Swiss humanist, priest, and admirer of Erasmus, Ulrich Zwingli (ZWIHN-glee) (1484–1531). Zwingli was convinced that the Scriptures were the pure words of God and the sole basis of religious truth, and he attacked indulgences, the Mass, the institution of monasticism, and clerical celibacy. In his gradual reform of the church in Zurich, he had the strong support of the city authorities, who had long resented the privileges of the clergy. The followers of Luther, Zwingli, and others who called for a break with Rome came to be called **Protestants**.

While not holding identical views, Luther, Zwingli, and other early Protestants agreed on many things. First, how is a person to be saved? Traditional Catholic teaching held

Protestant The name originally given to Lutherans, which came to mean all non-Catholic Western Christian groups.

The Ten Commandments Lucas Cranach the Elder, the court painter for the elector of Saxony, painted this giant illustration of the Ten Commandments (more than 5 feet by 11 feet) for the city hall in Wittenberg in 1516, just at the point that Luther was beginning to question Catholic doctrine. Cranach was an early supporter of Luther, and many of his later works depict the reformer and his ideas. Paintings were used by both Protestants and Catholics to teach religious ideas. (Lutherhalle, Wittenberg/The Bridgeman Art Library)

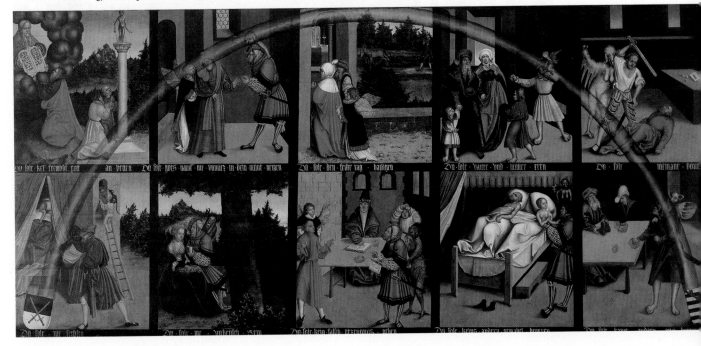

How did politics shape the course of the Reformation?

How did Protestantism spread beyond German-speaking lands?

How did the Catholic Church respond to the new religious situation?

Why did religious violence escalate in this period?

389

that salvation is achieved by both faith and good works. Protestants held that salvation comes by faith alone, irrespective of good works or the sacraments. God, not people, initiates salvation. (See "Listening to the Past: Martin Luther, *On Christian Liberty*," page 392.) Second, where does religious authority reside? Christian doctrine had long maintained that authority rests both in the Bible and in the traditional teaching of the church. For Protestants, authority rested in the Bible alone. On this basis, most Protestants rejected Catholic teachings about the sacraments—the rituals that the church had

▪ PICTURING THE PAST

Domestic Scene

The Protestant notion that the best form of Christian life was marriage and a family helps explain its appeal to middle-class urban men and women, such as those shown in this domestic scene. The engraving, titled "Concordia" (harmony), includes the biblical inscription of what Jesus called the greatest commandment — "You shall love the Lord your God with all your heart and all your soul and your neighbor as yourself" (Deuteronomy 6; Matthew 22) — on tablets at the back. The large covered bed at the back was both a standard piece of furniture in urban homes and a symbol of proper marital sexual relations. (Mary Evans Picture Library/The Image Works)

ANALYZING THE IMAGE What are the different family members doing? What elements of this image suggest that this is a pious, Christian family?

CONNECTIONS How do the various family roles shown here support the Protestant ideal of marriage and family?

To complete this activity online, go to the Online Study Guide at bedfordstmartins.com/mckaywestunderstanding.

Chapter 14
**Reformations and Religious
Wars • 1500–1600**

90

CHAPTER LOCATOR   What were the central beliefs of Protestant reformers?

defined as imparting God's benefits on the believer (see Chapter 10) — holding that only baptism and the Eucharist have scriptural support.

Third, what is the church? Protestants held that the church is a spiritual priesthood of all believers, an invisible fellowship not fixed in any place or person, which differed markedly from the Roman Catholic practice of a hierarchical clerical institution headed by the pope in Rome. Fourth, what is the highest form of Christian life? The medieval church had stressed the superiority of the monastic and religious life over the secular. Protestants disagreed and argued that every person should serve God in his or her individual calling.

The Appeal of Protestant Ideas

Pulpits and printing presses spread the Protestant message all over Germany, and by the middle of the sixteenth century people of all social classes had rejected Catholic teachings and had become Protestant. What was the immense appeal of Luther's religious ideas and those of other Protestants?

Educated people and many humanists were much attracted by Luther's ideas. He advocated a simpler personal religion based on faith, a return to the spirit of the early church, the centrality of the Scriptures in the liturgy and in Christian life, and the abolition of elaborate ceremonies — precisely the reforms the Christian humanists had been calling for. The Protestant insistence that everyone should read and reflect on the Scriptures attracted literate and thoughtful city residents. In addition, townspeople who envied the church's wealth and resented paying for it were attracted by the notion that the clergy should also pay taxes and should not have special legal privileges.

Scholars in many disciplines have attributed Luther's fame and success to the invention of the printing press, which rapidly reproduced and made known his ideas. Many printed works included woodcuts and other illustrations, so that even those who could not read could grasp the main ideas. Equally important was Luther's incredible skill with language. Luther's linguistic skill, together with his translation of the New Testament into German in 1523, led to the acceptance of his dialect of German as the standard written version of the German language.

Both Luther and Zwingli recognized that for reforms to be permanent, political authorities as well as concerned individuals and religious leaders would have to accept them. Zwingli worked closely with the city council of Zurich, and city councils themselves took the lead in other cities and towns of Switzerland and south Germany. They appointed pastors whom they knew had accepted Protestant ideas and oversaw their preaching and teaching.

Luther lived in a territory ruled by a noble — the elector of Saxony — and he also worked closely with political authorities, viewing them as fully justified in asserting control over the church in their territories. Indeed, he demanded that German rulers reform the papacy and its institutions, and he instructed all Christians to obey their secular rulers. Luther knew that a territory only became Protestant when its ruler, whether a noble or a city council, took practical steps toward reform. This happened in many of the states of the Holy Roman Empire during the 1520s.

The Radical Reformation and the German Peasants' War

While Luther and Zwingli worked with political authorities, some individuals and groups rejected the idea that church and state needed to be united. Beginning in the 1520s, they sought instead to create a voluntary community of believers, as they understood it to have existed in New Testament times. In terms of theology and spiritual practices, these individuals and groups varied widely, though they are generally termed "radicals" for their insistence on a more extensive break with prevailing ideas. Some adopted the

The idea of liberty has played a powerful role in the history of Western society and culture, but the meaning and understanding of liberty has undergone continual change and interpretation. In the Roman world, where slavery was a basic institution, liberty meant the condition of being a free man, independent of obligations to a master. In the Middle Ages possessing liberty meant having special privileges or rights that other persons or institutions did not have. A lord or a monastery, for example, might speak of his or its liberties, and citizens in London were said to possess the "freedom of the city," which allowed them to practice trades and own property without interference.

The idea of liberty also has a religious dimension, and the reformer Martin Luther formulated a classic interpretation of liberty in his treatise On Christian Liberty *(sometimes translated as* On the Freedom of a Christian*), arguably his finest piece. Written in Latin for the pope but translated immediately into German and published widely, it contains the main themes of Luther's theology: the importance of faith, the relationship of Christian faith and good works, the dual nature of human beings, and the fundamental importance of Scripture. Luther writes that Christians were freed from sin and death through Christ, not through their own actions.*

❝ A Christian man is the most free lord of all, and subject to none; a Christian man is the most dutiful servant of all, and subject to everyone. Although these statements appear contradictory, yet, when they are found to agree together, they will do excellently for my purpose. They are both the statements of Paul himself, who says, "Though I be free from all men, yet have I made myself a servant unto all" (I Corinthians 9:19) and "Owe no man anything but to love one another" (Romans 13:8). Now love is by its own nature dutiful and obedient to the beloved object. Thus even Christ, though Lord of all things, was yet made of a woman; made under the law; at once free and a servant; at once in the form of God and in the form of a servant.

Let us examine the subject on a deeper and less simple principle. Man is composed of a twofold nature, a spiritual and a bodily. As regards the spiritual nature, which they name the soul, he is called the spiritual, inward, new man; as regards the bodily nature, which they name the flesh, he is called the fleshly, outward, old man. The Apostle speaks of this: "Though our outward man perish, yet the inward man is renewed day by day" (II Corinthians 4:16). The result of this diversity is that in the Scriptures opposing statements are made concerning the same man, the fact being that in the same man these two men are opposed to one another; the flesh lusting against the spirit, and the spirit against the flesh (Galatians 5:17).

We first approach the subject of the inward man, that we may see by what means a man becomes justified, free, and a true Christian; that is, a spiritual, new, and inward man. It is certain that absolutely none among outward things, under whatever name they may be reckoned, has any influence in producing Christian righteousness or liberty, nor, on the other hand, unrighteousness or slavery. This can be shown by an easy argument. What can it profit to the soul that the body should be in good condition, free, and full of life, that it should eat, drink, and act according to its pleasure, when even the most impious slaves of every kind of vice are prosperous in these matters? Again, what harm can ill health, bondage, hunger, thirst, or any other outward evil, do to the soul, when even the most pious of men, and the freest in the purity of their conscience, are harassed by these things? Neither of these states of things has to do with the liberty or the slavery of the soul.

And so it will profit nothing that the body should be adorned with sacred vestment, or dwell in holy places, or be occupied in sacred offices, or pray, fast, and abstain from certain meats, or do whatever works can be done through the body and in the body. Something widely different will be necessary for the justification and liberty of the soul, since the things I have spoken of can be done by an impious person, and only hypocrites are produced by devotion to these things. On the other hand, it will not at all injure the soul that the body should be clothed in profane raiment, should dwell in profane places, should eat and drink in the ordinary fashion, should not pray aloud, and should leave undone all the things above mentioned, which may be done by hypocrites.

. . . One thing, and one alone, is necessary for life, justification, and Christian liberty; and that is the most Holy Word of God, the Gospel of Christ, as He says, "I am the resurrection and the life; he that believeth in me shall not die eternally" (John 9:25), and also, "If the Son shall make you free, ye shall be free indeed" (John 8:36), and "Man shall not live by bread alone, but by every word that proceedeth out of the mouth of God" (Matthew 4:4).

Let us therefore hold it for certain and firmly established that the soul can do without everything

baptism of believers—for which they were given the title of "Anabaptists" or rebaptizers by their enemies—while others saw all outward sacraments or rituals as misguided. Some groups attempted communal ownership of property. Some reacted harshly to members who deviated, but others argued for complete religious toleration and individualism.

On effective preaching, especially to the uneducated, Luther urged the minister "to keep it simple for the simple." (Church of St. Marien, Wittenberg/The Bridgeman Art Library)

except the Word of God, without which none at all of its wants is provided for. But, having the Word, it is rich and wants for nothing, since that is the Word of life, of truth, of light, of peace, of justification, of salvation, of joy, of liberty, of wisdom, of virtue, of grace, of glory, and of every good thing. . . .

But you will ask, "What is this Word, and by what means is it to be used, since there are so many words of God?" I answer, "The Apostle Paul (Romans 1) explains what it is, namely the Gospel of God, concerning His Son, incarnate, suffering, risen, and glorified through the Spirit, the Sanctifier." To preach Christ is to feed the soul, to justify it, to set it free, and to save it, if it believes the preaching. For faith alone, and the efficacious use of the Word of God, bring salvation. "If thou shalt confess with thy mouth the Lord Jesus, and shalt believe in thine heart that God hath raised Him from the dead, thou shalt be saved" (Romans 9:9); . . . and "The just shall live by faith" (Romans 1:17). . . .

But this faith cannot consist of all with works; that is, if you imagine that you can be justified by those works, whatever they are, along with it. . . . Therefore, when you begin to believe, you learn at the same time that all that is in you is utterly guilty, sinful, and damnable, according to that saying, "All have sinned, and come short of the glory of God" (Romans 3:23). . . . When you have learned this, you will know that Christ is necessary for you, since He has suffered and risen again for you, that, believing on Him, you might by this faith become another man, all your sins being remitted, and you being justified by the merits of another, namely Christ alone.

. . . [A]nd since it [faith] alone justifies, it is evident that by no outward work or labour can the inward man be at all justified, made free, and saved; and that no works whatever have any relation to him. . . . Therefore the first care of every Christian ought to be to lay aside all reliance on works, and strengthen his faith alone more and more, and by it grow in knowledge, not of works, but of Christ Jesus, who has suffered and risen again for him, as Peter teaches (I Peter 5). 〟

Source: *Luther's Primary Works*, ed. H. Wace and C. A. Buchheim (London: Holder and Stoughton, 1896). Reprinted in *The Portable Renaissance Reader*, ed. James Bruce Ross and Mary Martin McLaughlin (New York: Penguin Books, 1981), pp. 721–726.

QUESTIONS FOR ANALYSIS

1. What did Luther mean by liberty?
2. Why, for Luther, was Scripture basic to Christian life?

Religious radicals were often pacifists and refused to hold office or swear oaths. Both Protestant and Catholic authorities felt threatened by the social, political, and economic implications of their religious ideas, and by their rejection of a state church, which the authorities saw as key to maintaining order. In Saxony, in Strasbourg, and in the Swiss

How did politics shape the course of the Reformation?

How did Protestantism spread beyond German-speaking lands?

How did the Catholic Church respond to the new religious situation?

Why did religious violence escalate in this period?

cities, radicals were either banished or cruelly executed by burning, beating, or drowning. Their community spirit and heroism in the face of martyrdom, however, contributed to the survival of radical ideas, and eventually shaped the U.S. Constitution, which prohibited the establishment of an official state church.

Radical reformers sometimes called for social as well as religious change, a message that German peasants heard. In the early sixteenth century the economic condition of the peasantry was generally worse than it had been in the fifteenth century and was deteriorating. Crop failures in 1523 and 1524 aggravated an explosive situation. Nobles had aggrieved peasants by trying to squeeze even more crops, taxes, and labor from them. The peasants made demands that they believed conformed to the Scriptures, and they cited radical thinkers as well as Luther as proof that their demands did conform.

Luther initially sided with the peasants, blasting the lords for robbing their subjects. But when rebellion broke out, peasants who expected Luther's support were soon disillusioned. Freedom for Luther meant independence from the authority of the Roman church; it did not mean opposition to legally established secular powers. In response to the rebellion, Luther wrote the tract *Against the Murderous, Thieving Hordes of the Peasants:* "Let everyone who can smite, slay, and stab [the peasants], secretly and openly, remembering that nothing can be more poisonous, hurtful or devilish than a rebel."[2] The nobility ferociously crushed the revolt. Historians estimate that more than seventy-five thousand peasants were killed in 1525.

Marriage and Sexuality

Luther and Zwingli both believed that marriage brought spiritual advantages and so was the ideal state for nearly all human beings. Luther married a former nun, Katharina von Bora (1499–1532), and Zwingli married a Zurich widow, Anna Reinhart (1491–1538). Both women quickly had several children.

Though they denied that marriage was a sacrament, Protestant reformers stressed that it had been ordained by God as a "remedy" for the unavoidable sin of lust, provided a site for the pious rearing of God-fearing Christians, and offered husbands and wives companionship and consolation. A proper marriage was one that reflected both the spiritual equality of men and women and the proper social hierarchy of husbandly authority and wifely obedience.

Protestants did not break with medieval scholastic theologians in their idea that women were to be subject to men. Nonetheless, Protestants saw marriage as a contract in which each partner promised the other support, companionship, and the sharing of mutual goods. Because, in Protestant eyes, marriage was created by God as a remedy for human weakness, marriages in which spouses did not comfort or support one another physically, materially, or emotionally endangered their own souls and the surrounding community. The only solution might be divorce and remarriage, which most Protestants came to allow. Protestant allowance of divorce differed markedly from Catholic doctrine, which viewed marriage as a sacramental union that, if validly entered into, could not be dissolved. Although it was a dramatic legal change, divorce did not have a dramatic impact on newly Protestant areas. Because marriage was the cornerstone of society socially and economically, divorce was still seen as a desperate last resort.

As Protestants believed marriage was the only proper remedy for lust, they uniformly condemned prostitution. The licensed brothels that were a common feature of late medieval urban life (see Chapter 12) were closed in Protestant cities, and harsh punishments were set for prostitution. Many Catholic cities soon closed their brothels as well. Closing the official brothels did not end the exchange of sex for money, of course, but simply reshaped it. Smaller illegal brothels were established, or women moved to areas right outside city walls.

Martin Luther and Katharina von Bora Lucas Cranach the Elder painted this double marriage portrait to celebrate Luther's wedding in 1525 to Katharina von Bora, a former nun. The artist was one of the witnesses at the wedding and, in fact, had presented Luther's marriage proposal to Katharina. Using a go-between for proposals was very common, as was having a double wedding portrait painted. This particular couple quickly became a model of the ideal marriage, and many churches wanted their portraits. More than sixty similar paintings, with slight variations, were produced by Cranach's workshop and hung in churches and wealthy homes. (Uffizi, Florence/Scala/Art Resource, NY)

The Protestant Reformation clearly had a positive impact on marriage, but its impact on women was more mixed. Many nuns were in convents because their parents placed them there, and they did not have a strong sense of religious calling, but convents nevertheless provided women of the upper classes with scope for their literary, artistic, medical, or administrative talents if they could not or would not marry. The Reformation generally brought the closing of monasteries and convents, and marriage became virtually the only occupation for upper-class Protestant women. The Protestant emphasis on marriage made unmarried women (and men) suspect, for they did not belong to the type of household regarded as the cornerstone of a proper, godly society.

▼ How did politics shape the course of the Reformation?

The Holy Roman Empire included hundreds of largely independent states. Against this background of decentralization and strong local power, Martin Luther had launched a movement to reform the church. Two years after he published the "Ninety-five Theses," the electors of the Holy Roman Empire chose as emperor a nineteen-year-old Habsburg prince who ruled as Charles V (r. 1519–1556). The course of the Reformation was shaped by this election and by the political relationships surrounding it.

How did politics shape the course of the Reformation?

How did Protestantism spread beyond German-speaking lands?

How did the Catholic Church respond to the new religious situation?

Why did religious violence escalate in this period?

395

The Rise of the Habsburg Dynasty

Marriage was one of the key ways states increased their power in sixteenth-century Europe. Royal and noble sons and daughters were important tools of state policy. The benefits of an advantageous marriage stretched across generations, a process that can be seen most dramatically with the Habsburgs. The Holy Roman emperor Frederick III, a Habsburg who was the ruler of most of Austria, acquired a great deal of money with his marriage to Princess Eleonore of Portugal in 1452. He arranged for his son Maximilian to marry Europe's most prominent heiress, Mary of Burgundy, in 1477; she inherited the Netherlands, Luxembourg, and the County of Burgundy in what is now eastern France. Through this union with the rich and powerful duchy of Burgundy, the Austrian house of Habsburg, already the strongest ruling family in the empire, became an international power. The marriage of Maximilian and Mary angered the French, however, who considered Burgundy French territory. This inaugurated centuries of conflict between the Austrian house of Habsburg and the kings of France.

Maximilian learned the lesson of marital politics well, marrying his son and daughter to the children of Ferdinand and Isabella, the rulers of Spain, much of southern Italy, and eventually the Spanish New World empire. His grandson Charles V (1500–1558) fell heir to a vast and incredibly diverse collection of states and peoples, each governed in a different manner and held together only by the person of the emperor (Map 14.1).

Religious Wars in Switzerland and Germany

In the sixteenth century the practice of religion remained a public matter. The ruler determined the official form of religious practice in his (or occasionally her) jurisdiction. Almost everyone believed that the presence of a faith different from that of the majority represented a political threat to the security of the state.

Luther's ideas appealed to German rulers for a variety of reasons. Though Germany was not a nation, people did have an understanding of being German because of their language and traditions. Luther frequently used the phrase "we Germans" in his attacks on the papacy. Luther's appeal to national feeling influenced many rulers otherwise confused by or indifferent to the complexities of the religious matters. Some German rulers were sincerely attracted to Lutheran ideas, but material considerations swayed many others to embrace the new faith. The rejection of Roman Catholicism and adoption of Protestantism would mean the legal confiscation of church property. Thus many political authorities in the empire used the religious issue to extend their financial and political power and to enhance their independence from the emperor.

Charles V was a vigorous defender of Catholicism, so it is not surprising

Fresco of Pope Clement VII and the Emperor Charles V In this double portrait, artist Giorgio Vasari uses matching hand gestures to indicate agreement between the pope and the emperor, though the pope's red hat and cape make him the dominant figure. Charles V remained loyal to Catholicism, though the political situation and religious wars in Germany eventually required him to compromise with Protestants. (Palazzo Vecchio, Florence/Scala/Art Resource, NY)

Chapter 14
Reformations and Religious
396   Wars • 1500–1600

CHAPTER LOCATOR   What were the central beliefs of Protestant reformers?

that the Reformation led to religious wars. The first battleground was Switzerland, a loose confederation of thirteen largely autonomous territories called "cantons." Some cantons remained Catholic, and some became Protestant, and in the late 1520s the two sides went to war. Zwingli was killed on the battlefield in 1531, and both sides quickly decided that a treaty was preferable to further fighting. The treaty basically allowed each canton to determine its own religion and ordered each side to give up its foreign alliances.

Trying to halt the spread of religious division, Charles V called an Imperial Diet in 1530, to meet at Augsburg. The Lutherans developed a statement of faith, later called the Augsburg Confession, and the Protestant princes presented this to the emperor. Charles refused to accept it and ordered all Protestants to return to the Catholic Church and give up any confiscated church property. This demand backfired, and Protestant territories in the empire—mostly northern German principalities and southern German cities—formed a military alliance. The emperor could not respond militarily, as he was in the midst of a series of wars with the French: the Habsburg-Valois wars (1521–1559), fought in Italy along the eastern and southern borders of France and eventually in Germany.

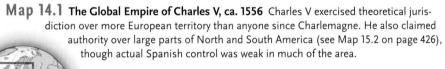

Map 14.1 **The Global Empire of Charles V, ca. 1556** Charles V exercised theoretical jurisdiction over more European territory than anyone since Charlemagne. He also claimed authority over large parts of North and South America (see Map 15.2 on page 426), though actual Spanish control was weak in much of the area.

How did politics shape the course of the Reformation?

How did Protestantism spread beyond German-speaking lands?

How did the Catholic Church respond to the new religious situation?

Why did religious violence escalate in this period?

397

The 1530s and early 1540s saw complicated political maneuvering among many of the powers of Europe. Various attempts were made to heal the religious split with a church council, but it became increasingly clear that this would not be possible and that war was inevitable. Charles V realized that he was fighting not only for religious unity, but also for a more unified state, against territorial rulers who wanted to maintain their independence.

Fighting began in 1546, and initially the emperor was very successful. This success alarmed both France and the pope, however, who did not want Charles to become even more powerful. The pope withdrew papal troops, and the Catholic king of France sent money and troops to the Lutheran princes. Finally, in 1555 Charles agreed to the Peace of Augsburg, which, "in order to bring peace into the holy empire," officially recognized Lutheranism. The political authority in each territory was permitted to decide whether the territory would be Catholic or Lutheran. Most of northern and central Germany became Lutheran, while the south remained Roman Catholic. There was no freedom of religion within the territories, however. Princes or town councils established state churches to which all subjects of the area had to belong. Dissidents had to convert or leave. Religious refugees became a common feature on the roads of the empire.

The Peace of Augsburg ended religious war in Germany for many decades. His hope of uniting his empire under a single church dashed, Charles V abdicated in 1556 and moved to a monastery, transferring power over his holdings in Spain and the Netherlands to his son Philip and his imperial power to his brother Ferdinand.

▼ How did Protestantism spread beyond German-speaking lands?

States within the Holy Roman Empire were the earliest territories to accept the Protestant Reformation, but by the later 1520s and 1530s religious change came to Denmark-Norway, Sweden, England, France, and eastern Europe. In most of these areas, a second generation of reformers built on Lutheran and Zwinglian ideas to develop their own theology and plans for institutional change.

Scandinavia

The first area outside the empire to officially accept the Reformation was the kingdom of Denmark-Norway under King Christian III (r. 1536–1559). In the 1530s the king officially broke with the Catholic Church, and most clergy followed. The process went smoothly in Denmark, but in northern Norway and Iceland (which Christian also ruled) there were violent reactions, and Lutheranism was only gradually imposed on a largely unwilling populace.

In Sweden, Gustavus Vasa (r. 1523–1560), who came to the throne during a civil war with Denmark, also took over control of church personnel and income. Protestant ideas spread, though the Swedish church did not officially accept Lutheran theology until later in the century.

Henry VIII and the Reformation in England

As on the continent, the Reformation in England had economic and political as well as religious causes. The impetus for England's break with Rome was King Henry VIII's (r. 1509–1547) desire for a new wife, though ultimately his own motives also combined personal, political, social, and economic elements.

398

Chapter 14
Reformations and Religious
Wars • 1500–1600

CHAPTER LOCATOR | What were the central beliefs of Protestant reformers?

Allegory of the Tudor Dynasty The unknown creator of this work intended to glorify the virtues of the Protestant succession; the painting has no historical reality. Henry VIII (seated) hands the sword of justice to his Protestant son Edward VI. The Catholic Queen Mary and her husband Philip of Spain (left) are followed by Mars, god of war, signifying violence and civil disorder. At right the figures of Peace and Plenty accompany the Protestant Elizabeth I, symbolizing England's happy fate under her rule. (Yale Center for British Art, Paul Mellon Collection/The Bridgeman Art Library)

Henry VIII was married to Catherine of Aragon, the daughter of Ferdinand and Isabella and widow of Henry's older brother Arthur. Marriage to a brother's widow went against canon law, and Henry had been required to obtain a special papal dispensation to marry Catherine. The marriage had produced only one living heir, a daughter, Mary. By 1527 Henry decided that God was showing his displeasure with the marriage by denying him a son, and he appealed to the pope to have the marriage annulled. He was also in love with a court lady-in-waiting, Anne Boleyn. Normally an annulment would not have been a problem, but the troops of Emperor Charles V were in Rome at that point, and Pope Clement VII was essentially their prisoner. Charles V was the nephew of Catherine of Aragon and thus was opposed to an annulment, which would have declared his aunt a fornicator and his cousin Mary a bastard.

When the pope failed to grant his request, Henry decided to remove the English church from papal jurisdiction. In a series of measures during the 1530s, Henry used Parliament to end the authority of the pope and make himself the supreme head of the church in England. When Anne Boleyn failed twice to produce a male child, Henry VIII charged her with adulterous incest and in 1536 had her beheaded. His third wife, Jane Seymour, gave Henry the desired son, Edward, but she died in childbirth. Henry went on to three more wives.

Theologically, Henry was conservative, and the English church retained many traditional Catholic practices and doctrines. Between 1535 and 1539, however, under the influence of his chief minister, Thomas Cromwell, Henry decided to dissolve the English monasteries because he wanted their wealth. Working through Parliament, the king dispersed England's monks and nuns and confiscated their lands. The proceeds enriched the royal treasury, and hundreds of properties were sold to the middle and upper classes, the very groups represented in Parliament. The dissolution of the monasteries did not

How did politics shape the course of the Reformation?

How did Protestantism spread beyond German-speaking lands?

How did the Catholic Church respond to the new religious situation?

Why did religious violence escalate in this period?

399

achieve a more equitable distribution of land and wealth; rather, the redistribution of land strengthened the upper classes and tied them to both the Tudor dynasty and the new Protestant church.

The nationalization of the church and the dissolution of the monasteries led to important changes in government administration. Vast tracts of formerly monastic land came temporarily under the Crown's jurisdiction, and new bureaucratic machinery had to be developed to manage those properties. As a result, Henry VIII's reign saw the growth of the modern centralized bureaucratic state.

Did the religious changes under Henry VIII have broad popular support? Some English people had been dissatisfied with the existing Christian church before Henry's measures. Traditional Catholicism exerted an enormously strong and vigorous hold over the imagination and loyalty of many people, however. Most clergy and officials accepted Henry's moves, but all did not quietly acquiesce. In 1536 popular opposition in the north to the religious changes led to the Pilgrimage of Grace, a massive rebellion that proved the largest in English history. The "pilgrims" accepted a truce, but their leaders were arrested, tried, and executed.

Loyalty to the Catholic Church was particularly strong in Ireland. Ireland had been claimed by English kings since the twelfth century, but in reality the English had firm control of only the area around Dublin, known as the Pale. In 1536, the Irish parliament, which represented only the English landlords and the people of the Pale, approved the English laws severing the church from Rome. The Church of Ireland was established on the English pattern, and the (English) ruling class adopted the new reformed faith. Most of the Irish people remained Roman Catholic, thus adding religious antagonism to the ethnic hostility that had been a feature of English policy toward Ireland for centuries (see Chapter 12).

Upholding Protestantism in England

In the short reign of Henry's sickly son, Edward VI (r. 1547–1553), Protestant ideas exerted a significant influence on the religious life of the country. Archbishop Thomas Cranmer simplified the liturgy, invited Protestant theologians to England, and prepared the first *Book of Common Prayer* (1549). The *Book of Common Prayer* included the order for all services and prayers of the Church of England.

The equally brief reign of Mary Tudor (r. 1553–1558) witnessed a sharp move back to Catholicism. Mary rescinded the Reformation legislation of her father's reign and restored Roman Catholicism. Mary's marriage to her cousin Philip II of Spain, son of the emperor Charles V, proved highly unpopular in England, and her execution of several hundred Protestants further alienated her subjects. Mary's death raised to the throne her sister Elizabeth, Henry's daughter with Anne Boleyn, who had been raised a Protestant. Her reign from 1558 to 1603 inaugurated the beginnings of religious stability.

Elizabeth chose a middle course between Catholicism and those who wanted a strict version of Protestantism, who were called "Puritans." She required her subjects to attend services in the Church of England or risk a fine, but she did not interfere with their privately held beliefs. As she put it, she did not "want to make windows into men's souls." The Anglican Church, as the Church of England was called, moved in a moderately Protestant direction. Services were conducted in English, monasteries were not reestablished, and clergymen were allowed to marry. But the church remained hierarchical, with archbishops and bishops, and services continued to be elaborate, with the clergy in distinctive robes, in contrast to the simpler services favored by many continental Protestants.

Toward the end of the sixteenth century Elizabeth's reign was threatened by European powers attempting to re-establish Catholicism. Philip II of Spain had hoped that his marriage to Mary Tudor would reunite England with Catholic Europe, but Mary's

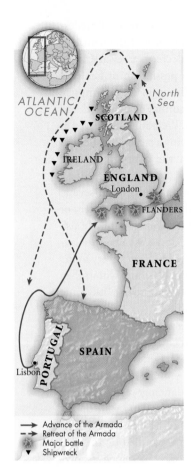

The Route of the Spanish Armada, 1588

death ended those plans. Another Mary—Mary, Queen of Scots—provided a new opportunity. Mary was Elizabeth's cousin, but she was Catholic and next in line to the English throne. In 1587 Mary became implicated in a plot to assassinate Elizabeth, a conspiracy that had Philip II's backing. When the English executed Mary, the Catholic pope urged Philip to retaliate.

Philip prepared a vast fleet to sail from Lisbon to Flanders, where a large army of Spanish troops was stationed because of religious wars in the Netherlands (see page 410). The Spanish ships were to escort barges carrying some of the troops across the English Channel to attack England. On May 9, 1588, a Spanish fleet composed of more than 130 vessels sailed from Lisbon harbor. The **Spanish Armada** met an English fleet in the channel before it reached Flanders. The English ships were smaller, faster, and more maneuverable, and many of them had greater firing power than their Spanish counterparts. A combination of storms and squalls, spoiled food and rank water, inadequate Spanish ammunition, and, to a lesser extent, English fire ships that caused the Spanish to scatter gave England the victory.

The battle in the English Channel had mixed consequences. Spain soon rebuilt its navy, and after 1588 the quality of the Spanish fleet improved. The war between England and Spain dragged on for years. Yet the defeat of the Spanish Armada prevented Philip II from reimposing Catholicism on England by force. In England the victory contributed to a David and Goliath legend that enhanced English national sentiment.

Spanish Armada The fleet sent by Philip II of Spain in 1588 against England as a religious crusade against Protestantism. Weather and the English fleet defeated it.

Calvinism

John Calvin (1509–1564) was born in Noyon in northwestern France. As a young man he studied law, which had a decisive impact on his mind and later his thought. In 1533 he experienced a religious crisis, as a result of which he converted to Protestantism.

Calvin believed that God had specifically selected him to reform the church. Accordingly, he accepted an invitation to assist in the reformation of the city of Geneva. There, beginning in 1541, Calvin worked to establish a Christian society ruled by God through civil magistrates and reformed ministers.

To understand Calvin's Geneva, it is necessary to understand Calvin's ideas. These he embodied in *The Institutes of the Christian Religion*. The cornerstone of Calvin's theology was his belief in the absolute sovereignty and omnipotence of God and the total weakness of humanity.

The Institutes of the Christian Religion Calvin's formulation of Christian doctrine, which became a systematic theology for Protestantism.

Calvin did not ascribe free will to human beings because that would detract from the sovereignty of God. Men and women cannot actively work to achieve salvation; rather, God in his infinite wisdom decided at the beginning of time who would be saved and who damned. This viewpoint constitutes the theological principle called **predestination**. Calvin explained his view:

predestination The teaching that God has determined the salvation or damnation of individuals based on his will and purpose, not on their merit or works.

> *Predestination we call the eternal decree of God, by which he has determined in himself, what he would have become of every individual. . . . For they are not all created with a similar destiny; but eternal life is foreordained for some, and eternal damnation for others. . . .*[3]

How did politics shape the course of the Reformation?

How did Protestantism spread beyond German-speaking lands?

How did the Catholic Church respond to the new religious situation?

Why did religious violence escalate in this period?

401

Young John Calvin This oil painting of the reformer as a young man captures his spiritual intensity and determination, qualities that the artist clearly viewed as positive. (Bibliothèque de Genève, Département iconographique)

Many people consider the doctrine of predestination to be a pessimistic view of the nature of God. But "this terrible decree," as even Calvin called it, did not lead to pessimism or fatalism. Rather, the Calvinist believed in the redemptive work of Christ and was confident that God had elected (saved) him or her. Predestination served as an energizing dynamic, giving a person the strength to undergo hardships in the constant struggle against evil.

In his reform of Geneva, Calvin had several remarkable assets, including complete mastery of the Scriptures and exceptional eloquence. He also established the Genevan Consistory, a body of laymen and pastors, "to keep watch over every man's life [and] to admonish amiably those whom they see leading a disorderly life" and provide "medicine to turn sinners to the Lord."[4]

Although all municipal governments in early modern Europe regulated citizens' conduct, none did so with the severity of Geneva's Consistory under Calvin's leadership. Absence from sermons, criticism of ministers, dancing, card playing, family quarrels, and heavy drinking were all investigated and punished by the Consistory. Serious crimes and heresy were handled by the civil authorities. Between 1542 and 1546 alone seventy-six persons were banished from Geneva, and fifty-eight were executed for heresy, adultery, blasphemy, and witchcraft (see page 411).

Religious refugees from France, England, Spain, Scotland, and Italy visited Calvin's Geneva, and many of the most prominent exiles from Mary Tudor's England stayed. Subsequently, the church of Calvin — often termed "Reformed" — served as the model for the Presbyterian church in Scotland, the Huguenot church in France (see page 409), and the Puritan churches in England and New England.

Calvinism became the compelling force in international Protestantism. The Calvinist ethic of the "calling" dignified all work with a religious aspect and encouraged an aggressive, vigorous activism, helping Calvinism become the most dynamic force in sixteenth-and seventeenth-century Protestantism.

Calvinism spread on the continent of Europe, and it also found a ready audience in Scotland. There as elsewhere, political authority was the decisive influence in reform. The monarchy was weak, and factions of virtually independent nobles competed for power. King James V and his daughter Mary, Queen of Scots (r. 1560–1567), staunch Catholics and close allies of Catholic France, opposed reform, but the Scottish nobles supported it. John Knox (1505?–1572) dominated the reform movement that led to the establishment of a state church.

Knox was determined to structure the Scottish church after the model of Geneva, where he had studied and worked with Calvin. In 1560 Knox persuaded the Scottish parliament, which was dominated by reform-minded barons, to end papal authority and rule by bishops, substituting governance by presbyters, or councils of ministers. The Presbyterian Church of Scotland was strictly Calvinist in doctrine, adopted a simple and dignified service of worship, and laid great emphasis on preaching.

CHAPTER LOCATOR   What were the central beliefs of Protestant reformers?

The Reformation in Eastern Europe

While political and economic issues determined the course of the Reformation in western and northern Europe, ethnic factors often proved decisive in eastern Europe, where people of diverse backgrounds had settled in the later Middle Ages. In Bohemia in the fifteenth century, a Czech majority was ruled by Germans. Most Czechs had adopted the ideas of Jan Hus, and the emperor had been forced to recognize a separate Hussite church (see Chapter 12). Yet Lutheranism appealed to Germans in Bohemia in the 1520s and 1530s, and the nobility embraced Lutheranism in opposition to the Catholic Habsburgs. The forces of the Catholic Reformation (see page 404) promoted a Catholic spiritual revival in Bohemia, and some areas reconverted. This complicated situation would be one of the causes of the Thirty Years' War in the early seventeenth century.

By 1500 Poland and the Grand Duchy of Lithuania were jointly governed by king, senate, and diet (parliament), but the two territories retained separate officials, judicial systems, armies, and forms of citizenship. The population of Poland-Lithuania was also very diverse; Germans, Italians, Tartars, and Jews lived with Poles and Lithuanians. Luther's ideas took root in Germanized towns but were opposed by King Sigismund I (r. 1506–1548) as well as by ordinary Poles, who held strong anti-German feeling. The Reformed tradition of John Calvin, with its stress on the power of church elders, appealed to the Polish nobility, however. Doctrinal differences among Calvinists, Lutherans, and other groups prevented united opposition to Catholicism, and a Counter-Reformation gained momentum. By 1650, due to the efforts of Stanislaus Hosius (1505–1579) and those of the Jesuits (see page 407), Poland was again staunchly Roman Catholic.

The Battle of Mohács Massed armies on both sides confront each other in this Turkish illustration of the battle of Mohács. In the right panel, Suleiman in a white turban sits on a black horse surrounded by his personal guard, while his soldiers fire muskets and large cannon at the enemy. In the left panel the Europeans are in disarray, and their weapons are clearly inferior. (Private Collection/Archives Charmet/The Bridgeman Art Library)

How did politics shape the course of the Reformation?

How did Protestantism spread beyond German-speaking lands?

How did the Catholic Church respond to the new religious situation?

Why did religious violence escalate in this period?

403

Hungary's experience with the Reformation was even more complex. Lutheranism was spread by Hungarian students who had studied at Wittenberg, and sympathy for it developed at the royal court of King Louis II in Buda. But concern about "the German heresy" by the Catholic hierarchy and among the high nobles found expression in a decree of the Hungarian diet in 1523 that "all Lutherans and those favoring them . . . should have their property confiscated and themselves punished with death as heretics."[5]

Before such measures could be acted on, a military event on August 26, 1526, had profound consequences for both the Hungarian state and the Protestant Reformation there. On the plain of Mohács in southern Hungary, the Ottoman sultan Suleiman the Magnificent inflicted a crushing defeat on the Hungarians, killing King Louis II. The Hungarian kingdom was then divided into three parts: the Ottoman Turks absorbed the great plains, including the capital, Buda; the Habsburgs ruled the north and west; and Ottoman-supported Janos Zapolya held eastern Hungary and Transylvania.

The Turks were indifferent to the religious conflicts of Christians, whom they regarded as infidels. Many Magyar (Hungarian) nobles accepted Lutheranism; Lutheran schools and parishes multiplied; and peasants welcomed the new faith. The majority of people were Protestant until the late seventeenth century, when Hungarian nobles recognized Habsburg (Catholic) rule and Ottoman Turkish withdrawal in 1699 led to Catholic restoration.

▼ How did the Catholic Church respond to the new religious situation?

Between 1517 and 1547 Protestantism made remarkable advances. Nevertheless, the Roman Catholic Church made a significant comeback. After about 1540 no new large areas of Europe, other than the Netherlands, accepted Protestant beliefs (Map 14.2). Many historians see the developments within the Catholic Church after the Protestant Reformation as two interrelated movements, one a drive for internal reform and the other a Counter-Reformation that opposed Protestants intellectually, politically, militarily, and institutionally. In both movements, the papacy, new religious orders, and the Council of Trent that met from 1545 to 1563 were important agents.

Papal Reform and the Council of Trent

Renaissance popes and their advisers were not blind to the need for church reforms, but they feared that any transformation would mean a loss of power, revenue, and prestige. This changed beginning with Pope Paul III (pontificate 1534–1549), when the papal court became the center of the reform movement rather than its chief opponent. Paul III and his successors supported improvements in education for the clergy, the end of simony (the selling of church offices), and stricter control of clerical life.

Holy Office The official Roman Catholic agency founded in 1542 to combat international doctrinal heresy.

In 1542 Pope Paul III established the Supreme Sacred Congregation of the Roman and Universal Inquisition, often called the Holy Office, with jurisdiction over the Roman Inquisition, a powerful instrument of the Catholic Reformation. The Roman Inquisition was a committee of six cardinals with the power to arrest, imprison, and execute suspected heretics. The Holy Office published the *Index of Prohibited Books*, a catalogue of forbidden reading that included works by Christian humanists such as Erasmus as well as by Protestants. Within the Papal States, the Inquisition effectively destroyed heresy, but outside the papal territories, its influence was slight.

Pope Paul III also called a general council, which met intermittently from 1545 to 1563 at Trent, an imperial city close to Italy. It was called not only to reform the Catholic

CHAPTER LOCATOR | What were the central beliefs of Protestant reformers?

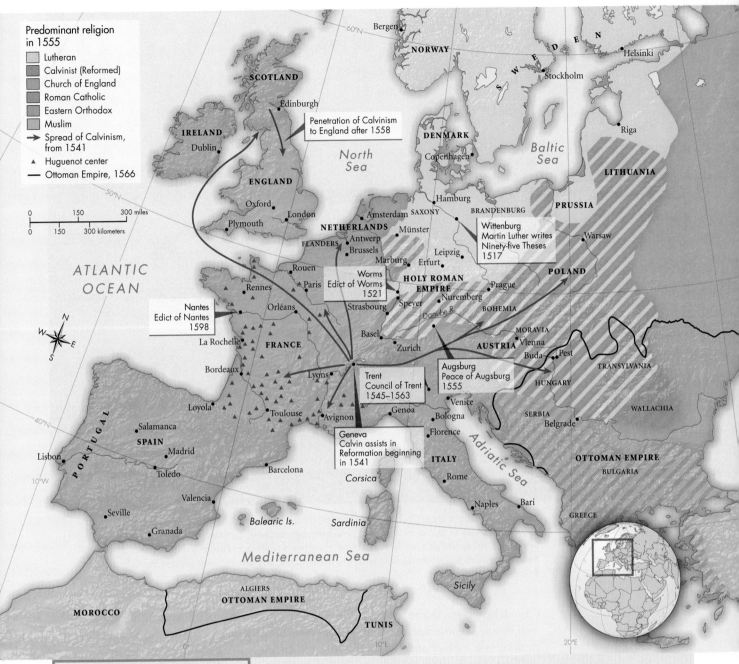

Predominant religion in 1555

- Lutheran
- Calvinist (Reformed)
- Church of England
- Roman Catholic
- Eastern Orthodox
- Muslim
- → Spread of Calvinism, from 1541
- ▲ Huguenot center
- — Ottoman Empire, 1566

Penetration of Calvinism to England after 1558

Wittenburg
Martin Luther writes Ninety-five Theses 1517

Worms
Edict of Worms 1521

Nantes
Edict of Nantes 1598

Trent
Council of Trent 1545–1563

Augsburg
Peace of Augsburg 1555

Geneva
Calvin assists in Reformation beginning in 1541

■ **MAPPING THE PAST**

Map 14.2 Religious Divisions in Europe, ca. 1555

The Reformations shattered the religious unity of Western Christendom. The situation was even more complicated than a map of this scale can show. Many cities within the Holy Roman Empire, for example, accepted a different faith than the surrounding countryside; Augsburg, Basel, and Strasbourg were all Protestant, though surrounded by territory ruled by Catholic nobles.

ANALYZING THE MAP Which countries were the most religiously diverse in Europe? Which were the least diverse?

CONNECTIONS Where was the first arena of religious conflict in sixteenth-century Europe, and why did it develop there and not elsewhere? To what degree can nonreligious factors be used as an explanation for the religious divisions in sixteenth-century Europe?

To complete this activity online, go to the Online Study Guide at bedfordstmartins.com/mckaywestunderstanding.

How did politics shape the course of the Reformation?	How did Protestantism spread beyond German-speaking lands?	**How did the Catholic Church respond to the new religious situation?**	Why did religious violence escalate in this period?	

Church of the Gesú Begun in 1568 as the mother church for the Jesuit order, the Church of the Gesú conveyed a sense of drama, motion, and power through its lavish decorations and shimmering frescoes. Gesú served as a model for Catholic churches elsewhere in Europe and the New World, their triumphant and elaborate style reflecting the dynamic and proselytizing spirit of the Catholic Reformation. (The Art Archive/Corbis)

Church but also to secure reconciliation with the Protestants. Lutherans and Calvinists were invited to participate, but their insistence that the Scriptures be the sole basis for discussion made reconciliation impossible. In addition, the political objectives of Charles V and France both worked against reconciliation: Charles wanted to avoid alienating the Lutheran nobility in the empire, and France wanted the Catholics and Lutherans to remain divided in order to keep Germany decentralized and weak.

Nonetheless, the decrees of the Council of Trent laid a solid basis for the spiritual renewal of the Catholic Church. It gave equal validity to the Scriptures and to tradition as sources of religious truth and authority. It reaffirmed the seven sacraments and the traditional Catholic teaching on transubstantiation. It required bishops to reside in their own dioceses, suppressed pluralism and simony, and forbade the sale of indulgences. Clerics who kept concubines were to give them up, and bishops were given greater authority. Moreover, the council required every diocese to establish a seminary for the education and training of the clergy. Seminary professors were to determine whether candidates for ordination had vocations, genuine callings to the priesthood. For the first time, great emphasis was laid on preaching and instructing the laity, especially the uneducated.

406

Chapter 14
**Reformations and Religious
Wars • 1500–1600**

CHAPTER LOCATOR

What were the central beliefs of Protestant reformers?

Although it did not achieve all of its goals, the Council of Trent composed decrees that laid a solid basis for the spiritual renewal of the church. The doctrinal and disciplinary legislation of Trent served as the basis for Roman Catholic faith, organization, and practice through the middle of the twentieth century.

New Religious Orders

The establishment of new religious orders within the church reveals a central feature of the Catholic Reformation. Most of these new orders developed in response to the need to raise the moral and intellectual level of the clergy and people. (See "Individuals in Society: Teresa of Ávila," page 408.) Education was a major goal of the two most famous orders.

The Ursuline order of nuns, founded by Angela Merici (1474–1540), attained enormous prestige for the education of women. Angela Merici worked for many years among the poor, sick, and uneducated around her native Brescia in northern Italy. In 1535 she established the first women's religious order concentrating exclusively on teaching young girls, with the goal of re-Christianizing society by training future wives and mothers. After receiving papal approval in 1565, the Ursulines rapidly spread to France and the New World.

The Society of Jesus, or **Jesuits**, founded by Ignatius Loyola (1491–1556) played a powerful international role in strengthening Catholicism in Europe and spreading the faith around the world. During a year spent in seclusion, prayer, and asceticism, Loyola gained insights that went into his great classic, *Spiritual Exercises* (1548). This work, intended for study during a four-week period of retreat, set out a training program of structured meditation designed to develop spiritual discipline and allow one to meld one's will with that of God.

Loyola was a man of considerable personal magnetism. After study at universities in Salamanca and Paris, he gathered a group of six companions and in 1540 secured papal approval of the new Society of Jesus. The first Jesuits saw the Reformation as a pastoral problem, its causes and cures related not to doctrinal issues but to people's spiritual condition. Their goal was not to reform the church, as Luther and Calvin understood that term, but rather "to help souls."

The Society of Jesus developed into a highly centralized, tightly knit organization. In addition to the traditional vows of poverty, chastity, and obedience, professed members vowed special obedience to the pope. Flexibility and the willingness to respond to the needs of time and circumstance formed the Jesuit tradition. The Jesuits carried Christianity to India and Japan before 1550 and to Brazil, North America, and the Congo in the seventeenth century. Within Europe the Jesuits brought southern Germany and much of eastern Europe back to Catholicism. Jesuit schools adopted the modern humanist curricula and methods, educating the sons of the nobility as well as the poor. As confessors and spiritual directors to kings, Jesuits exerted great political influence.

Jesuits Members of the Society of Jesus, founded by Ignatius Loyola, whose goal was the spread of the Roman Catholic faith.

▼ Why did religious violence escalate in this period?

In 1559 France and Spain signed the Treaty of Cateau-Cambrésis (CAH-toh kam-BRAY-sees), which ended the long conflict known as the Habsburg-Valois wars. A defeated France acknowledged Spanish dominance in Italy, where much of the fighting had taken place. However, true peace was elusive, and over the next century religious differences

How did politics shape the course of the Reformation?

How did Protestantism spread beyond German-speaking lands?

How did the Catholic Church respond to the new religious situation?

Why did religious violence escalate in this period?

407

INDIVIDUALS IN SOCIETY

Teresa of Ávila

HER FAMILY DERIVED FROM TOLEDO, CENTER
of the Moorish, Jewish, and Christian cultures in medieval Spain. Her grandfather, Juan Sanchez, made a fortune in the cloth trade. A New Christian (a convert from Judaism or Islam), he was accused of secretly practicing Judaism. He endured the humiliation of a public repentance and moved his family south to Ávila. Beginning again, he recouped his wealth and, perhaps hoping to hide his status as a convert, bought noble status. Juan's son Alzonzo Sanchez de Cepeda married a woman of thoroughly Christian background, giving his family an aura of impeccable orthodoxy. The third of their nine children, Teresa, became a saint and in 1970 was the first woman declared a Doctor of the Church, a title given to a theologian of outstanding merit.

At age twenty, inspired more by the fear of Hell than the love of God, Teresa (1515–1582) entered the Carmelite Convent of the Incarnation in Ávila. Most of the nuns were daughters of Ávila's leading citizens; they had entered the convent because of family decisions about which daughters would marry and which would become nuns. Their lives were much like those of female family members outside the convent walls, with good food, comfortable surroundings, and frequent visits from family and friends. Teresa was frequently ill, but she lived quietly in the convent for many years. In her late thirties, she began to read devotional literature intensely and had profound mystical experiences — visions and voices in which Christ chastised her for her frivolous life and friends. She described one such experience in 1560:

> It pleased the Lord that I should see an angel. . . .
> Short, and very beautiful, his face was so aflame that he appeared to be one of the highest types of angels. . . . In his hands I saw a long golden spear and at the end of an iron tip I seemed to see a point of fire. With this he seemed to pierce my heart several times so that it penetrated to my entrails. When he drew it out . . . he left me completely afire with the great love of God.*

Teresa responded with a new sense of purpose and resolved to found a reformed house. Four basic principles guided the new convent. First, poverty was to be fully observed, symbolized by the nuns' being barefoot, with charity and the nuns' own work supporting the community. Second, the convent must keep strict enclosure, with no visitors allowed, even if they were the convent's wealthy supporters. Third, the convent was to have an egalitarian atmosphere in which class distinctions were forbidden and all sisters, including those of aristocratic background, shared the manual chores. The discriminatory measures common in Spanish society that applied to New Christians were also not to be practiced. Fourth, like Ignatius Loyola and the Jesuits, Teresa placed great emphasis on obedience, especially to one's confessor.

Between 1562 and Teresa's death in 1582, she founded or reformed fourteen other houses of nuns, traveling widely to do so. Teresa thought of the new religious houses she founded as answers to the Protestant takeover of Catholic churches elsewhere in Europe. From her brother, who had obtained wealth in the Spanish colonies, she learned about conditions in Peru and instructed her nuns "to pray unceasingly for the missionaries working among the heathens." Through prayer, Teresa wrote, her nuns could share in the exciting tasks of evangelization and missionary work otherwise closed to women. Her books, along with her five hundred surviving letters, show her as a practical and down-to-earth woman as well as a mystic and a creative theologian.

Seventeenth-century cloisonné enamelwork illustrating Teresa of Ávila's famous vision of an angel piercing her heart. (By gracious permission of Catherine Hamilton Kappauf)

QUESTIONS FOR ANALYSIS

1. How did convent life in Ávila reflect the values of sixteenth-century society, and how did Teresa's reforms challenge these?
2. How is the life of Teresa of Ávila typical of developments in the Catholic Reformation? How is her life unusual?

*The Autobiography of St. Teresa of Ávila, trans. and ed. E. A. Peers (New York: Doubleday, 1960), pp. 273–274.

Chapter 14
Reformations and Religious
408 Wars • 1500–1600

CHAPTER LOCATOR | What were the central beliefs of Protestant reformers?

led to riots, civil wars, and international conflicts. Catholics continued to believe that Calvinists and Lutherans could be reconverted; Protestants persisted in thinking that the Roman church should be destroyed. Catholics and Protestants alike feared people of other faiths, whom they often saw as agents of Satan. Even more, they feared those who were explicitly identified with Satan: witches living in their midst. Such fears made this era the time of the most virulent witch persecutions in European history.

French Religious Wars

The costs of the Habsburg-Valois wars forced the French to increase taxes and borrow heavily. King Francis I (r. 1515–1547) also tried two new devices to raise revenue: the sale of public offices and a treaty with the papacy. The former proved to be only a temporary source of money: once a man bought an office he and his heirs were exempt from taxation. But the latter, known as the Concordat of Bologna (see page 377), gave the French crown the right to appoint all French bishops and abbots, ensuring a rich supplement of money and offices. Because French rulers possessed control over appointments and had a vested financial interest in Catholicism, they had no need to revolt against Rome.

Significant numbers of those ruled, however, were attracted to Calvinism. Initially, Calvinism drew converts from among reform-minded members of the Catholic clergy, industrious city dwellers, and artisan groups. Most French Calvinists (called **Huguenots**) lived in major cities. When King Henry II (r. 1547–1559) died in 1559, perhaps one-tenth of the population had become Calvinist.

The feebleness of the French monarchy was the seed from which civil violence sprang. The three weak sons of Henry II who occupied the throne could not provide leadership, and they were often dominated by their mother, Catherine de' Medici. The French nobility took advantage of this monarchical weakness. Just as German princes in the Holy Roman Empire had adopted Lutheranism as a means of opposition to Emperor Charles V, so French nobles frequently adopted Protestantism to advance their independence. Armed clashes between Catholic royalist lords and Calvinist antimonarchical lords occurred in many parts of France.

Politics was not, however, the only motive behind religious violence. Both Calvinists and Catholics saw the other as a danger to the community. Calvinist teachings called the power of sacred images into question, and mobs in many cities took down and smashed statues, stained-glass windows, and paintings, viewing this as a way to purify the church. Catholic mobs responded by defending images, and crowds on both sides killed their opponents, often in gruesome ways.

On Saint Bartholomew's Day, August 24, 1572, the king's sister Margaret of Valois was married to the Protestant Henry of Navarre. The marriage was intended to help reconcile Catholics and Huguenots. Instead, Huguenot wedding guests in Paris were massacred, and other Protestants were slaughtered by mobs. Religious violence spread to the provinces, where thousands were killed. This Saint Bartholomew's Day massacre led to a civil war that dragged on for fifteen years. Agriculture in many areas was destroyed and commercial life declined severely.

What ultimately saved France was a small group of moderates of both faiths, called *politiques*, who believed that only the restoration of strong monarchy could reverse the trend toward collapse. The politiques also favored accepting the Huguenots as an officially recognized and organized group. The death of Catherine de' Medici, followed by the assassination of King Henry III, paved the way for the accession of Henry of Navarre (the unfortunate bridegroom of the Saint Bartholomew's Day massacre), a politique who became Henry IV (r. 1589–1610).

Henry's willingness to sacrifice religious principles to political necessity saved France. He converted to Catholicism but also issued the **Edict of Nantes** in 1598, which granted

Huguenots French Calvinists.

politiques Moderates of both religious faiths who held that only a strong monarchy could save France from total collapse.

Edict of Nantes A document issued by Henry IV of France in 1598, granting liberty of conscience and of public worship to Calvinists, which helped restore peace in France.

How did politics shape the course of the Reformation?

How did Protestantism spread beyond German-speaking lands?

How did the Catholic Church respond to the new religious situation?

Why did religious violence escalate in this period?

409

liberty of conscience and liberty of public worship to Huguenots in 150 fortified towns. The reign of Henry IV and the Edict of Nantes prepared the way for French absolutism in the seventeenth century by helping restore internal peace in France.

The Netherlands Under Charles V

In the Netherlands, what began as a movement for the reformation of the church developed into a struggle for Dutch independence. Emperor Charles V had inherited the seventeen provinces that compose present-day Belgium and the Netherlands (see page 396). Each was self-governing and enjoyed the right to make its own laws and collect its own taxes.

Union of Utrecht The alliance of seven northern provinces (led by Holland) that declared its independence from Spain and formed the United Provinces of the Netherlands.

In the Low Countries as elsewhere, corruption in the Roman church and the critical spirit of the Renaissance provoked pressure for reform, and Lutheran ideas took root. Charles V had grown up in the Netherlands, however, and he was able to limit their impact. But Charles V abdicated in 1556 and transferred power over the Netherlands to his son Philip II, who had grown up in Spain. Protestant ideas spread.

The Netherlands, 1609

Iconoclasm in the Netherlands Calvinist men and women break stained-glass windows, remove statues, and carry off devotional altarpieces. Iconoclasm, or the destruction of religious images, is often described as a "riot," but here the participants seem very purposeful. Calvinist Protestants regarded pictures and statues as sacrilegious and saw removing them as a way to purify the church. (The Fotomas Index/The Bridgeman Art Library)

By the 1560s Protestants in the Netherlands were primarily Calvinists. Calvinism's intellectual seriousness, moral gravity, and emphasis on any form of labor well done appealed to urban merchants, financiers, and artisans. Whereas Lutherans taught respect for the powers that be, Calvinism tended to encourage opposition to political authorities who were judged to be ungodly.

When Spanish authorities attempted to suppress Calvinist worship and raised taxes in the 1560s, rioting and the destruction of Catholic churches ensued. Philip II sent twenty thousand Spanish troops under the duke of Alva to pacify the Low Countries. Alva interpreted "pacification" to mean ruthless extermination of religious and political dissidents. On top of the Inquisition, he opened his own tribunal, soon called the "Council of Blood." On March 3, 1568, fifteen hundred men were executed.

Between 1568 and 1578 civil war raged in the Netherlands between Catholics and Protestants and between the seventeen provinces and Spain. Eventually the ten southern provinces, the Spanish Netherlands, came under the control of Spanish forces. The seven northern provinces, led by Holland, formed the Union of Utrecht and in 1581 declared their independence from Spain. The north was Protestant; the south remained Catholic. Philip did not accept this, and war continued. England was even drawn into the conflict, supplying money and troops to the northern United Provinces. Hostilities ended

Chapter 14
Reformations and Religious
Wars • 1500–1600

410

CHAPTER LOCATOR | What were the central beliefs of Protestant reformers?

in 1609 when Spain agreed to a truce that recognized the independence of the United Provinces.

The Great European Witch-Hunt

The relationship between the Reformation and the upsurge in trials for witchcraft that occurred at roughly the same time is complex. Increasing persecution for witchcraft actually began before the Reformation in the 1480s, but it became especially common about 1560, and the mania continued until roughly 1660. Religious reformers' extreme notions of the Devil's powers and the insecurity created by the religious wars contributed to this increase. Both Protestants and Catholics tried and executed witches, with church officials and secular authorities acting together.

The heightened sense of God's power and divine wrath in the Reformation era was an important factor in the witch-hunts, but so was a change in the idea of what a witch was. Nearly all premodern societies believe in witches, who are understood to be people who use magical forces. In the late Middle Ages, however, many educated Christians added a demonological component to this notion of what a witch was. For them, the essence of witchcraft was making a pact with the Devil. Witches were no longer simply people who used magical power to get what they wanted, but rather people used by the Devil to do what he wanted. Some demonological theorists also claimed that witches were organized in an international conspiracy to overthrow Christianity. Witchcraft was thus spiritualized, and witches became the ultimate heretics.

Trials involving this new notion of witchcraft as diabolical heresy began in Switzerland and southern Germany in the late fifteenth century, became less numerous in the early decades of the Reformation when Protestants and Catholics were busy fighting each other, and then picked up again in about 1560. Scholars estimate that during the sixteenth and seventeenth centuries somewhere between 100,000 and 200,000 people were officially tried for witchcraft and between 40,000 and 60,000 were executed.

Between 75 and 85 percent of those tried and executed were women. Ideas about women and the roles women actually played in society were thus important factors shaping the witch-hunts. Some demonologists expressed virulent misogyny, or hatred of women. Most people viewed women as weaker and so more likely to give in to an offer by the Devil. Women were associated with nature, disorder, and the body, all of which were linked with the demonic. Women also had more contact with areas of life in which bad things happened unexpectedly, such as preparing food or caring for new mothers, children, and animals.

Legal changes also played a role in causing, or at least allowing for, massive witch trials. One of these was a change from an accusatorial legal procedure to an inquisitorial procedure. In the former, a suspect knew the accusers and the charges they had brought, and an accuser could in turn be liable for trial if the charges were not proven. In the latter, legal authorities themselves brought the case. This change made people much more willing to accuse others, for they never had to take personal responsibility for the accusation or face the accused person's relatives. Areas in Europe that did not make this legal change saw very few trials. Inquisitorial procedure involved intense questioning of the suspect, often with torture. Torture was also used to get the names of additional suspects, as most lawyers firmly believed that no witch could act alone.

The use of inquisitorial procedure did not always lead to witch-hunts. The most famous inquisitions in early modern Europe, those in Spain, Portugal, and Italy, were in fact very lenient in their treatment of people accused of witchcraft. Inquisitors believed in the power of the Devil and were no less misogynist than other judges, but they doubted very much whether the people accused of witchcraft had actually made pacts with the Devil that gave them special powers. They viewed such people not as diabolical Devil-worshipers but as superstitious and ignorant peasants who should be educated rather than executed.

How did politics shape the course of the Reformation?

How did Protestantism spread beyond German-speaking lands?

How did the Catholic Church respond to the new religious situation?

Why did religious violence escalate in this period?

411

Most witch trials began with a single accusation in a village or town. Individuals accused someone they knew of using magic to spoil food, make children ill, kill animals, raise a hailstorm, or do other types of harm. Tensions within families, households, and neighborhoods often played a role in these accusations.

Once a charge was made, the suspect was brought in for questioning. One German witch-pamphlet from 1587 described a typical case:

> *Walpurga Hausmännin . . . upon kindly questioning and also torture . . . confessed . . . that the Evil One indulged in fornication with her . . . and made her many promises to help her in her poverty and need. . . . She promised herself body and soul to him and disowned God in heaven. . . . She destroyed a number of cattle, pigs, and geese . . . and dug up [the bodies] of one or two innocent children. With her devil-paramour and other playfellows she has eaten these and used their hair and their little bones for witchcraft.*

Confession was generally followed by execution. In this case, Hausmännin was "dispatched from life to death by burning at the stake . . . her body first to be torn five times with red-hot irons."[6]

After the initial suspect had been questioned, and particularly if he or she had been tortured, the people who had been implicated were brought in for questioning. This might lead to a small hunt, involving from five to ten suspects, and it sometimes grew into a much larger hunt, what historians have called a "witch panic." Panics were most common in the part of Europe that saw the most witch accusations in general: the Holy Roman Empire, Switzerland, and parts of France. Most of this area consisted of very small governmental units that were jealous of each other and, after the Reformation, were divided by religion. The rulers of these territories often felt more threatened than did the monarchs of western Europe, and they saw persecuting witches as a way to demonstrate their piety and concern for order. Moreover, witch panics often occurred after some type of climatic disaster, such as an unusually cold and wet summer, and they came in waves.

In large-scale panics a wider variety of suspects were taken in—wealthier people, children, a greater proportion of men. Mass panics tended to end when it became clear to legal authorities, or to the community itself, that the people being questioned or executed were not what they understood witches to be, or that the scope of accusations was beyond belief.

Witch Pamphlet This printed pamphlet presents the confession of "Mother Waterhouse," a woman convicted of witchcraft in England in 1566, who describes her "many abominable deeds" and "execrable sorcery" committed over fifteen years, and asks for forgiveness right before her execution. Enterprising printers often produced cheap, short pamphlets during witch trials, knowing they would sell, sometimes based on the actual trial proceedings and sometimes just made up. They both reflected and helped create stereotypes about what witches were and did. (The Granger Collection, NY)

Chapter 14
Reformations and Religious
412 **Wars • 1500–1600**

CHAPTER LOCATOR | What were the central beliefs of Protestant reformers?

As the seventeenth century ushered in new ideas about science and reason, many began to question whether witches could make pacts with the Devil or engage in the wild activities attributed to them. Doubts about whether secret denunciations were valid or torture would ever yield truthful confessions gradually spread among the same type of religious and legal authorities who had so vigorously persecuted witches. Prosecutions for witchcraft became less common and were gradually outlawed. The last official execution for witchcraft in England was in 1682, though the last one in the Holy Roman Empire was not until 1775.

←LOOKING BACK LOOKING AHEAD→

ALONG WITH THE RENAISSANCE, the Reformation is often seen as a key element in the creation of the "modern" world. This radical change contained many elements of continuity, however. Sixteenth-century reformers looked back to the early Christian church for their inspiration, and many of their reforming ideas had been advocated for centuries. Most Protestant reformers worked with political leaders to make religious changes, just as early church officials had worked with Emperor Constantine and his successors as Christianity became the official religion of the Roman Empire in the fourth century. The spread of Christianity and the spread of Protestantism were both accomplished by preaching, persuasion, and teaching, but also by force and violence. The Catholic Reformation was carried out by activist popes, a church council, and new religious orders, just as earlier reforms of the church had been.

Just as they linked with earlier developments, the events of the Reformation were also closely connected with what is often seen as the third element in the "modern" world: European exploration and colonization. Only a week after Martin Luther stood in front of Charles V at the Diet of Worms declaring his independence in matters of religion, Ferdinand Magellan, a Portuguese sea captain with Spanish ships, was killed in a group of islands off the coast of southeast Asia. Charles V had provided the backing for Magellan's voyage, the first to circumnavigate the globe. Magellan viewed the spread of Christianity as one of the purposes of his trip, and later in the sixteenth century institutions created as part of the Catholic Reformation, including the Jesuit order and the Inquisition, would operate in European colonies overseas as well as in Europe itself. The islands where Magellan was killed were later named the Philippines, in honor of Charles's son Philip, who sent the ill-fated Spanish Armada against England. Philip's opponent Queen Elizabeth was similarly honored when English explorers named a huge chunk of territory in North America "Virginia" as a tribute to their "Virgin Queen." The desire for wealth and power was an important motivation in the European voyages and colonial ventures, but so was religious zeal. ■

- **For a list of suggested readings for this chapter, visit** *bedfordstmartins.com/mckaywestunderstanding*.

- **For primary sources from this period, see** *Sources of Western Society*, Second Edition.

- **For Web sites, images, and documents related to topics in this chapter, see Make History at** *bedfordstmartins.com/mckaywestunderstanding*.

How did politics shape the course of the Reformation?

How did Protestantism spread beyond German-speaking lands?

How did the Catholic Church respond to the new religious situation?

Why did religious violence escalate in this period?

Step 1

GETTING STARTED Below are basic terms about this period in the history of Western civilization. Can you identify each term below and explain why it matters? To do this exercise online, go to bedfordstmartins.com/mckaywestunderstanding.

TERMS	WHO (OR WHAT) AND WHEN	WHY IT MATTERS
anticlericalism, p. 386		
pluralism, p. 386		
indulgence, p. 387		
Protestant, p. 389		
Spanish Armada, p. 401		
The Institutes of the Christian Religion, p. 401		
predestination, p. 401		
Holy Office, p. 404		
Jesuits, p. 407		
Huguenots, p. 409		
politiques, p. 409		
Edict of Nantes, p. 409		
Union of Utrecht, p. 410		

Step 2

MOVING BEYOND THE BASICS The exercise below requires a more advanced understanding of the chapter material. Examine the implications of core Protestant beliefs by filling in the chart below with descriptions of each core belief, the way it differs from Catholic theology, and its larger implications for early modern life. When you are finished, consider the following questions: Why did Protestantism constitute an attack on both Catholic theology and the institutions of the Catholic Church? Why did Protestantism so quickly become entangled in political issues? To do this exercise online, go to bedfordstmartins.com/mckaywestunderstanding.

	DESCRIPTION OF BELIEF	CONTRAST WITH CATHOLICISM	POLITICAL, SOCIAL, AND CULTURAL IMPLICATIONS
Salvation by Faith Alone			
Sole and Absolute Authority of the Bible			
Church as a Spiritual Priesthood of All Believers			

PUTTING IT ALL TOGETHER
Now that you've reviewed key elements of the chapter, take a step back and try to see the big picture. Remember to use specific examples from the chapter in your answers. To do this exercise online, go to bedfordstmartins.com/mckaywestunderstanding.

THE GERMAN REFORMATION

- How did fifteenth-century criticism of the Catholic Church lay the foundation for the Reformation?

- How did Martin Luther differ from previous proponents of religious reform? Why did his efforts produce more dramatic results than those of his predecessors?

- What role did politics play in the spread of Protestantism in Germany? Would the Reformation have occurred without the competition between local rulers and the Holy Roman emperor for power and authority? Why or why not?

THE SPREAD OF PROTESTANT IDEAS

- What role did technology play in the spread of Protestant ideas? Is it going too far to say that the printing press made the Reformation possible?

- Why were political elites so important to the spread and entrenchment of Protestant ideas? What role did ordinary men and women play in the success of the Reformation?

THE CATHOLIC REFORMATION

- What were the most important outcomes of the Council of Trent? How did the pre-council church differ from the post-council church?

- How did the Catholic Church actively combat Protestantism? How much success did it have in rolling back the advance of Protestantism?

RELIGIOUS VIOLENCE

- In your opinion, was religion really at the heart of the French religious wars? If not, what was?

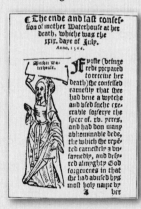

- Given the prevalence of belief in witchcraft throughout European history, how would you explain the witchcraft scares of the sixteenth and seventeenth centuries? Why did they begin and end when they did?

■ **In Your Own Words** Imagine that you must explain Chapter 14 to someone who hasn't read it. What would be the most important points to include and why?

15

European Exploration and Conquest

1450–1650

Before 1450 Europeans were relatively marginal players in a centuries-old trading system that linked Africa, Asia, and Europe. Elites everywhere prized Chinese porcelains and silks, while wealthy members of the Celestial Kingdom, as China called itself, wanted ivory and black slaves from Africa, and exotic goods and peacocks from India. African people wanted textiles from India and cowrie shells from the Maldives in the Indian Ocean. Europeans craved Asian silks and spices but they had few desirable goods to offer their trading partners.

The European search for better access to Asian trade led to a new overseas empire in the Indian Ocean and the accidental discovery of the Western Hemisphere. Within a few decades European colonies in South and North America would join this worldwide web. Europeans came to dominate trading networks and political empires of truly global proportions. The era of globalization had begun.

Global contacts created new forms of cultural exchange, assimilation, conversion, and resistance. Europeans struggled to comprehend the peoples and societies they found and sought to impose European cultural values on them. New forms of racial prejudice emerged, but so did new openness and curiosity about different ways of life. Together with the developments of the Renaissance and the Reformation, the Age of Discovery—as the period of European exploration and conquest from 1450 to 1650 is known—laid the foundations for the modern world. ■

Life in the Age of Discovery. A detail from an early-seventeenth-century Flemish painting depicting maps, illustrated travel books, a globe, a compass, and an astrolabe. The voyages of discovery revolutionized Europeans' sense of space and inspired a passion among the wealthy for collecting objects related to navigation and travel. (National Gallery, London/Art Resource, NY)

Chapter Preview

▶ **What were the limits of world contacts before Columbus?**

▶ **How and why did Europeans undertake voyages of expansion?**

▶ **What was the impact of conquest?**

▶ **How did Europe and the world change after Columbus?**

▶ **How did expansion change European attitudes and beliefs?**

▼ What were the limits of world contacts before Columbus?

Historians now recognize that a type of world economy, known as the Afro-Eurasian trade world, linked the products and people of Europe, Asia, and Africa in the fifteenth century. The West was not the dominant player before Columbus, and the European voyages derived from a desire to share in and control the wealth coming from the Indian Ocean.

The Trade World of the Indian Ocean

The Indian Ocean was the center of the Afro-Eurasian trade world. It was a crossroads for commercial and cultural exchange between China, India, the Middle East, Africa, and Europe (Map 15.1). From the seventh through the fourteenth centuries, the volume of this trade steadily increased, declining only during the years of the Black Death.

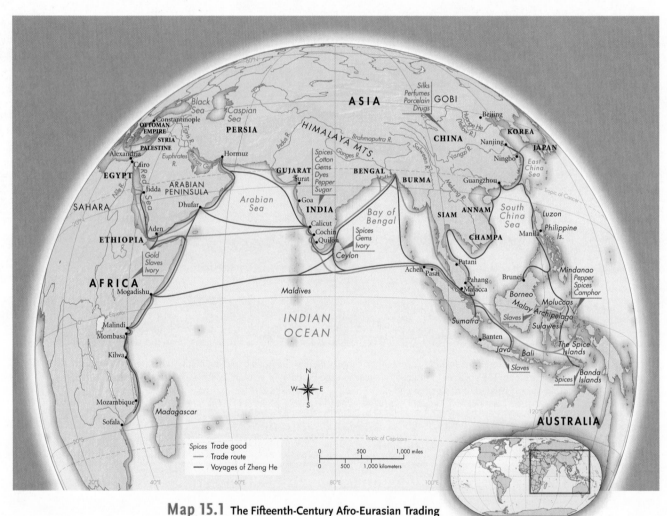

Map 15.1 The Fifteenth-Century Afro-Eurasian Trading World After a period of decline following the Black Death and the Mongol invasions, trade revived in the fifteenth century. Muslim merchants dominated trade, linking ports in East Africa and the Red Sea with those in India and the Malay Archipelago. Chinese Admiral Zheng He's voyages (1405–1433) followed the most important Indian Ocean trade routes, in the hope of imposing Ming dominance of trade and tribute.

Merchants congregated in a series of multicultural, cosmopolitan port cities strung around the Indian Ocean. The most developed area of this commercial web was in the South China Sea. In the fifteenth century the port of Malacca became a great commercial entrepôt (AHN-truh-poh), a trading post to which goods were shipped for storage while awaiting redistribution to other places.

The Mongol emperors opened the doors of China to the West, encouraging Europeans like the Venetian trader and explorer Marco Polo to do business there. Marco Polo's tales of his travels from 1271 to 1295 and his encounter with the Great Khan fueled Western fantasies about the Orient. After the Mongols fell to the Ming Dynasty in 1368, China entered a period of agricultural and commercial expansion, population growth, and urbanization. Historians agree that China had the most advanced economy in the world until at least the start of the eighteenth century.

China also took the lead in exploration, sending Admiral Zheng He's fleet along the trade web as far west as Egypt. From 1405 to 1433, each of his seven expeditions involved

The Port of Banten in Western Java Influenced by Muslim traders and emerging in the early sixteenth century as a Muslim kingdom, Banten evolved into a thriving entrepôt. The city stood on the trade route to China and, as this Dutch engraving suggests, in the seventeenth century the Dutch East India Company used Banten as an important collection point for spices purchased for sale in Europe. (Archives Charmet/The Bridgeman Art Library)

How and why did Europeans undertake voyages of expansion?

What was the impact of conquest?

How did Europe and the world change after Columbus?

How did expansion change European attitudes and beliefs?

hundreds of ships and tens of thousands of men. Court conflicts and the need to defend against renewed Mongol encroachment led to the abandonment of the expeditions after the deaths of Zheng He and the emperor. China's turning away from external trade opened new opportunities for European states to claim a decisive role in world trade.

Another center of trade in the Indian Ocean was India, the crucial link between the Persian Gulf and the Southeast Asian and East Asian trade networks. The subcontinent had ancient links with its neighbors to the northwest: trade between South Asia and Mesopotamia dates back to the origins of human civilization. Arab merchants who circumnavigated India on their way to trade in the South China Sea established trading posts along the southern coast of India, where the cities of Calicut and Quilon became thriving commercial centers. India was an important contributor of goods to the world trading system; much of the world's pepper was grown there, and Indian cotton textiles were highly prized.

The Trading States of Africa

Africa also played an important role in the world trade system before Columbus. By 1450 Africa had a few large and developed empires along with hundreds of smaller states. From 1250 until its defeat by the Ottomans in 1517, the Mamluk Egyptian empire was one of the most powerful on the continent. Its capital, Cairo, was a center of Islamic learning and religious authority as well as a hub for Indian Ocean trade goods. Sharing in Cairo's prosperity was the African highland state of Ethiopia, a Christian kingdom with scattered contacts with European rulers. On the east coast of Africa, Swahili-speaking city-states engaged in the Indian Ocean trade. Cities like Mogadishu and Mombasa were known for their prosperity and culture.

In the fifteenth century most of the gold that reached Europe came from Sudan in West Africa and from the Akan (AH-kahn) peoples living near present-day Ghana (GAH-nuh). Transported across the Sahara by Arab and African traders on camels, the gold was sold in the ports of North Africa. Other trading routes led to the Egyptian cities of Alexandria and Cairo, where the Venetians held commercial privileges.

Nations inland that sat astride the north-south caravan routes grew wealthy from this trade. In the mid-thirteenth century the kingdom of Mali emerged as an important player on the overland trade route. In later centuries the diversion of gold away from the trans-Saharan routes would weaken the inland states of Africa politically and economically.

Gold was one important object of trade; slaves were another. Slavery was practiced in Africa, as virtually everywhere else in the world, before the arrival of Europeans. Arabic and African merchants took West African slaves to the Mediterranean to be sold in European, Egyptian, and Middle Eastern markets and also brought eastern Europeans to West Africa as slaves. In addition, Indian and Arabic merchants traded slaves in the coastal regions of East Africa.

The Ottoman and Persian Empires

The Middle East served as an intermediary for trade between Europe, Africa, and Asia and was also an important supplier of goods for foreign exchange, especially silk and cotton. Two great rival empires, the Persian Safavids (sah-FAH-vidz) and the Turkish Ottomans, dominated the region.

The Persians' Shi'ite Muslim faith clashed with the Ottomans' adherence to Sunnism. Economically, the two competed for control over western trade routes to the East. Under Sultan Mohammed II (r. 1451–1481), the Ottomans captured Europe's largest city, Constantinople, in May 1453. Renamed Istanbul, the city became the capital of the Ottoman Empire. By the mid-sixteenth century the Ottomans controlled the sea trade

Chapter 15
**European Exploration and
Conquest • 1450–1650**

420

CHAPTER LOCATOR | What were the limits of world contacts before Columbus?

on the eastern Mediterranean, Syria, Palestine, Egypt, and the rest of North Africa, and their power extended into Europe as far west as Vienna.

Ottoman expansion frightened Europeans. In France in the sixteenth century, twice as many books were printed about the Turkish threat as about the American discoveries. The strength of the Ottomans helps explain some of the missionary fervor Christians brought to new territories. It also raised economic concerns. With trade routes to the east in the hands of the Ottomans, Europeans needed to find new trade routes.

Genoese and Venetian Middlemen

Compared to the East, Europe constituted a minor outpost in the world trading system. European craftsmen produced few products to rival those of Asia. In the late Middle Ages, the Italian city-states of Venice and Genoa controlled the European luxury trade with the East.

In 1304 Venice established formal relations with the sultan of Mamluk Egypt, opening operations in Cairo, the gateway to Asian trade. Venetian merchants specialized in expensive luxury goods like spices, silks, and carpets, which they obtained from middlemen in the eastern Mediterranean and Asia Minor.

The Venetians exchanged Eastern luxury goods for European products they could trade abroad, including Spanish and English wool, German metal goods, Flemish textiles, and silk cloth made by their own craftsmen using imported raw materials. Eastern demand for such goods was low. To make up the difference, the Venetians earned currency in the shipping industry and through trade in firearms and slaves.

Venice's ancient rival was Genoa. In the wake of the Crusades, Genoa dominated the northern route to Asia through the Black Sea. Expansion in the thirteenth and fourteenth centuries took the Genoese as far as Persia and the Far East. In 1291 they sponsored a failed expedition into the Atlantic in search of India. This voyage reveals the long roots of Genoese interest in Atlantic exploration.

In the fifteenth century, with Venice claiming victory in the spice trade, the Genoese shifted focus from trade to finance and from the Black Sea to the western Mediterranean. Located on the northwestern coast of Italy, Genoa had always been active in the western Mediterranean, trading with North African ports, southern France, Spain, and even England and Flanders through the Strait of Gibraltar. When Spanish and Portuguese voyages began to explore the western Atlantic (see pages 424–425), Genoese merchants, navigators, and financiers provided their skills to the Iberian monarchs.

A major element of both Venetian and Genoese trade was slavery. Merchants purchased slaves, many of whom were fellow Christians, in the Balkans. After the loss of the Black Sea—and thus the source of slaves—to the Ottomans, the Genoese sought new supplies of slaves in the West, taking the Guanches (indigenous peoples from the Canary Islands), Muslim prisoners and Jewish refugees from Spain, and by the early 1500s both black and Berber Africans. With the growth of Spanish colonies in the New World,

The Taking of Constantinople by the Turks, April 22, 1453 The Ottoman conquest of the capital of the Byzantine Empire in 1453 sent shock and despair through Europe. Capitalizing on the city's strategic and commercial importance, the Ottomans made it the center of their empire. (Bibliothèque nationale de France)

How and why did Europeans undertake voyages of expansion?　What was the impact of conquest?　How did Europe and the world change after Columbus?　How did expansion change European attitudes and beliefs?

421

Genoese and Venetian merchants would become important players in the Atlantic slave trade.

Italian experience in colonial administration, slaving, and international trade and finance served as a model for the Iberian states as they pushed European expansion to new heights. Mariners, merchants, and financiers from Venice and Genoa—most notably Christopher Columbus—played a crucial role in bringing the fruits of this experience to the Iberian Peninsula and to the New World.

▼ How and why did Europeans undertake voyages of expansion?

As we have seen, Europe was by no means isolated before the voyages of exploration and its "discovery" of the New World. But because they did not produce many products desired by Eastern elites, Europeans were modest players in the Indian Ocean trading world. As Europe recovered after the Black Death, new European players entered the scene with new technology, eager to spread Christianity and to undo Italian and Ottoman domination of trade with the East.

Causes of European Expansion

European expansion had multiple causes. By the middle of the fifteenth century, Europe was experiencing a revival of population and economic activity after the lows of the Black Death. This revival created demands for luxury goods, especially spices, from the East. The fall of Constantinople and subsequent Ottoman control of trade routes created obstacles to fulfilling these demands. Europeans needed to find new sources of precious metal to trade with the Ottomans, or trade routes that bypassed the Ottomans.

Religious fervor was another important catalyst for expansion. The passion and energy ignited by the Christian *reconquista* (reconquest) of the Iberian Peninsula encouraged the Portuguese and Spanish to continue the Christian crusade. Just seven months separated the Spanish conquest of Granada, the last remaining Muslim state on the Iberian Peninsula, and Columbus's departure across the Atlantic. Since the remaining Muslim states, such as the mighty Ottoman Empire, were too strong to defeat, Iberians turned their attention elsewhere.

Combined with eagerness for profits and to spread Christianity was the desire for glory and the urge to chart new waters. Scholars have frequently described the European discoveries as a manifestation of Renaissance curiosity about the physical universe. The detailed journals kept by European voyagers attest to their wonder and fascination with the new peoples and places they visited.

Individual explorers combined these motivations in unique ways. Christopher Columbus was a devout Christian who was increasingly haunted by messianic obsessions in the last years of his life. As Portuguese explorer Bartholomew Diaz put it, his own motives were "to serve God and His Majesty, to give light to those who were in darkness and to grow rich as all men desire to do." When the Portuguese explorer Vasco da Gama reached the port of Calicut, India, in 1498 and a native asked what he wanted, he replied, "Christians and spices."[1] The bluntest of the Spanish conquistadors, Hernando Cortés, announced as he prepared to conquer Mexico, "I have come to win gold, not to plow the fields like a peasant."[2]

Eagerness for exploration was heightened by a lack of opportunity at home. After the reconquista, young men of the Spanish upper classes found their economic and political opportunities greatly limited. The ambitious turned to the sea to seek their fortunes.

conquistador Spanish for "conqueror"; Spanish soldier-explorers, such as Hernando Cortés and Francisco Pizarro, who sought to conquer the New World for the Spanish crown.

Chapter 15
European Exploration and
422 **Conquest • 1450–1650**

CHAPTER LOCATOR | What were the limits of world contacts before Columbus?

Whatever the reasons, the voyages were made possible by the growth of government power. The Spanish monarchy was stronger than before and in a position to support foreign ventures. In Portugal explorers also looked to the monarchy, to Prince Henry the Navigator in particular (pages 424–425), for financial support and encouragement. Like voyagers, monarchs shared a mix of motivations, from the desire to please God to the desire to win glory and profit from trade. Competition among European monarchs was an important factor in encouraging the steady stream of expeditions that began in the late fifteenth century.

Ordinary sailors were ill paid, and life at sea meant danger, overcrowding, unbearable stench, and hunger. For months at a time, 100 to 120 people lived and worked in a space of 1,600 to 2,000 square feet. Men chose to join these miserable crews to escape poverty at home, to continue a family trade, to win a few crumbs of the great riches of empire, or to find better lives as illegal immigrants in the colonies.

The people who stayed at home had a powerful impact on the process. Royal ministers and factions at court influenced monarchs to provide or deny support for exploration. The small number of people who could read served as an audience for tales of fantastic places and unknown peoples. Cosmography, natural history, and geography aroused enormous interest among educated people in the fifteenth and sixteenth centuries.

The Travels of Sir John Mandeville The author of this tale claimed to be an English knight who traveled extensively in the Middle East and Asia from the 1320s to the 1350s. Although historians now consider the work a skillful fiction, it had a great influence on how Europeans understood the world at the time. This illustration, from an edition published around 1410, depicts Mandeville approaching a walled city on the first stage of his voyage to Constantinople (© British Library Board)

Technology and the Rise of Exploration

Technological developments in shipbuilding, weaponry, and navigation provided another impetus for European expansion. Since ancient times, most seagoing vessels had been narrow, open boats called galleys, propelled largely by slaves or convicts manning the oars. Though well suited to the placid waters of the Mediterranean, galleys could not withstand the rougher conditions in the Atlantic. The need for sturdier craft, as well as population losses caused by the Black Death, forced the development of a new style of ship that would not require much manpower to sail. In the course of the fifteenth century, the Portuguese developed the caravel, a small, light, three-mast sailing ship. The caravel held more cargo and was much more maneuverable than the galley. When fitted with cannon, it could dominate larger vessels.

Great strides in cartography and navigational aids were also made during this period. In 1406 Arab scholars reintroduced Europeans to Ptolemy's *Geography*. Written in the second century C.E., the work synthesized the geographical knowledge of the classical world. Ptolemy's work provided significant improvements over medieval cartography, showing the world as round and introducing the idea of latitude and longitude to plot position accurately. It also contained crucial errors. Unaware of the Americas, Ptolemy showed the world as much smaller than it is, so that Asia appeared not very distant from

caravel A small, maneuverable, three-mast sailing ship developed by the Portuguese in the fifteenth century that gave the Portuguese a distinct advantage in exploration and trade.

Ptolemy's *Geography*
A second century C.E. work that synthesized the classical knowledge of geography and introduced the concepts of longitude and latitude. Reintroduced to Europeans in 1406 by Arab scholars, its ideas allowed cartographers to create more accurate maps.

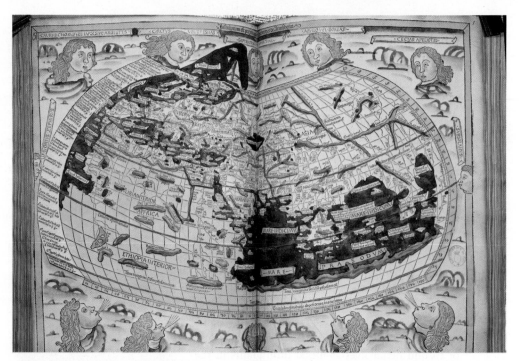

Ptolemy's *Geography* The recovery of Ptolemy's *Geography* in the early fifteenth century gave Europeans new access to ancient geographical knowledge. This 1486 world map, based on Ptolemy, is a great advance over medieval maps but contains errors with significant consequences for future exploration. It shows a single continent watered by a single ocean, with land covering three-quarters of the world's surface. Africa and Asia are joined with Europe, making the Indian Ocean a land-locked sea and rendering the circumnavigation of Africa impossible. The continent of Asia is stretched far to the east, greatly shortening the distance from Europe to Asia via the Atlantic. (Giraudon/Art Resource, NY)

Europe to the west. Based on this work, cartographers fashioned new maps that combined classical knowledge with the latest information from mariners.

The magnetic compass enabled sailors to determine their direction and position at sea. The astrolabe, an instrument invented by the ancient Greeks and perfected by Muslim navigators, was used to determine the altitude of the sun and other celestial bodies. It permitted mariners to plot their latitude, that is, their precise position north or south of the equator.

Like the astrolabe, much of the new technology that Europeans used on their voyages was borrowed from the East. Gunpowder, the compass, and the sternpost rudder were Chinese inventions. The lateen sail, which allowed European ships to tack against the wind, was a product of the Indian Ocean trade world and was brought to the Mediterranean on Arab ships. Advances in cartography also drew on the rich tradition of Judeo-Arabic mathematical and astronomical learning in Iberia. In exploring new territories, European sailors thus called on techniques and knowledge developed over centuries in China, the Muslim world, and the Indian Ocean.

The Portuguese Overseas Empire

Portugal had a long history of seafaring and navigation. Blocked from access to western Europe by Spain, the Portuguese turned to the Atlantic and North Africa, whose waters they knew better than did other Europeans.

In the early phases of Portuguese exploration, Prince Henry (1394–1460), a younger son of the king, played a leading role. A nineteenth-century scholar dubbed Henry "the

Chapter 15
European Exploration and
Conquest • 1450–1650

CHAPTER LOCATOR   What were the limits of world contacts before Columbus?

Navigator" because of his support for the study of geography and navigation and for the annual expeditions he sponsored down the western coast of Africa.

The objectives of Portuguese exploration policy included desires for military glory; crusades to Christianize Muslims and to locate a mythical Christian king of Africa, Prester John; and the quest to find gold, slaves, and an overseas route to the spice markets of India. Portugal's conquest of Ceuta, an Arab city in northern Morocco, in 1415 marked the beginning of European overseas expansion. In the 1420s, under Henry's direction, the Portuguese began to settle the Atlantic islands of Madeira (ca. 1420) and the Azores (1427). In 1443 they founded their first African commercial settlement at Arguin in North Africa. By the time of Henry's death in 1460, his support for exploration was vindicated by thriving sugar plantations on the Atlantic islands, the first arrival of enslaved Africans in Portugal (see page 439), and new access to African gold.

The Portuguese next established trading posts and forts on the gold-rich Guinea coast and penetrated into the African continent all the way to Timbuktu (Map 15.2). By 1500 Portugal controlled the flow of African gold to Europe.

The Portuguese then pushed farther south down the west coast of Africa. In 1487 Bartholomew Diaz rounded the Cape of Good Hope at the southern tip, but storms and a threatened mutiny forced him to turn back. A decade later Vasco da Gama succeeded in rounding the Cape while commanding a fleet in search of a sea route to India. With the help of an Indian guide, da Gama reached the port of Calicut in India. He returned to Lisbon loaded with spices and samples of Indian cloth, having proved the possibility of lucrative trade with the East via the Cape route. Thereafter, a Portuguese convoy set out for passage around the Cape every March.

Lisbon became the entrance port for Asian goods into Europe, but this was not accomplished without a fight. Muslim-controlled port city-states had long controlled the rich spice trade of the Indian Ocean, and they did not surrender it willingly. Portuguese cannon blasted open the port of Malacca in 1511, followed by Calicut, Ormuz, and Goa. The bombardment of these cities laid the foundation for Portuguese imperialism in the sixteenth and seventeenth centuries.

In March 1493, between the voyages of Diaz and da Gama, Spanish ships under a Genoese mariner named Christopher Columbus (1451–1506), in the service of the Spanish crown, entered Lisbon harbor. Spain also had begun the quest for an empire.

The Portuguese Fleet Embarked for the Indies This image shows a Portuguese trading fleet in the late fifteenth century bound for the riches of the Indies. Between 1500 and 1635 over nine hundred ships sailed from Portugal to ports on the Indian Ocean, in annual fleets composed of five to ten ships. (British Museum/HarperCollins Publishers/The Art Archive)

The Problem of Christopher Columbus

In order to understand Christopher Columbus in the context of his own time, we need to ask several questions. First, what kind of man was Columbus, and what forces or influences shaped him? Second, in sailing westward from Europe, what were his goals? Third, did he achieve his goals, and what did he make of his discoveries?

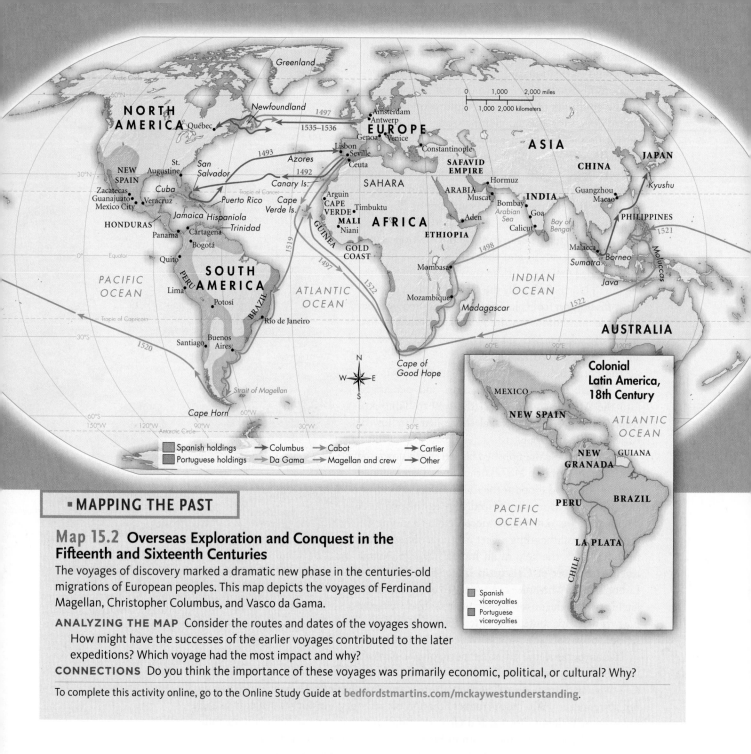

Scale: 0 1,000 2,000 miles / 0 1,000 2,000 kilometers

Map labels: Greenland, NORTH AMERICA, Québec, Newfoundland, 1497, 1535–1536, Amsterdam, Antwerp, EUROPE, Genoa, Venice, Lisbon, Seville, Constantinople, ASIA, JAPAN, CHINA, Kyushu, St. Augustine, San Salvador, Azores, 1493, NEW SPAIN, Zacatecas, Guanajuato, Mexico City, Veracruz, Cuba, Puerto Rico, 1492, Canary Is., Ceuta, Cape Verde Is., SAHARA, SAFAVID EMPIRE, ARABIA, Hormuz, Muscat, INDIA, Bombay, Arabian Sea, Goa, Guangzhou, Macao, PHILIPPINES, 1521, HONDURAS, Jamaica, Hispaniola, Trinidad, Cartagena, Panama, Bogotá, Quito, Cape Verde, ARGUIN, GUINEA, MALI, Timbuktu, Niani, AFRICA, GOLD COAST, ETHIOPIA, Aden, Calicut, Bay of Bengal, Malacca, Sumatra, Borneo, Moluccas, Java, PACIFIC OCEAN, Equator, Lima, PERU, SOUTH AMERICA, BRAZIL, 1519, 1497, ATLANTIC OCEAN, Potosí, Mombasa, 1498, 1522, INDIAN OCEAN, Mozambique, Madagascar, 1522, AUSTRALIA, Río de Janeiro, Tropic of Capricorn, 1520, Santiago, Buenos Aires, Strait of Magellan, Cape of Good Hope, Cape Horn, Antarctic Circle

Legend:
Spanish holdings — Columbus — Cabot — Cartier
Portuguese holdings — Da Gama — Magellan and crew — Other

Inset map: Colonial Latin America, 18th Century — MEXICO, NEW SPAIN, ATLANTIC OCEAN, NEW GRANADA, GUIANA, PACIFIC OCEAN, PERU, BRAZIL, CHILE, LA PLATA
Legend: Spanish viceroyalties / Portuguese viceroyalties

▪ MAPPING THE PAST

Map 15.2 Overseas Exploration and Conquest in the Fifteenth and Sixteenth Centuries

The voyages of discovery marked a dramatic new phase in the centuries-old migrations of European peoples. This map depicts the voyages of Ferdinand Magellan, Christopher Columbus, and Vasco da Gama.

ANALYZING THE MAP Consider the routes and dates of the voyages shown. How might have the successes of the earlier voyages contributed to the later expeditions? Which voyage had the most impact and why?

CONNECTIONS Do you think the importance of these voyages was primarily economic, political, or cultural? Why?

To complete this activity online, go to the Online Study Guide at bedfordstmartins.com/mckaywestunderstanding.

Columbus's westward voyages embodied a long-standing Genoese ambition to circumvent Venetian domination of eastward trade, which was now being claimed by the Portuguese. Columbus was very knowledgeable about the sea. He had worked as a mapmaker, and he was familiar with such fifteenth-century Portuguese navigational developments as *portolans*—written descriptions of the courses along which ships sailed—and the use of the compass as a nautical instrument. His successful thirty-three-day voyage to the Caribbean owed a great deal to his seamanship.

Columbus was also a deeply religious man. He began the *Journal* of his voyage to the Americas in the form of a letter to Ferdinand and Isabella of Spain:

Chapter 15
European Exploration and
426 Conquest • 1450–1650

CHAPTER LOCATOR   What were the limits of world contacts before Columbus?

On 2 January in the year 1492, when your Highnesses had concluded their war with the Moors who reigned in Europe, I saw your Highnesses' banners victoriously raised on the towers of the Alhambra, the citadel of the city, and the Moorish king come out of the city gates and kiss the hands of your Highnesses and the prince, My Lord. And later in that same month, on the grounds of information I had given your Highnesses concerning the lands of India . . . your Highnesses decided to send me, Christopher Columbus, to see these parts of India and the princes and peoples of those lands and consider the best means for their conversion.[3]

Columbus had witnessed the Spanish conquest of Granada and shared fully in the religious and nationalistic fervor surrounding that event. Like the Spanish rulers and most Europeans of his age, he understood Christianity as a missionary religion that should be carried to places where it did not exist.

What was the object of this first voyage? Columbus gave the answer in the very title of the expedition, "The Enterprise of the Indies." He wanted to find a direct ocean trading route to Asia. Rejected for funding by the Portuguese in 1483 and by Ferdinand and Isabella in 1486, the project finally won the backing of the Spanish monarchy in 1492. The Spanish crown named Columbus viceroy over any territory he might discover and gave him one-tenth of the material rewards of the journey. Based on Ptolemy's *Geography* and other texts, he expected to pass the islands of Japan and then land on the east coast of China.

How did Columbus interpret what he had found, and in his mind did he achieve what he had set out to do? Columbus's small fleet left Spain on August 3, 1492. He landed on an island in the Bahamas, which he christened San Salvador, on October 12, 1492. Columbus believed he had found some small islands off the east coast of Japan. In a letter he wrote to Ferdinand and Isabella on his return to Spain, Columbus described the natives as handsome, peaceful, and primitive people. Believing he was in the Indies, he called them "Indians," a name that was later applied to all inhabitants of the Americas. Columbus concluded that they would make good slaves and could quickly be converted to Christianity. (See "Listening to the Past: Columbus Describes His First Voyage," page 428.)

Scholars have identified the inhabitants of the islands as the Taino people, speakers of the Arawak language, who inhabited Hispaniola (modern-day Haiti and Dominican Republic) and other islands in the Caribbean. Columbus received reassuring reports from Taino villagers of the presence of gold and of a great king in the vicinity. From San Salvador, Columbus sailed southwest, believing that this course would take him to Japan or the coast of China. He landed instead on Cuba on October 28. Deciding that he must be on the mainland near the coastal city of Quinsay (now Hangzhou), he sent a small embassy inland with letters from Ferdinand and Isabella and instructions to locate the grand city.

The landing party found only small villages. Confronted with this disappointment, Columbus focused on trying to find gold or other valuables among the peoples he had discovered. The sight of Taino people wearing gold ornaments on Hispaniola seemed to prove that gold was available in the region. In January, confident that its source would soon be found, he headed back to Spain to report on his discovery.

Over the next decades, the Spanish would follow a policy of conquest and colonization in the New World. On his second voyage, Columbus forcibly subjugated the island of Hispaniola and enslaved its indigenous peoples. On this

Columbus's First Voyage to the New World, 1492–1493

LISTENING TO THE PAST

Columbus Describes His First Voyage

On his return voyage to Spain in January 1493, Christopher Columbus composed a letter intended for wide circulation and had copies of it sent ahead to Isabella and Ferdinand. Because the letter sums up Columbus's understanding of his achievements, it is considered the most important document of his first voyage. Remember that his knowledge of Asia rested heavily on Marco Polo's Travels, *published around 1298.*

❝ Since I know that you will be pleased at the great success with which the Lord has crowned my voyage, I write to inform you how in thirty-three days I crossed from the Canary Islands to the Indies, with the fleet which our most illustrious sovereigns gave me. I found very many islands with large populations and took possession of them all for their Highnesses; this I did by proclamation and unfurled the royal standard. No opposition was offered.

I named the first island that I found "San Salvador," in honour of our Lord and Saviour who has granted me this miracle. . . . When I reached Cuba, I followed its north coast westwards, and found it so extensive that I thought this must be the mainland, the province of Cathay.* . . . From there I saw another island eighteen leagues east-wards which I then named "Hispaniola.". . .†

Hispaniola is a wonder. The mountains and hills, the plains and meadow lands are both fertile and beautiful. They are most suitable for planting crops and for raising cattle of all kinds, and there are good sites for building towns and villages. The harbours are incredibly fine and there are many great rivers with broad channels and the majority contain gold.‡ The trees, fruits and plants are very different from those of Cuba. In Hispaniola there are many spices and large mines of gold and other metals.§ . . .

The inhabitants of this island, and all the rest that I discovered or heard of, go naked, as their mothers bore them, men and women alike. A few of the women, however, cover a single place with a leaf of a plant or piece of cotton which they weave for the purpose. They have no iron or steel or arms and are not capable of using them, not because they are not strong and well built but because they are amazingly timid. All the weapons they have are canes cut at seeding time, at the end of which they fix a sharpened stick, but they have not the courage to make use of these, for very often when I have sent two or three men to a village to have conversation with them a great number of them have come out. But as soon as they saw my men all fled immediately, a father not even waiting for his son. And this is not because we have harmed any of them; on the contrary, wherever I have gone and been able to have conversation with them, I have given them some of the various things I had, a cloth and other articles, and received nothing in exchange. But they have still remained incurably timid.

True, when they have been reassured and lost their fear, they are so ingenuous and so liberal with all their possessions that no one who has not seen them would believe it. If one asks for anything they have they never say no. On the contrary, they offer a share to anyone with demonstrations of heartfelt affection, and they are immediately content with any small thing, valuable or valueless, that is given them. I forbade the men to give them bits of broken crockery, fragments of glass or tags of laces, though if they could get them they fancied them the finest jewels in the world. . . .

I hoped to win them to the love and service of their Highnesses and of the whole Spanish nation and to persuade them to collect and give us of the things which they possessed in abundance and which we needed. They have no religion and are not idolaters; but all believe that power and goodness dwell in the sky and they are firmly convinced that I have come from the sky with these ships and people. In this be-lief they gave me a good reception everywhere, once they had overcome their fear; and this is not because they are stupid — far from it, they are men of great intelligence, for they navigate all those seas, and give a marvellously good account of every thing — but because they have never before seen men clothed or ships like these. . . .

In all these islands the men are seemingly content with one woman, but their chief or king is allowed more than twenty. The women appear to work more

and subsequent voyages, Columbus brought with him settlers for the new Spanish ter-ritories, along with agricultural seed and livestock. Columbus himself, however, had little interest in or capacity for governing. Revolt soon broke out against him and his brother on Hispaniola. A royal expedition sent to investigate returned the brothers to Spain in chains. Columbus was quickly cleared of wrongdoing, but he did not recover his authority over the territories.

Columbus was very much a man of his times. To the end of his life in 1506, he be-lieved that he had found small islands off the coast of Asia. He never realized the scope of his achievement: he found a vast continent unknown to Europeans, except for a fleeting

Chapter 15
European Exploration and
Conquest • 1450–1650

428

CHAPTER LOCATOR | What were the limits of world contacts before Columbus?

will give them as much gold as they require, if they will render me some very slight assistance; also I will give them all the spices and cotton they want. . . . I will also bring them as much aloes as they ask and as many slaves, who will be taken from the idolaters. I believe also that I have found rhubarb and cinnamon and there will be countless other things in addition. . . .

So all Christendom will be delighted that our Redeemer has given victory to our most illustrious King and Queen and their renowned kingdoms, in this great matter. They should hold great celebrations and render solemn thanks to the Holy Trinity with many solemn prayers, for the great triumph which they will have, by the conversion of so many peoples to our holy faith and for the temporal benefits which will follow, for not only Spain, but all Christendom will receive encouragement and profit.

This is a brief account of the facts. Written in the caravel off the Canary Islands.**

15 February 1493

At your orders   THE ADMIRAL 🙶

Christopher Columbus, by Ridolfo Ghirlandaio. Friend of Raphael and teacher of Michelangelo, Ghirlandaio (1483–1561) enjoyed distinction as a portrait painter, and so we can assume that this is a good likeness of the older Columbus. (Scala/ Art Resource, NY)

Source: From *The Four Voyages of Christopher Columbus*, edited and translated by J. M. Cohen (Penguin Classics, 1969). Copyright © J. M. Cohen, 1969. Reproduced by permission of Penguin Books, Ltd.

than the men and I have not been able to find out if they have private property. As far as I could see whatever a man had was shared among all the rest and this particularly applies to food. . . . In another island, which I am told is larger than Hispaniola, the people have no hair. Here there is a vast quantity of gold, and from here and the other islands I bring Indians as evidence.

In conclusion, to speak only of the results of this very hasty voyage, their Highnesses can see that I

QUESTIONS FOR ANALYSIS

1. How did Columbus explain the success of his voyage?
2. What was Columbus's view of the Native Americans he met?
3. Evaluate his statements that the Caribbean islands possessed gold, cotton, and spices.

*Cathay is the old name for China. In the logbook and later in this letter, Columbus accepts the native story that Cuba is an island that can be circumnavigated in something more than twenty-one days, yet he insists here and during the second voyage that it is part of the Asiatic mainland.

†Hispaniola is the second largest island of the West Indies. Haiti occupies the western third of the island, the Dominican Republic the rest.

‡This did not prove to be true.

§These statements are also inaccurate.

**Actually, Columbus was off Santa Maria in the Azores.

Viking presence centuries earlier. He could not know that the scale of his discoveries would revolutionize world power, raising issues of trade, settlement, government bureaucracy, and the rights of native and African peoples.

Later Explorers

The Florentine navigator Amerigo Vespucci (veh-SPOO-chee) (1454–1512) realized what Columbus had not. Writing about his discoveries on the coast of modern-day Venezuela, Vespucci stated: "Those new regions which we found and explored with the

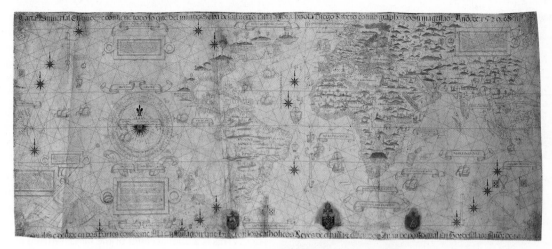

World Map of Diogo Ribeiro, 1529 This map integrates the wealth of new information provided by European explorers in the decades after Columbus's 1492 voyage. Working on commission for the Spanish king Charles V, mapmaker Diogo Ribeiro incorporated new details on Africa, South America, India, the Malay Archipelago, and China. Note the inaccuracy in his placement of the Moluccas, or Spice Islands, which are much too far east. This "mistake" was intended to serve Spain's interests in trade negotiations with the Portuguese. (Biblioteca Apostolica Vaticana)

fleet . . . we may rightly call a New World." In recognition of Amerigo's bold claim, the continent was named for him.

To settle competing claims to the Atlantic discoveries, Spain and Portugal turned to Pope Alexander VI. The resulting Treaty of Tordesillas (tor-duh-SEE-yuhs) in 1494 gave Spain everything to the west of an imaginary north-south line drawn down the Atlantic and Portugal everything to the east. This arbitrary division worked in Portugal's favor when in 1500 an expedition led by Pedro Alvares Cabral, en route to India, landed on the coast of Brazil, which Cabral claimed as Portuguese territory.

The search for profits determined the direction of Spanish exploration and expansion into South America. With insignificant profits from the Caribbean compared to the enormous riches that the Portuguese were reaping in Asia, Spain renewed the search for a western passage to Asia. In 1519 Charles V of Spain commissioned Ferdinand Magellan (1480–1521) to find a direct sea route to the spices of the Moluccas off the southeast coast of Asia. Magellan sailed southwest across the Atlantic to Brazil, and after a long search along the coast he located the treacherous straits that now bear his name (see Map 15.2). After passing through the straits, his fleet sailed north up the west coast of South America and then headed west into the Pacific toward the Malay Archipelago. Some of these islands were conquered in the 1560s and named the "Philippines" for Philip II of Spain.

Terrible storms, disease, starvation, and violence haunted the expedition. Sailors on two of Magellan's five ships attempted mutiny on the South American coast; one ship was lost, and another ship deserted and returned to Spain before even traversing the straits. Magellan himself was killed in a skirmish in the Philippines. The expedition had enough survivors to man only two ships, and one of them was captured by the Portuguese. One ship with only eighteen men returned to Spain from the east by way of the Indian Ocean, the Cape of Good Hope, and the Atlantic in 1522. The voyage — the first to circumnavigate the globe — had taken close to three years.

Despite the losses, this voyage revolutionized Europeans' understanding of the world by demonstrating the vastness of the Pacific. Although the voyage made a small profit in spices, the westward passage to the Indies was too long and dangerous for commercial purposes. Spain soon abandoned the attempt to oust Portugal from the Eastern spice trade and concentrated on exploiting her New World territories.

Treaty of Tordesillas The 1494 agreement giving Spain everything to the west of an imaginary line drawn down the Atlantic and giving Portugal everything to the east.

Chapter 15
**European Exploration and
Conquest • 1450–1650**

430

CHAPTER LOCATOR | What were the limits of world contacts before Columbus?

The English and French also set sail across the Atlantic during the early days of exploration in search of a northwest passage to the Indies. In 1497 John Cabot, a Genoese merchant living in London, discovered Newfoundland. The next year he returned and explored the New England coast. These forays proved futile, and the English established no permanent colonies in the territories they explored. Between 1576 and 1578, Martin Frobisher made three voyages in and around the Canadian bay that now bears his name. Frobisher hopefully brought a quantity of ore back to England with him, but it proved to be worthless.

Early French exploration of the Atlantic was equally frustrating. Between 1534 and 1541 Frenchman Jacques Cartier made several voyages and explored the St. Lawrence region of Canada, searching for a passage to the wealth of Asia. When this hope proved vain, the French turned to a new source of profit within Canada itself: trade in beaver pelts and other furs. French fisherman also competed with Spanish and English for the teeming schools of cod they found in the Atlantic waters around Newfoundland.

Spanish Conquest in the New World

In 1519 the Spanish sent an exploratory expedition from their post in Cuba to the mainland under the command of the conquistador Hernando Cortés (1485–1547). Accompanied by six hundred men, sixteen horses, and ten cannon, Cortés was to launch the conquest of the Mexica Empire. Its people were later called the Aztecs, but now most scholars prefer to use the term *Mexica* (meh-SHEE-kuh) to refer to them and their empire.

The Mexica Empire was ruled by Montezuma II (r. 1502–1520) from his capital at Tenochtitlán (tay-noch-teet-LAHN), now Mexico City. Larger than any European city of the time, it was the heart of a sophisticated civilization with advanced mathematics,

Mexica Empire Also known as the Aztec Empire, a large and complex Native American civilization in modern Mexico and Central America that possessed advanced mathematical, astronomical, and engineering technology.

The Aztec Capital of Tenochtitlán Occupying a large island, Tenochtitlán was laid out in concentric circles. The administrative and religious buildings were at the heart of the city, which was surrounded by residential quarters. Cortés himself marveled at the city in his letters: "The city is as large as Seville or Córdoba. . . . There are bridges, very large, strong, and well constructed, so that, over many, ten horsemen can ride abreast. . . . The city has many squares where markets are held. . . . There is one square . . . where there are daily more than sixty thousand souls, buying and selling. In the service and manners of its people, their fashion of living was almost the same as in Spain, with just as much harmony and order." (The Newberry Library)

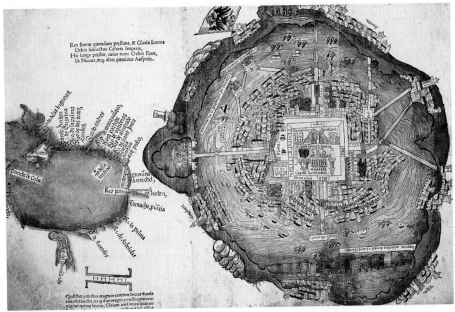

Doña Marina Translating for Hernando Cortés During His Meeting with Montezuma

In April 1519 Doña Marina (or La Malinche as she is known in Mexico) was among twenty women given to the Spanish as slaves. Fluent in Nahuatl (NAH-wah-tuhl) and Yucatec (YOO-kuh-tehk) Mayan (spoken by a Spanish priest accompanying Cortés), she acted as an interpreter and diplomatic guide for the Spanish. She had a close relationship with Cortés and bore his son, Don Martín Cortés, in 1522. This image was created by Tlaxcalan artists shortly after the conquest of Mexico and represents one indigenous perspective on the events. (The Granger Collection, NY)

ANALYZING THE IMAGE What role does Doña Marina (far right) appear to be playing in this image? Does she appear to be subservient or equal to Cortés (right, seated)? How did the painter indicate her identity as non-Spanish?

CONNECTIONS How do you think the native rulers negotiating with Cortés might have viewed her? What about a Spanish viewer of this image? What does the absence of other women here suggest about the role of women in these societies?

To complete this activity online, go to the Online Study Guide at bedfordstmartins.com/mckaywestunderstanding.

astronomy, and engineering, with a complex social system, and with oral poetry and historical traditions.

Cortés landed on the coast of the Gulf of Mexico on April 21, 1519. The Spanish camp was soon visited by delegations of unarmed Mexica leaders bearing gifts and news of

Chapter 15
European Exploration and

432   Conquest • 1450–1650

CHAPTER LOCATOR   What were the limits of world contacts before Columbus?

their great emperor. Cortés quickly realized that he could exploit internal dissension within the empire to his own advantage. The Mexica state religion necessitated constant warfare against neighboring peoples to secure captives for religious sacrifices and laborers for agricultural and building projects. Conquered peoples were required to pay tribute to the Mexica state through their local chiefs.

Cortés forged an alliance with the Tlaxcalas and other subject kingdoms, which chafed under the tribute demanded by the Mexicas. In October a combined Spanish-Tlaxcalan force occupied the city of Chollolan and massacred many thousand inhabitants. Strengthened by this display of power, Cortés made alliances with other native kingdoms. In November 1519, with a few hundred Spanish men and some six thousand indigenous warriors, Cortés marched on Tenochtitlán.

Montezuma refrained from attacking the Spaniards as they advanced toward his capital and welcomed Cortés and his men into Tenochtitlán. Other native leaders attacked the Spanish, but Montezuma relied on the advice of his state council, itself divided, and on the dubious loyalty of tributary communities. Montezuma's long hesitation proved disastrous. When Cortés—with incredible boldness—took Montezuma hostage, the emperor's influence over his people crumbled.

During the ensuing attacks and counter-attacks, Montezuma was killed. The Spaniards and their allies escaped from the city and began gathering forces and making new alliances against the Mexica. In May 1520 Cortés led a second assault on Tenochtitlán. Spanish victory in late summer 1521 was hard-won and greatly aided by the effects of smallpox, which had weakened and reduced the Mexica population. After the defeat of Tenochtitlán, Cortés and other conquistadors began the systematic conquest of Mexico. Over time, a series of indigenous kingdoms fell under Spanish domination, although not without decades of resistance.

More surprising than the defeat of the Mexicas was the fall of the remote Inca Empire. Perched more than 9,800 feet above sea level, the Incas were isolated from other indigenous cultures. Like the Mexicas, the Incas had created a civilization that rivaled the Europeans in population and complexity.

At the time of the Spanish invasion the Inca Empire had been weakened by disease and warfare. An epidemic of disease, possibly smallpox, had begun spreading among the people. Even worse, the empire had been embroiled in a civil war over succession. The Spanish conquistador Francisco Pizarro (ca. 1475–1541) landed on the northern coast of Peru on May 13, 1532, the very day Atahualpa (ah-tuh-WAHL-puh) won control of the empire after five years of fighting. As Pizarro advanced across the Andes toward Cuzco, Atahualpa was proceeding to the capital for his coronation.

Inca Empire The vast and sophisticated Peruvian empire centered at the capital city of Cuzco that was at its peak from 1438 until 1532.

Like Montezuma in Mexico, Atahualpa was aware of the Spaniards' movements. He sent envoys to greet the Spanish and invite them to meet him in the provincial town of Cajamarca. His plan was to lure the Spaniards into a trap, seize their horses and ablest men for his army, and execute the rest. Instead, the Spaniards ambushed and captured him, collected an enormous ransom in gold, and then executed him in 1533. The Spanish now marched on the capital of the empire itself, profiting once again from internal conflicts to form alliances with local peoples. When Cuzco fell in 1533, the Spanish plundered immense riches in gold and silver.

As with the Mexica, decades of violence and resistance followed the defeat of the Incan capital. Nevertheless, Spanish conquest opened a new chapter in European relations with the New World. It was not long before rival European nations attempted to forge their own overseas empires.

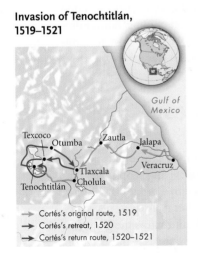

Invasion of Tenochtitlán, 1519–1521

Gulf of Mexico

Texcoco
Otumba • Zautla • Jalapa
Tlaxcala • Veracruz
Tenochtitlán • Cholula

→ Cortés's original route, 1519
→ Cortés's retreat, 1520
→ Cortés's return route, 1520–1521

Early French and English Settlement in the New World

For over a hundred years, the Spanish and the Portuguese dominated settlement in the New World. The first English colony was founded at Roanoke (in what is now North Carolina) in 1585. After a three-year loss of contact with England, the settlers were found to have disappeared; their fate remains a mystery. The colony of Virginia, founded at Jamestown in 1607, had better luck and gained a steady hold producing tobacco for a growing European market. While these colonies originated as bases for harassing Spanish shipping, settlement on the coast of New England was undertaken for different reasons. There, radical Protestants sought to escape Anglican repression in England and begin new lives. The small and struggling outpost of Plymouth (1620) was followed by Massachusetts (1630), which grew into a prosperous settlement. Religious disputes in Massachusetts itself led to the dispersion of settlers into the new communities of Providence, Connecticut, Rhode Island, and New Haven. Catholics acquired their own settlement in Maryland (1632) and Quakers in Pennsylvania (1681).

Where the Spanish established whole-scale dominance over Mexico and Peru, English settlements hugged the Atlantic coastline. This did not prevent conflict with the indigenous inhabitants over land and resources. The haphazard nature of English colonization also led to conflicts of authority within the colonies. As the English crown grew more interested in colonial expansion, efforts were made to acquire the territory between New England in the north and Virginia in the south. This would allow the English to unify their holdings and overcome French and Dutch competition on the North American mainland.

French navigator and explorer Samuel de Champlain founded the first permanent French settlement, at Quebec, in 1608. Ville-Marie, latter-day Montreal, was founded in 1642. The French were energetic and industrious traders and explorers. Following the waterways of the St. Lawrence, the Great Lakes, and the Mississippi, they ventured into much of North America. In 1682 French explorer LaSalle descended the Mississippi to the Gulf of Mexico, opening the way for French occupation of Louisiana.

While establishing their foothold in the north, the French slowly acquired new territories in the West Indies. These included Cayenne (1604), St. Christophe (1625), Martinique, Guadeloupe, and Saint-Domingue (1697) on the western half of the island of Hispaniola. These islands became centers of tobacco and then sugar production. French ambitions on the mainland and in the Caribbean sparked a century-long competition with the English that culminated in the Seven Years' War from 1756 to 1763. France lost Canada and Louisiana, but retained profitable colonies in the West Indies. France regained part of Louisiana by treaty in 1800 and sold it to the United States in 1803.

European involvement in the Americas led to profound transformation of pre-existing indigenous societies and the rise of a transatlantic slave trade. It also led to an acceleration of global trade and cultural exchange. Over time, the combination of indigenous, European, and African cultures gave birth to new societies in the New World. In turn, the profits of trade and the impact of cultural exchange greatly influenced European society.

▼ What was the impact of conquest?

The growing European presence in the New World transformed its land and its peoples forever. Violence and disease wrought devastating losses, while surviving peoples encountered new political, social, and economic organizations imposed by Europeans. The Columbian exchange brought infectious diseases to the Americas, but it also gave new crops to the Old World that altered consumption patterns in Europe and across the globe (see page 437).

Chapter 15
European Exploration and
434   **Conquest • 1450–1650**

CHAPTER LOCATOR

What were the limits of
world contacts before
Columbus?

Colonial Administration

In the sixteenth century the Spanish crown divided its New World territories into four **viceroyalties** or administrative divisions: New Spain, with the capital at Mexico City; Peru, with the capital at Lima; New Granada, with Bogotá as its administrative center; and La Plata, with Buenos Aires as the capital (see Map 15.2).

Within each territory, the viceroy, or imperial governor, exercised broad military and civil authority as the direct representative of Spain. The viceroy presided over the *audiencia* (ow-dee-EHN-see-ah), a board of twelve to fifteen judges that served as his advisory council and the highest judicial body. Later, King Charles III (r. 1759–1788) introduced the system of intendants to Spain's New World territories. These royal officials possessed broad military, administrative, and financial authority within their intendancies and were responsible not to the viceroy but to the monarchy in Madrid. The Portuguese governed their colony of Brazil in a similar manner. After the union of the crowns of Portugal and Spain in 1580, Spanish administrative forms were introduced.

Impact of European Settlement on the Lives of Indigenous Peoples

Before Columbus's arrival, the Americas were inhabited by thousands of groups of indigenous peoples with different languages and cultures. Their patterns of life varied widely, from hunter-gatherer tribes organized into tribal confederations to large-scale agriculture-based empires connecting bustling cities and towns. The best estimate is that the peoples of the Americas numbered around 50 million in 1492.

Their lives were radically transformed by the arrival of Europeans. In the sixteenth century perhaps two hundred thousand Spaniards immigrated to the New World. Conquistadors carved out vast estates called haciendas in temperate grazing areas and imported Spanish livestock for the kinds of ranching with which they were familiar. In coastal tropical areas, the Spanish erected huge plantations to supply sugar to the European market. Around 1550 silver was discovered in present-day Bolivia and Mexico. To work the cattle ranches, sugar plantations, and silver mines, the conquistadors first turned to the indigenous peoples.

The Spanish quickly established the **encomienda system**, in which the Crown granted the conquerors the right to employ groups of Native Americans as laborers or to demand tribute from them in exchange for providing food and shelter. In practice, the encomienda system was a legalized form of slavery.

The new conditions and hardships imposed by conquest and colonization resulted in enormous native population losses. The major cause of death was disease. Having little or no resistance to diseases brought from the Old World, the inhabitants of the New World fell victim to smallpox, typhus, influenza, and other illnesses. Another factor was overwork. Unaccustomed to forced labor, native workers died in staggering numbers. Moreover, forced labor diverted local people from agricultural work, leading to malnutrition, reduced fertility rates, and starvation. Women forced to work were separated from their infants, leading to high infant mortality rates in a population with no livestock to supply alternatives to breast milk. Malnutrition and hunger in turn lowered resistance to disease. Finally, many indigenous peoples also died through outright violence in warfare.[4]

The Franciscan Bartolomé de Las Casas (1474–1566) documented the brutal treatment of indigenous peoples at the hands of the Spanish:

> To these quiet Lambs . . . came the Spaniards like most c(r)uel Tygres, Wolves and Lions, enrag'd with a sharp and tedious hunger; for these forty years past, minding nothing else

viceroyalties The name for the four administrative units of Spanish possessions in the Americas: New Spain, Peru, New Granada, and La Plata.

encomienda system A system whereby the Spanish crown granted the conquerors the right to forcibly employ groups of Indians; it was a disguised form of slavery.

How and why did Europeans undertake voyages of expansion? | **What was the impact of conquest?** | How did Europe and the world change after Columbus? | How did expansion change European attitudes and beliefs?

435

Español con India,
Mestizo.

Mestizo con Española
Castizo.

5

6

Mulato con Española,
Morisco.

Morisco con Española
Chino.

9

10

Lobo con China
Gibaro.

Gibaro con Mulata
Albarazado

13

14

Sanbaigo con Loba
Calpamulato.

Calpamulato con Canbuja
Tente en el Aire.

Mixed Races The unprecedented mixing of peoples in the Spanish New World colonies inspired great fascination. An elaborate terminology emerged to describe the many possible combinations of indigenous, African, and European blood, which were known collectively as *castas*. This painting belongs to a popular genre of the eighteenth century depicting couples composed of individuals of different ethnic origin and the children produced of their unions. (Schalkwijk/Art Resource, NY)

but the slaughter of these unfortunate wretches, whom with divers kinds of torments neither seen nor heard of before, they have so cruelly and inhumanely butchered, that of three millions of people which Hispaniola itself did contain, there are left remaining alive scarce three hundred persons.[5]

Las Casas and other missionaries asserted that the Indians had human rights, and through their persistent pressure the Spanish emperor Charles V abolished the worst abuses of the encomienda system in 1531.

The pattern of devastating disease and population loss established in the Spanish colonies was repeated everywhere Europeans settled. The best estimate is that the native population declined from roughly 50 million in 1492 to around 9 million by 1700. It is important to note, however, that native populations and cultures did survive the conquest period, sometimes by blending with European incomers and sometimes by maintaining cultural autonomy.

For colonial administrators the main problem posed by the astronomically high death rate was the loss of a subjugated labor force to work the mines and sugar plantations. The search for fresh sources of labor gave birth to the new tragedy of the Atlantic slave trade (see page 440).

Life in the Colonies

Many factors helped to shape life in European colonies, including geographic location, religion, indigenous cultures and practices, patterns of European settlement, and the cultural attitudes and official policies of the European nations that claimed them as empire. Throughout the New World, Europeanized settlements were hedged by immense borderlands of European and non-European contact.

Women played a crucial role in the creation of new identities and the continuation of old ones. The first explorers formed unions with native women, through coercion or choice, and relied on them as translators and guides and to form alliances with indigenous powers. As settlement developed, the character of each colony was influenced by the presence or absence of European women. Where women and children accompanied men, as in the British colonies and the Spanish mainland

Chapter 15
European Exploration and
436   Conquest • 1450–1650

CHAPTER LOCATOR   What were the limits of world contacts before Columbus?

colonies, new settlements took on European languages, religion, and ways of life that have endured, with input from local cultures, to this day. Where European women did not, as on the west coast of Africa and most European outposts in Asia, local populations largely retained their own cultures, to which male Europeans acclimatized themselves.

Most women who crossed the Atlantic were Africans, constituting four-fifths of the female newcomers before 1800.[6] Wherever slavery existed, masters profited from their power to engage in sexual relations with enslaved women. One important difference among European colonies was in the status of children born from such unions. In some colonies, mostly those dominated by the Portuguese, Spanish, or French, substantial populations of free blacks descended from the freed children of such unions. In English colonies, masters were less likely to free children they fathered with female slaves.

The mixing of indigenous people with Europeans and Africans created whole new populations and ethnicities as well as complex self-identities. In Spanish America the word mestizo — *métis* in French — described people of mixed Native American and European descent. The blanket terms "mulatto" and "people of color" were used for those of mixed African and European origin. With its immense slave-based plantation agriculture system, large indigenous population, and relatively low Portuguese immigration, Brazil developed a particularly complex racial and ethnic mosaic.

The Columbian Exchange

The migration of peoples to the New World led to an exchange of animals, plants, and disease, a complex process known as the Columbian exchange. Columbus brought sugar plants on his second voyage; Spaniards also introduced rice and bananas from the Canary Islands, and the Portuguese carried these items to Brazil. Everywhere they settled, the Spanish and Portuguese brought and raised wheat with labor provided by the encomienda system. Grapes and olives brought over from Spain did well in parts of Peru and Chile.

Columbian exchange The exchange of animals, plants, and diseases between the Old and the New Worlds.

Apart from wild turkeys and game, Native Americans had no animals for food. Moreover, they did not domesticate animals for travel or to use as beasts of burden, except for alpacas and llamas in the Inca Empire. On his second voyage in 1493 Columbus introduced horses, cattle, sheep, dogs, pigs, chickens, and goats. The multiplication of these animals proved spectacular. In turn, Europeans returned home with many food crops that become central elements of their diet.

Disease was perhaps the most important form of exchange. The wave of catastrophic epidemic disease that swept the Western Hemisphere after 1492 can be seen as an extension of the swath of devastation wreaked by the Black Death in the 1300s, first on Asia and then on Europe. The world after Columbus was thus unified by disease as well as by trade and colonization.

▼ How did Europe and the world change after Columbus?

The centuries-old Afro-Eurasian trade world was forever changed by the European voyages of discovery and their aftermath. For the first time, a truly global economy emerged in the sixteenth and seventeenth centuries, and it forged new links among far-flung peoples, cultures, and societies. The ancient civilizations of Europe, Africa, the Americas, and Asia confronted each other in new and rapidly evolving ways. Those confrontations often led to conquest and exploitation, but they also contributed to cultural exchange and renewal.

INDIVIDUALS IN SOCIETY

Juan de Pareja

DURING THE LONG WARS OF THE RECONQUISTA, Muslims and Christians captured each other in battle and used the defeated as slaves. As the Muslims were gradually eliminated from Iberia in the fifteenth and sixteenth centuries, the Spanish and Portuguese turned to the west coast of Africa for a new supply of slaves. Most slaves worked as domestic servants, rather than in the fields. Some received specialized training as artisans.

Not all people of African descent were slaves, and some experienced both freedom and slavery in a single lifetime. The life and career of Juan de Pareja (pah-REH-huh) illustrates the complexities of the Iberian slave system and the heights of achievement possible for those who achieved freedom.

Pareja was born in Antequera, an agricultural region and the old center of Muslim culture near Seville in southern Spain. Of his parents

Velázquez, *Juan de Pareja* (1650). (The Metropolitan Museum of Art, Fletcher Fund, Rogers Fund, and Bequest of Miss Adelaide Milton de Groot [1876–1967], by exchange, supplemented by gifts from friends of the Museum, 1971. [1971.86]. Image © 1986 The Metropolitan Museum of Art)

we know nothing. Because a rare surviving document calls him a "mulatto," one of his parents must have been white and the other must have had some African blood. In 1630 Pareja applied to the mayor of Seville for permission to travel to Madrid to visit his brother and "to perfect his art." The document lists his occupation as "a painter in Seville." Since it mentions no other name, it is reasonable to assume that Pareja arrived in Madrid a free man. Sometime between 1630 and 1648, however, he came into the possession of the artist Diego Velázquez (1599–1660); Pareja became a slave.

How did Velázquez acquire Pareja? By purchase? As a gift? Had Pareja fallen into debt or committed some crime and thereby lost his freedom? We do not know. Velázquez, the greatest Spanish painter of the seventeenth century, had a large studio with many assistants. Pareja was set to grinding powders to make colors and to preparing canvases. He must have demonstrated ability because when Velázquez went to Rome in 1648, he chose Pareja to accompany him.

In 1650, as practice for a portrait of Pope Innocent X, Velázquez painted Pareja. The portrait shows Pareja dressed in fine clothing and gazing self-confidently at the viewer. Displayed in Rome in a public exhibition of Velázquez's work, the painting won acclaim from his contemporaries. That same year, Velázquez signed the document that gave Pareja his freedom, to become effective in 1654. Pareja lived out the rest of his life as an independent painter.

What does the public career of Pareja tell us about the man and his world? Pareja's career suggests that a person of African descent might fall into slavery and yet still acquire professional training and work alongside his master in a position of confidence. Moreover, if lucky enough to be freed, a former slave could exercise a profession and live his own life in Madrid. Pareja's experience was far from typical for a slave in the 1600s, but it reminds us of the myriad forms that slavery took in this period.

Sources: Jonathan Brown, *Velázquez: Painter and Courtier* (New Haven, Conn.: Yale University Press, 1986); *Grove Dictionary of Art* (New York: Macmillan, 2000); Sister Wendy Beckett, *Sister Wendy's American Collection* (New York: HarperCollins Publishers, 2000), p. 15.

QUESTIONS FOR ANALYSIS

1. Since slavery was an established institution in Spain, speculate on Velázquez's possible reasons for giving Pareja his freedom.
2. To what extent was Pareja a marginal person in Spanish society? Was he an insider or an outsider to Spanish society?

Chapter 15
European Exploration and
438 Conquest • 1450–1650

CHAPTER LOCATOR | What were the limits of world contacts before Columbus?

Sugar and Slavery

Throughout the Middle Ages slavery was deeply entrenched in the Mediterranean, but it was not based on race; many slaves were white. How, then, did black African slavery enter the European picture and take root in South and then North America? In 1453 the Ottoman capture of Constantinople halted the flow of white slaves from the eastern Mediterranean. The successes of the Iberian reconquista also meant that the supply of Muslim captives had drastically diminished. Cut off from its traditional sources of slaves, Mediterranean Europe then turned to sub-Saharan Africa, which had a long history of slave trading. (See "Individuals in Society: Juan de Pareja," left.) As Portuguese explorers began their voyages along the western coast of Africa, one of the first commodities they sought was slaves.

In the 1440s and 1450s, the first slaves were simply seized by small raiding parties. Portuguese merchants soon found that it was easier to trade with local leaders, who were accustomed to dealing in slaves captured through warfare with neighboring powers. From 1490 to 1530 Portuguese traders brought between three hundred and two thousand black slaves to Lisbon each year (Map 15.3).

Map 15.3 Seaborne Trading Empires in the Sixteenth and Seventeenth Centuries By the mid-seventeenth century, trade linked all parts of the world except for Australia. Notice that trade in slaves was not confined to the Atlantic but involved almost all parts of the world.

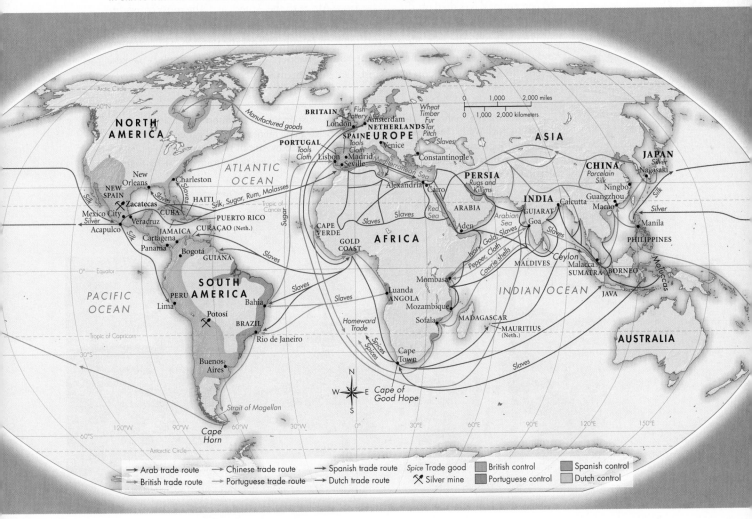

In this stage of European expansion, the history of slavery became intertwined with the history of sugar. Originally sugar was an expensive luxury that only the very affluent could afford, but population increases and monetary expansion in the fifteenth century led to increasing demand. The establishment of sugar plantations on the Canary and Madeira Islands in the fifteenth century testifies to this demand.

Sugar was a particularly difficult and demanding crop to produce for profit. Seed-stems were planted by hand, thousands to the acre. When mature, the cane had to be harvested and processed rapidly to avoid spoiling, forcing days and nights of work with little rest. Moreover, its growing season was virtually constant, meaning that there was no fallow period when workers could recuperate. The demands of sugar production were only increased with the invention of roller mills to crush the cane more efficiently. Yields could be augmented, but only if a sufficient labor force was found to supply the mills. Europeans solved the labor problem by forcing first native islanders and then enslaved Africans to provide the backbreaking work.

Sugar gave New World slavery its distinctive shape. The trans-Atlantic slave trade began in 1518 when the Spanish king Charles I authorized traders to bring African slaves to New World colonies. The Portuguese brought the first slaves to Brazil around 1550; by 1600 four thousand were being imported annually. After its founding in 1621, the Dutch West India Company transported thousands of Africans to Brazil and the Caribbean, mostly to work on sugar plantations. In the late seventeenth century, with the chartering of the Royal African Company, the English got involved.

Before 1700, when slavers decided it was better business to improve conditions, some 20 percent of slaves died on the voyage from Africa to the Americas.[7] The most common cause of death was from dysentery induced by poor quality food and water, intense crowding, and lack of sanitation. Men were often kept in irons during the passage, while women and girls were considered fair game for sailors. To increase profits, slave traders packed several hundred captives on each ship. On sugar plantations, death rates among slaves

A New World Sugar Refinery, Brazil Sugar was the most important and most profitable plantation crop in the New World. This image shows the processing and refinement of sugar on a Brazilian plantation. Sugar cane was grown, harvested, and processed by African slaves who labored under brutal and ruthless conditions to generate enormous profits for plantation owners. (The Bridgeman Art Library/Getty Images)

from illness and exhaustion were extremely high, leading to a constant stream of new shipments of slaves from Africa.

In total, scholars estimate that European traders embarked over 10 million African slaves across the Atlantic from 1518 to 1800 (of whom roughly 8.5 million disembarked), with the peak of the trade occurring in the eighteenth century.[8] By comparison, only 2 to 2.5 million Europeans migrated to the New World during the same period. Enslaved Africans worked in an infinite variety of occupations: as miners, soldiers, sailors, servants, and artisans and in the production of cotton, rum, indigo, tobacco, wheat, corn, and, most predominantly, sugar.

Spanish Silver and Its Economic Effects

The sixteenth century has often been called Spain's golden century, but silver mined in the Americas was the true source of Spain's incredible wealth. In 1545 the Spanish dis-covered an extraordinary source of silver at Potosí (poh-toh-SEE) (in present-day Bolivia) in territory conquered from the Inca Empire. By 1550 Potosí yielded perhaps 60 percent of all the silver mined in the world. From Potosí and the mines at Zacatecas (za-kuh-TAY-kuhs) and Guanajuato (gwah-nah-HWAH-toh) in Mexico, huge quantities of precious metals poured forth. Between 1503 and 1650, 35 million pounds of silver and over 600,000 pounds of gold entered Seville's port. Spanish predominance, however, proved temporary.

In the sixteenth century Spain experienced a steady population increase, creating a sharp rise in the demand for food and goods. Spanish colonies in the Americas also demanded consumer goods that were not pro-duced in the colonies, such as cloth and luxury goods. Since Spain had expelled some of its best farmers and businessmen—the Muslims and Jews—in the fifteenth century, the Spanish economy was suffering and could not meet the new demands. The excess of demand over supply led to widespread inflation. The result was a rise in production costs and a further decline in Spain's pro-ductive capacity.

Silver did not cause the initial inflation. It did, how-ever, exacerbate the situation, and, along with the ensu-ing rise in population, the influx of silver significantly contributed to the upward spiral of prices. Inflation se-verely strained government budgets. Several times be-tween 1557 and 1647, Spain's King Philip II and his successors wrote off the state debt, thereby undermining confidence in the government and leaving the economy in shambles. After 1600, when the population declined, prices gradually stabilized.

As Philip II paid his armies and foreign debts with silver bullion, Spanish inflation was transmitted to the rest of Europe. Between 1560 and 1600 much of Eu-rope experienced large price increases. Because money bought less, people who lived on fixed incomes, such as nobles, were badly hurt. Those who owed fixed sums of money, such as the middle class, prospered because in

Philip II, ca. 1533 This portrait of Philip II as a young man and crown prince of Spain is by the celebrated artist Titian, who was court painter to Philip's father, Charles V. After taking the throne, Philip became another great patron of the artist. (Prado, Madrid/Index/The Bridgeman Art Library.)

a time of rising prices, debts lessened in value each year. Food costs rose most sharply, and the poor fared worst of all.

In many ways, though, it was not Spain but China that controlled the world trade in silver. The Chinese demanded silver for their products and for the payment of imperial taxes. China was thus the main buyer of world silver, absorbing half the world's production. The silver market drove world trade, with New Spain and Japan being mainstays on the supply side and China dominating the demand side. The world trade in silver is one of the best examples of the new global economy that emerged in this period.

The Birth of the Global Economy

With the Europeans' discovery of the Americas and their exploration of the Pacific, the entire world was linked for the first time in history by seaborne trade. The opening of that trade brought into being three successive commercial empires: the Portuguese, the Spanish, and the Dutch.

The Portuguese were the first worldwide traders. In the sixteenth century they controlled the sea route to India (see Map 15.3). From their fortified bases at Goa on the Arabian Sea and at Malacca on the Malay Peninsula, ships carried goods to the Portuguese settlement at Macao in the South China Sea. From Macao Portuguese ships loaded with Chinese silks and porcelains sailed to the Japanese port of Nagasaki and to the Philippine port of Manila, where Chinese goods were exchanged for Spanish silver from New Spain. Throughout Asia the Portuguese traded in slaves. The Portuguese exported horses from Mesopotamia and copper from Arabia to India; from India they exported hawks and peacocks for the Chinese and Japanese markets. Back to Portugal they brought Asian spices that had been purchased with textiles produced in India and with gold and ivory from East Africa. They also shipped back sugar from their colony in Brazil, produced by African slaves whom they had transported across the Atlantic.

Coming to empire a few decades later than the Portuguese, the Spanish were determined to claim their place in world trade. The Spanish Empire in the New World was basically a land empire, but across the Pacific the Spaniards built a seaborne empire centered at Manila in the Philippines. The city of Manila served as the transpacific bridge between Spanish America and China. In Manila, Spanish traders used silver from American mines to purchase Chinese silk for European markets. After 1640, however, the Spanish silk trade declined in the face of stiff competition from Dutch imports.

In the seventeenth century the Dutch challenged the Spanish and Portuguese empires. Drawing on their commercial wealth and long experience in European trade, the Dutch emerged by the end of the century as the most powerful worldwide seaborne trading power. The Dutch Empire was built on spices. The Dutch East India Company was founded in 1602 with the stated intention of capturing the spice trade from the Portuguese.

The Dutch set their sights on gaining direct access to and control of the Indonesian sources of spices. The Dutch fleet, sailing from the Cape of Good Hope in Africa and avoiding the Portuguese forts in India, steered directly for Indonesia (see Map 15.3). In return for assisting Indonesian princes in local squabbles and disputes with the Portuguese, the Dutch won broad commercial concessions. Through agreements, seizures, and outright war, they gained control of the western access to the Indonesian archipelago in the first half of the seventeenth century. Gradually, they acquired political domination over the archipelago itself. By the 1660s the Dutch had managed to expel the Portuguese from Ceylon and other East Indian islands, thereby establishing control of the lucrative spice trade.

Not content with challenging the Portuguese in the Indian Ocean, the Dutch also aspired to a role in the Americas. Founded in 1621 in a period of war with Spain, the Dutch West India Company aggressively sought to open trade with North and South

Goods from the Global Economy After the discovery of the Americas, a wave of new items entered European markets. Spices from Southeast Asia were a driving force behind the new global economy and among the most treasured European luxury goods. They were used not only for cooking but also as medicines and health tonics. This fresco shows a fifteenth-century Italian pharmacist measuring out spices for a customer. (Alfredo Dagli Orti/The Art Archive)

America and capture Spanish territories there. The company captured or destroyed hundreds of Spanish ships, seized the Spanish silver fleet in 1628, and captured portions of Brazil and the Caribbean. The Dutch also successfully interceded in the transatlantic slave trade, bringing much of the west coast of Africa under Dutch control.

Dutch efforts to colonize North America were less successful. The colony of New Netherland, governed from New Amsterdam (modern-day New York City), was hampered by lack of settlement and weak governance and was easily captured by the British in 1664.

▼ How did expansion change European attitudes and beliefs?

The age of overseas expansion heightened Europeans' contacts with the rest of the world. These contacts gave birth to new ideas about the inherent superiority or inferiority of different races, in part to justify European participation in the slave trade.

Cultural encounter also inspired more positive views. The essays of Michel de Montaigne epitomized a new spirit of skepticism and cultural relativism, while the plays of William Shakespeare reflected his efforts to come to terms with the cultural complexity of his day.

New Ideas About Race

At the beginning of the transatlantic slave trade, most Europeans would have thought of Africans, if they thought of them at all, as savages—because of their eating habits, morals, clothing, and social customs—and as barbarians because of their language and methods of war. They grouped Africans into the despised categories of pagan heathens or Muslim infidels. Africans were certainly not the only peoples subject to such dehumanizing attitudes. Jews were also viewed as an alien group that was, like Africans, naturally given to sin and depravity. More generally, elite people across Europe were accustomed to viewing the peasant masses as a lower form of humanity.

As Europeans turned to Africa for new sources of slaves, they drew on and developed ideas about Africans' primitiveness and barbarity to defend slavery and even argue that enslavement benefited Africans by bringing the light of Christianity to heathen peoples. Over time, the institution of slavery fostered a new level of racial inequality. Africans gradually became seen as utterly distinct from and wholly inferior to Europeans. From rather vague assumptions about non-Christian religious beliefs and a general lack of civilization, Europeans developed increasingly rigid ideas of racial superiority and inferiority to safeguard the growing profits gained from plantation slavery. Black skin became equated with slavery itself as Europeans at home and in the colonies convinced themselves that blacks were destined by God to serve them as slaves in perpetuity.

Support for this belief went back to the Greek philosopher Aristotle's argument that some people are naturally destined for slavery and to biblical associations between darkness and sin. After 1700 the emergence of new methods of observing and describing nature led to the use of science to define race. From referring to a nation or an ethnic group, henceforth "race" would mean biologically distinct groups of people, whose physical differences produced differences in culture, character, and intelligence.

Michel de Montaigne and Cultural Curiosity

Racism was not the only possible reaction to the new worlds emerging in the sixteenth century. Decades of religious fanaticism, bringing civil anarchy and war, led both Catholics and Protestants to doubt that any one faith contained absolute truth. Added to these doubts was the discovery of peoples in the New World who had radically different ways of life. These shocks helped produce ideas of skepticism and cultural relativism in the sixteenth and seventeenth centuries. Skepticism is a school of thought founded on doubt that total certainty or definitive knowledge is ever attainable. Cultural relativism suggests that one culture is not necessarily superior to another, just different. Both notions found expression in the work of Frenchman Michel de Montaigne (duh mahn-TAYN) (1533–1592).

Montaigne developed a new literary genre, the essay—from the French *essayer*, meaning "to test or try"—to express his thoughts and ideas. Published in 1580, Montaigne's *Essays* consisted of short personal reflections. Intended to be accessible to ordinary people, Montaigne wrote in French rather than Latin and in an engaging conversational style.

Montaigne's essay "On Cannibals" reveals the impact of overseas discoveries on his consciousness. In contrast to the prevailing views of the time, he rejected the notion that one culture is superior to another. Speaking of native Brazilians, he wrote:

Chapter 15
**European Exploration and
Conquest • 1450–1650**

444

CHAPTER LOCATOR | What were the limits of
world contacts before
Columbus?

I find that there is nothing barbarous and savage in this nation [Brazil], . . . except, that everyone gives the title of barbarism to everything that is not according to his usage; as, indeed, we have no other criterion of truth and reason, than the example and pattern of the opinions and customs of the place wherein we live. . . . They are savages in the same way that we say fruits are wild, which nature produces of herself and by her ordinary course; whereas, in truth, we ought rather to call those wild whose natures we have changed by our artifice and diverted from the common order.[9]

In his own time and throughout the seventeenth century, few would have agreed with Montaigne's challenge to ideas of European superiority. The publication of his ideas, however, contributed to a basic shift in attitudes. Montaigne inaugurated an era of doubt.

William Shakespeare and His Influence

In addition to the essay as a literary genre, the period fostered remarkable creativity in other branches of literature. England—especially in the latter part of Queen Elizabeth I's reign and in the first years of her successor, James I (r. 1603–1625)—witnessed remarkable literary expression.

The undisputed master of the period was the dramatist William Shakespeare, whose genius lay in the originality of his characterizations, the diversity of his plots, his understanding of human psychology, and his unexcelled gift for language. Born in 1564, Shakespeare was a Renaissance man with a deep appreciation of classical culture, individualism, and humanism.

Titus Andronicus With classical allusions, fifteen murders and executions, a Gothic queen who takes a black lover, and incredible violence, this early Shakespearean tragedy (1594) was a melodramatic thriller that enjoyed enormous popularity with the London audience. The shock value of a dark-skinned character on the English stage is clearly shown in this illustration. (Reproduced by permission of the Marquess of Bath, Longleat House, Warminster, Wilts)

Like Montaigne, Shakespeare's work reveals the impact of the new discoveries and contacts of his day. The title character of *Othello* is described as a "Moor of Venice." In Shakespeare's day, the term *moor* referred to Muslims of Moroccan or North African origin, including those who had migrated to the Iberian Peninsula. It could also be applied, though, to natives of the Iberian Peninsula who converted to Islam or to non-Muslim Berbers in North Africa. To complicate things even more, references in the play to Othello as "black" in skin color have led many to believe that Shakespeare intended him to be a sub-Saharan African, and he is usually depicted as such in modern performances. This confusion in the play reflects the uncertainty in Shakespeare's own day about racial and religious classifications.

The character of Othello is both vilified in racist terms by his enemies and depicted as a brave warrior, a key member of the city's military leadership, and a man capable of winning the heart of an aristocratic white woman. In contrast to the prevailing view of Moors as inferior, Shakespeare presents Othello as a complex human figure. Shakespeare's play thus demonstrates both the intolerance of contemporary society and the possibility for some individuals to look beyond racial stereotypes.

Shakespeare's last play, *The Tempest*, displays a similar interest in race and race relations. The plot involves the stranding on an island of sorcerer Prospero and his daughter Miranda. There Prospero finds and raises Caliban, a native of the island, whom he instructs in his own language and religion. After Caliban's attempted rape of Miranda, Prospero enslaves him, earning the rage and resentment of his erstwhile pupil. Modern scholars often note the echoes between this play and the realities of imperial conquest and settlement in Shakespeare's day. It is no accident, they argue, that the poet portrayed Caliban as a monstrous dark-skinned island native who was best-suited for slavery. Shakespeare himself borrows words from Montaigne's essay "On Cannibals," suggesting that he may have intended to criticize, rather than endorse, racial intolerance. Shakespeare's work shows us one of the finest minds of the age grasping to come to terms with the racial and religious complexities around him.

446   Chapter 15
European Exploration and
Conquest • 1450–1650

CHAPTER LOCATOR | What were the limits of world contacts before Columbus?

←LOOKING BACK LOOKING AHEAD→

JUST THREE YEARS SEPARATED the posting of Martin Luther's "Ninety-five Theses" in 1517 from Ferdinand Magellan's discovery of the Pacific Ocean in 1520. Within a few short years, the religious unity of Western Europe and its notions of terrestrial geography were shattered. Old medieval certainties about Heaven and earth collapsed. In the ensuing decades, Europeans struggled to come to terms with religious difference at home and the multitudes of new peoples and places they encountered abroad. These processes were intertwined, as Puritans and Quakers fled religious persecution at home to colonize the New World and the new Jesuit order proved its devotion to the pope by seeking Catholic converts across the globe. While some Europeans were fascinated and inspired by this new diversity, too often the result was violence. Europeans endured decades of civil war between Protestants and Catholics, and indigenous peoples suffered massive population losses as a result of European warfare, disease, and exploitation. Tragically, both Catholic and Protestant religious leaders condoned the African slave trade that was to bring suffering and death to millions of Africans.

Even as the voyages of discovery contributed to the fragmentation of European culture, they also belonged to longer-term processes of state centralization and consolidation. The new monarchies of the Renaissance produced stronger and wealthier governments capable of financing the huge expenses of exploration and colonization. Competition to gain overseas colonies became an integral part of European politics. Spain's investment in conquest proved spectacularly profitable and yet, as we will see in Chapter 16, the ultimate result was a weakening of its power. Other European nations took longer to realize financial gain, yet over time the Netherlands, England, and France reaped tremendous profits from colonial trade, which helped them build modernized, centralized states. The path from medieval Christendom to modern nation-states led through religious warfare and global encounter. ▪

- **For a list of suggested readings for this chapter, visit** *bedfordstmartins.com/mckaywestunderstanding*.

- **For primary sources from this period, see** *Sources of Western Society*, Second Edition.

- **For Web sites, images, and documents related to topics in this chapter, see Make History at** *bedfordstmartins.com/mckaywestunderstanding*.

How and why did Europeans undertake voyages of expansion?

What was the impact of conquest?

How did Europe and the world change after Columbus?

How did expansion change European attitudes and beliefs?

Step 1

GETTING STARTED Below are basic terms about this period in the history of Western civilization. Can you identify each term below and explain why it matters? To do this exercise online, go to bedfordstmartins.com/mckaywestunderstanding.

TERMS	WHO (OR WHAT) AND WHEN	WHY IT MATTERS
conquistador, p. 422		
caravel, p. 423		
Ptolemy's *Geography*, p. 423		
Treaty of Tordesillas, p. 430		
Mexica Empire, p. 431		
Inca Empire, p. 433		
viceroyalties, p. 435		
encomienda system, p. 435		
Columbian exchange, p. 437		

Step 2

MOVING BEYOND THE BASICS The exercise below requires a more advanced understanding of the chapter material. Examine the nature and impact of European exploration and conquest by filling in the chart below. What were the motives behind expansion? Why did monarchs support overseas expeditions? Why did men like Columbus undertake such dangerous journeys? Identify key conquests and discoveries for each nation. Then, describe the impact of exploration and colonization in the Americas in both the New World, Europe, and Africa. When you are finished, consider the following question: What intended and unintended consequences resulted from European expansion? To do this exercise online, go to bedfordstmartins.com/mckaywestunderstanding.

EXPLORATION 1492–1600	MOTIVES FOR EXPLORATION AND SETTLEMENT	CONQUESTS AND DISCOVERIES	IMPACT IN NEW WORLD	IMPACT IN EUROPE	IMPACT IN AFRICA
Portugal					
Spain					
France					
England					

PUTTING IT ALL TOGETHER Now that you've reviewed key elements of the chapter, take a step back and try to see the big picture. Remember to use specific examples from the chapter in your answers. To do this exercise online, go to bedfordstmartins.com/mckaywestunderstanding.

WORLD CONTACTS BEFORE COLUMBUS

- How did trade connect the civilizations of Africa, Asia, and Europe prior to 1492? Which states were at the center of global trade? Which were at the periphery? Why?

- Why were Europeans at a trading disadvantage prior to 1492? How did geography limit European participation in world trade? What role did Europe's economy and material culture play in this context?

THE EUROPEAN VOYAGES OF DISCOVERY

- Why were Europeans so eager to gain better access to Asia and Asian trade? How did fifteenth-century economic and political developments help stimulate European expansion?

- Compare and contrast Spanish, French, and English exploration and colonization of the New World. What common motives underlay the efforts of all three nations? How would you explain the important differences you note?

THE IMPACT OF CONQUEST

- What kinds of societies and governments did Europeans seek to establish in the Americas? What light does the nature of colonial society shed on the motives behind European expansion and European views of the indigenous peoples of the Americas?

- What was the Columbian exchange? How did it transform both Europe and the Americas?

- How did European expansion give rise to new ideas about race?

EUROPE AND THE WORLD AFTER COLUMBUS

- What role did increasing demand for sugar play in shaping the economy and society of the New World? Why were sugar and slavery so tightly linked?

- If Europe was at the periphery of the global trading system prior to 1492, where was it situated by the middle of the sixteenth century? What had changed? What had not?

- How did expansion complicate Europeans' understanding of themselves and their place in the world?

■ **In Your Own Words** Imagine that you must explain Chapter 15 to someone who hasn't read it. What would be the most important points to include and why?

16

Absolutism and Constitutionalism in Europe

ca. 1589–1725

The seventeenth century was a period of transformation in Europe. Agricultural and manufacturing slumps meant that many people struggled to feed themselves and their families, and population rates stagnated or even fell. Religious and dynastic conflicts led to almost constant war and dramatic growth in the size of armies. To pay for these armies, governments created bureaucracies to collect greatly increased taxes. Despite these obstacles, European states succeeded in gathering more power. By 1680 much of the unrest that originated with the Reformation was resolved.

The crises of the seventeenth century were not limited to western Europe. Central and eastern Europe experienced even more catastrophic dislocation, with German lands serving as the battleground of the Thirty Years' War and borders constantly vulnerable to attack from the east. In Prussia and in Habsburg Austria absolutist states emerged in the aftermath of this conflict. Russia and the Ottoman Turks also developed absolutist governments. These empires seemed foreign and exotic to western Europeans, who saw them as the antithesis of their political, religious, and cultural values. Beneath the surface, however, these eastern governments shared many similarities with western ones.

While absolutism emerged as the solution to crisis in many European states, a small minority adopted a different path, placing sovereignty in the hands of privileged groups rather than the Crown. Historians refer to states where power was limited by law as "constitutional." The two most important seventeenth-century constitutionalist states were England and the Dutch Republic. Constitutionalism should not be confused with democracy. The elite rulers of England and the Dutch Republic pursued familiar policies of increased taxation, government authority, and social control. Nonetheless, they served as influential models to onlookers across Europe as a form of government that checked the power of a single ruler. ∎

Life in Absolutist France. King Louis XIV receives foreign ambassadors to celebrate a peace treaty. The king grandly occupied the center of his court, which in turn served as the pinnacle for the French people and, at the height of his glory, for all of Europe. (Erich Lessing/Art Resource, NY)

Chapter Preview

▸ What made the seventeenth century an "age of crisis"?

▸ Why did France rise and Spain fall in this period?

▸ What explains the rise of absolutism in Austria and Prussia?

▸ What was distinctive about Russia and the Ottoman Empire?

▸ Where and why did constitutionalism triumph?

▸ What developments do baroque art and music reflect?

▼ What made the seventeenth century an "age of crisis"?

Historians often refer to the seventeenth century as an "age of crisis." After the economic and demographic growth of the sixteenth century, Europe faltered into stagnation and retrenchment. This was partially due to climate changes, but it also resulted from religious divides, increased governmental pressures, and war. Overburdened peasants and city-dwellers took action to defend themselves, sometimes profiting from conflicts to obtain relief. In the long run, however, governments proved increasingly able to impose their will on the populace.

Peasant Life in the Midst of Economic Crisis

In the seventeenth century most Europeans lived in the countryside. The hub of the rural world was the small peasant village centered on a church and a manor. In western Europe, a small number of peasants in each village owned enough land to feed themselves and had the livestock and plows necessary to work their land. These independent farmers were leaders of the peasant village. They employed the landless poor, rented out livestock and tools, and served as agents for the noble lord. Below them were small landowners and tenant farmers who did not have enough land to be self-sufficient. These

An English Food Riot Nothing infuriated ordinary women and men more than the idea that merchants and landowners were withholding grain from the market in order to push high prices even higher. In this cartoon an angry crowd hands out rough justice to a rich farmer accused of hoarding. (Courtesy of the Trustees of the British Museum)

Chapter 16
Absolutism and Constitutionalism in Europe • ca. 1589–1725

452

CHAPTER LOCATOR   What made the seventeenth century an "age of crisis"?

families sold their best produce on the market to earn cash for taxes, rent, and food. At the bottom were the rural workers who worked as dependent laborers and servants. In eastern Europe, the vast majority of peasants toiled as serfs for noble landowners and did not own land in their own right (see the next section).

Rich or poor, east or west, bread was the primary element of the diet. Peasants paid stiff fees to the local miller for grinding grain into flour and sometimes to the lord for the right to bake bread in his oven. Bread was most often accompanied by a soup made of roots, herbs, beans, and perhaps a small piece of salt pork. An important annual festival in many villages was the killing of the family pig. The whole family gathered to help, sharing a rare abundance of meat with neighbors and carefully salting the extra and putting down the lard.

European rural society lived on the edge of subsistence. Because of the crude technology and low crop yield, peasants were constantly threatened by scarcity and famine. In the seventeenth century a period of colder and wetter climate throughout Europe, dubbed the "little ice age" by historians, meant a shorter farming season with lower yields. The result was recurrent famines that significantly reduced the population of early modern Europe. Most people did not die of outright starvation, but rather of diseases brought on by malnutrition and exhaustion.

Given the harsh conditions of life, industry also suffered. The output of woolen textiles, one of the most important European manufactures, declined sharply in the first half of the seventeenth century. Food prices were high, wages stagnated, and unemployment soared. This economic crisis was not universal: it struck various regions at different times and to different degrees. In the middle decades of the century, Spain, France, Germany, and England all experienced great economic difficulties; but these years were the golden age of the Netherlands.

The urban poor and peasants were the hardest hit. When the price of bread rose beyond their capacity to pay, they frequently expressed their anger by rioting. In towns they invaded bakers' shops to seize bread and resell it at a "just price." In rural areas they attacked convoys taking grain to the cities. Women often led these actions, since their role as mothers gave them some impunity in authorities' eyes. Historians have labeled this vision of a world in which community needs predominate over competition and profit a moral economy.

The Return of Serfdom in the East

While economic and social hardship was common across Europe, important differences existed between east and west. In the west the demographic losses of the Black Death allowed peasants to escape from serfdom as they acquired enough land to feed themselves as well as the livestock and ploughs necessary to work their land. In eastern Europe seventeenth-century peasants had largely lost their ability to own land independently. Eastern lords dealt with the labor shortages caused by the Black Death by restricting the

Chapter Chronology

ca. 1500–1650	Consolidation of serfdom in eastern Europe
1533–1584	Reign of Ivan the Terrible in Russia
1589–1610	Reign of Henry IV in France
1598–1613	Time of Troubles in Russia
1620–1740	Growth of absolutism in Austria and Prussia
1642–1649	English civil war, which ends with execution of Charles I
1643–1715	Reign of Louis XIV in France
1653–1658	Military rule in England under Oliver Cromwell (the Protectorate)
1660	Restoration of English monarchy under Charles II
1665–1683	Jean-Baptiste Colbert applies mercantilism to France
1670	Charles II agrees to re-Catholicize England in secret agreement with Louis XIV
1670–1671	Cossack revolt led by Stenka Razin
ca. 1680–1750	Construction of baroque palaces
1682	Louis XIV moves court to Versailles
1682–1725	Reign of Peter the Great in Russia
1683–1718	Habsburgs push the Ottoman Turks from Hungary
1685	Edict of Nantes revoked
1688–1689	Glorious Revolution in England
1701–1713	War of the Spanish Succession

Why did France rise and Spain fall in this period?

What explains the rise of absolutism in Austria and Prussia?

What was distinctive about Russia and the Ottoman Empire?

Where and why did constitutionalism triumph?

What developments do baroque art and music reflect?

453

Estonian Serfs in the 1660s The Estonians were conquered by German military nobility in the Middle Ages and reduced to serfdom. The German-speaking nobles ruled the Estonian peasants with an iron hand, and Peter the Great reaffirmed their domination when Russia annexed Estonia. (Mansell Collection/Time Life Pictures/Getty Images)

right of their peasants to move to take advantage of better opportunities elsewhere. Moreover, lords steadily took more and more of their peasants' land and arbitrarily imposed heavier and heavier labor obligations. By the early 1500s lords in many eastern territories could command their peasants to work for them without pay for as many as six days a week.

The power of the lord reached far into serfs' everyday lives. Not only was their freedom of movement restricted, but they required permission to marry or could be forced to marry. Lords could reallocate the lands worked by their serfs at will or sell serfs apart from their families.

Between 1500 and 1650 the consolidation of serfdom in eastern Europe was accompanied by the growth of commercial agriculture, particularly in Poland and eastern Germany. As economic expansion and population growth resumed after 1500, eastern lords increased the production of their estates by squeezing sizable surpluses out of the impoverished peasants. They then sold these surpluses to foreign merchants, who exported them to the growing cities of wealthier western Europe.

It was not only the peasants who suffered in eastern Europe. With the approval of kings, landlords systematically undermined the medieval privileges of the towns and the power of the urban classes. The population of the towns and the urban middle classes declined greatly. This development both reflected and promoted the supremacy of noble landlords in most of eastern Europe in the sixteenth century.

The Thirty Years' War

In the first half of the seventeenth century, the fragile balance of life was violently upturned by the ravages of the Thirty Years' War (1618–1648). The Holy Roman Empire was a confederation of hundreds of principalities, independent cities, duchies, and other polities loosely united under an elected emperor. The uneasy truce between Catholics and Protestants created by the Peace of Augsburg in 1555 deteriorated as the faiths of various areas shifted. Lutheran princes felt compelled to form the Protestant Union (1608), and Catholics retaliated with the Catholic League (1609). Each alliance was determined that the other should make no religious or territorial advance. Dynastic interests were also involved; the Spanish Habsburgs strongly supported the goals of their Austrian relatives: the unity of the empire and the preservation of Catholicism within it.

The war is traditionally divided into four phases. The first, or Bohemian, phase (1618–1625) was characterized by civil war in Bohemia between the Catholic League and the Protestant Union. In 1620 Catholic forces defeated Protestants at the Battle of the White Mountain. The second, or Danish, phase of the war (1625–1629)—so called because of the leadership of the Protestant king Christian IV of Denmark (r. 1588–1648)—witnessed additional Catholic victories.

Chapter 16
Absolutism and Constitutionalism
in Europe • ca. 1589–1725

454

CHAPTER LOCATOR | What made the seventeenth century an "age of crisis"?

The third, or Swedish, phase of the war (1630–1635) began with the arrival in Germany of the Swedish king Gustavus Adolphus (r. 1594–1632) and his army. Gustavus Adolphus intervened to support the empire's Protestants. The French chief minister, Cardinal Richelieu (ree-shuh-LYOO), subsidized the Swedes, hoping to weaken Habsburg power in Europe. Gustavus Adolphus won two important battles but was fatally wounded in combat. The final, or French, phase of the war (1635–1648) was prompted by Richelieu's concern that the Habsburgs would rebound after the death of Gustavus Adolphus. Richelieu declared war on Spain and sent military as well as financial assistance. Finally, in October 1648 peace was achieved.

The 1648 **Peace of Westphalia** that ended the Thirty Years' War marked a turning point in European history. Conflicts fought over religious faith ended. The treaties recognized the independent authority of more than three hundred German princes (Map 16.1), reconfirming the emperor's severely limited authority. The Augsburg agreement of 1555 became permanent, adding Calvinism to Catholicism and Lutheranism as legally permissible creeds.

Peace of Westphalia The name of a series of treaties that concluded the Thirty Years' War in 1648 and marked the end of large-scale religious violence in Europe.

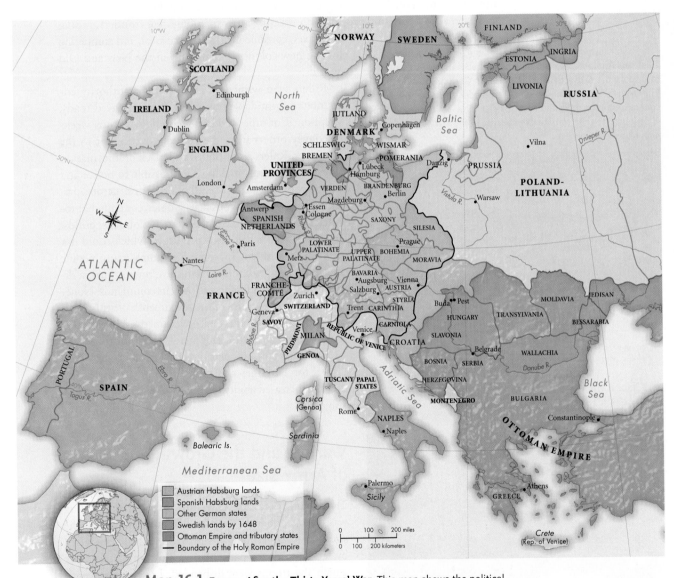

Map 16.1 Europe After the Thirty Years' War This map shows the political division of Europe after the Treaty of Westphalia (1648) ended the war. Which country emerged from the Thirty Years' War as the strongest European power? What dynastic house was that country's major rival in the early modern period?

Why did France rise and Spain fall in this period?

What explains the rise of absolutism in Austria and Prussia?

What was distinctive about Russia and the Ottoman Empire?

Where and why did constitutionalism triumph?

What developments do baroque art and music reflect?

The Thirty Years' War was probably the most destructive event for the central European economy and society prior to the world wars of the twentieth century. Perhaps one-third of urban residents and two-fifths of the rural population died, leaving entire areas depopulated. Trade in southern German cities was virtually destroyed. Agricultural areas suffered catastrophically. Many small farmers lost their land, allowing nobles to enlarge their estates and consolidate their control.[1]

Achievements in State-Building

In this context of economic and demographic depression, monarchs began to make new demands on their people. Traditionally, historians have distinguished between the "absolutist" governments of France, Spain, Central Europe, and Russia and the constitutionalist governments of England and the Dutch Republic. Whereas absolutist monarchs gathered all power under their personal control, English and Dutch rulers were obliged to respect laws passed by representative institutions. More recently, historians have emphasized commonalities among these powers. Despite their political differences, all these states shared common projects of protecting and expanding their frontiers, raising new taxes, consolidating central control, and competing for the new colonies opening up in the New and Old Worlds.

Rulers who wished to increase their authority encountered formidable obstacles. Without paved roads, telephones, or other modern technology, it took weeks to convey orders from the central government to the provinces. Rulers also suffered from lack of information about their realms, making it impossible to police and tax the population effectively. Local power structures presented another serious obstacle. Nobles, the church, provincial and national assemblies, town councils, guilds, and other bodies held legal privileges, which could not easily be rescinded. In some kingdoms many people spoke a language different from the Crown's, further diminishing their willingness to obey its commands. Nonetheless, over the course of the seventeenth century both absolutist and constitutional governments achieved new levels of central control. This increased authority focused in four areas in particular: greater taxation, growth in armed forces, larger and more efficient bureaucracies, and the increased ability to compel obedience from their subjects.

The Professionalization of the Swedish Army Swedish king Gustavus Adolphus, surrounded by his generals, gives thanks to God for the safe arrival of his troops in Germany during the Thirty Years' War. A renowned military leader, the king imposed constant training drills and rigorous discipline on his troops, which contributed to their remarkable success in the war. (Courtesy of The Army Museum, Stockholm)

Warfare and the Growth of Army Size

The driving force of seventeenth-century state-building was warfare, characterized by dramatic changes in the size and style of armies. Medieval armies had been raised by feudal lords for particular wars or campaigns, after which the troops were disbanded. In the seventeenth century monarchs took command of recruiting and maintaining armies — in peacetime as well as wartime. New techniques for training and deploying soldiers meant a rise in the professional standards of the army. Along with professionalization came an explosive growth in army size. The French took the lead, with the army growing from roughly 125,000 men in the Thirty Years' War to 340,000 at the end of the seventeenth century.[2] In response, France's neighbors greatly increased the size of their own armies and formed defensive coalitions for protection from French aggression.

Other European powers were quick to follow the French example. The rise of absolutism in central and eastern Europe led to a vast expansion in the size of armies. Great Britain followed a similar, albeit distinctive pattern. Instead of building a land army, the British focused on naval forces and eventually built the largest navy in the world.

Popular Political Action

In the seventeenth century increased pressures of taxation and warfare led to an increase in popular uprisings. Popular revolts were extremely common in England, France, Spain, Portugal, and Italy in the mid-seventeenth century. In 1640 Philip IV of Spain faced revolt in Catalonia, the economic center of his realm. At the same time he struggled to put down uprisings in Portugal and in the northern provinces of the Netherlands. In 1647 the city of Palermo, in Spanish-occupied Sicily, exploded in protest over food shortages caused by a series of bad harvests. Fearing public unrest, the city government subsidized the price of bread, attracting even more starving peasants from the countryside. When Madrid ordered an end to subsidies, municipal leaders decided to lighten the loaf rather than raise prices. Not fooled by this change, local women led a bread riot, shouting "Long live the king and down with the taxes and the bad government!" As riot transformed to armed revolt, the insurgency spread to the rest of the island and eventually to Naples on the mainland. Apart from affordable food, rebels demanded the suppression of extraordinary taxes and participation in municipal government. Some dreamed of a republic in which noble tax exemptions would be abolished. Despite initial successes, the revolt lacked unity and strong leadership and could not withstand the forces of the state.

In France urban uprisings became a frequent aspect of the social and political landscape. Beginning in 1630 and continuing on and off through the early 1700s, major insurrections occurred at Dijon, Bordeaux (bor-DOH), Montpellier, Lyons, and Amiens. All were characterized by deep popular anger and violence directed at outside officials sent to collect taxes. These officials were sometimes seized, beaten, and hacked to death.

Municipal and royal authorities often struggled to overcome popular revolt. They feared that stern repressive measures, such as sending in troops to fire on crowds, would create martyrs and further inflame the situation, while forcible full-scale military occupation of a city would be very expensive. The limitations of royal authority gave some leverage to rebels, allowing them to gain concessions.

By the beginning of the eighteenth century, this leverage had largely disappeared. Municipal governments were better integrated into the national structure, and local authorities had prompt military support from the central government. People who publicly opposed royal policies and taxes received swift and severe punishment.

▼ Why did France rise and Spain fall in this period?

Kings in absolutist states asserted that, as they were chosen by God, they were responsible to God alone. They claimed exclusive power to make and enforce laws, denying any other institution or group the authority to check their power. Louis XIV of France

Why did France rise and Spain fall in this period?   What explains the rise of absolutism in Austria and Prussia?   What was distinctive about Russia and the Ottoman Empire?   Where and why did constitutionalism triumph?   What developments do baroque art and music reflect?

457

is often seen as the epitome of an "absolute" monarch. In truth, his success relied on collaboration with nobles, and thus his example illustrates both the achievements and the compromises of absolutist rule.

As French power rose in the seventeenth century, the glory of Spain faded. Once the fabulous revenue from American silver declined, Spain's economic stagnation could no longer be disguised, and the country faltered under weak leadership.

The Foundations of Absolutism

Louis XIV's absolutism had long roots. In 1589 his grandfather Henry IV (r. 1589–1610), the founder of the Bourbon dynasty, acquired a devastated country. Civil wars between Protestants and Catholics had wracked France since 1561. Poor harvests had reduced peasants to starvation, and commercial activity had declined drastically.

Henry IV inaugurated a remarkable recovery by keeping France at peace during most of his reign. Although he had converted to Catholicism, he issued the Edict of Nantes, allowing Protestants the right to worship in 150 traditionally Protestant towns throughout France. He sharply lowered taxes and improved the infrastructure of the country, building new roads and canals and repairing the ravages of years of civil war. Despite his efforts at peace, Henry was murdered in 1610 by a Catholic zealot.

After the death of Henry IV his wife, the queen-regent Marie de' Medici, headed the government for the nine-year-old Louis XIII (r. 1610–1643). In 1628 Armand Jean du Plessis — Cardinal Richelieu (1585–1642) — became first minister of the French crown. Richelieu's maneuvers allowed the monarchy to maintain power within Europe and within its own borders despite the turmoil of the Thirty Years' War.

Cardinal Richelieu's domestic policies were designed to strengthen royal control. He extended the use of intendants, commissioners for each of France's thirty-two districts who were appointed directly by the monarch, to whom they were solely responsible. They recruited men for the army, supervised the collection of taxes, presided over the administration of local law, checked up on the local nobility, and regulated economic activities in their districts. As the intendants' power increased under Richelieu, so did the power of the centralized French state.

Under Richelieu, the French monarchy also acted to repress Protestantism. Louis personally supervised the siege of La Rochelle, an important port city and a major commercial center with strong ties to Protestant Holland and England. The fall of La Rochelle in October 1628 was one step in the removal of Protestantism as a strong force in French life.

Richelieu did not aim to wipe out Protestantism in the rest of Europe, however. His main foreign policy goal was to destroy the Catholic Habsburgs' grip on territories that surrounded France. Consequently, Richelieu supported Habsburg enemies, including Protestants. For the French cardinal, interests of state outweighed religious considerations.

Richelieu's successor as chief minister for the next child-king, the four-year-old Louis XIV, was Cardinal Jules Mazarin (1602–1661). Along with the regent, Queen Mother Anne of Austria, Mazarin continued Richelieu's centralizing policies. His struggle to increase royal revenues to meet the costs of war led to the uprisings of 1648–1653 known

the Fronde A series of violent uprisings during the early reign of Louis XIV triggered by growing royal control and oppressive taxation.

as the Fronde. In Paris, magistrates of the Parlement of Paris, the nation's most important court, were outraged by the crown's autocratic measures. These so-called robe nobles (named for the robes they wore in court) encouraged violent protest by the common people. As rebellion spread outside Paris and to the sword nobles (the traditional warrior nobility), civil order broke down completely. In 1651, when Anne's regency ended, much of the rebellion died away, and its leaders came to terms with the government.

The violence of the Fronde had significant results for the future. The twin evils of noble rebellion and popular riots left the French wishing for peace and for a strong monarch to reimpose order. This was the legacy that Louis XIV inherited when he assumed personal control of the government in 1661 after the death of Mazarin.

Chapter 16
Absolutism and Constitutionalism in Europe • ca. 1589–1725

458

CHAPTER LOCATOR   What made the seventeenth century an "age of crisis"?

■ PICTURING THE PAST

Hyacinthe Rigaud, *Louis XIV, King of France and Navarre*, 1701
This was one of Louis XIV's favorite portraits of himself. He liked it so much that he had many copies of the portrait made, in full and half-size format. (Scala/Art Resource, NY)

ANALYZING THE IMAGE Why do you think the king liked the portrait so much? What image of the king does it present to the viewer? What details does the painter include, and what impression do they convey?

CONNECTIONS How does this representation of royal power compare with the images of Peter the Great (page 471) and Charles I (page 477)? Which do you find the most impressive, and why?

To complete this activity online, go to the Online Study Guide at bedfordstmartins.com/mckaywestunderstanding.

Louis XIV and Absolutism

In the reign of Louis XIV (r. 1643–1715) the French monarchy reached the peak of absolutist development. Louis was a believer in the doctrine of the divine right of kings: God had established kings as his rulers on earth, and they were answerable ultimately to him alone. Kings were divinely anointed and shared in the sacred nature of divinity, but they could not simply do as they pleased. They had to obey God's laws and rule for the good of the people. To symbolize his central role in the divine order, when he was fifteen years old, Louis danced at a court ballet dressed as the sun, thereby acquiring the title of the "Sun King."

Louis worked very hard at the business of governing. He ruled his realm through several councils of state and insisted on taking a personal role in many of the councils' decisions. Despite increasing financial problems, Louis never called a meeting of the Estates General. The nobility, therefore, had no means of united expression or action. Nor did Louis have a first minister. In this way he kept himself free from worry about the inordinate power of a Richelieu.

Why did France rise and Spain fall in this period? | What explains the rise of absolutism in Austria and Prussia? | What was distinctive about Russia and the Ottoman Empire? | Where and why did constitutionalism triumph? | What developments do baroque art and music reflect?

459

Although personally tolerant, Louis hated division within the realm and insisted that religious unity was essential to his royal dignity and to the security of the state. He thus pursued the policy of Protestant repression launched by Richelieu. In 1685 Louis revoked the Edict of Nantes and took steps to suppress the Huguenots.

Despite his claims to absolute authority, there were multiple constraints on Louis's power. As a representative of divine power, he was obliged to rule in a way that seemed consistent with virtue and benevolent authority. He had to uphold the laws issued by his royal predecessors. Moreover, he also relied on the collaboration of nobles, who maintained social prestige and authority. Without their cooperation, it would have been impossible to extend his power throughout France or wage his many foreign wars. Louis's need to elicit noble cooperation led him to revolutionize court life at his palace at Versailles.

Life at Versailles

Through most of the seventeenth century, the French court had no fixed home, following the monarch to his numerous palaces and country residences. In 1682 Louis moved his court and government to the newly renovated palace at Versailles. The palace quickly

Pierre-Denis Martin, *View of the Chateau de Versailles, 1722* Versailles began as a modest hunting lodge built by Louis XIII in 1623. His son, Louis XIV, spent decades enlarging and decorating the original chateau. In 1682 the new palace became the official residence of the Sun King and his court. (Châteaux de Versailles et de Trianon, Versailles/Réunion des Musées Nationaux/Art Resource, NY)

Chapter 16
**Absolutism and Constitutionalism
in Europe • ca. 1589–1725**

460

CHAPTER LOCATOR | What made the seventeenth century an "age of crisis"?

became the center of political, social, and cultural life. The king required all great nobles to spend at least part of the year in attendance on him there. Since he controlled the distribution of state power and wealth, nobles had no choice but to obey and compete with each other for his favor at Versailles.

Louis further revolutionized court life by establishing an elaborate set of etiquette rituals to mark every moment of his day, from waking up and dressing in the morning to removing his clothing and retiring at night. He required nobles to serve him in these rituals, and they vied for the honor of doing so. Endless squabbles broke out over what type of chair one could sit on at court and the order in which great nobles entered and were seated in the chapel for Mass.

These rituals may seem absurd, but they were far from meaningless or trivial. The king controlled immense resources and privileges; access to him meant favored treatment for government offices, military and religious posts, state pensions, honorary titles, and a host of other benefits. Courtiers sought these rewards for themselves and their family members and followers. A system of patronage—in which a higher-ranked individual protected a lower-ranked one in return for loyalty and services—flowed from the court to the provinces. Through this mechanism Louis gained cooperation from powerful nobles.

Although they were denied public offices and posts, women played a central role in the patronage system. At court the king's wife, mistresses, and other female relatives recommended individuals for honors, advocated policy decisions, and brokered alliances between noble factions. Noblewomen played a similar role among courtiers, bringing their family connections to marriage to form powerful social networks.

Louis XIV was an enthusiastic patron of the arts. He commissioned many sculptures and paintings for Versailles as well as performances of dance and music. Louis XIV also loved the stage, and in the plays of Molière and Racine his court witnessed the finest achievements in the history of the French theater.

With Versailles as the center of European politics, French culture grew in international prestige. French became the language of polite society and international diplomacy, gradually replacing Latin as the language of scholarship and learning. The royal courts of Sweden, Russia, Poland, and Germany all spoke French. France inspired a cosmopolitan European culture in the late seventeenth century that looked to Versailles as its center.

French Financial Management Under Colbert

France's ability to build armies and fight wars depended on a strong economy. Fortunately for Louis, his controller general, Jean-Baptiste Colbert (1619–1683), proved to be a financial genius. Colbert's central principle was that the wealth and the economy of France should serve the state. To this end, from 1665 to his death in 1683, Colbert rigorously applied mercantilist policies to France.

Mercantilism is a collection of governmental policies for the regulation of economic activities by and for the state. It derives from the idea that a nation's international power is based on its wealth, specifically its supply of gold and silver. To accumulate wealth, a country always had to sell more goods abroad than it bought. To decrease the purchase of goods outside France, Colbert insisted that French industry should produce everything needed by the French people.

To increase exports, Colbert supported old industries and created new ones. Colbert enacted new production regulations, created guilds to boost quality standards, and encouraged foreign craftsmen to immigrate to France. To encourage the purchase of French goods, he abolished many domestic tariffs and raised tariffs on foreign products. In 1664 Colbert founded the Company of the East Indies with (unfulfilled) hopes of competing with the Dutch for Asian trade.

mercantilism A system of economic regulations aimed at increasing the power of the state based on the belief that a nation's international power was based on its wealth, specifically its supply of gold and silver.

Why did France rise and Spain fall in this period?

What explains the rise of absolutism in Austria and Prussia?

What was distinctive about Russia and the Ottoman Empire?

Where and why did constitutionalism triumph?

What developments do baroque art and music reflect?

461

Colbert also hoped to make Canada part of a vast French empire. He sent four thousand colonists to Quebec. Subsequently, the Jesuit Jacques Marquette and the merchant Louis Joliet sailed down the Mississippi River. Marquette and Joliet claimed possession of the land on both sides of the river as far south as present-day Arkansas. In 1684 French explorers continued down the Mississippi to its mouth and claimed vast territories for Louis XIV, naming the region "Louisiana."

During Colbert's tenure as controller general, Louis was able to pursue his goals without massive tax increases and without creating a stream of new offices. The constant pressure of warfare after Colbert's death, however, undid many of his economic achievements.

Louis XIV's Wars

Louis XIV kept France at war for thirty-three of the fifty-four years of his personal rule. François le Tellier, Marquis de Louvois—Louis's secretary of state for war—equaled Colbert's achievements in the economic realm. Louvois created a professional army in the employ of the French state. Uniforms and weapons were standardized, and a rational system of training and promotion was devised. As in so many other matters, Louis's model was followed across Europe.

Louis's goal was to expand France to what he considered its natural borders. His armies managed to extend French borders to include important commercial centers in the Spanish Netherlands and Flanders as well as the entire province of Franche-Comté between 1667 and 1678. In 1681 Louis seized the city of Strasbourg, and three years later he sent his armies into the province of Lorraine. At that moment the king seemed invincible. In fact, Louis had reached the limit of his expansion. The wars of the 1680s and 1690s brought no additional territories but placed unbearable strains on French resources. Colbert's successors resorted to desperate measures to finance these wars, including devaluation of the currency and new taxes.

Louis's last war was endured by a French people suffering high taxes, crop failure, and widespread malnutrition and death. In 1700 the childless Spanish king Charles II (r. 1665–1700) died. His will bequeathed the Spanish crown and its empire to Philip of Anjou, Louis XIV's grandson. The will violated a prior treaty by which the European powers had agreed to divide the Spanish possessions between the king of France and the Holy Roman emperor, both brothers-in-law of Charles II. Claiming that he was following both Spanish and French interests, Louis broke with the treaty and accepted the will, thereby triggering the War of the Spanish Succession (1701–1713).

In 1701 the English, Dutch, Austrians, and Prussians formed the Grand Alliance against Louis XIV. War dragged on until 1713. The **Peace of Utrecht**, which ended the war, allowed Louis's grandson Philip to remain king of Spain on the understanding that the French and Spanish crowns would never be united. France surrendered Newfoundland, Nova Scotia, and the Hudson Bay territory to England, which also acquired Gibraltar, Minorca, and control of the African slave trade from Spain (Map 16.2).

The Peace of Utrecht marked the end of French expansion. Thirty-five years of war had given France the rights to all of Alsace and some commercial centers in the north. But at what price? In 1714 an exhausted France hovered on the brink of bankruptcy. It is no wonder that when Louis XIV died on September 1, 1715, many subjects felt as much relief as they did sorrow.

Peace of Utrecht A series of treaties, from 1713 to 1715, that ended the War of the Spanish Succession, ended French expansion in Europe, and marked the rise of the British Empire.

The Acquisitions of Louis XIV, 1668–1713

Paris

FRANCHE-COMTÉ

FRANCE

Territory gained
■ 1668
■ 1678
■ 1713

Chapter 16
Absolutism and Constitutionalism in Europe • ca. 1589–1725

462

CHAPTER LOCATOR   What made the seventeenth century an "age of crisis"?

North America, 1714

HUDSON'S BAY COMPANY
Newfoundland
QUEBEC
NEW FRANCE
NOVA SCOTIA
LOUISIANA
THIRTEEN COLONIES
SP. FLORIDA

Claims
British
French
Spanish

Legend:
French Bourbon lands
Spanish Bourbon lands
Austrian Habsburg lands
Prussian lands
Great Britain
Russian Empire
— Boundary of the Holy Roman Empire

0 100 200 miles
0 100 200 kilometers

▪ MAPPING THE PAST

Map 16.2 Europe After the Peace of Utrecht, 1715

The series of treaties commonly called the Peace of Utrecht ended the War of the Spanish Succession and redrew the map of Europe. A French Bourbon king succeeded to the Spanish throne. France surrendered the Spanish Netherlands (later Belgium) to Austria and recognized the Hohenzollern (hoh-uhn-ZAH-luhrn) rulers of Prussia. Spain ceded Gibraltar to Great Britain, for which it has been a strategic naval station ever since. Spain also granted Britain the *asiento*, the contract for supplying African slaves to America.

ANALYZING THE MAP Identify the areas on the map that changed hands as a result of the Peace of Utrecht. How did these changes affect the balance of power in Europe?

CONNECTIONS How and why did so many European countries possess scattered or discontiguous territories? What does this suggest about European politics in this period? Does this map suggest potential for future conflict?

To complete this activity online, go to the Online Study Guide at **bedfordstmartins.com/mckaywestunderstanding**.

The Decline of Absolutist Spain in the Seventeenth Century

At the beginning of the seventeenth century, France's position appeared extremely weak. Struggling to recover from decades of religious civil war, France could not compete with Spain's European and overseas empire or its mighty military. Yet by the end of the century their positions were reversed.

Why did France rise and Spain fall in this period?

What explains the rise of absolutism in Austria and Prussia?

What was distinctive about Russia and the Ottoman Empire?

Where and why did constitutionalism triumph?

What developments do baroque art and music reflect?

Spanish Troops The long wars that Spain fought over Dutch independence, in support of Habsburg interests in Germany, and against France left the country militarily exhausted and financially drained by the mid-1600s. In this detail from a painting by Peeter Snayers, Spanish troops—thin, emaciated, and probably unpaid—straggle away from battle. (Prado, Madrid/Index/The Bridgeman Art Library)

By the early seventeenth century the seeds of Spanish disaster were sprouting. Between 1610 and 1650 Spanish trade with the colonies in the New World fell 60 percent due to competition from local industries in the colonies and from Dutch and English traders. At the same time, the mines that filled the empire's treasury started to run dry, and the quantity of metal produced steadily declined after 1620.

In Madrid, however, royal expenditures constantly exceeded income. To meet mountainous state debt, the Crown repeatedly devalued the coinage and declared bankruptcy, which resulted in the collapse of national credit. Meanwhile, manufacturing and commerce shrank. In contrast to the other countries of western Europe, Spain had a tiny middle class. The elite condemned moneymaking as vulgar and undignified. To make matters worse, the Crown expelled some three hundred thousand *Moriscos*, or former Muslims, in 1609, significantly reducing the pool of skilled workers and merchants. Those working in the textile industry were forced out of business by steep inflation that pushed their production costs to the point where they could not compete in colonial and international markets.[3]

Spanish aristocrats, attempting to maintain an extravagant lifestyle they could no longer afford, increased the rents on their estates. High rents and heavy taxes in turn drove the peasants from the land, leading to a decline in agricultural productivity. In cities wages and production stagnated.

The Spanish crown had no solutions to these dire problems. Philip III handed the running of the government over to the duke of Lerma, who used it to advance his personal and familial wealth. Philip IV left the management of his several kingdoms to Gaspar de Guzmán, Count-Duke of Olivares. Olivares did not lack energy and ideas, and he succeeded in devising new sources of revenue. But he clung to the belief that the solution to Spain's difficulties rested in a return to the imperial tradition of the sixteenth century. Unfortunately, the imperial tradition demanded the revival of war with the Dutch at the expiration of a twelve-year truce in 1622 and a long war with France over Mantua (1628–1659). These conflicts, on top of an empty treasury, brought disaster.

Chapter 16
Absolutism and Constitutionalism
464   **in Europe • ca. 1589–1725**

CHAPTER LOCATOR   What made the seventeenth century an "age of crisis"?

Spain's situation worsened with internal conflicts and fresh military defeats through the remainder of the seventeenth century. In 1640 Spain faced serious revolts in Catalonia and Portugal. In 1643 the French inflicted a crushing defeat on a Spanish army at Rocroi in what is now Belgium. By the Treaty of the Pyrenees of 1659, which ended the French-Spanish conflict, Spain was compelled to surrender extensive territories to France. In 1688 the Spanish crown reluctantly recognized the independence of Portugal. The era of Spanish dominance in Europe had ended.

▼ What explains the rise of absolutism in Austria and Prussia?

The rulers of eastern Europe also labored to build strong absolutist states in the seventeenth century. But they built on social and economic foundations far different from those in western Europe, namely serfdom and the strong nobility who benefited from it. The endless wars of the seventeenth century allowed monarchs to increase their power by building large armies, increasing taxation, and suppressing representative institutions. In exchange for their growing political authority, monarchs allowed nobles to remain as unchallenged masters of their peasants, a deal that appeased both king and nobility, but left serfs at the mercy of the lords.

The Austrian Habsburgs

Like all of central Europe, the Habsburgs emerged from the Thirty Years' War impoverished and exhausted. Their efforts to destroy Protestantism in the German lands and to turn the weak Holy Roman Empire into a real state had failed. Defeat in central Europe encouraged the Habsburgs to turn away from a quest for imperial dominance and to focus inward and eastward in an attempt to unify their diverse holdings.

Habsburg victory over Bohemia during the Thirty Years' War was an important step in this direction. Ferdinand II (r. 1619–1637) drastically reduced the power of the Bohemian Estates, the largely Protestant representative assembly. He also confiscated the landholdings of Protestant nobles and gave them to loyal Catholic nobles and to the foreign aristocratic mercenaries who led his armies. After 1650 a large portion of the Bohemian nobility was of recent origin and owed its success to the Habsburgs.

With the support of this new nobility, the Habsburgs established direct rule over Bohemia. Under their rule the condition of the enserfed peasantry worsened substantially and Protestantism was stamped out. These changes were important steps in creating absolutist rule in Bohemia.

Ferdinand III (r. 1637–1657) continued to build state power. He centralized the government in the empire's German-speaking provinces, which formed the core Habsburg holdings. For the first time, a permanent standing army was ready to put down any internal opposition.

The Habsburg monarchy then turned east toward Hungary, which had been divided between the Ottomans and the Habsburgs in the early sixteenth century. Between 1683 and 1699 the Habsburgs pushed the Ottomans from most of Hungary and Transylvania. The recovery of all the former kingdom of Hungary was completed in 1718.

The Hungarian nobility, despite its reduced strength, effectively thwarted the full development of Habsburg absolutism. Throughout the seventeenth century Hungarian nobles rose in revolt against the Habsburgs. They never triumphed decisively, but neither were they crushed. In 1703, with the Habsburgs bogged down in the War of the

Why did France rise and Spain fall in this period?

What explains the rise of absolutism in Austria and Prussia?

What was distinctive about Russia and the Ottoman Empire?

Where and why did constitutionalism triumph?

What developments do baroque art and music reflect?

465

Spanish Succession, the Hungarians rose in one last patriotic rebellion under Prince Francis Rákóczy.

Rákóczy and his forces were eventually defeated, but the Habsburgs agreed to restore many of the traditional privileges of the aristocracy in return for Hungarian acceptance of hereditary Habsburg rule. Thus Hungary was never fully integrated into a centralized, absolute Habsburg state.

Despite checks on their ambitions in Hungary, the Habsburgs made significant achievements in state-building elsewhere by forging consensus with the church and the nobility. A sense of common identity and loyalty to the monarchy grew among elites in Habsburg lands. German became the language of the state, and Catholicism helped fuse a collective identity. Vienna became the political and cultural center of the empire.

Prussia in the Seventeenth Century

In the fifteenth and sixteenth centuries, the Hohenzollern family had ruled parts of eastern Germany as the imperial electors of Brandenburg and the dukes of Prussia. When he came to power in 1640, the twenty-year-old Frederick William, later known as the "Great Elector," was determined to unify his three provinces and enlarge them by diplomacy and war. These provinces were Brandenburg; Prussia, inherited in 1618; and scattered holdings along the Rhine inherited in 1614 (Map 16.3). Each had its own estates, and

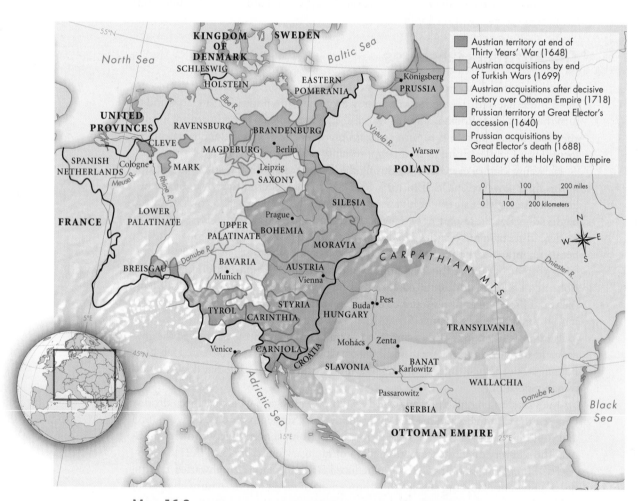

Map 16.3 The Growth of Austria and Brandenburg-Prussia to 1748 Austria expanded to the southwest into Hungary and Transylvania at the expense of the Ottoman Empire. It was unable to hold the rich German province of Silesia, however, which was conquered by Brandenburg-Prussia.

Chapter 16
Absolutism and Constitutionalism
466   in Europe • ca. 1589–1725

CHAPTER LOCATOR   What made the seventeenth century an "age of crisis"?

taxes could not be levied without their consent. The estates of Brandenburg and Prussia were dominated by the nobility and the landowning classes, known as the **Junkers**.

In 1660 Frederick William persuaded Junkers in the estates to accept taxation without consent in order to fund a permanent army. They agreed to do so in exchange for reconfirmation of their own privileges, including authority over the serfs. Having won over the Junkers, the king crushed potential opposition to his power from the towns. One by one, Prussian cities were eliminated from the estates and subjected to new taxes on goods and services.

Thereafter, the estates' power declined rapidly, for the Great Elector had both financial independence and superior force. State revenue tripled during his reign, and the army expanded drastically. In 1701 the elector's son, Frederick I, received the elevated title of king of Prussia (instead of elector) as a reward for aiding the Holy Roman emperor in the War of the Spanish Succession.

Junkers The nobility of Brandenburg and Prussia, they were reluctant allies of Frederick William in his consolidation of the Prussian state.

The Consolidation of Prussian Absolutism

Frederick William I, "the Soldiers' King" (r. 1713–1740), completed his grandfather's work, eliminating the last traces of parliamentary estates and local self-government. It was he who truly established Prussian absolutism and transformed Prussia into a military state. Frederick William summed up his life's philosophy in his instructions to his son: "A formidable army and a war chest large enough to make this army mobile in times of need can create great respect for you in the world, so that you can speak a word like the other powers."[4]

Frederick William and his ministers built an exceptionally honest and conscientious bureaucracy to administer the country and foster economic development. Twelfth in Europe in population, Prussia had the fourth largest army by 1740 and the best trained one.

Nevertheless, Prussians paid a heavy and lasting price for this achievement. Army expansion was achieved in part through forced conscription, which was declared lifelong in 1713. Desperate draftees fled the country or injured themselves to avoid service. Finally, in 1733 Frederick William I ordered that all Prussian men would undergo military training and serve as reservists in the army, allowing him to preserve both agricultural production and army size. To appease the Junkers, the king enlisted them to lead his growing army.

With all men harnessed to the war machine, Prussian civil society became rigid and highly disciplined. As a Prussian minister later summed up, "To keep quiet is the first civic duty."[5] Thus the policies of Frederick William I, combined with harsh peasant bondage and Junker tyranny, laid the foundations for a highly militaristic country.

A Prussian Giant Grenadier Frederick William I wanted tall, handsome soldiers. He dressed them in tight bright uniforms to distinguish them from the peasant population from which most soldiers came. He also ordered several portraits of his favorites, such as this one, from his court painter, J. C. Merk. Grenadiers wore the miter cap instead of an ordinary hat so that they could hurl their heavy grenades unimpeded by a broad brim. (The Royal Collection © 2010, Her Majesty Queen Elizabeth II)

Why did France rise and Spain fall in this period?

What explains the rise of absolutism in Austria and Prussia?

What was distinctive about Russia and the Ottoman Empire?

Where and why did constitutionalism triumph?

What developments do baroque art and music reflect?

467

▼ What was distinctive about Russia and the Ottoman Empire?

A favorite parlor game of nineteenth-century intellectuals was debating whether Russia was a Western (European) or non-Western (Asian) society. To this day, Russia differs from the West in some fundamental ways, though its history has paralleled that of the West in other aspects.

There was no question in the mind of Europeans, however, that the Ottomans were outsiders. Even absolutist rulers disdained Ottoman sultans as cruel and tyrannical despots. Despite stereotypes, the Ottoman Empire was in many ways more tolerant than its western counterparts, providing protection and security to other religions while maintaining the Muslim faith. The Ottoman state combined the Byzantine heritage of the territory it had conquered with Persian and Arab traditions. Flexibility and openness to other ideas and practices were sources of strength for the empire.

The Mongol Yoke and the Rise of Moscow

The two-hundred-year period of rule by the Mongol khan (king) set the stage for the rise of absolutist Russia. The Mongols, a group of nomadic tribes from present-day Mongolia, established an empire that, at its height, stretched from Korea to eastern Europe. In the thirteenth century, the Mongols forced the Slavic princes to submit to their rule. The princes of Moscow became particularly adept at serving the Mongols. Ivan III (r. 1462–1505), known as Ivan the Great, successfully expanded the principality of Moscow toward the Baltic Sea.

By 1480 Ivan III felt strong enough to stop acknowledging the khan as his supreme ruler and to cease paying tribute to the Mongols. To legitimize their new autonomy, the princes of Moscow modeled themselves on the Mongol khans. Like the khans, they declared themselves to be autocrats, meaning that they were the sole source of power. The Muscovite state also forced weaker Slavic principalities to render tribute and borrowed Mongol institutions such as the tax system, postal routes, and census. Loyalty from the highest-ranking nobles, or boyars, helped the Muscovite princes consolidate their power.

The Expansion of Russia to 1725

Another source of legitimacy lay in Moscow's claim to the political and religious inheritance of the Byzantine Empire. After the fall of Constantinople to the Turks in 1453, the princes of Moscow saw themselves as the heirs of both the caesars (or emperors) and of Orthodox Christianity. The title tsar, first taken by Ivan IV in 1547, is in fact a contraction of *caesar*. The tsars considered themselves rightful and holy rulers, an idea promoted by Orthodox churchmen. The marriage of Ivan III to the daughter of the last Byzantine emperor further enhanced Moscow's claim to inherit imperial authority.

boyars The highest-ranking members of the Russian nobility.

The Tsar and His People

Developments in Russia took a chaotic turn with the reign of Ivan IV (r. 1533–1584), the famous "Ivan the Terrible," who ascended to the throne at age three. His mother died, possibly poisoned, when he was eight, leaving Ivan to suffer insults and neglect

Chapter 16
Absolutism and Constitutionalism in Europe • ca. 1589–1725

468

CHAPTER LOCATOR | What made the seventeenth century an "age of crisis"?

Russian Peasant An eighteenth-century French artist visiting Russia recorded his impressions of the daily life of the Russian people in this etching of a fish merchant pulling his wares through a snowy village on a sleigh. Two caviar vendors behind him make a sale to a young mother standing at her doorstep with her baby in her arms. (From Jean-Baptiste Le Prince's second set of Russian etchings, 1765. Private Collection/www.amis-paris-petersbourg.org)

from the boyars at court. At age sixteen he suddenly pushed aside his hated advisers and crowned himself tsar.

Ivan's reign was successful in defeating the remnants of Mongol power, adding vast new territories to the realm, and laying the foundations for the huge, multiethnic Russian empire. After the sudden death of his beloved wife Anastasia Romanov, however, Ivan began a campaign of persecution against those he suspected of opposing him. Many were intimates of the court from leading boyar families, whom he had killed along with their families, friends, servants, and peasants. To further crush the power of the boyars, Ivan created a new service nobility, whose loyalty was guaranteed by their dependence on the state for noble titles and estates.

Ivan also moved toward making all commoners servants of the tsar. As landlords demanded more from the serfs who survived the wars and persecutions, growing numbers of peasants fled toward wild, recently conquered territories to the east and south. There they joined free groups and warrior bands known as **Cossacks** (KAH-sakz). The solution to the problem of peasant flight was to tie peasants ever more firmly to the land and to the noble landholders, who in turn served the tsar.

Simultaneously, Ivan bound urban traders and artisans to their towns and jobs so that he could tax them more heavily. The urban classes had no security in their work or property. These restrictions stood in sharp contrast to developments in western Europe. From nobles down to merchants and peasants, all of the Russian people were thus brought into the tsar's service. Ivan even made use of Cossack armies in forays to the southeast, forging a new alliance between Moscow and the Cossacks.

After the death of Ivan and his successor, Russia entered a chaotic period known as the "Time of Troubles" (1598–1613). While Ivan's relatives struggled for power, ordinary

Cossacks Free groups and outlaw armies originally comprising runaway peasants living on the borders of Russian territory from the fourteenth century onward. By the end of the sixteenth century they had formed an alliance with the Russian state.

Why did France rise and Spain fall in this period?　　What explains the rise of absolutism in Austria and Prussia?　　**What was distinctive about Russia and the Ottoman Empire?**　　Where and why did constitutionalism triumph?　　What developments do baroque art and music reflect?

469

Saint Basil's Cathedral, Moscow With its sloping roofs and colorful onion-shaped domes, Saint Basil's is a striking example of powerful Byzantine influences on Russian culture. According to tradition, an enchanted Ivan the Terrible blinded the cathedral's architects to ensure that they would never duplicate their fantastic achievement, which still dazzles the beholder in today's Red Square. (George Holton/Photo Researchers)

people suffered drought, crop failure, and plague. The Cossacks and peasants rebelled against nobles and officials, demanding fairer treatment. This social explosion from below brought the nobles together. They crushed the Cossack rebellion and elected Ivan's grandnephew, Michael Romanov, the new hereditary tsar (r. 1613–1645). (See "Listening to the Past: A German Account of Russian Life," page 472.)

Although the new tsar successfully reconsolidated central authority, he and his successors did not improve the lot of the common people. In 1649 a law extended serfdom to all peasants in the realm, giving lords unrestricted rights over their serfs and establishing penalties for harboring runaways. Social and religious uprisings among the poor and oppressed continued through the seventeenth century.

Despite the turbulence of the period, the Romanov tsars, like their Western counterparts, made several important achievements during the second half of the seventeenth century. After a long war, Russia gained land in Ukraine from Poland in 1667 and completed the conquest of Siberia by the end of the century. Territorial expansion was accompanied by growth of the bureaucracy and the army. Foreign experts were employed to help build and reform the Russian army, and Cossack warriors were enlisted to fight Siberian campaigns. The great profits from Siberia's natural resources funded the Romanovs' bid for Great Power status. Thus, Russian imperialist expansion to the east paralleled the western powers' exploration and conquest of the Atlantic world in the same period.

Chapter 16
**Absolutism and Constitutionalism
in Europe** • ca. 1589–1725

470

CHAPTER LOCATOR   What made the seventeenth century an "age of crisis"?

The Reforms of Peter the Great

Heir to Romanov efforts at state-building, Peter the Great (r. 1682–1725) embarked on a tremendous campaign to accelerate and complete these processes. Possessing enormous energy and willpower, Peter was determined to build and improve the army and to continue the tsarist tradition of territorial expansion.

Fascinated by weapons and foreign technology, the tsar led a group of 250 Russian officials and young nobles on an eighteen-month tour of western European capitals. Traveling unofficially to avoid lengthy diplomatic ceremonies, Peter met with foreign kings and experts. He was particularly impressed with the growing power of the Dutch and the English, and he considered how Russia could profit from their example.

Returning to Russia, Peter entered into a secret alliance with Denmark and Poland to wage a sudden war of aggression against Sweden with the goal of securing access to the Baltic Sea and opportunities for westward expansion. Peter and his allies believed that their combined forces could win easy victories because Sweden was in the hands of a new and inexperienced king.

Eighteen-year-old Charles XII of Sweden (r. 1697–1718) surprised Peter. He defeated Denmark quickly in 1700, then turned on Russia. His well-trained professional army attacked and routed unsuspecting Russians besieging the Swedish fortress of Narva on the Baltic coast. Peter and the survivors fled in panic to Moscow. The attack marked the beginning of the long and brutal Great Northern War, which lasted from 1700 to 1721.

Peter responded to this defeat with measures designed to increase state power, strengthen his armies, and gain victory. He required all nobles to serve in the army or

Peter the Great This compelling portrait by Grigory Musikiysky captures the strength and determination of the warrior-tsar in 1723, after more than three decades of personal rule. In his hand Peter holds the scepter, symbol of royal sovereignty, and across his breastplate is draped an ermine fur, a mark of honor. In the background are the battleships of Russia's new Baltic fleet and the famous St. Peter and St. Paul Fortress that Peter built in St. Petersburg. Peter the Great commissioned this magnificent new crown (left) for himself for his joint coronation in 1682 with his half-brother Ivan. (portrait: Kremlin Museums, Moscow/The Bridgeman Art Library; crown: Bildarchiv Preussischer Kulturbesitz/Art Resource, NY)

| Why did France rise and Spain fall in this period? | What explains the rise of absolutism in Austria and Prussia? | **What was distinctive about Russia and the Ottoman Empire?** | Where and why did constitutionalism triumph? | What developments do baroque art and music reflect? |

471

LISTENING TO THE PAST

A German Account of Russian Life

Seventeenth-century Russia remained a remote and mysterious land for western and even central Europeans, who had few direct contacts with the tsar's dominion. Westerners portrayed eastern Europe as more "barbaric" and less "civilized" than their homelands. Thus they drew on eastern Europe's undeniably harsher social and economic conditions to posit a very debatable cultural and moral inferiority.

Knowledge of Russia came mainly from occasional travelers who had visited Muscovy and sometimes wrote accounts of what they saw. The most famous of these accounts was by the German Adam Olearius (ca. 1599–1671), who was sent to Moscow on three diplomatic missions in the 1630s. These missions ultimately proved unsuccessful, but they pro- vided Olearius with a rich store of information for his Travels in Muscovy, *from which the following excerpts are taken. Published in German in 1647 and soon translated into several languages (but not Russian), Olearius's unflattering but well-informed study played a major role in shaping Euro- pean ideas about Russia.*

❝ The government of the Russians is what political theorists call a "dominating and despotic monarchy," where the sovereign, that is, the tsar or the grand prince who has obtained the crown by right of succes- sion, rules the entire land alone, and all the people are his subjects, and where the nobles and princes no less than the common folk — townspeople and peasants — are his serfs and slaves, whom he rules and treats as a master treats his servants. . . .

If the Russians be considered in respect to their character, customs, and way of life, they are justly to be counted among the barbarians. . . . The vice of drunkenness is so common in this nation, among people of every station, clergy and laity, high and low, men and women, old and young, that when they are seen now and then lying about in the streets, wallowing in the mud, no attention is paid to it, as something habitual. If a cart driver comes upon such a drunken pig whom he happens to know, he shoves him onto his cart and drives him home, where he is paid his fare. No one ever refuses an opportunity to drink and to get drunk, at any time and in any place, and usually it is done with vodka. . . .

The Russians being naturally tough and born, as it were, for slavery, they must be kept under a harsh and strict yoke and must be driven to do their work with clubs and whips, which they suffer without impa- tience, because such is their station, and they are accustomed to it. Young and half-grown fellows sometimes come together on certain days and train themselves in fisticuffs, to accustom themselves to receiving blows, and, since habit is second nature, this makes blows given as punishment easier to bear. Each and all, they are slaves and serfs. . . .

Because of slavery and their rough and hard life, the Russians accept war readily and are well suited to it. On certain occasions, if need be, they reveal them- selves as courageous and daring soldiers. . . .

Although the Russians, especially the common populace, living as slaves under a harsh yoke, can bear and endure a great deal out of love for their masters, yet if the pressure is beyond measure, then it can be said of them: "Patience, often wounded, finally turned into fury." A dangerous indignation results, turned not so much against their sovereign as against the lower authorities, especially if the people have been much oppressed by them and by their supporters and have not been protected by the higher authorities. And once they are aroused and enraged, it is not easy to appease them. Then, disregarding all dangers that may ensue, they resort to every kind of violence and behave like madmen. . . . They own little; most of them have no feather beds; they lie on cushions, straw, mats, or their clothes; they sleep on benches and, in winter, like the non-Germans [natives] in Livonia, upon the oven, which serves them for cooking and is flat on the top; here husband, wife, children, servants, and maids huddle together. In some houses in the country- side we saw chickens and pigs under the benches and the ovens. . . . Russians are not used to delicate food and dainties; their daily food consists of porridge, tur- nips, cabbage, and cucumbers, fresh and pickled, and in Moscow mostly of big salt fish which stink badly, because of the thrifty use of salt, yet are eaten with relish. . . .

The Russians can endure extreme heat. In the bath- house they stretch out on benches and let themselves be beaten and rubbed with bunches of birch twigs and wisps of bast (which I could not stand); and when they are hot and red all over and so exhausted that they can bear it no longer in the bathhouse, men and women rush outdoors naked and pour cold water over their bodies; in winter they even wallow in the snow and rub their skin with it as if it were soap; then they go back into the hot bathhouse. And since bathhouses are usually near rivers and brooks, they can throw themselves straight from the hot into the cold bath. . . .

in the civil administration — for life. Peter created schools and universities to produce skilled technicians and experts. One of his most hated reforms was requiring a five-year education away from home for every young nobleman. Peter established an interlocking military-civilian bureaucracy with fourteen ranks, and he decreed that all had to start at the bottom and work toward the top. Drawing on his experience abroad, Peter sought

Chapter 16
Absolutism and Constitutionalism
472   **in Europe • ca. 1589–1725**

CHAPTER LOCATOR | What made the seventeenth century an "age of crisis"?

The brutality of serfdom is shown in this illustration from Olearius's *Travels in Muscovy*. (University of Illinois Library, Champaign)

Generally noble families, even the small nobility, rear their daughters in secluded chambers, keeping them hidden from outsiders; and a bridegroom is not allowed to have a look at his bride until he receives her in the bridal chamber. Therefore some happen to be deceived, being given a misshapen and sickly one instead of a fair one, and sometimes a kinswoman or even a maidservant instead of a daughter; of which there have been examples even among the highborn. No wonder therefore that often they live together like cats and dogs and that wife-beating is so common among Russians. . . .

In the Kremlin and in the city there are a great many churches, chapels, and monasteries, both within and without the city walls, over two thousand in all. This is so because every nobleman who has some fortune has a chapel built for himself, and most of them are of stone. The stone churches are round and vaulted inside. . . . They allow neither organs nor any other musical instruments in their churches, saying: Instruments that have neither souls nor life cannot praise God. . . .

In their churches there hang many bells, sometimes five or six, the largest not over two hundredweights. They ring these bells to summon people to church, and also when the priest during mass raises the chalice. In Moscow, because of the multitude of churches and chapels, there are several thousand bells, which during the divine service create such a clang and din that one unaccustomed to it listens in amazement. 》

Source: "A Foreign Traveler in Russia" excerpt from pp. 249–251 in *A Source Book for Russian History from Early Times to 1917*, volume 1, *Early Times to the Late Seventeenth Century*, edited by George Vernadsky, Ralph T. Fisher, Jr., Alan D. Ferguson, Andrew Lossky, and Sergel Pushkarev, compiler. Copyright © 1972 by Yale University Press. Used with permission of the publisher.

QUESTIONS FOR ANALYSIS

1. How did Olearius characterize the Russians in general? What supporting evidence did he offer for his judgment?
2. How might Olearius's account help explain the social and religious uprisings of the seventeenth century (page 470)?
3. On the basis of these representative passages, why do you think Olearius's book was so popular and influential in central and western Europe?

talented foreigners and placed them in his service. These measures gradually combined to make the army and government more powerful and efficient.

Peter also greatly increased the service requirements of commoners. He established a regular standing army of more than two hundred thousand peasant-soldiers commanded by officers from the nobility. In addition, one hundred thousand men were brought

Why did France rise and Spain fall in this period?

What explains the rise of absolutism in Austria and Prussia?

What was distinctive about Russia and the Ottoman Empire?

Where and why did constitutionalism triumph?

What developments do baroque art and music reflect?

473

into the Russian army in special regiments of Cossacks and foreign mercenaries. To fund the army, taxes on peasants increased threefold during Peter's reign. Serfs were also arbitrarily assigned to work in the growing number of factories and mines that supplied the military.

Peter's new war machine was able to crush the army of Sweden in the Ukraine at Poltava in 1709, one of the most significant battles in Russian history. Russia's victory against Sweden was conclusive in 1721, and Estonia and present-day Latvia came under Russian rule for the first time. Russia became the dominant power in the Baltic and very much a European Great Power.

After his victory at Poltava, Peter channeled enormous resources into building a new Western-style capital on the Baltic to rival the great cities of Europe. The magnificent city of St. Petersburg was designed to reflect modern urban planning, with wide, straight avenues, buildings set in a uniform line, and large parks.

Peter the Great drafted twenty-five thousand to forty thousand men each summer to labor in St. Petersburg without pay. Many peasant construction workers died from hunger, sickness, and accidents. Nobles were ordered to build costly stone houses and palaces in St. Petersburg and to live in them most of the year. Merchants and artisans were also commanded to settle and build in the new capital. These nobles and merchants were then required to pay for the city's infrastructure. The building of St. Petersburg was, in truth, an enormous direct tax levied on the wealthy, with the peasantry forced to do the manual labor.

There were other important consequences of Peter's reign. For Peter, modernization meant westernization, and both Westerners and Western ideas flowed into Russia for the first time. He required nobles to shave their heavy beards and wear Western clothing. He obliged them to attend parties where young men and women would mix together and freely choose their own spouses. He forced a warrior elite to accept administrative service as an honorable occupation. From these efforts a new elite class of Western-oriented Russians began to emerge.

Peter's reforms were unpopular with many Russians. For nobles, one of Peter's most detested reforms was the imposition of unigeniture—inheritance of land by one son alone—cutting daughters and other sons from family property. For peasants, the reign of the tsar saw a significant increase in the bonds of serfdom, and the gulf between the enserfed peasantry and the educated nobility increased.

Peter's reforms were in some ways a continuation of Russia's distinctive history. He built on the service obligations of Ivan the Terrible and his successors, and his monarchical absolutism can be seen as the culmination of the long development of a unique Russian civilization. Yet the creation of a more modern army and state introduced much that was new and Western to Russia. This development paved the way for Russia to move somewhat closer to the European mainstream in its thought and institutions during the Enlightenment, especially under Catherine the Great.

The Growth of the Ottoman Empire

Most Christian Europeans perceived the Ottomans as the antithesis of their own values and traditions and viewed the empire as driven by lust for warfare and conquest. In their view the fall of Constantinople was a catastrophe and the taking of the Balkans a form of despotic imprisonment. To Ottoman eyes, the world looked very different. The siege of Constantinople liberated the city from its long decline under the Byzantines. Rather than being a despoiled captive, the Balkans became a haven for refugees fleeing the growing religious intolerance of Western Christian powers.

The Ottomans came out of Central Asia as conquering warriors, settled in Anatolia (present-day Turkey), and, at their peak in the mid-sixteenth century, ruled one of the

Chapter 16
Absolutism and Constitutionalism
474   in Europe • ca. 1589–1725

CHAPTER LOCATOR   What made the seventeenth century an "age of crisis"?

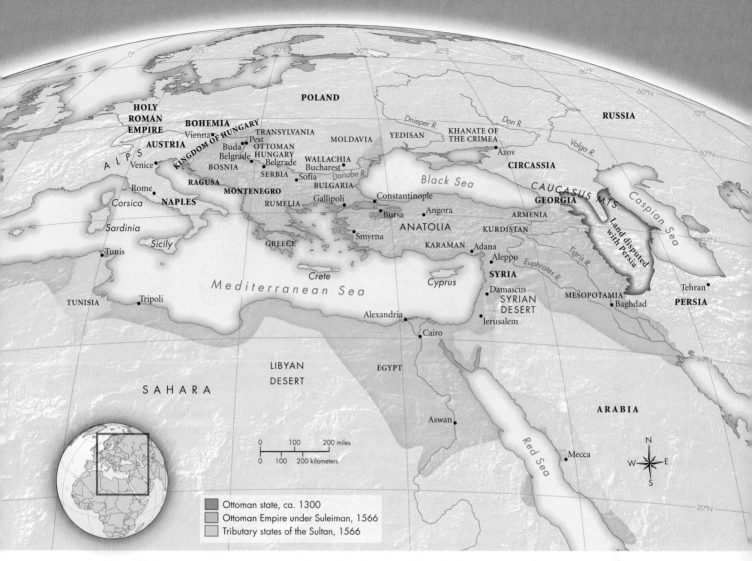

Map 16.4 The Ottoman Empire at Its Height, 1566 The Ottomans, like their great rivals the Habsburgs, rose to rule a vast dynastic empire encompassing many different peoples and ethnic groups. The army and the bureaucracy served to unite the disparate territories into a single state under an absolutist ruler.

Legend:
- Ottoman state, ca. 1300
- Ottoman Empire under Suleiman, 1566
- Tributary states of the Sultan, 1566

most powerful empires in the world (see Chapter 15). Their possessions stretched from western Persia across North Africa and into the heart of central Europe (Map 16.4).

The Ottoman Empire was originally built on a unique model of state and society. There was an almost complete absence of private landed property. Agricultural land was the personal property of the **sultan**, and peasants paid taxes to use the land. There was therefore no security of landholding and no hereditary nobility.

The Ottomans also employed a distinctive form of government administration. The top ranks of the bureaucracy were staffed by the sultan's slave corps. Because Muslim law prohibited enslaving other Muslims, the sultan's agents purchased slaves along the borders of the empire. Within the realm, the sultan levied a "tax" of one thousand to three thousand male children on the conquered Christian populations in the Balkans every year. These young slaves were raised in Turkey as Muslims and were trained to fight and to administer. The most talented Ottoman slaves rose to the top of the bureaucracy, where they might acquire wealth and power. The less fortunate formed the core of the sultan's army, the **janissary corps**. By 1683 service in the janissary (JAN-uh-sehr-ee) corps

sultan The ruler of the Ottoman Empire; he owned all the agricultural land of the empire and was served by an army and bureaucracy composed of highly trained slaves.

janissary corps The core of the sultan's army, composed of slave conscripts from non-Muslim parts of the empire; after 1683 it became a volunteer force.

Why did France rise and Spain fall in this period?

What explains the rise of absolutism in Austria and Prussia?

What was distinctive about Russia and the Ottoman Empire?

Where and why did constitutionalism triumph?

What developments do baroque art and music reflect?

475

Hürrem and Her Ladies in the Harem In Muslim culture *harem* means a sacred place or a sanctuary. The term was applied to the part of the household occupied by women and children and forbidden to men outside the family. The most famous member of the Ottoman sultan's harem was Hürrem (1505–1585), wife of Suleiman the Magnificent. Captured, according to tradition, in modern-day Ukraine in a Tartar raid and brought to the harem as a slave-concubine, she quickly won the sultan's trust and affection. Suleiman's love for Hürrem led him to break all precedents and marry his concubine, a decision that shocked some courtiers. (Bibliothèque nationale de France)

had become so prestigious that the sultan ceased recruitment by force, and it became a volunteer army open to Christians and Muslims.

The Ottomans divided their subjects into religious communities, and each *millet,* or "nation," enjoyed autonomous self-government under its religious leaders. The Ottoman Empire recognized Orthodox Christians, Jews, Armenian Christians, and Muslims as distinct millets. The millet system created a powerful bond between the Ottoman ruling class and religious leaders, who supported the sultan's rule in return for extensive authority over their own communities. Each millet (MIH-luht) collected taxes for the state, regulated group behavior, and maintained law courts, schools, houses of worship, and hospitals for its people.

Sultans married women of the highest social standing, while keeping many concubines of low rank. To prevent the elite families into which they married from acquiring influence over government, sultans procreated only with their concubines and not with official wives. They also adopted a policy of allowing each concubine to produce only one male heir. At a young age, each son went to govern a province of the empire accompanied by his mother. These practices were intended to stabilize power and prevent a recurrence of the civil wars of the late fourteenth and early fifteenth centuries.

Sultan Suleiman undid these policies when he boldly married his concubine, a former slave of Polish origin named Hürrem, and had several children with her. Starting with Suleiman, imperial wives began to take on more power. Marriages were arranged between sultans' daughters and high-ranking servants, creating powerful new members of the imperial household. Over time, the sultan's exclusive authority waned in favor of a more bureaucratic administration.

millet system A system used by the Ottomans whereby subjects were divided into religious communities with each millet (nation) enjoying autonomous self-government under its religious leaders.

476

Chapter 16
Absolutism and Constitutionalism in Europe • ca. 1589–1725

CHAPTER LOCATOR   What made the seventeenth century an "age of crisis"?

▼ Where and why did constitutionalism triumph?

While France, Prussia, Russia, and Austria developed the absolutist state, England and Holland evolved toward constitutionalism, which is the limitation of government by law. Constitutionalism also implies a balance between the authority and power of the government, on the one hand, and the rights and liberties of the subjects, on the other. By definition, all constitutionalist governments have a constitution. A nation's constitution may be embodied in one basic document, like the Constitution of the United States. Or it may be only partly formalized and include parliamentary statutes, judicial decisions, and a body of traditional procedures and practices, like the English and Dutch constitutions.

Despite their common commitment to constitutional government, England and the Dutch Republic represented significantly different alternatives to absolute rule. After decades of civil war and an experiment with republicanism, the English opted for a constitutional monarchy in 1688. England retained a monarch as the titular head of government but vested sovereignty in an elected parliament. Upon gaining independence from Spain in 1648, the Dutch rejected monarchical rule, adopting a republican form of government in which elected estates held supreme power.

constitutionalism A form of government in which power is limited by law and balanced between the authority and power of the government on the one hand, and the rights and liberties of the subject or citizen on the other hand; could include constitutional monarchies or republics.

republicanism A form of government in which there is no monarch and power rests in the hands of the people as exercised through elected representatives.

Absolutist Claims in England

In 1603 Queen Elizabeth I (r. 1558–1603) of England's Scottish cousin James Stuart succeeded her as James I (r. 1603–1625). King James was well educated and had thirty-five years' experience as king of Scotland. But he was not as interested in displaying the majesty of monarchy as Elizabeth had been. Urged to wave at the crowds who waited to greet their new ruler, James complained that he was tired and threatened to drop his breeches "so they can cheer at my arse."[6]

James's greatest problem, however, stemmed from his absolutist belief that a monarch has a divine right to his authority and is responsible only to God. James went so far as to lecture the House of Commons: "There are no privileges and immunities which can stand against a divinely appointed King." Such a view ran directly counter to the long-standing English idea that a person's property could not be taken away without due process of law. James I and his son Charles I considered such constraints a threat to their divine-right prerogative. Consequently, at every Parliament between 1603 and 1640, bitter squabbles erupted

Van Dyck, *Charles I at the Hunt*, ca. 1635 Anthony Van Dyck was the greatest of Rubens's many students. In 1633 he became court painter to Charles I. This portrait of Charles just dismounted from a horse emphasizes the aristocratic bearing, elegance, and innate authority of the king. Van Dyck's success led to innumerable commissions by members of the court and aristocratic society. He had a profound influence on portraiture in England and beyond; some scholars believe that this portrait influenced Rigaud's 1701 portrayal of Louis XIV (see page 459). (Scala/Art Resource, NY)

| Why did France rise and Spain fall in this period? | What explains the rise of absolutism in Austria and Prussia? | What was distinctive about Russia and the Ottoman Empire? | **Where and why did constitutionalism triumph?** | What developments do baroque art and music reflect? |

477

between the Crown and the Commons. Charles I's attempt to govern without Parliament (1629–1640) and to finance his government by emergency taxes brought the country to a crisis.

Religious Divides and the English Civil War

Religious issues also embittered relations between the king and the House of Commons. In the early seventeenth century increasing numbers of English people felt dissatisfied with the Church of England established by Henry VIII and reformed by Elizabeth. Many **Puritans** believed that the Reformation had not gone far enough. They wanted to "purify" the Anglican Church of Roman Catholic elements—elaborate vestments and ceremonials, bishops, and even the giving and wearing of wedding rings.

James I responded to such ideas by declaring, "No bishop, no king." For James, bishops were among the chief supporters of the throne. His son and successor, Charles I, further antagonized religious sentiments. Not only did he marry a Catholic princess, but he also supported the policies of the Archbishop of Canterbury William Laud (1573–1645). In 1637 Laud attempted to impose two new elements on church organization in Scotland: a new prayer book, modeled on the Anglican *Book of Common Prayer*, and bishoprics. The Presbyterian Scots rejected these elements and revolted. To finance an

Puritans Members of a sixteenth- and seventeenth-century reform movement within the Church of England that advocated purifying it of Roman Catholic elements, such as bishops, elaborate ceremonials, and wedding rings.

Puritan Occupations These twelve engravings depict typical Puritan occupations and show that the Puritans came primarily from the artisan and lower middle classes. The governing classes and peasants made up a much smaller percentage of the Puritans and generally adhered to the traditions of the Church of England. (Visual Connection Archive)

Chapter 16
Absolutism and Constitutionalism
in Europe • ca. 1589–1725

478

CHAPTER LOCATOR

What made the seventeenth century an "age of crisis"?

army to put down the Scots, King Charles was compelled to summon Parliament in November 1640.

Charles had ruled from 1629 to 1640 without Parliament, financing his government through extraordinary stopgap levies considered illegal by most English people. Most members of Parliament believed that such taxation without consent amounted to despotism. Consequently, they were not willing to trust the king with an army. Moreover, many supported the Scots' resistance to Charles's religious innovations. Accordingly, this Parliament, called the "Long Parliament" because it sat from 1640 to 1660, enacted legislation that limited the power of the monarch and made government without Parliament impossible.

In 1641 the Commons passed the Triennial Act, which compelled the king to summon Parliament every three years. The Commons impeached Archbishop Laud and then threatened to abolish bishops. King Charles, fearful of a Scottish invasion — the original reason for summoning Parliament — reluctantly accepted these measures.

The next act in the conflict was precipitated by the outbreak of rebellion in Ireland, where English governors and landlords had long exploited the people. In 1641 the Catholic gentry of Ireland led an uprising in response to a feared invasion by anti-Catholic forces of the British Long Parliament.

Without an army, Charles I could neither come to terms with the Scots nor respond to the Irish rebellion. After a failed attempt to arrest parliamentary leaders, Charles left London for the north of England where he recruited an army. In response, Parliament formed its own army, the New Model Army. During the spring of 1642 both sides prepared for war.

The English Civil War, 1642–1649

The English civil war (1642–1649) pitted the power of the king against that of the Parliament. After three years of fighting, Parliament's New Model Army defeated the king's armies at the battles of Naseby and Langport in the summer of 1645. Charles, though, refused to concede defeat. Both sides jockeyed for position, waiting for a decisive event. This arrived in the form of the army under the leadership of Oliver Cromwell, a member of the House of Commons and a devout Puritan. In 1647 Cromwell's forces captured the king and dismissed members of the Parliament who opposed his actions. In 1649 the remaining representatives, known as the "Rump Parliament," put Charles on trial for high treason. Charles was found guilty and beheaded on January 30, 1649.

Cromwell and Puritanical Absolutism in England

With the execution of Charles, kingship was abolished and a commonwealth, or republican government, was proclaimed. Theoretically, legislative power rested in the surviving members of Parliament, and executive power was lodged in a council of state. In fact, the army that had defeated the king controlled the government, and Oliver Cromwell controlled the army. Though called the **Protectorate**, the rule of Cromwell (1653–1658) constituted military dictatorship.

The army prepared a constitution, the Instrument of Government (1653), that invested executive power in a lord protector (Cromwell) and a council of state. It provided for triennial parliaments and gave Parliament the sole power to raise taxes. But after repeated disputes, Cromwell dismissed Parliament in 1655, and the instrument was never formally endorsed. Cromwell continued the standing army and proclaimed quasi-martial law. He divided England into twelve military districts, each governed by a major general.

Protectorate The English military dictatorship (1653–1658) established by Oliver Cromwell following the execution of Charles I.

Why did France rise and Spain fall in this period?   What explains the rise of absolutism in Austria and Prussia?   What was distinctive about Russia and the Ottoman Empire?   **Where and why did constitutionalism triumph?**   What developments do baroque art and music reflect?

479

"The Royall Oake of Brittayne" The chopping down of this tree, as shown in this cartoon from 1649, signifies the end of royal authority, stability, and the rule of law. As pigs graze (representing the unconcerned common people), being fattened for slaughter, Oliver Cromwell, with his feet in Hell, quotes Scripture. This is a royalist view of the collapse of Charles I's government and the rule of Cromwell. (Courtesy of the Trustees of the British Museum)

Reflecting Puritan ideas of morality, Cromwell's state forbade sports, kept the theaters closed, and rigorously censored the press.

On the issue of religion, Cromwell favored some degree of toleration, and the Instrument of Government gave all Christians except Roman Catholics the right to practice their faith. Cromwell had long associated Catholicism in Ireland with sedition and heresy, and he led an army there to reconquer the country in August 1649. Following Cromwell's reconquest, the English banned Catholicism in Ireland, executed priests, and confiscated land from Catholics for English and Scottish settlers. These brutal acts left a legacy of Irish hatred for England.

Cromwell adopted mercantilist policies similar to those of absolutist France. He enforced a Navigation Act (1651) requiring that English goods be transported on English ships. The act was a great boost to the development of an English merchant marine and brought about a short but successful war with the Dutch. Cromwell also welcomed the immigration of Jews because of their skills, and they began to return to England after four centuries of absence.

The Protectorate collapsed when Cromwell died in 1658 and his son succeeded him. Fed up with military rule, the English longed for a return to civilian government and, with it, common law and social stability. By 1660 they were ready to restore the monarchy.

The Restoration of the English Monarchy

The Restoration of 1660 brought to the throne Charles II (r. 1660–1685), eldest son of Charles I. Both houses of Parliament were also restored, together with the established

Chapter 16
**Absolutism and Constitutionalism
in Europe • ca. 1589–1725**

480

CHAPTER LOCATOR | What made the seventeenth century an "age of crisis"?

Anglican Church. The Restoration failed to resolve two serious problems, however. What was to be the attitude of the state toward Puritans, Catholics, and dissenters from the established church? And what was to be the relationship between the king and Parliament?

To answer the first question, Parliament enacted the Test Act of 1673 against those outside the Church of England, denying them the right to vote, hold public office, preach, teach, attend the universities, or even assemble for meetings. In politics Charles II was determined to work well with Parliament. This intention did not last, however. Finding that Parliament did not grant him an adequate income, in 1670 Charles entered into a secret agreement with his cousin Louis XIV. The French king would give Charles two hundred thousand pounds annually, and in return Charles would relax the laws against Catholics, gradually re-Catholicize England, and convert to Catholicism himself. When the details of this treaty leaked out, a great wave of anti-Catholic sentiment swept England.

When James II (r. 1685–1688) succeeded his brother, the worst English anti-Catholic fears were realized. In violation of the Test Act, James appointed Roman Catholics to positions in the army, the universities, and local government. And he went further. Attempting to broaden his base of support with Protestant dissenters and nonconformists, James granted religious freedom to all.

Seeking to prevent the return of Catholic absolutism, a group of eminent persons in Parliament and the Church of England offered the English throne to James's Protestant daughter Mary and her Dutch husband, Prince William of Orange. In December 1688 James II, his queen, and their infant son fled to France. Early in 1689 William and Mary were crowned king and queen of England.

Constitutional Monarchy

The English call the events of 1688 and 1689 the "Glorious Revolution" because it replaced one king with another with a minimum of bloodshed. It also represented the destruction, once and for all, of the idea of divine-right monarchy. The revolution of 1688 established the principle that sovereignty, the ultimate power in the state, was divided between king and Parliament and that the king ruled with the consent of the governed.

The men who brought about the revolution framed their intentions in the Bill of Rights, which was formulated in direct response to Stuart absolutism. Law was to be made in Parliament; once made, it could not be suspended by the Crown. Parliament had to be called at least once every three years. The independence of the judiciary was established, and there was to be no standing army in peacetime. Protestants could possess arms, but the Catholic minority could not. No Catholic could ever inherit the throne. Additional legislation granted freedom of worship to Protestant dissenters, but not to Catholics.

The Glorious Revolution and the concept of representative government found its best defense in political philosopher John Locke's *Second Treatise of Civil Government* (1690). Locke (1632–1704) maintained that a government that oversteps its proper function—protecting the natural rights of life, liberty, and property—becomes a tyranny. By "natural" rights Locke meant rights basic to all men because all have the ability to reason. Under a tyrannical government, the people have the natural right to rebellion.

The events of 1688 and 1689 did not constitute a democratic revolution. The revolution placed sovereignty in Parliament, and Parliament represented the upper classes. The age of aristocratic government lasted at least until 1832 and in many ways until 1928, when women received full voting rights.

England's brief and chaotic experiment with republicanism under Oliver Cromwell convinced its people of the advantages of a monarchy, albeit with strong checks on royal authority. The eighteenth-century philosopher David Hume went so far as to declare that he would prefer England to be peaceful under an absolute monarch than in constant civil war as a republic. These sentiments would have found little sympathy among the proud burgers of the Dutch Republic.

Test Act Legislation passed by the English parliament in 1673 to secure the position of the Anglican Church by stripping Puritans, Catholics, and other dissenters of the right to vote, preach, assemble, hold public office, and attend or teach at the universities.

Why did France rise and Spain fall in this period?

What explains the rise of absolutism in Austria and Prussia?

What was distinctive about Russia and the Ottoman Empire?

Where and why did constitutionalism triumph?

What developments do baroque art and music reflect?

481

INDIVIDUALS IN SOCIETY

Glückel of Hameln

IN 1690 A JEWISH WIDOW IN THE SMALL GERMAN town of Hameln in Lower Saxony sat down to write her autobiography. She wanted to distract her mind from the terrible grief she felt over the death of her husband and to provide her twelve children with a record "so you will know from what sort of people you have sprung, lest today or tomorrow your beloved children or grandchildren came and know naught of their family." Out of her pain and heightened consciousness, Glückel (1646–1724) produced an invaluable source for scholars.

She was born in Hamburg two years before the end of the Thirty Years' War. In 1649 the merchants of Hamburg expelled the Jews, who moved to nearby Altona, then under Danish rule. When the Swedes overran Altona in 1657–1658, the Jews returned to Hamburg "purely at the mercy of the Town Council." Glückel's narrative proceeds against a background of the constant harassment to which Jews were subjected — special papers, permits, bribes — and in Hameln she wrote, "And so it has been to this day and, I fear, will continue in like fashion."

When Glückel was "barely twelve," her father betrothed her to Chayim Hameln. She married at age fourteen. She describes him as "the perfect pattern of the pious Jew," a man who stopped his work every day for study and prayer, fasted, and was scrupulously honest in his business dealings. Only a few years older than Glückel, Chayim earned his living dealing in precious metals and in making small loans on pledges (pawned goods). This work required his constant travel to larger cities, markets, and fairs, often in bad weather, always over dangerous roads. Chayim consulted his wife about all his business dealings. As he lay dying, a friend asked if he had any last wishes. "None," he replied. "My wife knows everything. She shall do as she has always done." For thirty years Glückel had been his friend, full business partner, and wife. They had thirteen children, twelve of whom survived their father, eight then unmarried. As Chayim had foretold, Glückel succeeded in launching the boys in careers and in providing dowries for the girls.

Glückel's world was her family, the Jewish community of Hameln, and the Jewish communities into which her children married. Her social and business activities took her across Europe — from Amsterdam to Berlin, from Danzig to Vienna — so her world was neither narrow nor provincial. She took great pride that Prince Frederick of Cleves, later king of Prussia, danced at the wedding of her eldest daughter. The rising prosperity of Chayim's businesses allowed the couple to maintain up to six servants.

Glückel was deeply religious, and her culture was steeped in Jewish literature, legends, and mystical and secular works. Above all, she relied on the Bible. Her language, heavily sprinkled with scriptural references, testifies to a rare familiarity with the Scriptures.

Students who would learn about seventeenth-century business practices, the importance of the dowry in marriage, childbirth, Jewish life, birthrates, family celebrations, and even the meaning of life can gain a good deal from the memoirs of this extraordinary woman who was, in the words of one of her descendants, the poet Heinrich Heine, "the gift of a world to me."

QUESTIONS FOR ANALYSIS

1. Consider the ways in which Glückel of Hameln was both an ordinary and an extraordinary woman of her times. Would you call her a marginal or a central person in her society?
2. How might Glückel's successes be attributed to the stabilizing force of absolutism in the seventeenth century?

Source: *The Memoirs of Glückel of Hameln* (New York: Schocken Books, 1977).

Although no images of Glückel exist, Rembrandt's *The Jewish Bride* suggests the mutual devotion that Glückel and her husband felt for one another. (Rijksmuseum-Stichting Amsterdam)

Chapter 16
Absolutism and Constitutionalism
in Europe • ca. 1589–1725

482

CHAPTER LOCATOR   What made the seventeenth century an "age of crisis"?

The Dutch Republic in the Seventeenth Century

In the late sixteenth century the seven northern provinces of the Netherlands fought for and won their independence from Spain. The independence of the Republic of the United Provinces of the Netherlands was recognized in 1648 in the treaty that ended the Thirty Years' War. In this period, often called the "golden age of the Netherlands," Dutch ideas and attitudes played a profound role in shaping a new and modern worldview. At the same time, the United Provinces developed its own distinctive model of a constitutional state.

Rejecting the rule of a monarch, the Dutch established a republic, a state in which power rested in the hands of the people and was exercised through elected representatives. An oligarchy of wealthy businessmen called "regents" handled domestic affairs in each province's Estates (assemblies). The provincial Estates held virtually all the power. A federal assembly, or States General, handled foreign affairs and war, but it did not possess sovereign authority. All issues had to be referred back to the local Estates for approval, and each of the seven provinces could veto any proposed legislation.

In each province, the Estates appointed an executive officer, known as the **stadholder**, who carried out ceremonial functions and was responsible for military defense. Although in theory freely chosen by the Estates, in practice the reigning prince of Orange usually held the office of stadholder in several of the seven provinces of the Republic. This meant that tensions always lingered between supporters of the House of Orange and those of the staunchly republican Estates, who suspected the princes of harboring monarchical ambitions. When one of them, William III, took the English throne in 1688 with his wife, Mary, the republic simply continued without stadholders for several decades.

> **stadholder** The executive officer in each of the United Provinces of the Netherlands, a position often held by the princes of Orange.

The political success of the Dutch rested on their commercial prosperity (see Chapter 15). The moral and ethical bases of that commercial wealth were thrift, frugality, and religious toleration. Jews enjoyed a level of acceptance and assimilation in Dutch business and general culture unique in early modern Europe. (See "Individuals in Society: Glückel of Hameln," left.) In the Dutch Republic, toleration paid off: it attracted a great deal of foreign capital and investment.

The Dutch came to dominate the shipping business by putting profits from their original industry—herring fishing—into shipbuilding. They boasted the lowest shipping rates and largest merchant marine in Europe, allowing them to undersell foreign competitors. Trade and commerce brought the Dutch the highest standard of living in Europe, perhaps in the world.

▼ What developments do baroque art and music reflect?

Rome and the revitalized Catholic Church of the later sixteenth century played an important role in the early development of the baroque style. The papacy and the Jesuits encouraged the growth of an intensely emotional, exuberant art. They wanted artists to appeal to the senses and thereby touch the souls and kindle the faith of ordinary churchgoers while proclaiming the power and confidence of the reformed Catholic Church. In addition to this underlying religious emotionalism, the baroque drew its sense of drama, motion, and ceaseless striving from the Catholic Reformation.

Taking definite shape in Italy after 1600, the baroque style in the visual arts developed with exceptional vigor in Catholic countries. Yet baroque art was more than just "Catholic art" in the seventeenth century and the first half of the eighteenth. Protestants

Why did France rise and Spain fall in this period? | What explains the rise of absolutism in Austria and Prussia? | What was distinctive about Russia and the Ottoman Empire? | Where and why did constitutionalism triumph? | **What developments do baroque art and music reflect?**

483

Rubens, *Garden of Love*, 1633–1634 This painting is an outstanding example of the lavishness and richness of baroque art. Born and raised in northern Europe, Peter Paul Rubens trained as a painter in Italy. Upon his return to the Spanish Netherlands, he became a renowned and amazingly prolific artist, patronized by rulers across Europe. Rubens was a devout Catholic, and his work conveys the emotional fervor of the Catholic Reformation. (Scala/Art Resource, NY)

accounted for some of the finest examples of baroque style, especially in music. The baroque style spread partly because its tension and bombast spoke to an agitated age that was experiencing great violence and controversy in politics and religion.

In painting, the baroque reached maturity early with Peter Paul Rubens (1577–1640), the most outstanding and most representative of baroque painters. Studying in his native Flanders and in Italy, Rubens developed his own rich, sensuous, colorful style, which was characterized by animated figures, melodramatic contrasts, and monumental size. Rubens excelled in glorifying monarchs such as Queen Mother Marie de' Medici of France. He was also a devout Catholic; nearly half of his pictures treat Christian subjects. Yet one of Rubens's trademarks was fleshy, sensual nudes who populate his canvases as Roman goddesses, water nymphs, and remarkably voluptuous saints and angels.

In music, the baroque style reached its culmination almost a century later in the dynamic, soaring lines of the endlessly inventive Johann Sebastian Bach (1685–1750). Organist and choirmaster of several Lutheran churches across Germany, Bach was equally at home writing secular concertos and religious cantatas. Bach's organ music combined the baroque spirit of invention, tension, and emotion in an unforgettable striving toward the infinite.

Chapter 16
**Absolutism and Constitutionalism
in Europe** • ca. 1589–1725

484

CHAPTER LOCATOR   What made the
seventeenth century an
"age of crisis"?

←LOOKING BACK LOOKING AHEAD→

THE SEVENTEENTH CENTURY represented a difficult passage between two centuries of dynamism and growth. On one side lay the sixteenth century of religious enthusiasm and strife, overseas expansion, rising population, and vigorous commerce. On the other side stretched the eighteenth-century era of renewed population growth, economic development, and cultural flourishing. The first half of the seventeenth century was marked by the spread of religious and dynastic warfare across Europe, resulting in the death and dislocation of many millions. This catastrophe was compounded by recurrent episodes of crop failure, famine, and epidemic disease, all of which contributed to a stagnant economy and population loss. In the middle decades of the seventeenth century, the very survival of the European monarchies established in the Renaissance appeared in doubt.

With the re-establishment of order in the second half of the century, maintaining political and social stability appeared of paramount importance to European rulers and elites. In western and eastern Europe, a host of monarchs proclaimed their God-given and "absolute" authority to rule in the name of peace, unity, and good order. Rulers' ability to impose such claims in reality depended a great deal on compromise with local elites, who acquiesced to state power in exchange for privileges and payoffs. In this way, absolutism and constitutionalism did not always differ as much as they claimed. Both systems relied on political compromises forged from decades of strife.

The eighteenth century was to see this status quo thrown into question by new Enlightenment aspirations for human society, which themselves derived from the inquisitive and self-confident spirit of the scientific revolution. By the end of the century, demands for real popular sovereignty challenged the very bases of political order so painfully achieved in the seventeenth century. ∎

■ **For a list of suggested readings for this chapter, visit** *bedfordstmartins.com/mckaywestunderstanding*.

■ **For primary sources from this period, see** *Sources of Western Society*, Second Edition.

■ **For Web sites, images, and documents related to topics in this chapter, see Make History at** *bedfordstmartins.com/mckaywestunderstanding*.

Why did France rise and Spain fall in this period?   What explains the rise of absolutism in Austria and Prussia?   What was distinctive about Russia and the Ottoman Empire?   Where and why did constitutionalism triumph?   What developments do baroque art and music reflect?

Chapter 16 Study Guide

Online Study Guide
bedfordstmartins.com/mckaywestunderstanding

Step 1

GETTING STARTED Below are basic terms about this period in the history of Western civilization. Can you identify each term below and explain why it matters? To do this exercise online, go to bedfordstmartins.com/mckaywestunderstanding.

TERMS	WHO (OR WHAT) AND WHEN	WHY IT MATTERS
Peace of Westphalia, p. 455		
the Fronde, p. 458		
mercantilism, p. 461		
Peace of Utrecht, p. 462		
Junkers, p. 467		
boyars, p. 468		
Cossacks, p. 469		
sultan, p. 475		
janissary corps, p. 475		
millet system, p. 476		
constitutionalism, p. 477		
republicanism, p. 477		
Puritans, p. 478		
Protectorate, p. 479		
Test Act, p. 481		
stadholder, p. 483		

Step 2

MOVING BEYOND THE BASICS The exercise below requires a more advanced understanding of the chapter material. Examine the growth of state power in France, Prussia, Austria, and England by filling in the chart below with descriptions of developments in four areas where these seventeenth-century governments achieved new levels of control: taxation, the armed forces, bureaucracies, and the ability to compel obedience from subjects. When you are finished, consider the following questions: Why did seventeenth-century governments place so much emphasis on increasing their military power? How did the need to maintain large armies shape other aspects of government? How did the growth of the state in England differ from the growth of the state in absolutist France, Prussia, and Austria? To do this exercise online, go to bedfordstmartins.com/mckaywestunderstanding.

STATE	TAXATION	ARMED FORCES	BUREAUCRACIES	CONTROL OVER SUBJECTS
France				
Prussia				
Austria				
England				

PUTTING IT ALL TOGETHER Now that you've reviewed key elements of the chapter, take a step back and try to see the big picture. Remember to use specific examples from the chapter in your answers. To do this exercise online, go to bedfordstmartins.com/mckaywestunderstanding.

THE AGE OF CRISIS

- How did life for Europe's peasants change during the seventeenth century? Why was peasant life harder in eastern Europe than in western Europe?

- What conflicts and tensions underlay the warfare of the seventeenth century?

ABSOLUTISM

- How and why did Louis XIV try to co-opt and control the French aristocracy? In practice, how "absolute" was his rule?

- Compare and contrast absolutism in Austria, Prussia, and Russia. What common problems and challenges did would-be absolutist rulers face in each of these three states?

- How did the Ottoman absolutist state differ from its European counterparts? To what do you attribute these differences?

CONSTITUTIONAL STATES

- Why did the efforts of English monarchs to build an absolutist state fail? What groups and institutions in English society were most responsible for the triumph of constitutionalism?

- Compare and contrast the constitutional governments of England and the Netherlands. What role did merchant elites and commercial interests play in each state?

BAROQUE ART AND MUSIC

- What role did religion play in the cultural developments of the seventeenth century? What do cultural developments tell us about the religious life of seventeenth-century Europeans?

- Why was baroque art and music so appealing to seventeenth-century Europeans? To what groups did it appeal the most? Why?

■ **In Your Own Words** Imagine that you must explain Chapter 16 to someone who hasn't read it. What would be the most important points to include and why?

17

Toward a New Worldview

1540–1789

The intellectual developments of the seventeenth and eighteenth centuries created the modern worldview that the West continues to hold—and debate—to this day. In the seventeenth century fundamentally new ways of understanding the natural world emerged. Those leading the changes saw themselves as philosophers and referred to their field of study as "natural philosophy." In the nineteenth century scholars hailed these achievements as a "scientific revolution" that produced modern science as we know it. The new science created in the seventeenth century entailed the search for precise knowledge of the physical world based on the union of experimental observations with sophisticated mathematics. Whereas medieval scholars looked to authoritative texts like the Bible or the classics, seventeenth-century natural philosophers performed experiments and relied on increasingly complex mathematical calculations. The resulting conception of the universe and its laws remained in force until Einstein's discoveries in the first half of the twentieth century.

In the eighteenth century philosophers extended the use of reason from the study of nature to the study of human society. They sought to bring the light of reason to bear on the darkness of prejudice, outmoded traditions, and ignorance. Self-proclaimed members of an "Enlightenment" movement, they wished to bring the same progress to human affairs as their predecessors had brought to the understanding of the natural world. While the scientific revolution ushered in modern science, the Enlightenment created concepts of human rights, equality, progress, universalism, and tolerance that still guide Western societies today. At the same time, some people used their new understanding of reason to explain their own superiority, thus rationalizing such attitudes as racism and male chauvinism. ■

Life During the Scientific Revolution. This 1768 painting by Joseph Wright captures the popularization of science and experimentation during the Enlightenment. Here, a scientist demonstrates the creation of a vacuum by withdrawing air from a flask, with the air-deprived cockatoo serving as shocking proof of the experiment. (National Gallery, London/The Bridgeman Art Library)

Chapter Preview

▶ **How did European views of nature change in this period?**

▶ **What were the core principles of the Enlightenment?**

▶ **What did enlightened absolutism mean?**

▼ How did European views of nature change in this period?

The emergence of modern science was a development of tremendous long-term significance. With the scientific revolution, which lasted roughly from 1540 to 1690, Western society began to acquire its most distinctive traits.

Scientific Thought in 1500

The term *science* as we use it today only came into use in the nineteenth century. Prior to the scientific revolution, many different scholars and practitioners were involved in aspects of what came together to form science. One of the most important disciplines was **natural philosophy**, which focused on fundamental questions about the nature of the universe, its purpose, and how it functioned. In the early 1500s natural philosophy was still based primarily on the ideas of Aristotle. Medieval theologians such as Thomas Aquinas brought Aristotelian philosophy into harmony with Christian doctrines. According to the revised Aristotelian view, a motionless earth was fixed at the center of the universe, and it was encompassed by ten separate concentric crystal spheres in which were embedded the moon, sun, planets, and stars. Beyond the spheres was Heaven, with the throne of God and the souls of the saved. Angels kept the spheres moving in perfect circles.

Aristotle's cosmology made intellectual sense, but it could not account for the observed motions of the stars and planets. The great second-century Greek scholar Ptolemy (see Chapter 15) offered a solution to this dilemma. According to Ptolemy, the planets moved in small circles, called epicycles, each of which moved in turn along a larger circle or deferent. Ptolemaic astronomy was less elegant than Aristotle's neat nested circles and required complex calculations, but it provided a surprisingly accurate model for predicting planetary motion.

Aristotle's views, revised by medieval philosophers, also dominated thinking about physics and motion on earth. Aristotle had distinguished sharply between the world of the celestial spheres and that of the earth—the sublunar world. The spheres consisted of a perfect, incorruptible "quintessence," or fifth essence. The sublunar world, however, was made up of four imperfect, changeable elements: air, fire, water, and earth. Aristotle and his followers also believed that a uniform force moved an object at a constant speed and that the object would stop as soon as that force was removed.

Aristotle's ideas about astronomy and physics were accepted for two thousand years because they offered a commonsense

natural philosophy An early modern term for the study of the nature of the universe, its purpose, and how it functioned; it encompassed what we would call "science" today.

The Aristotelian Universe as Imagined in the Sixteenth Century A round earth is at the center, surrounded by spheres of water, air, and fire. Beyond this small nucleus, the moon, the sun, and the five planets were embedded in their own rotating crystal spheres, with the stars sharing the surface of one enormous sphere. Beyond, the heavens were composed of unchanging ether. (Image Select/Art Resource, NY)

explanation for the natural world and fit neatly with Christian doctrines placing humans on earth at the center of creation, with God and the angels in the eternal heavens above.

Origins of the Scientific Revolution

Why did Aristotelian teachings give way to new views about the universe? The scientific revolution drew on long-term developments in European culture, as well as borrowings from Arabic scholars. The first important development was the university. By the thirteenth century permanent universities with professors and large student bodies had been established in western Europe. In the universities, medieval philosophers developed a limited but real independence from theologians and a sense of free inquiry.

In the fourteenth and fifteenth centuries leading universities established new professorships of mathematics, astronomy, and physics (natural philosophy) within their faculties of philosophy. Although the prestige of the new fields was low, critical thinking was now applied to scientific problems by a permanent community of scholars.

The Renaissance also stimulated scientific progress. Many ancient works were recovered, often through Arabic translations of the original Greek and Latin. In fields such as mathematics, the translations were accompanied by learned Arabic commentaries that went beyond ancient learning. Renaissance patrons played a role in funding scientific investigations, as they did for art and literature. In addition, Renaissance artists' turn toward realism and their use of geometry to convey three-dimensional perspective encouraged scholars to practice close observation and to use mathematics to describe the natural world. The rise of printing provided a faster and less expensive way to circulate knowledge across Europe.

The navigational problems of long sea voyages in the age of overseas expansion were another factor in the scientific revolution. Navigational problems were critical in the development of many new scientific instruments, such as the telescope, barometer, thermometer, pendulum clock, microscope, and air pump. Better instruments, which permitted more accurate observations, often led to important new knowledge.

Recent historical research has also focused on the contribution to the scientific revolution of practices now relegated far beyond the realm of science. For most of human history, interest in astronomy was inspired by belief that the changing relationships between planets and stars influenced events on earth. Many of the most celebrated astronomers were also astrologers. Used as a diagnostic tool in medicine, astrology formed a regular part of the curriculum of medical schools. Centuries-old practices of magic and alchemy also remained important traditions for participants in the scientific revolution. The idea that objects possessed hidden or "occult" qualities that allowed them to affect other objects was a particularly important legacy of the magical tradition.

The Copernican Hypothesis

The first great departure from the medieval system was the work of the Polish cleric Nicolaus Copernicus (koh-PUHR-nih-kuhs) (1473–1543). After studies at the university of Kraków, Copernicus departed for Italy, where he studied astronomy, medicine,

Chapter Chronology

ca. 1540–1690	Scientific revolution
ca. 1690–1789	Enlightenment
ca. 1700–1789	Growth of book publishing
1720–1780	Rococo style in art and decoration
1740–1748	War of Austrian Succession
1740–1780	Reign of the empress Maria Theresa
1740–1786	Reign of Frederick the Great of Prussia
ca. 1740–1789	French salons led by elite women
1756–1763	Seven Years' War
1762–1796	Reign of Catherine the Great of Russia
1765	Philosophes publish *Encyclopedia: The Rational Dictionary of the Sciences, the Arts, and the Crafts*
1780–1790	Reign of Joseph II of Austria
1791	Establishment of the Pale of Settlement

CHAPTER LOCATOR   **How did European views of nature change in this period?**   What were the core principles of the Enlightenment?   What did enlightened absolutism mean?

491

and church law at the famed universities of Bologna, Padua, and Ferrara. In his studies of astronomy, Copernicus came to believe that Ptolemy's cumbersome and occasionally inaccurate rules detracted from the majesty of a perfect creator. He preferred an ancient Greek idea: that the sun, rather than the earth, was at the center of the universe.

Finishing his university studies and returning to a church position in East Prussia, Copernicus worked on his hypothesis from 1506 to 1530. Without questioning the Aristotelian belief in crystal spheres or the idea that circular motion was divine, Copernicus theorized that the stars and planets, including the earth, revolved around a fixed sun. Fearing the ridicule of other astronomers, Copernicus did not publish his *On the Revolutions of the Heavenly Spheres* until 1543, the year of his death.

Copernican hypothesis
The idea that the sun, not the earth, is the center of the universe.

The Copernican hypothesis presented a revolutionary view of the universe and brought sharp attacks from religious leaders, especially Protestants, who objected to the idea that the earth moved but the sun did not. Protestant leaders John Calvin and Martin Luther condemned Copernicus. Luther noted that the theory was counter to the Bible: "as the Holy Scripture tells us, so did Joshua bid the sun stand still and not the earth."[1] Catholic reaction was milder at first. The Catholic Church had never held to literal interpretations of the Bible, and not until 1616 did it officially declare the Copernican hypothesis false.

Other events were almost as influential in creating doubts about traditional astronomical ideas. In 1572 a new star appeared and shone very brightly for almost two years. The new star, which was actually a distant exploding star, seemed to contradict the idea that the heavenly spheres were unchanging and therefore perfect. In 1577 a new comet suddenly moved through the sky, cutting a straight path across the supposedly impenetrable crystal spheres. It was time, as a sixteenth-century scientific writer put it, for "the radical renovation of astronomy."[2]

Hevelius and His Wife Portable sextants were used to chart a ship's position at sea by measuring the altitude of celestial bodies above the horizon. Astronomers used much larger sextants to measure the angular distances between two bodies. Here, Johannes Hevelius makes use of the great brass sextant at the Danzig observatory, with the help of his wife Elisabetha. Six feet in radius, this instrument was closely modeled on the one used by Tycho Brahe. (Houghton Library, Harvard College Library)

Brahe, Kepler, and Galileo: Proving Copernicus Right

One astronomer who agreed with Copernicus was the Danish astronomer Tycho Brahe (TEE-koh BRAH-hee) (1546–1601). Brahe established himself as Europe's leading astronomer with his detailed observations of the new star of 1572. Aided by grants from the king of Denmark, Brahe built the most sophisticated observatory of his day.

Upon the king's death, Brahe acquired a new patron in the Holy Roman emperor Rudolph II and built a new observatory in Prague. In return for the emperor's support, he pledged to create new and improved tables of planetary motions, dubbed the *Rudolfine Tables*. For twenty years Brahe observed the stars and planets with the naked eye, compiling much more complete and accurate data than ever before. His limited understanding of mathematics and his sudden death in 1601, however, prevented him from making much sense out of his mass of data.

It was left to Brahe's young assistant, Johannes Kepler (YO-hah-nihs KEH-pluhr) (1571–1630), to rework Brahe's mountain of observations. A brilliant mathematician, Kepler was inspired by belief that the universe was built on mystical mathematical relationships and a musical harmony of the heavenly bodies.

Kepler's examination of his predecessor's findings convinced him that they could not be explained by Ptolemy's astronomy. Abandoning the notion of epicycles and deferents, Kepler developed three new and revolutionary laws of planetary motion. First, he demonstrated that the orbits of the planets around the sun are elliptical rather than circular. Second, he demonstrated that the planets do not move at a uniform speed in their orbits. When a planet is close to the sun it moves more rapidly, and it slows as it moves farther away from the sun. Finally, Kepler's third law stated that the time a planet takes to make its complete orbit is precisely related to its distance from the sun.

Kepler's contribution was monumental. Whereas Copernicus had speculated, Kepler proved mathematically the precise relations of a sun-centered (solar) system. His work demolished the old system of Aristotle and Ptolemy, and in his third law he came close to formulating the idea of universal gravitation (see page 495). In 1627 he also fulfilled Brahe's pledge by completing the Rudolfine Tables begun so many years earlier. These tables were used by astronomers for many years.

Kepler was not, however, the consummate modern scientist that his achievements suggest. His duties as court mathematician included casting horoscopes, and his own diary was based on astrological principles. He also wrote at length on cosmic harmonies and explained, for example, elliptical motion through ideas about the beautiful music created by the combined motion of the planets. His career exemplifies the complex interweaving of ideas and beliefs in the emerging science of his day.

While Kepler was unraveling planetary motion, a young Florentine named Galileo Galilei (ga-luh-LEE-oh ga-luh-LAY) (1564–1642) was challenging all

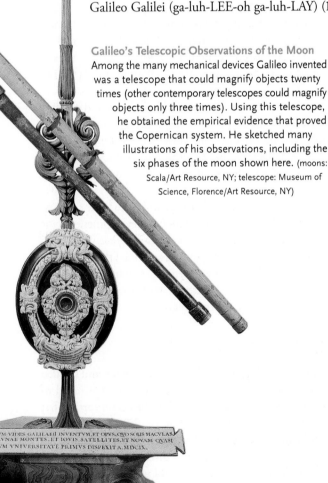

Galileo's Telescopic Observations of the Moon
Among the many mechanical devices Galileo invented was a telescope that could magnify objects twenty times (other contemporary telescopes could magnify objects only three times). Using this telescope, he obtained the empirical evidence that proved the Copernican system. He sketched many illustrations of his observations, including the six phases of the moon shown here. (moons: Scala/Art Resource, NY; telescope: Museum of Science, Florence/Art Resource, NY)

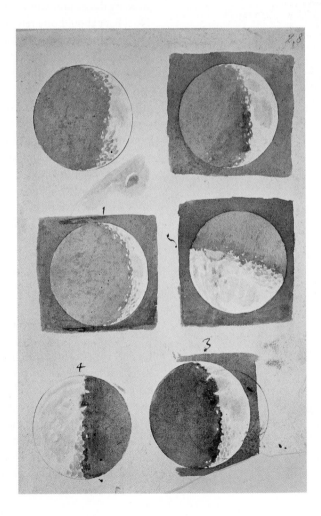

CHAPTER LOCATOR | **How did European views of nature change in this period?** What were the core principles of the Enlightenment? What did enlightened absolutism mean?

493

experimental method The approach, pioneered by Galileo, that the proper way to explore the workings of the universe was through repeatable experiments rather than speculation.

law of inertia A law formulated by Galileo that states that motion, not rest, is the natural state of an object, that an object continues in motion forever unless stopped by some external force.

the old ideas about motion. Galileo's great achievement was the elaboration and consolidation of the experimental method. That is, rather than speculate about what might or should happen, Galileo conducted controlled experiments to find out what actually did happen.

In some of his experiments Galileo measured the movement of a rolling ball across a surface, repeating the action again and again to verify his results. In his famous acceleration experiment, he showed that a uniform force—in this case, gravity—produced a uniform acceleration. Through another experiment, he formulated the law of inertia (ih-NUR-shuh). Rest was not the natural state of objects. Rather, an object continues in motion forever unless stopped by some external force. His discoveries proved Aristotelian physics wrong.

Galileo also applied the experimental method to astronomy. On hearing details about the invention of the telescope in Holland, Galileo made one for himself. He quickly discovered the first four moons of Jupiter, which clearly suggested that Jupiter could not possibly be embedded in any impenetrable crystal sphere as Aristotle and Ptolemy maintained. This discovery provided new evidence for the Copernican theory, in which Galileo already believed. Galileo then pointed his telescope at the moon. He wrote in 1610 in *Siderus Nuncius*:

> By the aid of a telescope anyone may behold [the Milky Way] in a manner which so distinctly appeals to the senses that all the disputes which have tormented philosophers through so many ages are exploded by the irrefutable evidence of our eyes, and we are freed from wordy disputes upon the subject.[3]

Reading these famous lines, one feels a crucial corner in Western civilization being turned. No longer should one rely on established authority. A new method of learning and investigating was being developed, one that proved useful in any field of inquiry. A historian investigating documents of the past, for example, is not so different from a Galileo studying stars and rolling balls.

As early as 1597, when Johannes Kepler sent Galileo an early publication defending Copernicus, Galileo wrote back agreeing with his position and confessing he lacked the courage to follow Kepler's example. Within the Catholic world, expressing public support for Copernicus was increasingly dangerous. In 1616 the Holy Office placed the works of Copernicus and his supporters, including Kepler, on a list of books Catholics were forbidden to read.

Out of caution Galileo silenced his beliefs for several years, until in 1623 he saw new hope with the ascension of Pope Urban VIII, a man sympathetic to developments in the new science. However, Galileo's 1632 *Dialogue on the Two Chief Systems of the World* went too far. Published in Italian and widely read, this work openly lampooned the traditional views of Aristotle and Ptolemy and defended those of Copernicus. Galileo was tried for heresy by the papal Inquisition. Imprisoned and threatened with torture, the aging Galileo recanted, "renouncing and cursing" his Copernican errors.

Newton's Synthesis

Despite the efforts of the church, by about 1640 the work of Brahe, Kepler, and Galileo had been largely accepted by the scientific community. But the new findings failed to explain what forces controlled the movement of the planets and objects on earth. That challenge was taken up by English scientist Isaac Newton (1642–1727).

Newton was born into the lower English gentry in 1642 and he enrolled at Cambridge University in 1661. A genius who united the experimental and theoretical-mathematical sides of modern science, Newton was fascinated by alchemy and was also intensely religious. Like Kepler and other practitioners of the scientific revolution, he was far from being the perfect rationalist so glorified by writers in the eighteenth and nineteenth centuries.

Newton arrived at some of his most basic ideas about physics between 1664 and 1666. During this period, he later claimed to have discovered his law of universal gravitation as well as the concepts of centripetal force and acceleration. Not realizing the significance of his findings, the young Newton did not publish them, and upon his return to Cambridge he took up the study of optics. It was in reference to his experiments in optics that Newton outlined his method of scientific inquiry most clearly, explaining the need for scientists "first to enquire diligently into the properties of things, and to establish these properties by experiment, and then to proceed more slowly to hypotheses for the explanation of them."[4]

In 1684 Newton returned to physics and the preparation of his ideas for publication. The result appeared three years later in *Philosophicae Naturalis Principia Mathematica* (Mathematical Principles of Natural Philosophy). Newton's work presented a single explanatory system that could integrate the astronomy of Copernicus, as corrected by Kepler's laws, with the physics of Galileo and his predecessors. *Principia Mathematica* laid down Newton's three laws of motion, using a set of mathematical laws that explain motion and mechanics.

The key feature of the Newtonian synthesis was the **law of universal gravitation**. According to this law, every body in the universe attracts every other body in the universe in a precise mathematical relationship, whereby the force of attraction is proportional to the quantity of matter of the objects and inversely proportional to the square of the distance between them. The whole universe was unified in one coherent system. Newton's synthesis of mathematics with physics and astronomy prevailed until the twentieth century and established him as one of the most important figures in the history of science.

Isaac Newton This portrait suggests the depth and complexity of Isaac Newton. Is the powerful mind behind those piercing eyes thinking of science or of religion, or perhaps of both? (Scala/Art Resource, NY)

law of universal gravitation Newton's law that all objects are attracted to one another and that the force of attraction is proportional to the object's quantity of matter and inversely proportional to the square of the distance between them.

Bacon, Descartes, and the Scientific Method

The creation of a new science was not accomplished by a handful of brilliant astronomers working alone. Scholars in many fields sought answers to long-standing problems, sharing their results in a community that spanned Europe. One of the keys to the achievement of a new worldview in the seventeenth century was the development of better ways of obtaining knowledge about the world. Two important thinkers, Francis Bacon (1561–1626) and René Descartes (day-KAHRT) (1596–1650), were influential in describing and advocating for improved scientific methods based, respectively, on experimentation and mathematical reasoning.

The English politician and writer Francis Bacon was the greatest early propagandist for the new experimental method. Rejecting the Aristotelian and medieval method of using speculative reasoning to build general theories, Bacon argued that new knowledge had to be pursued through empirical research. The researcher who wants to learn more about leaves or rocks, for example, should not speculate about the subject but should rather collect a multitude of specimens and then compare and analyze them to derive general principles. Bacon's contribution was to formalize the empirical method, which had already been used by Brahe and Galileo, into the general theory of inductive reasoning known as **empiricism**.

empiricism A theory of inductive reasoning that calls for acquiring evidence through observation and experimentation rather than reason and speculation.

CHAPTER LOCATOR | **How did European views of nature change in this period?** | What were the core principles of the Enlightenment? | What did enlightened absolutism mean?

495

On the continent, more speculative methods retained support. As a twenty-three-year-old soldier serving in the Thirty Years' War, the French philosopher René Descartes experienced a life-changing intellectual vision one night in 1619. Descartes saw that there was a perfect correspondence between geometry and algebra and that geometrical spatial figures could be expressed as algebraic equations and vice versa. A major step forward in the history of mathematics, Descartes's discovery of analytic geometry provided scientists with an important new tool.

Descartes used mathematics to elaborate a highly influential vision of the workings of the cosmos. Drawing on ancient Greek atomist philosophies, Descartes developed the idea that matter was made up of identical "corpuscles" that collided together in an endless series of motions. All occurrences in nature could be analyzed as matter in motion and, according to Descartes, the total "quantity of motion" in the universe was constant. Descartes's mechanistic view of the universe depended on the idea that a vacuum was impossible, so that every action had an equal reaction, continuing in an eternal chain reaction. Although Descartes's hypothesis about the vacuum was proved wrong, his notion of a mechanistic universe intelligible through the physics of motion proved highly influential.

Descartes's greatest achievement was to develop his initial vision into a whole philosophy of knowledge and science. The Aristotelian cosmos was appealing in part because it corresponded with the evidence of the human senses. When the senses were proven to be wrong, Descartes decided it was necessary to doubt them and everything that could reasonably be doubted, and then, as in geometry, to use deductive reasoning from self-evident principles to ascertain scientific laws. Descartes's reasoning ultimately reduced all substances to "matter" and "mind" — that is, to the physical and the spiritual. Descartes believed that God had endowed man with reason for a purpose and that rational speculation could provide a path to the truths of creation. His view of the world as consisting of two fundamental entities is known as Cartesian dualism. Descartes's thought was highly

Cartesian dualism
Descartes's view that all of reality could ultimately be reduced to mind and matter.

▪ Major Contributors to the Scientific Revolution

Nicolaus Copernicus (1473–1543)	*On the Revolutions of the Heavenly Spheres* (1543); theorized that the sun, rather than the earth, was the center of the galaxy
Andreas Vesalius (1514–1564)	*On the Structure of the Human Body* (1543)
Tycho Brahe (1546–1601)	Built observatory and compiled data for the Rudolfine Tables, a new table of planetary data
Francis Bacon (1561–1626)	Advocated experimental method, formalizing theory of inductive reasoning known as empiricism
Galileo Galilei (1564–1642)	Used telescopic observation to provide evidence for Copernican hypothesis; experimented to formulate laws of physics, such as inertia
Johannes Kepler (1571–1630)	Used Brahe's data to mathematically prove the Copernican hypothesis; his new laws of planetary motion united for the first time natural philosophy and mathematics; completed the Rudolfine Tables in 1627
William Harvey (1578–1657)	Discovery of circulation of blood (1628)
René Descartes (1596–1650)	Used deductive reasoning to formulate the theory of Cartesian dualism
Robert Boyle (1627–1691)	Boyle's law (1662) governing the pressure of gases
Isaac Newton (1642–1727)	*Principia Mathematica* (1687); set forth the law of universal gravitation, synthesizing previous findings of motion and matter

influential in France and the Netherlands, but less so in England, where experimental philosophy won the day.

Both Bacon's inductive experimentalism and Descartes's deductive mathematical reasoning had their faults. Bacon's inability to appreciate the importance of mathematics and his obsession with practical results clearly showed the limitations of antitheoretical empiricism. Likewise, some of Descartes's positions—he believed, for example, that it was possible to deduce the whole science of medicine from first principles—demonstrated the inadequacy of rigid, dogmatic rationalism. Although insufficient on their own, Bacon's and Descartes's extreme approaches are combined in the modern scientific method, which began to crystallize in the late seventeenth century.

Science and Society

The rise of modern science had many consequences. First, it went hand in hand with the rise of a new and expanding social group—the international scientific community. Members of this community were linked together by common interests and shared values as well as by journals and learned scientific societies. Second, as governments intervened to support and sometimes direct research, the new scientific community became closely tied to the state and its agendas. National academies of science were created under state sponsorship in London in 1662, Paris in 1666, Berlin in 1700, and later across Europe. At the same time, scientists developed a critical attitude toward established authority that would inspire thinkers to question traditions in other domains as well.

Some things did not change in the scientific revolution. New "rational" methods for approaching nature did not question traditional inequalities between the sexes—and may have worsened them in some ways. When Renaissance courts served as centers of learning, talented noblewomen could find niches in study and research. The rise of a professional scientific community raised barriers for women because the new academies that furnished professional credentials did not accept female members.

There were, however, a number of noteworthy exceptions. In Italy, universities and academies did offer posts to women. Women across Europe were allowed to work as makers of wax anatomical models and as botanical and zoological illustrators. Women were also very much involved in informal scientific communities, attending salons, participating in scientific experiments, and writing learned treatises. Some female intellectuals were recognized as full-fledged members of the philosophical dialogue. In England, Margaret Cavendish, Anne Conway, and Mary Astell all contributed to debates about Descartes's mind-body dualism, among other issues.

The scientific revolution had few consequences for economic life and the living standards of the masses until the late eighteenth century. Thus the scientific revolution of the seventeenth century was first and foremost an intellectual revolution. For more than a hundred years its greatest impact was on how people thought and believed.

Finally, there is the question of the role of religion in the development of science. Just as some historians have argued that Protestantism led to the rise of capitalism, others have concluded

Metamorphoses of the Caterpillar and Moth Maria Sibylla Merian (1647–1717), the stepdaughter of a Dutch painter, became a celebrated scientific illustrator in her own right. Her finely observed pictures of insects in the South American colony of Surinam introduced many new species. For Merian, science was intimately tied with art: she not only painted but also bred caterpillars and performed experiments on them. Her two-year stay in Surinam, accompanied by a teenage daughter, was a daring feat for a seventeenth-century woman. (Bildarchiv Preussischer Kulturbesitz/Art Resource, NY)

CHAPTER LOCATOR | **How did European views of nature change in this period?**   What were the core principles of the Enlightenment?   What did enlightened absolutism mean?

497

that Protestantism was a fundamental factor in the rise of modern science. According to this view, Protestantism, particularly in its Calvinist varieties, made scientific inquiry a question of individual conscience, not of religious doctrine. The Catholic Church, in contrast, supposedly suppressed scientific theories that conflicted with its teachings and thus discouraged scientific progress. The truth is more complicated. All Western religious authorities—Catholic, Protestant, and Jewish—opposed the Copernican system to a greater or lesser extent until about 1630, by which time the scientific revolution was definitely in progress. The Catholic Church was initially less hostile than Protestant and Jewish religious leaders, and Italian scientists played a crucial role in scientific progress right up to the trial of Galileo in 1633. Thereafter, the Counter-Reformation church became more hostile to science, a change that helped account for the decline of science in Italy (but not in Catholic France) after 1640. At the same time, Protestant countries such as the Netherlands, Denmark, and England became quite "pro-science," especially countries that lacked a strong religious authority capable of imposing religious orthodoxy on scientific questions.

Medicine, the Body, and Chemistry

The scientific revolution, which began with the study of the cosmos, soon inspired renewed study of the microcosm of the human body. For many centuries the ancient Greek physician Galen's explanation of the body carried the same authority as Aristotle's account of the universe. According to Galen, the body contained four humors: blood, phlegm, black bile, and yellow bile. Illness was believed to result from an imbalance of humors.

Swiss physician and alchemist Paracelsus (1493–1541) was an early proponent of the experimental method in medicine and pioneered the use of chemicals and drugs to address what he saw as chemical, rather than humoral, imbalances. Another experimentalist, Flemish physician Andreas Vesalius (1516–1564) studied anatomy by dissecting human bodies. In 1543, the same year Copernicus published *On the Heavenly Revolutions*, Vesalius issued *On the Structure of the Human Body*. Its two hundred precise drawings revolutionized the understanding of human anatomy. The experimental approach also led English royal physician William Harvey (1578–1657) to discover the circulation of blood through the veins and arteries in 1628. Harvey was the first to explain that the heart worked like a pump and to explain the function of its muscles and valves.

Irishman Robert Boyle (1627–1691) founded the modern science of chemistry. Following Paracelsus's lead, he undertook experiments to discover the basic elements of nature, which he believed was composed of infinitely small atoms. Boyle was the first to create a vacuum, thus disproving Descartes's belief that a vacuum could not exist in nature, and he discovered Boyle's law (1662), which states that the pressure of a gas varies inversely with volume.

▼ What were the core principles of the Enlightenment?

Enlightenment The influential intellectual and cultural movement of the late seventeenth and eighteenth centuries that introduced a new worldview based on the use of reason, the scientific method, and progress.

The scientific revolution was the single most important factor in the creation of the new worldview of the eighteenth-century Enlightenment. This worldview grew out of a rich mix of diverse and often conflicting ideas. For the writers who espoused them, these ideas competed vigorously for the attention of a growing public of well-educated readers, who remained a minority of the population.

Despite the diversity, three central concepts stand at the core of Enlightenment thinking. The most important and original idea was that the methods of natural science could and should be used to examine and understand all aspects of life. This was what intellectuals meant by *reason*, a favorite word of Enlightenment thinkers. Nothing was to be accepted on faith; everything was to be submitted to rationalism, a secular, critical way of thinking. A second important Enlightenment concept was that the scientific method was capable of discovering the laws of human society as well as those of nature. This second concept led to the third key idea, that of progress. Armed with the proper method of discovering the laws of human existence, Enlightenment thinkers believed, it was at least possible for human beings to create better societies and better people.

rationalism A secular, critical way of thinking in which nothing was to be accepted on faith, and everything was to be submitted to reason.

The Emergence of the Enlightenment

Loosely united by certain key ideas, the European Enlightenment (ca. 1690–1789) gained strength gradually and did not reach its maturity until about 1750. Yet it was the generation that came of age between the publication of Newton's *Principia* in 1687 and the death of Louis XIV in 1715 that tied the crucial knot between the scientific revolution and a new outlook on life. Talented writers of that generation popularized hard-to-understand scientific achievements for the educated elite.

A new generation came to believe that the human mind itself is capable of making great progress. Medieval and Reformation thinkers had been concerned primarily with the abstract concepts of sin and salvation. The humanists of the Renaissance had emphasized worldly matters (especially art and literature), but their inspiration came from the classical past. Enlightenment thinkers came to believe that their era had gone far beyond antiquity and that intellectual progress was very possible.

The excitement of the scientific revolution also generated doubt and uncertainty, contributing to a widespread crisis in late-seventeenth-century European thought. In the wake of the devastation wrought by the Thirty Years' War, some people asked whether ideological conformity in religious matters was really necessary. Others skeptically asked if religious truth could ever be known with absolute certainty and concluded that it could not.

The most famous of these skeptics was the French Huguenot Pierre Bayle (1647–1706). Bayle critically examined the religious beliefs and persecutions of the past in his *Historical and Critical Dictionary* (1697). Demonstrating that human beliefs had been extremely varied and very often mistaken, he concluded that nothing can ever be known beyond all doubt, a view known as skepticism.

Some Jewish scholars participated in the early Enlightenment movement. The philosopher Baruch Spinoza (1632–1677) was excommunicated by the relatively large Jewish community of Amsterdam for his controversial religious ideas. Spinoza believed that mind and body are united in one substance and that God and nature were

Popularizing Science The frontispiece illustration of Fontenelle's *Conversations on the Plurality of Worlds* (1686) invites the reader to share the pleasures of astronomy with an elegant lady and an entertaining teacher. The drawing shows the planets revolving around the sun. (© Roger-Viollet/The Image Works)

CHAPTER LOCATOR | How did European views of nature change in this period? | **What were the core principles of the Enlightenment?** | What did enlightened absolutism mean?

499

two names for the same thing. He envisioned a deterministic universe in which good and evil were merely relative values. Few of Spinoza's radical writings were published during his lifetime, but he is now recognized as among the most original thinkers of the early Enlightenment.

The rapidly growing travel literature on non-European lands and cultures was another cause of questioning among thinkers. In the wake of the great discoveries, Europeans were learning that the peoples of China, India, Africa, and the Americas all had their own very different beliefs and customs. Travel accounts helped change the perspective of educated Europeans. They began to look at truth and morality in relative, rather than absolute, terms. If anything was possible, who could say what was right or wrong?

Out of this period of intellectual turmoil came John Locke's *Essay Concerning Human Understanding* (1690), often viewed as the first major text of the Enlightenment. In this work Locke (1632–1704) set forth a new theory about how human beings learn and form their ideas. Whereas Descartes based his deductive logic on the conviction that certain first premises, or innate ideas, are imbued in all humans by God, Locke insisted that all ideas are derived from experience. The human mind at birth is like a blank tablet, or tabula rasa (tah-byuh-luh RAH-zuh) on which the environment writes the individual's understanding and beliefs. Human development is therefore determined by education and social institutions, for good or for evil. Locke's essay contributed to the theory of sensationalism, the idea that all human ideas and thoughts are produced as a result of sensory impressions. The *Essay Concerning Human Understanding* passed through many editions and translations and, along with Newton's *Principia*, was one of the dominant intellectual inspirations of the Enlightenment.

The Influence of the Philosophes

By the time Louis XIV died in 1715, many of the ideas that would soon coalesce into the new worldview had been assembled. Yet Christian Europe was still strongly attached to its established political and social structures and its traditional spiritual beliefs. By 1775, however, a large portion of western Europe's educated elite had embraced many of the new ideas. This acceptance was the work of the **philosophes**, a group of influential intellectuals who proudly proclaimed that they were bringing the light of knowledge to their ignorant fellow creatures.

Philosophe is the French word for "philosopher," and it was in France that the Enlightenment reached its highest development. There were at least three reasons for this. First, French was the international language of the educated classes in the eighteenth century, and France was still the wealthiest and most populous country in Europe. Second, although French intellectuals were not free to openly criticize either church or state, they were not as strongly restrained as intellectuals in eastern and east-central Europe. Third, the French philosophes made it their goal to reach a larger audience of elites, many of whom were joined together in the eighteenth-century concept of the "republic of letters" — an imaginary transnational realm of the well-educated.

To appeal to the public and get around the censors, the philosophes wrote novels and plays, histories and philosophies, dictionaries and encyclopedias, all filled with satire and double meanings to spread their message. One of the greatest philosophes, the baron de Montesquieu (1689–1755), pioneered this approach in *The Persian Letters*, an extremely influential social satire published in 1721. This work consisted of letters supposedly written by two Persian travelers, Usbek and Rica, who as outsiders see European customs in unique ways and thereby allow Montesquieu a vantage point for criticizing existing practices and beliefs.

Like many Enlightenment philosophes, Montesquieu saw relations between men and women as representative of the overall social and political system. He used the oppression of women in the Persian harem, described in letters from Usbek's wives, to symbolize

philosophes A group of French intellectuals who proclaimed that they were bringing the light of knowledge to their fellow creatures in the Age of Enlightenment.

Voltaire and Philosophes This painting belongs to a series commissioned by Catherine the Great to depict daily life at the philosopher's retreat at Ferney in Switzerland. It shows Voltaire seated at the dinner table surrounded by his followers, including *Encyclopedia* editors Diderot and d'Alembert. The scene is imaginary, for Diderot never visited Ferney. (Photo by permission of the Voltaire Foundation, University of Oxford)

Eastern political tyranny. At the end of the book, the rebellion of Usbek's harem against the cruel eunuchs he left in charge demonstrates that despotism must ultimately fail.

Having gained fame by using wit as a weapon against cruelty and superstition, Montesquieu settled down on his family estate to study history and politics. His interest was partly personal. He was disturbed by the growth in royal absolutism under Louis XIV. But Montesquieu was also inspired by the example of the physical sciences, and he set out to apply the critical method to the problem of government in *The Spirit of Laws* (1748). The result was a comparative study of republics, monarchies, and despotisms.

Showing that forms of government were shaped by history, geography, and customs, Montesquieu focused on the conditions that would promote liberty and prevent tyranny. Admiring greatly the English balance of power among the king, the houses of Parliament, and the independent courts, he argued for a separation of powers, with political power divided and shared by a variety of classes and legal estates holding unequal rights and privileges. Apprehensive about the uneducated poor, Montesquieu was no democrat, but his theory of separation of powers had a great impact on the constitutions of the young United States in 1789 and of France in 1791.

The most famous and in many ways most representative philosophe was François Marie Arouet, who was known by the pen name Voltaire (1694–1778). In his long career, Voltaire wrote more than seventy witty volumes, hobnobbed with kings and queens, and died a millionaire because of shrewd business speculations. His early career, however, was turbulent, and he was arrested on two occasions for insulting noblemen. Voltaire moved to England for three years in order to avoid a longer prison term in France, and there he came to share Montesquieu's enthusiasm for English liberties and institutions.

CHAPTER LOCATOR | How did European views of nature change in this period? | **What were the core principles of the Enlightenment?** | What did enlightened absolutism mean?

501

Madame du Châtelet The marquise du Châtelet was fascinated by the new world system of Isaac Newton. She helped spread Newton's ideas in France by translating his *Principia* and by influencing Voltaire, her companion for fifteen years until her death. (Giraudon/Art Resource, NY)

Returning to France and soon threatened again with prison in Paris, Voltaire met Gabrielle-Emilie Le Tonnelier de Breteuil, marquise du Châtelet (SHAH-tuh-lay) (1706–1749), a gifted woman from the high aristocracy with a passion for science. Inviting Voltaire to live in her country house at Cirey in Lorraine and becoming his long-time companion, Madame du Châtelet studied physics and mathematics and published scientific articles and translations, including the first—and only—translation of Newton's *Principia* into French.

While living at Cirey, Voltaire wrote various works praising England and popularizing English scientific progress. Newton, he wrote, was history's greatest man, for he had used his genius for the benefit of humanity. "It is," wrote Voltaire, "the man who sways our minds by the prevalence of reason and the native force of truth, not they who reduce mankind to a state of slavery by force and downright violence . . . that claims our reverence and admiration."[5] In the true style of the Enlightenment, Voltaire mixed the glorification of science and reason with an appeal for better individuals and institutions.

Yet, like almost all of the philosophes, Voltaire was a reformer, not a revolutionary, in social and political matters. He pessimistically concluded that the best one could hope for in the way of government was a good monarch, since human beings "are very rarely worthy to govern themselves." Nor did Voltaire believe in social and economic equality in human affairs. The only realizable equality, Voltaire thought, was that "by which the citizen only depends on the laws which protect the freedom of the feeble against the ambitions of the strong."[6]

Voltaire's philosophical and religious positions were much more radical than his social and political beliefs. Voltaire believed in God, but his was a distant, deistic God. Drawing on Newton, he envisioned a mechanistic universe in which God acted like a great clockmaker who built an orderly system and then stepped aside and let it run. Above all, Voltaire and most of the philosophes hated all forms of religious intolerance, which they believed often led to fanaticism and savage, inhuman action.

The ultimate strength of the philosophes lay in their number, dedication, and organization. The philosophes felt keenly that they were engaged in a common undertaking that transcended individuals. Their greatest and most representative intellectual achievement was a group effort—the seventeen-volume *Encyclopedia: The Rational Dictionary of the Sciences, the Arts, and the Crafts*, edited by Denis Diderot (deh-nee DEE-duh-roh) (1713–1784) and Jean le Rond d'Alembert (dah-lum-BEHR) (1717–1783). The two men set out in 1751 to find coauthors who would examine the rapidly expanding whole of human knowledge. Even more fundamentally, they set out to teach people how to think critically and objectively about all matters.

The *Encyclopedia* survived initial resistance from the French government and the Catholic Church. Completed in 1765, it contained hundreds of thousands of articles by leading scientists, writers, skilled workers, and progressive priests, and it treated every aspect of life and knowledge. Science and the industrial arts were exalted, religion and immortality questioned. Intolerance, legal injustice, and out-of-date social institutions were openly criticized. The encyclopedists were convinced that greater knowledge would result in greater human happiness, for knowledge was useful and made possible economic, social, and political progress. Summing up the new worldview of the Enlightenment, the *Encyclopedia* was widely read, especially in less-expensive reprint editions, and it was extremely influential.

The Enlightenment Outside of France

Historians now recognize the existence of important strands of Enlightenment thought outside of France. They have identified distinctive Enlightenment movements in eighteenth-century Italy, Spain, Greece, the Balkans, Poland, Hungary, and Russia. Different areas developed different forms of Enlightenment thinking. In England and Germany, scholars have described a more conservative Enlightenment that tried to integrate the findings of the scientific revolution with religious faith. After the Act of Union with England and Ireland in 1707, Scotland was freed from political crisis to experience a vigorous period of intellectual growth. The Scottish Enlightenment, centered in Edinburgh, was marked by an emphasis on pragmatic and scientific reasoning. Intellectual revival there was stimulated by the creation of the first public educational system in Europe.

The most important figure in Edinburgh was David Hume (1711–1776), whose carefully argued religious skepticism had a powerful impact at home and abroad. Building on Locke's teachings on learning, Hume argued that the human mind is really nothing but a bundle of impressions. These impressions originate only in sense experiences and our habits of joining these experiences together. Since our ideas ultimately reflect only our sense experiences, our reason cannot tell us anything about questions that cannot be verified by sense experience, such as the origin of the universe or the existence of God. Paradoxically, Hume's rationalistic inquiry ended up undermining the Enlightenment's faith in the power of reason.

Urban Culture and Life in the Public Sphere

A series of new institutions and practices encouraged the spread of Enlightenment ideas in the late seventeenth and the eighteenth centuries. First, the European production and consumption of books grew significantly between 1700 and 1789. Moreover, the types

▪ Major Figures of the Enlightenment

Baruch Spinoza (1632–1677)	Early Enlightenment thinker excommunicated from the Jewish religion for his concept of a deterministic universe
John Locke (1632–1704)	*Essay Concerning Human Understanding* (1690)
Pierre Bayle (1647–1706)	*Historical and Critical Dictionary* (1697)
Montesquieu (1689–1755)	*The Persian Letters* (1721); *The Spirit of Laws* (1748)
Voltaire (1694–1778)	Renowned French philosophe and author of more than seventy works
David Hume (1711–1776)	Central figure of the Scottish Enlightenment; *Of Natural Characters* (1748)
Jean-Jacques Rousseau (1712–1778)	*The Social Contract* (1762)
Denis Diderot (1713–1784) and Jean le Rond d'Alembert (1717–1783)	Editors of *Encyclopedia: The Rational Dictionary of the Sciences, the Arts, and the Crafts* (1765)
Immanuel Kant (1724–1804)	*What Is Enlightenment?* (1784); *On the Different Races of Man* (1775)

CHAPTER LOCATOR | How did European views of nature change in this period? | **What were the core principles of the Enlightenment?** | What did enlightened absolutism mean?

503

of books people read changed dramatically. The proportion of religious and devotional books published in Paris declined after 1750; history and law held constant; the arts and sciences surged.

reading revolution The transition in Europe from a society where literacy consisted of patriarchal and communal reading of religious texts to a society where literacy was commonplace and reading material was broad and diverse.

Reading more books on many more subjects, the educated public in France and throughout Europe increasingly approached reading in a new way. The result was what some scholars have called a **reading revolution**. The old style of reading in Europe had been centered on a core of sacred texts. Reading had been patriarchal and communal, with the father of the family slowly reading the text aloud. Now reading involved a broader field of books that constantly changed. Reading became individual and silent, and texts

▪ PICTURING THE PAST

Enlightenment Culture

An actor performs the first reading of a new play by Voltaire at the salon of Madame Geoffrin in this painting from 1755. Voltaire, then in exile, is represented by a bust statue. (Réunion des Musées Nationaux/Art Resource, NY)

ANALYZING THE IMAGE Which of these people do you think is the hostess, Madame Geoffrin, and why? Using details from the painting to support your answer, how would you describe the status of the people shown?

CONNECTIONS What does this image suggest about the reach of Enlightenment ideas to common people? To women? Does the painting of the coffeehouse on page 506 suggest a broader reach? Why?

To complete this activity online, go to the Online Study Guide at bedfordstmartins.com/ mckaywestunderstanding.

could be questioned. Subtle but profound, the reading revolution ushered in new ways of relating to the written word.

Conversation, discussion, and debate also played a critical role in the Enlightenment. Paris set the example, and other French and European cities followed. In Paris from about 1740 to 1789, a number of talented, wealthy women presided over regular social gatherings named after their elegant private drawing rooms, or **salons**. There they encouraged the exchange of observations on literature, science, and philosophy with great aristocrats, wealthy middle-class financiers, high-ranking officials, and noteworthy foreigners. Talented hostesses, or *salonnières* (sah-lahn-ee-EHRZ), mediated the public's examination of Enlightenment thought. As one philosophe described his Enlightenment hostess and her salon:

> She could unite the different types, even the most antagonistic, sustaining the conversation by a well-aimed phrase, animating and guiding it at will. . . . Politics, religion, philosophy, news: nothing was excluded. Her circle met daily from five to nine. There one found men of all ranks in the State, the Church, and the Court, soldiers and foreigners, and the leading writers of the day.[7]

As this passage suggests, the salons created a cultural realm free from religious dogma and political censorship. There a diverse but educated public could debate issues and form its own ideas. Through their invitation lists, salon hostesses brought together members of the intellectual, economic, and social elites. In such an atmosphere, the philosophes, the French nobility, and the prosperous middle classes intermingled and influenced one another.

Elite women also exercised great influence on artistic taste. Soft pastels, ornate interiors, sentimental portraits, and starry-eyed lovers protected by hovering cupids were all hallmarks of the style they favored. This style, known as **rococo** (ruh-KOH-koh), was popular throughout Europe in the period from 1720 to 1780. It has been argued that feminine influence in the drawing room went hand in hand with the emergence of polite society and the general attempt to civilize a rough military nobility. Similarly, some philosophes championed greater rights and expanded education for women, claiming that the position and treatment of women were the best indicators of a society's level of civilization and decency.[8]

While membership at the salons was restricted to the well-born, the well-connected, and the exceptionally talented, a number of institutions emerged for the rest of society. Lending libraries served an important function for people who could not afford their own books. The coffeehouses that first appeared in the late seventeenth century became meccas of philosophical discussion. In addition to these institutions, book clubs, Masonic lodges (groups of Freemasons, a secret egalitarian society that existed across Europe), and journals all played roles in the creation of a new **public sphere** that celebrated open debate informed by critical reason. The public sphere was an idealized space where members of society came together as individuals to discuss issues relevant to the society, economics, and politics of the day.

What of the common people? Did they participate in the Enlightenment? Enlightenment philosophes did not direct their message to peasants or urban laborers. They believed that the masses had no time or talent for philosophical speculation and that elevating them would be a long, slow, potentially dangerous process.

There is some evidence, however, that the people were not immune to the words of the philosophes. At a time of rising literacy, book prices were dropping in cities and towns, and many philosophical ideas were popularized in cheap pamphlets. Moreover, even illiterate people had access to written material through the practice of public reading. Although they were barred from salons and academies, ordinary people were nonetheless exposed to the new ideas in circulation.

salons Regular social gatherings held by talented and rich Parisian women in their homes, where philosophes and their followers met to discuss literature, science, and philosophy.

rococo A popular style in Europe in the eighteenth century, known for its soft pastels, ornate interiors, sentimental portraits, and starry-eyed lovers protected by hovering cupids.

public sphere An idealized intellectual space that emerged in Europe during the Enlightenment, where the public came together to discuss important issues relating to society, economics, and politics.

CHAPTER LOCATOR | How did European views of nature change in this period? | **What were the core principles of the Enlightenment?** | What did enlightened absolutism mean?

505

Seventeenth-Century English Coffeehouse By the seventeenth century, coffeehouses were popular throughout Europe and helped spread the ideas and values of the scientific revolution and the Enlightenment. (The Granger Collection, NY)

Race and the Enlightenment

If philosophers did not believe the lower classes qualified for enlightenment, how did they regard individuals of different races? In recent years, historians have found in the scientific revolution and the Enlightenment a crucial turning point in European ideas about race. A primary catalyst for new ideas about race was the urge to classify nature unleashed by the scientific revolution's insistence on careful empirical observation. As scientists developed more elaborate taxonomies of plant and animal species, they also began to classify humans into hierarchically ordered "races" and to investigate the origins of race. The Comte de Buffon (komt duh buh-FOHN) argued that humans originated with one species that then developed into distinct races due largely to climatic conditions.

Enlightenment thinkers such as David Hume and Immanuel Kant (see page 510) helped popularize these ideas. In *Of Natural Characters* (1748), Hume wrote:

> *I am apt to suspect the negroes and in general all other species of men (for there are four or five different kinds) to be naturally inferior to the whites. There never was a civilized nation of any other complexion than white, nor even any individual eminent amongst them, no arts, no sciences. . . . Such a uniform and constant difference could not happen, in so many countries and ages if nature had not made an original distinction between these breeds of men.*[9]

Kant shared and elaborated Hume's views about race in *On the Different Races of Man* (1775), claiming that there were four human races, each of which had derived from a supposedly original race of "white brunette" people. According to Kant, the closest descendants of the original race were the white inhabitants of northern Germany. In deriving new physical characteristics, the other races had degenerated both physically and culturally from this origin.

Using the word *race* to designate biologically distinct groups of humans was new. Previously, Europeans grouped other peoples into "nations" based on their historical, political, and cultural affiliations, rather than on supposedly innate physical differences. Unsurprisingly, when European thinkers drew up a hierarchical classification of human species, their own "race" was placed at the top. Europeans had long believed they were culturally superior. Now emerging ideas about racial difference taught them they were biologically superior as well. In turn, scientific racism helped legitimate and justify the tremendous growth of slavery that occurred during the eighteenth century. If one "race" of humans was fundamentally different and inferior, its members could be seen as particularly fit for enslavement.

Racist ideas did not go unchallenged. *Encyclopedia* editor Denis Diderot penned a scathing critique of European arrogance and exploitation in the voice of Tahitian villagers. (See "Listening to the Past: Denis Diderot's 'Supplement to Bougainville's Voyage,'" page 508.) Scottish philosopher James Beattie (1735–1803) responded directly to claims of white superiority by pointing out that Europeans had started out as savage as nonwhites and that many non-European peoples in the Americas, Asia, and Africa had achieved high levels of civilization. German thinker Johann Gottfried von Herder (1744–1803) criticized Kant, arguing that humans could not be classified into races based on skin color and that each culture was as intrinsically worthy as any other.

Scholars are only at the beginning of efforts to understand links between Enlightenment ideas about race and its notions of equality, progress, and reason. There are clear parallels, though, between the use of science to propagate racial hierarchies and its use to defend social inequalities between men and women. Swiss philosopher Jean-Jacques

Encyclopedia **Image of the Cotton Industry** This romanticized image of slavery in the West Indies cotton industry was published in Diderot and d'Alembert's *Encyclopedia*. It shows enslaved men, at right, gathering and picking over cotton bolls, while the woman at left mills the bolls to remove their seeds. The *Encyclopedia* presented mixed views on slavery; one article described it as "indispensable" to economic development, while others argued passionately for the natural right to freedom of all mankind. (Courtesy, Dover Publications)

CHAPTER LOCATOR | How did European views of nature change in this period? | **What were the core principles of the Enlightenment?** | What did enlightened absolutism mean?

507

Denis Diderot's "Supplement to Bougainville's Voyage"

Denis Diderot (1713–1784) was born in a provincial town in eastern France and educated in Paris. Rejecting careers in the church and the law, he devoted himself to literature and philosophy. In 1749, sixty years before Charles Darwin's birth, Diderot was jailed by Parisian authorities for publishing an essay questioning God's role in the creation and suggesting the autonomous evolution of species. Following these difficult beginnings, Diderot's editorial work and writing on the Encyclopedia were the crowning intellectual achievements of his life and, according to some, of the Enlightenment itself.

Like other philosophes, Diderot employed numerous genres to disseminate Enlightenment thought, ranging from scholarly articles in the Encyclopedia, to philosophical treatises, novels, plays, book reviews, and erotic stories. His "Supplement to Bougainville's Voyage" (1772) was a fictional account of a European voyage to Tahiti inspired by the writings of traveler Louis-Antoine de Bougainville. In this passage, Diderot expresses his own loathing of colonial conquest and exploitation through the voice of an elderly Tahitian man. The character's praise for his own culture allows Diderot to express his Enlightenment idealization of "natural man," free from the vices of civilized societies.

❝ He was the father of a numerous family. At the time of the Europeans' arrival, he cast upon them a look that was filled with scorn, though it revealed no surprise, no alarm and no curiosity. They approached him; he turned his back on them and retired into his hut. His thoughts were only too well revealed by his silence and his air of concern, for in the privacy of his thoughts he groaned inwardly over the happy days of his people, now gone forever. At the moment of Bougainville's departure, when all the natives ran swarming onto the beach, tugging at his clothing and throwing their arms around his companions and weeping, the old man stepped forward and solemnly spoke:

"Weep, wretched Tahitians, weep—but rather for the arrival than for the departure of these wicked and grasping men! The day will come when you will know them for what they are. Someday they will return, bearing in one hand that piece of wood you see suspended from this one's belt and in the other the piece of steel that hangs at the side of his companions. They will load you with chains, slit your throats and enslave you to their follies and vices. Someday you will be slaves to them, you will be as corrupt, as vile, as wretched as they are. . . ."

Then, turning to Bougainville, he went on: "And you, leader of these brigands who obey you, take your vessel swiftly from our shores. We are innocent and happy, and you can only spoil our happiness. We follow the pure instinct of nature, and you have tried to efface her imprint from our hearts. Here all things are for all, and you have preached to us I know not what distinctions between mine and thine. . . .

". . . You are not slaves; you would suffer death rather than be enslaved, yet you want to make slaves of us! Do you believe, then, that the Tahitian does not know how to die in defense of his liberty? This Tahitian, whom you want to treat as a chattel, as a dumb animal—this Tahitian is your brother. You are both children of Nature—what right do you have over him that he does not have over you?

"You came; did we attack you? Did we plunder your vessel? Did we seize you and expose you to the arrows of our enemies? Did we force you to work in the fields alongside our beasts of burden? We respected our own image in you. Leave us our own customs, which are wiser and more decent than yours. We have no wish to barter what you call our ignorance for your useless knowledge. We possess already all that is good or necessary for our existence. Do we merit your scorn because we have not been

Rousseau used women's "natural" passivity to argue for their passive role in society, just as other thinkers used non-Europeans' "natural" inferiority to defend slavery and colonial domination. The new powers of science and reason were thus marshaled to imbue traditional stereotypes with the force of natural law.

Late Enlightenment

After about 1770 a number of thinkers and writers began to attack the Enlightenment's faith in reason, progress, and moderation. The most famous of these was the Swiss Jean-Jacques Rousseau (1712–1778). Like other Enlightenment thinkers, Rousseau was passionately committed to individual freedom. Unlike them, however, he attacked rationalism and civilization as destroying, rather than liberating, the individual. Warm, spontaneous

able to create superfluous wants for ourselves? When we are hungry, we have something to eat; when we are cold, we have clothing to put on. You have been in our huts — what is lacking there, in your opinion? You are welcome to drive yourselves as hard as you please in pursuit of what you call the comforts of life, but allow sensible people to stop when they see they have nothing to gain but imaginary benefits from the continuation of their painful labors. If you persuade us to go beyond the bounds of strict necessity, when shall we come to the end of our labor? When shall we have time for enjoyment? We have reduced our daily and yearly labors to the least possible amount, because to us nothing seemed more desirable than leisure. Go and bestir yourselves in your own country; there you may torment yourselves as much as you like; but leave us in peace, and do not fill our heads with a hankering after your false needs and imaginary virtues." 🗩

Source: From Denis Diderot, *Supplement to Bougainville's Voyage*, edited by Jacques Barzun (Upper Saddle River, N.J.: Prentice-Hall, 1965. © 2010 by Jacques Barzun. All rights reserved, c/o Writers Representatives LLC, New York, NY, 10011, permissions@writersrep.com.

QUESTIONS FOR ANALYSIS

1. On what grounds does the speaker argue for the Tahitians' basic equality with the Europeans?
2. What is the good life according to the speaker, and how does it contrast with the European way of life? Which do you think is the better path?
3. In what ways could Diderot's thoughts here be seen as representative of Enlightenment ideas? Are there ways in which they are not?
4. How realistic do you think this account is? Does it matter? How might defenders of colonial expansion respond to Diderot's criticism?

This image depicts the meeting of French explorer Louis-Antoine de Bougainville with Tahitians in April 1768. Of his stay on the island, Bougainville wrote: "I felt as though I had been transported to the Garden of Eden. . . . Everywhere reigned hospitality, peace, joy, and every appearance of happiness." Diderot's philosophical tract was a fictional sequel to Bougainville's account. (Unknown artist, Tahitians presenting fruit to Bougainville attended by his officers. PIC T2996 NK5066 LOC7321, National Library of Australia)

feeling had to complement and correct cold intellect. Moreover, the basic goodness of the individual and the unspoiled child had to be protected from the cruel refinements of civilization. Rousseau's ideals greatly influenced the early romantic movement, which rebelled against the culture of the Enlightenment in the late eighteenth century.

Rousseau also called for a rigid division of gender roles. According to Rousseau, women and men were radically different beings. Destined by nature to assume a passive role in sexual relations, women should also be passive in social life. Women's love for displaying themselves in public, attending salons, and pulling the strings of power was unnatural and had a corrupting effect on both politics and society. Rousseau thus rejected the sophisticated way of life of Parisian elite women. His criticism led to broader calls for privileged women to renounce their frivolous ways and stay at home to care for their children.

CHAPTER LOCATOR | How did European views of nature change in this period? | **What were the core principles of the Enlightenment?** | What did enlightened absolutism mean?

509

Rousseau's contribution to political theory in *The Social Contract* (1762) drew less attention at first but proved to be highly significant. His contribution was based on two fundamental concepts: the general will and popular sovereignty. According to Rousseau, the general will is sacred and absolute, reflecting the common interests of all the people, who have displaced the monarch as the holder of sovereign power. The general will is not necessarily the will of the majority, however. At times the general will may be the authentic, long-term needs of the people as correctly interpreted by a farseeing minority. Little noticed before the French Revolution, Rousseau's concept of the general will appealed greatly to democrats and nationalists after 1789. Rousseau was both one of the most influential voices of the Enlightenment and, in his rejection of rationalism and social discourse, a harbinger of reaction against Enlightenment ideas.

As the reading public developed, it joined forces with the philosophes to call for the autonomy of the printed word. Immanuel Kant (1724–1804), a professor in East Prussia and the greatest German philosopher of his day, posed the question of the age when he published a pamphlet in 1784 entitled *What Is Enlightenment?* Kant answered, "*Sapere Aude* (dare to know)! 'Have the courage to use your own understanding' is therefore the motto of enlightenment." He argued that if serious thinkers were granted the freedom to exercise their reason publicly in print, enlightenment would almost surely follow. Kant was no revolutionary; he also insisted that in their private lives, individuals must obey all laws, no matter how unreasonable, and should be punished for "impertinent" criticism. Kant thus tried to reconcile absolute monarchical authority with a critical public sphere. This balancing act characterized experiments with "enlightened absolutism" in the eighteenth century.

▼ What did enlightened absolutism mean?

How did the Enlightenment influence political developments? To this important question there is no easy answer. Most Enlightenment thinkers outside of England and the Netherlands, especially in central and eastern Europe, believed that political change could best come from above — from the ruler — rather than from below. Royal absolutism was a fact of life. Therefore, the philosophes and their sympathizers realistically concluded that a benevolent absolutism offered the best opportunities for improving society.

Many government officials were interested in philosophical ideas. Their daily involvement in complex affairs of state made them naturally attracted to ideas for improving human society. Encouraged and instructed by these officials, some absolutist rulers tried to reform their governments in accordance with enlightenment ideals — what historians have often called the enlightened absolutism of the later eighteenth century. The most influential of the new-style monarchs were in Prussia, Russia, and Austria. Their example illustrates both the achievements and the great limitations of enlightened absolutism.

enlightened absolutism
Term coined by historians to describe the rule of eighteenth-century monarchs who, without renouncing their own absolute authority, adopted Enlightenment ideals of rationalism, progress, and tolerance.

Frederick the Great of Prussia

Frederick II (r. 1740–1786), commonly known as Frederick the Great, built masterfully on the work of his father, Frederick William I (see Chapter 16). Although in his youth he embraced culture and literature rather than the life of the barracks championed by his father, by the time he came to the throne Frederick was determined to use the army that his father had left him.

When the young Maria Theresa of Austria inherited the Habsburg dominions upon the death of her father Charles VI, Frederick pounced. He invaded her rich, mainly German province of Silesia (sigh-LEE-zhuh), defying solemn Prussian promises to respect the Pragmatic Sanction, a diplomatic agreement that had guaranteed Maria Theresa's

The War of Austrian Succession, 1740–1748

succession. In 1742, as other greedy powers vied for her lands in the European War of the Austrian Succession (1740–1748), Maria Theresa was forced to cede almost all of Silesia to Prussia. In one stroke Prussia had doubled its population to 6 million people and become a European Great Power.

Though successful in 1742, Frederick had to fight against great odds to save Prussia from total destruction after the ongoing competition between Britain and France for colonial empire brought another great conflict in 1756. Maria Theresa, seeking to regain Silesia, formed an alliance with the leaders of France and Russia. The aim of the alliance during the resulting Seven Years' War (1756–1763) was to conquer Prussia and divide up its territory. In the end Frederick was miraculously saved: Peter III came to the Russian throne in 1762 and called off the attack against Frederick, whom he greatly admired.

The terrible struggle of the Seven Years' War tempered Frederick's interest in territorial expansion and brought him to consider how more humane policies for his subjects might also strengthen the state. Thus he tolerantly allowed his subjects to believe as they wished in religious and philosophical matters. He promoted the advancement of knowledge, improving his country's schools and permitting scholars to publish their findings. Moreover, Frederick tried to improve the lives of his subjects more directly. As he wrote his friend Voltaire, "I must enlighten my people, cultivate their manners and morals, and make them as happy as human beings can be, or as happy as the means at my disposal permit."

The legal system and the bureaucracy were Frederick's primary tools. Prussia's laws were simplified, torture of prisoners was abolished, and judges decided cases quickly and impartially. Prussian officials became famous for their hard work and honesty. After the Seven Years' War ended in 1763, Frederick's government energetically promoted the reconstruction of agriculture and industry in his war-torn country.

Frederick's dedication to high-minded government went only so far, however. While he condemned serfdom in the abstract, he accepted it in practice and did not free the serfs on his own estates. He accepted and extended the privileges of the nobility, who remained the backbone of the army and the entire Prussian state. In reforming Prussia's bureaucracy, Frederick drew on the principles of **cameralism**, the German science of public administration that emerged in the decades following the Thirty Years' War. Influential throughout the German lands, cameralism held that monarchy was the best of all forms of government, that all elements of society should be placed at the service of the state, and that, in turn, the state should make use of its resources and authority to improve society.

cameralism View that monarchy was the best form of government, that all elements of society should serve the monarch, and that, in turn, the state should use its resources and authority to increase the public good.

Catherine the Great of Russia

Catherine the Great of Russia (r. 1762–1796) was one of the most remarkable rulers of her age, and the French philosophes adored her. Catherine was a German princess from Anhalt-Zerbst (AHN-hahlt ZEHRBST), an insignificant principality sandwiched between Prussia and Saxony. Her father commanded a regiment of the Prussian army, but her mother was related to the Romanovs of Russia.

At the age of fifteen Catherine's Romanov connection made her a suitable bride for the heir to the Russian throne. When her husband Peter III came to power during the Seven Years' War, his decision to withdraw Russian troops from the coalition against

CHAPTER LOCATOR   How did European views of nature change in this period?   What were the core principles of the Enlightenment?   **What did enlightened absolutism mean?**

511

Catherine the Great Strongly influenced by the Enlightenment, Catherine the Great cultivated the French philosophes and instituted moderate reforms, only to reverse them in the aftermath of Pugachev's rebellion. This equestrian portrait now hangs above her throne in the palace throne room in St. Petersburg. (Musée des Beaux-Arts, Chartres/The Bridgeman Art Library)

Prussia alienated the army. Catherine profited from his unpopularity to form a conspiracy to depose her husband. In 1762 Catherine's lover Gregory Orlov and his three brothers murdered Peter, and the German princess became empress of Russia.

Never questioning that absolute monarchy was the best form of government, Catherine set out to rule in an enlightened manner. She had three main goals. First, she worked hard to continue Peter the Great's effort to bring the culture of western Europe to Russia (see Chapter 16). To do so, she imported Western architects, sculptors, musicians, and intellectuals. She bought masterpieces of Western art and patronized the philosophes. Moreover, this intellectual ruler, who wrote plays and loved good talk, set the tone for the entire Russian nobility. Peter the Great westernized Russian armies, but it was Catherine who westernized the imagination of the Russian nobility.

Catherine's second goal was domestic reform, and she began her reign with sincere and ambitious projects. In 1767 she appointed a special legislative commission to prepare a new law code. This project was never completed, but Catherine did restrict the practice of torture and allowed limited religious toleration. She also tried to improve education and strengthen local government. The philosophes applauded these measures and hoped more would follow.

Such was not the case. In 1773 a common Cossack soldier named Emelian Pugachev (PYOO-gah-chehv) sparked a gigantic uprising of serfs. Proclaiming himself the true tsar, Pugachev issued orders abolishing serfdom, taxes, and army service. Thousands joined his cause, slaughtering landlords and officials over a vast area of southwestern Russia. Pugachev's untrained forces eventually proved no match for Catherine's noble-led army, and Pugachev was captured and executed.

Pugachev's rebellion put an end to any intentions Catherine might have had about reforming the system. The peasants were clearly dangerous, and her empire rested on the support of the nobility. After 1775 Catherine gave the nobles absolute control of their serfs, and she extended serfdom into new areas. In 1785 she formalized the nobility's privileged position, freeing nobles forever from taxes and state service. Under Catherine the Russian nobility attained its most exalted position, and serfdom entered its most oppressive phase.

Catherine's third goal was territorial expansion, and in this respect she was extremely successful. Her armies subjugated the last descendants of the Mongols and the Crimean Tartars and began the conquest of the Caucasus (KAW-kuh-suhs). Her greatest coup was the partition of Poland (Map 17.1). When, between 1768 and 1772, Catherine's armies scored unprecedented victories against the Turks and thereby threatened to disturb the balance of power between Russia and Austria in eastern Europe, Frederick of Prussia came forward with a deal. He proposed that Turkey be let off easily and that Prussia, Austria, and Russia each compensate itself by taking a slice of Polish territory. The first partition of Poland took place in 1772. Subsequent partitions in 1793 and 1795 gave away the rest of Polish territory, and Poland vanished from the map.

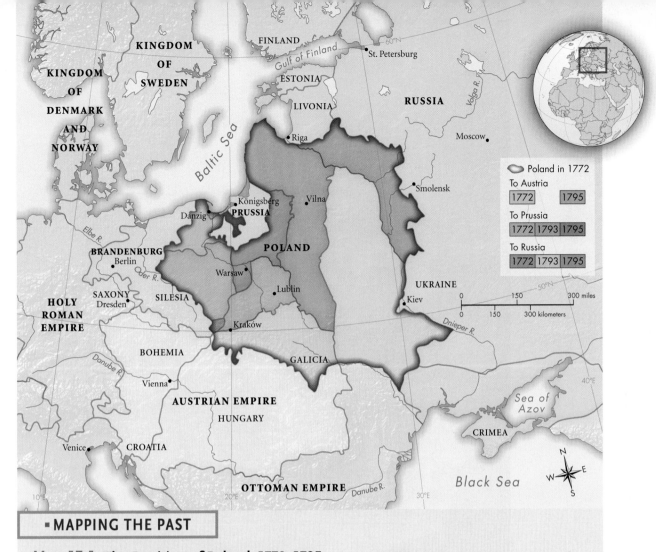

MAPPING THE PAST

Map 17.1 The Partition of Poland, 1772–1795

In 1772 war between Russia and Austria threatened over Russian gains from the Ottoman Empire. To satisfy desires for expansion without fighting, Prussia's Frederick the Great proposed that parts of Poland be divided among Austria, Prussia, and Russia. In 1793 and 1795 the three powers partitioned the remainder, and the ancient republic of Poland vanished from the map.

ANALYZING THE MAP Of the three powers that divided the kingdom of Poland, which benefited the most? How did the partition affect the geographical boundaries of each state, and what was the significance? What border with the former Poland remained unchanged? Why do you think this was the case?

CONNECTIONS Why was Poland vulnerable to partition in the latter half of the eighteenth century? What does it say about European politics at the time that a country could simply cease to exist on the map? Could that happen today?

To complete this activity online, go to the Online Study Guide at **bedfordstmartins.com/mckaywestunderstanding**.

The Austrian Habsburgs

Maria Theresa (r. 1740–1780) of Austria also set out to reform her nation, although traditional power politics was a more important motivation for her than were Enlightenment teachings. Maria Theresa was a remarkable but old-fashioned absolutist. Her more radical son, Joseph II (r. 1780–1790), drew on Enlightenment ideals, earning the title of "revolutionary emperor."

CHAPTER LOCATOR | How did European views of nature change in this period? | What were the core principles of the Enlightenment? | **What did enlightened absolutism mean?**

513

Maria Theresa The empress and her husband pose with eleven of their sixteen children at Schönbrunn palace in this family portrait by court painter Martin Meytens (1695–1770). Joseph, the heir to the throne, stands at the center of the star on the floor. Wealthy women often had very large families, in part because they, unlike poor women, seldom nursed their babies. (Réunion des Musées Nationaux/Art Resource, NY)

Emerging from the long War of the Austrian Succession in 1748 with the loss of Silesia, Maria Theresa was determined to introduce reforms that would make the state stronger and more efficient. First, she introduced measures aimed at limiting the papacy's political influence in her realm. Second, a whole series of administrative reforms strengthened the central bureaucracy, smoothed out some provincial differences, and revamped the tax system, taxing even the lands of nobles, previously exempt from taxation. Third, the government sought to improve the lot of the agricultural population, cautiously reducing the power of lords over their hereditary serfs and their partially free peasant tenants.

Coregent with his mother from 1765 onward and a strong supporter of change, Joseph II moved forward rapidly when he came to the throne in 1780. Most notably, Joseph abolished serfdom in 1781, and in 1789 he decreed that peasants could pay landlords in cash rather than through compulsory labor on their land. This measure was rejected not only by the nobility but also by the peasants it was intended to help, because they lacked the necessary cash. When Joseph died prematurely at forty-nine, the entire Habsburg empire was in turmoil. His brother Leopold II (r. 1790–1792) canceled Joseph's radical edicts in order to re-establish order.

Despite differences, Joseph II and the other eastern European absolutists of the later eighteenth century combined old-fashioned state-building with the culture and critical thinking of the Enlightenment. In doing so, they succeeded in expanding the role of the state in the life of society. Their failure to implement policies we would recognize as humane and enlightened—such as abolishing serfdom—may reveal inherent limitations in Enlightenment thinking about equality and social justice, rather than in their execution of Enlightenment programs. The fact that leading philosophes supported rather than criticized eastern rulers' policies suggests some of the blinders of the era.

Jewish Life and the Limits of Enlightened Absolutism

Perhaps the best example of the limitations of enlightened absolutism are the debates surrounding the possible emancipation of the Jews. Europe's small Jewish populations lived under highly discriminatory laws. For the most part, Jews were confined to tiny, overcrowded ghettos, were excluded by law from most business and professional activities, and could be ordered out of a kingdom at a moment's notice. Still, a very few did manage to succeed and to obtain the right of permanent settlement, usually by performing some special service for the state.

In the eighteenth century, an Enlightenment movement known as the Haskalah emerged from within the European Jewish community, led by the Prussian philosopher Moses Mendelssohn (MEN-dul-suhn) (1729–1786). (See "Individuals in Society: Moses Mendelssohn and the Jewish Enlightenment," page 516.) Christian and Jewish Enlightenment philosophers, including Mendelssohn, began to advocate for freedom and civil rights for European Jews. In an era of reason, tolerance, and universality, they argued, restrictions on religious grounds could not stand.

Arguments for tolerance won some ground. The British Parliament passed a law allowing naturalization of Jews in 1753, but later repealed the law due to public outrage. The most progressive reforms took place under Austrian emperor Joseph II. His liberal edicts included measures intended to integrate Jews more fully into society, including eligibility for military service, admission to higher education and artisanal trades, and removal of requirements for special clothing or emblems. Welcomed by many Jews, these reforms raised fears among traditionalists of assimilation into the general population.

Many monarchs refused to entertain the idea of emancipation. Although he permitted freedom of religion to his Christian subjects, Frederick the Great of Prussia firmly opposed any general emancipation for the Jews. Catherine the Great, who acquired most of Poland's large Jewish population when she annexed part of that country in the late eighteenth century, similarly refused. In 1791 she established the Pale of Settlement, a territory including parts of modern-day Poland, Latvia, Lithuania, Ukraine, and Belorussia, in which most Jews were required to live.

The first European state to remove all restrictions on the Jews was France under the French Revolution. Over the next hundred years, Jews gradually won full legal and civil rights throughout the rest of western Europe. Emancipation in eastern Europe took even longer and aroused more conflict and violence.

Haskalah The Jewish Enlightenment of the second half of the eighteenth century, led by the Prussian philosopher Moses Mendelssohn.

The Pale of Settlement, 1791

CHAPTER LOCATOR | How did European views of nature change in this period? | What were the core principles of the Enlightenment? | **What did enlightened absolutism mean?**

515

INDIVIDUALS IN SOCIETY

Moses Mendelssohn and the Jewish Enlightenment

IN 1743 A SMALL, HUMPBACKED JEWISH BOY WITH a stammer left his poor parents in Dessau (DEH-sow) in central Germany and walked eighty miles to Berlin, the capital of Frederick the Great's Prussia. According to one story, when the boy reached the Rosenthaler (ROH-zuhn-tah-luhr) Gate, the only one through which Jews could pass, he told the inquiring watchman that his name was Moses and that he had come to Berlin "to learn." The watchman laughed and waved him through. "Go Moses, the sea has opened before you."*

In Berlin the young Mendelssohn studied Jewish law and eked out a living copying Hebrew manuscripts in a beautiful hand. But he was soon fascinated by an intellectual world that had been closed to him in the Dessau ghetto. There, like most Jews throughout central Europe, he had spoken Yiddish—a mixture of German, Polish, and Hebrew. Now, working mainly on his own, he mastered German; he learned Latin, Greek, French, and English; and he studied mathematics and Enlightenment philosophy. Word of his exceptional abilities spread in Berlin's Jewish community (the dwelling of 1,500 of the city's 100,000 inhabitants). He began tutoring the children of a wealthy Jewish silk merchant, and he soon became the merchant's clerk and later his partner. But his great passion remained the life of the mind and the spirit, which he avidly pursued in his off hours.

Gentle and unassuming in his personal life, Mendelssohn was a bold thinker. Reading eagerly in Western philosophy since antiquity, he was, as a pious Jew, soon convinced that Enlightenment teachings need not be opposed to Jewish thought and religion. He concluded that reason could complement and strengthen religion, although each would retain its integrity as a separate sphere.† Developing his idea in his first great work, "On the Immortality of the Soul" (1767), Mendelssohn used the neutral setting of a philosophical dialogue between Socrates and his followers in ancient Greece to argue that the human soul lived forever. In refusing to bring religion and critical thinking into conflict, he was strongly influenced by contemporary German philosophers who argued similarly on behalf of Christianity. He reflected the way the German Enlightenment generally supported established religion, in contrast to the French Enlightenment, which attacked it.

Mendelssohn's treatise on the human soul captivated the educated German public, which marveled that a Jew could have written a philosophical masterpiece. In the excitement, a Christian zealot named Lavater challenged Mendelssohn in a pamphlet to accept Christianity or to demonstrate how the Christian faith was not "reasonable." Replying politely but passionately, the Jewish philosopher affirmed that his studies had only strengthened him in his faith, although he did not seek to convert anyone not born into Judaism. Rather, he urged toleration in religious matters and spoke up courageously against Jewish oppression.

Orthodox Jew and German philosophe, Moses Mendelssohn serenely combined two very different worlds. He built a bridge from the ghetto to the dominant culture over which many Jews would pass, including his novelist daughter Dorothea and his famous grandson, the composer Felix Mendelssohn.

QUESTIONS FOR ANALYSIS

1. How did Mendelssohn seek to influence Jewish religious thought in his time?
2. How do Mendelssohn's ideas compare with those of the French Enlightenment?

*H. Kupferberg, *The Mendelssohns: Three Generations of Genius* (New York: Charles Scribner's Sons, 1972), p. 3.

†D. Sorkin, *Moses Mendelssohn and the Religious Enlightenment* (Berkeley: University of California Press, 1996), pp. 8 ff.

Lavater (right) attempts to convert Mendelssohn, in a painting of an imaginary encounter by Moritz Oppenheim. (Collection of the Judah L. Magnes Museum, Berkeley)

⬅ LOOKING BACK **LOOKING AHEAD** ➡

HAILED AS THE ORIGINS of modern thought, the scientific revolution must also be seen as a product of its past. Medieval universities gave rise to important new scholarship, and the ambition and wealth of Renaissance patrons nurtured intellectual curiosity. Religious faith also impacted the scientific revolution, inspiring thinkers to understand the glory of God's creation, while bringing censure and personal tragedy to others. Natural philosophers following Copernicus pioneered new methods of observing and explaining nature while drawing on centuries-old traditions of astrology, alchemy, and magic.

The Enlightenment ideas of the eighteenth century were a similar blend of past and present; they could serve as much to bolster authoritarian regimes as to inspire revolutionaries to fight for individual rights and liberties. Although the Enlightenment fostered critical thinking about everything from science to religion, the majority of Europeans, including many prominent thinkers, remained devout Christians.

The achievements of the scientific revolution and the Enlightenment are undeniable. Key Western values of rationalism, human rights and open-mindedness were born from these movements. With their new notions of progress and social improvement, Europeans would embark on important revolutions in industry and politics in the century that followed. Nonetheless, others have seen a darker side. For these critics, the mastery over nature permitted by the scientific revolution now threatens to overwhelm the earth's fragile equilibrium, and the Enlightenment belief in the universal application of reason can lead to arrogance and intolerance, particularly intolerance of other people's spiritual, cultural, and political values. Such vivid debate about the legacy of these intellectual and scientific developments testifies to their continuing importance in today's world. ◾

- **For a list of suggested readings for this chapter, visit** *bedfordstmartins.com/mckaywestunderstanding*.

- **For primary sources from this period, see** *Sources of Western Society*, Second Edition.

- **For Web sites, images, and documents related to topics in this chapter, see Make History at** *bedfordstmartins.com/mckaywestunderstanding*.

CHAPTER LOCATOR | How did European views of nature change in this period? | What were the core principles of the Enlightenment? | **What did enlightened absolutism mean?**

517

Chapter 17 Study Guide

Step 1

GETTING STARTED Below are basic terms about this period in the history of Western civilization. Can you identify each term below and explain why it matters? To do this exercise online, go to bedfordstmartins.com/mckaywestunderstanding.

TERMS	WHO (OR WHAT) AND WHEN	WHY IT MATTERS
natural philosophy, p. 490		
Copernican hypothesis, p. 492		
experimental method, p. 494		
law of inertia, p. 494		
law of universal gravitation, p. 495		
empiricism, p. 495		
Cartesian dualism, p. 496		
Enlightenment, p. 498		
rationalism, p. 499		
philosophes, p. 500		
reading revolution, p. 504		
salons, p. 505		
rococo, p. 505		
public sphere, p. 505		
enlightened absolutism, p. 510		
cameralism, p. 511		
Haskalah, p. 515		

Step 2

MOVING BEYOND THE BASICS The exercise below requires a more advanced understanding of the chapter material. Examine the contributions of key figures of the scientific revolution by filling in the chart below with descriptions of the major contributions of key people. Be sure to include both concrete discoveries and contributions to the development of the scientific method. When you are finished, consider the following questions: How did these thinkers build off of each other's discoveries and insights? What common goals did they share? To do this exercise online, go to bedfordstmartins.com/mckaywestunderstanding.

	DISCOVERIES AND CONTRIBUTIONS
Nicolaus Copernicus	
Tycho Brahe	
Johannes Kepler	
Francis Bacon	
René Descartes	
Galileo Galilei	
Isaac Newton	

PUTTING IT ALL TOGETHER Now that you've reviewed key elements of the chapter, take a step back and try to see the big picture. Remember to use specific examples from the chapter in your answers. To do this exercise online, go to bedfordstmartins.com/mckaywestunderstanding.

THE SCIENTIFIC REVOLUTION

- What was revolutionary about the scientific revolution? How did the study of nature in the sixteenth century differ from the study of nature in the Middle Ages?

- How did Newton's ideas build on the contributions of his predecessors? Is it fair to describe his work as the culmination of the scientific revolution? Why or why not?

- How did religious belief both stimulate and hinder scientific inquiry?

THE ENLIGHTENMENT

- How did the scientific revolution contribute to the emergence of the Enlightenment? What new ideas about the power and potential of human reason were central to both developments?

- In what ways did the Enlightenment influence eighteenth-century European society and politics? In what ways was its influence limited?

- How did Enlightenment thinkers deal with issues of gender and race? What does this tell us about the nature of the Enlightenment?

ENLIGHTENED ABSOLUTISM

- Why did many Enlightenment thinkers see absolute monarchy as a potential force for good? What light do the political views of the philosophes shed on the nature and limits of Enlightenment thinking?

- How did Enlightenment ideas contribute to the expansion of the role of the state in central and eastern European society? What existing social and economic structures were least susceptible to enlightened reform? Why?

■ **In Your Own Words** Imagine that you must explain Chapter 17 to someone who hasn't read it. What would be the most important points to include and why?

Chapter Endnotes

Chapter 1

1. Quoted in J. B. Pritchard, ed., *Ancient Near Eastern Texts*, 3d ed. (Princeton, N.J.: Princeton University Press, 1969), p. 44. *Note:* John Buckler is the translator of all uncited quotations from a foreign language in Chapters 1–6 of *Understanding Western Society: A Brief History*.
2. Ibid., p. 104.
3. Ibid., p. 372.
4. Quoted in A. H. Gardiner, "Ramesside Texts Relating to the Taxation and Transport of Corn," *Journal of Egyptian Archaeology* 27 (1941), pp. 19–20.
5. Manetho, *History of Egypt*, frag. 42, pp. 75–77.

Chapter 2

1. James H. Breasted, *Ancient Records of Egypt*, vol. 4 (Chicago: University of Chicago Press, 1907), para. 398.

Chapter 3

1. G. Tarditi, *Archilochus Fragmenta* (Rome: Edizioni dell'Ateno, 1968), frag. 112.
2. W. Barnstable, *Sappho* (New York: Garden City, 1965), frag. 24.

Chapter 4

1. Plutarch, *Moralia* 328E.

Chapter 5

1. Polybius, *The Histories* 1.1.5.
2. Plutarch, *Pyrrhos* 21.14.
3. Sallust, *War with Catiline* 10.1–3.
4. Ovid, *Fasti* 2.535–539.
5. Plutarch, *Life of Tiberius Gracchus* 9.5–6.

Chapter 6

1. Virgil, *Aeneid* 6.851–853.
2. Horace, *Odes* 4.15.
3. Pliny, *Natural History* 29.8.18, 21.
4. Text in Mary Johnston, *Roman Life* (Chicago: Scott, Foresman, and Co., 1957), p. 172.

Chapter 7

1. R. C. Petry, ed., *A History of Christianity: Readings in the History of Early and Medieval Christianity* (Englewood Cliffs, N.J.: Prentice Hall, 1962), p. 70.

Chapter 8

1. Quoted in R. McKitterick, *The Frankish Kingdoms Under the Carolingians, 751–987* (New York: Longman, 1983), p. 77.
2. Quoted in B. D. Hill, ed., *Church and State in the Middle Ages* (New York: John Wiley & Sons, 1970), pp. 46–47.
3. Quoted in R. Pipes, *Russia Under the Old Regime* (New York: Charles Scribner's Sons, 1974), p. 48.

Chapter 9

1. *Hrosvithae Liber Tertius, a Text with Translation*, ed. and trans. Mary Bernardine Bergman (Covington, Ky.: The Sisters of Saint Benedict, 1943), pp. 45 and 53.

2. J. Johns, *Arabic Administration in Norman Sicily: The Royal Dīwān* (New York: Cambridge University Press, 2002), p. 293.
3. H. T. Riley, ed., *Memorials of London* (London: Longmans Green, 1868).
4. Quotations related to the dispute between Henry and Gregory are all from E. F. Henderson, ed., *Select Historical Documents of the Middle Ages* (London: George Bell and Sons, 1892), pp. 372–373, 376–377, 385–387.
5. Fulcher of Chartres, *A History of the Expedition to Jerusalem, 1095–1127*, trans. Frances Rita Ryan, ed. Harold S. Fink (Knoxville: University of Tennessee Press, 1969), pp. 121–123.
6. Quoted in Jo Ann H. Moran Cruz and Richard Gerberding, *Medieval Worlds: An Introduction to European History 300–1492* (Boston: Houghton Mifflin, 2004), p. 305.

Chapter 10

1. Honorius of Autun, "Elucidarium sive Dialogus de Summa Totius Christianae Theologiae," in *Patrologia Latina*, ed. J. P. Migne (Paris: Garnier Brothers, 1854), vol. 172, col. 1149.
2. Translated and quoted in Susan C. Karant-Nunn, *The Reformation of Ritual: An Interpretation of Early Modern Germany* (London: Routledge, 1997), p. 77.
3. Honorius of Autun, "Elucidarium sive Dialogus," vol. 172, col. 1148.
4. William of Malmesbury, *Chronicle*, in James Bruce Ross and Mary Martin McLaughlin, eds., *The Portable Medieval Reader* (New York: Viking, 1949), pp. 57–58.

Chapter 11

1. Quoted in J. H. Mundy, *Europe in the High Middle Ages, 1150–1309* (New York: Basic Books, 1973), pp. 474–475.

Chapter 12

1. Christos S. Bartsocas, "Two Fourteenth-Century Descriptions of the 'Black Death,'" *Journal of the History of Medicine*, October 1966, p. 395.
2. Giovanni Boccaccio, *The Decameron*, trans. Mark Musa and Peter Bordanella (New York: W. W. Norton, 1982), p. 9.
3. Florence Warren, ed., *The Dance of Death* (Oxford: Early English Text Society, 1931), p. 8. Spelling modernized.
4. W. P. Barrett, trans., *The Trial of Jeanne d'Arc* (London: George Routledge, 1931), pp. 165–166.
5. Quoted in J. H. Smith, *The Great Schism, 1378: The Disintegration of the Medieval Papacy* (New York: Weybright & Talley, 1970), p. 15.
6. Quoted in Katharina M. Wilson, ed., *Medieval Women Writers* (Athens: University of Georgia Press, 1984), p. 245.
7. Quoted in R. Bartlett, *The Making of Europe: Conquest, Colonization and Cultural Change, 950–1350* (Princeton, N.J.: Princeton University Press, 1993), p. 239.

Chapter 13

1. In James Bruce Ross and Mary Martin McLaughlin, *The Portable Renaissance Reader* (New York: Penguin, 1953), p. 480–481, 482, 492.
2. Niccolò Machiavelli, *The Prince*, trans. Leo Paul S. de Alvarez (Prospect Heights, Ill.: Waveland Press, 1980), p. 101.
3. Ibid., p. 149.

4. Quoted in F. Seebohm, *The Oxford Reformers* (London: J. M. Dent & Sons, 1867), p. 256.

5. Quoted in Lauro Martines, *Power and Imagination: City-States in Renaissance Italy* (New York: Vintage Books, 1980), p. 253.

Chapter 14

1. Quoted in Owen Chadwick, *The Reformation* (Baltimore: Penguin Books, 1976), p. 55.

2. Quoted in S. E. Ozment, *The Age of Reform, 1250–1550: An Intellectual and Religious History of Late Medieval and Reformation Europe* (New Haven, Conn.: Yale University Press, 1980), p. 284.

3. J. Allen, trans., *John Calvin: The Institutes of the Christian Religion* (Philadelphia: Westminster Press, 1930), bk. 3, chap. 21, paras. 5, 7.

4. Quoted in E. William Monter, *Calvin's Geneva* (New York: John Wiley & Sons, 1967), p. 137.

5. Quoted in David P. Daniel, "Hungary," in *The Oxford Encyclopedia of the Reformation*, vol. 2, ed. H. J. Hillerbrand (New York: Oxford University Press, 1996), p. 273.

6. From *The Fugger News-Letters*, ed. Victor von Klarwell, trans. P. de Chary (London: John Lane, The Boley Head Ltd., 1924), quoted in James Bruce Ross and Mary Martin McLaughlin, *The Portable Renaissance Reader* (New York: Penguin, 1968), pp. 258, 260, 262.

Chapter 15

1. Quoted in C. M. Cipolla, *Guns, Sails, and Empires: Technological Innovation and the Early Phases of European Expansion, 1400–1700* (New York: Minerva Press, 1965), p. 132.

2. Quoted in F. H. Littell, *The Macmillan Atlas: History of Christianity* (New York: Macmillan, 1976), p. 75.

3. J. M. Cohen, ed. and trans., *The Four Voyages of Christopher Columbus* (New York: Penguin Books, 1969), p. 37.

4. Thomas Benjamin, *The Atlantic World: Europeans, Africans, Indians, and Their Shared History, 1400–1900* (Cambridge, U.K.: Cambridge University Press, 2009), pp. 35–59.

5. Quoted in C. Gibson, ed., *The Black Legend: Anti-Spanish Attitudes in the Old World and the New* (New York: Knopf, 1971), pp. 74–75.

6. Cited in Geoffrey Vaughn Scammell, *The First Imperial Age: European Overseas Expansion, c. 1400–1715* (London and New York: Routledge, 2002), p. 432.

7. Herbert S. Klein, "Profits and the Causes of Mortality," in David Northrup, ed., *The Atlantic Slave Trade* (Lexington, Mass.: D. C. Heath and Co., 1994), p. 116.

8. Voyages: The Trans-Atlantic Slave Trade Database, http://www.slavevoyages.org/tast/assessment/estimates.faces (accessed May 9, 2009).

9. C. Cotton, trans., *The Essays of Michel de Montaigne* (New York: A. L. Burt, 1893), pp. 207, 210.

Chapter 16

1. H. Kamen, "The Economic and Social Consequences of the Thirty Years' War," *Past and Present* 39 (April 1968): 44–61.

2. John A. Lynn, "Reconstructing French Army Growth," in *The Military Transformation of Early Modern Europe*, ed. Clifford J. Rogers (Boulder, Colo.: Westview Press, 1995), p. 125.

3. J. H. Elliott, *Imperial Spain, 1469–1716* (New York: Mentor Books, 1963), pp. 306–308.

4. H. Rosenberg, *Bureaucracy, Aristocracy, and Autocracy: The Prussian Experience, 1660–1815* (Boston: Beacon Press, 1966), p. 43.

5. Ibid., *Bureaucracy, Aristocracy, and Autocracy*, p. 40.

6. For a revisionist interpretation, see J. Wormald, "James VI and I: Two Kings or One?" *History* 62 (June 1983): 187–209.

Chapter 17

1. Quoted in A. G. R. Smith, *Science and Society in the Sixteenth and Seventeenth Centuries* (New York: Harcourt Brace Jovanovich, 1972), p. 97.

2. Quoted in Butterfield, *The Origins of Modern Science* (New York: Macmillan, 1951), p. 47.

3. Ibid., p. 120.

4. Quoted in John Freely, *Aladdin's Lamp: How Greek Science Came to Europe Through the Islamic World* (New York: Knopf, 2009), p. 217.

5. Quoted in L. M. Marsak, ed., *The Enlightenment* (New York: John Wiley & Sons, 1972), p. 56.

6. Quoted in G. L. Mosse et al., eds., *Europe in Review* (Chicago: Rand McNally, 1964), p. 156.

7. Quoted in G. P. Gooch, *Catherine the Great and Other Studies* (Hamden, Conn.: Archon Books, 1966), p. 149.

8. See E. Fox-Genovese, "Women in the Enlightenment," in *Becoming Visible: Women in European History*, 2d ed., ed. R. Bridenthal, C. Koonz, and S. Stuard (Boston: Houghton Mifflin, 1987), esp. pp. 252–259, 263–265.

9. Quoted in Emmanuel Chukwudi Eze, ed., *Race and the Enlightenment: A Reader* (Oxford: Blackwell, 1997), p. 33.

Index

Cannon, in Hundred Years' War, 334
Canon law, 171, 244, 304
    Roman law and, 304
Canon of Medicine (Avicenna), 204
Canossa, Henry IV at, 243
Canterbury, 187
    Becket in, 239
Canterbury Tales (Chaucer), 347
Cantons (Switzerland), religion in, 397
Canute, 231
Cape of Good Hope, 425
Capetian dynasty (France), 233, 329
Capitalism, 342
    mercantile, 298
    Protestantism and, 497
Capitoline Hill (Rome), 116
Caravan trade, 100–101, 198, 420
Caravel, 423
Careers. *See also* Labor
    in Rome, 151, 152
Caribbean region. *See also* West Indies
    French in, 434
    slaves in, 440
Carmelite nuns, 408
Carolingian Empire, 206–210, 207*(m)*
    division of, 215, 222
    fiefs in, 223
    Vikings and, 215–221
Carolingian minuscule, 211, 212*(i)*
Carolingian Renaissance, 211–215
Cartesian dualism, 496
Carthage, 35, 62, 115, 122–124, 122*(i)*, 123*(m)*
Cartier, Jacques, 431
Cartography, 423
Castiglione, Baldassare, 360–361, 360*(i)*
Castile, 237. *See also* Ferdinand and Isabella
    (Spain); Spain
Catacombs, near Rome, 159, 160*(i)*
Catalonia, 457, 465
Cateau-Cambrésis, Treaty of, 407
Cathars. *See* Albigensian heresy
Cathedrals
    in Córdoba, 237*(i)*
    medieval, 172, 308–313
    schools in, 211, 212, 302
Catherine de' Medici, 409
Catherine of Aragon, 377, 399
Catherine the Great (Russia), 474, 511–512, 512*(i)*, 515
Catholic, use of term, 244
Catholic Church. *See also* Christianity;
        Councils (Christian); Counter-
        Reformation; Papacy; Protestantism
    in American colonies, 434
    Babylonian Captivity of, 335
    baroque art and, 483–484
    Carolingians and, 211, 212
    Copernican hypothesis and, 492, 494
    criticisms of, 336–337, 336*(i)*
    Crusades and, 245
    in England, 187, 399–400, 478
    feudal, 223
    in France, 458

Galileo and, 494
    Great Schism in, 335–336, 335*(m)*
    in Hungary, 404
    in Ireland, 400, 479, 480
    in late Middle Ages, 335–340
    lay piety and, 338–340
    in Low Countries, 410
    in Moravia, 220
    vs. Orthodox Christianity, 245
    reforms in, 404–407
    science and, 498
Catholic League, 454
Catholic Reformation, 403, 404–407, 413, 483
Cato the Elder (Marcus Cato), 125–128
Caucasus region, 512
Causa et Curae (Hildegard of Bingen), 284*(b)*
Cavendish, Margaret, 497
Cayenne, 434
Celibacy
    Christianity and, 174, 175
    of clergy, 242
    Judaism and, 39
    Luther on, 388
Cellini, Benvenuto, 358*(i)*
Celtic peoples, 177, 180–181, 181*(i)*. *See also*
        Gaul and Gauls
    Rome and, 117, 153
Censors (Rome), 119
Central America, 6
    agriculture in, 6
Central Asia, Seleucids and, 98
Central Europe
    in High Middle Ages, 234–235
    immigrants to, 291
Centralization, of governments, 228, 230–237
Central Middle Ages. *See* High Middle Ages;
        Middle Ages
Ceremonies
    in Italian cities, 355
    religious, 275
Ceuta, Morocco, 425
Ceylon, 442
Chaeronea, battle at, 82–83
Chaldeans, 32, 46
Chamber of Accounts (France), 234
Champlain, Samuel de, 434
Chancery, papal, 244
Chansons de geste, 308
Chariots
    Assyrian, 44
    Roman, 152
Charlemagne, 207–210, 208*(i)*, 234
    Carolingian Renaissance and, 211–215
    conquests by (768–814), 207–208, 207*(m)*
    coronation of, 210
    empire after death, 215
Charles I (England), 477*(i)*, 478
Charles I (Spain), 440
Charles I at the Hunt (Van Dyck), 477*(i)*
Charles II (England), 480–481
Charles II (Spain), 462

Charles III (Spain), 435
Charles IV (France), 329
Charles V (Holy Roman Empire; **Charles I
        of Spain**), 358, 380, 395, 396, 396*(i)*, 406, 436
    abdication by, 410
    Catherine of Aragon and, 399
    empire of, 397*(m)*
    Luther and, 389
    Magellan and, 430
    Netherlands under, 410–411
    religion and, 396–398
Charles VI (Austria), 510
Charles VI (France), 334
Charles VII (France), 332, 333, 376
Charles VIII (France), 357
Charles XII (Sweden), 471
Charles Martel, 206, 223
Charles the Bald, 215, 215*(m)*, 217
Charles the Bold (Burgundy), 377
Charles the Great. *See* Charlemagne
Charles the Simple (Franks), 217
Chartres Cathedral, 312, 312*(i)*
Châtelet, marquise de, 502, 502*(i)*
Chaucer, Geoffrey, 347
Chedworth, Britain, Roman villa at, 153*(i)*
Chemistry, 498
Chieftains, of barbarian tribes, 178
Childbirth. *See also* Midwives
    in Athens, 75
    Bridget of Sweden and, 338
    deaths from, 108*(i)*
    in Middle Ages, 268–269
    separation of women after, 275
Childhood, of medieval aristocrats, 277
Children
    abandonment of, 268–269, 269*(i)*
    peasant, 265
    in Rome, 125, 151
Chilperic II (Merovingian), 206
China
    agriculture in, 6
    Black Death in, 324
    trade and, 100, 295, 418, 442
Chivalry, 276–277
Choir monks, 283
Chollolan, 433
Chrétien de Troyes, 308
Christ. *See* Jesus of Nazareth
Christendom, 255–256
Christian III (Denmark), 398
Christian IV (Denmark), 454
Christian church. *See* Christianity;
        Church(es); Protestant Reformation;
        Reformation
Christian humanists, 364–367, 364*(i)*
Christianity, 156–161. *See also* Cathedrals;
        Church(es); Jesus of Nazareth;
        Orthodox Christianity; Reformation;
        Saint(s)
    appeal of, 159–160
    astronomy and, 490
    in Baltic region, 254–255, 254*(m)*

in Christian Mass, 270
Franks and, 183
humanist studies and, 358–359
literature in, 145–146
Romance languages and, 152–153
scientific works in, 491
Latin people, Rome and, 117, 120–121
Latin West, 169. *See also* Western Roman Empire
Latium, 114*(m)*, 115, 116, 117, 120, 123
Latvia, 474
Laud, William, 478, 479
Laura de Dianti (Titian), 374*(i)*
Law(s). *See also* Canon law; Law codes; Mosaic law; Natural law
barbarian, 178–179
canon, 171, 244
church, 244
in daily life, 240–241
in England, 239, 240–241, 377
of Hammurabi, 16–17
in High Middle Ages, 238–241
Mosaic, 39, 42
Roman, 118, 119, 120, 179, 183
Salic, 178–179, 329
in Sumer, 13
sumptuary, 299–300
university study of, 302, 303–304
witchcraft trials and, 411
Law (scientific)
of inertia, 494
of planetary motion (Kepler), 493
of universal gravitation, 495
Law codes
of Draco, 64
of Hammurabi, 16–17
of Jews, 39, 42
of Justinian, 189–190, 303
of Salian Franks, 178–179
study of, 303–304
Law of the Twelve Tables (Rome), 120
Lay investiture, 234, 242, 243–244
Lay piety, 338–340
Leagues, Greek, 60, 81
Learning. *See also* Education; Intellectual thought; Schools; Universities
Muslim, 202, 203–204
nuns and, 214–215, 214*(i)*
Lechfeld, Battle of, 221, 234
Legal dualism (pluralism), 346
Legal system. *See* Law(s)
Legions and legionnaires, 117, 121*(b)*, 129, 131, 141, 145*(i)*, 163
culture spread by, 154*(b)*, 154*(i)*
under Hadrian, 150
Legislation. *See also* Law(s)
in Athens, 65
Legnano, battle at, 235, 235*(m)*
Leisure, in Rome, 127–128, 128*(i)*
Leo I (Pope), 172, 182
Leo III (Pope), 210
Leo IX (Pope), 242, 245
Leo X (Pope), 377, 387

León, Spain, 237
Leonardo da Vinci, 370, 372*(b)*, 372*(i)*
Leonidas, 67*(i)*
Leopold II (Holy Roman Empire), 515
Lepidus (Rome), 135
Leprosy, hospitals for, 285
Lerma, duke of, 464
Lesbians. *See also* Homosexuality
origins of term, 76
Lesbos, 76
Le Tellier, François. *See* Louvois, marquis de
Letters of exchange, 297
Leuctra, battle at, 82
Lex Canuleia (Rome), 120
Lex Hortensia (Rome), 120
Liberty(ies), in medieval towns, 291
Libraries
in Alexandria, 106
Muslim, 202
Libya and Libyans, 34
Licinian-Sextian laws (Rome), 120
Licinius (Rome), 120
Life after death, in Christianity, 158, 161
Lifespan, in Middle Ages, 212
Lifestyle. *See also* Children; Families; Health; Marriage; Middle class(es)
in American colonies, 436–437
in Athens, 74–75, 74*(b)*, 74*(i)*
in Babylon, 16–17
of barbarian groups, 177–178
Carolingian, 209–210
Christian, 172–173, 269–271
Dutch, 483
in early Middle Ages, 197*(i)*
in Egypt, 3*(i)*, 20–23, 22*(b)*
in Greece, 55*(i)*
of Hebrews, 40–42
of Hellenistic Greeks, 87*(i)*, 96–97
in High Middle Ages, 229*(i)*, 260–285, 261*(i)*
of indigenous Americans, 435
law and, 240–241
on manors, 263–264
in medieval cities, 289*(i)*, 298–301
in Middle Ages, 229*(i)*, 321*(i)*
Minoan, 56
monastic, 173–174, 282–285
Muslim, 200–201
Neolithic, 6–8
of nuns, 282, 282*(i)*
Paleolithic, 6
religious violence and, 385*(i)*
in Renaissance, 353*(i)*, 354–355
Roman, 113*(i)*, 129, 150–156
of sailors, 423
of university students, 306–307
Ligugé, monastery of, 186
Lima, Spanish in, 435
Lindisfarne, Gospel of, 214, 214*(i)*
Linen, 265
Lisbon, 425
Literacy, 8. *See also* Writing
in 18th century, 8

in Greece, 57
of laypeople, 348
Merovingian, 205
in Middle Ages, 308, 347–348
of nobility, 277
printing and, 366–367
Literature. *See also* Philosophy; Poets and poetry; specific works and writers
Byzantine, 190–191
essay as, 444–445
Latin, 145–146
in Middle Ages, 307–308
of philosophes, 500
Lithuania, 403
"Little ice age," 322, 453
Liturgy, Protestantism and, 391
Lives of the Most Excellent Painters, Sculptors and Architects, The (Vasari), 359
Livia (Rome), 147, 147*(i)*
Livy (historian), 146
Locke, John, 481, 500, 503
Logic, Abelard on, 305
Loire River region, 217
Lollards, 336–337
Lombards, 184, 186, 206
Lombardy, Charlemagne and, 207
Longbow, 330, 331
Long-distance trade, 294–295, 294*(m)*
Long Parliament (England), 479
Lord protector (England), Cromwell as, 479
Lords. *See* Nobility
Lorraine, 462
Lost Gospels, 158
Lothar, 215, 215*(m)*
Louis II (Hungary), 404
Louis VI (France), 233
Louis IX (France), 247, 329
Louis XI "Spider King" (France), 376–377
Louis XII (France), 377
Louis XIII (France), 458
Louis XIV (France), 459*(i)*, 499
absolutism of, 451*(i)*, 458, 459–462
acquisitions of, 462*(m)*
Charles II (England) and, 481
Versailles and, 460–461
wars of, 462
Louisiana, 434, 462
Louis the German, 215, 215*(m)*
Louis the Pious, 215
Louvois, marquis de (François le Tellier), 462
Love. *See also* Marriage; Sex and sexuality
courtly, 308
in Greece, 76
Low Countries, 410. *See also* Belgium; Holland; Netherlands
Christian humanism in, 364
cities in, 291
Hundred Years' War in, 330
in late Middle Ages, 323
merchant guilds in, 292–293
Lower classes. *See* Class; Peasant(s)
Loyalty oaths, 223

Production, Hellenistic, 100
Professionalization, of armies, 456–457, 456(i)
Promised Land, Israel as, 37
Property. *See also* Inheritance
  of Muslim women, 201
  women's rights and, 64, 75
Prophets, 199(i). *See also* Muhammad
Propylaea (gateway), 70, 71, 72(i)
Prosperity
  in Italian Renaissance, 354–355
  Neolithic, 7
Prostitutes and prostitution
  clothing for, 299–300
  in Greece, 76
  Hammurabi's code on, 17
  in late Middle Ages, 344–345, 344(i)
  Protestants on, 394
  in Rome, 128
Protectorate, in England, 479–480
Protest(s). *See* Revolts and rebellions; Revolution(s)
Protestant, use of term, 389
Protestantism. *See also* Christianity; Edict of Nantes; Huguenots; Lutheranism
  appeal of, 391
  baroque art and, 484
  Calvin and, 401–402
  capitalism and, 497
  in England, 398–401
  in English colonies, 434
  in France, 398, 402, 409–410, 458, 459
  in Germany, 391–394, 465
  in Holy Roman Empire, 395–398
  science and, 498
  spread of, 398–404
  thought about, 389–391
  Zwingli and, 389
Protestant Reformation
  Calvinism and, 401–402
  in eastern Europe, 403–404
  in England, 398–401
  Puritans and, 400
Protestant Union, 454
Provence, France, 253, 377
Providence, 434
Provinces. *See also* Colonies and colonization
  French, 234
  Roman, 124, 141, 152–156
Prussia. *See also* Brandenburg-Prussia; Frederick II the Great (Prussia); Germany
  absolutism in, 467, 510–511
  bureaucracy in, 511
  in 17th century, 466–467
  Silesia and, 511
  Teutonic Knights and, 255–256
Psalters, 212–214
Ptah (god), 99(i)
Ptolemais (city), 98
Ptolemies (Egypt), 91. *See also* Egypt
  Greek culture and, 98
  Ptolemy II, Arsinoe II, and, 95(i)

Ptolemy III and, 106
Ptolemy V and, 99(i)
Ptolemy XIII, 133
Rome and, 124
trade and, 100
Ptolemy, Claudius (scientist), 105, 423–424, 424(i), 490, 492
Publicans (tax collectors), 156
Public education. *See* Education
Public health. *See also* Health care
  in Middle Ages, 268
Public sphere, 505
Pugachev, Emelian, 512
Punic Wars, 122–125, 145
Punishment. *See also* Crime and criminals; Law codes
  for adultery, 240(i)
  in Hammurabi's code, 16, 17
  in High Middle Ages, 240–241
  medieval stocks as, 283(i)
Purgatory, 275–276, 387
Puritans, 400, 402
  Anglican Church and, 478
"Purity of blood" laws (Spain), 380
Pyramids, in Egypt, 20, 21(i)
Pyrenees, Treaty of the, 465
Pyrrhic victory, 122
Pyrrhus (Epirus), 122
Pythia (priestess), 75
Pythian games, 79

Quaestors (Rome), 119
Quakers, in Pennsylvania, 434
Quebec, 434, 462
Queens. *See also* Monarchy
  in Renaissance, 375
Quilon, India, 420
Quirini, Lauro, 362–363(b)
Qur'an, 198–199, 200, 201
  death, afterlife, and, 276
  Judeo-Christian scriptures and, 202

Ra (god), 19, 19(i)
Rabbinic academies, 304
Rabbis, 304
Race and racism. *See also* Ethnic groups; Slaves and slavery
  anti-Semitism and, 380
  Enlightenment and, 506–508
  ethnicity, religion, and, 347
  European attitudes and, 443, 444, 445–446
  ideas about, 444
  mixed-race populations and, 436(i), 437
  Renaissance use of term, 373
Racine, Jean, 461
Radical Reformation, 391–394
al-Rahman, Abd (Caliph), 203
Rákóczy, Francis, 466
Ramadan, 201
Rameses II (Egypt), 27
Ranching, Spanish American, 435

Rape
  in Hellenistic wars, 108
  in Middle Ages, 345
Raphael (Raphael Sanzio), 370
Rationalism, 499
  of Hume, 503
Rats, Black Death and, 324
Ravenna, Ostrogoths in, 183
Raw materials
  in Egypt, 18
  in Hellenistic world, 100
Reading. *See also* Education; Literacy
  revolution in, 504
Reason. *See also* Enlightenment
  Descartes and, 496–497
  inductive reasoning and, 495
Rebellions. *See* Revolts and rebellions
Reconquista (Spain), 237(i), 238, 238(m), 245, 272(b), 380
  exploration and, 422
  slavery and, 438(b), 439
Rede, Edmund, 264(i)
Redemption, Augustine on, 175
Red Sea region
  Arabs and, 198
  Egypt and, 35
Reform(s). *See also* Protestant Reformation; Reformation; Revolts and rebellions; Revolution(s)
  in Athens, 65
  in Austria, 513–515
  of Christian Church, 384, 386–394
  Gregorian, 242, 313
  monastic, 280–282
  in Rome, 120, 129, 130, 168
  in Russia, 471–474, 512
Reformation, 384. *See also* Counter-Reformation; Protestant Reformation
  Catholic, 403, 404–407, 413, 483
  of Christian church, 384, 386–395
  in England, 398–400
  radical, 391–394
  witchcraft trials and, 411–413
Reformed Church, 402
Refugees
  to Geneva, 402
  religious, in Holy Roman Empire, 398
Regents, Dutch, 483
Regular clergy, 173
Reinhart, Anna, 394
Relics, of saints, 167(i), 188, 270
Religion(s). *See also* Crusades; Cults; Gods and goddesses; specific groups
  Athenian drama and, 72–73
  in Babylon, 16
  barbarian, 179
  Black Death and, 327
  Chaldean, 46
  Crusades and, 245–246
  death and, 275–276
  in Egypt, 18–19, 25, 26, 98
  in England, 398–401, 480
  in Europe (ca. 1555), 405(m)

invasions by, 215–221, 216(m)
in Slavic areas, 220
Villa (Roman country estate), 153, 153(i), 169
Villages. *See also* Cities and towns; Manors and manorialism
barbarian, 177
feudal, 223, 225
in High Middle Ages, 262–269
Neolithic, 6, 7
Roman, 162
Ville-Marie. *See* Montreal
Vinland, 218(b)
Violence. *See also* Revolts and rebellions; Wars and warfare
against Jews, 273
religious, 245, 407–413
Virgil, 139, 145, 146(i), 347
Virginia, 413, 434
Virgin Mary. *See* Mary (mother of Jesus)
Virtù, 359, 361
Virtue, Roman, 125, 146–147
Viscounts, 208
Visigoths, 176, 177, 177(i), 182, 186, 201
Voltaire, 501–502, 501(i), 503, 504(i)
Vortigern (Celts), 181
Voting and voting rights, in Rome, 117, 130(i)
Voyages. *See also* Exploration
of Columbus, 427–429, 427(m), 428–429(b)
European voyages of discovery, 421, 422–431, 425(i), 426(m)
of Zheng He, 418(m), 419–420

Wages. *See also* Income
in medieval cities, 300
Waldensians, 313
Waldo, Peter, 313, 314
Walled cities
medieval, 299
Neolithic, 7–8
War of the Austrian Succession, 511, 511(m), 514
War of the Spanish Succession, 462, 465–466
Warriors
Greek, 61(i)
Mycenaean, 57
nobility as, 245, 277
Russian Cossacks as, 469
saints as, 245
Viking, 221
Wars and warfare. *See also* Civil war(s); Military; Navy; Weapons; specific battles and wars
army size and, 456–457
barbarian, 177
Greco-Macedonian style of, 96
Hellenistic, 107–108
nobility and, 278–279
Roman, 116–117, 120, 122–124, 128
Sparta-Messenia, 63
training in, 277

Warships. *See* Ships and shipping
Wars of the Roses (England), 377
Water pollution, 299
Wealth. *See also* Class
in Athenian society, 65
in commercial revolution, 298
in England, 232
in France, 461
in Hellenistic world, 100
hierarchy of classes by, 374–375
in Renaissance, 354–355, 374–375
Weapons
Assyrian, 44
of barbarians, 177
siege machines as, 107
Weather. *See* Climate
Weaving. *See* Textile industry
Weddings. *See also* Marriage
medieval, 274, 274(i)
peasant, 274
Weekdays, naming of, 179
Wends people, 220
Wenzeslas (Czech king), 175(i)
Wergeld (monetary value), 179
Wessex, 231
West, the. *See* Western world
West Africa, gold trade and, 420
Western Christian church. *See* Catholic Church
Western civilization, 4, 5. *See also* Western world
Western Europe, Roman expansion into, 142–145, 144(m)
Western Hemisphere. *See* Americas; New World
Westernization, of Russia, 474
Western Roman Empire, 166, 169(m), 172. *See also* Byzantine Empire; Roman Empire
barbarians in, 178, 179, 184
emperors in, 183
end of, 188
Middle Ages and, 196
Western world
Charlemagne and, 207–208
defined, 4–5
Russia and, 468, 471
West Indies, 434
Westphalia, Peace of, 455, 455(m)
West Slavs, 217, 220
What Is Enlightenment? (Kant), 510
Whitby, monastery of, 215
White Mountain, Battle of the, 454
Widows, 264, 293, 343. *See also* Women
William and Mary (England), 481, 483
William of Malmesbury, 280
William of Normandy (the Conqueror), 231–232, 242
William of Occam. *See* Occam, William of
William of Orange (king of England), 481, 483
William the Pious (Aquitaine), 280
Wilusa kingdom, 27

Witches and witchcraft, 411–413
Wittenberg, Luther at, 387, 388, 389(i)
Wives. *See also* Women
of Charlemagne, 208(i), 209
in Islam, 201
Women. *See also* Gender and gender issues; Homosexuality; Marriage; Midwives; Nuns; Prostitutes and prostitution
age at marriage, 344
in American colonies, 436–437
in Athens, 75–76
celibacy of male clergy and, 242
Christianity and, 159, 174–175
as clergy, 173
in clerical orders, 282
craft guilds and, 293
in Crusades, 247
in Egypt, 23
in Enlightenment, 500–501, 505
in feudal society, 223
food riots and, 453
in French court, 461
Hammurabi's code on, 17
Hellenistic, 97
in High Middle Ages, 264, 265, 267(i), 268
as humanists, 360, 362
in Judaism, 39, 41–42
in medieval Europe, 264, 265
Merovingian, 205
monasticism and, 172
Montesquieu on, 500–501
in Northumbrian Christian culture, 214–215
in Paleolithic society, 6
in Protestantism, 395
in Renaissance, 370–371, 375–376, 375(i)
in Rome, 125, 146–147, 151
Rousseau on, 508, 509
in sciences, 497, 497(i)
Spartan, 64
in Sumer, 13
as troubadours, 308
witchcraft and, 411–413
as workers, 435
Woodblock printing, 365
Woolen industry. *See also* Textile industry
Hundred Years' War and, 330, 334
in late Middle Ages, 323
trade and, 295
Work. *See also* Labor; Peasant(s); Workers
of peasants, 264–266
Workers. *See also* Labor; Peasant(s)
for medieval architecture, 311–312
Workforce. *See* Labor; Workers
Worldview, of Enlightenment, 498–499, 500
Worms
conference at (1122), 243
Diet of (1521), 389
Jews of, 272
Wright, Joseph, 489(i)
Writ (England), 232

Writing, 8. *See also* Alphabet; Literature
in barbarian society, 176*(i)*, 177
Carolingian minuscule as, 211, 212*(i)*
cuneiform, 10–11, 11*(f)*, 29, 45
Syrian, 28
Wyclif, John, 336

Xenophon (historian), 45
Xerxes (Persia), 48, 66, 89

Yahweh (God), 37, 40–41*(b)*, 41, 50*(b)*, 156,
158
Yangshao culture, 6

Year of the four emperors (Rome), 148
Yom Kippur, 272
York
house of, 377
schools in, 348
Young people, of nobility, 277–278
Ypres, 294
Yucatec Mayan language, 432*(i)*

Zacatecas, 441
Zacharias (Pope), 206
Zama, battle at, 124
Zannanza (Hittites), 25

Zarathustra. *See* Zoroaster and
Zoroastrianism
Zealots, 156
Zeno (Cyprus), 104–105
Zeno (Rome), 183
Zeus (god), 59, 78, 102, 126
Zheng He, voyages of, 418*(m)*, 419–420
Ziggurats, Mesopotamian, 11, 12*(i)*
Zoroaster and Zoroastrianism, 49,
49*(i)*, 51
Zwingli, Ulrich, 389, 394

About the Authors

John P. McKay (Ph.D., University of California, Berkeley) is professor emeritus at the University of Illinois. He has written or edited numerous works, including the Herbert Baxter Adams Prize–winning book *Pioneers for Profit: Foreign Entrepreneurship and Russian Industrialization, 1885–1913*.

Bennett D. Hill (Ph.D., Princeton University), late of the University of Illinois, published *English Cistercian Monasteries and Their Patrons in the Twelfth Century*, *Church and State in the Middle Ages*, and numerous articles and reviews. A Benedictine monk of St. Anselm's Abbey in Washington, D.C., he was also a visiting professor at Georgetown University.

John Buckler (Ph.D., Harvard University), late of the University of Illinois, published numerous books, including *Theban Hegemony, 371–362 B.C.*; *Philip II and the Sacred War*; and *Aegean Greece in the Fourth Century B.C.* With Hans Beck, he most recently published *Central Greece and the Politics of Power in the Fourth Century*.

Clare Haru Crowston (Ph.D., Cornell University) teaches at the University of Illinois, where she is currently associate professor of history. She is the author of *Fabricating Women: The Seamstresses of Old Regime France, 1675–1791*, which won the Berkshire and Hagley Prizes. She edited two special issues of the *Journal of Women's History*, has published numerous journal articles and reviews, and is a past president of the Society for French Historical Studies.

Merry E. Wiesner-Hanks (Ph.D., University of Wisconsin–Madison) taught first at Augustana College in Illinois, and since 1985 at the University of Wisconsin–Milwaukee, where she is currently UWM Distinguished Professor in the department of history. She is the coeditor of the *Sixteenth Century Journal* and the author or editor of more than twenty books, most recently *The Marvelous Hairy Girls: The Gonzales Sisters and Their Worlds* and *Gender in History*.

Joe Perry (Ph.D., University of Illinois at Urbana-Champaign) is associate professor of modern German and European history at Georgia State University. He has published numerous articles and is author of the recently published book, *Christmas in Germany: A Cultural History*. His current research interests include issues of consumption, gender, and television in East and West Germany after World War II.

About the Cover Art

At the Market, Joachim Beuckelaer, 1564

In the late sixteenth century, Antwerp was the richest city in Europe because of its role in world trade and a thriving textile industry. This painting, by local Flemish artist Joachim Beuckelaer (ca. 1533–ca. 1574), reflects the abundance of fresh food found in the city's markets and the high standard of living enjoyed by its inhabitants. Such scenes of everyday life became increasingly popular in the sixteenth century with urban residents who hung the paintings in their increasingly comfortable homes. The city's wealth also allowed it to become a center of humanist scholarship, printing, and the performing arts.

(The Bridgeman Art Library)